ACCOUNTING
INFORMATION
SYSTEMS

ACCOUNTING INFORMATION SYSTEMS

SECOND EDITION

John F. Nash

East Tennessee State University

PWS-KENT PUBLISHING COMPANY

Boston

PWS–KENT
Publishing Company

© 1989 by PWS-KENT Publishing Company; © 1984 by
Macmillan Publishing Company. All rights reserved. No part of
this book may be reproduced, stored in a retrieval system, or
transcribed, in any form or by any means, electronic, mechanical,
photocopying, recording, or otherwise, without the prior written
permission of the publisher, PWS-KENT Publishing Company,
20 Park Plaza, Boston, Massachusetts 02116.

PWS-KENT Publishing Company is a division of Wadsworth, Inc.

Printed in the United States of America

1 2 3 4 5 6 7 8 9   92 91 90 89 88

Macmillan Publishing Company
866 Third Avenue, New York, New York 10022

Collier Macmillan Canada, Inc.

Library of Congress Cataloging-in-Publication Data

Nash, John F. (John Francis), 1937–
    Accounting information systems / John F. Nash. —2nd ed.

        p. cm.
    Includes index.
    ISBN 0-534-91798-4
    1. Information storage and retrieval systems—Accounting.
2. Accounting—Data processing. I. Title.
HF5679.N329 1988
657′.028′5—dc19
                                            88-23490
                                            CIP

Printing: 1 2 3 4 5 6 7 8   Year: 9 0 1 2 3 4 5 6 7 8

Preface

Accounting Information Systems is intended to meet the needs of a first course in accounting systems, at either the undergraduate or graduate level. It may also be used as a review text in second or subsequent courses in this same area. The book provides a blend of the conceptual aspects of the subject and practical guidance for applying those concepts. As future members of the accounting profession, students must prepare to interact with accounting information systems in write-up work, in tax, in external and internal auditing, and in management advisory services and consulting. The concepts are interesting in their own right but are more important insofar as they provide a basis for understanding, developing, evaluating, and using practical accounting systems.

The first edition of the book was tested over a period of years in many different institutions throughout North America and elsewhere. The experience of the large number of instructors using the first edition demonstrated that the original decisions on basic structure and topic coverage were sound. The second edition seeks to build on this success by retaining the same structure and broad topic content while upgrading the material to incorporate improvements and to reflect technological and other advances in the subject. The greater part of the text has been rewritten for this purpose.

Since the first edition appeared, several important developments have occurred that influence the requirements for of a modern accounting information systems text. First, many more schools now offer at least one course in accounting information systems, and a substantial number require such a course for accounting majors. Indeed, the American Assembly of Collegiate Schools of Business (AACSB) now insists on coverage of accounting systems in all accredited accounting programs in the United States. Second, interaction among

instructors and discussion at professional meetings and elsewhere have considerably increased the consensus on course content. As a result, the scope of the first course in accounting information systems—and to a lesser extent that of more advanced courses—is now more clearly defined than hitherto.

Third, on a more formal level, the American Accounting Association (AAA) Committee on Contemporary Approaches to Teaching Accounting Information Systems has made an in-depth study of the accounting system course. The committee identified a common body of knowledge relating to accounting information systems which includes the following nine areas:

- data base concepts
- internal control
- the technology of information systems, including computer hardware and software, applications programming, and data communications
- the use of systems technology
- accounting information systems applications
- management uses of information
- management of information systems
- systems analysis and design
- auditing of accounting information systems

Clearly there is a need for flexibility in any given course—and in any given textbook—for differences in emphasis on particular areas. However, the committee's conclusion was that all accounting programs should include a minimum level of coverage in each of these nine areas. The present text offers the desirable flexibility but covers, in substantial accordance with the committee's recommendations, all of the topic areas listed.

In its recommendations, the AAA Committee emphasized the role of computerization in accounting information systems. The authors of AICPA Statement on

Auditing Standards No. 48 also pointed out that automated accounting systems must now be regarded as the norm. The pace of technological change has been maintained, or even has increased over the last several years, demanding corresponding changes in textbook coverage. Some technologies, such as data base management systems, networks, and telecommunications, have emerged to the point of major significance to accountants. Other technologies, such as manual processing, have declined to the point that extensive coverage can no longer be justified.

Because of the advance of computer technology, some of the material in a textbook like this is obviously technical, but the accountant must have a basic appreciation of this material in order to deal with all but the most elementary systems. In the future, accountants will be confronted by advanced computerized systems in almost every aspect of their work. The intent of this text is not to try to turn accounting students into computer specialists but to acquaint them with the most important terms, concepts, and techniques needed for success in the accounting profession. Students are entering college, and certainly are entering courses in accounting information systems, with a higher level of computer literacy than ever before. The often-cited fear that students will be unable to grasp the fundamental issues of computers has largely given way to concern that *instructors* may have difficulty in keeping up with their students.

The book consists of 22 chapters divided into five parts (one fewer than in the first edition). Part I, *Introduction to Accounting Information Systems,* provides the background necessary to understand information systems and the accounting information system. This part has been strengthened by increased emphasis on the structure of the major accounting subsystems, the transaction cycles and applications. Part I now also includes chapters covering a number of practical topics, including flowcharting, communication of information between people and machines, and the nature and techniques of data storage. These chapters also discuss modern innovations such as computer-aided flowcharting and forms design.

Part II, *The Role of Computers in Accounting Information Systems,* provides a user-oriented exploration of modern computerized systems, including computer hardware and software and end-user computing. The material has been completely revised to reflect advances in computer technology. The chapter on data-base management systems now includes additional material on relational data base concepts, and a new chapter has been added on the growing field of telecommunications. Part III, *The Life Cycle of Accounting Information Systems,* covers the analysis, design, and implementation of accounting information systems. The chapter on systems design expands the coverage of structured design methods. And a whole chapter is now devoted to systems implementation, including the acquisition of computer hardware and software, organizational changes, conversion from the old to the new system, and cost considerations in computerized information systems.

Part IV, *Control of Accounting Information Systems,* discusses internal controls in accounting systems. The material on controls has been updated to reflect the developing professional and legal environment of internal control and also to avoid the somewhat artificial distinctions among certain major categories of controls. Such distinctions are rapidly becoming obsolete. Part VI, *Accounting Applications,* is a "guidebook" to the transaction cycles and the major accounting applications into which they can be divided. The popularity of this material, among both instructors and students, has prompted the addition of a new chapter dealing with the planning and control cycle and the reporting cycle.

Each chapter starts with a set of learning objectives and ends with a summary of the chapter's highlights. A bibliography for further reading is included and discussion questions and problems allow students to apply the concepts and techniques learned in the chapter. A major objective of the problems at the end of each chapter is to integrate the material covered in earlier chapters. Through these exercises, students can see how to apply the methods and techniques learned in one chapter to the issues encountered in another.

Exercises of varying degrees of difficulty are included, allowing instructors to match assignments to students' capabilities and their level in the accounting curriculum. Some of the exercises are sufficiently challenging to be used for take-home exams or small projects. Some exercises are theoretical, but many require students to design components of accounting systems—files, screen or paper forms, processing tasks, computer hardware or software specifications, internal controls—in keeping with the text's practical emphasis.

Acknowledgments

Many people contributed to this book, and I am greatly indebted to them. I gratefully acknowledge the contribution of Dr. Martin B. Roberts, coauthor of the first edition. Dr. Roberts was unable to serve as an author of the second edition because of responsibilities of his growing business, but his ideas and practical methods survive in this edition. I am also indebted to the many instructors who offered comments on the first edition, which were important to the development of the second edition.

I am indebted to the many helpful comments and suggestions made by the reviewers of the second edition: James V. Hansen, Brigham Young University; Cynthia Heagy, University of Georgia; Howard W. Pullman, Youngstown State University; and William O. Van Dongen, University of Wisconsin. Any remaining weaknesses are mine alone.

I acknowledge, with thanks, the following companies and institutions that graciously gave permission for the inclusion of proprietary material in the book: Clark Truck Lines; Compaq Computer Corporation; Control Data Corporation; Coopers and Lybrand; Delta Transport, Inc.; Digital Equipment Corporation; General Dynamics Corporation; General Electric Corporation; Healthdyne, Inc.; Honeywell Corporation; International Business Machines Corporation; Management Science America, Inc.; McBee Division of Litton Business Systems, Inc.; Memorex Corporation; Microdata Corporation; Winn-Dixie Stores, Inc.; Zep Manufacturing Company; and a large industrial enterprise that prefers to remain anonymous.

Finally, I am indebted to four accounting students at East Tennessee State University who contributed many hours of help in preparing the manuscript: Louise Beck, now at Emory and Henry College in Virginia; Charles Daniel, now with the state government of Tennessee; Deborah Hess, now with Coopers and Lybrand; and Pamela Prince, now with Texas Instruments, Inc.

J.F.N.

Dedicated to my students

Contents

PART   THREE

THE LIFE CYCLE OF ACCOUNTING INFORMATION SYSTEMS

PART FOUR

CONTROL OF ACCOUNTING INFORMATION SYSTEMS

PART FIVE

ACCOUNTING
APPLICATIONS

PART ONE

INTRODUCTION TO ACCOUNTING INFORMATION SYSTEMS

Part I provides a general introduction to the subject of business information systems and a more specific introduction to the accounting information system. It also introduces some of the many tools and techniques used in information systems and information processing.

Modern information systems are combinations of people, facilities, data, and media, together with the expertise necessary to put them to work in support of organizational goals. Business information systems embrace a number of functions, including the one central to our present concern, the accounting function. Chapter 1 discusses the business information system from a number of different viewpoints and introduces the basic concepts of systems, data, and information. Chapter 2 continues this discussion with an introduction to the nature, structure, and activities of the accounting information system. Chapter 3 deals with the preparation and use of flowcharts and other graphical models of the information system. Chapter 4 addresses the concept of communication between users and the system—at input and output—and stresses the need for careful design of information formats for effective and efficient transfer of information. Chapter 5 explores the notion of data storage and retrieval, through which the accounting data base is accumulated, and introduces the basic types of file processing, including posting, file maintenance, sorting, and merging.

1

Business Information Systems

LEARNING OBJECTIVES

After you have studied this chapter you should be able to

- Discuss the nature of the business information system, with its dual role of operational data processing and decision support.
- Describe the involvement of people and machines in the information system, and the synergistic relationship between them.
- Explain some useful concepts and terminology from general systems theory.
- Discuss the nature of information and its effects on people and their behavior.

CHAPTER OUTLINE

THE ROLE OF INFORMATION SYSTEMS IN BUSINESS

What Is an Information System?

Virtually every business enterprise has an information system of some kind. But attempts to define a business information system frequently fall prey to the kinds of problems faced by the blind men trying to describe an elephant. Because an information system has so many different facets, it is difficult to derive a simple definitional formula that in any sense does it justice.

One possible definition would state that a business information system is a combination of people, data, facilities, technology, media, procedures, and controls intended to maintain essential channels of communication, process certain routine types of transactions, alert management and others to significant internal and external events, support managerial planning and control, and provide a basis for informed decision making. We may note that this definition says a little about what an information system *is*, but more about what it *does*. An information system is a *process* rather than an entity, or thing, and is understood more readily from that standpoint.

The functions of the business information system can be divided into routine and nonroutine functions. The routine function is referred to as *operational data processing* and includes the traditional accounting functions. The nonroutine function is referred to as *decision support* and provides managers with information to help them make decisions. Modern business information systems are normally complex, computerized systems whose influence extends throughout the organization and beyond. They may interface with other automated business systems in administration, building maintenance, engineering, manufacturing, and marketing. In some cases it may be difficult to decide where the business information system ends and where one of these other systems begins. On a smaller scale, the same is true of the accounting information system; there are no clear lines demarcating the boundaries of the accounting system, and some of its functions overlap with those of other components of the business information system.

But before discussing modern business information systems, it will be helpful to explore briefly how the systems we know today came into existence.

Historical Perspective

The emergence of information systems as an identifiable element in the theory and practice of business organizations occurred well into the present century, and the study of systems as a discipline worthy of significant attention in its own right is no more than a few decades old. Before that time, businesses and institutions were organized; accounting data were collected, processed, and communicated; decisions were made; and controls were implemented. But the people engaging in these activities did so without ever being aware that what they were doing might be of interest or concern beyond their immediate purpose. The procedures that people followed and the paperwork that they used evolved almost haphazardly. But the approaches that were followed were adequate in the relatively simple business environment that existed at that time.

The situation started to change at about the time of World War II, and it has been changing at an increasing pace ever since. The changes were provoked by several factors. First, business enterprises and institutions became bigger and more complex, and divisionalized enterprises, conglomerates, multinational organizations, and giant government agencies became the rule rather than the exception. In turn, size and complexity demanded more formal methods of internal communication. Individual managers and entrepreneurs could no longer keep abreast of operating conditions on an informal basis. And when professional managers assumed positions of authority, they brought with them an emphasis on new methods of internal reporting, performance evaluation, and decision making. The new field of decision science grew up, stressing the need for rational analysis of information and quantitative modeling. Decision science may not have had the impact that some of its early proponents originally envisioned. The proper role of subjective factors in decision making has been reasserted. But decision support through the provision of relevant information has increasingly been recognized as an essential ingredient of successful management.

Second, along with the increased size and complexity of modern business there has been a steady increase in its tempo. The pace of business has accelerated so that the time to respond to opportunities and react to threats has shortened. The need for timely information alerting management to developments inside and outside the organization has become more and more pressing.

Third, the social environment in which businesses and institutions operate has changed. The trend has been toward increasing government regulation and increasing demand for disclosure of information. Requirements for public disclosure of financial and operating data are at a level that would have been unthinkable a generation ago; many of the data required to be published today would have been judged to be nobody else's business. Furthermore, "ethical" behavior in business is now required by law. A growing body of legislation, including the monumental Foreign Corrupt Practices Act, mandates that people do business in a socially acceptable manner and that a framework of controls be established to ensure compliance. Internal control has become a matter of concern to the public, whereas it used to be of interest only to the organization, its owners, and the external auditors.

Finally, the technology of information processing has changed beyond recognition. In place of manual systems, adding machines, and primitive bookkeeping systems, sophisticated computer equipment is now the norm, even in the smallest organization. The revolution in information systems, which started in the early 1950s when the first business computers became available, is still in progress. Large mainframe computers were followed by smaller minicomputers and, later, by even smaller (but increasingly powerful) microcomputers. Personal computers today can outperform the largest computers of 20 to 30 years ago and cost less than 1 percent of their forebears. Communications systems can link computers with other machines, either on the next desk or halfway around the world. Innovations in automated information processing continue to be announced year by year and month by month.

Operational Data Processing

The routine function of operational data processing includes payroll processing, customer billing and collections, purchasing and materials requirements, inventory management, production control, and budget tracking. It produces the material for the external financial statements and generates the typically large volume of internal management reports. Operational data processing supports many routine, structured decisions at the lower and middle levels of management, and it provides much of the input to the routine performance evaluation of individuals and groups within the organization.

The operational data-processing system is of obvious importance to the enterprise; it forms the ''nervous system'' of the business, and most organizations would literally die within a few days without it. But the operational system is expected to carry out its tasks without the need for upper management's day-to-day concern.[1] As we shall see later, top management should be closely involved in the system development process. But when the development is complete and the information system has been deployed, it should be so reliable that top management can safely forget about it and devote its energies and attention to more pressing issues. Management should be completely confident that the payroll will be processed, customers will be billed, production will be controlled, and so on. The system should behave like a trusted servant, ever at hand to do the job but always maintaining a discreetly low profile.

Decision Support

Decision support underlies management's decision-making and problem-solving activities and has characteristics essentially different from those of operational data processing. Instead of handling routine functions, the decision support system is specifically designed to respond to requests for information as and when the need arises. And instead of keeping a discreetly low profile,

it enjoys a high level of visibility in the eyes of upper management; the system plays its most vital role at the very times when top management is faced with its most important decisions.

The purpose of the decision support system is three-fold:[2]

- To assist management in the decision process
- To support managerial judgment
- To improve the effectiveness of decision making

The decision support system has its biggest impact in situations that have enough structure to permit the use of computational methods but in which human judgment is still essential to the problem. In this context, ''structure'' refers to the ability to formulate a problem in quantitative terms, to measure the associated parameters, and to define the objectives as a basis for evaluating candidate solutions. Problems that are completely structured, the so-called programmed decisions, can be solved by a machine. Those that are completely *unstructured* may have to be solved by inspiration rather than by judgment. Decision support systems are most important in the middle ground between these two extremes. No attempt is made to automate the decision or replace the human manager; rather, the emphasis is on giving the human decision maker the best available *support* to supplement the normal managerial faculties of informed judgment and reasoned choice.

Common Data Base

Distinguishing between the two major functions of the business information system should not be taken to mean that there should be two separate information systems. Conceivably, an organization could develop and maintain two systems, but to do so would be highly inefficient, as there would be a duplication of people, facilities, equipment, and effort, and also of data. More commonly, organizations seek to develop a single information system capable of serving both types of needs.

---

[1] However, an individual at top management level, often referred to as the chief information officer, will normally have overall responsibility for the information system, including the operational data-processing function.

[2] P. G. W. Keen and W. S. Scott Morton, *Decision Support Systems* (Reading, Mass.: Addison-Wesley, 1978).

Operational data processing and decision support are complementary functions and, in most cases, can be integrated successfully.

A key component of the integrated information system is a common data base. The information required by the decision support system and that required by the operational system come largely from the same source: accounting transactions. Payroll data may form the basis of a decision regarding personnel levels; cost accounting data may provide input to a decision to add a new product or to discontinue an existing one; and accounts receivable data may support a decision concerning credit policy. In the case of the operational system, the processing of information is routine; in the case of the decision support system, the corresponding processes are nonroutine.

Management requests for decision support information are met by extracting the relevant data from the data base, analyzing them, and communicating the results to the users. The ability to respond properly to management's needs depends on the comprehensiveness of the data base and on the facilities available for extracting, assembling, and processing the information in the form required for the particular purpose. But most of the data become part of the data base as the result of routine recording, classifying, and storing of day-to-day transactions.

INFORMATION SYSTEMS, PEOPLE, AND COMPUTERS

Modern business information systems are normally automated and rely heavily on computer equipment providing for the input, processing, storage, communication, and output of data. But regardless of the level of automation, such systems also depend heavily on people. People plan, implement, maintain, operate, and use information systems. Virtually everyone in the organization—as well as many outside people—interact with the system or are affected by it in some way. It will be helpful to identify the various individuals and groups involved with the business information system and to explore some of the human factors that arise because of this involvement.

Involved Groups

The list of involved groups starts with management. Top management probably has the most vital interest of any group in the effectiveness of the information system. This group applies resources to the development, maintenance, and operation of the system and is responsible for the outcome. If the job has been well done, the company and top management can enjoy the benefits of the system as it effectively supports both routine operations and nonroutine decision making and problem solving. If the job has not been well done, the company and top management will suffer the consequences. It is not an exaggeration to say that the business information system can make or break a company—or make or break top management.

Lower and middle management bear the ongoing responsibility for the operation and use of the information system and the supervision of the rank-and-file users. They also have the responsibility for seeing that organizational policies and procedures relating to the system are properly carried out. These levels of management bear a particularly heavy burden when system changes are introduced. They must implement any necessary organizational changes, adjust to any associated differences in hierarchical status, and help their subordinates adapt to new forms, new equipment, new procedures, and new ways of doing their jobs.

The users of the information system include both "active" and "passive" users. Active users, those who directly use the system, comprise a large proportion of the people in the organization. Besides managers at all levels, there are many others whose jobs are more or less dependent on the information system: people in accounts receivable, production control, purchasing, sales analysis, and so forth. Passive users are those who interface with the system only indirectly but nonetheless benefit from it in one way or another. They include everybody who receives a paycheck, a W-2 form, a statement of benefits, or a credit union report. Passive users also include the customers who receive invoices and monthly statements, the vendors who receive purchase orders and payment checks, the taxation authorities that receive tax returns and deposits, the government agencies that receive regulatory reports, and the stockholders who receive the annual financial report and dividend checks.

Most types of accountants are closely involved with the information system. Internal accountants are involved in the system because it furnishes the means by which they accumulate, process, and communicate accounting data. Internal auditors are involved because of their responsibility of ensuring that controls are properly implemented and functioning. External auditors attest to the fairness of the output from the information system as it is presented in the annual report, and they also are involved in related activities, including examination of the internal controls. Accountants of all types are becoming increasingly involved in the development of information systems.

Personnel in operations research have a strong interest in the information system. The operations research function is similar to, and runs parallel to, the accounting function, particularly in its decision support role. The only differences lie in the scope of its activities and in the processing tools employed.

Data-processing professionals are heavily involved because of their training and expertise in the development, maintenance, and operation of information systems, particularly computerized systems. These professionals include consultants, systems analysts and designers, computer specialists and programmers, documentation specialists, data librarians, data base administrators, telecommunications specialists, data-entry personnel, and equipment maintenance technicians. It would also be fair to include computer manufacturers, software "houses," computer retail stores, user groups, publishers of technical journals and books, service bureaus—organizations that sell computer services, independent equipment maintenance organizations, contractors who specialize in the design and construction of computer rooms, data-processing supply companies, and transportation companies that specialize in moving sophisticated data-processing equipment. A vast industry has grown up to support the modern information system and its users.

Last but not least in this list of involved groups comes the public. Everybody is involved in information systems in today's world. We all carry driver's licenses and social security cards. We receive credit card statements, utility bills, tax assessments, census forms, and mass mailings. We fill out questionaires and application forms. We read reports, listen to news bulletins, watch documentaries, and attend briefings. We are the targets of a huge network of citizen, consumer, professional, and interest group information systems, and our five senses are continually bombarded with their output.

Human Factors

Anything that involves so many different kinds of people as an information system does can be expected to exhibit problems in human attitudes and responses. These problems have tended to increase with the spread of automated systems. People's attitudes toward information systems range from intense excitement and deep personal fulfillment, at one end of the spectrum, to open hostility and fear, at the other. Between these two extremes lie the attitudes of most people who interact with such systems and work with them. The majority of people accept the necessity of information systems but occasionally grumble about their inadequacies—no matter how effective, reliable, and easy to use those systems may be.

Much has been done to make the information systems themselves less threatening. Considerable advances have been made in the development of "user-friendly" systems; these are designed to be used by the layperson and help to break down the mystique that surrounds computers. Frequent contact with computers and computer-controlled devices of many different types in school, in the home, and elsewhere are also helping in this regard. For those people who come into contact only with the output from information systems, much can be done to alleviate feelings of impersonality through the design of pleasing information formats, a tasteful choice of wording, and an accent on "the personal touch."

Significant problems also arise in interpersonal relations in information systems. If systems are to be successful, people of different backgrounds, levels of education and training, organizational positions, and personal attitudes must work together as a team. Unfortunately, the team spirit is not always easy to engender. Computer professionals have a habit of trying to impress others with their expertise—creating an "in group," talking the same jargon, and sharing anecdotes that only they understand—rather than helping one another and trying to solve their problems. Accountants and managers often dismiss the computer specialists as arrogant eggheads who make no attempt to understand the real world; they may also experience interpersonal difficulties with one another. Lower-level employees may adopt a ''we-they'' attitude, seeing all other groups as part of an ongoing conspiracy to make them work ever harder for a smaller return.

These problems demand our attention too. Here, the best prospect for improvement lies in communication and education. Systems professionals, including accountants, must talk more to one another—and listen more to one another—and to other people in the system. Communications should be improved with the rank-and-file users; their contribution should be acknowledged and their personal worth emphasized so as to eliminate any feelings of alienation. Professionals should listen to their comments and solicit their input on ways to improve the system; often relatively minor and inexpensive changes can make their responses more positive and their jobs easier. Wherever possible, the system should be tailored to reduce the difficulty or tedium of routine work. Systems developers frequently overlook the stress imposed on a data entry clerk who is forced to use a badly designed keyboard or look at a glaring, flickering screen. They may also overlook the stress imposed on managers who are inundated with paper but who still cannot obtain the information they need.

Automation of the Information System

Automation of the business information system requires the use of electronic equipment to support the tasks of operational data processing as well as to provide for the more sophisticated analysis and communication processes used in decision support. The use of a hand calculator or a bookkeeping machine represents a low level of automation; higher levels of automation are provided by computer facilities. In most modern business information systems, computers are used to carry out most of the processing, storage, retrieval, and output functions according to programmed instructions. These programmed instructions take the place of the clerical procedures on which manual systems are based.

One of the primary motivations in the development of computers for business data-processing applications was the need to handle the ever-growing volume of data that has to be digested by the modern organization. Manual processing is slow, expensive, and error prone. Moreover, the physical limitations of manual processing place severe constraints on the amount and type of processing that can be carried out. In the days of manual systems, the level of analysis to be performed was frequently dictated by labor constraints instead of by the users' needs. Managers were often forced to compromise their informational needs in the interests of feasibility and timeliness, and the prospects for deploying an effective decision support system based on manual processing were slim. The advent of business computers offered a means of removing all or most of these constraints. Computers are fast, accurate, and relatively inexpensive—and have become dramatically cheaper over the last twenty years. They can carry out the most tedious processing operations promptly and reliably and can respond with decision support information in a time frame consistent with management's needs. Managers can ask for the information they require without having to be so concerned about the burden imposed by their requests. Computers have already revolutionized information processing, and their potential as tools of data capture, storage, processing, communication, and output is far from being exhausted.

People–Computer Synergy

When automation was first introduced, the natural approach was to reproduce faithfully the functions previously preformed by hand. Later it became evident that this approach was not taking proper advantage of the computer and that better systems could be designed that exploited its special strengths. Today, most systems designed with the computer in mind are quite different from what they would be if manual operation were intended.

The principal strengths of computers are their speed, accuracy, and capacity to store and retrieve large volumes of data. On the other hand, despite widely publicized work on artificial intelligence and ''fifth-generation'' programming languages, computers' innate level of ''thinking'' is very low. Most computers have to be instructed in minute detail how to perform even the most elementary operations. In artificial intelligence systems, computers' ability to make logical decisions according to preprogrammed rules simulates to some extent the functioning of the human brain, but there is still a wide gap between the computer and the brain, and many experts believe that the gap will never be bridged completely.

Fortunately, however, computers' strengths correspond to weaknesses in manual processing, and vice versa. Those types of processing that people generally do not do well computers handle superbly. Computers have superhuman memories and capacities for fast processing, and ordinarily they do not make mistakes. Conversely, people think intelligently and creatively, whereas computers "think" (to the extent that they think at all) in conventional, stereotyped ways. Thus computers and people complement each other very effectively. Out of this realization of the synergistic relationship between computers and their users has emerged the potential for information processing at a level of effectiveness that could scarcely have been imagined thirty years ago. And again, the potential for even more effective interaction is far from being exhausted.

One rather conspicuous difference between manual and computerized information systems lies in the media in which the data reside. In manual systems, the data reside in paper media: journals, ledgers, and reports. But in automated systems, paper media are of more limited value because the data cannot easily be read by machines. To overcome this problem, most data and computerized systems are stored in "machine-readable" media. Punched cards and punched paper tape were two of the earliest machine-readable media. Today, magnetic media such as magnetic tapes and magnetic disks, and optical media such as laser disks, are used for permanent storage of data, and semiconductor devices are typically used for temporary storage while processing is in progress. The data must be transcribed, or "encoded," onto machine-readable media for processing. During processing, the data are manipulated in the form of electrical pulses. When the processing has been completed, the information must be returned to human-readable form. This "decoding" process may be performed by a printer, which produces paper output, by a video device, which produces a screen display, or by some other device.

THEORETICAL BASIS OF INFORMATION SYSTEMS

Our treatment of business information systems is intended to be practical. On the other hand, it will be useful to examine briefly some theoretical concepts that will enhance the understanding of information systems and information itself. Some important concepts regarding information systems emerge from the discipline known as *general systems theory*.

General Systems Theory

General systems theory is a discipline that has evolved over the last several decades in response to the need to study complex things, activities, and situations. It consists of a set of concepts that provides a format or structure for rational analysis—a way of looking at things. Systems theory is intended to be general and interdisciplinary, and it has been applied to problems as diverse as microorganisms and space vehicles. The theory has also been applied successfully to business activities and situations. In parallel with systems theory, people speak of the "systems approach" which has proved particularly successful in the analysis and solution of business problems. The systems approach refers to a pragmatic, but rational and "systematic," approach to solving such problems, using concepts that have emerged mainly from general systems theory.

A *system* is defined in the theory as an assemblage of interacting components forming a complex whole and united (at least to some degree) in pursuit of common goals. If the system is a business enterprise, the components may be the various departments organized to help achieve management's objectives. The system exists in some kind of environment, but there may or may not be any interaction with the environment. A *closed* system is one that is assumed to be effectively isolated from its environment so that there is no external interaction. An *open* system is one in which external interaction is assumed to be significant. Closed systems are rare in the real world, and virtually all business systems have to be regarded as open. They affect, and are affected by, their particular environments—which include the industry, the economy, and the society in which they operate.

FIGURE 1.1 A system and its environment. The inputs and outputs provide the interaction between a system and its environment.

Environment

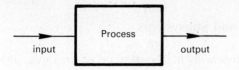

FIGURE 1.2 Signal inputs and control inputs. Signal inputs are required in order for the output to be produced. Control inputs govern the way in which the process works.

Environment

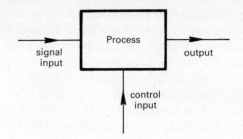

The interaction between an open system and its environment takes place through the system's inputs and outputs. The inputs represent the influence of the environment on the system; the outputs represent the influence of the system on its environment. One of the inputs to a business system is labor, and the outputs may include manufactured products or service rendered to customers. Within the system, some activity or process takes place through which the inputs are converted into outputs or give rise to the outputs (Figure 1.1). The recognition of the three elements of inputs, process, and outputs is fundamental to the study of systems of any kind. Accordingly, systems analysis requires, among other things, identification of the inputs and outputs of a given system.

Frequently, particularly in business systems, the inputs can be divided into two types, the *signal* inputs and the *control* or *maintenance* inputs (Figure 1.2). The signal inputs are the tangible or intangible inputs that directly stimulate the process to produce the outputs or that are required by the process to generate the outputs. The control inputs determine *how* the system will process the signal inputs. If the system is conceptualized as a "black box" the control inputs represent the "knobs" on the front of the box. Typically, control inputs do one of two things: They communicate the objectives of the system—what it is intended to do—or they provide constraints on the way in which it operates.

To illustrate, suppose that the system is a television set. Its signal inputs are the electricity supply and the electromagnetic waves that carry the audio and video transmissions. And its outputs are the sound and picture. The control inputs are the switch and knob settings that turn the receiver on, select the channel, and adjust the volume and picture quality.

Business systems, however, are typically more complex and have a longer list of inputs and outputs. For example, an accounting practice, regarded as a system, may be analyzed as follows:

Signal Inputs	*Control Inputs*	*Outputs*
Capital	Goals and policies of the practice	Client services:
Personnel	Generally accepted accounting	Write-up work
Client firms	principles	Tax services
Accounting	Professional ethics	Auditing
skills	The law	Consulting
Good judgment	Peer evaluation	Earnings
	Demand for services	Taxes
		Client satisfaction
		Professional pride
		Trash

Control inputs often limit the output from the system. A low demand for client services, for example, will limit an accounting firm's performance. But sometimes this limitation of output is imposed in the interests of improving the *quality* of the output. Generally accepted accounting principles and professional ethics serve as "quality constraints" on the firm's work. Because of these constraints, the firm's short-run performance may be less than it would be in an unconstrained environment, but over the long term, the improved quality may substantially enhance performance.

Furthermore, it is interesting to note that not all the outputs are "desirable" from the standpoint of the system's objectives; for example, taxes and trash may be considered undesirable "by-products" of the system.

Sometimes part of the input from a system is fed back to form a control input or even a signal input; this is the basis of the so-called feedback system. If a feedback system is properly arranged, it can be self-regulating and can serve as a control device (Figure 1.3). A familiar example is a thermostatically controlled heating system. The input is the power supply, and the output is heat. Part of the heat output is diverted to activate a thermostat that turns the heat on when the room gets too cold or turns it off when the room gets too hot. The objective is to maintain the temperature of the room at, or close to, some desired level—the "setting" of the thermostat.

FIGURE 1.3 Feedback system. Part of the output is fed back to provide input to the system. Feedback systems can be self-regulating.

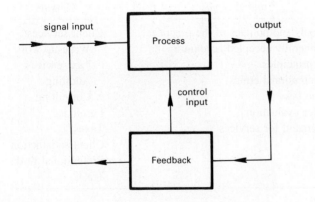

Management control systems function in an analogous manner. Output from the information system is fed back to control the business and to keep operations in step with management's plans.

Systems and Subsystems

The components of a system are referred to as *subsystems*. A subsystem is a "system within a system." In turn, within any one of the subsystems it may be possible to identify *sub-subsystems*. However, in the other direction, the original system may be identified as being a component of some larger, encompassing *suprasystem*. An accounting firm may have departmental subsystems such as auditing, tax, and management advisory services (MAS). In turn, the tax department subsystem may include component sub-subsystem groups specializing in tax planning and tax compliance. However, the firm itself might be regarded as being part of a larger suprasystem: the accounting profession (Figure 1.4). Thus a hierarchy exists in which the entities at any one level are made up of subsystems at the next lower level, but they themselves are components of the entities at the next higher level. The level in the hierarchy to which the label *system* is assigned is purely arbitrary and corresponds to our focus of attention at any one time. Later, our focus might change, and an entity at a different level might be selected as the system. A system can be treated as a subsystem or suprasystem if it is viewed from above or below.

The subsystems that comprise any given system have their own inputs, controls, and outputs. These inputs, controls, and outputs provide the means by which the subsystems interact with one another and the means by which subsystems near the boundaries of the system can interact with the external environment.

The control inputs of the overall system include inputs representing the objectives of the system, and the same is true of each subsystem. Some important lessons can be learned from the relationship between the objectives of individual subsystems and the objectives of the overall system. In order to achieve optimal performance, the objectives of the subsystems should be closely coordinated. The objective of each subsystem in a business system should be the subset of the organization's overall

FIGURE 1.4 **Hierarchy of subsystems.** A given entity may be a subsystem of the entity above it or the suprasystem of the one below it.

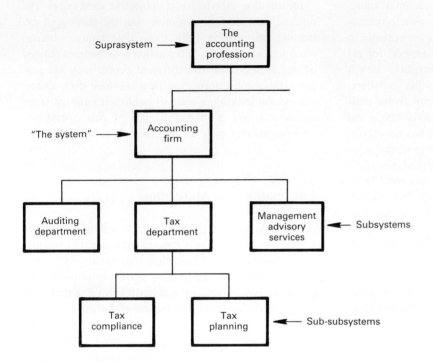

objectives that pertains to its particular task within the organization. Thus the objective of the accounting department, for example, should not be to become the world's best accounting department; rather, it should be to support the objectives of the organization in the area of accounting. Narrow, parochial objectives lead to suboptimal performance, whereas broad, organization-oriented objectives can greatly help achieve optimal performance for the system.

The Nature of Information

The information system, of course, produces information. Information is elusive but potentially of considerable value. A Frenchman, Louis Joinet, shrewdly observed: "Information is power, and economic information is economic power." The value of information depends on its content, timeliness, and "newsworthiness;" on the needs of the recipients to whom it is com-

municated; and on the way in which it is presented to them.

Information should be distinguished from data; these two terms are often confused, but they have essentially different meanings. Data are potentially useful but have no immediate value. Information, on the other hand, is a subset of data that is useful for some identifiable purpose. Information is extracted from the available data to meet a need. The content of a telephone directory represents data, but the number that a person looks up becomes useful information.

Many attempts have been made to measure the value of information. The field of knowledge known as *information theory*, which was primarily the work of the American mathematician Claude Elwood Shannon, attaches a value to the information contained in a message in relation to the recipient's degree of surprise upon receiving the message. The degree of surprise, in turn, is measured by the improbability of the reported event. For example, a 50 percent increase of sales from one month to the next is ordinarily judged to be very improbable; the news that it had just occurred would therefore be assigned a correspondingly high informational value. Shannon's work has had a great impact on telecommunications technology, but relatively little on business in general. Information theory provides a method for assigning a quantitative value to the information content of a message, but it does not express the value in dollars. Business people recognize that the economic value must depend both on the recipient's informational needs and on the surprise element. If the recipient has no use for the data in the message or is indifferent to it, the news will have little value, no matter how surprising it is.

A more direct attempt to measure the economic value of information is made in decision theory. Here, information is related to the reduction of risk in decision making. Under conditions of uncertainty, it is not possible to make firm projections of the consequences of any one of the available alternatives. At best, an expected, or mean, estimate can be made, for instance, the expected contribution to profits. This expected value falls below its maximum potential level as the degree of uncertainty—or risk—increases. But if additional information can be acquired that will reduce the degree of uncertainty, the expected profit will be increased. Decision theory directly relates the value of the information to this increase. Decision theory considers the ideal of "perfect" information, which removes all uncertainty from the decision, and also "imperfect" information, which reduces, but does not eliminate, the element of uncertainty. The theory is elegant, but unfortunately it does not have a wide application; decisions can rarely be formulated with the required level of detail. Good conceptual notions, but (except in rare instances) not meaningful dollar figures, can be derived from this theory.

In a more qualitative sense, information has economic value because it helps people make better decisions. It helps the decision maker identify and evaluate the available choices in terms of their projected consequences and helps assess risk. Clearly, information also has a time value. Timely information often enables the decision maker to take advantage of choices that may not be available at a later time. As time passes and the choices narrow, the economic potential for exploiting gain or avoiding loss usually becomes less favorable. Without timely information, the decision maker may have to react to events rather than plan them.

Information clearly has a subjective dimension. The original data may be objective, but the process of extracting information from those data requires human interpretation. In fact, information is sometimes defined as interpreted data. But different people may not perceive the same information in a common data source: one person looking at a set of published financial statements may see a dismal picture of past operations, whereas another may see enormous future potential.

Information and Motivation

The link between the information and the decision is a vital one, not just in a conceptual sense, but because it emphasizes that information remains of little value until it produces some form of *action*. Information that is only of passing interest has much less value than does information that results in meaningful change or influences somebody's behavior. Accordingly, the responsibility for the development and operation of an information system does not stop at delivering printed output. Particularly in the case of managerial accounting, in which the identity and needs of the users are known, that responsibility—on the part of accountants and other systems professionals—extends to the user's response to the information and the effect it has in motivating people to act and act in the right way.

Information plays a vital role in motivating people to do things. In business situations, results are achieved through people, and people must be suitably motivated to work toward attaining the company's goals. The effectiveness of this motivational process depends heavily on what information is communicated to the various individuals and on the manner in which it is communicated. Obviously, information must be accurate and should be communicated clearly and in a manner that is easily understood. But there is a further element that has to do with people's behavioral responses to the information. The receipt of information may produce a strong, positive response and evoke effective action. Conversely, virtually the same information can produce a negative response and destroy interest and morale. The difference in response depends on the way in which the information is presented.

Context is an important aspect of this phenomenon. For example, the statement "You are to receive a 10 percent pay raise" would normally evoke a positive response, whereas the extended statement "You are to receive a 10 percent pay raise, but everyone else will get 20 percent" would probably be received in a totally different manner. Contextual data may completely change the message as it is perceived by the recipient. Similarly, the message "Last week, your department had a 2 percent unfavorable materials usage variance" would have a different connotation if the speaker added "and was the lowest in the plant."

Whenever possible, information should be presented in a positive rather than a negative light. The statement

FIGURE 1.5 Information formats communicate standards of quality in the organization.

Bage	NAme	reg	Over	3/31/9
1234	Harold Black	40	0	
2345	Joe Green	35		
3456	Betty Blue	40	5	
4567	Pink, tom	40		
5678	cherly White	40	8	

(a) Poorly designed information formats communicate an expectation of low standards of work.

XYZ Company

Date: 3/31/99   LABOR HOUR SUMMARY   Page 1

Badge No.	Name	Regular Hrs.	Overtime Hrs.
1234	Black, Harold	40	0
2345	Green, Joe	35	0
3456	Blue, Betty	40	5
4567	Pink, Tom	40	0
5678	White, Cheryl	40	8

Form No. 98756

(b) Well-designed formats communicate an expectation of high standards of work.

"We came within 20 percent of achieving our sales quota last year" has more motivational appeal than does "We failed by 20 percent to achieve our sales quota." It is better to say that the cup is half-full than to say that it is half-empty. Accountants often take the view that information is information and that it is not their concern how the recipient responds to it. But that attitude is partly responsible for the human problems in information systems referred to earlier.

Another aspect of successful information presentation is the format in which it is communicated. Figure 1.5 shows two versions of a hypothetical management report, both containing the same data. In the first version, no attempt has been made to design a pleasing format, and there are several mistakes in the legends; possibly the computer program that produced the report was never fully debugged. It conveys the subliminal message "Quality is not important in this organization; any kind of sloppy work is good enough." The second version presents a well-designed report format and conveys a totally different message: "In this organization, high standards of quality are taken for granted; your work is expected to be of a similarly high standard." The need for quality in material sent to customers is readily accepted, but many organizations forget the motivational effect of good information formats when the material is intended for internal consumption. In the long run, creating the right internal image may be as important as is showing the right image to the outside world.

SUMMARY

The purpose of this first chapter has been to provide a general background to the study of information systems and their role in the organization. Business information systems are a dynamic amalgam of people, computers, data, and media, together with the technology or "know-how" to put these components to work.

The role of the information system has progressively increased as businesses have become more complex and have been forced to operate in a more complex economic, political, technological, and social environment. The information system interfaces with most other activities in the modern business, from manufacturing and marketing to office automation. Two vital roles are operational data processing, which satisfies routine, day-to-day data-processing requirements, and decision support, which attempts to satisfy the need for nonroutine input to management decision making. Operational data processing includes the traditional accounting function, and decision support may include some of the more modern aspects of accounting. The two roles do not require separate information systems; rather, they can and should be integrated into a single system accessing a common data base. Decision support information is drawn largely from the data base of accumulated transaction data.

Modern business information systems typically are automated and depend for their effectiveness on the use of computers. But they also depend on people. Individuals and organizational groups are involved in the planning, implementation, maintenance, operation, and use of the information system. Indeed, this involvement extends, directly or indirectly, to virtually everyone in the organization as well as to many people outside it.

People are a vital part of the information system, and so great care must be taken to ensure that the system truly helps rather than hinders their work and properly contributes to the goals of the user organization. Automation of the business information system seeks to support the human content of the system with computer facilities whose processing speed and accuracy characteristics exceed those of their human counterparts. These characteristics combine with the cognitive and judgmental skills of the human elements to provide the potent synergy of modern information systems.

Among the theoretical underpinnings of information systems are general systems theory and the theory of information. General systems theory assists our understanding of the basic concepts underlying business information systems and also helps in the analysis and design of information systems. It lays the conceptual foundation for much of the later material covered in this book.

Information should be regarded as a major resource of the organization. The value of information can be measured both in economic terms and in terms of influence on its recipients. Information is an elusive commodity whose value extends to considerations of surprise or ''newsworthiness.'' But its value also depends strongly on the recipient's perceptions and responses and on the extent to which it influences behavior. The end product of the information system is not data—or even information—but influence over the actions of decision makers. Ultimately, the success of the information system must be evaluated in terms of its support for people and its favorable effects on their decisions.

BIBLIOGRAPHY

Ackoff, Russell L. ''Towards a Systems of Systems Concepts.'' *Management Science*, vol. 17, no. 11, July 1971, pp. 661–671.

Alter, Steven L. *Decision Support Systems: Current Practice and Continuing Challenge*. Reading, Mass.: Addison-Wesley, 1980.

American Accounting Association. ''Report of the Committee on Accounting and Information Systems.'' *The Accounting Review*, vol. 46, supplement, 1971, pp. 287–350.

Churchill, Neil C., and Andrew C. Stedry. ''Extending the Dimensions of Accounting Measurement.'' *Management Services,* April–May 1967, pp. 15–22.

Cleland, David I., and William R. King. *Systems, Organizations, Analysis, Management: A Book of Readings*. New York: McGraw-Hill, 1969.

Davis, James R., and Barry E. Cushing. *Accounting Information Systems: A Book of Readings with Cases*. Reading, Mass.: Addison-Wesley, 1980.

Firmin, Peter A. ''The Potential of Accounting as a Management Information System.'' *Management International Review*, February 1966, pp. 45–55.

Goldman, Stanford. *Information Theory*. New York: Dover, 1953.

Johnson, Richard A. *The Theory and Management of Systems*. New York: McGraw-Hill, 1967.

Keen, P. G. W., and W. S. Scott Morton. *Decision Support Systems*. Reading, Mass.: Addison-Wesley, 1978.

Martin, E. W., Jr. ''The Systems Concept.'' *Business Horizons*, Spring 1966, pp. 63–64.

Riley, M. J. *Management Information Systems*, 2nd ed. San Francisco: Holden-Day, 1981.

Turban, Efraim, and Jack Meredith. *Fundamentals of Management Science*. Dallas: Business Publications, 1981.

DISCUSSION QUESTIONS AND PROBLEMS

1. Define and discuss the following concepts:

- Data •
- Decision support system
- Decision theory
- Feedback
- Control input
- Feedback system
- General systems theory
- Information
- Input
- Open and closed systems
- Output
- Signal input
- Subsystem
- Subsystem structure
- Suprasystem
- Synergy between people and computers
- System

2. Identify and discuss the potential uses of the following types of accounting data in (a) the operational system and (b) the decision support system:

- Employee time-card data
- Product cost data
- Accounts payable data
- Customer purchase order data
- Customer invoice data

3. Discuss the involvement of internal accountants in the information system from the standpoints of

- Their roles as accountants
- Their roles as employees
- Their potential roles as managers in the accounting department
- Their roles as individuals and consumers

4. Why must business systems be regarded as open? Try to envision a closed business system. Discuss the ways in which the following systems interact with their environments:

- A school or university
- General Motors Corporation
- A farm

5. What are the signal inputs and control inputs of

- An automobile
- A sports team
- An airline

6. Identify and list the signal inputs, control inputs, and outputs of

- A laundry
- A bank
- A hospital
- A church

7. Identify the signal inputs, control inputs, and outputs of the following systems. Try to develop as all-embracing a picture as possible. Classify the outputs as "desirable" or "undesirable."

- Your own school or college
- The news media
- The U.S. Army

8. List the control inputs that apply to a large charitable organization, such as United Way. Divide them into objective and constraint control inputs. Identify those controls that help maintain or improve the quality of the output, even when this is achieved at the expense of short-run performance.

9. Identify the various levels of subsystems in your school or college. Is there more than one way in which the system could be analyzed into subsystems? Try to explore as many different types of subsystem structures as you can.

10. Analyze the following systems, identifying their purpose, the environment in which they operate, and their main subsystem structure:

- A manufacturing firm
- A law firm
- The Internal Revenue Service

11. Identify and discuss the purpose, environment, and structure of the following organizational segments or activities in a mail-order business:

- The mail room
- The warehouse
- The accounts receivable department
- The data-processing department

12. Discuss the value of information from the following standpoints:

• Degree of surprise
• Reduction of uncertainty
• Improvement of decision making

13. Discuss ways in which information systems can be made less threatening to those who come in contact with them. Does the responsibility for monitoring and improving the "image" of the system rest with the system's developers, or does it extend to others, including accountants?

14. The accounting function in a medium-sized independent department store had always been performed manually. There were no complaints about its effectiveness, but because of increasing competition from large retail chains and shrinking profit margins, upper management started considering the automation of part of the accounting system. Specifically, a proposal was made to computerize the servicing of the customer revolving credit system, which essentially was an in-house credit card system.

When the controller learned of the proposal she was sharply critical of management's plans. "If you get a computer in here, I will quit my job the same day, and so will most of my people. I have worked for many years to build up a good accounting department. The one thing that has kept this company alive has been the accuracy of our statements, the personal service we provide to our customers, and the understanding we show when the customers are slow in paying their bills. With a computer, we shall be locked into the same impersonal and inflexible billing service that the national credit card people offer. I don't like computers, and I don't trust them; they're always going wrong and making mistakes. I'm not going to be the one who has to tell a customer, 'I'm so sorry, that was a computer error,' My people haven't made a mistake to speak of in five years. Besides, if we have a computer here, we'll be overrun by smooth-talking programmers lording it over us. Let's keep accounting in the hands of the accountants."

Required

Evaluate the controller's criticisms and suggest ways in which top management might try to overcome the resistance to automation in this company.

15. This chapter claims that the value of information, and indeed the value of the information system, depends on its ability to bring about meaningful change or to provoke action by the information's recipients. Evaluate the truth of this claim by examining the following situations involving the receipt of information provided by the accounting system and the likely changes or actions produced:

• Receipt by middle management of an internal report on labor productivity
• Receipt by stockholders of the annual financial statements
• Receipt by a labor union of the external financial statements
• Receipt by a government agency of a regulatory report
• Receipt by the Internal Revenue Service of a corporate tax return

16. The message conveyed by the following statements is clear and could be expected to have a positive motivational effect on the recipients. But additional (not necessarily extraneous) content could profoundly alter the motivational response. Suggest some such additions to the following statements, and discuss the effects they would have:

• "You have completed your work on schedule nine times out of ten."
• "The waste of material in this department has been reduced to 2 percent."
• "Costs are now within 1 percent of our current target."
• "This division's sales have increased by 30 percent over the same period last year."
• "Your travel budget has been increased to $100,000 for next year."

2

Overview of the Accounting Information System

LEARNING OBJECTIVES

After studying this chapter you should be able to

- Discuss the role of the accounting information system.
- Divide the accounting system into transaction cycles and applications.
- Identify the flow of transactions through the accounting system.
- Describe the objectives and methods of transaction coding.
- Discuss the nature and content of the accounting data base.
- Identify the basic activities of the accounting system: input, processing, output, and control.

CHAPTER OUTLINE

**THE ROLE OF THE ACCOUNTING
INFORMATION SYSTEM**

**THE STRUCTURE OF THE ACCOUNTING
INFORMATION SYSTEM**

Transaction Cycles
Accounting Applications
The Flow of Transactions
Integration of the Accounting Applications

THE ACCOUNTING DATA BASE

Information for Multiple Purposes

Transaction Coding
Data Files

THE ACTIVITIES OF INFORMATION PROCESSING

The Input Function
The Processing Function
The Output Function
The Control Function

**SUMMARY
BIBLIOGRAPHY
DISCUSSION QUESTIONS AND PROBLEMS**

THE ROLE OF THE ACCOUNTING INFORMATION SYSTEM

Accounting can be defined as a service function that seeks to provide quantitative information to a user constituency. The accounting information system is the delivery system that makes possible the accomplishment of that service function. As noted in Chapter 1, the accounting system forms part of the larger business information system.

The classical accounting system was concerned almost exclusively with recording and processing financial transaction data and with preparing external financial statements. To the extent that the data might also be of interest to managers, the system played a second role, that of management support; but this second role was considered incidental and peripheral. Today, the situation is quite different. The accounting function in most organizations is now heavily oriented toward management support, and a great volume of information is directed specifically to internal users. This information is intended to help in planning and controlling the enterprise, in evaluating individuals and groups within the enterprise, and in solving business problems. External

reporting in its various forms is still a crucial function; indeed, it has become a progressively larger one as a result of increasing government regulation. But it occupies a much smaller proportion of the total accounting effort.

To accommodate these broader functions, the accounting system has moved away from an exclusive focus on financial transaction data to embrace data from other sources and data measured in nonmonetary terms. Today, accounting systems commonly accept inputs from a variety of sources, from both inside and outside the enterprise. They also deal with labor hours, units of production, ratios, percentage changes, and other statistics, in addition to data in traditional dollar terms. Much analysis may be performed on the data before the output is delivered to its recipients, and it may be delivered in media and through channels other than the traditional paper report characteristic of classical accounting. A manager may, for instance, retrieve data on a screen or may request data on a floppy diskette for further analysis on a personal computer. Even some types of external reporting to agencies, including the Securities and Exchange Commission and the Internal Revenue Service, can now be accomplished electronically.

20

The expanded role of accounting and the increasing role of automated information-processing technologies have led to difficulties in properly defining the boundaries of either accounting or the accounting information system. Several activities, including decision support, operations research, modeling, information management, and planning and implementation of information systems, are ''gray areas'' in which the responsibilities of accountants may overlap those of other professionals. Commentators differ in their assessment of whether or not these areas lie within the proper boundaries of the accounting discipline.

However, for many years, leaders of the accounting profession have taken a broad view of the function of accounting. For example, in 1969 a committee of the American Accounting Association expressed its support for accounting involvement in such decision support areas as modeling and forecasting. And in 1971, another committee of the association included the design and management of accounting systems in a list of the accountant's principal and ''traditional'' responsibilities. The 1971 committee also expressed the following opinion:

The Committee believes that accounting in the broad sense of the term can and should rise to the challenge and opportunities of the developing information technologies and take the lead in information management. In the narrowest sense of the term, the accountant is only a part of the organization's formal information system and hence is both a user of information and a part of the operating and design group concerned with information as a whole.[1]

As technology continues to advance and as the demands for information from managers and others increase, there will no doubt be further pressures to redefine the boundaries of accounting. Accounting is not a static profession, and accountants must be able to adopt new methods and new modes of thinking as the need arises. A major purpose of this book is to help emerging members (and present members) of the accounting profession acquire the skills necessary to fulfill their responsibilities in the

[1] American Accounting Association, ''Report of the Committee on Accounting and Information Systems,'' *The Accounting Review* 46 (supplement) (1971): 344.

provision, management, use, and control of business information in an expanding business environment.

THE STRUCTURE OF THE ACCOUNTING INFORMATION SYSTEM

Accounting systems are established to serve the needs of both their host organizations and external parties to which the organizations may be obliged to report. There are almost as many types of accounting systems as there are organizations. Analysis of the accounting system is complicated by these nonuniformities as much as by the complexity of the accounting systems themselves. A subsystem existing in one accounting system may have no counterpart in another. For example, service organizations normally have no inventory; merchandising organizations have no production operations; nonprofit institutions have no owners; and so forth.

Transaction Cycles

In the face of these difficulties of complexity and diversity, several attempts have been made to simplify the understanding of accounting systems and to establish a common framework to unify the essential elements of different systems. One of the most successful of these attempts produced the notion of *transaction cycles*. The term *cycle* denotes something that repeats itself over and over again. In one sense, all business operations can be regarded as cycles; money is invested in the enterprise and finances various activities that in turn generate more money. But more specifically, the transaction cycles are identified with broadly defined components of the accounting system. The transaction cycles are normally associated with the operational aspects of the accounting system (it is possible, although more difficult, to identify them with the decision support aspects). The six cycles are (Figure 2.1):

1. The purchasing, procurement, acquisition, or expenditure cycle
2. The production or conversion cycle
3. The revenue cycle
4. The planning/control cycle
5. The reporting cycle
6. The investment, financial, or treasury cycle

FIGURE 2.1   Transaction cycles within the accounting information system. The purchasing, production, and revenue cycles are collectively referred to as the *operating cycles*.

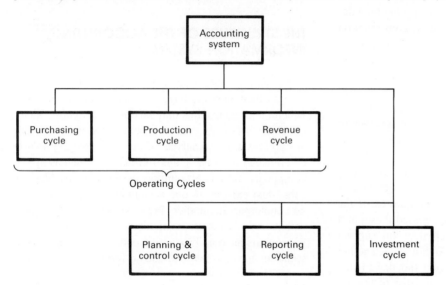

The first three are collectively referred to as the *operating cycles* because of their close association with the enterprise's operations. The other three play a supporting role.[2]

The purchasing cycle, sometimes referred to as the procurement, acquisition, or expenditure cycle, refers to the acquisition from external parties of resources in the form of goods and services and the disbursement of funds in exchange for those resources. It includes the function of purchasing in the narrower and more conventional sense of the word but extends to a wider range of "purchasing" activities, such as the personnel and payroll functions. The production cycle, sometimes called the conversion cycle, refers to the accumulation, use, and transformation of resources. It includes the functions of production control and inventory management as well as cost accounting. The conversion or transformation of resources can be seen most clearly in manufacturing or construction companies. But the management of inventories is of obvious concern to merchandising organizations, and cost accounting is of concern to service organizations ranging from automobile

repair shops to banks. The revenue cycle pertains to the distribution of resources to the customers and others and the collection of revenues earned from those distributed resources. The revenue cycle includes the functions of shipping, sales, and accounts receivable (including billing and collection) as well as such activities as screening credit applicants.

The planning and control cycle is somewhat different from the others insofar as it does not directly involve transactions; rather, its effect is to determine what transactions will take place in the other cycles and how they will be handled and controlled. Planning activities include both long-term and short-term planning. A large part of the short-term planning activities centers on the preparation of the annual budget; the subsequent tracking of the budget is the corresponding control activity. In manufacturing firms the establishment of cost standards may form part of the activities of this cycle. The implementation and maintenance of internal controls are major components of the planning and control cycle. The reporting cycle refers primarily to external financial, tax, and regulatory reporting. The preparation of company-wide internal reporting, such as in a responsibility accounting system, can also be regarded as part of the reporting cycle. The preparation of other types of internal reports, particularly those closely related to one or

---

[2] For a good account of transaction cycles, see Arthur Andersen & Co., *A Guide for Studying and Evaluating Internal Accounting Controls*. Publ. No. 2880, Item 1 (Chicago: Arthur Andersen & Co., January 1978).

other of the operating cycles, can more conveniently be regarded as part of the cycle with which they are associated. The investment, financial, or treasury cycle has to do with the acquisition of capital resources from owners and creditors and with the custody of those resources. It includes the management of cash, working capital, investment portfolios, pension funds, fixed assets, and other types of assets. The investment cycle also includes debt management and equity financing.

Accounting Applications

The transaction cycles comprise the first- or highest-level subsystems of the accounting information system.

The second-level subsystems take the form of the accounting *applications*. But whereas the cycles were defined in general terms, so as to have the broadest possible relevance, the applications are defined more narrowly and may have relevance in only certain types of enterprise. The principal applications, classified according to their relationship to the transaction cycles, are as follows (Figure 2.2):

I. *Applications Within the Purchasing Cycle*
   A. *Purchasing* deals with the issuance of purchase orders for the procurement of raw materials or merchandise inventory; it may also extend to the procurement of services from vendors and to the placement of subcontracts.

FIGURE 2.2   The accounting applications and their relationships to the transaction cycles.

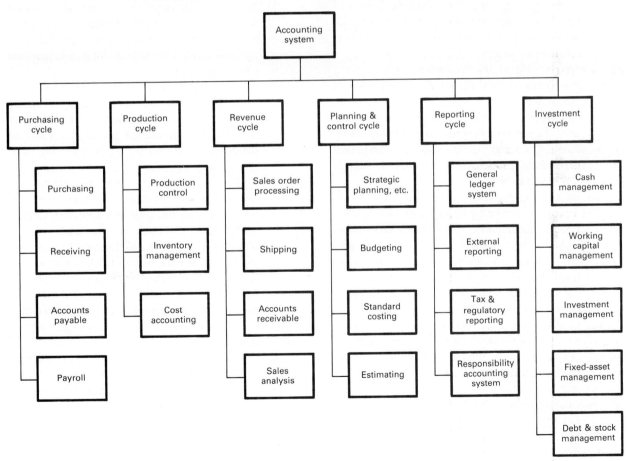

B. *Receiving* refers to the inspection and acceptance of goods delivered to the organization from outside vendors. It includes the recording of the receipt of the goods, and the disposition of the goods within the enterprise.

C. *Accounts payable* is concerned with the payment for goods and services procured from outside vendors. It involves the processing of invoices received from vendors, the maintenance of records of the associated liabilities, and the preparation for the disbursement of cash.

D. *Payroll* refers to the payment of wages and salaries, and sometimes sales commissions, to employees of the company and to the related withholding of taxes and other deductions. It involves the custody and disposition of liabilities arising from amounts withheld from employee earnings. It also involves the deposit of tax withholdings and the reporting of withholding data to the relevant federal, state, and local revenue authorities.

II. *Applications Within the Production Cycle*

A. *Production control* deals with the initiation of production orders within the factory and with the tracking and control of production operations. In addition, the preparation of bills of materials, labor and machine schedules, and product routing through the factory all are part of this application.

B. *Inventory management* (or *inventory control*) refers to the accounting for raw materials, finished goods, merchandise, and supplies inventories, including the maintenance of perpetual inventory records. Inventory control extends to the regulation of stock levels to provide for consistent supply while avoiding the extremes of stockouts or excessive inventory levels.

C. *Cost accounting* is concerned with the accumulation of product costs in a manufacturing organization. It includes the monitoring of work-in-process inventories and may interface with a standard cost system.

III. *Applications Within the Revenue Cycle*

A. *Sales order processing* is concerned with the processing of orders received from customers for goods or services provided by the organi-

zation. It may include the establishment of credit terms, the recording of sales tax data, and the determination of sales representatives' commissions.

B. *Shipping* is the location and retrieval of products from merchandise or finished goods warehouses and the preparation of the goods and accompanying paperwork for shipment. It may extend to the identification of appropriate modes of shipment and negotiation with common carriers.

C. *Accounts receivable* is concerned with the preparation of customer invoices and periodic customer statements. It includes the maintenance of records of customer indebtedness and collection activities. Accounts receivable is sometimes divided into two applications: billing and collection.

D. *Sales analysis* is primarily a decision support activity dealing with the routine or nonroutine analysis of historical sales data to provide management with information for marketing and similar purposes.

IV. *Applications Within the Planning and Control Cycle*

A. *Strategic, tactical, and operational planning* are the establishment of long-term goals and objectives for the organization at every level and the determination of the means of achieving those goals and objectives.

B. *Budgeting*, including budget preparation and budget tracking, represents the primary vehicle for short-term financial planning and control. The budget expresses the financial goals to which management commits itself for the coming period. It must be consistent within its own time period with the longer-term strategic, tactical, and operational planning. Tracking the budget, that is, comparing budget and actual costs and revenues, forms a strong basis for management control.

C. *Standard costing* is closely allied with the budgeting system. Standards are established as part of the budget preparation exercise for materials, labor, and overhead costs of production. Determination of variances from the standards and analysis of these variances both run parallel to the process of budget tracking.

D. *Estimating* refers to the process of predicting the costs of manufacturing custom goods or providing nonstandard services. The usual purpose is to determine bid prices.

V. *Applications Within the Reporting Cycle*

A. *General ledger system* provides for the traditional accumulation and processing of accounting transactions and the preparation of the trial balance. This application includes the maintenance of the various journals as well as the general ledger itself. Journal entries may be made directly into the general ledger system or may be transferred from other applications such as accounts receivable. Adjusting and reversing entries may be generated internally.

B. *External reporting* involves preparation of the customary external financial statements, including the balance sheet, income statement, statement of cost of goods manufactured, statement of retained earnings, and statement of changes in financial position. Frequently the external reporting application is combined with the general ledger system.

C. *Tax and regulatory reporting* is concerned with complying with statutory obligations to report to the relevant revenue and regulatory bodies at federal, state, and local levels. Deposits of various tax payments may also be involved.

D. *Responsibility accounting system* is a system of internal reporting tailored to the authority and responsibilities of the reports' recipients. Emphasis is on those items of revenue and expense that the recipients can control and for which they are held responsible. Responsibility accounting reports frequently contain budget comparisons.

VI. *Applications Within the Investment Cycle*

A. *Cash management* is the short-term control of cash to minimize cash balances while providing for coverage of the enterprise's obligations. Cash management is normally integrated with control of marketable securities and other short-term investment instruments.

B. *Working capital management* is related to cash management but is concerned with the various components of working capital, including cash, accounts and notes receivable, prepaid expenses, inventory, accounts and notes payable, and accrued expenses. This application interfaces with applications in several other transaction cycles.

C. *Management of long-term investments* is the management of investment portfolios maintained for various purposes. In-house pension funds may comprise a large portion of the portfolios.

D. *Fixed-asset management* deals with the keeping of records relating to the valuation, custody, physical maintenance, and eventual disposal of productive assets: property, plant, and equipment. It may extend to similar activities relating to natural resources.

E. *Management of long-term debt and capital stock* is the issuance and retirement of bond and stock instruments; issuance and redemption of options, warrants, and stock rights; payment of interest and dividends; management of treasury stock accounts; and maintenance of the bondholders' and stockholders' ledgers.

The Flow of Transactions

The recording of transactions forms a major part of operational data processing. Transactions are the basic quanta of business operations. To understand the working of an accounting system, it is necessary to have a working knowledge of how transactions are created and flow through the accounting system. The steps in the flow of transactions are independent of the processing methodology and therefore are essentially the same in both manual and automated systems.

The process starts with the occurrence of economic events, either inside or outside the organization. Some events are initiated by personnel in the organization: purchase agents, production managers, salespersons, employees at large, and the like, acting within the framework of authority established by management. Occasionally an event may be initiated outside this framework of authority, in which case it is regarded as an irregularity. In modern accounting systems, events may be initiated by a computer in accordance with programmed instructions. Other events are triggered by outside bodies such as taxation or regulatory agencies. Still others are associated with the passage of time, such as depreciation or accrual of interest.

In every case the event must first be recognized, which can be done by one of several methods, including observation, notification, agreement, or judgment. Upon recognition, the event is captured on a paper source document or some other medium and may be keyed into a computer. It is quantified—traditionally as a dollar amount—and must also be classified in order to relate it to some account entity that can serve as a focus for subsequent processing. Thus a transaction involving cash is related to the cash account, and one involving a particular customer is related to the appropriate customer account in the subsidiary ledger. The chart of accounts and the subsidiary ledgers provide the usual basis for transaction classification.

Transactions may be accumulated in batches and stored for processing all at one time. This type of processing is referred to as *batch processing*. Alternatively, transactions may be processed immediately upon entry into the system. This type of processing is called *real-time*, or *event-driven*, processing. The processed data may also be stored for future use. The raw transaction data and the partially or completely processed data comprise the accounting data base. From the data base, a transaction may be retrieved as needed for further processing, for reporting purposes, or possibly to answer a decision support query.

The transaction may be reported individually, or it may contribute to aggregate, or summary, information, such as an account balance. Individual transactions may be reported to customers, vendors, or employees; for example, an invoice reports a particular sale made to that customer. Aggregate transaction data provide the basis for preparing the financial statements and reports addressed to groups such as the stockholders, the government, or management; most reporting is of this type.

FIGURE 2.3   Integration of typical subsystems in an accounting information system.

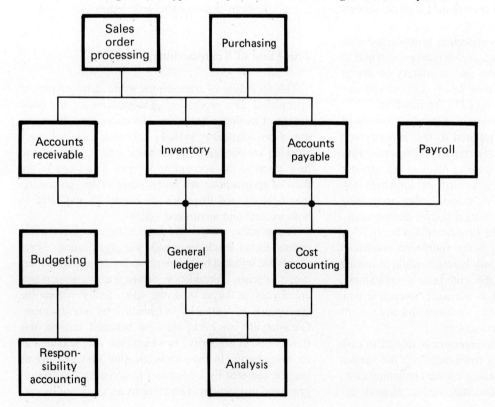

The transaction's final resting place is ordinarily some form of archive file. In such a file the transaction awaits its eventual destruction at a time governed by the company's record retention policies or by applicable legal requirements.

The flow of transactions from their point of origin to their final destination must be clearly understood by the developers and managers of the accounting information system and by those persons whose job it is to ensure that the system is performing satisfactorily. In the latter category are the internal and external auditors. The path of transactions through the system, evidenced by printed output or equivalent electronic means, is referred to as an *audit trail*.

Integration of the Accounting Applications

The accounting applications are not stand-alone subsystems. Rather, they are highly integrated with one another, sharing data and transferring data from one to another. Figure 2.3 shows the relationships among some of the applications. Sales order transactions originate in the sales order processing application, and the transaction data subsequently are transferred to accounts receivable and inventory. The purchase of materials and services originates in the purchasing application, and purchase transaction data subsequently flow to inventory and accounts payable. Accounts receivable, inventory, accounts payable, and payroll provide input data to the general ledger and possibly to cost accounting. The responsibility accounting and budgeting applications are related to the general ledger application. Finally, data analysis, providing decision support information, may interface with general ledger and cost accounting.

The relationship between the general ledger application and the other accounting applications is a strong one. The principal file in the general ledger application is the chart of accounts which involves the five major classifications of accounts: assets, liabilities, owners' equity, expense, and revenue. Three applications—accounts receivable, inventory, and accounts payable—are particularly closely related to the general ledger system because of their position in the chart of accounts. Indeed, their files form special journals and subsidiary ledgers.

FIGURE 2.4   The major accounting applications and their relationship to the general ledger.

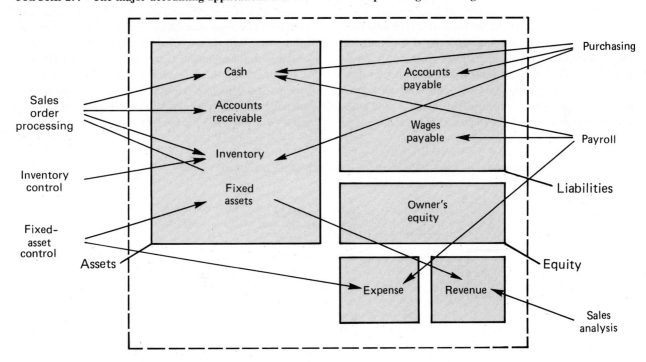

Several of the other applications interface either with these three applications or with other accounts within the general ledger (Figure 2.4).

THE ACCOUNTING DATA BASE

Information for Multiple Purposes

The accounting data base contains numbers (dollar amounts, quantities, and labor hours), account codes, dates, narrative or textual data (names, addresses, product descriptions, explanations, instructions, and so forth), and many other types of data. The data base provides for timing differences among input, processing, communication, and output of data. Inputs originating from different points in the system and entered at different times can be accumulated and combined to produce types of output that would not otherwise be possible.

The accounting data base supports both the operational and the decision support functions (Figure 2.5). As already noted, data find their way into the data base—primarily via the operational data-processing system—as a result of the routine capture of transactions. Information can subsequently be retrieved from the data base as needed to satisfy the requirements of the system's users. In the case of the operational function, retrieval is routine. What data are needed and the form, or *configuration*, in which they must be delivered are known in advance and can be planned. In the case of the decision support function, the requests are nonroutine, and

their specific nature may be difficult or impossible to plan; they will depend on what management needs at the time. The data base must be maintained in a state of readiness, and the system must be ready to respond to the requests as and when they are made.

In order to provide for the various kinds of requests for information, the data must be stored in meaningful structures. The traditional and still most common data structure is the data file. Files consist of collections of records, each of which may contain several data elements. For example, an employee file typically consists of a collection of records, one for each employee; in turn, each record might contain the employee's name, social security number, pay rate, and year-to-date earnings. Conventional files are stored in the configurations in which the data will later be retrieved.

As an alternative to storing information in the configuration in which it will ultimately be needed, provision can be made—as in data base management systems—to assemble the individual elements of data into the required configuration at retrieval time. Prior to retrieval the data elements may be in some other form, perhaps one that better matches the characteristics of the physical storage medium. Because of their capability for real-time assembly of data configurations, data base management systems offer more flexibility to respond to a variety of information requests, including unexpected ones associated with management's decision support activities.

In either case the data must be labeled to provide for prompt and effective retrieval for whatever purpose is intended. A properly coded time-card entry can supply input to a paycheck, a product cost, a financial state-

FIGURE 2.5 The accounting data base. The data base supports both the operational and the decision support functions.

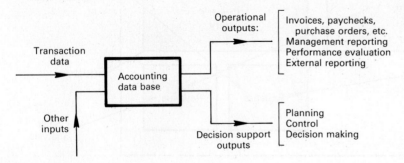

ment, a management report, or an on-line query. Retrieval of information from a data base of labeled data elements is limited only by the flexibility of the retrieval system and the imagination of the users. Data elements are labeled in the first instance through transaction coding. Subsequently, new labels may be assigned as data are extracted, processed into other forms, and returned to the data base.

Transaction Coding

Transactions are coded in order to classify them for subsequent processing. Codes also "tag" the transaction during processing and help preserve the audit trail. The chart of accounts provides the principal method of classification or coding. Figure 2.6 is a typical chart of accounts, including a coding system for the accounts. The first digit denotes the primary account classification: 1 = assets, 2 = liabilities, and so forth; and the second digit denotes the secondary classification: 11 = current assets, 12 = property, plant, and equipment; and so forth. Additional digits can be given specific meanings as desired. Account numbers from four to six digits are commonly used to provide coding flexibility and to accommodate variations of account density within the classifications, even though most of the available numbers

FIGURE 2.6 Sample chart of accounts with account numbers. The first two digits in the account numbers are used for coding purposes.

	Assets			Revenue
1110	Cash		4110	Sale of goods
1120	Marketable securities		4115	Returns and allowances
1130	Accounts receivable		4210	Sale of services
1135	Allowance for bad debts		4310	Other income
1140	Inventory			Expense
1150	Prepaid expense		5110	Cost of goods sold
1210	Equipment		5210	Wages and salaries
1215	Accum. deprec. - eqpt.		5220	Payroll expense
1220	Buildings		5230	Travel
1225	Accum. deprec. - bldg.		5240	Transportation
1230	Land		5250	Entertainment
1310	Intangibles		5260	Advertising
1410	Other assets		5310	Rent
	Liabilities		5320	Utilities
2110	Accounts payable		5340	Telephone
2120	Notes payable (short term)		5350	Supplies
2130	Accrued liabilities		5360	General administration
2140	Wages payble		5410	Interest expense
2150	Taxes payable		5420	Taxes
2160	Current portion of long-term debt		5430	Depreciation expense
2210	Notes payable (long term)		5440	Amortization expense
2220	Bond payable		5450	Miscellaneous expense
2225	Discount on bonds payable			
	Stockholders' Equity			
3110	Common stock			
3115	Premium of common stock			
3120	Other contributed capital			
3210	Current earnings			
3220	Retained earnings			

are never used. Sometimes, account number extensions are used to represent the organizational segment or responsibility center from which the transaction originated. For example, the account numbers 5350.35 and 5350.49 might represent supplies consumed by departments 35 and 49, respectively. Responsibility accounting systems frequently employ a comprehensive coding system for tracking transactions, possibly based on a hierarchical scheme such as illustrated in Figure 2.7. In such a system, the retrieval of all transactions of a given type, relating, say, to a particular branch, department, or team within the organization, is straightforward.

Individual transactions are often identified by a source code and reference number. The source code refers to the source—often the special journal—from which the transaction originated. For example, all entries in the general journal might be coded GJ, and those in the cash disbursement journal might be coded CD. The reference number provides a unique identifier for the given source code. The reference number is sometimes chosen to be the same as the number on the corresponding source document, for example, the check number.

Other types of coding systems refer to inventory items, customers, vendors, production jobs, employees, or similar entities. Composite code numbers may be used to represent several pieces of information. For example, an inventory part number might have the following structure:

12986 — A13 — VIN

item   bin   vendor
number

FIGURE 2.7 **Hierarchical coding system for a responsibility accounting system.**

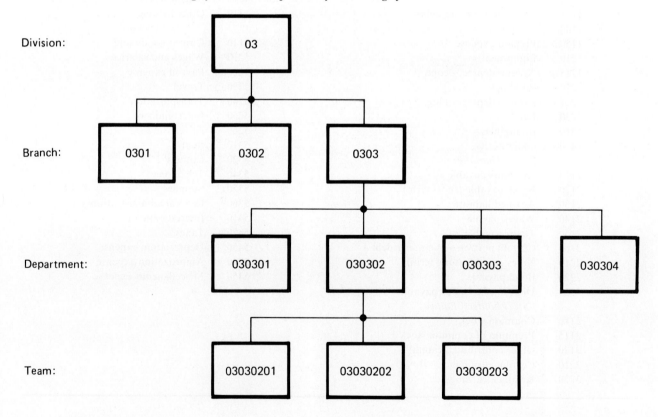

Similarly, an employee number might be structured as follows:

```
            01      02      34971
            /       |        \
       division  salaried  employee
```

The component parts of the number may or may not be separated by spaces, hyphens, or other delimiters. Such composite numbers provide a useful basis for identification and analysis of transaction data.

A variation on the structuring of inventory part numbers provides a system for identifying the components in a bill-of-materials explosion. The bill of materials lists the raw materials and other items required to assemble a particular manufactured product. Suppose, for example, that there are three levels of components: raw materials, subassemblies, and finished products. These three levels can be represented by the three segments of a composite inventory number. Thus, part number 36-01-03 might represent a raw material required for subassembly number 36-01-00, which, in turn, would form part of finished product number 36-00-00 (or sim-

ply 36). This kind of coding scheme is illustrated in Figure 2.8.

Data Files

The concept of the data file is a powerful one. Even in data base management systems, users may still validly think of the data as being stored in files; files provide models of the stored data, regardless of the data's actual physical arrangement.

Data files used in accounting systems (as well as other types of business information systems) are of two main types: transaction files and master files. Transaction files correspond to the paper journals or registers in manual accounting systems. *Transaction file* is simply the generic term for a journal. A set of transaction files is established to suit the major types of transactions in the system: general journal transactions, purchases, payments, sales, collections, employee hours and earnings, inventory receipts and issuances, and so forth.

Transaction files capture, or "journalize," detailed transaction data, usually in chronological order, providing a kind of diary of the organization's financial activ-

FIGURE 2.8 Inventory part numbers coded for a bill-of-materials explosion.

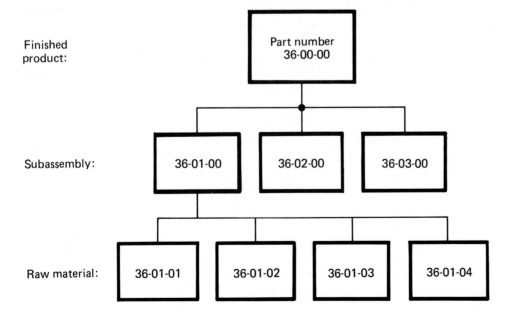

FIGURE 2.9 Sample entries in a general journal. The account numbers correspond to the chart of accounts shown in Figure 2.1.

GENERAL JOURNAL

Date	Source/Ref.	Narrative	Acct.	Amount Debit	Amount Credit
7/31/99	GJ/8207311	Depreciation on equipment	5430	520.00	
			1215		520.00
7/31/99	GJ/8207312	Depreciation on buildings	5430	985.00	
			1225		985.00
7/31/99	GJ/8207313	Expiration of prepayments	5360	32.50	
			1150		32.50
7/31/99	GJ/8207314	Amortization of bond discount	5410	123.00	
			2225		123.00

ities. In manual systems, the transaction files usually take the form of paper journals. Figures 2.9 and 2.10 show examples of a general journal and a special journal. In computerized systems the transaction files are more commonly maintained on a machine-readable medium such as magnetic disk or magnetic tape. However, their content corresponds closely to the content of paper journals. Typical components of the records in a transaction file are the transaction date, one or more amounts, and a reference to some entity such as an account, a customer, a vendor, an employee, or an inventory item. Useful additional information is an explanation and some unique identifier for the transaction, such as the source code and reference number mentioned earlier.

Master files correspond to the general ledger and subsidiary ledgers in traditional accounting systems. The records in master files normally refer to such entities as accounts, customers, vendors, employees, inventory items, jobs in progress in the factory, and unfilled purchase or sales orders. Each record typically contains a number and name, a dollar balance, and various supporting data relevant to the particular type of entity involved. The records in inventory files usually contain the quantity on hand as well as the dollar balance. Those in customer files may contain not just the outstanding balance but also a division of the balance into several age categories: current, 30 days overdue, 60 days overdue, and so forth. Records in employee files usually contain pay rate, marital status, number of dependents, and year-to-date earnings and withholding data.

The sum of the dollar balances in the master file may correspond to the control balance in one of the accounts in the general ledger. For instance, the sum of the balances in the customer file—which are the amounts owed by each customer—is equal to the accounts receivable control balance. A control balance is one supported by a detailed breakdown in a subsidiary ledger. Other relationships of this type are as follows:

Master File	*Interpretation of Individual Balances*	*Interpretation of Balance Total*
Inventory file	Dollar equivalent of each item on hand	Inventory control balance
Vendor file	Amounts owed to each vendor	Accounts payable control balance
Employee file	Accrued wages and benefits owed to each employee	Wages payable control and other payroll liabilities

FIGURE 2.10 Sample cash disbursements journal. The transaction reference is a composite of the voucher number and the check number.

CASH DISBURSEMENTS JOURNAL

Date	Sce / Vch / Chk	Name of Payee	Cash Credit	Discount Credit	Acc. Pay. Debit	Misc. Acct.	Amount
9/1/99	CD / 1234 / 531	J. G. Brown, Co.	2,329.00		2,329.00		
9/1/99	CD / 1237 / 532	Orange Associates	513.50			2120	513.50
9/2/99	CD / 1238 / 533	Bright Red Corporation	1,778.25	55.00	1,833.25		
9/2/99	CD / 1240 / 534	Pitch Black Bros.	31.00		31.00		
9/2/99	CD / 1235 / 535	White, Inc.	1,176.00	24.00	1,200.00		
9/3/99	CD / 1236 / 536	Green County Rev. Dept.	830.00			2150	830.00
9/4/99	CD / 1241 / 537	Sky Blue, Inc.	536.75		536.75		
9/4/99	CD / 1242 / 538	H. F. Pink Company	5,445.00	55.00	5,500.00		
9/5/99	CD / 1244 / 539	Magenta Trucking Co.	1,234.80	25.20	1,260.00		

These relationships confirm the earlier comment that the master files in question are, in effect, subsidiary ledgers of the general ledger application. These master files serve as the connecting links between the general ledger application and other accounting applications.

THE ACTIVITIES OF INFORMATION PROCESSING

The Input Function

The input function is one of the two principal interfaces between the users and the information system. Data are captured and fed into the system for subsequent processing. In traditional systems, data are captured in the form of *source documents*. Documents are items of paperwork (or sometimes other media) that provide the permanent or semipermanent record of single transactions or small groups of transactions that are processed as a unit. Documents can be classified either as source, or input, documents or as output documents. A source document records the initiation of a transaction and enters new data into the information system. Time cards, work orders, receiving tickets, customer purchase orders, invoices from suppliers, and expense claims all are examples of source documents.

In manual systems, transaction data from the source documents are usually copied into journals for subsequent processing. The data remain in human-readable form throughout the processing operations. But in computerized systems the data must ordinarily be transcribed, or encoded, into machine-readable form before processing can commence. Data entry clerks key the data from the source documents into a keyboard that is connected either directly to the computer or to a separate data preparation device that prepares an intermediate, machine-readable medium to be read later by the computer.

Keying of the input data is particularly vulnerable to errors. One of the most common errors is a transposition error in which two digits in a number are inadvertently interchanged; thus 12345 might be keyed in as 12435. Accordingly, the keyed data must be verified to ensure (to the extent possible) that erroneous data will not be processed into erroneous output. Such data may be verified by edit programs, by visual checking, or by a combination of both. In batch systems, an edit program is often run after the whole batch of transactions has been keyed in. The edit program generates an *edit listing* that identifies obvious errors, omissions, duplications, and other kinds of invalid data that the computer is programmed to recognize. It may also provide a human-readable listing of the input transactions that can be com-

FIGURE 2.11 **Verification of input data in a batch system.** The edit program screens the keyed data for validity, according to predetermined criteria, and produces the edit listing indicating possible problems. The edit listing is compared with the original source documents, and invalid data are rekeyed.

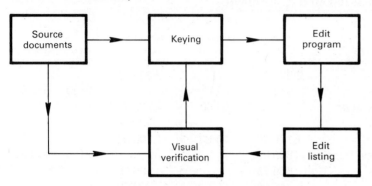

pared visually with the source documents (Figure 2.11). The errors can then be corrected and rekeyed. When the batch of transactions has been verified, it is available for processing.

In real-time systems, in which transactions are processed immediately upon entry, verification must be performed by the computer alone at the point of entry. Programmed controls will screen each element of data as it is entered and will reject the element and display a diagnostic message if the data element fails to ''pass'' certain tests of acceptability. Correction and reentry can be done at once.

In modern systems it is becoming increasingly common to bypass source documents and capture the transaction data directly in machine-readable form. Examples of direct transaction capture include electronic time clocks, electronic point-of-sale registers, and automatic bank teller machines. Alternatively, scanning devices can sometimes be used to read printed (or even hand-written) data on source documents. Optical pattern recognition systems, which make this type of operation possible, are still in their infancy but have improved greatly in reliability over the last several years.

The direct capture of data eliminates the task of manual transcription, saving time, effort, and cost, and greatly reduces the risk of errors. On the other hand, even with direct data capture, some degree of human contact with the data is desirable. Owing to a system malfunction or possibly some type of irregularity, the electronic record may not be correct, and in the absence

of human screening, the erroneous record may pass undetected through programmed edit checks and be processed.

The Processing Function

Data are processed in a variety of forms, with some of the most common as follows. More complex forms of processing may be built up from combinations of these basic forms.

- *Classification*, or the separation of data into categories. Transactions are usually classified according to the accounting application to which they relate. For example, inventory transaction data may be classified into receipts, issuances, and backorders. General ledger accounts are classified into balance sheet and income statement accounts. Classification is usually indicated by transaction coding.
- *Comparison* of two data elements to determine whether they are similar or whether one is in some sense larger than the other. A comparison is made when the name of a prospective customer is checked against a list of individuals or firms to whom credit terms have been extended. A comparison is also made when a check is made to determine whether an employee's year-to-date earnings are high enough to have reached the FICA tax ceiling.
- *Sorting*, or the ordering of lists of data elements. Sorting is arranging lists of data elements into meaningful

sequences, usually in either ascending or descending order of an appropriate attribute of the data, or *key*. A chronological file is one whose component records are sorted by date. Vendor files may be sorted in alphabetical order of the vendor names, or in ascending order of the corresponding vendor numbers.

• *Merging* of ordered lists of data elements. Merging is combining two (or more) lists of data elements, each of which is already sorted in a similar manner, to provide a single ordered list. Two inventory files, each prepared by a regional warehouse and each sorted by part number, might, for instance, be combined into a single companywide inventory file, also sorted by part number.

• *Summarization*, or the aggregation of data. Summarization is adding together a list of numbers to produce a total that represents the overall characteristics of the original list. For example, the amounts of cash disbursements recorded in the cash disbursements journal might be added together to produce a daily summary total. A file of daily summary totals might then be maintained separate from the detail journal containing the original transactions.

• *Posting*, or the process in which transaction data are used to update the balances in the master file or ledger records. For example, cash receipt and cash disbursement amounts are posted to the cash account in the general ledger to produce an updated cash balance. The new cash balance is equal to the original balance, plus the cash receipts and less the cash disbursements. The process is illustrated in Figure 2.12. Posting is one of the most common data-processing activities, playing a central role in most of the accounting applications.

In traditional batch systems, the transactions are accumulated in batches for periodic posting, once per day, week, month, or quarter, or even once per year. The balances in the master file are correct immediately after posting, but at other times they are "out of date." However, in real-time systems, posting is performed immediately upon data entry, and consequently the balances are essentially current at all times. Real-time processing has great advantages in situations in which data currency must be preserved in the master files.

• *Calculation*, or computation, is a process involving the mathematical manipulation of numbers. A very simple example is the multiplication of a unit cost by a quantity to provide the extended cost. More complex examples may be the determination of payroll withholdings, purchase or sales discounts, and sales commissions. Some quantitative models, which are used in decision support applications, involve large numbers of complex calculations.

• *Analysis* is a general type of processing commonly involving the extraction of information from a body of data in order to meet a particular need. Analysis may be either routine or nonroutine. A routine analysis of

FIGURE 2.12 Illustration of the posting process. In this manual system the transactions are transferred to the general ledger as a basis for updating the ledger balance. In an automated system, the ledger balance would be updated, but the transactions themselves would probably not be transferred to the ledger.

GENERAL JOURNAL

Date	Account	Debit	Credit
1/2/99	Cash	5,000	
	Sales		5,000
1/3/99	Inventory	2,000	
	Cash		2,000
1/4/99	Wages Expense	4,000	
	Cash		4,000

GENERAL LEDGER
Ledger Account : Cash

Date	Debit	Credit
Beg. balance	15,000	
1/2/99	5,000	
1/3/99		2,000
1/4/99		4,000
	20,000	6,000
End. balance	14,000	

sales transactions might be performed in order to provide data for marketing purposes. A nonroutine analysis, possibly arising in a decision support application, might be performed in order to prepare a list of all customers with balances over 90 days old, whose names lie in the range A through G and who have made year-to-date purchases of less than $100,000. Analysis is also used extensively by auditors. During an engagement, for example, an auditor might wish to analyze transaction records to identify all transactions that involve a selected sample of inventory items and relate them to reported changes in the corresponding on-hand balances. Or an auditor might analyze transaction data to determine how often time cards were processed containing claims for more than 50 hours' work in a single workweek. In the auditing context, this type of analysis is referred to as the *analytical review*.

Processing can be performed manually or by a computer. In either case, instructions must be provided to ensure that the data are processed correctly. In manual systems the instructions take the form of clerical procedures to be followed by the accounting clerks. The procedures typically refer to specific tasks, telling the clerks what to do and how to do it. The procedures also may refer to such tasks as entering transaction data into journals, posting journal data to ledgers, using worksheets, and preparing financial statements and other reports. Other procedures might pertain to processing the payroll, preparing invoices and payables vouchers, or reconciling bank statements. An example of a simple clerical procedure is shown in Figure 2.13.

Some manual accounting systems are designed as *one-write* systems. In such systems, the various items of paperwork—journals, ledgers, documents, and so forth—are placed one above the other, with interleaving carbons. Each transaction is recorded simultaneously on all of them by means of a single entry (Figure 2.14), thereby achieving a rare kind of "real-time" manual processing. One-write systems avoid the need for duplication of data entry and realize substantial gains in efficiency and—more important—accuracy.

In computer-based systems, processing instructions take the form of applications software, or applications programs. Programs intended to perform specific types of processing related to payroll, accounts receivable, and

FIGURE 2.13 **A simple clerical procedure for the journalization of credit sales transactions.**

Procedure: Journalization of credit sales transactions

Personnel: Accounting clerks

Related paperwork: Sales order forms, sales journal

General description: Credit sales transactions must be entered into the sales journal in chronological order. Each entry must be on a new line. Data to be recorded in the journal include the date, customer name, sales order number, amount of sale, and terms. Amounts are to be totaled for each page of the journal.

Detailed instructions:
1. Enter date in column 1.
2. Enter customer name in column 2.
3. Enter sales order in column 3.
4. Enter amount of sale in column 4.
5. Enter terms in column 5.
6. When the page is full, add up the amounts for that page and enter the total in column 4.

other applications are written in a programming language. A popular programming language for business purposes is COBOL, and a portion of such a program might contain the following:

```
WRITE-HEADINGS
    ADD 1 TO WS-PAGE-COUNT
        GIVING WS-PAGE-COUNT
    MOVE HEADER-LINE-1 TO PRINT-RECORD
    PERFORM WRITE-NEW-PAGE
    MOVE HEADER-LINE-2 TO PRINT-RECORD
    PERFORM WRITE-REPORT-LINE
    MOVE HEADER-LINE-3 TO PRINT-RECORD
    MOVE 1 TO LINE-SPACING
    PERFORM WRITE-REPORT-LINE
    MOVE SPACES TO PRINT-RECORD
    PERFORM WRITE-REPORT-LINE
WRITE-NEW-PAGE
    WRITE PRINT-RECORD
        AFTER ADVANCING PAGE
    MOVE 1 TO LINES-USED
WRITE-REPORT-LINE
    WRITE PRINT-RECORD
        AFTER ADVANCING LINE-SPACING LINES
    ADD LINE-SPACING TO LINES-USED
```

Before being executed, the programmed instructions are subsequently *compiled*, or translated, into a form that the computer can "understand." In their final compiled

FIGURE 2.14 **A one-write manual accounting system.** (Courtesy of McBee Systems Division of Litton Industries.)

PAYROLL/CASH DISBURSEMENTS

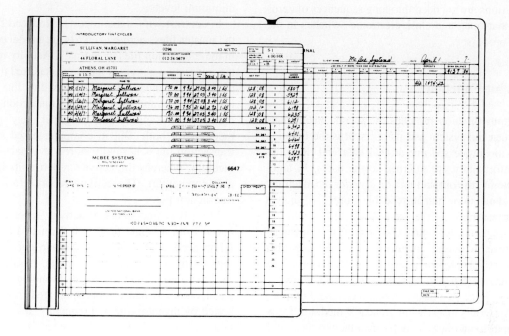

CASH DISBURSEMENTS

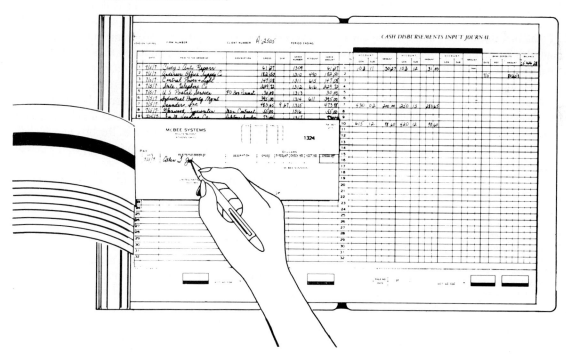

form, usually referred to as *object code* or *machine code*, the instructions are encoded into long sequences of zeros and ones that open and close electronic switches in the computer processor.

The Output Function

The output function provides the second main interface between the system and its users. It is the function in which the processed operational data and decision-making information are returned to the users. In automated systems, the output function *decodes* the machine-readable data into human-readable form so that it becomes meaningful to the users.

The output may be a financial statement, a management report, an output document such as a customer invoice or paycheck,[3] or a chart or graph. The output medium may be paper, microfilm, a video screen image, or possibly voice synthesis. Sometimes, the "output" from the system is in a machine-readable medium, forming the input to another computer, and the interface with an end-user is deferred to some later processing stage. The broad range of available media enables systems designers to meet a correspondingly wide variety of user needs.

The financial statements and many of the management reports are examples of *status reports*. Status reports focus on the balances recorded in the master files or ledgers after posting has been completed. Thus the balance sheet lists the asset, liability, and owners' equity accounts in the chart of accounts and their associated balances. The income statement presents the equivalent information for the revenue and expense accounts.[4] Some management reports list only a small subset of the total number of records in the file; an example is an inventory reorder report that identifies only those items whose on-hand balances have fallen below prescribed minimum levels.

In contrast with status reports, produced from data in the master files, *activity reports* are produced from data in the transaction files or journals. Activity reports show the transaction activities that have occurred over a period of time. In manual systems the dividing line between an activity report and its associated transaction file may be blurred; the same piece of paper may provide the medium for both. But in computer-based systems, the transaction file is normally stored in a machine-readable medium, whereas the activity report is its human-readable counterpart. The activity report is a *listing* of the transaction file.

More than one status or activity report may be produced from a single file, each formatted to meet a different need. The contents of a report may be sorted differently from the records in the file. A sales transaction file would normally be ordered chronologically, whereas an inventory issuance report prepared from it might be sorted by inventory item. Frequently, a report may contain information additional to what is contained in its principal companion file. This additional information may be retrieved from another file containing historical data, or it may be deduced from calculation. For example, a purchases activity report may show both the vendor number and the vendor name; the report is essentially a listing of the purchases transaction file, but the vendor names may have to be retrieved from the vendor master file because they were never recorded in the transaction file. In other situations, data may be derived from calculations either based on historical data or originating from some other source. Reports may include estimates or projections of what might happen if a certain course of action were followed.

An important element of the output process is the formatting of the information for communication to the user. The format selected depends on the medium of presentation: paper, screen, or audio, as the case may be; but in all cases its principal objective is to provide for the effective, efficient transfer of information to the human user. Paper reports, containing tables of figures, have been the traditional medium of communication for accounting data. Screen displays, typical of modern computer-based systems, often present data in tabular form also. Tabular presentation seems likely to continue

---

[3] Invoices and paychecks do more than just provide information. Besides performing their information functions, invoices trigger payment transactions in the customers' accounting systems, and checks disburse cash. Invoices and the like are sometimes referred to as *action documents*, and checks as *negotiable documents*.

[4] The description of the income statement as a status report may be surprising. However, the reader should recall that the revenue and expense balances are set to zero at the beginning of the period. Hence the balances, "as of" some later point in time, in fact reflect the performance of the enterprise throughout the intervening period.

to be the principal output format for the foreseeable future. However, other media and formats, including the graphical representation of data, are gaining in popularity. Graphics output provides less quantitative detail than do tables of figures but offer improved qualitative comprehension and "feel" for the underlying meaning of the data. Accordingly, information specialists increasingly are turning to multimedia (and multiformat) communications in which the same data may be communicated to the users in more than one form. For example, a table of figures may be supplemented by a chart or graph, or a screen display may be supplemented by synthesized voice output.

The output from the accounting information system either meets or fails to meet the users' needs. Meeting the users' informational requirements is the chief justification for the investment in developing, maintaining, and operating the accounting information system. To this end, systems developers seek not only to provide useful information but also to provide it in a timely, effective, and easy-to-understand manner. Ultimately, the information should provoke action of some kind or influence somebody's behavior. If it fails to do either, the value of the output—and the justification for the information system—is in doubt.

The Control Function

The accounting information system is controlled by both external and internal factors. *External controls* include the various legal, regulatory, and professional rules imposed on the system from outside the enterprise. The Internal Revenue Service, for example, has established minimum standards for recording and processing the accounting data used in preparing tax returns. The Financial Accounting Standards Board has established similar standards relating to the external reporting function.

Internal controls are incorporated into the accounting system to ensure that the system performs in accordance with management's expressed wishes. The major objectives of internal controls are promoting efficiency, encouraging compliance with management policies and procedures, protecting the integrity of the accounting information, and safeguarding the organization's assets.

Verification of the input data, which has already been mentioned, is an example of an internal-control measure designed to help protect the integrity of the accounting information. There is normally no conflict between external and internal controls. In the area of overlap (primarily concerning the integrity of the data), both serve to ensure that the accounting records properly reflect the enterprise's underlying economics and that the processing and communication of information are accurate, complete, timely, and reliable.

Establishment and maintenance of internal controls are management's responsibility. But the external auditors also have a direct interest in the internal controls because the controls have a bearing on the credibility of the financial statements produced by the accounting system. If the controls are ineffective, the whole burden of the auditors' opinion must be borne by substantive testing of the accounting records. The test program must then be extensive, and the audit will be expensive. On the other hand, if the controls are found to be effective, the auditors can place some degree of reliance on them and correspondingly reduce the level of required testing.

SUMMARY

The debate over the proper boundaries of accounting has continued for many years, the issues being complicated by rapid change in the business and technological environments. The boundaries of the accounting information system are similarly ill defined and seem likely to remain so for the foreseeable future. Nonetheless, a measure of consensus has emerged that views the accounting system as a broadly based information-providing function, supplying both routine and nonroutine information and possibly overlapping the functions of other components of the overall business information system.

The accounting information system can be divided into six transaction cycles: the purchasing, production, revenue, planning and control, reporting, and investment cycles. These six cycles provide a framework for analysis that is sufficiently general to transcend the differences between the accounting systems in different types of organizations. The transaction cycles form the first, or highest, level of subsystems in an analysis of the accounting information system. The second level of subsystems corresponds to the familiar accounting applications, including accounts receivable, accounts payable, purchasing, sales order processing, payroll, inventory management, and the general ledger. The nature, function, and even the existence of each of the subsystems in this second level depend on the nature of the enterprise. In any event, the applications incorporated into any given accounting system are highly integrated, sharing common data and transferring data from one to another.

Much can be learned about the accounting information system by tracing the flow of transactions through the system and by examining the nature and content of the accounting data base. The data base supports both the routine operational and the nonroutine decision support aspects of the accounting system. Coding transactions establishes a verifiable audit trail. It also facilitates efficient and effective retrieval of data from the data base to meet both the routine and the nonroutine requirements of the users.

The basic building blocks of information processing are the activities of data input, processing, output, and control. The input and output functions form the two main interfaces with the users, in which data are fed into the system for processing and subsequently returned to the users in processed form. The preparation of input data is vulnerable to errors, and so verification is necessary to reduce the risk that contaminated data will be processed further. The output must effectively and efficiently communicate real information to the users. The success of the accounting system can be measured by its ability to supply users with the right outputs, at the right time, and in the right form. A wide range of media is available to help achieve this objective.

The accounting system is controlled by both agencies outside the enterprise, such as the external auditors and the Securities and Exchange Commission, and internal controls inside the enterprise. The control function seeks to ensure that information is processed in accordance with accepted norms and that management's goals for the enterprise are properly served. It is an area of traditional concern to accountants.

BIBLIOGRAPHY

Arthur Andersen & Co. *A Guide for Studying and Evaluating Internal Accounting Controls*, Publ. no. 2880, Item I. Chicago: Arthur Andersen & Co., 1978.

Burch, John G., Felix R. Strater, and Gary Grudnitski. *Information Systems: Theory and Practice*, 3rd ed. New York: Wiley, 1984.

Davis, William, S. *Information Processing Systems*, 2nd ed. Reading, Mass.: Addison-Wesley, 1981.

Dolan, Kathleen. *Business Computer System Design* Santa Cruz, Calif.: Mitchell, 1984.

Matz, Adolph, and Milton F. Usry. *Cost Accounting: Planning and Control*, 7th ed. Cincinnati: South-Western, 1980.

McLeod, Raymond, Jr. *Management Information Systems*, 2nd ed. Chicago: Science Research Associates, 1983.

Moscove, Stephen A., and Mark G. Simkin. *Accounting Information Systems: Concepts and Practice for Effective Decision Making*. New York: Wiley, 1981.

DISCUSSION QUESTIONS AND PROBLEMS

1. Define and discuss the following terms:

- Action document
- Activity report
- Application
- Classification
- Comparison
- Data base
- Data capture
- Data verification
- Display
- Document
- Encoding
- File
- Information media
- Journal
- Ledger
- Merging
- Posting
- Report
- Sorting

- Source document
- Status report
- Summarization
- Transaction cycle
- Transaction coding

2. Under which transaction cycle would each of the following accounting activities fall?
a. Production control
b. Shipping
c. Accounts payable
d. Accounts receivable
e. Cash management
f. Inventory management
g. Budget preparation
h. Short-term borrowing
i. Cost accounting
j. Receiving

3. Identify the accounting applications that might be included in the revenue cycle in each of the following types of organizations:
a. A large manufacturing firm that produces automobiles and trucks
b. A large insurance company offering life, accident, health, and liability policies
c. A federal government agency
d. A charity organization involved in African famine relief

4. Trace the paths through the accounting information system taken by transactions originating from the following types of source documents. Identify the files, documents, or reports encountered on each transaction path.
a. A time card
b. A purchase order received from a customer
c. A check received from a customer
d. An expense claim submitted by an employee
e. An invoice received from a supplier
f. An assessment for back taxes received from the Internal Revenue Service

5. Develop a coding system applicable to the recording of expense items in a multisegment organization. The intention is to provide for the future retrieval of data in the following configurations:

- Companywide totals of an individual expense item
- Divisional totals of an individual item
- Departmental totals of an individual item
- Divisional totals of aggregate expense
- Departmental totals of aggregate expense

The company has 4 divisions, and the maximum number of departments in any one division is 15. There are 500 different expense items.

6. The data in the table on p. 42 refer to sales transactions in a divisionalized organization. The first three digits of the account numbers, "300," designate "sales" in the chart of accounts. The fourth digit designates the type of sale:

1 = cash sale
2 = credit sale (30-day terms)
3 = installment sale
4 = miscellaneous

The fifth and sixth digits designate the division in which the sale originated.

Required
a. Determine the total sales in division 10.
b. Determine companywide cash sales.
c. Determine the total of credit sales and installment sales in division 20.
d. Identify those divisions in which installment sales exceed credit sales.
e. Identify those divisions that have no miscellaneous sales.

7. Identify at least 20 different purposes for which data files are established. Which would you expect to find

- In the home
- In a service enterprise
- In a merchandising enterprise
- In a manufacturing enterprise
- In a nonprofit institution

8. In how many different ways might an inventory file be sorted? Identify those that might be useful in an accounting information system.

Data for Problem 6

Data	Account No.	Amount of Sales
1/1/19A	300120	$ 250.00
1/2/19A	300140	650.00
1/3/19A	300310	1,125.00
1/4/19A	300220	75.00
1/5/19A	300240	560.00
1/6/19A	300130	2,500.00
1/7/19A	300410	125.00
1/8/19A	300120	500.00
1/9/19A	300440	35.00
1/10/19A	300210	120.00
1/11/19A	300240	1,050.00
1/12/19A	300330	380.00
1/13/19A	300110	130.00
1/14/19A	300120	200.00
1/15/19A	300410	85.00
1/16/19A	300220	900.00
1/17/19A	300230	3,750.00
1/18/19A	300320	400.00
1/19/19A	300140	120.00
1/20/19A	300410	25.00
1/21/19A	300310	310.00
1/22/19A	300330	160.00
1/23/19A	300220	1,450.00
1/24/19A	300130	600.00
1/25/19A	300330	2,750.00
1/26/19A	300220	675.00
1/27/19A	300310	1,200.00
1/28/19A	300210	340.00
1/29/19A	300420	550.00
1/30/19A	300110	300.00
1/31/19A	300230	1,500.00

9. Identify 20 different uses for a screen display. Could any of them be replaced by printed output? What would be the advantages and disadvantages of doing so?

10. Design a sales journal suitable for the manual recording of cash sales and credit sales in a retail merchandising company. Provision should be made for recording the product identification number, the quantity, the unit price, the extended price, and a 4 percent sales tax. Appropriate daily totals are required for accounting purposes.

11. Design a register for recording the acquisition of equity and bond securities by a portfolio manager. The register should include columns for the type and name of the security, the number of shares, the dollar value, any premium or discount on the bonds, the investment objective (short- or long-term, yield or growth, and so on), and any relevant remarks about the securities in question.

12. Red Company maintains a perpetual inventory system for the raw materials used in its manufacturing process. The table on p. 43 shows some entries in the purchases journal (recording receipt of inventory items) and some entries in the materials requisitions journal (recording issuances to production).

Required
a. Design an inventory subsidiary ledger card for Part A12, and post the entries to it.
b. Determine the quantity on hand and the total dollar value for Part A12 by day and at the end of the month. Assume that 150 units are on hand at the beginning of the month, with a unit cost of $2.00.

13. The following is a general description of a clerical procedure pertaining to the retrieval of product items from a warehouse and the preparation of these items for shipment to customers:

Items are to be retrieved from the warehouse according to authorized sales orders provided from the sales department. The location of items on the shelves can be found in the weekly stock status report. Items are to be weighed and then packed in cardboard containers for shipment. A packing slip is to be prepared, listing the items and quantities enclosed and indicating the customer name, destination, and mode of shipment. Items with a net weight of less than 30 lb. are to be shipped by parcel service, whereas heavier items are to be sent by common carrier. Orders that are designated ''Expedite'' are to be sent by air freight.

Data for Problem 12
Purchase Journal

Date	Part No.	Description	Quantity	Unit Cost	Ext. Cost.
7/1/XX	A12	Right-hand widget	100	$2.00	$200.00
7/4/XX	B06	Threaded widget	150	3.50	525.00
7/9/XX	A24	Left-hand widget	20	2.00	40.00
7/13/XX	A12	Right-hand widget	100	2.00	200.00
7/14/XX	C36	Heavy-duty widget	50	5.00	250.00
7/20/XX	A12	Right-hand widget	200	2.00	400.00
7/26/XX	A12	Right-hand widget	100	2.00	200.00

Materials Requisitions Journal

Date	Part No.	Department	Job No.	Quantity
7/1/XX	A06	22	122-G	30
7/2/XX	C12	24	108-P	25
7/5/XX	A12	16	124-J	120
7/12/XX	B06	08	121-G	1,000
7/19/XX	A12	22	98-B	70
7/22/XX	C36	18	130-A	5
7/26/XX	A12	16	124-K	20
7/29/XX	A12	02	116-A	160

Required

Translate this narrative description into a sequence of detailed tasks to be performed by the personnel concerned. Clearly define the tasks so that the stores clerks will know what is expected of them.

14. A manual inventory system involves the weekly posting of receipts and issuances of inventory items; this posting process is performed every Friday just before the close of business.

The demand for item 12345 is stable at a rate of 5 units per day, five days per week. Purchases are made every three weeks in quantities of 75 units, and deliveries are normally made first thing Monday morning. On Friday evening, January 29, the inventory level of item 12345 in the warehouse was 10 units, and the perpetual inventory records were verified as being correct. A delivery was scheduled for the following Monday.

Required

Perform a simulation for the month of February to determine the maximum discrepancy between the actual quantity of item 12345 on hand and the balance shown on the ledger card. (Set up a table with a line for each day in the month, and calculate the quantity on hand corresponding to the stated pattern of receipts and issuances. Also calculate the net transaction activity posted to the ledger on each posting date and the resulting balance in the perpetual inventory records.)

15. The acquisition, custody, and disposition of resources, in the form of goods and services, are the subject of the purchasing, production, and revenue cycles. The acquisition, custody, and disposition of *capital resources* all are contained in the investment cycle.

Required

a. Draw appropriate parallels between the applications in the investment cycle and those in the three operating cycles.

b. What does such a study of the handling of the two types of resources suggest about the classification of applications in the conventional transaction cycle analysis, as described in the text and summarized in Figure 2.2? Might some of the applications have been misclassified?

3

Graphical Representation of Information Systems

CHAPTER OUTLINE

LEARNING OBJECTIVES

After you have studied this chapter you should be able to

- Identify the major approaches to graphical representation or modeling of information systems and their purposes.
- Discuss the objectives of systems flowcharting.
- Identify the standard flowcharting symbols and explain their usage.
- Analyze systems flowcharts and evaluate the information systems represented.
- Prepare systems flowcharts for typical accounting applications.
- Discuss the use of computer aids to flowcharting.

OVERVIEW OF GRAPHICAL REPRESENTATION TECHNIQUES

The use of graphical representations of information systems is based on the reasoning that "a picture is worth a thousand words." Showing someone a picture of some object ordinarily conveys more—and does so with less effort and in a shorter time—than does describing the object in words. Most people are visually oriented, and so pictures, diagrams, and other visual aids can communicate concepts that are difficult or inefficient to convey by other means. Similarly, providing a diagram or "picture" of an information system helps people understand the system better. And on the basis of this understanding, people can analyze the system, evaluate it, identify problems, and seek solutions. They can try to improve the system or to adapt it to a new set of requirements. No information system continues to meet the needs of its users forever, and sooner or later it must be updated or replaced to reflect changes in the enterprise or its environment.

Diagrams are also useful in providing a permanent record of the information system and the way it operates. They may document the underlying structure of the system, how it was designed, its operating procedures, the computer programs, the maintenance requirements, its internal controls, and other aspects of the system. Documentation is essential to people who have to work with the system, and diagrams of various kinds are important components of documentation.

Graphical representations are models of the real object or process. They portray certain aspects of reality, and intentionally omit others, in order to make a point. The user's attention is focused at least temporarily on the aspects of interest and away from distracting aspects. In Chapters 1 and 2, block diagrams were used to represent accounting systems in an attempt to convey to the reader the purpose and construction of the systems in question and the concepts underlying them. Block diagrams form one type of graphical representation. They are particularly simple; each entity—process, activity, organizational unit, and the like—is represented by a rectangle, and connecting lines represent the association of one entity with another. More complex graphical models are used when greater detail is required. Different symbols may be used to depict different types of entity, and the symbols may be arranged according to agreed-upon rules.

Accountants, like other business people, need to be able to understand the various types of graphical representation of information systems and to construct them. Accountants are most likely to have to deal with systems flowcharts; consequently, this chapter concentrates on understanding and constructing flowcharts. Nevertheless, familiarity with other types is useful too, and so we now shall briefly describe the principal types of representation.

Block Diagrams

Block diagrams are used for various purposes. Organization charts are a familiar example in which the blocks comprising them correspond to people in the organization, and the lines connecting them indicate the lines of authority and responsibility. Block diagrams are also used to represent accounting information systems. Block diagrams are commonly used to provide an overview of a system in terms of its major component subsystems. They are easy to draw and easy to understand.

Two types of block diagrams are noteworthy. One is the "horizontal" block diagram in which the blocks represent the various subsystems and the connecting lines represent the information flows among them. Figures 3.1 and 3.2 illustrate this type of block diagram. The first shows a production planning process, and the second, which is more elaborate, shows the processing activities and principal documents making up the three operating cycles: the purchasing cycle, the production cycle, and the revenue cycle. Block diagrams of this type are frequently drawn as a preliminary step in the preparation of a systems flowchart. Figure 3.2 has already progressed in this direction because it contains document symbols in addition to the rectangular blocks that ordinarily are the only symbols from which block diagrams are constructed.

A second type of block diagram is the hierarchical block diagram that was illustrated in Chapter 2. Hierarchical block diagrams show the division of a system into successive levels of component subsystems or, alternatively, the synthesis of individual components into a coherent and purposeful whole. Thus, the revenue cycle may be broken down into the applications of sales, shipping, and accounts receivable. In turn, sales may be divided into order taking and order processing, and accounts receivable into billing and collections (Figure 3.3). The connecting lines in hierarchical block diagrams represent not the flow of information but interlevel associations, which take the form of "parent–child" relationships. Hierarchical block diagrams, often referred to as *structure charts*, are commonly used in systems development activities to provide a general overview of an information system and its component cycles and applications.

Two other kinds of block diagrams, often used in conjunction with hierarchical block diagrams, are the *overview diagram* and *detail diagram*, which will be discussed in Chapter 14. Both types depict the inputs, processes, and outputs of accounting subsystems.

Data Flow Diagrams

Data flow diagrams provide a more detailed representation of an information system than does a block diagram. However, they are free from many of the rules attached to the more formal systems flowcharts and consequently can be drawn—and redrawn as necessary—with a minimum of effort. The simplest kind of data flow diagram, the *bubble chart*, uses only one symbol, a circle or "bubble," to represent all component entities, with connecting lines representing the relationships among them. The usual objective is to depict the flow of information without regard for the nature of the entities (people, computers, documents, and the like) involved and without regard for the logic of individual processing activities. This kind of data flow diagram is illustrated in Figure 3.4. Using its wider repertoire of symbols, a more complicated kind of data flow diagram distinguishes between processing activities and repositories of data such as files. Figure 3.5 shows a typical example.

FIGURE 3.1 Horizontal block diagram of a production-planning process.

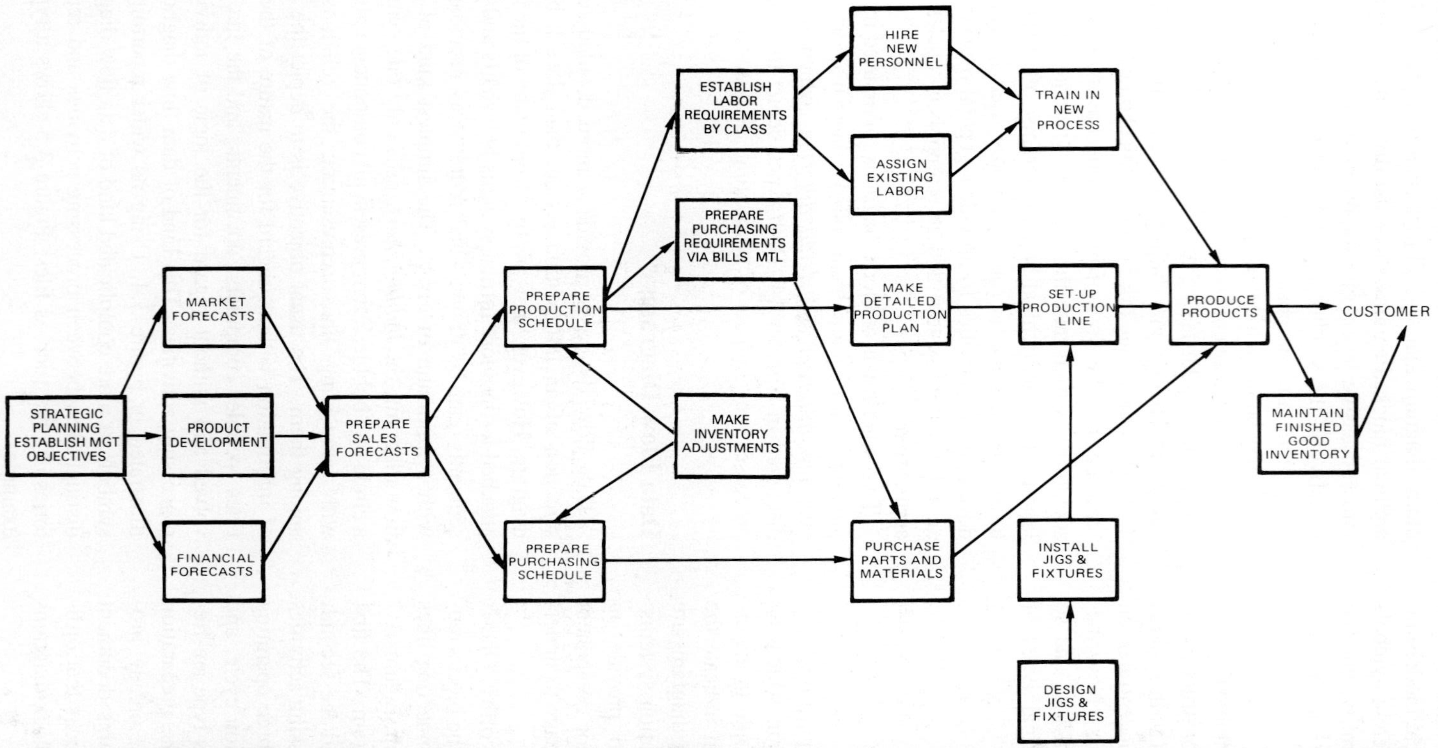

FIGURE 3.2 Horizontal block diagram of the purchasing cycle. In this "block diagram," some additional flowcharting symbols have been introduced.

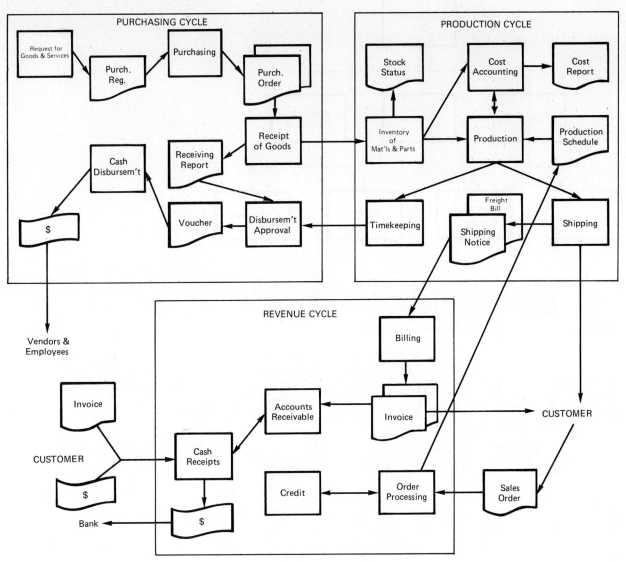

FIGURE 3.3   **Hierarchical block diagram showing analysis of the revenue cycle.**

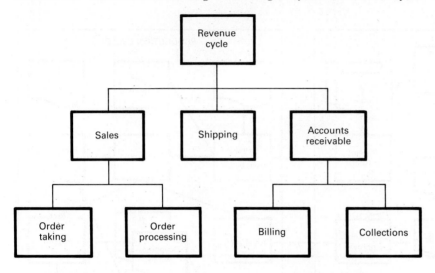

FIGURE 3.4   **Bubble chart.** A bubble chart is a type of data flow diagram using only one symbol.

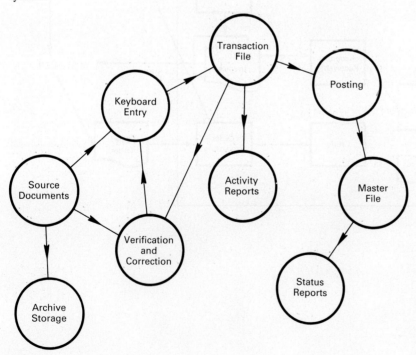

FIGURE 3.5 Data flow diagram using multiple symbols.

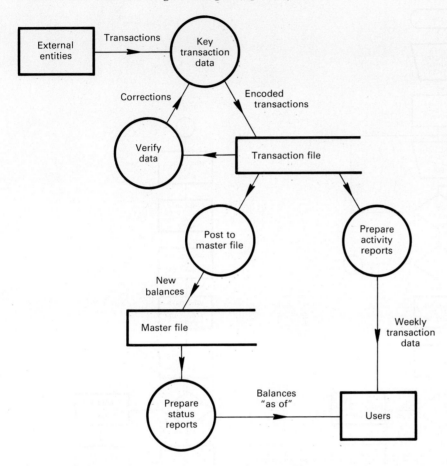

Data flow diagrams are frequently prepared in the early stages of a systems analysis or design, when the details are still fluid. Most accountants prefer to convert the data flow diagrams into systems flowcharts as the design crystallizes; however, a small but increasing number treat data flow diagrams as permanent documentation. The main disadvantage of data flow diagrams lies in the limited range of symbols used and in the consequent difficulty or inability to represent points of detail.

Program Flowcharts

Program flowcharts depict the detailed logic used in an information-processing activity. Figure 3.6 shows an example for processing an investment credit application. Program flowcharts were once used extensively as aids to the development of computer software. (Figure 3.6 contains references to COBOL language instructions.) But with the increasing popularity of structured approaches to computer programming, program flowcharts now are secondary to the newer tools, including pseudocode, Nassi-Schneiderman diagrams, Chapin charts, and Warnier diagrams. For a discussion of these tools, the reader is referred to any text on structured programming.

Program flowcharts are frequently confused with systems flowcharts, and the decreasing popularity of the former is sometimes mistakenly offered as evidence that systems flowcharts are obsolete. But the intent of the

FIGURE 3.6 Program flowchart for simplified investment credit application.

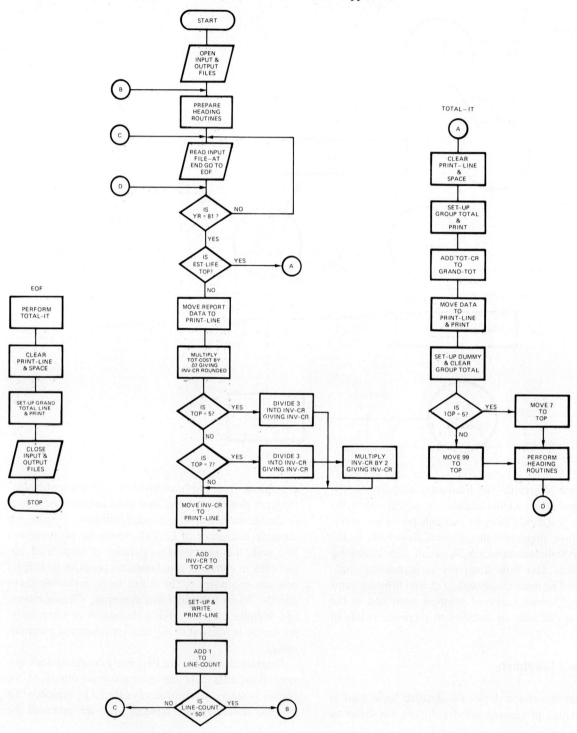

two kinds of flowcharts is quite different. Program flowcharts normally describe the logical steps within a single processing activity, whereas systems flowcharts describe the flow of information among the various processing activities and other components of the system. A whole program flowchart might refer to an activity depicted by a single symbol in the corresponding systems flowchart. Program flowcharts contain ''start'' and ''stop'' symbols that are not found in a systems flowchart. They also contain decision symbols corresponding to the end of an iterative loop, for example, one involving a test for an end-of-file condition. Such a test would not be represented in a systems flowchart.

Document Flowcharts

Document flowcharts depict the flow of paperwork through an information system. Normally the only symbol they contain is the document symbol, which can refer to a document, a journal, or a report. Connecting flow lines show the movement of information from one item of paperwork to another or the distribution of copies of paperwork (for example, copies of a multipart invoice) to a number of destinations. Document flowcharts are frequently arranged in columnar form, each column corresponding to an organizational unit within the enterprise or possibly to an external entity such as a customer or vendor. The objective is to draw attention to each unit's responsibilities for generating, transmitting, or receiving each item of paperwork. A simple example of a document flowchart is shown in Figure 3.7. This figure illustrates a commonly adopted convention in which a descriptive legend appears only in those symbols corresponding to the point of origination of a particular item of paperwork. Symbols corresponding to copies of the item, distributed to other organizational units are left blank. An alternative convention includes the legends in all copies of a document but numbers the copies 1, 2, 3 . . . to avoid the impression that they might be different documents.

Document flowcharts are easy to prepare and to understand, but they depict only one aspect of the system. They were more useful in the days of manual systems,

FIGURE 3.7   Example of a simple columnar document flowchart.

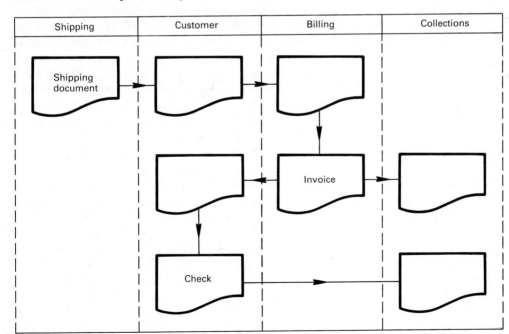

when paperwork comprised a more important component of accounting systems than it does now. Today, document flowcharts are normally used in conjunction with other kinds of flowcharts that show complementary aspects of the system.

Systems Flowcharts

Systems flowcharts depict the detailed flow of data through an information system. They contain distinct symbols representing paperwork, files, processing activities, and other aspects of the system. The symbols also distinguish between manual operations and computerized processing activities. An example is shown in Figure 3.8.

Systems flowcharts can be as simple or as complicated as is necessary to convey the intended description of the system. Perhaps only an overview flowchart may be needed as a visual aid for a presentation to upper management. Its purpose may be to show how the system cuts across organizational boundaries, how it affects management responsibilities, and what kinds of coordination are required. On the other hand, a detailed representation may be necessary, for example, to communicate a completed systems design to the programmers who will write the associated software. Frequently, a set of related flowcharts is prepared, each providing a different view of the system and incorporating a different level of detail.

Systems flowcharting thus provides a great deal of flexibility in systems representation for multiple purposes. Systems flowcharts are the most common type of graphical representation that accountants use. They are featured in systems development and enhancement (including the design of internal controls), systems evaluation, auditing, and many other types of work.

Systems flowcharts are sometimes arranged in columnar form, and such flowcharts may resemble the document flowcharts described earlier. However, columnar systems flowcharts use the whole range of flowcharting symbols and not just the document symbol. The intention of columnar systems flowcharts is to highlight the portions of the system—particularly the processing activities—corresponding to the functional responsibilities of each organizational unit. An example, depicting a

manual purchasing system, is shown in Figure 3.9. It illustrates the convention, mentioned earlier, of numbering copies of the same document.

In contrast with other types of graphical representation, systems flowcharting is governed by national and international standards. The purpose of these standards is to provide a level of uniformity that will minimize misinterpretation among users of systems flowcharts throughout the world. Flowcharting is by no means a science; individual style, particularly as it helps achieve a clear, orderly, pleasing layout, is most welcome. But adherence to the accepted rules helps reduce ambiguities and makes flowcharts more useful.

USES OF FLOWCHARTS

Who Uses Flowcharts?

Systems flowcharts are used by a variety of people, including accountants, auditors, information-processing specialists, and managers. Managers are constantly faced with changing operational requirements, bottlenecks in processing functions, unbalanced work loads, and other problems that systems flowcharts can help solve. Managers who can flowchart a process or understand a flowchart prepared by someone else have an advantage over those who do not have that skill. The flowchart provides a graphic model of the business activities and aids in posing "what if" questions as various alternative solutions are suggested, thought through, and conceptually tested. Managers also use flowcharts as training aids and aids in communicating systems details at meetings and presentations.

Accountants are often asked to help solve operating problems and, consequently, have largely the same flowcharting needs. They also coordinate systems activities with others, or they may be responsible for designing or assisting in the design of business systems. Another major responsibility of accountants is designing and monitoring system controls. Flowcharts are used extensively to document the system, including its internal controls, and to help accountants evaluate these controls.

Auditors use flowcharts as an essential tool in their audit examinations. They often flowchart the system under review to gain an understanding of how it works.

FIGURE 3.8 Systems flowchart of an inventory control system.

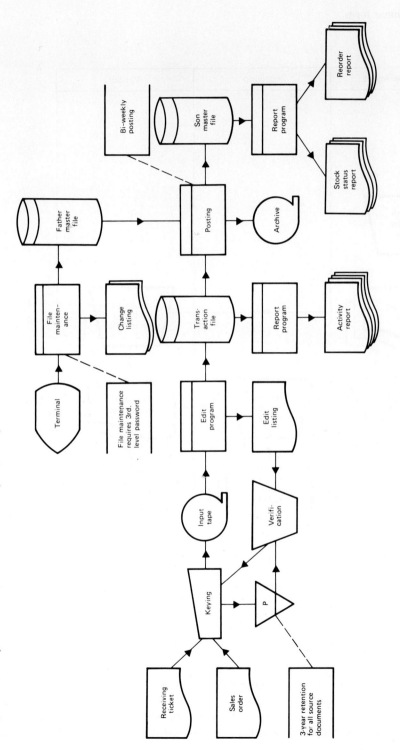

FIGURE 3.9 Systems flowchart in columnar form.

Manual Purchasing System

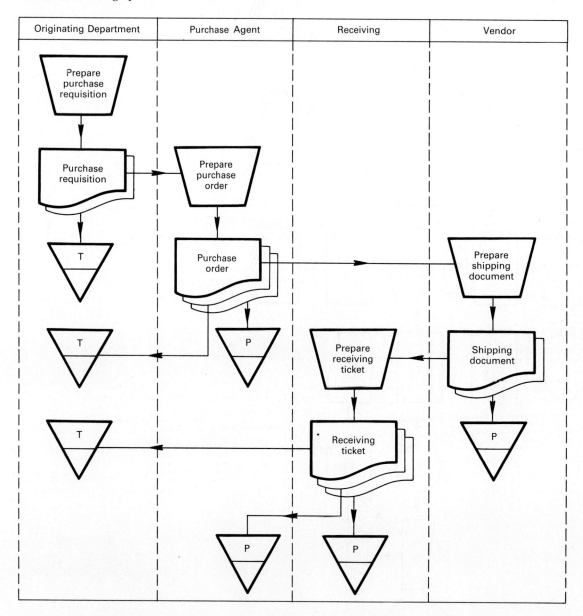

They also use the flowcharts to analyze the internal controls and to evaluate the adequacy of the controls as they contribute to the system's overall integrity.

In most large organizations, the prime responsibility for designing new systems or improving existing ones is assigned to the systems staff in the information services department. Personnel in this capacity use both systems flowcharts and program flowcharts to help design, analyze, and revise the systems with which they work. One other important function they perform is properly documenting each system; flowcharts again are a major component of systems documentation.

How Are Flowcharts Used?

The previous section explained who uses systems flowcharts and for what broad purposes. This section expands on the ways in which flowcharts are used. Five principal types of usage can be identified. But this should not imply that a different kind of flowchart is needed for each purpose. In many cases a single flowchart may be useful for a variety of purposes; indeed, the possibility of multiple use is an important advantage of flowcharting.

The principal uses of flowcharts are as follows:

- *Communications Vehicle*: for data gathering, training, and reviewing system details with others.
- *Problem-solving Tool*: for analyzing the details of an existing or proposed system, documenting alternative solutions, and serving as a paper model of the physical activities.
- *Design Tool*: for describing the details of a system to guide development. The flowchart serves the same purpose for information systems as a blueprint does for a machine.
- *Evaluation Medium*: for identifying and highlighting control points and control techniques so that they can be compared with desired control objectives and evaluated. Flowcharts may also be used to evaluate system performance.
- *Documentation Medium*: for recording details of an existing or proposed system as evidence of its contents, construction, and operation.

Flowcharting is an excellent way to understand the inner workings of a business system. The process of gathering data and converting them into a systems flowchart is a quick and effective means of checking that the assembled details are complete and learning how they are interrelated. Gaps in the information will be readily apparent, and possible improvements may suggest themselves. As the analyst pieces together the jigsaw puzzle, further questions come to mind that can be discussed with those who do the daily tasks or processing. By combining the preparation of flowcharts with the gathering of data, the analyst gains insights into the system that would be difficult to obtain in any other way.

Flowcharts, like flip charts, can provide a pictorial focus for training purposes or management presentations. In training sessions, operating procedures can be cross-referenced to details of the flowcharts; in this way more information is communicated to the trainees, and their understanding is improved. A flowchart can be used in meetings for guiding discussions on operating matters. The flowchart establishes the factual situation being discussed and often eliminates conjecture and misunderstanding. The more complex the activities are, the more helpful a flowchart will be.

The traditional approach to solving problems starts with defining the problem. When a problem exists in a business system, flowcharting, along with the necessary data gathering, is an excellent way of defining the problem. The flowchart defines the problem area graphically, giving a picture of each step in the process and its related components. Key data such as document volumes, file media, and people's names can be recorded on the flowchart next to the symbols to which they refer. Notes and references to other material can provide whatever additional details are needed to define the problem.

When the problem has been adequately defined, the analysis can begin. The flowchart provides a worksheet for this analysis. Each step in the process is examined as to what is being done, why, by whom, when, where, and how. Questions can be posed such as "What would happen if this step were eliminated?" or "Would time be saved by combining that step with this one?" Each facet of the problem is dissected and investigated, and notes can be made as ideas are generated. Thus the flowchart may stimulate creative ideas and serve as a medium for recording these ideas for further consideration.

When the problem has been thoroughly analyzed, the process of synthesis and the development of a solution start. Usually several alternative solutions are investigated before deciding on the best one. Flowcharts play a major role in defining each alternative and acting as a recording medium for trying out new ideas and redesigns. Each proposed solution is flowcharted and analyzed to check its validity and consistency and generally to determine its attractiveness.

In a similar fashion, a flowchart can be made from a new set of specifications. As each part of the system is developed, the details are recorded on the flowchart. The system is designed part by part, and the completed design is examined and tested conceptually, using the flowchart as an evaluation mechanism prior to any implementation efforts. By analyzing the flowchart, errors or omissions may be identified, and the design can be improved. By using the flowchart, the designer can manipulate and rearrange the various portions of the system while exploring the consequences of alternative designs.

The systems flowchart is one of the chief tools in accumulating and recording the specific details of the system required to evaluate its internal controls. The flowchart helps identify control strengths and weaknesses. A critical portion of the review of internal controls is identifying and appraising the audit trail; the existence of a clear audit trail is essential to the auditability of the accounting system.

More generally, flowcharts, and indeed any type of graphical representation of an information system, provide a means of evaluating a system from the standpoints

FIGURE 3.10 The most commonly used flowcharting symbols.

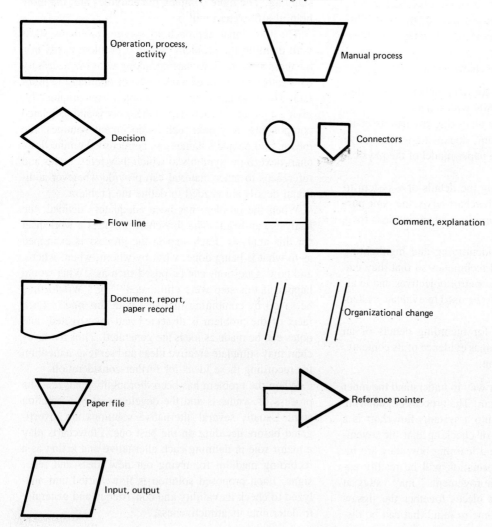

Operation, process, activity

Manual process

Decision

Connectors

Flow line

Comment, explanation

Document, report, paper record

Organizational change

Paper file

Reference pointer

Input, output

of effectiveness and efficiency. For example, bottle-necks, which can cause serious delays in processing, may become apparent from studying a flowchart.

FLOWCHARTING SYMBOLS AND THEIR USE

Standard Flowcharting Symbols

The applicable standards for flowcharting symbols were established by the International Organization for Standardization (ISO) and the American National Standards Institute (ANSI). There are few differences between the two sets of standards, and here we shall refer principally to the ANSI standards which were for-

mulated in 1970.[1] Figure 3.10 shows the most common flowcharting symbols from the ANSI bulletin, together with a few others that, although not recognized in the standards, have become de facto standards through their wide usage. Some of the symbols listed in the ANSI bulletin have fallen into disuse because of technological advances, for example, the symbol for collating related primarily to punched-card bookkeeping machines that are now obsolete.

Flowcharting symbols should be drawn using a flow-charting template. Commercially available templates conform to the ANSI standards and help to produce uni-

[1] *Flowcharting Symbols and Their Usage in Information Processing*, ANSI X3.5 (1970). Published by the American National Standards Institute, 1430 Broadway, New York, N.Y. 10018.

FIGURE 3.10   (Continued)

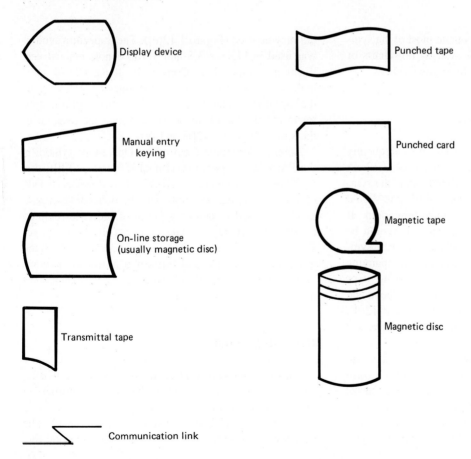

Display device

Punched tape

Manual entry keying

Punched card

On-line storage (usually magnetic disc)

Magnetic tape

Transmittal tape

Magnetic disc

Communication link

FIGURE 3.11 Flowchart template. (Courtesy of International Business Machines Corporation)

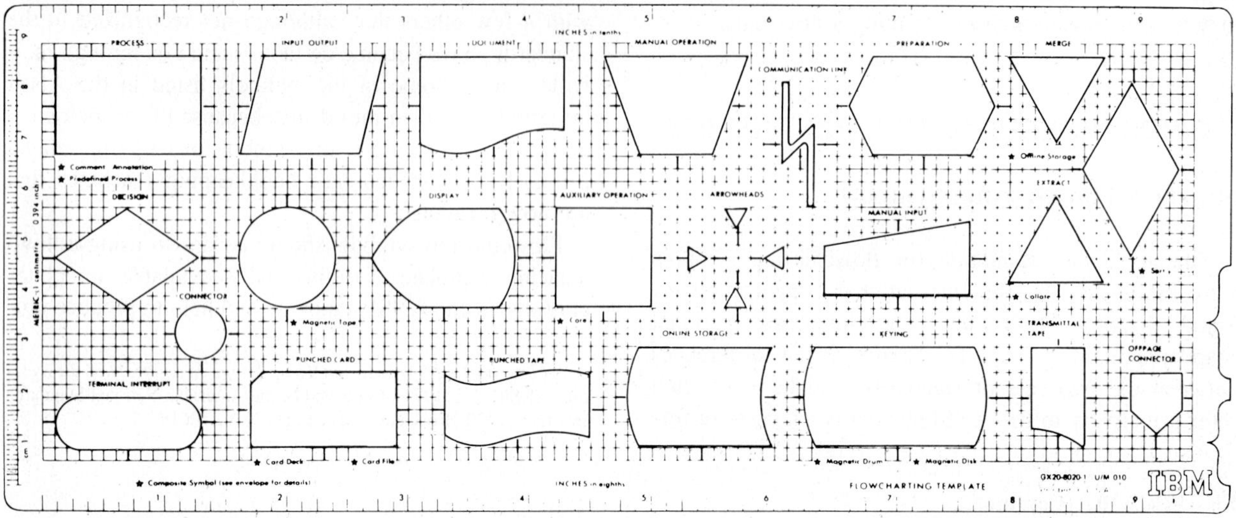

formity of usage; they normally contain most of the symbols required in order to prepare systems flowcharts of all kinds. An example is shown in Figure 3.11.

Operation or Process Symbol

The Operation symbol is one of the most frequently used symbols. Its use is illustrated in Figure 3.12. A brief description of the process is printed within the symbol's boundaries. A telegraphic or keyword style should be adopted because of the obvious space limitations. If a more extensive explanation is required, it should be placed elsewhere, either in an attached Comment symbol, in a footnote to the flowchart, or in accompanying documentation. Often the symbols or processing steps are numbered, and the number can be written above and to the left of the symbol, as shown in Figure 3.12(d). This same convention applies to all other flowcharting symbols.

According to the ANSI standards, the rectangular Operations symbol may represent either a manual or a computerized process. But when it is necessary to emphasize the manual nature of the process, for example, if a manual operation is embedded in an otherwise automated process, the optional trapezium Manual Operation sym-

bol may be used (Figure 3.12[e]). The trapezium symbol was used in Figures 3.8 and 3.9 to denote manual verification of input data. Conversely, if the fact of automation is to be emphasized, a stripe may be drawn across the top of the rectangular symbol. Pertinent information regarding the hardware or software may be inserted in the stripe (Figure 3.12[f] and [g]).

Another derivative form of the Operations symbol is the Predefined Operation symbol (Figure 3.12[h]); this is formed by drawing a vertical stripe down each side of the rectangular symbol. The Predefined Operation symbol is used to denote a group of processes defined in detail elsewhere—perhaps on an accompanying page. The objective is normally to avoid repeating the same group of symbols several times in a flowchart. A common example is the file maintenance operations associated with several master files.

Decision Symbol

The diamond-shaped Decision symbol is used when a decision is necessary or when the flow of information divides into separate processing paths according to a stated criterion. Its use is illustrated in Figure 3.13. The decision criterion is formulated as a brief question and

FIGURE 3.12 Examples of usage of operations symbols.

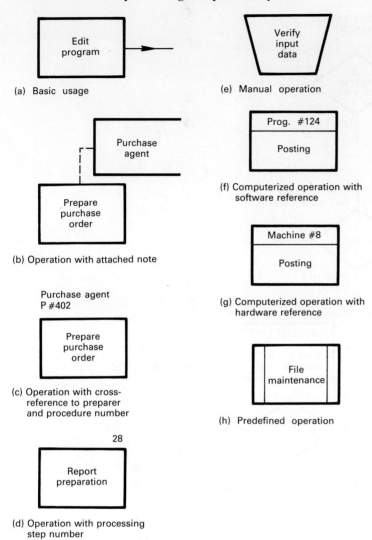

(a) Basic usage

(b) Operation with attached note

(c) Operation with cross-reference to preparer and procedure number

(d) Operation with processing step number

(e) Manual operation

(f) Computerized operation with software reference

(g) Computerized operation with hardware reference

(h) Predefined operation

is printed inside the symbol. Additional information may be contained in an attached Comment symbol, in a footnote, or in accompanying documentation.

There must be at least two possible outcomes of the decision, although there may be more. Up to three outcomes can be accommodated by flow lines exiting from the "corners" of the symbol. If there are additional outcomes, the exits can be stacked, as shown in Figure 3.13(d). Because of space limitations, it may be necessary to use Connector symbols to link some of the outcomes to their respective processes elsewhere on the page or on another page.

The decision criteria should be examined to ensure that there are no logical gaps or overlaps. For example, there is a gap in the choices "Sales < $1,000" and "Sales > $1,000." (What happens if sales are exactly equal to $1,000?) An example of an overlap is the following account-aging criteria: "0-30 days," "30-60

FIGURE 3.13 **Examples of usage of the decision symbol.**

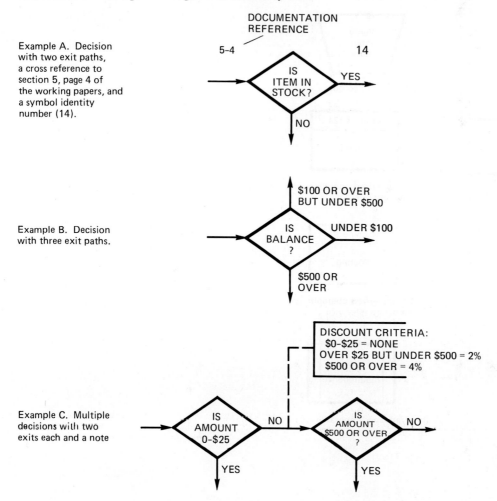

Example A. Decision with two exit paths, a cross reference to section 5, page 4 of the working papers, and a symbol identity number (14).

Example B. Decision with three exit paths.

Example C. Multiple decisions with two exits each and a note

days,'' ''Over 60 days''; that is, the handling of cases in which the account is exactly 30 or 60 days old is ambiguous.

File Symbols

The ANSI standards provide for a range of file symbols, each pertaining to a particular file medium. The most common ones are illustrated in Figure 3.14. The triangular Manual File symbol (Figures 3.14[a] and [b]) is used to show the storage of documents, reports,

memos, and other paper records. The records might be physically located on a post binder or in a Kardex file, ''in'' or ''out'' tray, filing cabinet, desk drawer, or fire-proof vault. A ''T'' or ''P'' printed inside the symbol designates whether the file is a temporary or a permanent one. An ''R'' can be printed in the symbol to designate a file used for reference purposes, for example, a file containing shipping instructions. Because the symbol is so small, there is little space to accommodate a descriptive legend inside the symbol. Instead, the nature of the file, the retention period, and other brief, pertinent information can be written above or below the symbol.

FIGURE 3.13 (Continued)

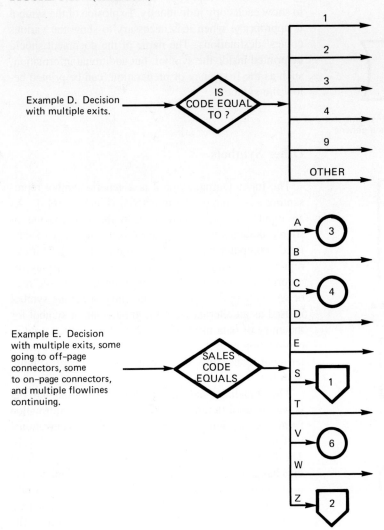

Example D. Decision with multiple exits.

Example E. Decision with multiple exits, some going to off-page connectors, some to on-page connectors, and multiple flowlines continuing.

The Punched Card symbol may be used either for an individual card or, if modified to make it three-dimensional, for a card file (Figure 3.14[c] and [d]). But this symbol is becoming obsolete, as are the punched cards themselves. The On-Line File symbol (Figure 3.14[e]) refers to any file that can be accessed by a processor device without human intervention. But this symbol is also used widely as a generic file symbol, denoting any file, manual or computerized; it is used in that sense in this book. The Magnetic Disk and Magnetic Tape File symbols (Figure 3.14[f] and [h]) designate files on those respective media. Floppy diskette files are sometimes designated by the nonstandard symbol shown in Figure 3.14(g). All the descriptions of the computer-oriented files can be shown by a name printed inside the symbol. Other brief, pertinent information, such as the arrangement of records, can be printed under the symbol, as shown in Figure 3.14(d).

FIGURE 3.14 **Examples of usage of file symbols.**

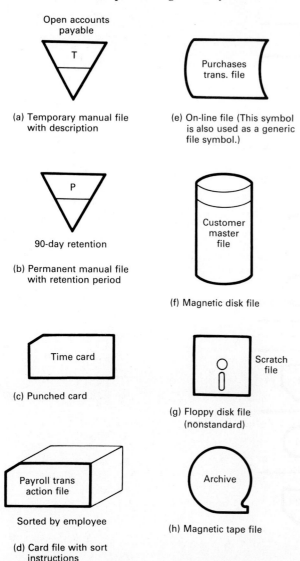

(a) Temporary manual file with description

(b) Permanent manual file with retention period

(c) Punched card

(d) Card file with sort instructions

(e) On-line file (This symbol is also used as a generic file symbol.)

(f) Magnetic disk file

(g) Floppy disk file (nonstandard)

(h) Magnetic tape file

Document Symbol

The Document symbol may represent a document, a report, or any similar kind of paperwork. Its use is illustrated in Figure 3.15. Multiple copies of a document can be represented by a single symbol; alternatively, the symbols can be exploded (as in Figure 3.15[b] and [c]) to show each copy individually. Explosion of the symbol is appropriate when it is necessary to show the various copies' destinations. The name of the document should be printed inside the symbol, but additional information, such as the frequency of preparation, can be printed below the symbol.

Other Symbols

The Input–Output symbol is a generic symbol representing any input or output activity (Figure 3.16[a]). As an input symbol, it can refer to the transcription of source documents into a journal or to the entry of data into a computer keyboard. As an output symbol, it can represent the output of data to a document, display, or report. The symbol can also be used to show file read or write operations. The manual entry or keying symbol is used as an alternative to the Input–Output symbol for the entry of data through a keyboard. It is often used in conjunction with the display symbol to represent a video terminal consisting of screen and keyboard (Figure 3.16[b]).

The Organizational Change symbol is nonstandard but is widely used to represent the movement of information from one location to another or from one organizational unit to another. Its usage is shown in Figure 3.16[c]). The Organizational Change symbol draws attention to the change of responsibility for the associated processing operations. When depiction of processing responsibilities is important, this symbol may provide a convenient alternative to the adoption of the columnar format. The Organizational Change symbol is often used to designate transfer of information—by courier, mail, or electronic means—between a branch or divisional office and headquarters. The point of origin or destination is printed between the double hash marks forming the symbol.

The On-Page and Off-Page Connector symbols (Figure 3.16[d]) are nonstandard but are widely used to show the flow of information to another part of the flowchart. The use of On-Page connectors is helpful when long flow lines or crossing flow lines would otherwise be necessary. However, such connectors should be used spar-

FIGURE 3.15 Examples of document symbol usage.

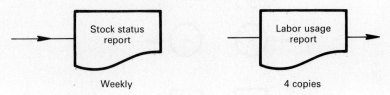

(a) Single symbols may represent
    multiple-copy documents.

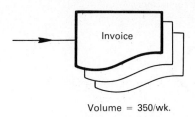

(b) Multiple symbols may represent
    multipart forms.

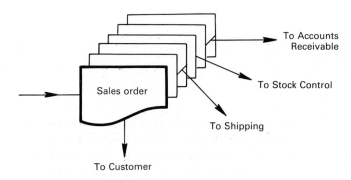

(c) Multipart forms may have continuing
    flow lines.

ingly, or the flowchart may become disjointed. The connectors are ordinarily used in pairs and are labeled accordingly. Off-Page connectors should bear the number of the page where their partners occur. Arrows should be used to show the direction of the flow of information and to distinguish between entry and exit connectors.

The Reference Pointer symbol (Figure 3.16[e]) is another nonstandard symbol used to emphasize or reference a particular part of a flowchart. Reference pointers are usually numbered and referred to in accompanying documentation. They are frequently used to designate control points, or the lack thereof, in a review of internal controls. They may also be used to identify an audit trail.

FIGURE 3.16   **Examples of usage of miscellaneous symbols.**

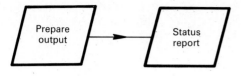

(a) Input/output symbol

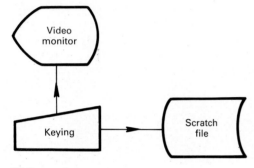

(b) Keyboard entry

(c) Organizational change symbol

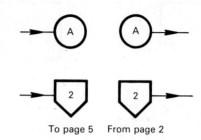

(d) On-page and off-page connectors

(e) Reference pointer symbol

Flow Lines

Flow lines are used to link symbols, to show the flow of information through the system, and to show the sequence of operations. The usage of flow lines is illustrated in Figure 3.17. There is a convention that the flow should be from left to right and from top to bottom; but it is not always possible to conform to this convention, and arrows should always be used to avoid ambiguity.

Ideally, the flow lines connecting the symbols should be as short as possible and should not cross one another, and efforts should be made to arrange the symbols to achieve this objective. However, the objective is not always attainable because of the nature of the system being flowcharted. Connector symbols can be used to avoid long flow lines, but, as noted earlier, they should be used sparingly; rearrangement of the symbols is a better solution than is excessive use of connectors. There also is the danger that crossing flow lines may be confused with connecting ones. The ANSI standards expressly state that flow lines that cross one another are assumed to make no mutual connections (Figure 3.17[a]). Connecting flowlines should be shown by offset lines with arrows, as shown in Figure 3.17(b). But some analysts allow the lines to cross and simply add a dot at the point of connection (resembling a blob of solder connecting two wires) to show that a connection is intended. A nonstandard but helpful way of emphasizing the *absence* of a connection between crossing flow lines is to leave small gaps in one of the lines, suggesting that it passes under the other flow line (Figure 3.17[d]).

FIGURE 3.17 Examples of flow line usage.

Example A. Flow lines with
no connections.

Example B. Connecting flow
lines.

Example C. Long flow lines
using on-page connectors.

Example D. Nonstandard
methods often used to show
crossing flow lines with no
connections. The form on
the right is preferred.

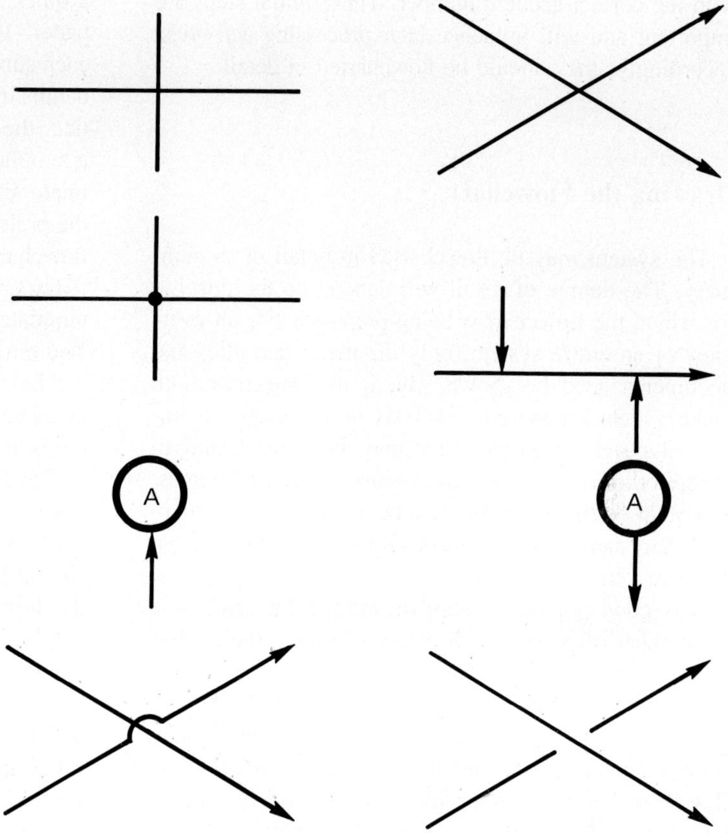

FLOWCHART PREPARATION

What Should Be Included

Systems flowcharts of business activities normally chart the flow of data through the various processes that make up the system. They are "pictures" of the data flow through the system, showing the documents involved, the files used, and the reports and displays generated.

In most cases, the flow of data begins with the input from a transaction document and ends as the data finally come to rest as part of a file, an output document, or a report. En route, the data may be checked, extended, summarized, transcribed to other media, formatted, filed and retrieved, and filed again. The flowchart shows the details of these activities. Transaction data are encoded, filed, and posted to a master file. Management reports; documents such as invoices or checks, and external financial statements may be prepared. The processing steps may be performed by clerks, supervisors, machines, or combinations thereof.

The flowchart should show the processing steps in their proper operational sequence, just as they are performed. Processing activities are normally triggered by the receipt or preparation of an input document: a sales order, a purchase requisition, an invoice, a timekeeping record, or some other document. The document may be received or prepared locally or at a remote location. Subsequent processing may be manual or computerized, but even in the latter case some manual activities are usually necessary to get the documents completed, time-stamped, arranged in proper sequence, batched, or coded with the correct account number. These initial steps are important and will influence later processing activities; accordingly, they should be flowcharted in detail.

Drawing the Flowchart

The system may be flowcharted in detail or in summary. The degree of detail will depend on the purpose for which the flowchart is being prepared. For an overview of an entire system, only the major activities and documents need be shown. But if the objective is to make a detailed systems analysis or to design an improved system, then each step must be charted, and all exception routines, files, documents, reference sources, and other pertinent details must be included. A summary flowchart can always be made from a detailed one, but not vice versa.

It is good practice to start drawing a flowchart on a large sheet of paper. With plenty of space, the analyst can concentrate on the system being charted and on how best to show its component features. Otherwise, the material may have to be selected according to the availability of space. The readability and even the accuracy of flowcharts suffer when the layout is cramped. In general, single page flowcharts are preferable to multipage flowcharts. If the whole system is represented on one page, all of its features and relationships will be visible and can be analyzed and evaluated. When different components are shown on different pages, important relationships may be misunderstood or overlooked. On the other hand, it may be impossible to show all the details of systems activities on a single flowchart. In that case, several flowcharts, each focusing on a different area of activity, will be clearer and more effective. Too much detail in a single flowchart will make it look cluttered and crowded.

A rough preliminary sketch is usually made early in a study. It can be drawn as data are gathered or as a design begins to take shape. It helps to identify gaps in the design or in the analyst's understanding of the existing system; undefined exits from a decision, lack of information on the distribution of a report, and illogical processing activities all will be obvious even in a rough

flowchart. This preliminary flowchart gives the analyst a quick overview of what the system will look like on paper. It also shows the amount of space required for each subsystem, where the flow lines must go, and other details that will affect the final layout. After a little practice, the symbols can be drawn freehand, without using a template; but it is a good idea to duplicate the approximate size of the template symbols so that the scale of the preliminary sketch will be similar to that of the final flowchart.

Except when making a rough preliminary sketch, a template should always be used to draw the symbols. The template provides uniform shape and size[2] for the symbols and gives the flowchart a neat, balanced appearance. Also, properly drawn symbols are easily recognized by other analysts and avoid confusion.

The lettering on flowcharts for symbol descriptions, notes, references, and so on should follow the same conventions used in preparing blueprints. All lettering should be printed and should be readable when holding the flowchart in its normal position, or from the right side view (i.e., with the page rotated 90 degrees). All lettering on the body of the flowchart should be of approximately the same size, except possibly in the case of lengthy notes that might require smaller print to conserve space. Titles should be several times larger and preferably in boldface. All flowcharts should have a descriptive title and should show the date of preparation and the initials or name of the analyst. The date and initials are normally in small print and are placed in the lower right-hand corner of the flowchart or centered under the title. The flowchart should be drawn in ink if photographic reproduction or reduction is anticipated.

The symbols should be drawn with approximately the same line thicknesses shown in Figure 3.10. Flow lines are often about one third the thickness of the symbol lines. This technique makes the symbols stand out on the flowchart, emphasizing the more important processing steps. In regard to symbols representing multicopy documents, it is usually preferable to draw the first copy with the standard symbol thickness and the others about one half as thick.

---

[2] The symbols shown in some of the illustrations in this book are not of standard size but have been reduced to conserve space.

In some situations, it may be desirable to number, or in some other way identify, each symbol or processing step on the flowchart. Particular processing steps can then be referenced in the supporting documentation. Also, when flowcharts are used as training aids, instructors may wish to refer to each step in the process as the system is described. There is no standard coding system for this purpose, and the analyst can devise any convenient scheme that seems appropriate. A numbering scheme is often used, in which the identifying number is placed outside the upper right-hand corner of the symbol. Alternatively, some analysts use a coordinate scheme similar to that used for street maps, dividing the page into squares, each designated by a letter and a number, such as E6.

Guidelines for Effective Flowcharting

Exhibit 3.1 presents a series of guidelines that are a working summary of the suggestions already discussed. They are not hard-and-fast rules, but they will help the analyst present a system more clearly and make the flowchart easier to understand.

Several common errors or pitfalls in flowchart construction, noted in Figure 3.18, should be avoided. Example (a) illustrates the confusion between the techniques of systems flowcharting and those of program flowcharting. A systems flowchart would not contain "Start" and "Stop" (or "Beginning" and "End") symbols, nor would it contain a Decision symbol with the question "End of file?"

EXHIBIT 3.1   Guidelines for Effective Systems Flowcharting

1. Start with the entry of the input document(s) or data into the system you are flowcharting.

2. Show the source and disposition of all major documents and copies of those documents.

3. Show all working files. Try to show a file on the flowchart just as it exists in the working environment. For example, if a file exists only once, try to arrange the layout of activities so that it is shown only once on the flowchart.

4. Use a template for symbols.

5. Separate exception routines from the path of major flow. The major flow is normally from left to right; an error-correction process, for example, should be shown above or below the major flow path.

6. Use connectors sparingly. An overuse of connectors indicates poor layout and makes the flowchart hard to follow. Usually a maximum of three or four pairs of connectors is sufficient.

7. Put the entire system on one page unless it is impractical to do so.

8. Place title, date drawn, and preparer's name or initials on all pages of the flowchart. Number pages—page *x* of *n*—so that reader will know when the flowchart is complete.

9. When abbreviating is necessary, use standard abbreviations only, or use a note or legend to explain nonstandard abbreviations.

10. Print, don't write. Use a telegraphic, keyword active style in the words on the flowchart, leaving out *a, an, the, with,* and other nonessential words.

11. Don't assume flow; use arrowheads on all flow lines.

12. Don't leave dangling branches. A dangling branch occurs when a process suddenly stops on the flowchart, but obviously other activities are necessary to complete the process. Explain with a note; show data going into another system, or whatever happens. Don't leave the reader wondering.

FIGURE 3.18 **Common errors in flowchart construction.**

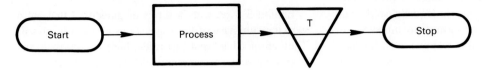

(a) Confusion with program flowcharting techniques

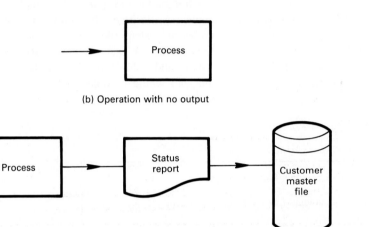

(b) Operation with no output

(c) Break in machine-readable data path

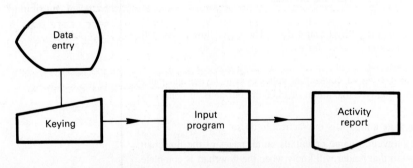

(d) Unintended "real-time" processing

Example (b) shows an operation with no output. (One wonders what its purpose could be!) Example (c) illustrates a common mistake in which a flow line connects a paper document or report to a machine-readable file. If data really were to be transferred from a report to a magnetic-disk file, the data would have to be entered through a keyboard or to be read by a scanning device; in either case additional symbols would be required in the flowchart. But the preparer of the flowchart probably intended the input to the file to come from data generated by the preceding operation that were already in machine-readable form. In that case, the flow line leading to the file should come from the operation and not from the report.

Example (d) appears to show the printing of an activity report in real time. In some situations the printed output would be generated at the very moment that the input data were entered; an example is the generation of an invoice for a walk-in customer. More generally, however, transactions are stored in a transaction file and printed later. Preparers of flowcharts may forget to include the transaction file, thereby implying unintended real-time printing.

Computer Aids to Flowchart Preparation

Flowcharting can be tedious, and accountants and analysts who need to prepare numerous flowcharts in the course of their jobs are naturally interested in any tools that can speed up the process and improve productivity. Some measure of automation has long been regarded as a desirable ideal. Obviously the preparation of systems flowcharts cannot be fully automated[3] because judgment is necessary in deciding which symbols should be used and where they should be located. But recently, several computer programs have been marketed that partially automate the preparation of systems flowcharts, and some of them work very well.

These flowcharting software packages allow the flowchart to be designed and edited on a screen and then to be printed. Flowcharts can be stored in machine-readable files and retrieved for future use. Video monitors with graphics capability may be required, and either graphics printers or plotters are needed to produce high-quality paper copies. Because of space limitations, only a portion of the flowchart appears on the screen at any one time. Sometimes the capability is provided to enlarge, or "zoom in" on, details of the flowchart.

Typical software packages provide representations of the standard ANSI symbols and a few of the more widely used nonstandard symbols. The placement of symbols is controlled by the user by moving a screen cursor. Individual symbols and/or groups of symbols can often be moved around to improve the flowchart's layout. Place-

ment of the symbols is usually not completely arbitrary; rather, the symbols can be placed at the intersections of imaginary "grid lines" and thus are arranged in regular rows and columns. This removes some flexibility but nevertheless helps preserve an ordered appearance. Flow lines connecting the symbols are entered under cursor control, or they may be inserted automatically by the program. In some cases the flow lines are automatically rerouted as symbols are moved from one location to another. Titles, legends, footnotes, and other textual material can be added as needed. An example of a flowchart prepared using a commercially available software package is shown in Figure 3.19. Several of the other flowcharts—and block diagrams—in this textbook were initially prepared in the same manner but were then redrawn for reproduction.

Computer-assisted preparation of flowcharts is much faster than manual preparation. Moreover, editing can be done quickly and efficiently without the need to redraw the whole flowchart. Production quality is good, although some of the features that can easily be incorporated in manual preparation may not be available. One, already mentioned, is the ability to place a symbol in any position within the flowchart. Another is the ability to draw the symbols with a pen thicker than that with which the flow lines are drawn. A third is the ability to vary the print size of textual material, particularly titles. Some of these problems can be overcome by manual retouching of completed flowcharts, which is still much faster than unassisted manual preparation.

Deficiencies in the currently available packages are likely to be removed as the software products mature. But even at this time, flowcharting software packages offer a major breakthrough in productivity, and they are likely to become increasingly popular in the future.

SUMMARY

The purpose of this chapter has been to give the student a grasp of the concepts, techniques, and uses of graphical modeling of information systems, with an emphasis on systems flowcharting.

Many types of graphical models are used to represent

---

[3] Software packages are available that fully automate the production of *program flowcharts* from computer program source code.

FIGURE 3.19 Computer-assisted flowchart preparation. This example was prepared using Interactive Easy Flow, a product of Haven Tree Software Ltd. It shows one strategy for verifying transaction entry to the accounting information system.

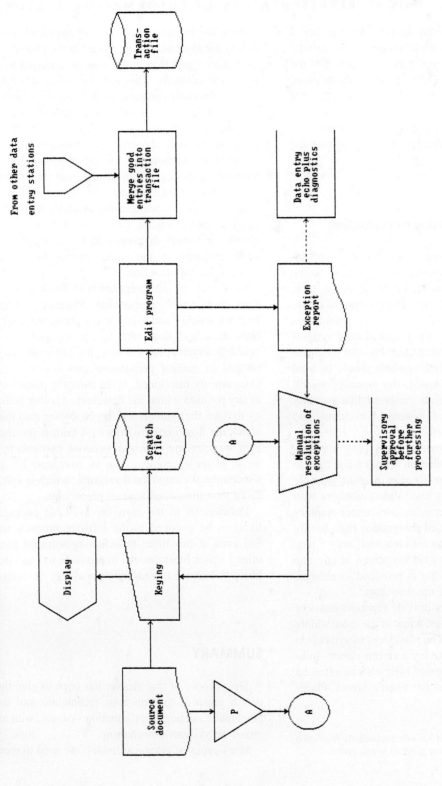

information systems and to make them easier to understand. Block diagrams, data flow diagrams, document flowcharts, and systems flowcharts are frequently used as visual aids in various systems-related activities ranging from design to personnel training. Graphical representations do not replace other descriptions of information systems, such as narrative descriptions, but supplement them effectively and efficiently.

Although there have been inroads from competing types of graphical modeling, systems flowcharting, which is regulated by national and international standards, remains one of the primary visual tools used by accountants. Systems flowcharts describe the flow of information through accounting systems. They relate the inputs, processes, files, communications, and outputs and show transaction paths and internal controls. Systems flowcharts are used in systems analysis and design, in the documentation of information systems, in the solution of systems problems, and in the evaluation of accounting information systems. Systems flowcharts are widely used to assist in the gathering of systems data, to assist in the conceptual testing of proposed solutions to systems problems, and as a basis for evaluating the adequacy of systems controls. The analysis of systems flowcharts plays a large role in the review of internal controls, performed as part of the external audit.

Systems flowcharts should be prepared in conformity with applicable national and international standards. In this way their usefulness is enhanced, and the possibility of ambiguities is reduced. Some derivative forms of systems flowcharts, including block diagrams and document flowcharts, depart from established flowcharting standards but nevertheless are useful in systems work.

The preparation and use of flowcharts are not activities to be left to professional systems analysts and designers. Flowcharts are essential tools for accountants, managers, and others who are involved with the information system in the conduct of their work and who may have to interact with analysts and designers when new systems are being developed. To fulfill their mission, accountants should acquire the basic skills necessary to prepare, evaluate, and use flowcharts. Computer aids to flowchart preparation make the task considerably easier. They take much of the tedium out of flowcharting and free the preparer to concentrate on the more creative aspects of the work.

BIBLIOGRAPHY

American National Standards Institute. *Flowchart Symbols and Their Usage in Information Processing*, Publ. no. ANSI X3.5. New York: American National Standards Institute, 1970.

Barton, Larry M. "How to Prepare a Flowchart." *The Practical Accountant*, November-December 1977, pp. 53-58.

Ernst & Whinney. *Evaluating Internal Control: Guide to Flowcharting*, Publ. no. 39080. Cleveland: Ernst & Whinney, 1979.

Farina, Mario V. *Flowcharting*. Englewood Cliffs, N.J.: Prentice-Hall, 1970.

Powers, Michael J., David R. Adams, and Harlan D. Mills. *Computer Information Systems Development: Analysis and Design*. Cincinnati: South-Western, 1984.

Radio Corporation of America. *Flowcharting Standards for Information Processing*, Publ. no 97-05-001. New York: Radio Corporation of America, January 1967.

U.S. Army. *AMC Information and Data Systems*. Vol. 5: *Flowcharting and Symbology*, Publ. no. AMCR 18-5. Washington, D.C.: U.S. Army Material Command, 1969.

DISCUSSION QUESTIONS AND PROBLEMS

1. Define and discuss the following terms:

· ANSI (American National Standards Institute) flow-charting standards
· Block diagram
· Bubble chart
· Columnar flowchart
· Data flow diagram
· Document
· Document flowchart
· Documentation
· Program flowchart
· Reference pointer
· Systems flowchart
· Telegraphic style

2. List several reasons that flowcharts are prepared by systems analysts and others. Which of these are of particular interest to managers or accountants?

3. Identify and discuss the main uses of systems flow-charts by
a. Systems analysts and designers
b. Managers
c. Internal accountants
d. External auditors

4. Draw the correct flowcharting symbol for each of the following processing activities, and include the corresponding legend in some suitable manner:

Manual processes:
a. Prepare invoice.
b. Make bank deposit (First National Bank).
c. Verify transaction entries (assistant controller).
d. Post transactions to the ledger (reference E29).

Automated processes:
e. Sort the customer file alphabetically.
f. Retrieve all open accounts (program #RTVOPN).
g. Copy the production order transaction file (Model 16B microcomputer).
h. Perform file maintenance on inventory file (operator reference, J-2).

5. Show the flowcharting symbol appropriate to the following decision situations, and include any notes that may be required.
a. Does the account have a zero balance?
b. Is the quantity on hand less than or greater than the reorder point? (What will happen if they are equal?)
c. Is the age of the account less than 30 days old, between 31 and 60 days old, or over 60 days old?
d. Is this sales representative's monthly sales total less than $100,000, between $100,001 and $300,000, between $300,001 and $1,000,000, or more than $1,000,000?

6. Draw the correct form of the document symbol to represent
a. A monthly open order report.
b. A four-part stores requisition form, of which all four copies go to the stores clerk.
c. A five-part invoice form distributed as follows: copies 1 and 2 to the customer, copy 3 to accounting, copy 4 to sales, and copy 5 to shipping.

7. Show the flowcharting symbol appropriate to the following types of files:

a. A manual open order file (temporary)
b. A manual closed order file (permanent)
c. An inventory file maintained on magnetic tape
d. An employee file maintained on a floppy diskette
e. A sales transaction file stored on a magnetic disk cartridge

8. You are the partner in charge of an audit engagement and have assigned an entry-level staff person to prepare a systems flowchart depicting part of the client's accounting system. The next day, the staff person presents you with the flowchart on the opposite page. Find the errors in the flowchart, and explain the correct usage of the symbols in question.

9. The accounts receivable function at Bayes Farm Products Company is divided into four areas: billing, preparation of monthly statements, collection, and delinquency follow-up. Billing activities start with the receipt of a sales order from the sales personnel. An invoice is cut, and the amount due is recorded in the customer ledger. Monthly statements are prepared from data in the customer ledger. When cash is received, a record of the collection is made in the cash receipts journal, and the customer ledger is credited with the amount. Delinquency procedures are initiated in cases in which an account has been outstanding for more than 90 days. A delinquency notice, or "dun," is sent to the customer. If the customer fails to respond, the account will be turned over to a collections agency.

Required
a. Prepare a hierarchical block diagram showing the relationships among the various levels of subsystems. Thus "invoice preparation" would be a component of "billing," which in turn would be a component of the accounts receivable system as a whole.
b. Prepare a "horizontal" block diagram of the same system, showing the flow of information among components at the lowest level, which includes "invoice preparation," "cash receipt," and "transfer to collections agency."

10. In a manual sales order–processing system, sales orders are prepared in triplicate by the sales personnel and are routed to accounting. There, a four-part invoice and a four-part shipping document are prepared. One

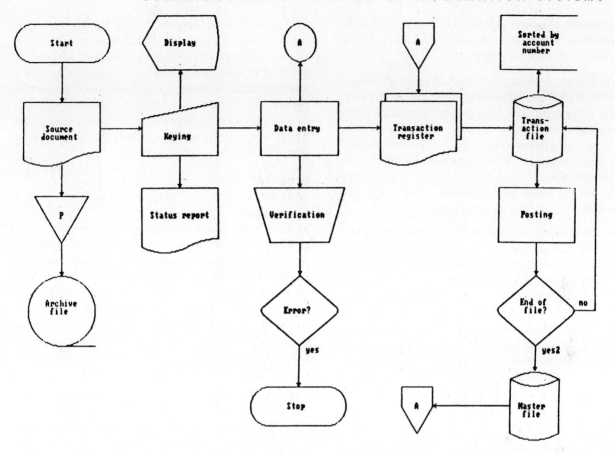

copy of each is returned to the salesperson together with one copy of the sales order form. A second copy of the order form is stapled to two copies of the shipping document and is sent to dispatching. Two copies of the invoice are sent to the customer. The remaining copies of the order form, invoices, and shipping document are placed in a permanent file in the accounting department. A record of all transactions is made in a sales ledger.

Required

Prepare a system flowchart of this sales order–processing system.

11. Jones Company operates an automated payroll system. Machine-readable time cards are batched and input to the payroll calculation program (PAYCALC). The employee master file, which contains the name, address, pay rate, marital status, and number of dependents

of each employee, is kept on magnetic tape. The file is accessed by the program, along with a file containing the tax-withholding tables that also resides on magnetic disk. Paychecks are prepared automatically, and a two-part payroll register is printed. One part of the register is sent to accounting. After the paychecks are cashed, the canceled checks are reconciled to the payroll register in the accounting department. This reconciliation is done manually.

Required

Construct a systems flowchart for this simplified payroll system.

12. Draw a horizontal block diagram showing the major subsystems in the engineering department of Red Corporation. The subsystems are research and development (R&D), advanced development, routine product development, computer support, and drafting. Show the relationships among the subsystems and the principal information flows among them.

13. Prepare a hierarchical block diagram showing a division of your own educational institution into its component subsystems. The highest-level subsystems might be administrative, academic, and athletic. In turn the academic subsystem could be divided into sub-subsystems corresponding to the various schools and colleges in the institution. Continue your analysis at least down to the level of academic departments. Also analyze the administrative and athletic subsystems.

14. Draw a document flowchart to represent the examination and grading processes at a university. The instructors return graded examination papers to the students and submit grades to the registrar, with copies to their own department and college. The registrar mails the grade report forms to the students and sends selected copies to scholarship agencies and to the Veterans Association. Permanent records of student grades are maintained by both the dean of the college and the registrar. Individual department chairpersons do not maintain permanent records but review the grades each semester to monitor examination standards and to help evaluate individual instructors.

15. Discuss the role of computer software packages in the preparation of systems flowcharts and other types of graphical representation of information systems. What are the main advantages and disadvantages of such packages? What do you think will be the future development of such packages?

16. Aquamarine Company, a manufacturer of heavy machinery, uses a system of stores requisitions to control the release of raw materials to production. Four-part requisition forms are prepared by production personnel, authorized by shop supervisors, and taken to the stores. At the stores window, the stores clerk stamps the requisition forms FILLED, returns one copy of the form to the requestor, and helps load the appropriate materials onto a forklift truck. A second copy of the requisition form is returned independently to the supervisor of the originating department; another copy is retained in the stores; and the fourth copy is forwarded to cost accounting. The stores copy is used to update perpetual inventory records and to prepare a daily materials issuance report, which is circulated to shop supervisors and the factory superintendent. The copy received by cost accounting is used (along with other inputs) to prepare a weekly production report that is distributed to production control, the factory superintendent, and the vice-president of operations. A monthly materials usage variance report is also prepared and distributed to shop supervisors and the factory superintendent.

Required
a. Draw a data flow diagram of the process just described.
b. Draw a document flowchart of the process.
c. Prepare a detailed systems flowchart of the process, using the Organizational Change symbol to denote transfers of processing responsibility.
d. Prepare a columnar systems flowchart of the process.
e. A manager is trying to understand the workings of the system. The manager's only source of information about the system is one of the four graphical representations that you have prepared. Which one would the manager choose?

17. Adam Company employs a work-in-process system to keep track of the 2,000 jobs that typically are in the factory at any one time. Details of labor and materials costs expended on jobs are encoded daily from job cards onto magnetic tapes. Each week, the tapes produced are merged into a transaction file maintained in chronological order on magnetic disk. A program is then run to apply overhead to all jobs as a percentage of direct labor expended. After this program is run, the transaction file is sorted by job number, and the data are posted to the work-in-process master file, which is also maintained on magnetic disk.

Several management reports are prepared from the work-in-process file. One lists all current jobs in the factory by job number; another lists jobs by the date on which they were placed in production; and a third lists the jobs by the target completion date.

Required
Draw a systems flowchart of the work-in-process system described here. Show all merging and sorting operations (using Operations symbols), and add footnotes explaining each step in the transaction processing.

4

Input–Output Formats and Communication of Accounting Information

---

LEARNING OBJECTIVES

After you have studied this chapter you should be able to

- Explain the basic issue of person–person, person–machine, and machine–person communication.
- Identify the role of forms and forms media.
- Discuss the basic principles of forms design.
- Discuss the relationship between effectiveness and aesthetics in forms design.
- Explain the use of block and tabular formats.
- Explain the use of graphs and charts in presenting accounting information.
- Design a range of screen and paper forms.

CHAPTER OUTLINE

THE NATURE OF INFORMATION FORMATS

Formats and Comprehension

As information flows through the information system, it must cross numerous interfaces between adjacent components of the system. These interfaces may connect two computer devices, a person and a machine, or two or more people. When two machines—such as an input terminal and a processor device—communicate with each other, the format of the data must be specified, but that format does not have to satisfy any kind of quality requirement. No matter how "jumbled up" the data may be and no matter how "messy" the format may be, any recipient machine containing a minimal amount of processing logic can normally assimilate and "understand" the data. For instance, the following communication would be entirely clear to a machine once it was instructed to ignore every second character:

Tahbicsd eifsg hai jmkelsmsnaogpeq.

But data transfer takes on a special dimension when the human element is involved. When two people—or one person and a machine—communicate, the information format must be structured so that they can understand each other. If the format is carefully designed, the data will readily be understood, and the people involved will be able to communicate effectively and efficiently. But if it is poorly designed, comprehension will be impaired; efficiency will be lost; errors may be made; and motivation may be adversely affected. In the example just given, the information is presented to us, but we have difficulty recognizing it even when we know the formatting rules.

In information systems terminology, information formats are referred to as *forms*. The word *form* is not (as in everyday usage) restricted to a paper document but pertains to any information medium used for visual, person-person, person-machine, or machine-person communication. In fact, even in the case of a paper document, the "form" refers to the spatial configuration of the information on the paper, not to the piece of paper itself.

Communications Media

Traditionally, accounting data were communicated on paper media. Paper source documents captured the transaction data; the data were transcribed into paper journals and subsequently posted to paper ledgers; and finally, the processed financial statements were printed on paper for distribution to their recipients. Today, the paper media are supplemented by other types, including microfilm, screen displays, and voice synthesizers, as well as a variety of machine-readable media. When human interfaces are involved and when the communications media are visual, the same basic principles of forms design apply, although the techniques by which those principles are applied may vary according to the particular medium involved. An example of a screen form is shown in Figure 4.1. The subject of "forms design" extends to the design of paper documents and reports, microfilm materials, screen displays, and any other relevant visual media. It does not extend to magnetic or electronic media, because they are not human readable, nor does it extend to voice synthesis because this is not a visual

medium. Analogous considerations might apply to non-visual media, but they do not use a spatial configuration of data.

Types of Information Formats

In the past, most accounting data were communicated in either block formats or tabular formats. Block formats are used widely for document and screen forms. A block format is one in which a descriptive legend is attached to each item of data; examples are:

```
Name: Susan Jenkins
Amount received: $239,400
Units on hand: 120
```

Reports are usually presented in tabular formats, that is, as columns of figures. The balance sheet and income statement are familiar examples of tabular presentations, and most internal management reports are also formatted as tables of data. Tables provide an ideal format for presenting quantitative data when the recipient will refer

FIGURE 4.1 Screen form for an interactive computer system. (Courtesy of BPI Systems, Inc.)

```
                    BPI Systems, Inc.
              General Accounting - Version 1.10
                    Menu 2 - Posting

  1 Run Queue                2 Erase Queue
  3 Change/Exit BPI System   4 Enter Company Code and Dates
  5 Change Menu              6 Print on  Screen /Printer


  31 Post Ledgers            41 Process End-of-Month
  32 Print Income Statement  42 Process End-of-Quarter
  33 Print Trial Balance     43 Process End-of-Year
  34 Print Balance Sheet     44 Process End-of-Fourth-Quarter


   Data Drive:    B
   Company Code: XXXXXX     As-Of   Date: MM/DD/YY
   Password    : XXXXXX     Today's Date: MM/DD/YY

  Command Queue: Empty

  Enter Command Number ==>
```

to details of the data, that is, will "look up" selected numbers in the table. For example, the recipient of a balance sheet might be interested in the balance of long-term investments. The person would find the value stated to a high degree of precision and, assuming that the financial statements were audited, would have considerable confidence that the value was correct.

The recipient of data presented in a tabular format might also be interested in the range, mean, trend, and other statistics and might extract such data formally by means of a calculation or informally by judgment. An experienced credit manager can scan a table of customer balances and infer valuable information about the impact of the company's credit policies, particularly if the data are sorted by account balance (Figure 4.2[a]). However, inferences of qualitative characteristics obtained from scanning a table of data may not be of as high a quality as could be obtained from alternative information formats. For instance, a bar chart showing the number of

accounts in each of several balance categories (Figure 4.2[b]) would probably give a better overall picture of the data. Graphics formats—charts and graphs—are not intended to provide numerical precision. But they clearly show the qualitative characteristics; that is, they show "at a glance" selected qualitative features of interest to their recipients.

Forms can be classified as either input or output forms according to which of the two main interfaces, person–machine or machine–person, is being considered. Block and tabular formats are appropriate to both input and output forms. However, graphics formats are normally appropriate only to output forms. Information processing ordinarily demands a level of precision in the input data that cannot be achieved from graphics formats. In certain industrial situations, accounting data are measured using on-line analog devices and are converted to numerical form upon input to the information system; but in these cases, the data are fed directly into the system, and no human interface is involved.

Some input forms elicit a dialogue with the user. One example is an application document consisting of questions to which the user responds. Another example is an input screen display consisting of prompts for data. Other types of forms, including most output forms, simply communicate information in one direction.

FIGURE 4.2 Alternative formats for the same data.
Tabular formats (a) communicate quantitative precision, whereas charts or graphs (b) emphasize the qualitative characteristics of the data.

Customer No.	Account Balance
15819	42.25
09281	50.00
41120	71.85
74574	169.30
67494	409.50
-----	------
-----	------
55031	8,551.00
00995	12,345.40
72451	20,766.75

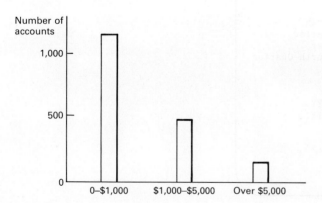

GENERAL PRINCIPLES OF FORMS DESIGN

Forms design is the arrangement of information symbols on a plane surface. The symbols include data elements and descriptive legends that explain the data. Forms design is one part of the broader field of spatial design that extends to commercial and fine art.

Effective forms design requires some creativity and knowledge of certain generally accepted guidelines. Most people are creative enough to do an acceptable job, although some are obviously better than others. Inherent creativity can be enhanced by using the traditional rules and guidelines of spatial design. The objective is not to produce an artistic masterpiece; rather, it is to produce something functional, easy to use, and aesthetic. Many forms are in constant use, and the performance of the individuals working with the forms depends—sometimes critically—on the effectiveness of the forms design.

The rules and guidelines for effective forms design focus on the following factors:

• Clarity of presentation
• Grouping and logical flow of data
• Effective use of space
• Ease of use
• Size and proportion
• Use of special effects

Clarity

Clarity is of obvious importance. The whole notion of forms centers on the need for easy understanding and effective communication of information. The clearer the form is, the more impact it will have, and the less likely it will be to produce confusion and misunderstanding. Perhaps the best way to achieve clarity is to select carefully the data to be presented on the form. A form containing relatively few data may convey much useful information and have substantial impact, whereas one containing a great deal of data may give the user mental indigestion and convey little real information. Irrelevant data create confusion and distract from important material and should be omitted so as to allow the principal message to come through.

Grouping and Logical Flow

Grouping data is important when the form refers to several different concepts. The form should be divided into regions, each dealing with a particular concept and containing data that have a common element. Allowing data elements relating to one idea to become interspersed with those relating to other ideas causes concept fragmentation and loss of impact.

The arrangement of the major conceptual groupings on a form, as well as the arrangement of data elements within a given group, should preserve a logical flow of ideas so as to avoid mental dissonance. Such dissonance occurs when we are forced to jump from one idea to another; it offends our sense of aesthetics and also reduces the performance of those who must work with the form. To give an example, Exhibit 4.1 contains a list of questions that might be addressed to a credit applicant. In the first case the questions are arranged randomly,

resulting in serious dissonance; that is, the user has to "shift gears" between each question to attend to the different kinds of information being requested. In the second case, the questions are arranged into logical groups and are sequenced to produce a satisfying flow of ideas.

Use of Space

The effective use of space also pertains to the arrangement of material within the available space of the page or screen. Newspaper editors face a similar problem in designing the optimal layout of news items on the pages of a newspaper. The objective should be to arrange the major data groupings to fill the available space and still have suitable margins; large areas of blank space should be avoided. The width of the margins should be adequate to provide for typical usage of the material; for instance, it may be necessary to punch holes in documents or reports for insertion into ring binders. On the other hand, screen displays may need no margins.

Considerations of space utilization extend to detailed data elements. Some data elements are of variable length, and so enough space must be provided to accommodate the maximum length likely to be encountered. The amount of space provided must also reflect how the data entry is to be made. Handwritten entries typically occupy more space than do printed entries, particularly if they are to be made using crude writing implements such as felt-tip markers. Input documents often do not allow enough space for effective completion in the environment in which they will be used. Examples are the following:

```
Address (street, city, state, zip) _____
```

on a form offering some open-ended invitation:

```
List all manuals you wish to
receive _____
Write any complaints here [    ]
```

or on a form to be filled out on the loading bay:

```
Name of trucking company _____
Description of shipment _____
```

Exhibit 4.1   Logical Grouping and Flow of Information

(a) Random arrangement of data causing mental dissonance

```
CREDIT APPLICATION

Annual salary
Street address
Middle initial
Other income
Number of dependents
First name
City, state, zip
Employer
Other credit references
Last name
Length of time at present address
Credit cards held (with balances)
Marital status
Financial commitments
Name of bank
```

(b) Arrangement of data to preserve the logical flow of ideas and to avoid mental
dissonance

```
CREDIT APPLICATION
Biographical Data:
    First name
    Middle initial
    Last name
    Street address
    City, state, zip
    Length of time at present address
    Telephone number
    Marital status
    Number of dependents

Employment and Financial Data:
    Employer
    Annual salary
    Other income
    Financial commitments

Credit History:
    Name of bank
    Other credit references
    Credit cards held (with balances)
```

Ease of Use

Ease of use depends greatly on the type of form involved. Manually completed input forms should use check-off boxes wherever possible to reduce the amount of writing involved. Check-off boxes also force the user to provide the information in a preferred style, thereby reducing the variability of the responses. But care should be taken to avoid overrestricting the user; for example, the following request excludes an important segment of the population (widowed persons) as well as people engaging in nontraditional life-styles:

```
Marital status: S [ ], M [ ], D [ ]
```

For safety, options like this should also provide a catch-all category:

```
Other [  ], specify: _____
```

Instructions should be clear but should not overwhelm the other contents of the form. Instructions such as "Today's date" and "Your name" are preferable to "Date" and "Name." But lengthy instructions should be removed from the vicinity of the associated data element and placed elsewhere, perhaps in accompanying documentation.

Written instructions relating to the distribution of copies of a document can be supplemented by numbering or coloring the copies:

```
          Copy #1 to customer
          Copy #2 to Sales
          Copy #3 to Accounting
```

or

```
          Pink copy to employee
          Yellow copy to Personnel
          Blue copy to Labor Department
```

Size and Proportion

The size and proportion of forms largely depend on practical considerations. Among the most obvious factors that must be taken into account are the volume of data to be included, the capacity of the device used to produce the forms, the need for compatibility with related items such as binders and envelopes, and the availability of standard paper stock.

The standard computer printer has a maximum usable width of 132 characters, at a pitch of 10 characters per inch. Narrow-carriage printers have a width of 80 characters, at 10 characters per inch, but may have variable pitch to provide either expanded or condensed type. Typewriters usually have a pitch of either 10 or 12 characters per inch. The standard vertical pitch, for both printers and typewriters, is 6 lines per inch, with double spacing corresponding to 3 lines per inch. Some printers have a range of vertical pitches.

The standard screen on a video terminal or monitor can display numbers and text over a width of 80 characters and a height of 24 or 25 lines. However, both the vertical and the horizontal pitch may vary from one device to another. Screens are available providing greater capacity, but they are considerably more expensive. Monitors designed for graphics output offer finer screen resolution and/or color capability.

Many output forms are printed on plain paper. Standard bond typing paper measures $8\frac{1}{2}$ in. x 11 in., providing a maximum of 66 lines at a vertical pitch of 6 lines per inch. Legal-size paper measures $8\frac{1}{2}$ in. x 14 in. and provides for a maximum of 84 lines at 6 lines per inch. Standard computer paper measures either $8\frac{1}{2}$ (or $9\frac{1}{2}$ including the perforations) or 18 in. x 11 in. and, again, provides for a maximum of 66 lines at 6 lines per inch.

Paper forms can be ordered in nonstandard sizes. Many "special" forms, such as checks, invoices, and purchase orders, are preprinted and are designed to fit into envelopes or conform to other constraints. But the cost of forms of nonstandard sizes will rise abruptly if they cannot be cut from rolls of standard stock paper. Accordingly, there is an economic incentive to make special forms conform to standard sizes whenever possible. Many check forms, for example, are $8\frac{1}{2}$ in. in width, even though their height may be much less than 11 in.

Aside from practical considerations, the size and proportion of forms become largely a matter of aesthetics. It has long been recognized that certain proportions (width versus height) are aesthetically more pleasing

FIGURE 4.3   Proportions of several familiar forms, all drawn within the same area.

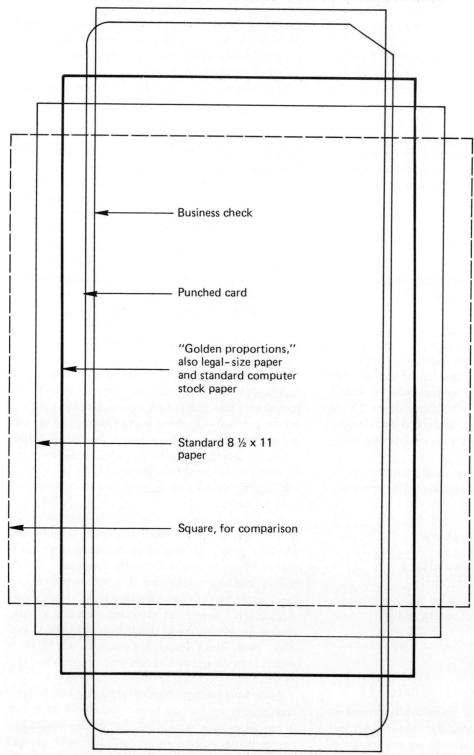

Business check

Punched card

"Golden proportions,"
also legal-size paper
and standard computer
stock paper

Standard 8 ½ x 11
paper

Square, for comparison

than others. The Greeks observed the rule of "golden proportions" or "divine proportions." Lucas Pacioli later placed this rule on a theoretical basis. (He also proposed the principles of double-entry bookkeeping.) A rectangle with the golden proportions has sides in a ratio of 0.618 to 1.[1] This ratio is very close to the proportions of legal-size paper (0.607) and computer stock paper (0.611); it is more elongated than regular bond typing paper (0.773) but is much less elongated than a standard punched card (0.441) or a check (0.35 to 0.45). These proportions are compared in Figure 4.3.

Aesthetics should not be the overriding concern in forms design. On the other hand, centuries of support for guidelines such as the golden proportions should not be ignored. Forms seem to "look right" when their proportions are somewhere between 2:3 and 3:5 (0.667 and 0.6, respectively). Many design publications recommend these proportions not only for the forms themselves but also for major items of content such as tables and charts.

Special Effects

Special effects include the use of artwork, logos, and other techniques offering visual or aesthetic appeal. Most organizations choose to incorporate the company logo or the company name, in an ornamental typeface, on output documents such as checks, purchase orders, and invoices. Special effects can be useful in enhancing the impact of a form and are often used for promotional purposes. They seek to convey something of the corporate image. On the other hand, most organizations keep special effects to a minimum on internal forms, such as employee expense claims and materials requisitions; these forms are considered to be purely functional in nature and are designed accordingly.

The best advice with regard to special effects is to use them sparingly and to exercise good taste. The excessive use of special effects or tasteless gimmicks detracts from the image of the organization and is not likely to improve the communication of information, which is the form's primary purpose.

Examples of Good Forms Design

Some examples of effective forms design are presented in Figures 4.4(a) through (e).[2] The first two are input forms and the last three are output forms. The first

FIGURE 4.4 Some examples of effective form design.

(a) Time sheet.

WINN-DIXIE STORES, INC.

Name ______________________

Store or Market No. ______________________

Job Classification ______________________

Social Security No. ______________________

Week Ending ______________ 19 ______

IN	OUT	IN	OUT	IN	OUT

I CERTIFY THIS CARD ACCURATELY RECORDS ALL TIME WORKED BY ME.

EMPLOYEE'S SIGNATURE ______________________

____
DEPT. MANAGER'S SIGNATURE

____
MANAGER'S SIGNATURE

SPEEDISET ® MOORE BUSINESS FORMS, INC., A Raleigh, N. C.

[1] The exact value is $(5^{1/2} - 1)/2$.

[2] These forms are reproduced by courtesy of Winn-Dixie Stores, Inc., General Dynamics, Zep Manufacturing Company, Delta Transport, Inc., and Clark Truck Line.

FIGURE 4.4 (Continued) (b) Sales order form.

PRESS HARD YOU ARE MAKING SEVERAL COPIES

SPEEDISET® MOORE BUSINESS FORMS, INC., ABILENE, TEX. - N 379321443

GENERAL DYNAMICS
Abilene Facility
P.O. Box 1401 – 300 Wall St., Abilene, Texas 79604 · (915) 692-0122

S.O. NO._____ CHG. NO._____

BATES NO._____

ECT NO._____

DATE_____ / ___ / _____

SALES ORDER NUMBER
_____

CUSTOMER_____ PART NO._____

P.O. NO._____ CHG. NO._____ GSI REQ_____ ☐

REASON FOR CHANGE	
SCHEDULE_____ ☐	E.D._____ ☐
CONFIGURATION_____ ☐	MFG. INSTRUCTIONS_____ ☐
PRICE_____ ☐	OTHER_____ ☐

ROUTING AND APPROVAL

☐ **ACCOUNTING**

ITEM NO._____ ASSY. NO._____ PROJ. NO._____ APPROVED:_____

ITEM NO._____ ASSY. NO._____ PROJ. NO._____ DATE:_____

☐ **ENGINEERING** RECEIVED_____

PLANNING CHG'D ☐ YES ☐ NO BY: (DATE)_____ ITEM_____ PLNG CHG ☐

COMMENTS_____ ITEM_____ PLNG CHG ☐

REVIEWED _____ APPROVED _____

DATE_____ DATE _____

☐ **PRODUCTION CONTROL** RECEIVED:_____

☐ MASTER SCHEDULE NOTED ☐ SCHEDULE O.K. ☐ SCHEDULE NOT O.K.

COMMENTS_____

REVIEWED_____ DATE_____ APPROVED_____ DATE_____

☐ **CONTRACTS** RECEIVED_____
COMMENTS _____

APPROVED _____ DATE _____

☐ **MANAGEMENT**

APPROVED _____ DATE _____

GENERAL COMMENTS:

_____
_____
_____
_____
_____
_____
_____
_____
_____
_____

CONTRACTS FILE COPY

FIGURE 4.4 (Continued) (c) Invoice.

BILL TO:

SHIP TO:

CUSTOMER'S COPY

ZeP MANUFACTURING COMPANY
A DIVISION OF NATIONAL SERVICE INDUSTRIES, INCORPORATED

First ... in maintenance and sanitation

6567565
INVOICE NUMBER

P.O. BOX 299
10 FADEM ROAD
SPRINGFIELD, NEW JERSEY 07081
201 - 379-6545
For your Convenience . . .

PLANTS and OFFICES from COAST to COAST

U.S.A. - CANADA - MEXICO

CUSTOMER NUMBER	BRANCH CODE	SALESMAN		ACTIVITY CODE	INVOICE NUMBER	DATE			ORDERED BY	TERMS
		NAME	CODE			MTH.	DAY	YR.		NET – 30 DAYS
	365				6567565					

ROUTING VIA	TRANSPORTATION TYPE	CUSTOMER'S ORDER NUMBER	OUR ORDER NUMBER	GOODS RETURNED WITH-OUT OUR AUTHORITY WILL NOT BE ACCEPTED.

UNIT QUANTITY	UNIT OF ISSUE	EXTENDED QUANTITY	PRICE PER MEASURE	ITEM DESCRIPTION	EXTENDED AMOUNT

TAXABLE AMOUNT	SALES TAX		SUB - TOTAL	TRANSPORTATION CHARGES	TRANS SALES TAX		PAY THIS AMOUNT	INVOICE TOTAL
	PERCENT	AMOUNT			PERCENT	AMOUNT		

ALL ORDERS TO SALESMAN ARE SUBJECT TO APPROVAL OF THE HOME OFFICE. QUOTATIONS SUBJECT TO CHANGE WITHOUT NOTICE. ALL CLAIMS FOR ERROR OR ADJUSTMENT OF ANY KIND MUST BE MADE FIVE DAYS AFTER RECEIPT OF GOODS.

"WE HEREBY CERTIFY THAT THESE GOODS WERE PRODUCED IN COMPLIANCE WITH ALL APPLICABLE REQUIREMENTS OF SEC. 6-7 AND 12 OF FAIR LABOR STANDARDS ACT AS AMENDED, AND OF REGULATIONS AND ORDERS OF THE UNITED STATES DEPARTMENT OF LABOR ISSUED UNDER SEC. 14 THEREOF."

PLEASE RETURN ATTACHED REMITTANCE COPY WITH YOUR PAYMENT. THANK YOU.

example is a time sheet used by a large retail grocery chain. It is simple and to the point, soliciting input data together with the necessary authorizations. The second is a sales order form used by a branch of a large manufacturing firm. It provides for the review of orders by several organizational groups and solicits input both via checkmarks and in the form of narrative comments. The form is in six parts, five of which are to be retained by the various departments and the sixth used for follow-up.

The third example is an invoice form used by another manufacturing firm and is also in six parts, two of which go to the customer. A substantial amount of material has been included on this form, but the arrangement of items avoids a cluttered appearance. Also, because this is an output form directed to customers, special effects have

FIGURE 4.4 (Continued) (d) Paycheck with stub.

DELTA TRANSPORT, INC.
ROUTE 2, BOX 221X
SAN ANTONIO, TEXAS 78229

5310

DATE

PAY

DOLLARS $

TO THE ORDER OF

DELTA TRANSPORT, INC.
PAYROLL ACCOUNT

SOUTHWEST TEXAS NATIONAL BANK
SAN ANTONIO, TEXAS 78229

⑆1140⑈0050⑆ ⑈0 009 326⑈

DELTA TRANSPORT, INC. • San Antonio, Texas PAYEE: DETACH THIS STATEMENT BEFORE DEPOSITING CHECK.

EMPLOYEE'S NAME

S.S. NO.

PAY PERIOD ENDING	HOURS	RATE	GROSS EARNINGS	DEDUCTIONS					NET EARNINGS PAID
				F.I.C.A.	W.H.	Insurance			
	REG. TIME								
	OVERTIME								

been used freely. These would have been out of place on an input form such as the time sheet. The fourth and fifth examples, a payroll check and a shipping document, also use promotional symbols. Both use space effectively and have attractive layouts. The paycheck is in two parts, and the shipping document is in six parts.

The proportions of these five forms are

Time sheet	0.61
Sales order form	0.72
Invoice	0.77
Paycheck:	
alone	0.41
with stub	0.82
Shipping document	0.65

Two of them, the time sheet and the shipping document, lie in the aesthetic range of 2:3 to 3:5, whereas the others have evidently been chosen according to practical considerations; nevertheless they have a width of 8 in. and thus conform to the dimensions of envelopes and binders.

BLOCK AND TABULAR FORMATS

Block Formats

As already noted, a block format or layout is one in which descriptive captions, legends, and/or prompts are placed next to the data elements to which they refer (Figure 4.5). Captions are usually to the left, or sometimes above, their associated data elements. Figure 4.5

FIGURE 4.4 (Continued) (e) Shipping document.

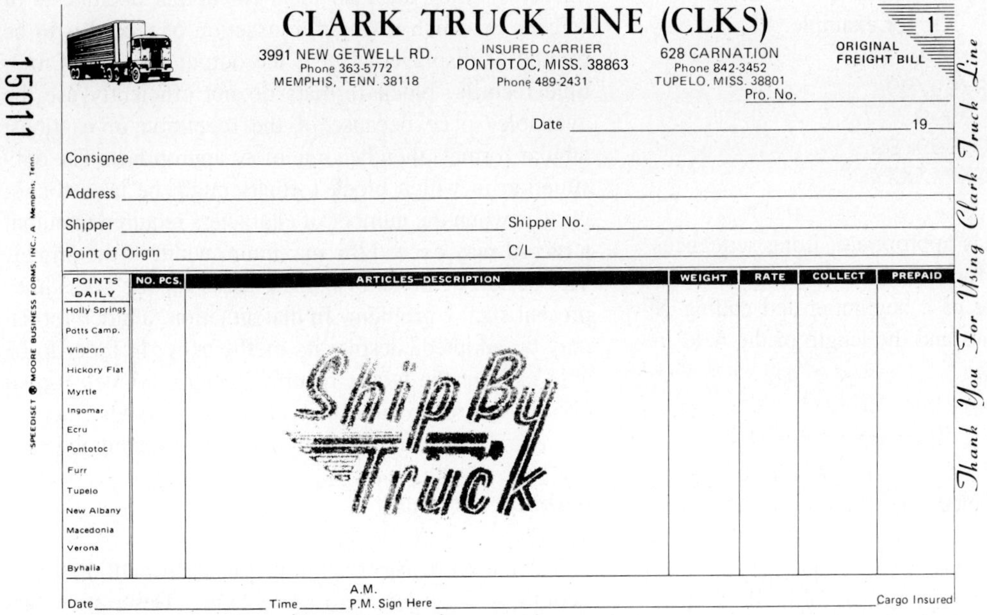

15011

SPEEDISET ® MOORE BUSINESS FORMS, INC. A Memphis, Tenn.

CLARK TRUCK LINE (CLKS)

3991 NEW GETWELL RD.
Phone 363-5772
MEMPHIS, TENN. 38118

INSURED CARRIER
PONTOTOC, MISS. 38863
Phone 489-2431

628 CARNATION
Phone 842-3452
TUPELO, MISS. 38801

1

ORIGINAL FREIGHT BILL

Pro. No. ______

Date ______ 19___

Consignee ______

Address ______

Shipper ______ Shipper No. ______

Point of Origin ______ C/L ______

POINTS DAILY	NO. PCS.	ARTICLES—DESCRIPTION	WEIGHT	RATE	COLLECT	PREPAID
Holly Springs						
Potts Camp.						
Winborn						
Hickory Flat						
Myrtle						
Ingomar						
Ecru						
Pontotoc						
Furr						
Tupelo						
New Albany						
Macedonia						
Verona						
Byhalia						

Ship By Truck

Date ______ Time ______ A.M. P.M. Sign Here ______ Cargo Insured

Thank You For Using Clark Truck Line

FIGURE 4.5 Example of block format used for a screen form.

```
                GENERAL JOURNAL ENTRY

Enter:
  Transaction date (MM/DD/YY)        99/99/99
  Source code & reference            XX/99999
  Debit account number               9999
  Amount                            $999999.99
  ...
  ...
  Credit account number              9999
  Amount                            $99999.99
  ...
  ...
  Explanation        X------------(30)------------X

Continuation option:
  (Next, Edit, Abort, Menu)          X
```

shows a documentation convention in which numeric data elements are shown by a series of 9s, and alphanumeric data elements by Xs; for example:

99/99/99
9999
$99,999.99
XXXXXXXXXX

Punctuation is inserted as appropriate. Long sequences of Xs, as required here for the explanation field, can be replaced by a composite of a beginning and ending X enclosing a row of dashes and the length of the field in parentheses; for example:

All forms should be labeled, and the one in the figure has a descriptive title.

Block formats are appropriate when there are few data elements, as on a document or screen form. Block formats are ideal for source documents or for input screen forms, in which the components of each transaction are entered in turn and where data entry personnel need the reinforcement provided by the prompts so as to avoid mistakes. They are also ideal for output documents or screens in which a single transaction or record is to be printed or displayed. But if the output consists of multiple records, block formats do not efficiently use the available space because of the repetition of captions; tabular formats then become more appropriate. The only situation in which block formats might be used for reports is when the number of characters required to output a record may exceed the maximum width of the printer. The design of inventory stock status reports sometimes present such a problem. In that situation, a block format may be adopted, despite its inefficiency, in order to be able to print the whole record. Because a block format divides the record into data elements or fields, there is no natural limit on the length that can be accommodated.

Tabular Formats

Tabular formats are appropriate when multiple transactions or records are to be included. Descriptive captions are confined to headings, resulting in a more efficient use of space than is possible with block formats. Tables comprise the principal content of accounting re-

FIGURE 4.6 **General layout for a table.**

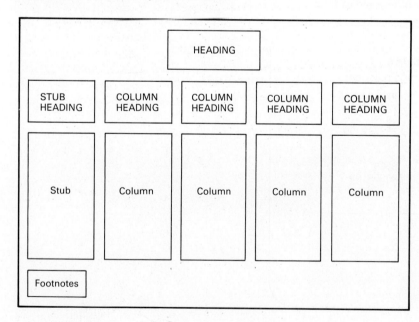

ports, but they may also appear on documents or screen displays.

The general layout of a table is shown in Figure 4.6. The content of a table includes

- Heading (title, subtitle, headnote)
- Stub and stub caption, or heading
- Columns and column captions, or headings
- Column subtotals and totals
- Footnotes

The main heading normally contains the title of the table and possibly a table number. It may also contain a subtitle and headnote. The title and subtitle describe the subject of the material presented in the table, the time or time period to which it applies, and sometimes the scope of the data. An example is

The word *Balance* applies to more than one column and is sometimes called a multicolumn caption or heading.

In the case of printed reports, the table will frequently occupy more than one page, and the stub and column captions should be repeated at the top of each new page. However, in order to economize on space, the main heading normally appears only on the first page. If the table is likely to become dissected in use, then it may be necessary to include a brief reference, such as the table or report number, on each page; this could be placed on the same line as the page number. For example

```
(Report 129, continued).
```

The repeated rows of data, comprising the table's stub and columns, are often referred to as *detail lines*, *print*

```
Title:               GREEN CORPORATION
             SCHEDULE OF AGED ACCOUNTS RECEIVABLE
    ──────────────────────────────────────────────────
Subtitle:               As of 99/99/9999
                      Southeastern Division
```

The date represents a data element and is documented using 9s as variables. A headnote usually indicates limitations on or qualifications of the generality of the data. One accompanying our example could be

```
(Excluding U.S. Government Customers)
```

The stub and columns comprise the main body of the table and consist of repeated rows of data. The stub defines the subject of the detail line: the customer name and probably also the customer number. The columns present the data applicable to that customer: the aged balances in that customer's account. The stub caption, or stub heading, and the column captions, or column headings, explain the subject of the stub and of each column. In our example, the stub caption might be

```
    ... Customer ...
   Number      Name
```

and the column captions would consist of

lines, or *line items*. In our example, there would typically be one detail line for each customer. The stub and columns are documented by 9s and Xs, showing the width of each field. There must be adequate spacing between adjacent stub and columns. A minimum of one character space must be allowed, but the spacing would need to be greater if either the column headings or the column totals were wider than the columns themselves. Once the intercolumn spacing has been determined, the total length of the detail line must be checked to see that it will fit into the width of the paper or screen.

Column totals are presented when they are meaningful. In the accounts receivable example, all the columns contain dollar balances, and so totals should be shown for all of them. Some tables may include not only a grand total but also one or more levels of subtotals. Subtotals may, for example, be included for groups of customers in the same territory or serviced by the same sales representative. Each subtotal is presented at a *break point* corresponding to the end of a related block of detail lines. In our example, a break point would be defined

```
....................... Balance .......................
 Total   Current   30-60 days   61-90 days   Over 90 days
```

as the point where a change occurred in the sales representative's identification number, from one record to the next. Each block of detail lines may be preceded by a block caption, or subtitle, usually placed near the left-hand margin; for example:

```
Territory: X————(18)————X
```

The stub and column captions may or may not be repeated after a block caption.

Footnotes are added to explain the meaning of certain items appearing in the body of the table. For example:

```
*These accounts will be written off
during the next period unless payment
is received.
```

The complete table, forming the accounts receivable aging report, is shown in Figure 4.7.

Sometimes the desired detail line is too long to fit into the width of the paper or screen and some means must be found to shorten it. The width of certain columns, particularly those containing textual or narrative material, may be reduced and the contents abbreviated or truncated. It may be possible to reduce the intercolumn spacing, if necessary, abbreviating the column captions or staggering the column totals:

```
$999,999.99          $999,999.99

    $999,999.99          $999,999.99
```

Another strategy is to stagger the fields and their captions in the detail line; for example:

```
Part #        Description   Location   .......
      On hand        On order      On reserve .......
9999999       X——( )——X X——( )——X
        99,999        99,999        99,999
```

This mode of presentation lacks the clarity of the standard tabular format, but it may be necessary in certain situations.

Another strategy is to try to divide the table into two smaller ones. If none of these strategies reduces the length of the detail line sufficiently, it may be necessary to adopt a block format.

FIGURE 4.7   Example of tabular format used for a report form.

```
Report #129                          GREEN CORPORATION                              Page 99
                          SCHEDULE OF AGED ACCOUNTS RECEIVABLE
                                  As of 99/99/9999
                                  Southeastern Division
                          (Excluding U.S. Government Customers)

Number          Name           Total        Current      30-60 days    60-90 days   Over 90 days
--------------------------------------------------------------------------------------------------
Territory:  X------(18)------X
999999  X-------------(30)-------------X  999,999.99   999,999.99   999,999.99   999,999.99   999,999.99*


           Subtotal, this territory  $9,999,999.99 $9,999,999.99 $9,999,999.99 $9,999,999.99 $9,999,999.99

           Total                     $9,999,999.99 $9,999,999.99 $9,999,999.99 $9,999,999.99 $9,999,999.99


    * These accounts will be written off during the next period unless payment is received.
```

GRAPHIC PRESENTATION OF ACCOUNTING DATA

Charts have increasingly been recognized for the role they play in the communication of data—either by themselves or in conjunction with associated printed material. Frequently, charts are presented to enhance the impact of data appearing in more detail in a table; the table communicates the data more accurately, but the chart communicates the highlights in a form that is more readily digested and understood. Charts may be prepared by hand; they may be generated by means of a printer or plotter; or they may be displayed on a video screen.

Several types of charts are in common use:

• Graphs
• Bar or column charts
• Pie charts

Graphs, Bar Charts, and Pie Charts

Graphs depict the relationship between a dependent and (usually one) independent variable. "Three-dimensional" graphs are sometimes constructed in which there is more than one independent variable, but they do not lend themselves so readily to representation on a flat surface. Frequently, but not always, there is assumed to be a causal relationship between the variables, so that a change in the independent variable(s) is responsible for corresponding changes in the dependent variable. In business applications, the independent variable is often time or some measure of volume—sales volume, production volume, number of orders, number of employees, number of labor hours expended, and so forth.

The data in a graph may be shown as discrete data points or as a line or a curve if the relationship between the variables can be expressed as a continuous mathematical function. When discrete points are plotted, they may be connected by line or curve segments. This is usually done for visual effect; it may or may not be possible to derive intermediate values by interpolation. Graphs of continuous functions arise from modeling techniques more often than from business data processing. In scientific and engineering applications, data

sometimes emerge in the form of a continuous analog signal; but in business and economic fields, observed data are almost always obtained and communicated in the form of discrete values and are plotted in the same manner. A line or curve is often drawn for comparison with the data points. It may arise from a model that is believed to explain the underlying behavior of the data; a regression line exemplifies such a model. Alternatively, the line or curve may be purely subjective and intended to focus the viewer's attention on some aspect of the data and away from other aspects such as the dispersion of the data. In other cases, the objective may be to draw attention to the scatter in the data, and then only discrete points are shown. Examples of the different types of graphs are presented in Figure 4.8.

Bar charts are a familiar method of depicting a variable's discrete values. The length of the bar is understood to correspond to the value of the variable. Bar charts may be drawn with either vertical or horizontal bars; when the bars are vertical, the chart is sometimes referred to as a *column chart*. In some cases, there is a real independent variable, as in a graph. In other cases, there is no independent variable in the ordinary sense, and the separate bars correspond to different organizational units, locations, or situations. Figure 4.9 illustrates both types. Often, two bar charts are superimposed so that information is communicated about the relative values of the two variables (Figure 4.10). Bar charts are often preferred to graphs because of their greater impact. The height or length of the bars seem to be grasped more easily than is the position of a data point above the axis.

Circular diagrams, popularly referred to as *pie charts*, are convenient aids for depicting allocations or distributions of some global total. They are frequently seen in business magazines, material prepared for meetings and presentations, and management reports. The idea is to show how the total "pie" is divided up into its component parts. Budgets are often illustrated by this means. On one side, the revenue pie is divided into its component sources; on the other, the expense pie is divided up among competing natural, functional, divisional, or program-related expenditures. An example of this usage appears in Figure 4.11. More than one such diagram relating to the same total may be shown if it is intended to compare different types of allocations. For example,

FIGURE 4.8   Examples of graphs.

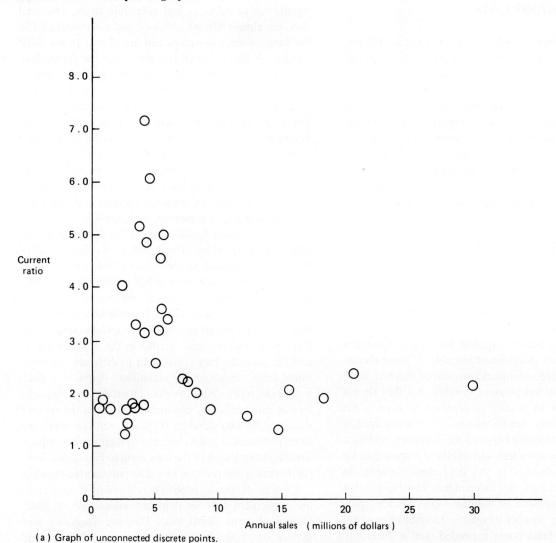

(a) Graph of unconnected discrete points.

FIGURE 4.8 (continued)

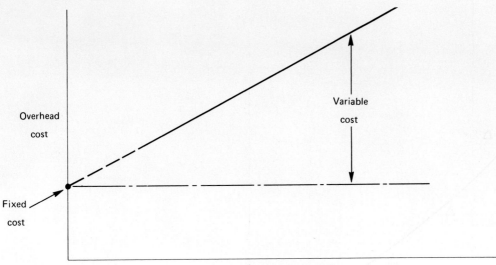

(b) Graph of a continuous function derived from a well-known model.

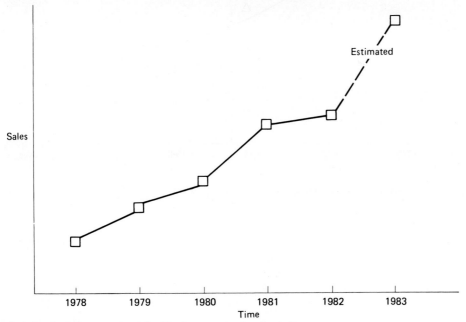

(c) Graph of discrete points joined by line segments for visual effect.

FIGURE 4.8 (continued)

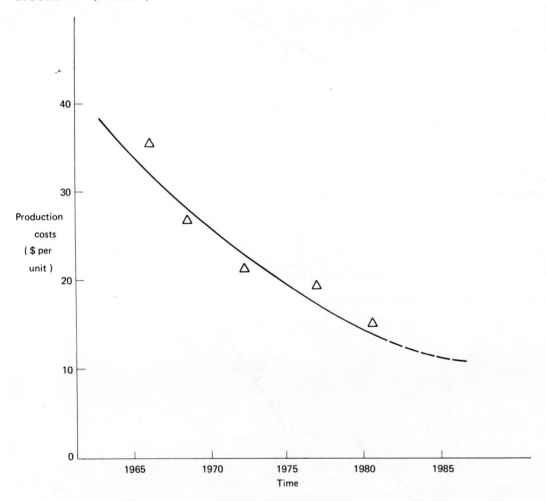

(d) Graph of discrete points with subjectively drawn trend line.

FIGURE 4.9 Examples of two types of bar charts.

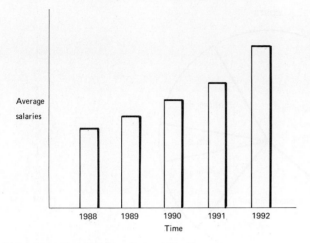

(a) Bar chart with a real independent variable—time.

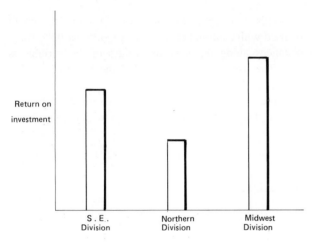

(b) Bar chart without a real independent variable.

FIGURE 4.10   Superposition of two bar charts for comparison.

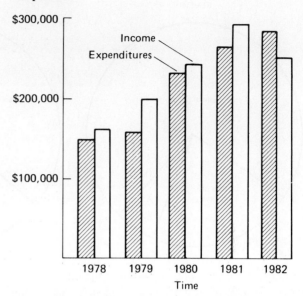

one diagram may present the division of total expenses into "natural" categories, such as labor, materials, and utilities; another may present the same expense total distributed among divisional segments of the organization. Similarly, one diagram may show divisional contributions to total revenue, and another the contributions from different products.

Scales

Distances measured along the horizontal and vertical axes of a graph correspond to values of the independent and dependent variables, respectively. Normally, equal spatial intervals along each of the axes correspond to equal intervals of the variables, and the scales are said to be linear (Figure 4.12). Occasionally, however, a nonlinear scale is adopted because it is considered to be more suitable for the data in question; scales of this type will be discussed later.

In the simplest case, an axis starts with the value zero; this is appropriate when only positive (or possibly, only negative) values of the variable are of interest. In other cases, both positive and negative values are to be plotted, and the value zero lies somewhere along the length of the axis. Normally, the two axes intersect where each takes the value zero, and the point of intersection is called the *origin* of the graph. Theoretically, the axes extend to infinity in both directions, and so every graph with linear scales has an origin somewhere. However,

FIGURE 4.11 Typical application of pie charts.

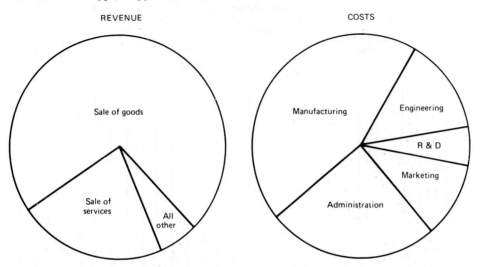

in practice, because only a portion of the total range of each axis is of interest and is to be plotted, that portion may or may not include the origin. If the portion of the axis that is plotted contains the origin, the axis is said to have a "true" origin; otherwise, it is said to have a "false" origin.

A false origin can scarcely be avoided if the axis cor- responds to the date. But otherwise false origins should be used with caution because the proportionality between distances along the axis and values of the variable is lost. The use of a false origin has the effect of empha- sizing the differences between neighboring values of the variable and diminishing the emphasis on their absolute values. This may be helpful in certain situations, but it

FIGURE 4.12 Different types of scales for use in plotting graphs.

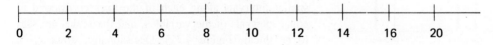

(a) Linear scale with a true origin

(b) Linear scale with a false origin

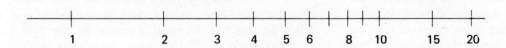

(c) Logarithmic scale

FIGURE 4.13 Distortion of information by use of false origins.

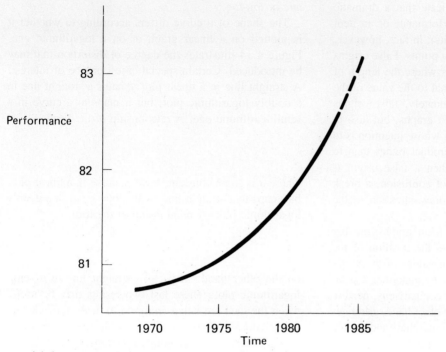

(a) Graphs with false origins may mislead the user.

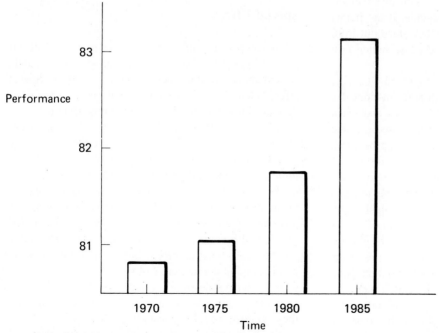

(b) False origins should never be used on bar charts.

can be misleading. Figure 4.13(a) illustrates a situation in which the graph seems to indicate that a dramatic increase is taking place in the performance of an item (measured in some appropriate units); in fact, however, the change is only a few percentage points. False origins should never be used in bar charts where the length of the bar is assumed to be proportional to the value of the variable [Figure 4.13(b)]. Unfortunately, false origins are a common feature, not only in graphs, but also in bar charts, in promotional material whose intention is to exaggerate some feature of the product rather than to convey unbiased information. When a false origin is used and there is any possibility of confusion, a break in the axis should be shown to draw attention to the absence of proportionality.

Grid lines are sometimes drawn on graphs and bar charts to help the viewer associate the position of the data points with the corresponding values of the variables. This is particularly helpful when quantitative data, and not just qualitative trends and comparisons, need to be extracted from the chart. On the other hand, grid lines can obscure the other material on the chart and should therefore be kept to a minimum. Grid lines should be avoided, if possible, when the device used to prepare the charts is not capable of printing with different intensities. A close grid may be acceptable if the points can be printed in bold type, so that they stand out from the grid, but not if the points may get lost among grid lines of comparable intensity.

Nonlinear scales are sometimes employed when the density of the data points is far from uniform along the applicable range of one or both of the axes and when the points would otherwise be unduly clustered near the origin. A range of scale transformations can be used, but the most common is a logarithmic transformation. On a logarithmic scale, equal intervals of distance correspond not to equal intervals of the variable but to equal *ratios* of the variable. For example, 1 in. might correspond to a factor of 2. Because the logarithm of zero is equal to minus infinity, the value zero cannot be plotted, and so all logarithmic scales have false origins. Care may have to be taken to avoid confusion about the point where the axes intersect; this point is chosen purely as a matter of convenience. In some cases, only one of the axes has a logarithmic scale; graphs of this type are referred to as *semilogarithmic*. When both scales are logarithmic, the graph is referred to as *doubly logarithmic* or *log-log*.

The shape of a curve differs according to whether it is plotted on a linear graph or on a logarithmic one. Figure 4.14 illustrates the degree of distortion that may be introduced. Certain special cases may be of interest. A straight line in a linear plot remains a straight line in a doubly logarithmic plot, but it maps to a curve in a semilogarithmic one. A relationship of the form

$$y = x^a$$

where a is some constant, forms a curve in a linear plot, but maps to a straight line (with slope $= a$) in a doubly logarithmic plot. A relationship of the form

$$y = a^x$$

on the other hand, maps to a straight line in a semilogarithmic plot. These last two results may be useful when the data are being analyzed to determine whether the relationship between two variables can be modeled by one of these two algebraic functions.

Special Effects

The preparation of charts that make appropriate impact and that hold the viewer's attention is an art, and a certain amount of flair goes into producing them. Special effects clearly can be overused, but on the other hand, they are important to this area of forms design.

Colors are perhaps the major vehicles for visual emphasis and, when the particular medium (or technology) permits their use, they are always helpful. No more than three colors, in addition to black and white, should normally be used, however, and care should be taken to avoid dissonance among them. Primary colors are appropriate in most cases: Red, yellow, green and red, green, and blue are familiar combinations. More subtle combinations such as green, brown, and gold may add a tone of quiet distinction. Colors such as red and orange or blue and purple should usually not be placed next to each other, either because they lack contrast or because they produce visual dissonance.

As alternatives to color, particularly when the avail-

FIGURE 4.14   The same curves plotted on linear scale (above) and semilogarithmic scale (below). The linear function is $y = 10x$, the quadratic function is $y = 1.5x^2$, and the exponential function is $y = 1.5^x$.

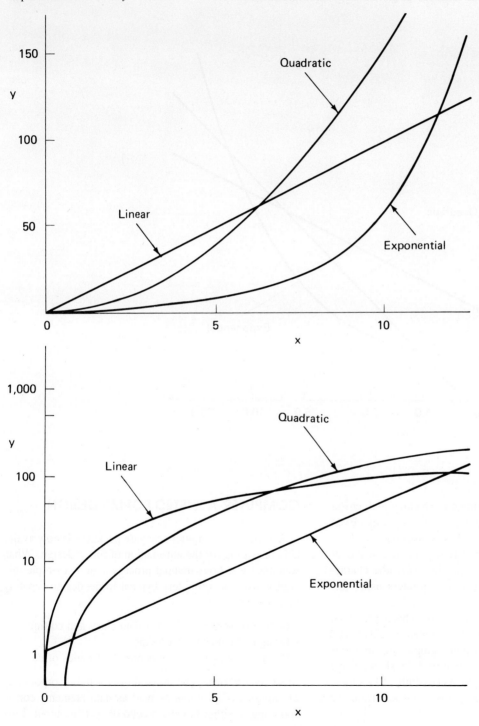

FIGURE 4.14 (continued) **The same curves plotted on double logarithmic scales.**

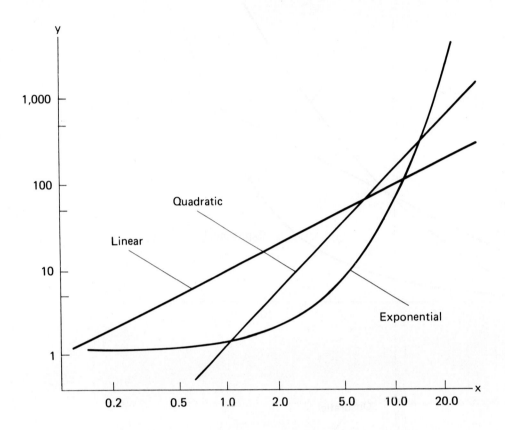

able technology is more limited, shading and cross-hatching are sometimes used to vary emphasis. Even when charts are being prepared on something as inflexible as a line printer, some variation of intensity over surface areas is possible by repeating particular characters. Cartoons are prepared on line printers using this kind of technique.

Another special effect seen in many charts presented in magazines is implied three-dimensionality. Bar charts, pie charts, and sometimes graphs are drawn as though they have thickness. Figure 4.15 shows some examples that have been used successfully. The objective here is to make the diagrams stand out from the paper.

COMPUTER-ASSISTED FORMS DESIGN

A variety of computer software packages is now available providing for the automation of forms design. What was once a tedious manual process is now a simple operation using a computer. Typical forms design capabilities are the

- Design of screen forms for data entry and editing
- Design of paper report forms
- Design of graphics layouts based on tables of data

Most screen form generators allow for the incorporation of captions or prompts as well as data elements corresponding to either keyboard echo or system output. Fig-

FIGURE 4.15(a)   Use of implied three-dimensionality to add impact to bar charts. The included angle of the wedges on the left should not exceed about 10 degrees.

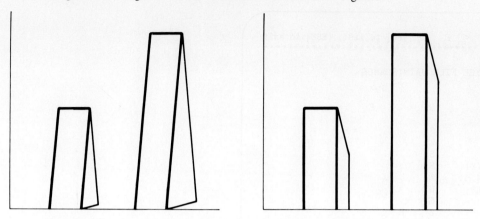

(b)   Use of implied three-dimensionality to add impact to graphs and charts. The "thickness" of the figures should not be so great as to distort the other proportions.

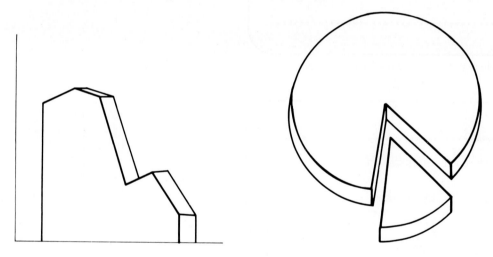

ure 4.16 shows the design process, using a popular data base management software package operated on a personal computer; screen form design is one of its peripheral features. The location and length of each data element is indicated on the form by the "S...E" symbols (S stands for "start" and E for "end"). These data elements and also the captions can be moved around on the face of the screen until the designer is satisfied with the layout. A limited range of special effects can be achieved by using characters such as asterisks.

Report form design is similar to screen form design, except that more information must be specified. Figure 4.17 shows an example using the same data base management package as before. In addition to the locations of the captions and data elements, the design requires specification of the report and page headings, block headings, detail lines, totals and subtotals (including break points), and page and report footings. These data are specified by the column of coded symbols down the extreme left-hand side of the form.

FIGURE 4.16 Computer-aided screen form design. This example was prepared using R:BASE 5000, a product of Microrim, Inc.

```
                   < 1, 1>  [F3] to list, [ESC] to exit
*********************************************************
*                                                       *
*               EMPLOYEE FILE MAINTENANCE                *
*                                                       *
*                                                       *
*   Employee S/S number       S           E             *
*   Employee name:                                      *
*     First name              S               E         *
*     Middle initial          E                         *
*     Last name               S               E         *
*   Date hired (MM/DD/YY)      S      E                  *
*   Marital status (S,M,H)     E                         *
*   Number of dependents      SE                         *
*   Department                S    E                     *
*   Pay rate                  S    E                     *
*                                                       *
*                                                       *
*       Press <Esc> and then select [Add] to save record *
*                                                       *
*                                                       *
*********************************************************
```

(a) Definition of the form. The positions of the data elements are defined by S (start) and E (end) symbols.

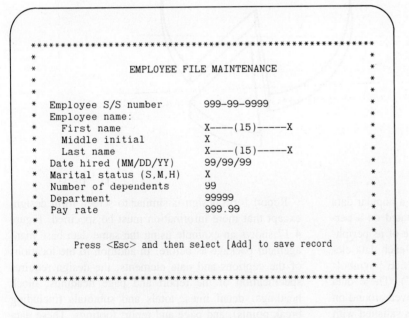

```
*********************************************************
*                                                       *
*               EMPLOYEE FILE MAINTENANCE                *
*                                                       *
*                                                       *
*   Employee S/S number       999-99-9999                *
*   Employee name:                                      *
*     First name              X----(15)-----X            *
*     Middle initial          X                          *
*     Last name               X----(15)-----X            *
*   Date hired (MM/DD/YY)      99/99/99                   *
*   Marital status (S,M,H)     X                          *
*   Number of dependents      99                          *
*   Department                99999                       *
*   Pay rate                  999.99                      *
*                                                       *
*       Press <Esc> and then select [Add] to save record *
*                                                       *
*********************************************************
```

(b) Documentation of the form design, using 9 to designate numeric data elements and X to designate alphanumeric data elements.

FIGURE 4.17 Computer-aided report form design. This example was prepared using R:BASE 5000, a product of Microrim, Inc. The positions of the data elements are defined by S (start) and E (end) symbols. The symbols down the left-hand edge of the form are HR = report heading, HP = page heading, D = detail line, Fl = block footing, and FR = report footing.

```
----------------------------------------------------------------------------------------
                                                                < 1,  1>  [F3] to list,
HR                                   GREAT AMERICAN COMPANY
HR                                   PAYROLL DEDUCTION REPORT
HR                                   For Period Ending S      E                 Page SE

HP                   ..........Name..........    Gross       Tax       Other      Net
HP   Empl #        Last    MI      First          pay     withhold.  deductions    pay
HP--------------------------------------------------------------------------------------
D S        E S              E E S             E S      . E S      . E S      . E S      . E

Fl                                          ------------  ------------  ------------  ------------
Fl              Total                       S      . E S      . E S      . E S      . E
Fl                                          ============  ============  ============  ============

FR Report # 9876
```

FIGURE 4.18 Computer-generated graphics. These examples were prepared using Lotus 123, a product of Lotus Development Corporation.

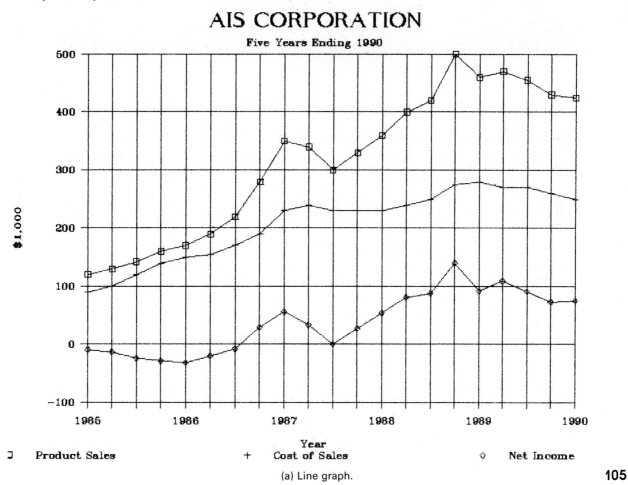

(a) Line graph.

105

FIGURE 4.18 (Continued)

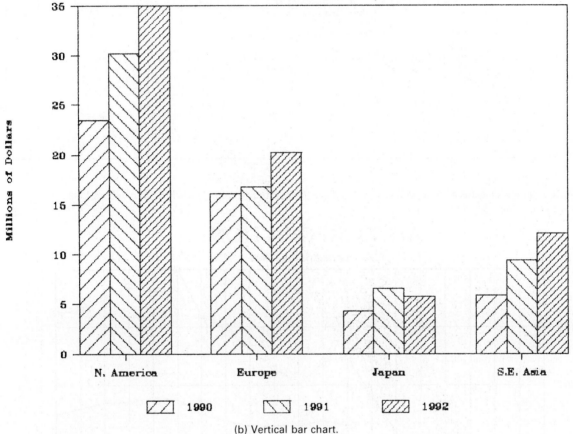

(b) Vertical bar chart.

The computer generation of graphics output is different insofar as the charts and graphs are generated for a given set of data. Instead of providing a framework for the future output of data, they present an existing data set in graphical form. The output can either be displayed on a screen or be printed on a graphics printer. Figure 4.18 shows some graphics output generated by a popular spreadsheet software package. It includes illustrations of line graphs, bar charts, and pie charts.

The availability of computer aids to forms design has streamlined the preparation of various forms. But the need for good forms design remains as important as ever. Accountants and others must understand the principles of effective forms design and will increasingly be called upon to develop presentation-quality graphics to supplement the more traditional types of accounting output.

SUMMARY

Information transferred from one component of an information system to another can be characterized by content and format. Computers are essentially indifferent to the format in which data are transmitted, as long as that format is defined. In contrast, if people are involved,

FIGURE 4.18 (Continued)

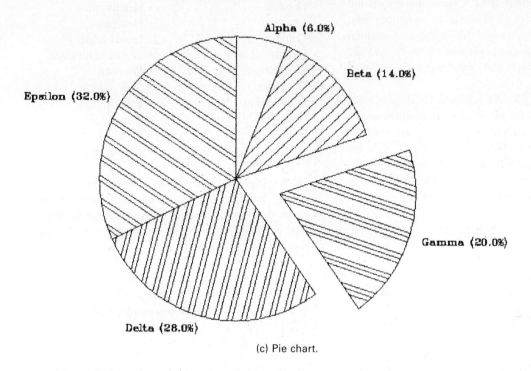

SALES BY PRODUCT

2nd Quarter 1999

Alpha (6.0%)

Beta (14.0%)

Epsilon (32.0%)

Gamma (20.0%)

Delta (28.0%)

(c) Pie chart.

formats must be designed to promote a clear transfer of information and to facilitate related processes of mental assimilation and comprehension. Consequently, the choice of information formats must be considered carefully, and accountants, who seek to communicate with a variety of information users, should be acquainted with the issues involved.

The basic vehicle for communication of information to and from the human operator is the "form." The traditional topic of forms design is still important, but now it deals less with document design than with the design of report layouts and screen displays. In systems terminology, a "form" refers to the configuration of the information on a particular medium rather than to a paper document. It applies to any interface: report, screen display, tables, chart, or whatever, between people and

machines or between two or more people. Forms are part of the input and output of data from the system and may be involved in the interfaces between one part of an information system and another.

Forms design is vital to the system's overall design. The primary objectives of good form layout are clarity, grouping and logical flow of data, effective use of space, and ease of use. Size and proportion are important aesthetic considerations, although they may compete with more practical concerns. The use of special effects can enhance forms design but should be used with caution to preserve an authoritative, professional image.

This chapter outlined the design of forms for major accounting applications, with emphasis on block, tabular, and graphics formats. Block and tabular formats are the staples of document, report, and screen forms. Tables and graphs are useful complements; tables can present large amounts of data in quantitative form for detailed reference, whereas charts and graphs can present the material in a more qualitative form for easy comprehension and assimilation. Graphics techniques are playing an increasingly important role in the communication of accounting data. Charts and graphs are used widely in presentations made to audiences who need to grasp the "big picture." Multimedia information formats are becoming more common in which data are presented in both tabular and complementary graphical form.

The availability of personal computers and specialized software has brought the preparation of good forms design, including graphics materials, within easy reach of many accountants and other business people. On the other hand, the availability of such technological aids does not eliminate the need to understand the basics of the effective communication of information.

BIBLIOGRAPHY

Anderson, Anker V. *Graphing Financial Information: How Accountants Can Use Graphs to Communicate.* New York: National Association of Accountants, 1983.

Awad, Elias M. *Systems Analysis and Design.* Homewood, Ill: Irwin, 1979.

Fisher, Edward M. "A Graphic Change for PCs." *Datamation*, January 15, 1987, pp. 44–50.

Koral, Jonathan K. "Graphical Perception and the Representation of Financial Information." *Georgia Journal of Accounting*, Spring 1986, pp. 147–157.

"Management Warms Up to Computer Graphics." *Business Week*, August 13, 1984, pp. 96–101.

Mason, Robert D. *Statistical Techniques in Business and Economics.* Homewood, Ill.: Irwin, 1974.

U.S. Office of Training Development and Productivity *Presenting Data in Graphs, Charts and Tables.* Washington, D.C.: U.S. Government Printing Office, 1975.

van Dam, Adries. "Computer Software for Graphics." *Scientific American*, September 1984, pp. 146–161.

DISCUSSION QUESTIONS AND PROBLEMS

1. Define and discuss the following terms:

• Bar chart	• Graph
• Block layout	• Graphics
• Caption	• Heading
• Chart	• Headnote
• Column	• Linear scale
• Column chart	• Logarithmic scale
• Dissonance	• Pie chart
• Document	• Stub
• False origin	• Subtitle
• Footnote	• Table
• Form	• Title
• Format	• True origin

2. Explain why form design is important to communications involving human beings but is relatively insignificant in communications between computer components. Is there any need to specify the data format in intermachine communications?

3. Applicants for employment at a large manufacturing firm are requested to complete a form asking for biographical data and previous employment history. The following information is requested:

• Date of birth	• Marital status
• Physical handicaps	• Highest education level reached
• Last name	• Signature of applicant
• Age	• Middle initial
• Street address	• First name
• Military service record	• Today's date
• Zip code	• Position at last place of employment
• Height	
• City/state	• Professional licenses
• Criminal record	• Place of birth
• Length of time with previous employer	• Weight
• Union membership(s)	• Number of dependents
• Major illnesses during the last five years	• Annual salary at previous place of employment
• Telephone number	
• Name of last employer	

Required

Classify the data into related groups. Arrange the groups and the material in them to produce an effective logical flow of ideas.

4. Design an input document to solicit the data referred to in Problem 3.

5. Assume that the data in Problem 3 are to be entered through a video terminal. The screen size is 80 columns by 24 rows. As characters are typed on the keyboard, they appear on the screen next to the caption or prompt. Design the necessary screen form(s).

6. Design an invoice form for Summit Products Corporation, a small merchandising enterprise. The firm's address is 2000 Boulevard Place, Hicksville, NM 59599.

Provision must be made for four-line customer billing and shipping addresses and also for the sales representative's name. The invoice must allow for six product line items, and for each, the product number, description, quantity, unit price, and extended price should be shown. The standard credit terms are 2/10, n/30. A promotional message—"We serve the best, to the best"— should appear on the invoice.

7. a. Design a table listing the chapters of this book, the chapter titles, the beginning and ending page numbers, and the number of pages in the chapter. Include a total indicating the total number of pages in the book. Suggest an appropriate heading consisting of a title, subtitle, and headnote and at least one footnote.

b. What would be the maximum width of the table, in characters, allowing for a suitable gap between each column?

8. Suppose that the data in Figure 4.7 had to be compressed into a maximum width of 40 characters. Suggest alternative ways of presenting the data, and show detailed layouts for each.

9. Draw a vertical bar (column) chart to supplement the following table of data relating to an analysis of accounts receivable balances:

Size of Account	Number of Accounts	Total Balance
0 to $100	17,882	$ 919,834
$101 to $500	1,995	586,092
$501 to $2,000	352	322,108
$2,001 to $10,000	29	153,640
Over $10,000	7	91,371
Total	20,265	$2,073,045

10. Your supervisor has asked you to prepare a graph of the following data for use in a presentation to be made to upper management:

Year	Sales
19A	$300,420
19B	366,930
19C	448,170
19D	547,390
19E	668,590
19F	816,620

Required

Draw a graph according to each of the following conventions:

a. Linear scale, true origin on the vertical scale
b. Linear scale, with the vertical scale covering the range $300,000 and up
c. Logarithmic vertical scale

11. The officers of St. Paul's Church have asked you to help them design the church's annual financial report to the congregation. The report consists of a balance sheet, a statement of income and expenditures, supporting schedules showing the sources of income (pledges, other donations and contributions, legacies, interest, and so on) and the distribution of expenditures among the various church programs (worship, ministry, missions, administration, debt service, and so forth). A comparative schedule is also included showing income and expenditures for the last five years.

One of the objectives of the design is easy understanding of the financial data by the members of the congregation who, for the most part, are intelligent people but are not trained accountants, business people, or financial analysts. Clearly, the members would resent being "talked down to." But the church officers wisely recognize that the members' commitment to giving can be fostered by presenting the financial information in a simple, straightforward manner, without sacrificing accounting rigor.

Required

Design a set of financial statements and supporting materials—tables, charts, graphs—to present the church's financial condition and results of operations.

12. Agate Company has been approached by a large corporation with a tentative merger offer. The stockholders and directors of Agate are excited about the prospects of realizing an immediate monetary gain on their holdings in the company and also of obtaining the support of a large parent corporation to provide much-needed funds for research and development and for advertising.

A meeting is scheduled at which time the directors of Agate are to make a presentation to a high-level team from the prospective merger partner. First on the agenda for the meeting is a discussion of Agate's financial position and operating performance for the five years since its formation. Some data provided by Agate's controller are shown in the table at the end of the questions and problems section.

Required

Prepare material to be handed out at the meeting that will demonstrate the sound financial state, rapid growth, and future prospects of Agate Company. The budget for 19F calls for expenditures of $30,800 on research and development and $21,500 on advertising. Budgeted sales are $300,000. The gross margin ratio and ratio of general operating expenses to sales are expected to be about the same as in 19E.

13. Stead Manufacturing Company operates a job order costing system. There were no jobs in process as of January 1, 19A. But Jobs 1706 through 1715 were active

during the year 19A. Materials costs and labor hours charged to these jobs were as follows:

Job No.	Materials	Labor hours
1706	$20,300	150
1707	14,700	260
1708	19,800	190
1709	30,500	90
1710	23,100	290
1711	9,800	330
1712	12,300	180
1713	21,500	240
1714	6,000	260
1715	15,600	100

All labor is charged at a rate of $9.00 per hour. Overhead is applied at the rate of 200 percent of direct labor cost. Jobs 1706, 1707, and 1709 were completed and shipped to customers. Jobs 1708, 1710, and 1711 were completed and transferred to finished goods inventory. All other jobs were "open," that is, were still in process, at the end of the year.

Required

a. Design an open job report for Stead Manufacturing Company. The report should list the job number, job description, materials cost, labor hours and cost, overhead cost, and estimated percentage completion. In addition to showing the columns (fields) in the approved manner, illustrate a detail line of the report with data from one of the open jobs. Invent any data not provided. Be sure to identify your report heading, page headings, and any totals included.

b. Prepare a bar chart showing the relative total costs of the open jobs as of 12/31/19A.

c. Prepare pie charts showing (i) a comparison of the dollar balances of work in process, finished goods, and cost of goods sold and (ii) a breakdown of work in process among materials, labor, and overhead costs.

14. How can computer software help in the preparation of screen and paper forms and graphics materials? What are the advantages and disadvantages of such computer software packages? What future developments do you foresee for computer-assisted forms design?

15. A computer program has been designed to generate a screen display on screens of different sizes. To accommodate this flexibility the screen locations of the various messages to be displayed are contained in a small machine-readable file. The structure of this file is as follows:

Message No.	X	Y
(1)	.	.
(2)	.	.
.	.	.

On a video screen, the origin of the coordinates is at the top left-hand corner; X is measured horizontally to the right, and Y is measured vertically downward. The value of X in the parameter file should correspond to the first character of the message in question. The messages to be displayed are

(1) SOUTHWESTERN WIDGET COMPANY [centered near the top of the screen and underlined with == signs on the line below]

(2) This system provides the following functions: [centered below the title]

(3) A: Budget Preparation [items 3 through 5 to form a table near the middle of the screen]

(4) B: Budget Tracking

(5) C: Report Preparation

(6) Enter Selection > [starting under *This* of item 2, near the bottom of the screen]

Required
Design the content of the file to provide a pleasing layout

a. On a standard screen of size 80 columns × 24 rows
b. On a screen of size 64 columns × 15 rows
c. On a screen of size 90 columns × 30 rows

Data for Problem 12

| Item | Year | | | | |
	19A	19B	19C	19D	19E
Sales	$25,305	$29,667	$80,024	$144,712	$243,801
Cost of sales	7,946	14,432	28,113	42,559	60,293
Operating expenses	8,355	12,004	23,278	59,240	119,402
Research and development	14,141	11,935	15,004	18,882	24,994
Advertising	5,438	7,678	10,843	12,668	15,452
Current assets	11,964	9,045	13,226	19,552	36,293
Current liabilities	9,123	9,551	8,737	9,044	10,084
Total assets	35,217	33,884	48,292	60,366	81,456
Total liabilities	12,864	15,033	14,267	23,981	35,330

5

Files and File Processing

LEARNING OBJECTIVES

After you have studied this chapter you should be able to

- Identify the major types of files and their purposes.
- Identify the principal types of file media and their advantages and disadvantages.
- Identify the principal types of data files and explain how they are used.
- Explain the distinction between the logical and physical data structures.
- Explain the notions of data type, field length, and record layout.
- Analyze the principal methods of data retrieval and their strengths and weaknesses.
- Explain the nature of the routine posting process.
- Identify the steps in the classical posting cycle.
- Discuss the nature of file maintenance.
- Explain the concepts of file sorting and merging.
- Describe some simple methods of evaluating sorting procedures.

CHAPTER OUTLINE

THE NATURE AND USE OF FILES

What Is a File?

A file is a collection of data stored together in one place for future use. Files can be classified by function, content, application, type of storage medium, internal structure, mode of access, and so forth. A useful classification is by function, that is, by the role that files play in the information process:

- Data files
- Index files
- Text files
- Program files

Data files, as their name implies, contain data—account codes, quantities, dollar amounts, balances, wage rates, names, addresses, and the like. They will be the subject of considerable further discussion, and we shall return to them shortly.

Index files assist in finding a record in a related data file. The index at the end of a book helps the reader locate the page on which an item of interest appears; an index file helps to locate a particular item of data in the same manner. Text files contain narrative or textual material. A text file might be a set of engineering specifications, a clerical procedure, or a report on a potential new product. It might include tables of figures and charts as well as descriptive material. Text files play a major role in word processing systems. Program files, which appear in automated systems, contain the computer programs, or software, necessary to perform particular processing tasks.

Other types of files found in computerized systems include parameter files and command files. Parameter files contain lists of the parameters needed for associated processing operations. Command files contain short lists of coded instructions—typically ones that control a larger number of subordinate instructions. Command files often take the form of addenda to program files.

For example, a computer program designed to sort a data file might be written in general terms, leaving details such as identity of the data file and the manner in which it is to be sorted to be supplied at run time. The details would be supplied in a user-specified parameter and/or command file.

File Media

Perhaps the most familiar example of a file is a collection of documents in a manila folder residing in a file cabinet. Many businesses maintain such files on their customers, vendors, products, or employees. The manila folder and its contents represents one kind of file medium. It is a convenient one for many purposes, especially for text material. Variations on the manila folder include hanging files in a file drawer or on a rack. Other examples of file media include the following:

- Printed cards
- Magnetic tape
- Magnetic disk
- Microfilm

Printed cards are used in many types of files featured in manual systems. They are also used widely for customer files, vendor files, inventory files, fixed asset files, student files, and many other applications. Card files are ideal when the contents change often. New cards can easily be inserted, or existing ones can be removed or updated. The cards are typically kept in order of some appropriate key such as customer number or name, facilitating record retrieval. The cards can be housed in a file drawer, or they can be attached to a rack. Several kinds of racks, designed for easy access to the cards, are commercially available; in rotary card files, the cards are hinged along one edge and radiate out from a central spindle (see Figure 5.1). Card files are convenient, but they are difficult to copy or duplicate. Their potential for use in computerized systems is limited. Data can be read by an optical scanner, and some types of cards have a magnetic stripe that contains coded data that can be read by a magnetic scanning device. But in both cases the process is slow.

Several types of file media, including magnetic tape and magnetic disk, are machine readable and are in-

FIGURE 5.1 A rotary card file.

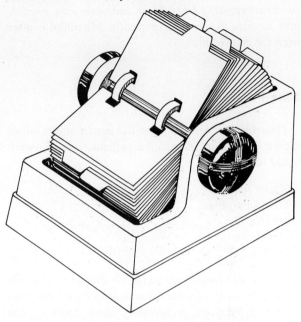

tended for use in computerized systems. Magnetic tape is the cheapest machine-readable file medium, but it is not good for files whose contents change often or for files that are frequently used. This is because the retrieval of data may be slow, since magnetic tape files can only be read sequentially (i.e., from one end of the tape to the other) and updating them normally means preparing a new tape. Magnetic-disk media are more expensive but avoid both of these limitations. Fast, random access to records is possible, and individual records can be updated without affecting the data in neighboring records. The characteristics of magnetic tape and disk media are discussed further in Chapter 7.

Magnetic media have the important quality of being machine readable. But unfortunately, they cannot be read by a human user, and so the data must be verified by some other means, such as via listings made with the help of electromagnetic or electronic equipment.

Microfilm is an important type of file medium in which human readability is required and large volumes of data are accumulated. Microfilm files occupy only a small fraction of the space needed for their paper counterparts. Unfortunately, the records cannot be altered (without preparing a new film), and so they are not suitable for files that change frequently. Microfilm is often used for archive files.

Data Files

Data files, which represent the largest subset of all files appearing in information systems, can be subdivided further into

- Master files
- Transaction files
- Archive files
- Scratch files
- Backup files

A master file contains permanent or semipermanent data relating to entities such as general ledger accounts, customers, employees, or inventory items, together with their account balances. It corresponds to a ledger in the traditional accounting system. In manual systems, master files sometimes contain detailed transaction data supporting the ending balances. But in computerized systems, master files contain, at most, summarized data, such as year-to-date activity.

Master files are found in virtually all accounting applications (and indeed in virtually all information systems); a partial list includes the following:

Application	Master File
General ledger	Chart of accounts
	General ledger file
Accounts receivable	Customer file
	Accounts receivable master file
Accounts payable	Vendor file
	Accounts payable master file
Inventory	Product file
	Inventory master file
Payroll	Employee file
	Payroll master file
Job cost	Job master file
	Work-in-process master file

The pairs of names indicate that there may be differences in the names of particular files. They also indicate that some systems may use two master files instead of one. For example, some systems maintain a customer master file containing just biographical data on the customers and also an accounts receivable master file containing the account balances. However, most automated systems combine both types of data into a single file.

Transaction files are designed to capture the detailed transaction data. They are usually maintained in chronological order, and records relating to new transactions are added to the end of the file as the transactions occur. Some examples of transaction files for the preceding applications are:

Application	Transaction File
General ledger	General journal file
	Special journal file (e.g., cash receipts file, cash disbursements file)
Accounts receivable	Sales file
	Collections file
Accounts payable	Purchases file
	Payment or check file
Inventory management	Receipts or purchases file
	Issuances or sales file
Payroll	Payroll transaction file
	Check file
Job cost	Production cost file
	Completed job file

Accounting applications often require two or more transaction files to capture different types of transactions. For example, in an inventory management application, there may be one transaction file for receipts of inventory items, a second for issuances, and possibly a third for adjustments to inventory values to reflect breakages, deterioration, obsolescence, and so forth. Alternatively, all types of transactions may be accommodated in a single transaction file; however, in this case, designing the file is more difficult, and the design may use storage capacity less efficiently.

Furthermore, as in the preceding list, a particular transaction file may appear in more than one application. For example, the purchases transaction file is listed as part of both accounts payable and the inventory management application. This sharing of transaction files reflects the high degree of integration of the accounting applications. Dividing transactions of different types into separate transaction files may be a matter of convenience, but it also facilitates the process of sharing. If, for example, both purchases and payment records were included in a single accounts payable transaction file, the posting process would have to distinguish between the two types when posting data to the inventory master file.

Transaction files are temporary files. The data are periodically summarized in order to update the corresponding master file; this is the function of the posting operation. After the posting has been completed, the transaction files are ''purged,'' or emptied, and then reused. If permanent records of transactions need to be kept, they will be placed in archive files, which can be transferred to a cheaper medium and location. Archived records can always be retrieved if needed.

Scratch files are set up during a processing operation and are purged when the operation is completed. They are very temporary files that aid in the operation with which they are associated, but they do not have any lasting importance. Sometimes scratch files are used to collect data before they are inserted into a master file or transaction file. Scratch files are also used to hold records duplicated from another file but sorted in some other way, perhaps for the preparation of a report. If a vendor file is normally maintained in alphabetical order, but a report is required in order of increasing dollar purchasing volume, it may be convenient to set up a scratch file for sorting and analysis.

Backup files are duplicate copies of a file, usually made for security reasons. They are placed in some safe location for use in case the original file is damaged or destroyed. Often, backup files can be in some cheaper medium than the original file because they do not need to be accessed frequently.

Measures of File Activity

The files are established, the data are put into them and are changed from time to time, and the data are accessed or retrieved as necessary. The design of a file must take account of the type and frequency of usage it will receive. Two useful measures of the usage of a file are its activity ratio and its volatility ratio.

The activity ratio of a file is equal to the fraction of the total records that are accessed in a standard time period—an hour, a day, a week, or, perhaps, one posting period:

$$\text{Activity ratio} = \frac{\text{no. of records accessed per unit time}}{\text{total number of records}}$$

The activity ratio might be expressed in such units as percentage per week. To illustrate, suppose that, on average, 200 records in a certain file are accessed each week. If the total number of records is 1,000, then the activity ratio will be equal to 20 percent per week.

A file's volatility ratio measures how often the file's contents are changed. Such changes include additions, deletions, or record updates. The volatility ratio is defined as

$$\text{Volatility ratio} =$$
$$\frac{\text{no. of additions, deletions, and updates per unit time}}{\text{total number of records}}$$

For example, if in a typical week, 2 new records are added, 1 record is deleted, and 10 records are updated, then the volatility ratio of the 1,000 record file will be equal to $(2 + 1 + 10)/1{,}000 = 13/1{,}000 = 1.3\%$ per week.

A well-used telephone directory may have a high activity ratio, but it has relatively low volatility. The low volatility allows the telephone company to publish a new directory only about once per year; if telephone numbers had greater volatility, the familiar bound volume would have to be replaced by a loose-leaf book or a card file.

Another important parameter of file usage, although one that cannot be quantified as easily as activity or volatility can, is the file's accessibility. This accessibility has to do with the ease or difficulty of data storage and retrieval, as measured by the time (or perhaps the cost) of entering or retrieving a record. Files lying on the user's desktop are clearly more accessible than are those stored in a basement vault. On the other hand, there may be good reasons for storing files in a vault, and in such cases, trade-offs have to be made between accessibility and competing factors such as security and cost. Trade-offs often have to be made as well between accessibility and the volume of data in a file. There is some limit to the number of files that can be kept on the desktop; above that limit, some of the files must be removed and stored in a filing cabinet, even though the user would like to have them all equally accessible. The accessibility of a file is closely connected with the medium in which the data are stored. That is, the user could retain a much larger volume of file data on his or her desk if the data were on microfilm than if they were in printed reports.

File Listings

It is often convenient to have a printed copy of a file's contents. Such a document is called a *file listing*. The listing presents the content of a file in a different medium that may be more appropriate to the purpose at hand. When files are maintained on a machine-readable medium, such as magnetic tape, listings play an important role in translating the data into human-readable form. This may be necessary for verification or simply for user access to the file's contents.

There is flexibility with regard to what data are included in the listing and the order in which the records are printed. A full listing includes all the data on the original file; a partial listing might be restricted to just some of the records or to a part of each record. The listing might be printed in the same order in which the original records are physically stored, or the data could be sorted in some other manner. A partial listing of an inventory file might correspond to parts supplied by a particular vendor, or parts whose on-hand quantity had fallen below the reorder point. The latter would correspond to a reorder report; it could be sorted by part number, but alternatively it might be sorted by vendor.

FILE STRUCTURE

Logical and Physical Structures

Data files can be divided into records, and records, in turn, can be divided into fields. Each record contains one or more retrieval keys and a number of fields containing data related to those keys. For example, in a vendor master file, the primary retrieval key might be the vendor number; a secondary key—used less often—might be the vendor name; and the related fields might be provided for the vendor's mailing address and telephone number, the account balance (possibly broken down into age categories), and other miscellaneous data. The content of a field is referred to as a *data element*. A data element is the smallest meaningful unit of data. It is composed of characters, digits, or other symbols, which are even smaller; however, these do not have individual meaning or significance. Records and files and other assemblages of data elements are referred to as *data aggregates*. The way in which the data elements are arranged within the particular data aggregate is referred to as the *data structure*.

Data structures can be viewed from either the perspective of the user or that of the physical storage medium. The user's perspective is referred to as the *logical data structure* and may be distinguished from the *physical data structure*. The logical structure of a record in a vendor master file may be represented as follows:

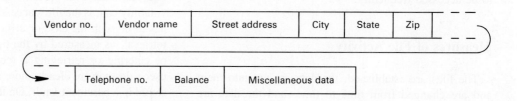

Vendor no.	Vendor name	Street address	City	State	Zip	

Telephone no.	Balance	Miscellaneous data

Similarly, the logical structure of a file can often be represented by a table in which the rows correspond to records and the columns correspond to fields:

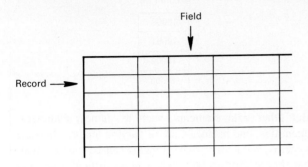

This example illustrates the simplest case, in which each record contains the same number of fields and all the fields are of the same length. Such a file is referred to as a *flat file*. In other cases, the number of fields varies from one record to another, and the fields may be of varying lengths.

Often the physical data structure is entirely different from the logical structure, particularly when the file resides on a machine-readable medium. Each logical record may occupy more than one physical record; this is common when the physical record is short, as it is in the case of a punched card. Alternatively, two or more logical records may occupy a single physical record. Furthermore, the arrangement of records may be quite different. For example, if a flat file were stored on magnetic tape, the records would be arranged one after the other, in a linear sequence, rather than one below the other. Or if the file were stored on magnetic disk, each record would be stored within one or more sectors of a circular "track" on the disk (see Chapter 7). Successive records might not necessarily be stored in adjacent sectors but might be scattered about the face of the disk in an apparently random manner. The disk directory retrieves them in the correct order when needed. As users, designers, or evaluators of accounting information systems, we are primarily interested in logical data structures and are interested in physical structures only insofar as these may help us understand the characteristics of particular physical media.

Data Type

Data elements can be classified according to data type. The concept of data type is closely related to that of data format. The principal data types are

- Numeric data
- Dates
- Alphabetic data
- Alphanumeric data
- Flags or control symbols

Numeric data consist only of numbers, together with a small number of related punctuation symbols or delimiters (. , + −). Examples of numeric data are 2, 10, 1.25, 135,289, and 10^6. Some quantity data elements can have both positive and negative values and must be accompanied by a sign. "Trailing" signs are most often used in file data; that is, the sign is placed after the numeric value to which it applies; for example, 150+ or 144,000−. Similarly, dollar balances may be either debit or credit balances. One common convention is to designate debit balances by a plus sign and credits by a minus sign. Examples are

$125.50+ (debit balance of $125.50)

$79.25− (credit balance of $79.25)

One interesting and useful property of this scheme is that the grand total of all the balances in the chart of accounts should be zero. This result makes possible a simple routine check on the integrity of the trial balance.

Alphabetic data consist of the letters of the alphabet (uppercase and lowercase); examples are people's names. Data elements or fields are rarely specified as alphabetic. Unless there is some good reason to exclude nonalphabetic characters, the more inclusive alphanumeric data type is specified. Alphanumeric data consist of both numbers and letters and also a wide variety of punctuation marks and other symbols. Examples of alphanumeric data are

Bob, Customer #9876, P/O #1234, 1/21/99, 3M Company, and "The Willows"

Flags or control symbols are single characters (or sometimes two or more characters) that provide information in highly stereotyped, coded formats. One example is the check mark which may stand for a statement ("This record may not be updated"), the answer to a question ("Yes, this invoice has been paid"), or a selection ("Male or female, check one"). Some control symbols represent an instruction: "Check this box if you wish to donate your kidneys (K), eyes (E), or any internal organ (A), in the event of a fatal accident," or "Archive this record at the end of the month."

Sometimes a given data element can be described by alternative data types. A numeric data element would normally be stored in a data file as a numeric value, but it might also be stored in a text file (e.g., a word-processing file) as a sequence of alphanumeric characters, or *string*. Strings are simply collections of symbols. Thus the number 155,900 might be stored as the string "155,900." The repertoire of subsequent processing operations would differ according to the mode of storage. Strings are manipulated according to a set of rules different from that governing numeric data elements. Several strings can be combined—or *concatenated*—into a single longer one; for example:

"Joe" + "(space)" + "Doe" = "Joe Doe"

Alternatively, a string can be divided up into a number of shorter ones:

"1234567890" = "1234" + "567890"

But such manipulations performed on numeric strings are not equivalent to adding or subtracting the numerical values. Furthermore, one string is not ordinarily multiplied or divided by another.[1]

Field Length

The fields must be long enough to contain the data elements to be placed in them. Specification of field length will be straightforward if all the data elements to

be placed in the corresponding fields in each record are of the same prescribed length. This is usually the case with account numbers, for example:

Account no.

10000
10001
10002
10003

But other data elements, such as names, addresses, quantities, and balances, are of varying lengths. In some systems, fields of variable lengths can be incorporated, but this feature usually proves more difficult than it is worth. Instead, common practice is to design the file so that the corresponding fields are of the same length and long enough to accommodate the longest data element likely to occur. The penalty paid for this practice is that most of the fields will not be filled by their resident data elements, and so file space will be wasted; for example:

Vendor name

Watkins, Inc.
David Hall
S.W. Illinois Wholesale Corp.
Bruce Bros.
Savage, Jenkins, Brown, and Domingo

To save file space, numeric data elements are often "depunctuated," and the punctuation is restored upon output of the data element on a document, report, or screen. Thus the dollar balance $1,243,508.23 might be stored as 1243508.23 or even as 124350823 if the number of decimal places were standardized at 2. In this way, a balance of up to $9,999,999.99, for example, or a signed balance (debit or credit) of $999,999.99± could be accommodated in a field length of 9 digits. More space can be saved if all dollar amounts are rounded to the nearest dollar or to the nearest 100 or 1,000 dollars. The maximum field length ever likely to be needed for a dollar data element is 16 digits, which can accommodate a signed balance (including dollars and cents) of just under $10 trillion.

[1] In "string arithmetic" this is done, but only with very rigid conventions attached to the meaning of such operations.

Some quasi-numeric data types include telephone numbers, code numbers, and dates. These, too, are ordinarily depunctuated. Thus the telephone number (615) 929–4432 and the social security number 123–45–6789 would be stored, respectively, as 6159294432 and 123456789. Dates are expressed in various formats; for example, July 4, 1999, 4 July 1999, 7/4/99, or (in some countries) 4/7/99. In a file, this date would most likely be stored as either 070499 or 990704. The advantage of the latter format is that the date "numbers" increase monotonically with time and, accordingly, can serve as sort keys if the file has to be sorted chronologically. Standard North American telephone numbers require a field width of 10 digits, social security numbers require 9 digits; and dates require only 6 digits.

Record Layout

The record layout can conveniently be documented by means of a table listing each field, its data type, and its length. The same information can be contained in a parameter file. Each record in the parameter file corresponds to one field in the main data file. Parameter files of this type are frequently used in generalized computer software, as discussed in Chapter 8.

The following might represent the record layout for a simplified general ledger master file:

Field No.	Field Name	Data Type	Length*
1	Account number	Numeric	5
2	Account name	Alphanumeric	25
3	Account type	Alphabetic	1
4	Beginning balance	Numeric	14
5	Ending balance	Numeric	14
		Record length	59

* Characters or digits.

Numeric data types are often designated by the abbreviations N(2), N(4), and so on, which indicate the number of implied decimal places. A common abbreviation for alphanumeric is A/N.

Figure 5.2 shows how the first few lines in the data file might look. The line consisting of 9s and Xs documents the field's position and length, and the several example lines show typical record content. Thus "Allowance for bad debts" has a credit balance. The total record length of the file is 59 characters. If provision is made for a maximum of 1,000 records (i.e., a maximum of 1,000 accounts), the total size of the file will be 59 × 1,000 = 59,000 characters. Details of how such a file size translates into a storage device's capacity are described in Chapter 7.

FIGURE 5.2   General ledger master file.

Record no.	Acct. no.	Account name	Type	Beginning balance	Ending balance
	0 1 2 3 4 5				
	123456789012345678901234567890123456789012345678901234567890				
	99999X----------------(25)----------------XX9999999999999-9999999999999-				
1	11100Cash		A	2724321	2837109
2	11200Marketable securities		A	16109872	15992335
3	11300Accounts receivable		A	19332108	24587617
4	11350Allowance for bad debts		A	386642-	491752-
5	11400Merchandise inventory		A	89211655	84759832

Repeated Fields

In some instances, a field may occur more than once within the same record. For example, a sales order record may contain fields referring to several items, with their respective quantities and prices, to be shipped to the same customer. Since the number of items on sales orders varies, the designer does not know how many fields to include in the record; and the total length of the record cannot be specified. For the purposes of the logical design of the file, the record may be divided into two portions, or *subrecords*, one referring to the fields that appear only once, and the other referring to the repeated fields. The physical arrangement of the record in the storage medium can be determined later. An example of the documentation of such a record is

Subrecord A:
Field

No.	Field Name	Data Type	Length
1	Sales order number	N	10
2	Date of order	N	6
3	Customer number	A/N	8
4	Terms	A/N	5
5	Shipping instructions	A/N	30
		Subrecord length	59

Subrecord B:
Field

No.	Field Name	Data Type	Length
1	Stock number	N	14
2	Quantity	N(0)	6
3	Unit price	N(2)	7
		Subrecord length	27

DATA STORAGE AND RETRIEVAL

Data storage is performed solely as a matter of convenience for the users. The design of data structures has to consider primarily how the data will be later retrieved. Storage of data is relatively straightforward, but finding the data later may be difficult and time-consuming.

Serial Files

The simplest way to build a file is in "arrival order": New records are simply added to the end of the file. It is the natural approach if, for example, the file is made up of sheets of ledger paper; each new entry is made on the next line. Such an approach gives rise to a "serial file," and transaction files often take this form. The cash disbursements file in the following example will illustrate:

Cash Disbursement Journal

Date of Entry	Check No.	Payee	Amount
Jan. 1	100	James Company	$260
	101	Brown Brothers	175
Jan. 2	103	Green Associates	300
Jan. 3	104	Fox Industries	950
	105	A. B. Wolfe, Inc.	123
	106	Smith, Inc.	444
Jan. 4	108	W. W. Cox Co.	80

Note that the records are chronological according to the date of entry into the file. If the bookkeeper discovered on January 5 that checks #102 and #107 had been omitted, these entries would have to be added to the end of the file, and the records would no longer be chronological with respect to the issuance of the checks. Serial files do not provide for insertion of records within the body of the file, except by rebuilding the file.

Serial files are easily built, but retrieving data from them may be difficult, particularly if the file is a long one. Suppose, in the example just given, that it was fairly common for checks to be entered in the cash disbursements file "out of sequence." It might then be necessary to look through the whole file to find the record relating to a given check number—*or to determine that the record was missing.* Another example might make the point even more dramatically. Suppose that telephone directories were arranged in the order in which subscribers' telephones were installed; it would take a very long time to search for a given person's number, even if there were no possibility of inadvertently passing over the person's name.

Clearly some other approach must be adopted if retrieval of the data is to be made easy, and many different schemes have been proposed. A few of the more popular ones are described here.

Ordered Files

Some files, such as the telephone directory, are almost always accessed via the name of the person or institution whose number is required. The name forms the retrieval "key," and the telephone number and address form the data associated with that key. It is convenient to maintain such files in order of the primary key—the key most often used for retrieval—just as the telephone directory is maintained in alphabetical order. However, a problem that arises with this strategy is that it is more difficult to add new records. Either the file has to be rebuilt each time, or some method needs to be found for inserting new records in the body of the file. A card file obviously provides for insertion, but a ledger sheet does not; it would have to be rewritten to include any new entries that did not, by chance, fall at the end of the file because of "high" values of their corresponding keys.

If a file is maintained in order of the retrieval key, it is usually unnecessary to search all the way through to find a given record or to verify the existence of the record; one does not need to look beyond the "D" entries to find Joe Doe in a telephone directory. On the other hand, searching sequentially through part of a long file may still be intolerably time-consuming, even for a computer. In fact, despite their speed, computers are at somewhat of a disadvantage compared with people because computers cannot use intuitive clues as to the probable location of a record, for instance, that the "W" entries are close to the end of the telephone directory.

A technique that has been developed to aid computers in searching through ordered files is the binary search procedure. It is a process of sampling to locate the desired record. Assume, for example, that the record containing the key *Indigo* is to be retrieved from the following file:

```
                                    Sample No.:
Record No.   Key          1   2   3   4
    1        Blue  ----------------◁
    2        Brown
    3        Green ------------------◁
    4        Indigo ----------------------◁
    5        Orange -------◁
    6        Pink
    7        Red
    8        Yellow
    9        Violet
```

The file is first sampled at its midpoint (the fifth record) yielding the key *Orange*. This key is "higher" than *Indigo*, indicating that the target record lies in the upper half of the file. The first record is then sampled, producing *Blue*. This is lower than *Indigo*, showing that the target record lies somewhere between the first and the fifth record. The third sample is taken one fourth of the way through the file, producing *Green*. This is again lower than *Indigo*, indicating that the target record is somewhere between one fourth and halfway through the file. The fourth, and in this case final, sample is taken three eighths of the way through the file, producing the record containing the desired key. Each successive sample in a binary search is made halfway between the previous two.

Clearly the number of samples likely to be needed to retrieve a given record increases with the length of the file. It can be shown that maximum number of samples required to locate any record in the file is given by

$$\text{Number of samples} = \log_2(n - 1) + 1$$

where *n* is the number of records in the file. Thus a maximum of 11 samples would be needed in a file containing 1,000 records and 21 samples in a file of 1,000,000 records. For comparison, the maximum number of samples to retrieve a record by a sequential search would be 1,000 and 1,000,000, respectively. The binary search procedure is obviously much more efficient. It does assume, however, that the file is ordered on the retrieval key and also that random access to the file is provided.

Retrieval of a record containing a desired key is an example of *retrieval by content*. In contrast, retrieval of a record at a given location is referred to as *retrieval by address*. Retrieval by content is generally more difficult than is retrieval by address and normally requires an iterative, or trial-and-error, process. The binary search procedure essentially converts retrieval by content into an acceptably short sequence of retrievals by address.

Index Files

Another method of retrieval that makes this conversion is the construction of a secondary file called an *index file*. The index file contains only two fields: a key and the address of the corresponding record in the main data file. The index is ordered in the key, whereas the main file generally is not; the records in the file may, for example, be stored in arrival order.

The following illustration shows how the index file is used. The main file contains the signs of the zodiac in order of their positions in the heavens, together with other data. The index file contains the signs in alphabetical order.

Index File		Main File		
Key	Address	Record No.	Key	Other Data
Aquarius	11	1	Aries	. . .
Aries	1	2	Taurus	. . .
Cancer	4	3	Gemini	. . .
Capricorn	10	4	Cancer	. . .
Gemini	3	5	Leo	. . .
Leo	5	6	Virgo	. . .
Libra	7	7	Libra	. . .
Pisces	12	8	Scorpio	. . .
Sagittarius	9	9	Sagittarius	. . .
Scorpio	8	10	Capricorn	. . .
Taurus	2	11	Aquarius	. . .
Virgo	6	12	Pisces	. . .

If the record pertaining to Capricorn is required, for example, the index file will be searched (if necessary, using a binary search or other efficient procedure), and the address "record 10" retrieved. Then, record 10 is retrieved directly from the main file.

One advantage of the use of an index file is that when new records are added, only the key file needs to be rebuilt; the main file, which may contain much longer records and therefore is more cumbersome, can be left unchanged except for the new records appended to it. Another, possibly more important advantage is that more than one index file can be constructed for a given main data file. An inventory master file, for example, might be stored in the order in which the items were added to stock. One index file might be sorted by part number, another by part description, and a third by the name of the vendor who supplied the part.

Sometimes, the main file is ordered in a primary key, and an index file is built to provide access via a secondary key—one that is used less frequently than the primary key is. In an accounts receivable master file, the primary key might be customer number and the secondary key customer name:

Main File

Record No.	Customer No.	Name	Other Data
1	1001	Florida Co.	. . .
2	1002	Alabama Co.	. . .
3	1003	California Co.	. . .
4	1004	Georgia Co.	. . .
5	1005	Nebraska Co.	. . .
6	1006	Iowa Co.	. . .

Index File

Name	Address
Alabama Co.	2
California Co.	3
Florida Co.	1
Georgia Co.	4
Iowa Co.	6
Nebraska Co.	5

An index file associated with a main file sorted on another key is often called an *inverted file*; the file is inverted with respect to the index.

Record No.	Customer No.	Name	Other Data	[1st = 2] Pointer
1	1001	Florida Co.	. . .	4
2	1002	Alabama Co.	. . .	3
3	1003	California Co.	. . .	1
4	1004	Georgia Co.	. . .	6
5	1005	Nebraska Co.	. . .	—
6	1006	Iowa Co.	. . .	5

Linked Lists

In the index files just described, one field in each record contains the address of a record in the main file. The data element providing this address is often referred to as a *pointer*, because it points, so to speak, to the record in question. Sometimes pointers are contained not in a separate index file, but in the records of the main file themselves. A common application of this technique is to locate the "next" record in terms of some key other than any primary one on which the file might be ordered. The preceding customer file could be structured as shown above.

The information that *Alabama Co.* is the first key in the alphabetical sequence must be stored in some appropriate place. Its record points to the second key, *California Co.*, which in turn points to *Florida Co.*, and so on. Record 5 containing *Nebraska Co.* does not have a value assigned to the pointer because it corresponds to the last key in the sequence. The collection of data elements forming the pointers are referred to as a *linked list*. The linked list in the present example is made up of *forward pointers*, where *forward* denotes that they point to the *next* key in sequence. It is also possible to have *backward* or *reverse* pointers, which indicate the *previous* key. Sometimes files contain both forward and reverse pointers. If the last record in a linked list contains a pointer to the first record, a continuous loop will be formed; this is referred to as a *ring* or *chain* structure.

Indexed Sequential Files

The problem of inserting new records in an ordered file has already been mentioned. A fairly common data structure that seeks to overcome this problem is the ISAM file (Indexed Sequential Access Method). In an ISAM file, the records are grouped into blocks within which the records are ordered (or may possibly be associated with one another, say, by the use of a linked list). The address of the start of each block is separately referenced by an indexed file. The color file discussed earlier in this chapter may be used to illustrate:

Index File			Main File		
Key	Address		Record No.	Key	Other Data
Blue	1		1	Blue	. . .
Orange	17		2	Brown	. . .
			3	Green	. . .
			4	Indigo	. . .
			.	.	. . .
			.	.	. . .
			.	.	. . .
			17	Orange	. . .
			18	Pink	. . .
			19	Red	. . .
			20	Yellow	. . .
			21	Violet	. . .

The first block starts with record 1, the second with record 17. A search through the index file (which is ordered in the primary key) indicates the block in which the target record resides; *Indigo*, for instance, lies between *Blue* and *Orange* and therefore lies in block 1. A search through block 1 then produces the desired record.

Spare records are often provided for in each block to allow for insertion of new records; some of the existing records may need to be repositioned within the block as part of the process. If many new records are added, however, the block may be filled. When this occurs, subsequent additions are placed in an "overflow" area, usually located at the end of the file. Appropriate pointers are set to allow for the retrieval of these records. There is no limit to how many records can be placed in the overflow area (except its own capacity limit). But retrieval becomes increasingly inefficient, and at some stage it is desirable to rebuild the whole file. Utility programs are generally provided in automated systems for doing this.

The ISAM concept is a powerful one. An analogy that helps explain it is the search for someone's home. The first step is to find the street (the block) on which the person lives, and the second step is to find the particular house (the record) on that street.

Computed Addressing

All the retrieval methods discussed so far depend on multiple sampling to locate the target record. A method that avoids this inefficiency is called *computed addressing, randomizing* or *hashing*. In this method, the records are stored at locations specified according to the values of their primary keys. Each key is translated into a record number, or address, by means of some suitable algorithm. Retrieval, in turn, means translating the target key into its corresponding record number and then using this information to retrieve the record directly. The physical order of the records in the file is essentially random, but this is of no concern because the records can always be retrieved with the help of the translation algorithm.

In the case of numeric keys, the form of the algorithm is arithmetic and is chosen to distribute the records as uniformly as possible through the available file space. One possible form is referred to as *remaindering*. Suppose, for instance, that a file is to contain 2,000 records and that a particular key is account 4321. The numeric key is divided by 2,000, yielding an integer quotient of 2 and a remainder of 321. The computed address is then determined by adding 1 to the remainder, and the record would be stored at location 322. In the case of alphanumeric keys, the algorithm must be more complicated because it has to translate the keys into numbers as well

as produce a satisfactory distribution of records in the file; sometimes an arithmetic operation is performed on the ASCII equivalents of the characters comprising the key. The ASCII code is described in Chapter 6.

To illustrate the use of computed addressing, suppose that the translation algorithm[1] converted alphabetic keys into addresses as follows:

Key	Record No.
Blue	27
Brown	8
Green	3
Indigo	19
Orange	35
Pink	11
Red	17
Yellow	8
Violet	6

The nine records containing those keys would be stored at the addresses indicated. There are some gaps between the records, which might or might not be filled by new records added in the future. On the other hand, there are two keys, *Brown* and *Yellow*, that translate into the same address: record 8. Such keys are referred to as *synonyms*, and obviously only one of them can be stored at the particular address. The conflict is usually resolved by storing the first occurrence of the synonym at the computed address and then arranging other occurrences in an overflow area as a linked list. Retrieval will then necessitate multiple sampling, but the required number of samples (as well as the incidence of conflicts) can usually be kept manageably small. Careful design of the translation algorithm will minimize the number of conflicts and also the number of unused record locations.

Computed addressing is one of the fastest retrieval methods. Unfortunately, it does not provide an obvious means of locating—or even identifying—the next (or

---

[1] The precise algorithm that might perform this translation is not important here.

previous) key in a sequence; it is useful solely for storing and retrieving individual keyed records.

THE POSTING PROCESS

Posting is the process in which master files are updated to reflect accumulated transaction activity. The process involves a master file and at least one transaction file. The posting of journal entries to the general ledger is probably the best-known example, but the posting process extends to other situations, including

- Posting of current earnings data to an employee master file
- Posting of purchases and sales to a merchandise inventory master file
- Posting of billings and collections to a customer master file
- Posting of vouchers and check data to a vendor master file
- Posting of materials, labor, and overhead costs to a work-in-process master file

Routine File Update

In all cases, the process is essentially the same. The transaction file contains records that pertain to particular master file records: a general ledger account, an employee, a customer, a vendor, a job order, and so forth. The master file record contains a balance—in dollars or some other units—that must be updated to reflect the transactions that have occurred since posting was last performed. Some of the balances will increase; others will decrease; and still others may remain unchanged. In a general ledger system, transactions involving a debit to cash result in an increase of the cash balance, whereas those involving a credit to cash result in a decrease. Similarly, receipts of an inventory item (purchases in the case of a merchandise inventory) increase the balance on hand, whereas issuances (or sales) reduce it.

In general, the updated balance of a master file account is given by

$$\text{Updated balance} = \text{initial balance} + \text{total additions} - \text{total deductions}^2$$

In the case of the general ledger system, the additions may be identified with debits and the deductions with credits; this assumes (as is customary in automated systems) that negative balances are interpreted as credit balances. In an inventory system, the additions are interpreted as receipts and the deductions as issuances.

The new balance is entered in the master file record in place of the value that had remained there since the last posting operation. After posting has been completed for all master file records for which there has been transaction activity, the transaction file can be purged or archived and a new one established for the next period.

In automated systems, it is customary to leave the original version of the master file intact until posting is completed and has been verified. The updated balances are written to a new version of the file. This technique is adopted for control reasons, and it has the advantage that the process can be rerun in the event of erroneous or incomplete posting. After verification, the old version of the file (or ''father'') is purged or archived, and the new version (or ''son'') is released for general use. Figure 5.3 illustrates the relationship between the transaction file and the two versions of the master file. In more complicated situations, there may be two or more transaction files involved in the posting process.

The term *posting* recalls primitive accounting systems that were modeled after operations in a post office. Rows of pigeonholes were provided, one for each account, into which related source documents were placed. Updated balances were then determined by analyzing the source documents accumulated for each account. The distribution of source documents among the various pigeonholes is a sorting process, and sorting has remained an essential ingredient of posting up to the present day. The

---

[2] This result is an application of the well-known bathtub model. The model states that the final amount of water in the bath is equal to the amount there initially plus the amount added through the faucet and less the amount that goes down the drain.

FIGURE 5.3 System flowchart showing the use of "father" and "son" master files.

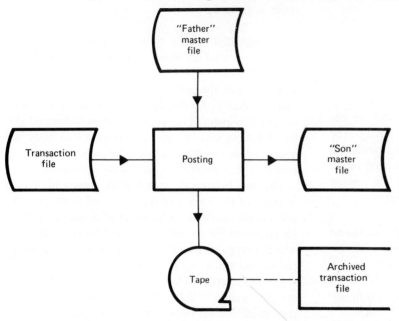

objective is to bring together all transactions relating to each master file record so as to facilitate the determination of the updated balance. For example, in an accounts receivable system, the transactions are first sorted to bring together the records relating to each customer. The sales and collections can then readily be tallied to determine the new outstanding balance. Figure 5.4 illustrates the same process applied to an inventory system; Figure 5.4(a) shows the sorting process—this time by inventory part number—and Figure 5.4(b) shows the update of the inventory master file.

Figure 5.4 provides examples of the three possible effects that posting can have on a master file record: The balance can be changed as a result of the transaction activity; it can remain unchanged because there is no transaction activity affecting that record; or it can remain unchanged despite relevant transaction activity because the additions and deductions fortuitously happen to cancel each other.

These three possibilities must be recognized when procedures are designed to check the completeness and accuracy of the posting process. In automated systems, particularly, such procedures are important to ensure that

all transactions actually are posted and that none is "lost." One reason that transaction records can be lost is that they reference a nonexistent master file record, as when they reference an invalid account number, employee, or inventory item. The existence of such transactions often is revealed when the sorted transaction file is compared with the corresponding master file.

One method of verifying the completeness of the posting process is to generate control totals: one for the transactions file and one for the master file. In the inventory example, shown in Figure 5.4, a control total would be formed for total receipts less total issuances—over *all* the records, not just those referencing a certain inventory item. A second control total would be formed from the master file, equal to the sum of the updated quantities on hand and less that of the old quantities on hand. The results are as follows:

$$\begin{aligned} \text{Total receipts} &= 340 \\ \text{Total issuances} &= 299 \\ \hline \text{First control total} &= 41 \end{aligned}$$

FIGURE 5.4 **Posting in an inventory management system.**

Transaction file in normal chronological order:

Date	Part #	Receipts	Issuances
Jan. 1	12345		20
Jan. 1	45678	30	
Jan. 1	23456		10
Jan. 2	56789		200
Jan. 2	12345	100	
Jan. 3	23456		15
Jan. 3	45678		5
Jan. 3	34567	5	
Jan. 4	34567		1
Jan. 4	12345		30
Jan. 5	23456		8
Jan. 5	56789	200	
Jan. 5	34567	5	
Jan. 5	12345		10

Transaction file sorted by part number:

Date	Part #	Receipts	Issuances
Jan. 1	12345		20
Jan. 2	12345	100	
Jan. 4	12345		30
Jan. 5	12345		10
Jan. 1	23456		10
Jan. 3	23456		15
Jan. 5	23456		8
Jan. 3	34567	5	
Jan. 4	34567		1
Jan. 5	34567	5	
Jan. 1	45678	30	
Jan. 3	45678		5
Jan. 2	56789		200
Jan. 5	56789	200	

Total activity:
Receipts – 100
Issuances = 60
Net change = +40

(a) Sorting of an inventory transaction file prior to posting.

Master file before posting:

Part #	Description	Quantity on hand
12345	Small widget	90
23456	Short widget	110
34567	Medium widget	0
45678	Large widget	8
56789	Long widget	339
67890	Super widget	15

—Net change→
= +40

Master file after posting:

Part #	Description	Quantity on hand
12345	Small widget	130
23456	Short widget	77
34567	Medium widget	9
45678	Large widget	33
56789	Long widget	339
67890	Super widget	15

(b) Update of the inventory master file as the result of posting the transactions.

$$\begin{aligned}\text{Total updated quantities on hand} &= 603\\\text{Total old quantities on hand} &= 562\\\hline\text{Second control total} &= 41\end{aligned}$$

If the two control totals are not equal to each other, the posting operation has not been successful. The use of control totals verifies that all transactions have been duly posted, but it does not guarantee that they have been posted to the right master file records. Errors can arise if the master file reference (account number, employee number, and the like) was a valid one in the sense that it was listed in the master file but was incorrect. This possibility emphasizes that there is no substitute for careful checking on the transaction data, either at the time of entry or between data entry and posting.

The Posting Cycle

Posting is a regularly recurring periodic operation. A general ledger system requires posting to be done at least once per year, in time for the closing of the books and the preparation of the annual financial statements, but often it is done more frequently to provide for interim statements and budget tracking. Other systems, such as accounts receivable and account payable, require posting at least once per month and possibly weekly. A payroll system would probably involve posting once per pay period: weekly, monthly, or semimonthly, as the case may be. An inventory system would probably require the most frequent posting to control inventory levels properly; daily posting of inventory transactions is not uncommon.

Posting can usefully be understood in terms of a posting cycle. It consists of the following steps (see Figure 5.5):

- Establishment of a transaction file
- Accumulation of transaction records
- Posting of transaction data to the master file
- Archiving of the transaction records
- Purging of the transaction file

The posting operation can be verified for completeness. This is the classical posting cycle, and it is followed, without modification, in numerous practical situations. In other cases, however, deviations from the classic pat-

FIGURE 5.5 The posting cycle.

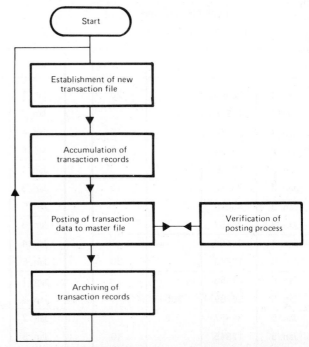

tern are accommodated to serve better the purposes of the information system and the needs of its users.

One common departure from the classic pattern eliminates the purging of the transaction records at the end of the cycle. Instead, the transaction file is kept open permanently, and individual records are deleted upon completion of some significant economic event. An example is the open-invoice accounts receivable system. Here, invoice records are retained in the transaction file until payment is received; at that point, they are deleted and archived. Because not all the payments are received simultaneously, there is no time at which the whole transaction file can be purged and reestablished. If the transaction file remains open indefinitely, posting to the master file will have a somewhat different significance. In some cases, the transaction records are summarized only when needed—say, to prepare the customer statements—and they are summarized each time from the transaction file, without any entry made to the master file. In other cases, the summary figure is written to the master file, but only to provide a control balance, and the detail remains in the transaction file. Individual transactions may remain in the transaction file during several "postings," and some means is adopted for avoiding their being counted more than once; one commonly used technque is to "flag" the transactions that they have already been included in the summary total. Open-invoice accounts receivable systems are probably more common than are balance forward systems, which do conform to the classical posting pattern.

Another variation from classical posting is found in some FIFO and LIFO inventory systems. Here, the cost "layers" may be preserved in the form of semipermanent transaction records rather than in the inventory master file. This is an advantage in some automated systems that do not provide for variable length records. Because there is no way of predicting how many cost layers will be required, it is difficult to design a master file capable of accommodating all the necessary layers without wasting a considerable amount of file space. At the time that those cost layers are liquidated, by being matched against an issuance record, the cost records are deleted from the transaction file. Back orders are also sometimes retained in the transaction file (possibly separate from the file or files established to accept receipts and issuances) until the orders can be filled; at that time, they are deleted or archived.

Perhaps the most far-reaching departure from the classic posting pattern is found in real-time systems and data base management systems. In real-time systems (see Chapter 6), the master files are updated immediately rather than at the end of the posting period. This is mandatory to control fast-moving inventories and to reserve airline seats and hotel rooms. The transaction records usually are retained for audit purposes and to help reconstruct the master file data in the event of a machine malfunction. However, there is no subsequent "posting" operation involving routine update of the master file. In data base systems (see Chapter 9), the distinction between transaction files and master files itself becomes blurred. Rather, there are transaction records, or groups of transaction data elements, and master records or groups. Relationships are established between the transaction data elements and the master data elements that permit summary data to be extracted whenever a user may need such data. "Posting" is no longer a periodic operation, but a continuous—and automatic—process of maintaining the relationships among corresponding data elements.

FILE MAINTENANCE

File maintenance is the process of changing a file's content by direct intervention of the user rather than as the result of posting the accumulated transaction data. It is basically an editing process, and typically it is carried out on master files (although the editing of transaction files, for error correction, is substantially similar). File maintenance can be considered nonroutine, in the sense that it is performed only when the need arises: when new customers are added, when employees terminate, when vendor addresses have to be changed, and so forth.

File maintenance consists of three types of operations (see Figure 5.6):

- Addition or insertion of new records
- Deletion of old records
- Update of existing records

In some instances new records are simply added to the end of the file. This is appropriate, for example, when the system automatically assigns the next available customer number to each new addition; the latest customer added would lie at the end of the file and would have the highest number of assigned to date. In other cases, particularly in which the records are sorted by some key such as customer name, the new records are inserted into their proper places within the file.

Updating of existing records is usually done on fields that are not the target of a posting process. In a general ledger file, for example, the account description might be changed from "noncurrent assets" to "long-term assets," but it would be unusual to modify an account balance by means of a file maintenance operation; indeed, there would be adverse control implications if this were to be permitted. Many automated systems have such fields write protected expressly to prevent alteration—either intentional or inadvertent—during file maintenance activity. There could also be control implications if it were permissible to delete a record that had an active balance; again, some computerized systems are designed to check critical balance fields before the delete request is carried out.

File maintenance is potentially far-reaching in its implications, and suitable controls have to be established in addition to those already mentioned, to ensure that all changes are properly authorized and executed. Among

FIGURE 5.6   **Illustration of file maintenance on an employee file.**

File before
maintenance:

Name	S/S #	Date hired	Dept.	Marital status
Abraham, A.	123 - 45 - 6789	1/10/75	Manuf.	D
Cain, C.	234 - 56 - 7890	6/5/72	Acctg.	S
David, D.	345 - 67 - 8901	12/3/76	Acctg.	M
Hadar, H.	456 - 78 - 9012	11/10/80	Mktg.	M
Jacob, J.	567 - 89 - 0123	5/3/79	Manuf.	M
Moses, M.	678 - 90 - 1234	7/21/80	Finance	S

Records updated

Record deleted

File after
maintenance:

Name	S/S #	Date hired	Dept.	Marital status
Abraham, A.	123 - 45 - 6789	1/10/75	Manuf.	D
Cain, C.	234 - 56 - 7890	6/5/72	Finance	S
David, D.	345 - 67 - 8901	12/3/76	Acctg.	M
Esau, E.	789 - 01 - 2345	6/1/82	Manuf.	D
Hadar, H.	456 - 78 - 9012	11/10/80	Mktg.	M
Jacob, J.	567 - 89 - 0123	5/3/79	Manuf.	D
Zebah, Z.	890 - 12 - 3456	6/10/82	Acctg.	M

Records added

other control measures, a log should be kept of all file maintenance activities, listing which records have been altered and the nature of the alteration. Systems that permit a record to be changed—and possibly changed back after some process has been run—without leaving a tangible record of what has been done, exhibit a major control weakness.

SORTING AND MERGING OF DATA FILES

It was shown earlier that it is easier to retrieve data records if the file is maintained in order of the primary key or if an ordered index file is constructed. The process of ordering a file according to a given key (i.e., arranging the records in the "proper" order—alphabetical, chronological, numerically monotonic, as the case may be) is called *sorting*. A common application of sorting is to the posting process; the association of transaction records with their corresponding master records is easier if the transaction file is first sorted by the same key as the master file. Another application is to the preparation of management reports; several reports may be prepared from the same data, each sorted on a different key. For instance, the data in a sales file might be sorted by customer in one version of a sales analysis report, by sales representative in another version, and by product type in a third.

Sorting is one of the most familiar data-processing operations and also one of the most time-consuming. It has been estimated that some 30 percent of all data-processing effort is expanded on sorting. This is an interesting observation because sorting does not change the data as such, but only their arrangement or configuration. One of the advantages of the data base management system, discussed in Chapter 9, is that data can often be retrieved in different configurations without the need to sort the associated files.

Merging is a complementary process in which two or more existing files are combined into a single new file. Normally *merging* is understood to refer to the situation in which the original files are already ordered on the same key as the desired new file; otherwise, sorting is required first. When new records are being added to an existing master file in a file maintenance procedure, it is customary to sort the new records and then merge them into the master file.

Merging is a conceptually simple processing operation. All that is needed is to make parallel passes through the relevant files, selecting the "next" record in the desired sequence and writing it to the new file. The following example will illustrate:

Files to be merged.

Record No.	Key		Record No.	Key
File 1:			*File 2:*	
1	101		1	103
2	102		2	105
3	107		3	108
4	114		4	112
5	120			

New file,

Record No.	Key
1	101
2	102
3	103
4	105
5	107
6	108
7	112
8	114
9	120

There is little difference between one method of merging and another, and no sophisticated strategies are normally required to ensure efficiency. In contrast, sorting can be quite complex, and great care needs to be taken, particularly with long files, to avoid excessive processing times, even on large powerful computers. The remainder of this section will discuss some of the issues in sorting and in the development of effective and efficient sort procedures.

Insertion Sorting

Probably the most elementary method of sorting is insertion sorting, which is constructing a new file record by record. The original file is read sequentially, and a copy of each record (or possibly the record itself) is added to a new file by inserting it in its appropriate position. The procedure is the one that would be adopted if a deck of cards were being sorted by hand. To illustrate, consider the following simplified file:

Record No.	Key
1	107
2	101
3	112
4	114
5	102
6	105
7	120
8	103
9	108

A total of nine insertions will be required to build the new file (one for each record), the first five of which are

Record No.	Insertion No.				
	1	*2*	*3*	*4*	*5*
1	107	101	101	101	101
2		107	107	107	102
3			112	112	107
4				114	112
5					114
6					

The particular record inserted is shown underlined. Note that there must be provision for the insertion of records in the body of the new file and the corresponding displacement of records previously added.

The method of successive insertion is effective, but it is highly inefficient. The efficiency of a sorting technique is usually measured (at least in part) by the average necessary number of comparisons between keys. This method requires an average of

$$\frac{n(n + 1)}{4}$$

comparisons,[3] where n is the number of records in the file. This number rapidly increases as the file grows larger.

Insertion sorting is a special case of a broader series of methods referred to as *successive merging*.

Exchange Sorting

Exchange sorting can be adopted in order to sort the records in a file physically. If a separate sorted file is required, a copy of the original one will be made first.

The simplest version of exchange sorting is called *bubble sorting*. Successive passes are made through the file, and adjacent pairs of keys are compared. If a pair is out of sequence, the order is reversed. Eventually the whole file will be ordered on the particular key. The first five passes through the numerical file described earlier will result in the following:

Original File	Passes				
	1	*2*	*3*	*4*	*5*
107	101	101	101	101	101
101	107	107	102	102	102
112	112	102	105	105	103
114	102	105	107	103	105
102	105	112	103	107	107
105	114	103	108	108	108
120	103	108	112	112	112
103	108	114	114	114	114
108	120	120	120	120	120

After five passes, the sorting of this particular file is complete. Note that the largest key "sinks to the bottom" of the file during the first pass, the next largest during the second pass, and so on.[4] As a consequence, each pass can be shorter than the previous one, down to the dashed line drawn across the table.

The average number of comparisons in the bubble sorting method is

$$\frac{n(n - 1)}{4}$$

which is nearly as large as the corresponding number for insertion sorting. On the other hand, bubble sorting is superior insofar as it does not require the insertions and the rewriting of records that insertion usually implies. Bubble sorting is more widely used, but it is still far too inefficient to be suitable for large files.

Efficient Sorting Methods

It can be shown theoretically that the minimum average number of comparisons required in even the most efficient sort of procedure is given by the formula

Minimum average number of comparisons $= n \log_e n$

This number is considerably smaller than the corresponding figures for insertion or bubble sorting—6,908 for a file of 1,000 records as compared with 250,250 for insertion and 249,750 for bubble sorting—and demonstrates the potential for developing more efficient methods. The ideal can rarely be achieved, but several methods do substantially better than do the simple ones just described.

One popular method (or group of methods) is *tree sorting*. It resembles insertion sorting, except that the

[3] This is the theoretical expected value for a file initially in random order. The worst case is one in which the file is in the *reverse* of the desired order; sorting of such a file requires twice the number of comparisons.

[4] If the file is read from the last record forward, the smallest key will immediately "rise to the top" of the file—perhaps more in keeping with the notion of the "bubble sort."

records themselves are not rewritten each time an insertion is made. Instead, a "tree" of pointers is built first, and the file is subsequently reconstructed in a single operation. A tree is a data structure that serves a purpose similar to that of an index file, but it is more complex. A simple binary tree starts with a "root" and splits into two "branches"; each branch then splits into two more branches, and so on.

The development of a binary tree for the numeric keys discussed earlier is represented by the following; the first table shows the tree after four insertions, and the second shows the completed tree:

Level	Tree
1 (root)	107
2	101 112
3	102

Level	Tree
1 (root)	107
2	101 112
3	102 114
4	105 120
5	103 108

The best tree-sorting procedures can achieve an average number of comparisons of

$$2.4n \log_2 n \quad \text{or} \quad 3.46n \log_e n$$

which is equal to 23,873 for a file of 1,000 records.

Another popular group of methods includes *quick sort* and *quicker sort*. In common with bubble sorting, it exchanges pairs of keys, but instead of working with the whole file, it divides up the file into a number of smaller ones. This is usually advantageous; sorting two files of

500 records each, by the bubble method, for example, would require only one half the number of comparisons as would sorting a single file of 1,000 records. The methods in this group usually divide up the original file into a large number of small subfiles and achieve greater reductions. The numeric key file mentioned earlier would initially be divided into two:

Original File		Subfiles	
Record No.	Key	Record No.	Key
1	107	1	101
2	101	2	102
3	112	3	105
4	114	4	103
5	102	--------	--------
6	105	1	107
7	120	2	112
8	103	3	114
9	108	4	108
		5	120

in which the largest key in the first subfile is 105 and the smallest key in the second is 107. Further divisions would then be made until the set of subfiles adds up to the desired ordered file.

The best methods in this group achieve average numbers of comparisons of

$$2n \log_e n$$

or 13,816 for a 1,000-record file. This is only twice as large as the theoretical minimum and indicates the efficiency of methods of this type.

SUMMARY

Files are collections of related pieces of data stored with the intention of subsequent retrieval and use. Data files are established to hold accounting data or other quantitative material. They normally have a well-defined structure consisting of records which, in turn, are composed of individual data elements or fields. Other types of files, which may be less rigidly structured, are established to store record locations, computational parameters, processing instructions, computer programs, or text. Such files are important to automated information systems and word-processing systems.

In manual systems, data files take the form of paper documents, journals, registers, ledgers, printed cards, or microfilm. In computerized systems, files normally reside in electrostatic or magnetic media which are machine readable but which unfortunately cannot be read directly by human operators. The most important types of data files are transaction files, which contain detailed records of recent transaction events, and master files, which contain account balances and semipermanent data such as account descriptions. Transaction files correspond to the journals, and master files to the ledgers, in traditional accounting systems.

Data elements are the building blocks of records, files, and data bases, the latter being examples of data aggregates. The arrangement of the data elements in a record, file, or data base, and the manner in which data elements are stored and retrieved are referred to as the data structure. There may be more than one way of looking at a data structure; the view taken by the user or programmer is referred to as the logical structure, and the actual arrangement of data elements in the physical storage medium is referred to as the physical structure.

Data are stored in files with the objective of subsequent retrieval, but the manner in which they are stored requires a trade-off between storage effort and retrieval effort. Some data structures require more storage effort but provide for easier retrieval. Such an arrangement may be justified if frequent retrieval—say for decision support purposes—is anticipated. The binary search method and computed addressing are two efficient methods of retrieval, each applicable to particular situations.

Operational data processing consists largely of routine file manipulation, including transaction posting and file maintenance. In batch systems, posting is performed at regularly scheduled intervals whose length is chosen to provide a balance between processing effort and information currency. Transaction data are accumulated in transaction files and are periodically summarized as a basis for updating balances in related master files. The classical pattern of the posting cycle provides a point of reference for almost any type of information system, although the extent to which the pattern is followed may vary from one system to another. The greatest degree of departure from the classical pattern is found in real-time systems and data base management systems. In real-time systems, master files are updated immediately upon entry of a transaction; real-time systems avoid problems of poor data currency that commonly plague batch systems.

File maintenance is a common nonroutine file-processing activity. File maintenance allows a file's contents to be modified by the direct intervention of the user. The main application of file maintenance is to the addition, editing, and deletion of records in a master file.

The sorting and merging of data files require a significant processing effort in many modern information systems. Many sorting techniques are available, but their efficiency varies greatly. The time taken to sort a long file can often be reduced by one or more orders of magnitude by using a more efficient method. Merging presents less of a processing problem, but still not a trivial one.

BIBLIOGRAPHY

Davis, William S. *Information Processing Systems.* Reading, Mass.: Addison-Wesley, 1978.

Knuth, D. E. *The Art of Computer Programming.* Vol. 3, *Sorting and Searching.* Reading, Mass.: Addison-Wesley, 1973.

Lewis, T. G., and M. Z. Smith. *Applying Data Structures.* Boston: Houghton Mifflin, 1976.

Meadow, Charles T. *Applied Data Management.* New York: Wiley, 1976.

Palmer, Ian R. *Data Base Systems: A Practical Approach.* Wellesley, Mass.: Q.E.D. Information Sciences, 1975.

Powers, Michael J., David R. Adams, and Harlan D. Mills. *Computer Information Systems Development: Analysis and Design.* Cincinnati: South-Western, 1984.

Silver, G. A., and J. B. Silver. *Data Processing for Business.* Orlando, Fla.: Harcourt Brace Jovanovich, 1981.

DISCUSSION QUESTIONS AND PROBLEMS

1. Define and discuss the following terms:

- Accessibility
- Activity ratio
- Backup file
- Binary search
- Chain structure
- Command file
- Data aggregate
- Data element
- Exchange sorting
- File
- File listing
- File maintenance
- File medium
- File volatility
- Hashing
- Index file
- Insertion sorting
- Inverted file
- ISAM file
- Linked list
- Logical record
- Master file
- Ordered file
- Parameter file
- Physical record
- Primary key
- Posting
- Posting cycle
- Program file
- Record
- Ring structure
- Scratch file
- Secondary key
- Sequential search
- Serial file
- Text file
- Transaction file

2. Identify the data elements you would expect to find in the master file and transaction file(s) used in the following applications:
a. General ledger
b. Accounts receivable

c. Job cost
d. Sales order processing
e. Inventory management

3. Identify the data elements that would be found in the master file in an inventory application designed for an automobile dealer. Assume that every car or truck in stock is unique in some way and that costs are assigned on a specific identification basis. No transaction file is maintained.

4. A survey has been made to measure the file activity in several files used in a particular application. The results obtained are as follows:

File	Total Records	Activity per Week Records Accessed	Records Changed
Master file	1,000	500	3
Transaction file	5,000	1,250	1,250
Scratch file	5,000	5,000	5,000
Archive file	5,000	0	1,250
Index file	1,000	5,000	3
Parameter file	10	50	0

Required
a. Determine the activity ratio and volatility ratio of each file.
b. Comment on the required accessibility of the various files.
c. What types of file media would be most suitable for the files?

5. a. Design a master file to hold student records in a university. The following information should be specified: file name, storage medium, method of access, activity ratio,* volatility ratio,* field name, field length, and field data type. No transcript data are to be included in the file.
b. If there are 10,000 students in the university, how much storage capacity will be required for the master file?

* Indicate "high," "low," and so forth, as the case may be.

6. a. Design a transaction file suitable for recording customer payments received by a credit card company. Provide file name, storage medium, access method, and field definitions.

b. There are 500,000 active customers, and on the average one half make a payment each month. The company has a policy of retaining transaction records on line for three months after payment is received, after which the records are archived. How much storage capacity must be provided for the transaction file?

7. The table below shows the transaction file and master file in a simplified accounts payable system. Sort the transaction file by vendor number, and post the data to the master file. Verify that the total change in the accounts payable balance is equal to the dollar total of vouchers, less payments.

8. Design an open purchase order file for use in a computerized information system. A purchase order may be placed for a single item or for several items all purchased from the same vendor. Accordingly, the file should be able to accept purchase order records with an arbitrary number of line items. Each line item should be identified by an in-house product number and also by the vendor's catalog number; the quantity, unit of measure, and list price of each item should be included. Purchase orders specify a requested delivery date and the suggested mode of shipment. The paper purchase-order forms are prenumbered, and the purchase order number should be referenced in the computerized record.

In your design, distinguish the fields that appear only once in each purchase order record from those that may appear several times, once for each line item. What is the total length of (a) the subrecord containing the fields that appear once and (b) the subrecord containing the fields that may be repeated?

Data for Problem 7

	Transaction File						Master File		
Date	Vendor No.	Voucher No.	Voucher Amount	Check No.	Check Amount		Vendor No.	Name	Balance
3/1/19XX	305	961	$375.00				300	Elm Company	0
3/2/19XX	301	962	105.00				301	Apple, Inc.	$150.00
3/5/19XX	310	963	260.00				302	Yew & Sons	360.00
3/6/19XX	302	964	50.00				303	Pine Associates	0
3/9/19XX	312	965	85.00				304	Oak Company	0
3/11/19XX	301	966	325.00				305	Cedar, Inc.	50.00
3/12/19XX	302	967	140.00				306	Peach, Bros.	210.00
3/15/19XX	301			146	$255.00		307	Maple Enterprises	112.00
3/15/19XX	302			147	410.00		308	Fir, Inc.	23.00
3/15/19XX	310			148	260.00		309	Cyprus Company	0
3/15/19XX	312			149	585.00		310	Fig Bros.	48.00
3/17/19XX	304	968	400.00				311	Pear Associates	0
3/21/19XX	301	969	130.00				312	Plum Company	500.00
3/25/19XX	311	970	45.00						
3/28/19XX	303	971	92.00						
3/31/19XX	301			150	325.00				
3/31/19XX	305			151	200.00				
3/31/19XX	307			152	80.00				

9. An automated accounts receivable system contains an open invoice file in which invoices are recorded until they are paid. Specifically, invoice records are written to the file at the time that sales are made. When payment is received, the corresponding record is accessed and flagged "paid." A weekly purging program is executed in which all records flagged in this manner are archived and are deleted from the file. Immediately before this purging program is run, the data in new sales records and payment records are posted to the customer master file, which contains the appropriate balance fields.

Required
a. Comment on the use of the open invoice file from the standpoint of the classical posting cycle.
b. What special provisions would need to be made to ensure that sales records were not posted to the master file more than once? How could this be accomplished?
c. The open invoice file has a record length of 100 characters. A total of 200 sales are concluded per 5-day working week, each resulting in an invoice record, and the average payment period is 35 days. What is the average size of the file?

10. A designer is trying to choose among a serial file, an ordered file, and an ISAM file for a number of applications. Select the most suitable type for the following:
a. A general journal transaction file
b. A customer master file in which records are retrieved by customer number and new customers are assigned the next highest number
c. An alphabetical employee file with low volatility
d. An alphabetical vendor file with high volatility
e. An alphabetical vendor file with low volatility but a high activity ratio
f. An archive file

11. a. Indicate the sequence of sampling iterations required to extract the key 102 from the following list, using a binary search procedure: 101, 102, 103, 104, 105, 106, 107, 108, 109, 110, 111, 112, 113, 114, 115, 116, 117
b. How would the binary search procedure be modified to handle the situation in which the number of keys (less 1) is not a power of 2? Extend the list in (a)

through the key 124, and check the validity of your proposed solution.

12. Part of an employee master file, ordered on employee number, is as follows:

Record No.	Employee	Name	Other Data
1	101	Hawkins, Charles	. . .
2	102	Thompson, Mandy	. . .
3	103	Baker, Terry	. . .
4	105	Montgomery, Jack	. . .
5	108	Caplan, Betty	. . .
6	109	Winter, Alice	. . .
7	112	Wilson, Tracy	. . .
8	113	Smith, Mary	. . .
9	115	McKinley, John	. . .
10	118	Greenfield, Karen	. . .

There are several applications in which it would be desirable to be able to choose retrieval either by employee number or by employee name. You have been asked to develop a procedure for retrieval by name (other than a sequential search through the whole file).

Required
a. Build an index file ordered by employee name, with appropriate pointers to the records in the main file. How would the desired name be located in the index file?
b. Add forward and reverse pointers to the records in the main file to establish an alphabetical linked list. Would retrieval using a linked list be faster, on the average, than retrieval by a sequential search? What is the main advantage of the linked list?
c. Retrieval of records by employee number would have been easier if the employee numbers in the file had been contiguous (there would then have been a unique relationship between the employee number and the record address). What is the likely reason for the gaps in the assigned employee numbers? Could the numbers be made contiguous?

13. An accounts receivable master file contains customer records ordered on customer number. The following is a sample of the records in the main file:

Record Number	Customer Number	Customer Name	Other Data
1	1002	Brown & Co.	. . .
2	1004	Allen Bros.	. . .
3	1005	Magenta Enterprises	. . .
4	1007	Wolf, Inc.	. . .
5	1008	Blacksburg Co.	. . .
6	1011	Green & Sons	. . .
7	1012	Smithson, Inc.	. . .
8	1014	Baker, Inc.	. . .
9	1015	Grouper Gifts	. . .
10	1018	Young & Co.	. . .
11	1019	Dennis Bros.	. . .
12	1020	Howard Co.	. . .
13	1024	North Pole Products	. . .
14	1025	East Tennessee State Univ.	. . .
15	1026	Cousins, Inc.	. . .
16	1028	Thomas Enterprises	. . .
17	1029	Zebra Co.	. . .

Ordinarily, records are retrieved by customer number. But customer service personnel occasionally need to retrieve records by customer name for query purposes.

Required

a. Establish an index file providing for the efficient retrieval of records by customer name.

b. Show how the record for Dennis Brothers would be retrieved using a binary search through the index file.

14. The customer master file, forming part of an accounts receivable system, is structured as an ISAM file as shown in the table at the bottom of this page. Subsequent file maintenance activity calls for the addition and deletion of records. Initially, the overflow area is empty. The file is not reorganized between each file maintenance operation.

Required

a. Add records for Ayin Enterprises, Mem Corporation, and Yod Brothers.

b. Delete the records corresponding to Daleth Brothers, Gimel Brothers, and Teth Company.

c. Add records for Nun Corporation, Qoph Associates, Resh Brothers, and Vau Enterprises.

Data for Problem 14

Index File		Main Data File		
Customer	Record No.	Record No.	Customer	Other Data
Aleph Corp.	1	1	Aleph Corp.	. . .
Gimel Bros.	6	2	Beth Assoc.	. . .
Samekh & Sons	10	3	Daleth Bros.	. . .
		4	(empty)	
		5	(empty)	
		6	Gimel Bros.	. . .
		7	Kaph Company	. . .
		8	Lamed Bros.	. . .
		9	(empty)	
		10	Samekh & Sons	. . .
		11	Shin Corp.	. . .
		12	Teth Company	. . .

15. The open purchase order file to be incorporated into a new computerized information system has a record layout defined as follows:

Field No.	Description	Data Type	Length
1	Purchase order #	N	6
2	Date of issuance	N	6
3	Vendor #	A/N	8
4	Total $ amount	$(2)	8
5	Number of items	N	5
6	Date of receipt	N	6
7	Partial/complete	A/N	1
8	Shipping instructions	A/N	20
9	Inventory item #	A/N	10*
10	Unit of measure	A/N	2*
11	Unit price	$(4)	8*
12	Quantity	N	5*

* Repeated for each P/O line item.

Purchase orders containing up to 10 line items are issued. A survey of issuances during the last 12 months indicated the following data:

Number of Line Items	Number of P/Os Issued
1	265
2	490
3	623
4	585
5	318
6	209
7	160
8	97
9	51
10	8

Required

The file is to be stored on a magnetic-disk device that is restricted to fixed-length physical records. Design a physical record layout that minimizes the required storage capacity. Assume that the device can accommodate any prescribed record length so long as it is the same for all physical records. Do not subdivide the A and B subrecords, as defined in the chapter.

16. A computed addressing, or hashing, scheme is being developed for use with an inventory management system. The system uses five-digit numeric part numbers, and the hashing algorithm consists of multiplying the individual digits together. The resulting number is used as the address of the record in question. For example, for part 12345, multiplication of the digits results in $1 \times 2 \times 3 \times 4 \times 5 = 120$, and accordingly the item is stored at record address 120.

Required

a. Determine the record address assigned to the following inventory items, and identify any synonyms:

    11111
    12345
    23456
    34567
    45678
    76543
    99999

b. What is the average number of synonyms for each record address?

c. Consider other types of algorithms for translating the key into a record address. What types of algorithms would be suitable for alphanumeric keys?

17. Sort the following file alphabetically, using (a) the insertion sorting method, (b) bubble sort method, and (c) the tree sort method:

Record No.	Primary Key	Other Data
1	January	. . .
2	February	. . .
3	March	. . .
4	April	. . .
5	May	. . .
6	June	. . .

Record No.	Primary Key	Other Data
7	July	. . .
8	August	. . .
9	September	. . .
10	October	. . .
11	November	. . .
12	December	. . .

18. The posting of materials requisition transaction data to the inventory master file requires monthly sorting of an average of 10,000 transaction records. You are trying to select an appropriate sort procedure, taking into account the complexity of the method and the computation time. As part of your analysis, you decide to calculate the average number of comparisons in some of the candidate methods.

Required

Determine the average number of comparisons required to sort the transaction file, using the following:

a. The bubble sort method
b. The theoretically "ideal" method
c. A tree sort method in which the number of comparisons is given by
$3n \log_2 n$.
d. A method of the quick-sort family in which the number of comparisons is given by $3n \log_e n$.

19. A general ledger master file is to be established with storage and retrieval based on computed addressing. The file is to provide for a maximum of 1,000 records. Four-digit numeric account numbers are used, providing for a coding scheme in which the first digit indicates that account classification: 1 = assets, 2 = liabilities, 3 = stockholders' equity, 4 = revenue, 5 = direct costs, and 6 = indirect costs.

The randomizing algorithm uses the method of remaindering. Specifically, the account number is divided by 1,000, leaving a remainder; the computed record number is then given by adding 1 to this remainder.

Required

a. Compute the record addresses corresponding to the following accounts:

Cash	1010
Accounts receivable	1110
Allowance for bad debts	1155
Furniture and fixtures	1510
Accumulated depreciation	1515
Accounts payable	2110
Bonds payable	2310
Common stock	3010
Premium on common stock	3020
Sales	4010
Sales returns	4015
Direct labor	5010
Direct materials	5110
Depreciation expense	6010
Indirect labor	6110
Indirect materials	6210

b. Identify the synonyms in the keys listed in (a). What other synonyms would be expected to occur?
c. Suggest possible ways of avoiding the conflicts arising with the coding scheme and the randomizing algorithm.

PART TWO

THE ROLE OF COMPUTERS IN ACCOUNTING INFORMATION SYSTEMS

Part II addresses the broad subject of computerized information systems. Chapter 6 introduces computerized information processing and its historical development, discussing the various modes of operation of computer systems from the standpoint of processing objectives and efficiency. Chapter 7 explores computer hardware components, including input, storage, processing, data communications, and output devices. Simple performance parameters are presented, forming the basis for a range of useful design calculations. Chapter 8 introduces computer instructions and the development of systems, applications, and end-user software. Chapter 9 deals with data base management systems and discusses alternative structural models of the data contained in such systems. Chapter 10 introduces computer networks and data communications and explains the concepts of network topology and telecommunications media.

6

Introduction to Computerized Information Systems

LEARNING OBJECTIVES

After you have studied this chapter you should be able to

- Describe the nature and purpose of modern digital computers.
- Explain briefly how computers work.
- Discuss the historical development of computer hardware and software.
- Explain modern computers' principal modes of operation.
- Discuss the principles of batch processing and its uses.
- Discuss the principles of real-time processing and its uses.
- Explain the notion of multitasking.
- Discuss the role of end-user computing.
- Describe the principal numbering systems used in computer technology.
- Explain how to convert from one numbering system to another.

THE BASICS OF COMPUTERS

In the broadest sense, a computer is a mechanical, electrical, or electronic device that can process data in a prescribed manner. Today virtually all computers are digital electronic devices that can input, store, process, transmit, and output data according to instructions provided in advance by their users. A brief history of computers presented later in this chapter shows that the idea of computers originated long ago. But computers have developed to the point that they can influence business information processing only as a result of advances in electronics since World War II. However, these advances have been so rapid that computers have risen from having a barely perceptible impact to their present dominant impact in only 40 to 50 years.

In order for accountants to be able to use computerized information systems, they must understand how computers work. In this section we shall examine how data are represented in modern digital computers, how computers process information, and what hardware and software are necessary.

Representation of Data in Computers

The processing capability of modern digital computers resides in logic devices that operate by counting electrical pulses. These pulses correspond to binary digits, or *bits*, consisting of zeros and ones. Data that are meaningful to the user, such as dollar amounts, account numbers, names, and addresses, must be converted into binary form before they can be processed. Moreover, these processing instructions must also be presented to the processing device in binary form.

Numeric data can be represented in binary form in two ways. First, every decimal number has its equivalent in the binary numbering system; for example, the binary representation of the decimal number 75 is 1001011. This kind of representation is often referred to as *pure binary*. Binary numbers tend to be much longer than decimal numbers, and bits are typically grouped into aggregates of eight, or *bytes*, or into aggregates of four, sometimes called *nibbles*. Each nibble corresponds to a hexadecimal number, and the latter numbering system provides a convenient shorthand for cumbersome binary words. Thus the decimal number 75 can be expressed in pure binary as 01001011 or in hexadecimal shorthand (because 0100 = 4 and 1011 = B) as 4B.

Decimal numbers can be converted into pure binary form by means of standard algorithms, and many hand calculators can also do this. Appendix 1 discusses numbering systems and presents some conversion algorithms applicable to the binary system and the octal and hexadecimal systems, which are important in computer technology. Appendix 2 contains a table showing the binary (as well as the octal and hexadecimal) equivalents of the first 255 decimal numbers.

Both numbers and alphanumeric characters can be represented by standard codes of symbols. Two such codes are the American Standard Code for Information Interchange (ASCII) and the Extended Binary Coded Decimal Interchange Code (EBCDIC). The former is used extensively in microcomputers and telecommunications systems. The latter is used extensively in large mainframe computers. A complete list of the ASCII and EBCDIC codes and their binary equivalents is shown in Appendix 2. The ASCII and EBCDIC codes should be viewed as codes of symbols, or *alphabets*, and not as systems of numerical representation. The numbers 0 through 9 do not occupy positions 0 through 9 in the tables. Instead, they correspond to character numbers 48 through 57 in the ASCII code and numbers 240 through 249 in the EBCDIC code. As a result, performing arithmetic in ASCII or EBCDIC, although possible, is fairly complicated. Computers normally perform arithmetic operations in pure binary.

A number may be stored in a computer in pure binary form, as the binary equivalent of its ASCII character number, or as the binary equivalent of its EBCDIC character number. Thus the number 5 (ASCII #53, EBCDIC #245) may be stored (in an eight-bit word length) in any of three ways:

Pure binary: 00000101, or 05_{16} (the binary equivalent of 5)

ASCII: 01100101, or 35_{16} (the binary equivalent of 53)

EBCDIC: 11110101, or $F5_{16}$ (the binary equivalent of 245)

A multidigit decimal number is expressed digit by digit in ASCII or EBCDIC. For example, the decimal number 250 (which can be represented by one byte in pure binary: 11111010, or FA_{16}) would be represented by three bytes:

ASCII

2	5	0
00110010	00110101	00110000
32_{16}	35_{16}	30_{16}

EBCDIC

2	5	0
11110010	11110101	11110000
$F2_{16}$	$F5_{16}$	$F0_{16}$

ASCII or EBCDIC representation, in which every character is associated with a whole byte, takes up more storage space than does pure binary representation. On the other hand, the conversion back and forth from human-readable decimal form is much easier—it can be accomplished, character by character, by means of a simple table look-up. There are other types of representation of numeric characters, including *compressed decimal* in which two decimal digits are stored in each byte.

Switch Settings

Logic devices associate binary words with the settings of internal switches, which in turn generate patterns of electrical pulses. Specifically, a binary digit of 1 turns a switch to ''on,'' resulting in an electrical pulse, while a binary digit of 0 turns the switch to ''off,'' resulting in the absence of a pulse. For example, the equivalent of the decimal number 6 in the binary numbering system is 0110. This number can be represented by a row of four switches with the following settings, and a signal pattern consisting of two pulses and two gaps, or "absent" pulses:

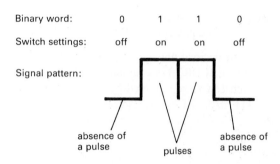

Other representations of numeric and alphanumeric characters are illustrated in Figure 6.1. Although a number such as 6 can be represented by a 4-bit word, larger numbers require more bits, and alphanumeric characters require up to 8. Most computer processors are designed with standardized word lengths, such as 16 or 32 bits, and leading 0s are inserted to added to fill the unused portion of each word.

The electromechanical computers of 50 years ago employed small relays that opened and closed as the data were processed. Modern computers use electronic switches etched into silicon chips, which are much smaller and more reliable and operate much faster. Nevertheless, the principle is the same, and the relationship between binary digits and switch settings is precisely the same.

Binary Arithmetic

As noted earlier, computers perform all arithmetic operations in the binary numbering system. The basic arithmetic function is addition. To illustrate, suppose that the computer has to add the numbers 3 and 5. The numbers are stored in binary form,

$$3 = 0000\ 0011_2$$
$$5 = 0000\ 0101_2$$

assuming an 8-bit word length.[1] Their sum is found by successive addition of the binary digits, starting from the right (in the same way that a decimal addition would be performed), and "carry digits" are accumulated as necessary[2]:

$$
\begin{array}{r}
0000\ 0011 \\
\underline{0000\ 0101}
\end{array}
$$

Result:	0000 1000
Carry digits:	111

The result, $0000\ 1000_2$, is, of course, equal to 8.

Binary subtraction is more difficult for digital computers and is handled by converting the operation into one of addition. The first step is to determine the "twos complement" of the subtrahend (the number to be subtracted). The twos complement is found by changing all the "zeros" in the number to "ones," and vice versa, and then adding 1 to the result.

Suppose, for example, that we want to subtract 4 (i.e., $0000\ 0100_2$) from 6 ($0000\ 0110_2$). The twos complement of 4 is determined as follows:

Original subtrahend:	0000 0100
Interchanging 0's and 1's:	1111 1011
Adding 1:	1111 1100

The second step is to add the twos complement to the minuend (the number from which the subtrahend is to be subtracted):

Original minuend:	0000 0110
Twos complement of subtrahend:	1111 1100
Result (by addition):	0000 0010
Carry digits:	(1)1111 11

---

[1] An 8-bit word length is chosen for convenience here. The arithmetic operations described in this section would be essentially similar for binary words of any length.

[2] Note that $1 + 1 = 10$ in binary arithmetic.

FIGURE 6.1 **Representation of numeric and alphanumeric characters by switch settings and patterns of electrical pulses.**

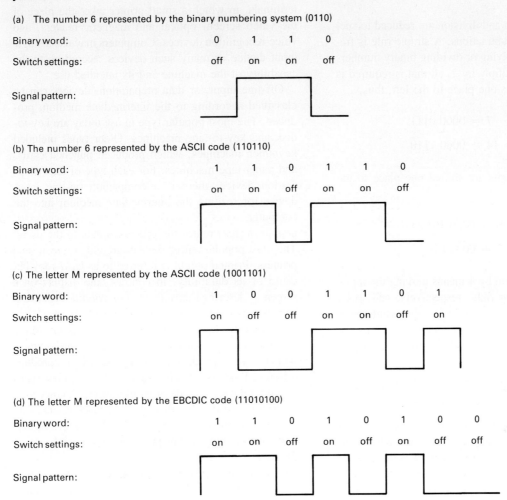

(a) The number 6 represented by the binary numbering system (0110)

Binary word:

Switch settings:

Signal pattern:

(b) The number 6 represented by the ASCII code (110110)

Binary word:

Switch settings:

Signal pattern:

(c) The letter M represented by the ASCII code (1001101)

Binary word:

Switch settings:

Signal pattern:

(d) The letter M represented by the EBCDIC code (11010100)

Binary word:

Switch settings:

Signal pattern:

The final carry digit (on the left) is ignored. The result, as expected, is equal to 2.

Sometimes subtraction results in a negative number: For example, if 6 is subtracted from 4, the result will be -2. If the foregoing procedure is carried out for computing the difference, the result will be $1111\ 1110_2$, which normally is interpreted as 254. However, the convention is adopted that the first (high-order) bit indicates the sign of the number: 0 indicates a positive and 1 a negative number. Thus the binary number just men-tioned is interpreted not as 254 but as $254 - 256 = -2$ (256 is the total number of combinations possible in an 8-bit word system). To avoid ambiguity between numbers such as -2 and 254, which would have the same binary equivalent, the range of acceptable positive numbers is usually restricted to 2^{n-1}, where n is the word length (i.e., to 128 for an 8-bit word length) instead of 2^n (or 256 for an 8-bit word length), leaving the other half of the available range to correspond to negative numbers. An advantage of this convention for representing negative numbers is that the procedure for subtraction is the same whether or not the result is positive or negative.

Binary multiplication and division are reduced to successive additions and subtractions. A simple rule is frequently used for multiplying or dividing binary numbers by powers of 2. To multiply by 2, all that is required is to shift the binary digits one place to the left; thus,

$$7 = 0000\ 0111$$

$$7 \times 2 = 14 = 0000\ 1110$$

To divide by 2, the digits are shifted one place to the right, for example,

$$10 = 0000\ 1010$$

$$10/2 = 5 = 0000\ 0101$$

Multiplication or division by 4 means moving the digits *two* places to the left or right, respectively, and so on for higher powers of 2. These rules are the counterparts of the familiar rule in decimal arithmetic of shifting the decimal point to multiply or divide by powers of 10.

Computer Hardware

The two most important aspects of a computer system are the hardware and software. The hardware is the computing equipment, and the software provides the instructions that "tell" the equipment what tasks the user wants it to perform. The principal components of computer hardware parallel the processing activities of input, output, storage, processing, and data communications (Figure 6.2).

• *Input devices* accept data from the users and encode it into machine-readable form in readiness for processing. They include *on-line* input devices, which are connected to and are under the control of the computer, as well as *off-line* input devices, sometimes called *data preparation* devices, which encode the data onto an intermediate medium which is fed into the computer (via an on-line device) at a later time. The principal type of on-line input device in use today is the video

display terminal (VDT), consisting of a keyboard and a screen. Other types of input devices include printer terminals, in which a small printer takes the place of the video screen, optical and magnetic readers, and voice-recognition devices. Computers may use a single input device or many such devices, according to the capability of the machine and its intended use.

Off-line input, or data preparation, devices can be classified according to the intermediate medium produced. The most popular type in use today are key-to-disk and key-to-tape machines. Older types included keypunch machines, which produced punched cards, and paper-tape machines. For each type of data preparation device, there is a companion on-line input device for reading the intermediate medium into the computer.

• *Output devices* return the processed data to the users. The most popular output devices are video screens and printers. Printed output is referred to as *hard copy* because of its durability. In contrast, the display on a screen is described as *soft copy* or *volatile* because it vanishes as soon as the power is turned off or as soon as another display is brought up onto the screen. Many different types of printers are available, providing a wide range of speed, print quality, ability to reproduce different kinds of material, and so forth. Other types of output device include microfilm printers, voice synthesizers, and devices that produce machine-readable output that can be read by another computer. Again, a computer may have just one or several output devices.

Storage devices provide for the accumulation of material in a data base. Numbers, textual material, logical values, programs, and other data can be stored for later retrieval and use. Computers typically incorporate more than one level of storage. *Main memory*, or *primary storage*, is built into the processor unit and provides fast, addressable, random access to its contents. Main-memory storage is normally volatile, holding the data currently being operated upon, together with the programmed instructions for performing those operations. For example, during execution of a payroll program, one employee's data at a time are usually loaded into main memory; when that employee's data have been processed, another employee's data will be loaded, and so forth.

FIGURE 6.2   The principal components of a computer system.

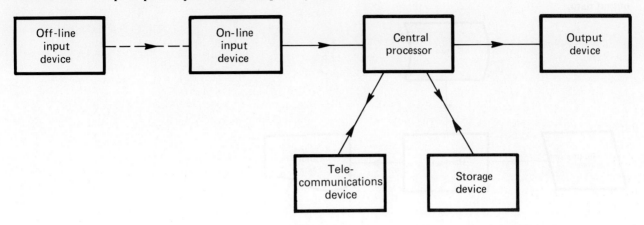

Secondary storage provides for more permanent storage of data and software not immediately in use. While the payroll is being processed, an accounts receivable program or an inventory file may reside in secondary storage. The most popular secondary storage medium is magnetic disk. Several types of magnetic disk are available, ranging from small, flexible ("floppy") disks, of relatively small capacity, up to large "fixed," or "hard," disks capable of holding much larger volumes of data. Magnetic disk media all offer random access to the data. Other kinds of secondary storage media include optical disk, which also permits random access, and magnetic tape, which permits only sequential access. Secondary storage is on line in the sense that the data are available upon issuance of a command by the processor. Operator intervention may be required to exchange floppy disks or hard disk cartridges or to mount reels of tape, but once in place the media are on line to the processor.

Tertiary storage is sometimes available in order to back up secondary storage. The files in secondary storage are periodically copied to tertiary storage media as a security measure. If the data in secondary storage are lost, the most recent copy is reloaded from tertiary storage. Tertiary storage also provides a cheaper medium for archive purposes. Tertiary storage devices need not allow random access, and they are not necessarily on line to a processor device. Operator action may be required in order to transfer data back and forth between secondary and tertiary storage, although some large modern systems provide for automated transfer of data in the interest of minimizing storage costs. The most common tertiary storage medium, providing machine-readable capability, is magnetic tape. If machine readability is not necessary, microfilm or even paper printout may suffice.

• *Processor devices* provide the capability for the actual processing of data. Processing may be the arithmetic and logical manipulation of numerical data or the editing of textual material. Processor devices also control the system's operation: starting, monitoring, and stopping the execution of programs; keeping track of data; maintaining communications with other devices; and so forth. In most computer systems designed up till the late 1970s, all of the processing capability was concentrated in a *central processor unit* (CPU). The other devices—called *peripheral devices*—were passive and simply carried out commands issued by the central processor. More recently the trend has been toward distributing the processing capability throughout the system. Small, special-purpose processors are incorporated into the input, output, storage, and other devices, so as to share the work of processing and system control. The burden on the central processor is thereby reduced, either permitting a smaller central processor to be used or increasing the system's operating speed. Peripheral devices, which contain significant processing capability of their own, are referred to as "smart" or "intelligent" devices. In some systems, this trend is taken to its logical conclusion, and all the

FIGURE 6.3 Relationship among computer hardware and software, and input and output data.

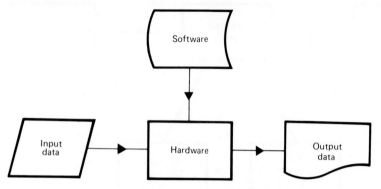

processing capability is distributed, with the result that the central processor can be eliminated. All that is necessary is some mechanism to allow the various devices to "talk" to one another and to pass data back and forth among them. Distributed processing systems of this type offer good performance and reliability characteristics. Whereas conventional systems are completely dependent on the continued operation of the central processor, distributed processing systems consist only of autonomous "peripheral" devices whose failure is merely a local problem; the processing "eggs" are no longer all placed in one basket.

- *Telecommunications devices* provide for the electronic transmission of data over a distance, which may range anywhere from a few feet to several thousand miles. Telecommunications hardware includes the actual medium of the channel—telephone lines, coaxial cable, fiber optic cable, microwave link, or satellite, as the case may be—and also the equipment that must be located at the "nodes" where the channels intersect.

Telecommunications systems are becoming increasingly important in view of the growth of distributed systems, which may be confined to a single location such as a building but which often cover a large geographical area. With many types of transmission media, it is inefficient to transmit the data in their original digital form; over all but short distances and at slow transmission speeds, there is an intolerable loss of signal strength, and the data are distorted by "noise." The solution is to convert the data into analog form, in which the discrete pulses of digital signals are changed into a signal with a continuous waveform. At the other end of the communications channel the signal is converted back to digital form.

Computer Software

Modern business computers invariably have the capability to store the sets of instructions—the programs, or software—that determine how the data are to be processed. Software is loaded into main memory to perform a particular processing task and then is replaced by other software to perform another task; when not currently in use the software resides in secondary or tertiary storage (Figure 6.3). Software has been compared to the human mind with its thought patterns and learned responses, whereas the hardware corresponds to the brain with its cells and neurons.[3]

Software is customarily divided into systems software and applications software. Systems software includes the operating system, drivers for interfacing with the various peripheral devices, utility programs, and program language translators. The operating system, the most important component of systems software, supervises the operation of the central processor, allocates space in main memory, maintains contact—via the driver interfaces—with the peripheral devices, and provides an operating environment for the applications software.

[3] Douglas R. Hofstadter, *Godel, Escher, Bach* (New York: Vintage Books, 1980).

Utility programs include data base management systems, query languages, report generators, and standardized processing functions for such tasks as copying, editing, and sorting files. Utility programs may be operated from a terminal or may be invoked by another program before or during execution. Language translators are used during the preparation of applications software.

Systems software is usually prepared for a particular type of processor and usually cannot be operated on another type. However, in the case of microcomputers, several manufacturers often use the same processor chip, and it may be possible to run the same systems software on any of them.

Applications software performs the tasks of direct interest to the user: processing invoices, printing checks, updating ledger accounts, preparing financial statements, and so forth. Applications software is less closely related to a particular processor design, and programs can often be transported from one machine to another with minimal modification.

Some users write their own applications software. Others have software written by professional programmers or buy it in the form of "canned packages" from software "houses." Most applications software is written using "high-level" programming languages, such as COBOL, FORTRAN, Pascal, and BASIC. These programs must then be translated into "low-level" binary instructions that turn electronic switches on and off in the central processor. Language translators used for this purpose include assemblers, compilers, and interpreters. They differ from one another in the types of language that they can translate and the timing of translation relative to the execution of the programs. Interpreters translate the programs at the time that they are executed, whereas asssemblers and compilers translate the programs only one time, resulting in more efficient operation.

In recent years, much software has been developed with the end user in mind. Such software is designed to be "user friendly"; that is, it can be operated by lay people with little or no formal computer training, and it is distributed in the form of "canned packages" together with instruction manuals. Such end-user packages are primarily for accountants, managers, professional people, and others who operate personal computers. Perhaps the best-known package of this kind is the electronic spreadsheet, the electronic analog of the columnar worksheet. Spreadsheet packages have wide application, and millions of copies have been sold. Other end-user packages include file management and data base management systems, word-processing systems, graphics packages, and combinations of two or more of these into "integrated packages."

EVOLUTION OF THE COMPUTER

Mechanical Computation

Mechanical aids to computation are not a modern innovation. The earliest form of hand calculator—supplementing people's ability to count on their fingers—was probably the abacus. There is little doubt that the abacus dates from the middle of the first millenium B.C. when it was used in both China and Egypt, and there is some evidence that it existed in the Tigris–Euphrates Valley as early as 5000 B.C. The abacus consists of a frame strung with wires representing the positional value of the numbers being manipulated; beads sliding on the wires represent the absolute values. An adaptation of the abacus was used by the Romans in which small stones took the place of the beads; the stones were called *calculi*, providing the origin of our word *calculation*. The abacus and its various derivatives were essentially "general-purpose calculators."

More specialized computational capability has been attributed to certain ancient monuments. It is claimed, for instance, that Stonehenge, which dates at least to 2000 B.C., was used for astronomical calculations, including predictions of eclipses of the sun and moon.[4] The calculations are supposed to have been performed by moving small portable stones around a large circle of stationary ones.

During the first 1,500 years of our era, many mechanical devices were constructed for performing astronomical calculations as well as for telling the time.

---

[4] See, for example, G. S. Hawkins and J. B. White, *Stonehenge Decoded* (New York: Dell, 1965).

These devices date from the time of the great scholastic center in Alexandria and were subsequently developed by the Arab astronomers who eventually brought them to Europe. Machines, which today we call general-purpose calculators and which provided greater capability than the abacus did, are thought to have originated about 1,000 years ago. The earliest known machine of this type was constructed by the Apraphulians of New Guinea in the ninth century.[5] This "computer" consisted of ropes and pulleys contained (literally) in black boxes and was capable of performing an impressive range of digital processing operations. Motive power is believed to have been provided by teams of elephants.

In Europe, general purpose mechanical computers became of interest during the Renaissance and the centuries that followed. Several such machines were developed by John Napier, Blaise Pascal, Gottfried Leibniz, the third Earl of Stanhope, and other gentleman scientists of the fourteenth through the eighteenth centuries. In the early part of the nineteenth century, Charles Babbage devoted much of his life (and considerable personal fortune) to the development of mechanical computers of even more significant capability. His most ambitious project was the "analytical engine," which was to have been driven by steam; unfortunately, it was never completed. Babbage proposed the idea of the memory device and the use of punched cards as an input medium, anticipating by several years their more successful use by Herman Hollerith. Hollerith is generally regarded as the "father" of the punched card.

Babbage's computational machines, along with many of the earlier devices, used the rotational position of gear wheels to represent numbers. The teeth on the gear wheels perhaps were the more modern analog of the stationary stones in the Stonehenge "astronomical computer." Much later, digits were represented by the opening and closing of relays in electromechanical devices and then by the opening and closing of electronic switches in the form of vacuum tubes or solid-state devices.

[5] A. K. Dewdney. "An Ancient Rope-and-Pulley Computer Is Unearthed in the Jungles of Apraphul." *Scientific American* (April 1988), pp. 118–121.

Electronic Computation

One of the most significant events in the development of computers was the invention of the vacuum tube: the diode by Ambrose Fleming in 1904 and the triode by Lee de Forest in 1908. But it took many years before vacuum tubes were developed into successful switching devices, leading to their use in digital computing equipment in place of mechanical relays. The invention of the cathode ray tube (CRT), by William Crookes also had a profound influence on computers by making possible the concept of video displays.

The first general-purpose computer to use vacuum tubes was the ENIAC (Electronic Numerical Integrator and Calculator) developed during World War II. It cost $400,000 to develop, weighed 30 tons, and contained 18,000 vacuum tubes that dissipated 150 kilowatts of heat. It could perform 5,000 calculations per second but usually would not run for more than about 20 minutes without failure. The first commercially available computer using vacuum tubes was the UNIVAC I, developed by Remington Rand in 1950.

The invention of the transistor by John Bardeen, Walter Brattain, and William Shockley made possible modern computing as we know it. Solid-state electronics—based initially on transistors and later on integrated circuits—offered dramatic reductions in the size of components, in power consumption, in cooling demands, and in cost; moreover, there were comparably dramatic increases in operating speed. Transistorized computers first became available in 1959, with the appearance of the IBM 1401 machine. The 1401 was the first "low-cost" computer to be marketed to medium-sized businesses.

Miniaturization of electronic components continued through the 1960s and produced the "chip" and the microprocessor. Today's chip, about the size of a small fingernail, can hold hundreds of thousands of memory locations; it can also perform an incredible number of functions. The microcomputer is essentially a whole computer on a chip. Even large computers are now based almost entirely on microelectronic components.

From the microprocessor to the powerful supercomputers, which can perform tens of millions of computations per second, an enormous range of processing capability is now available. And substantial capability is available at low cost. The ENIAC computer can now be outperformed by machines costing only a few hundred dollars. There is no evidence that the pace of technological developments has slowed, and increases in capability as well as the emergence of many more innovations can be expected in the future.

Computer Software

There is debate as to who was the first computer programmer. Some authorities attribute this honor to Ada Countess Lovelace, an associate of Charles Babbage, after whom the programming language Ada was named. But programming as we know it had to wait for the development of the notion of stored software. This development is due largely to the work of John von Neumann in connection with the ENIAC. Prior to his innovation, instructions for the particular problem had to be wired into the computer, as had been necessary with electromechanical bookkeeping machines. Von Neumann showed that by using preprogrammed instructions, which could be read into the computer along with the data, the process could be speeded up enormously. With this development, the rapid deployment of computers for multiple uses was made possible.

The earliest computer software was written in machine code. Writing a program in machine code required the programmer to select the actual sequences of ones and zeros necessary to turn on and off the electronic switches in the computer processor. Although this procedure was preferable to physical wiring of the processor, it was still highly inefficient. Later, assemblers, compilers, and interpreters were developed that allowed programs to be written in high-level programming languages, using symbols more closely related to the arithmetic and logical processes being represented. The programs could subsequently be translated into machine code in readiness for processing. With the availability of high-level languages, during the 1950s and 1960s, software development soon became much more efficient. Applications programming, as we now know it, dates from that time.

Systems software evolved rapidly, in response to increasingly sophisticated computer hardware technology.

Multitasking operating systems, capable of running more than one processing task at a time, date from the late 1950s. Interactive systems and data base management systems date from the 1960s. In the mid-1970s, end-user software started to emerge. The development of the electronic spreadsheet by Daniel Bricklin and Robert Frankton was possibly the most significant event in this regard.

Many commentators now predict the decline of applications programming. There are now so many programs available for the common accounting and other business purposes that there is simply no need for any more. The only remaining need is to update software to adapt it to improved computer systems. Today, much of the emphasis in software development is on producing systems software for new computer systems and on developing innovative end-user packages.

A second area of emphasis is on the development of so-called artificial intelligence systems. The software for these systems is intended to mimic some of the cognitive and problem-solving activities of the human mind. Whereas conventional computers are programmed to operate in a precisely predictable manner, artificial intelligence systems are able to act in less structured ways. Work in this area is still in its infancy, but some significant advances have been made. One of the more successful innovations has been the development of *expert systems*, which were first applied to medical diagnosis. Symptom data are entered into the computer, and as part of an interactive dialogue, the machine asks questions of the physician-user, soliciting more symptom clues. Finally, on the basis of an analysis of the data, the system suggests possible diagnoses for the physician's consideration. Other "diagnostic" applications of expert systems have been proposed, such as the interrogation of legal case history, the tax code, and FASB pronouncements.

Computer Generations

Many commentators on the evolution of computers refer to distinct generations of machines, or distinguishable phases in their development. According to this classification, the first generation of machines included the ENIAC and the other early machines that used vacuum tubes. The second generation, dating from the late 1950s, saw the introduction of solid-state transistors as the active electronic switching devices. Also during this generation, high-level programming languages became established, with FORTRAN being the first to win wide acceptance in the United States, and ALGOL in Europe. The third generation dated from the mid-1960s and marked the introduction of integrated electronic circuitry. Advanced processing concepts also emerged during the third generation, including interactive processing, time sharing, and data base management systems.

In about 1980, the fourth generation began. The fourth generation is supposedly characterized by large-scale circuit integration, increasing miniaturization of compo-

FIGURE 6.4 Pure batch processing. Source documents are keyed off line into the transaction file which, in this particular system, is on magnetic tape. The transaction file is subsequently loaded onto the computer for posting to the master file, which is also on magnetic tape. A father–son system is used to protect the master file. After posting, the transaction data are archived. The activity and status reports are simply listings of the transaction and master files, respectively.

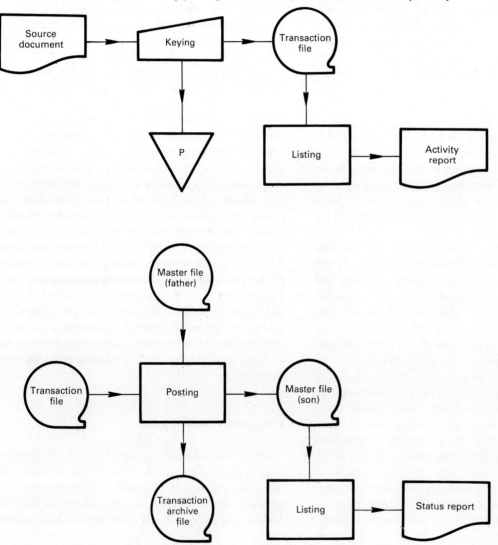

nents, the growth of data communications systems, and the emergence of "code generators" that automate some routine programming tasks. The easier access to computer systems by nonspecialists is also claimed to be a distinguishing feature. Today, advances in interactive processing, the emergence of "plain English" query languages allowing users to interrogate large data bases, the widespread availability of microcomputers, and the development of user-friendly software including the spreadsheet all have contributed to the end-user computing revolution.

Some commentators suggest that we have already entered the fifth generation. This latest generation is identified with the growth of expert systems and other forms of artificial intelligence software. What other developments will be included remains to be seen.

MODES OF PROCESSING

Batch Processing

The processing mode refers to the way in which the computer is used to process the data and to the degree of interaction (if any) between the user and the machine. The simplest processing mode is *batch processing*; it was adopted on the earliest computers and is still used widely today. With batch processing, transaction data are accumulated into batches for processing all at one time. It conforms closely to the classical posting cycle, and its steps are

- Preparation of input data
- Loading of programs and files
- Input of data
- Execution of the programs
- Printing (or other delivery) of output
- Distribution of output to the users

In "pure" batch processing, which is widely used on large mainframe computers, transaction data are prepared off line, on a freestanding device that is not connected to the computer. The data are encoded onto a machine-readable medium (magnetic tape, floppy diskettes, and the like) and are verified before being loaded into the computer. Programs and master files, which may

also reside on magnetic tape or magnetic disk, are loaded into the computer in readiness for the programs' execution. Several batches of data may be run using the same programs (and possibly the same master files). Figure 6.4 shows a flowchart of the updating of the files in a pure batch system.

The output may be printed (or delivered in some other manner) while processing is actually in progress. Alternatively, the output may be stored for subsequent, "offline" printing. The advantage of off-line printing is that processing is not delayed by the printer's relatively slow speed; the output can be written much faster to some medium, such as magnetic tape, and printing can be done at some convenient later time. In some machines, the operating system provides for the sets of output to be placed in a queue—usually on magnetic disk—to be printed in turn, and the printer runs continuously until the printing is completed. This arrangement is referred to as *spooling*. Strictly speaking, it cannot be regarded as off-line printing because the central processor schedules the flow of jobs to the printer and maintains communications among the various devices in use.

Batch processing has both advantages and disadvantages relative to other modes of processing, and the most important of these are listed in Exhibit 6.1. Batch processing is well suited to routine accounting functions: the general ledger, customer billings, vendor payments, payroll, and control of slow-moving inventories. In large companies in particular, batch processing is used predominantly for these functions. But batch processing is not suitable when a quick response is essential, for instance, in airline reservation systems. There are many accounting applications in which fast response is needed, including sales order and inventory-processing systems. Often it is necessary to interrogate the files and, on the basis of the information obtained, to initiate a transaction that must be processed immediately. For such applications, real-time processing is the answer.

Interactive Processing

Interactive processing involves a dialogue between the user and the machine. It is more complicated conceptually than is pure batch processing, and it requires a more sophisticated operating system and hardware. Not

---

EXHIBIT 6.1.   Advantages and Disadvantages of Pure Batch Processing

Advantages:
- Conceptually simple
- Consistent with classical posting model
- Requires relatively simple hardware configuration and operating system
- Facilitates scheduling of jobs for efficient utilization of computer resources
- Can accept job prioritization
- Lends itself well to the design of effective controls

Disadvantages:
- Slow turnaround
- No means of file interrogation
- Processing out of the control of users
- No provision for any user–machine dialogue

---

surprisingly, interactive processing developed later than did pure batch processing, but it has developed rapidly, and today, a substantial proportion of business data processing is done in an interactive mode.

In interactive processing, the distinct steps that could be identified in batch processing become blurred. The encoding, processing, and output of the data all are done on line and may be integrated with one another. The user is in control of both the input and the output devices. The programs and files may already be on line and ready to be accessed, or if they have to be loaded, they remain on line and under the user's control until the processing is completed.

The main advantage of interactive processing lies in its fast response. Even when there is speed degradation in a time-sharing environment, owing to heavy usage, response is measured in minutes rather than in hours or days. With many modern interactive systems, response is virtually instantaneous. The user is also able to monitor progress of the run and may be able to alter the course of processing in the light of the results. The user may be able to select, at some key decision point, one of several different processing options. One of the options may be to abort the run to save the cost and time of continued unsuccessful processing.

Interactive processing typically offers a number of important aids to effective operator–machine dialogue. One of these is the screen *menu*, from which different processing selections can be selected. The menu for part of an accounts receivable system might look like the following:

```
        ACCOUNTS RECEIVABLE SYSTEM
    Processing options available:
        1.   Enter invoice data
        2.   Verify and edit invoice data
        3.   Print invoice preview report
        4.   Print invoices
        5.   Print customer statements
        6.   Perform end-of-period closing
    Enter selection number >
```

There are two common methods by which the user selects the desired option from the menu. In some systems the user enters the number of the selection, as in the illustration; in others the user moves the screen cursor to the desired selection and presses the "enter" key on the keyboard. In either case, the computer automatically loads and executes the desired program module. When processing is completed, the system returns to the menu

FIGURE 6.5 Master menu for an interactive computer system. (Courtesy of Management Science America, Inc.)

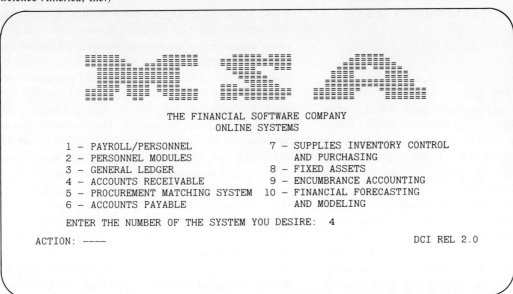

```
                    M S A
             THE FINANCIAL SOFTWARE COMPANY
                    ONLINE SYSTEMS

    1 - PAYROLL/PERSONNEL      7 - SUPPLIES INVENTORY CONTROL
    2 - PERSONNEL MODULES          AND PURCHASING
    3 - GENERAL LEDGER         8 - FIXED ASSETS
    4 - ACCOUNTS RECEIVABLE    9 - ENCUMBRANCE ACCOUNTING
    5 - PROCUREMENT MATCHING SYSTEM 10 - FINANCIAL FORECASTING
    6 - ACCOUNTS PAYABLE           AND MODELING

    ENTER THE NUMBER OF THE SYSTEM YOU DESIRE:  4

  ACTION: ----                              DCI REL 2.0
```

and awaits the user's next selection. Some machines automatically display a master menu—a menu of menus—when the system is turned on; in this way the user is relieved of having to learn systems commands necessary to load and execute programs. Figure 6.5 shows a master menu designed by a major software house. The ideal of the completely menu-driven system has not entirely been realized, but there have been enormous strides in this direction.

Another important aid to operator–machine dialogue is the input prompt. It is used in interactive systems to prompt the user to enter each item of input data. For example, if a date has to be entered, the program may display a prompt such as

```
Enter today's date (MM/DD/YY) > --------
```

The symbols MM/DD/YY indicate the format required: month, day, and year, each having two digits. The row of dashes may indicate the number of characters of input that are expected (in this case eight). Most input devices automatically backspace so that the screen echo of the data entered through the keyboard appears on the line of dashes.

Another example of input prompts, requesting entry of an accounts payable transaction, might look like this:

```
Today's date (MM/DD/YY)      _____
Vendor number               _____
Voucher number              _____
Amount                   $  _____
Due date (MM/DD/YY)         _____
Remarks                     _____
                            _____
```

The "Remarks" field permits the entry of any narrative information that the user wants to append to the voucher record for future reference.

Many interactive systems provide for point-of-entry editing of input data. There are many types of editing provided, but a typical one compares the input data with the expected format of the particular data item. Suppose, for example, that in response to the date prompt shown, the user entered the following:

```
Enter today's date (MM/DD/YY): > 125.50
```

The system might compare the "125.50" with the required date format and conclude that the input was invalid. A message might then be displayed such as

```
Invalid date. Please reenter: _____
```

Menus and input prompts reduce operator training time, improve accuracy, and reduce the need for extensive editing of the data subsequent to entry. On the other hand, the prompts may reduce the speed of data input; there may be a delay while the prompt is being displayed and the operator has to wait before entering the data. If this delay is appreciable, the efficiency of data input may be substantially reduced. The problem of delays in an interactive system is part of the larger problem of matching the resources of the system to the needs of the users.

In an interactive mode, data are entered at a speed that is much lower than that of devices such as tape drives that accept machine-readable data prepared beforehand. Furthermore, the operator may have to pause to interpret output returned to the terminal before entering more data. In some cases, the operator may have to think about the data and consider what to do next, and there may be long pauses between the operator's successive actions. As a result, the terminal typically may use only a small part of the resources available from the central processor. The answer to the problem, of course, lies in time sharing, in which a number of terminals are tied into a single processor. In some large systems, more than 100 terminals may be supported by a single central processor. On the other hand, the use of time sharing solves only part of the total problem, the other part being the inability to schedule jobs for maximum efficiency. Whereas the jobs in a batch system can, if necessary, be scheduled throughout the three shifts, all the users of an interactive time-sharing system expect a response whenever they want to use the system (typically during the normal workday). Accordingly, there is a peak-load problem with interactive systems, and unless alternative batch jobs can be scheduled during the other two shifts, the system may lie idle for much of the 24-hour day. Some organizations sell computer time to outside users during off hours, in an attempt to achieve better utilization of the facilities.

Real-Time Processing

Interactive processing normally implies on-line or direct access to data files for query purposes; for example, a user may access a file from an interactive terminal and examine its contents. Or in a file maintenance operation, a user may add a new record, delete an unwanted one, or modify the content of an existing record. On the other hand, an on-line system may or may not provide for real-time transaction processing. The distinction lies in the timing of the update of the master files to reflect the transaction. In "interactive" batch systems, widely used on micro- and minicomputers, transaction data are keyed into an on-line file via a terminal device under the control of the computer; but thereafter the data are processed as in a pure batch system (Figure 6.6). In real-time systems, the master files are updated immediately to reflect the transaction activity. Real-time systems are a subset of on-line systems. All real-time systems are on line, but not all on-line systems are real time. Most real-time systems involve data base management systems, but it is also possible to operate in a real-time mode using a conventional file structure.

Real-time systems may not use transaction files at all. Because the appropriate master file is updated at once, upon entry of the transaction, the transaction record loses its importance as the repository of information for subsequent processing. On the other hand, it retains its importance as a key link in the audit trail, and it may be required if, for any reason, the master records need to be reconstructed from their status at an earlier time.

Real-time systems have overwhelming advantages in certain types of applications, but they also have disadvantages relative to other modes of processing (Exhibit 6.2). They require more intelligent use, and more things can go wrong. An unsophisticated user may be able to understand and use a batch system effectively but might be out of his or her depth with a real-time system. In small computer systems, real-time systems may be more trouble than they are worth, although greater experience in the design and implementation of "canned" data base systems—complete with controls—is bringing on-line systems more within the reach of the small machine and the nonspecialist user.

FIGURE 6.6 Interactive batch processing. Source documents are keyed on line into a transaction file which in this case is on magnetic disk. Posting is still performed on a batch basis, and the father–son system is still used to protect the master file, which is also on magnetic disk. After posting, the transaction data are archived onto magnetic tape. The activity report is a listing of the transaction file, but data such as account names, which may not appear in the transaction file, are retrieved from the master file.

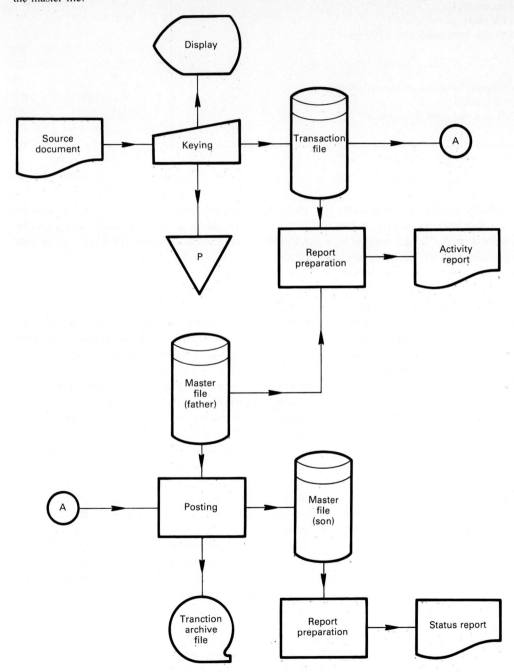

EXHIBIT 6.2.   Advantages and Disadvantages of Real-Time Processing

Advantages:
- Fast turnaround
- Immediate update of master files
- Supports meaningful file query
- Can exploit potential of data base management systems

Disadvantages:
- Complexity
- Greater demands on computer hardware and systems software
- Need for more stringent controls
- Possible error contamination and error propagation
- Unclear audit trails

Another problem with real-time systems arises in situations when more than one user attempts to process the same master record simultaneously. This can happen in a sales order-processing system, as, for example, when two order entry clerks access the same inventory record and observe that there are 20 units of a particular inventory item on hand; one accepts an order for 15 of the units, and the other simultaneously accepts an order for 12. Confusion and ill will are likely to be caused by accepting orders and subsequently having to cancel them. This problem is usually overcome by having an ''intent-to-update'' flag in the master record. The flag is set by the first interactive user who contemplates entering a transaction affecting that record; it then alerts all other users that a conflict could occur and automatically rejects conflicting entries. A time limit may be set, at the end of which the flag will be removed if the transaction has not yet been completed.

Figure 6.7 shows the file-processing arrangement in a real-time processing system. This figure may be compared and contrasted with Figure 6.5 for pure batch processing and with Figure 6.6 for interactive batch processing.

Multitasking

In modern computer systems—both batch and interactive—it is common for several jobs or tasks to be processed concurrently. Some large mainframe computers have multiple processor devices and can actually process several tasks at once (a mode of processing referred to as *multiprocessing*). However, most machines simply give the impression of simultaneous processing by dividing their time among the various jobs. This mode of processing is termed *time sharing* or *multitasking*.

In the case of interactive time-sharing systems, a major justification for multitasking has already been mentioned: the fact that a single terminal can rarely use the resources of the central processor efficiently. But even with batch systems, multitasking is an attractive feature. It can compensate for the difference in the operating speeds of the central processor and the peripheral devices. During execution of typical processing tasks, there is frequent communication with peripheral devices; for example, data may be read from or written to a storage device. While the peripheral device is responding to the particular command, the processor is idle; and if only one task is executed at a time, the central processor may be idle for a substantial portion of the run. Multitasking is a means for leveling out the processor's work load by making it attend to the needs of two or more jobs being run in parallel. Because of the gaps in central processor activity, which would otherwise occur while peripheral device commands are being carried out, several tasks can often be executed almost as fast as a single task can (Figure 6.8). Any delay in the execution of any given task is the cause of the speed degradation experienced

FIGURE 6.7 Real-time processing. Source documents are keyed on line, and the master file is immediately updated to reflect the transaction activity. Balances in the master file are current and can support on-line query from a user terminal. The status of the transaction file is downgraded to that of a transaction log, used for preparing the activity report and providing a basis for recovery from loss of data in the master file. The transaction file can be conveniently maintained on magnetic tape.

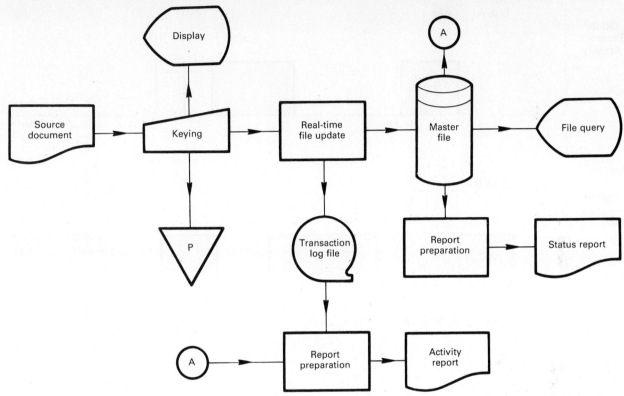

in time-sharing systems. The degradation may be insignificant if only a few tasks are being executed concurrently, but it can become intolerable if many jobs are competing for the available processor resources.

The model of multitasking presented in Figure 6.8 is actually a considerable oversimplification of the way in which modern computer systems normally operate. It implies that control by a particular task is not relinquished until a peripheral-device command is issued; meanwhile the other tasks are dormant. Although such a situation might be acceptable in a batch system, it could lead to intolerable delays in an interactive system if one task happened to make few requests for communication with a peripheral device. The problem is overcome by what is usually called *round-robin scheduling*: The processor is instructed to attend to a particular task

for no more than a prescribed interval of time and then to pass control to the next task in the queue. In this way, each task receives regular attention, even if only for a short time, regardless of the processing requirements of the others.

The procedure by which time is allocated among the competing tasks is referred to as *time slicing*, and it is carried out automatically by the operating system. The objective of efficient time slicing is to optimize the allocation of the central processor's resources and to minimize the average run time of each task. The time interval devoted to each task in turn rarely exceeds one second, and on high-speed machines it may be considerably less.

Time slicing can be modified according to a priority system by increasing the time interval allotted to the higher-priority tasks and reducing it for the lower-prior-

FIGURE 6.8 **Principle of multitasking.** Multitasking can improve central processor utilization.

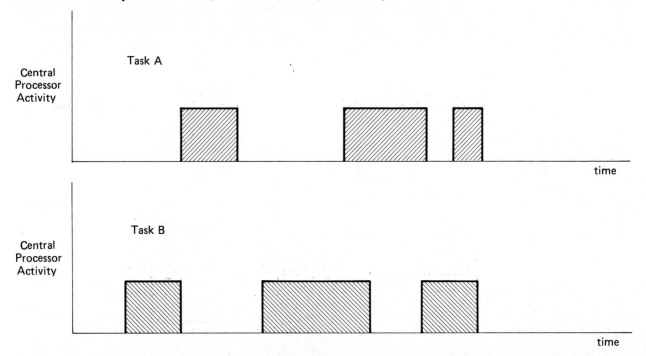

(a) Central processor activity with two tasks run independently

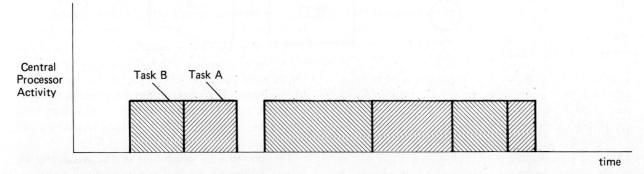

(b) Central processor activity with the two tasks run in a multitasking mode

ity ones. In practice, however, the problem may be more complicated because some tasks, even high-priority ones, may have to wait until some other system resource, such as a larger share of main memory, can be made available. The need to handle contingencies of this kind contributes to the complexity of modern multitasking operating systems.

END-USER COMPUTING

The Role of End-User Computing

Perhaps the most significant development in automated data processing over the last several years is end-user, or personal, computing. End-user computing is a mode of processing in which the user is in essential control of the hardware, software, data, and processing operations. End-user computing bypasses the traditional functions of the data-processing department staffed by computer professionals. Instead of submitting specifications for new applications to the computer department and then sending batches of data to be processed, users process the data themselves, using software packages that can be implemented and operated by laypersons. Starting in the 1970s with the proliferation of on-line terminals, the revolution gained momentum with the advent of personal computers that were powerful and reliable enough to handle business tasks. But other reasons for the growth of end-user computing are dissatisfaction with the turnaround time on primary data-processing facilities, the long lead times and high cost of software development by professional programmers, the inability to express requirements in advance, the need for processing experimentation, difficulties in communicating with data-processing personnel, and excessive levels of bureaucracy surrounding formal systems development.

Today, end-user computing includes

- Use of a stand-alone microcomputer
- Use of an interactive terminal connected to a host computer in a time-sharing environment
- Use of a microcomputer optionally connected to a host computer
- Use of several microcomputers connected to one another in a clustered system or network

The capability for networking personal computers and for interfacing business microcomputers with mini- and large mainframe computers has opened up new avenues of data processing, eclipsing the advantages of either the stand-alone microcomputer or the passive interactive terminal. It is becoming common to connect numbers of microcomputers to one another in a cluster or local area network (LAN). The objective may be to access a common peripheral device such as a hard disk drive or a printer, or it may be to provide the capability for transferring files or messages from one work station to another.

Individual microcomputers, or local area networks, may also be connected to larger host computers. Two main types of operations are possible:

- Terminal operation with a host computer
- Downloading and uploading of files

Terminal operation simply turns the personal computer into an interactive work station as an alternative to its normal mode of operation as a stand-alone machine. Downloading files transfers data from the data base of a host computer into the secondary storage of a microcomputer. Uploading is the reverse process, in which data originating in a microcomputer are transferred to the host computer's data base.

The need for downloading files from an organization's in-house data base arose in connection with spreadsheets, statistical models, graphics, and other software packages marketed for microcomputers. Although the volume of data required for these packages is not large by mainframe computer standards, it is often far more than users would wish to key in from printed reports. Most users are not expert typists and would waste valuable time or might make frequent mistakes in entering the data. Transmitting the data directly from the main data base to the microcomputer is an attractive possibility. But downloading data into a personal computer involves more than simply providing output ports on the mainframe and stringing interconnecting wiring. The problems include differences in data representation (most microprocessors use the ASCII code, whereas many mainframe computers use EBCDIC), incompatibilities in communications protocols, and the size of typical files in the main data base; these files may be much larger than the capacity of secondary storage on the microcomputer. Finally, there are serious control problems in downloading data, and still more serious ones in uploading data.

End-User Computing Applications

End users typically use canned software packages, and an impressive array of packages is now offered for sale, including electronic spreadsheets, word-processing packages, statistical packages, graphics packages, data management systems, query languages, modeling packages, and report generators. These software packages are offered individually and also as components of "integrated packages" that combine several functions. The various functions can be performed on the same data, and sometimes the results of two or more can be displayed simultaneously on the screen or combined for output to a printer.

The purpose and use of the various types of end-user software packages will be discussed in more detail in Chapter 8. Meanwhile, to illustrate the type of processing that end users might undertake—and some of the problems that can arise—we shall present two typical business scenarios.

Scenario 1

The credit manager at ABC Corporation is preparing to review commercial credit policies at his organization and to report his findings to top management. The manager puts his personal computer in a terminal mode and logs onto the mainframe computer. He calls up a query language on the mainframe and, by means of interactive commands, requests the data base management system (DBMS) to identify all the invoice records that have been closed during the last 90 days. A few moments later, a message appears on the screen stating that 18,500 such records have been identified. The manager then enters commands instructing the DBMS to retrieve the following data items from each record:

- Customer number
- Customer type
- Invoice amount
- Terms
- Collection lead time
- Discount taken (if any)

The query language provides for alternative modes of output. The output can be displayed on the screen; it can be sent to a line printer; or it can be written to a scratch file. Because further analysis is necessary, the manager selects the third option and specifies a file name to which the data will be written. But as a backup, the manager also selects the second option and enters formatting instructions into a report generator that prepares the data for hard-copy output.

The manager wants the content of the scratch file to be downloaded to the personal computer for analysis, but it is too large to fit in secondary storage. Instead, the manager calls up a statistical package on the mainframe and extracts a 10-percent random sample of the records; at the same time, population and sample statistics are computed for later reference. The sampled records are written to a second scratch file, sorted by customer number. This file is now converted from EBCDIC to ASCII, by a utility program on the mainframe, and the data await transmittal to the manager's personal computer.

The manager exits from the terminal mode, in which the microcomputer controls a task on the mainframe, and selects a communications mode. After the appropriate parameters in the communications software are selected, the sample file is downloaded. The data file now resides in secondary storage and can be accessed and processed by the personal computer operating in a stand-alone mode.

First, a statistical package is called up, and various statistical parameters are calculated. Some of these merely duplicate the computations performed on the mainframe and are intended to verify the integrity of the data downloaded onto the microcomputer. Other calculations yield a series of frequency distributions relating to collection lead times. The results are printed out on a dot-matrix printer.

Next, the manager wishes to perform a spreadsheet analysis of the data. The content of the scratch file is read into prescribed cells of the worksheet, and a few headings are inserted for reference. The manager performs various extensions of the data and also computes such quantities as the inputed interest costs for alternative annual rates. Summary data are computed for the whole sample, and individual records are identified that satisfy certain exception criteria. These records are intended to provide information for forthcoming reviews of individual credit ratings. A series of printouts is made of selected portions of the worksheet, and a copy of the worksheet is saved on disk for future retrieval and reference.

Finally, the manager wishes to generate some charts and graphs showing various aspects of the data. The spreadsheet package interfaces with a graphics package and can access the same files. Several bar charts and graphs are prepared showing the collection patterns for different customer groups, for different invoice amount categories, and so forth. A number of graphs is also produced. The charts and graphs are printed on the dot-matrix printer which has a graphics option.

The manager intends to include the graphics material in a report being prepared for the vice-president for finance. The text for this report is being assembled using a word-processing package, but unfortunately the available software does not allow insertion of graphics within the text. The manager settles for cutting and pasting the final version of the report and resolves to buy an integrated version of the software out of next year's supplies budget.

Scenario 2

XYZ Corporation, a medium-sized service organization, is preparing its budget for the coming year. Because the company uses a participatory budgeting system, budget preparation starts several months before the start of the fiscal year. After upper management has issued its overall budget guidelines, department managers throughout the organization submit their proposed departmental expense budgets and, where applicable, their revenue estimates. For several years, because most departments had personal computers, budget inputs were prepared on electronic spreadsheets and submitted to the budget committee on floppy disks. In order to be able to do this, all the departments were required to use the same spreadsheet package and a standardized spreadsheet template (program) so as to eliminate inconsistencies among the inputs. The pattern has been the same each year. Staff personnel attached to the committee transfer the inputs onto one large spreadsheet that can be used for summarization and analysis. As the committee considers budget priorities, resolves conflicts, and makes funding allocation decisions, the staff people incorporate the necessary changes on the master spreadsheet. Finally, after the completed budget is approved by top management, extracts from the master spreadsheet are distributed on floppy disks to the department managers.

This year, the same procedures are to be followed, except that the departmental personal computers are now networked, eliminating the need to transfer floppy disks. Now, when each manager has completed his or her departmental budget, a suitably labeled file containing the inputs is transmitted to a common hard disk drive. An interoffice memo announcing its arrival is also transmitted electronically to a personal computer operated by a budget committee staff person. When all of the inputs have arrived, the staff personnel can load each input file onto the master spreadsheet, as before. The intention is to distribute the final budget by transmitting extracts over the network to the department managers.

Even though the principles underlying the modified system were sound, several practical problems arose. First, there was a fault in the hard disk drive after most of the departmental inputs had been transmitted. The contents were lost, and each department had to retransmit its budget inputs. One department had inadvertently erased its own floppy disk, and its data had to be keyed in again. Second, a department manager learned that another department, with which it was competing for funds, had managed to access its budget file, gaining information considered to be confidential. A dispute arose, and some "feathers became ruffled." Finally, when the completed budget extracts were being transmitted back to the departments, one portion was erroneously transmitted to the wrong department, enabling the unintended recipient to learn of the higher salaries being paid to certain individuals elsewhere in the organization. As a result of the mix-up, a disgruntled manager, who had for two years been pressing unsuccessfully for a raise, quit her job.

Members of the project team who had designed and installed the network system bemoaned the inadequacy of internal controls in commercially available network products and resolved to introduce some additional controls to deal with the confidentiality problems. "It is strange," one of the accountants on the team observed, "that the problems involved unauthorized *intracompany* data access. We put all our efforts into stopping people *outside* the company from breaking into the system." As for the loss of data on the disk drive, the internal auditors wrote a memo to the budget committee complaining that routine backup procedures had not been followed. The following year, the system worked without any "glitches."

$$
\begin{aligned}
3 \times 10^3 &= 3 \times 1{,}000 = 3{,}000 \\
0 \times 10^2 &= 0 \times 100 = 0 \\
2 \times 10^1 &= 2 \times 10 = 20 \\
6 \times 10^0 &= 6 \times 1 = 6 \\
2 \times 10^{-1} &= 2 \times \tfrac{1}{10} = .2 \\
5 \times 10^{-2} &= 5 \times \tfrac{1}{100} = .05 \\
& \text{Total} = 3{,}026.25
\end{aligned}
$$

APPENDIX 1: NUMBERING SYSTEMS

Decimal System

The conventional numbering system is the decimal system. It is said to have a "base" of 10, and it is thought to have originated from the fact that we have ten fingers. The decimal system uses the ten symbols 0 through 9, which are called its "absolute values." Larger numbers are derived from aggregates of these symbols according to a well-defined set of rules. The rules involve "positional values," which are exponential powers of the base 10. Every number can be represented as the sum of the products of the absolute values and the positional values. As an example, the number 3,026.25 is equivalent to the mathematical expansion

$$(3 \times 10^3) + (0 \times 10^2) + (2 \times 10^1) + (6 \times 10^0)$$
$$+ (2 \times 10^{-1}) + (5 \times 10^{-2}) = 3{,}026.25$$

The numbers 3, 0, 2, 6, 2, and 5 are the absolute values, and the powers of 10 are the positional values. The same series expansion can be written in the form

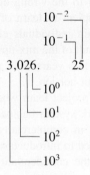

Binary, Octal, and Hexadecimal Systems

The decimal system is convenient for hand calculations, primarily because we are so familiar with it, but it is not the most efficient numbering system in computer technology. Instead, in their internal processing, computers typically use binary, octal, or hexadecimal systems. When the processing is completed, the results are translated (automatically) into decimal form for output. The binary system has a base of 2; the octal system has a base of 8; and the hexadecimal system uses a base of 16.

The binary system uses only two absolute values, 0 and 1, and the octal system uses the values 0 through 7 (the number of absolute value symbols is always equal to the base of the numbering system). The hexadecimal system requires 16 symbols, and conventionally these are chosen to be the numbers 0 through 9, together with the letters A through F (i.e., 0, 1, 2, 3, 4, 5, 6, 7, 8, 9, A, B, C, D, E, and F). As an example of the equivalents between the various numbering systems, the decimal number 28 is represented as 11100 in the binary system, as 34 in the octal system, and as 1C in the hexadecimal system.

To denote a number in a system other than the decimal one, it is customary to attach a subscript to the number to indicate its base. For example, the octal number 120 (which is equal to 96 in the decimal system) is written as 120_8 to distinguish it from the decimal number "one hundred twenty."

The positional values are composed of powers of the particular base: powers of 2 in the binary system, powers of 8 in the octal system, and powers of 16 in the hexadecimal system. These can be represented as follows:

Binary:

$$2^{-3}$$
$$2^{-2}$$
$$2^{-1}$$
$$\longleftarrow \text{X X X. X X X} \longrightarrow$$
$$2^{0}$$
$$2^{1}$$
$$2^{2}$$

Octal:

$$8^{-3}$$
$$8^{-2}$$
$$8^{-1}$$
$$\longleftarrow \text{X X X. X X X} \longrightarrow$$
$$8^{0}$$
$$8^{1}$$
$$8^{2}$$

Hexadecimal:

$$16^{-3}$$
$$16^{-2}$$
$$16^{-1}$$
$$\longleftarrow \text{X X X. X X X} \longrightarrow$$
$$16^{0}$$
$$16^{1}$$
$$16^{2}$$

Conversion from One Numbering System to Another

It is sometimes necessary to convert numbers in one system to their equivalents in another system (i.e., to change the base of a number). There are many different methods for performing the conversion; the one described here is simple and straightforward.

First, to convert a number to any base different from 10 into a decimal number, the number is simply expanded as the sum of products of the absolute values times the corresponding positional values. The calculation is done using decimal arithmetic. Some examples are as follows:

(1) $120_8 = 1 \times 8^2 + 2 \times 8^1 + 0 \times 8^0$

$\qquad\quad = 1 \times 64 + 2 \times 8 + 0 \times 1$

$\qquad\quad = 64 + 16 + 0$

$\qquad\quad = 80_{10}$

(2) $111001.101_2 = 1 \times 2^5 + 1 \times 2^4 + 1 \times 2^3 + 0 \times 2^2 + 0 \times 2^1 + 1 \times 2^0 + 1 \times 2^{-1} + 0 \times 2^{-2} + 1 \times 2^{-3}$

$\qquad\qquad\quad = 32 + 16 + 8 + 0 + 0 + 1 + \frac{1}{2} + 0 + \frac{1}{8}$

$\qquad\qquad\quad = 32 + 16 + 8 + 1 + 5 + .125$

$\qquad\qquad\quad = 57.625_{10}$

(3) $4BD3.A_{16} = 4 \times 16^3 + B \times 16^2 + D \times 16^1 + 3 \times 16^0 + A \times 16^{-1}$

$\qquad\qquad\quad = 4 \times 16^3 + 11 \times 16^2 + 13 \times 16 + 3 \times 16^0 + 10 \times 16^{-1}$

$\qquad\qquad\quad = 4 \times 4096 + 11 \times 256 + 13 \times 16 + 3 \times 1 + \frac{10}{16}$

$\qquad\qquad\quad = 16384 + 2816 + 208 + 3 + .625$

$\qquad\qquad\quad = 19411.625_{10}$

To convert a decimal number into one with a different base is slightly more complicated. The integer and the fractional portions of the decimal number must be converted separately. To convert the integer portion of the decimal number, it is repeatedly divided (again using decimal arithmetic). The integer is successively divided by the desired base until an integer quotient is no longer possible. At each step, the remainder in the division is saved, and the sequence of remainders makes up the absolute values of the converted number. The first remainder forms the low-order digit of the converted number, and the last remainder forms the high-order digit. Some examples of the process are as follows:

(1) 80_{10} to octal

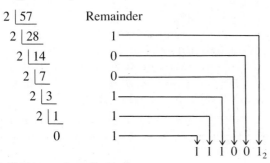

```
8 | 80        Remainder
8 | 10           0
8 | 1            2
    0            1
                      1  2  0₈
```

(2) 57_{10} to binary

```
2 | 57        Remainder
2 | 28           1
2 | 14           0
2 | 7            0
2 | 3            1
2 | 1            1
    0            1
                    1  1  1  0  0  1₂
```

(3) 19411_{10} to hexadecimal

```
16 | 19411      Remainder
16 | 1213          3
16 | 75            13
16 | 4             11
     0             4
                        4  B  D  3₁₆
```

Then, to convert the fractional portion of the decimal number, the decimal fraction is repeatedly multiplied by the desired base, and the integer portion of the products is saved. Two examples illustrate the procedure:

(1) $.625_{10}$ to binary

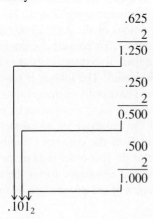

```
         .625
            2
        1.250

         .250
            2
        0.500

         .500
            2
        1.000

    .101₂
```

(2) $.625_{10}$ to hexadecimal

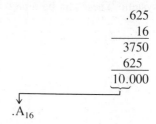

```
           .625
            16
          3750
           625
        10.000

    .A₁₆
```

Note that when a number is being converted to hexadecimal form, it is sometimes necessary to substitute the absolute value symbols A through F, for the decimal remainders, or the integer product (in the case of the fractional portion of the number), 10 through 15.

Sometimes it is necessary to convert back and forth between the binary and either the octal or the hexadecimal system. This could be done by converting to decimal as an intermediate step, but a convenient shortcut is available. To illustrate, if the octal number 567_8 has to be converted into binary, all that is necessary is to write down the three-digit binary equivalents of 5, 6, and 7 and lay them end to end:

$$567_8 = 101110111_2$$

Similarly, if the binary number 010111111010_2 must be converted to hexadecimal, it is divided up into four-digit groups:

$$0101 \ 1111 \ 1010$$

and the hexadecimal character substituted for each group:

$$5FA_{16}$$

This rule demonstrates that the octal and hexadecimal systems serve as a kind of shorthand for writing binary numbers. Each octal character stands for three bits, and each hexadecimal character stands for four bits of the corresponding number. This is precisely the way in which these two numbering systems are used in computer systems.

APPENDIX 2: BINARY, OCTAL, AND HEXADECIMAL EQUIVALENTS AND THE ASCII AND EBCDIC CODES

Decimal	Binary	Octal	Hexadecimal	ASCII	EBCDIC
0	0	0	0	NUL	NUL
1	1	1	1	SOH	SOH
2	10	2	2	STX	STX
3	11	3	3	ETX	ETX
4	100	4	4	EOT	SEL
5	101	5	5	ENQ	HT
6	110	6	6	ACK	RNL
7	111	7	7	BEL	DEL
8	1000	10	8	BS	GE
9	1001	11	9	HT	SPS
10	1010	12	A	LF	RPT
11	1011	13	B	VT	VT
12	1100	14	C	FF	FF
13	1101	15	D	CR	CR
14	1110	16	E	SO	SO
15	1111	17	F	SI	SI
16	10000	20	10	DLE	DLE
17	10001	21	11	DC1	DC1
18	10010	22	12	DC2	DC2
19	10011	23	13	DC3	DC3
20	10100	24	14	DC4	RES
21	10101	25	15	NAK	NL
22	10110	26	16	SYN	BS
23	10111	27	17	ETB	POC
24	11000	30	18	CAN	CAN
25	11001	31	19	EM	EM
26	11010	32	1A	SUB	UBS
27	11011	33	1B	ESC	CU1
28	11100	34	1C	FS	IFS
29	11101	35	1D	GS	IGS
30	11110	36	1E	RS	IRS
31	11111	37	1F	US	ITB
32	100000	40	20		DS
33	100001	41	21	!	SOS
34	100010	42	22	"	FS
35	100011	43	23	#	WUS
36	100100	44	24	$	BYP

Decimal	Binary	Octal	Hexadecimal	ASCII	EBCDIC
37	100101	45	25	%	LF
38	100110	46	26	&	ETB
39	100111	47	27	'	ESC
40	101000	50	28	(	SA
41	101001	51	29	)	SFE
42	101010	52	2A	*	SM
43	101011	53	2B	+	CSP
44	101100	54	2C	,	MFA
45	101101	55	2D	-	ENQ
46	101110	56	2E	.	ACK
47	101111	57	2F	/	BEL
48	110000	60	30	0	SYN
49	110001	61	31	1	IR
50	110010	62	32	2	PP
51	110011	63	33	3	TRN
52	110100	64	34	4	NBS
53	110101	65	35	5	EOT
54	110110	66	36	6	SBS
55	110111	67	37	7	IT
56	111000	70	38	8	RFF
57	111001	71	39	9	CU3
58	111010	72	3A	:	DC4
59	111011	73	3B	;	NAK
60	111100	74	3C	<	SUB
61	111101	75	3D	=	space
62	111110	76	3E	>	
63	111111	77	3F	?	
64	1000000	100	40	@	
65	1000001	101	41	A	
66	1000010	102	42	B	
67	1000011	103	43	C	
68	1000100	104	44	D	
69	1000101	105	45	E	
70	1000110	106	46	F	
71	1000111	107	47	G	
72	1001000	110	48	H	
73	1001001	111	49	I	
74	1001010	112	4A	J	¢
75	1001011	113	4B	K	.
76	1001100	114	4C	L	<
77	1001101	115	4D	M	(

Decimal	Binary	Octal	Hexadecimal	ASCII	EBCDIC
78	1001110	116	4E	N	+
79	1001111	117	4F	O	¦
80	1010000	120	50	P	&
81	1010001	121	51	Q	
82	1010010	122	52	R	
83	1010011	123	53	S	
84	1010100	124	54	T	
85	1010101	125	55	U	
86	1010110	126	56	V	
87	1010111	127	57	W	
88	1011000	130	58	X	
89	1011001	131	59	Y	
90	1011010	132	5A	Z	!
91	1011011	133	5B	[	$
92	1011100	134	5C	\	*
93	1011101	135	5D	]	)
94	1011110	136	5E	^	;
95	1011111	137	5F	_	
96	1100000	140	60	¨	-
97	1100001	141	61	a	/
98	1100010	142	62	b	
99	1100011	143	63	c	
100	1100100	144	64	d	
101	1100101	145	65	e	
102	1100110	146	66	f	
103	1100111	147	67	g	
104	1101000	150	68	h	
105	1101001	151	69	i	
106	1101010	152	6A	j	¦
107	1101011	153	6B	k	,
108	1101100	154	6C	l	%
109	1101101	155	6D	m	-
110	1101110	156	6E	n	>
111	1101111	157	6F	o	?
112	1110000	160	70	p	
113	1110001	161	71	q	
114	1110010	162	72	r	
115	1110011	163	73	s	
116	1110100	164	74	t	
117	1110101	165	75	u	
118	1110110	166	76	v	

Decimal	Binary	Octal	Hexadecimal	ASCII	EBCDIC
119	1110111	167	77	w	
120	1111000	170	78	x	
121	1111001	171	79	y	\
122	1111010	172	7A	z	:
123	1111011	173	7B	{	#
124	1111100	174	7C	¦	@
125	1111101	175	7D	}	'
126	1111110	176	7E	~	=
127	1111111	177	7F	DEL	"
128	10000000	200	80		a
129	10000001	201	81		b
130	10000010	202	82		c
131	10000011	203	83		d
132	10000100	204	84		e
133	10000101	205	85		f
134	10000110	206	86		g
135	10000111	207	87		h
136	10001000	210	88		i
137	10001001	211	89		
138	10001010	212	8A		
139	10001011	213	8B		
140	10001100	214	8C		
141	10001101	215	8D		
142	10001110	216	8E		
143	10001111	217	8F		
144	10010000	220	90		
145	10010001	221	91		j
146	10010010	222	92		k
147	10010011	223	93		l
148	10010100	224	94		m
149	10010101	225	95		n
150	10010110	226	96		o
151	10010111	227	97		p
152	10011000	230	98		q
153	10011001	231	99		r
154	10011010	232	9A		
155	10011011	233	9B		
156	10011100	234	9C		
157	10011101	235	9D		
158	10011110	236	9E		

Decimal	Binary	Octal	Hexadecimal	ASCII	EBCDIC
159	10011111	237	9F		
160	10100000	240	A0		
161	10100001	241	A1		~
162	10100010	242	A2		s
163	10100011	243	A3		t
164	10100100	244	A4		u
165	10100101	245	A5		v
166	10100110	246	A6		w
167	10100111	247	A7		x
168	10101000	250	A8		y
169	10101001	251	A9		z
170	10101010	252	AA		
171	10101011	253	AB		
172	10101100	254	AC		
173	10101101	255	AD		
174	10101110	256	AE		
175	10101111	257	AF		
176	10110000	260	B0		
177	10110001	261	B1		
178	10110010	262	B2		
179	10110011	263	B3		
180	10110100	264	B4		
181	10110101	265	B5		
182	10110110	266	B6		
183	10110111	267	B7		
184	10111000	270	B8		
185	10111001	271	B9		
186	10111010	272	BA		
187	10111011	273	BB		
188	10111100	274	BC		
189	10111101	275	BD		
190	10111110	276	BE		
191	10111111	277	BF		
192	11000000	300	C0		{
193	11000001	301	C1		A
194	11000010	302	C2		B
195	11000011	303	C3		C
196	11000100	304	C4		D
197	11000101	305	C5		E
198	11000110	306	C6		F

Decimal	Binary	Octal	Hexadecimal	ASCII	EBCDIC
199	11000111	307	C7		G
200	11001000	310	C8		H
201	11001001	311	C9		I
202	11001010	312	CA		
203	11001011	313	CB		
204	11001100	314	CC		S
205	11001101	315	CD		
206	11001110	316	CE		Y
207	11001111	317	CF		
208	11010000	320	D0		}
209	11010001	321	D1		J
210	11010010	322	D2		K
211	11010011	323	D3		L
212	11010100	324	D4		M
213	11010101	325	D5		N
214	11010110	326	D6		O
215	11010111	327	D7		P
216	11011000	330	D8		Q
217	11011001	331	D9		R
218	11011010	332	DA		
219	11011011	333	DB		
220	11011100	334	DC		
221	11011101	335	DD		
222	11011110	336	DE		
223	11011111	337	DF		
224	11100000	340	E0		
225	11100001	341	E1		
226	11100010	342	E2		S
227	11100011	343	E3		T
228	11100100	344	E4		U
229	11100101	345	E5		V
230	11100110	346	E6		W
231	11100111	347	E7		X
232	11101000	350	E8		Y
233	11101001	351	E9		Z
234	11101010	352	EA		
235	11101011	353	EB		
236	11101100	354	EC		
237	11101101	355	ED		
238	11101110	356	EE		

Decimal	Binary	Octal	Hexadecimal	ASCII	EBCDIC
239	11101111	357	EF		
240	11110000	360	F0		0
241	11110001	361	F1		1
242	11110010	362	F2		2
243	11110011	363	F3		3
244	11110100	364	F4		4
245	11110101	365	F5		5
246	11110110	366	F6		6
247	11110111	367	F7		7
248	11111000	370	F8		8
249	11111001	371	F9		9
250	11111010	372	FA		¦
251	11111011	373	FB		
252	11111100	374	FC		
253	11111101	375	FD		
254	11111110	376	FE		
255	11111111	377	FF		EO

SUMMARY

Automation has become the norm for all but the smallest business information system. Virtually all accounting systems in use today are powered by computer systems of some level of sophistication, all the way from small desktop machines to large multiprocessor mainframe computers. Accountants thus must acquire a basic understanding of computers and how they work.

The computer is an electronic device capable of capturing, storing, processing, and communicating data in response to stored instructions. Automated information processing has deep roots in history, but their "time" has come only in the last few decades, and during this brief period there has been a phenomenal growth of computer technology.

Digital logic devices process data by opening and closing electronic switches; by this means they can perform a range of arithmetic and logical operations. The ability of logic devices to carry out these operations quickly and accurately has helped make the computer an essential tool in modern business. Logic devices form the main ingredient of the central processing unit which is the heart of the computer system. The central processor interfaces with peripheral devices that carry out the functions of input, storage, output, and communications.

At the basic electronic level, all arithmetic and logical operations are carried out in the form of binary "words" that correspond to sets of electronic switch settings. Binary words comprise not only the data to be processed but also the instructions for doing so. In conventional general-purpose machines, the instructions are supplied by the user in the form of computer programs, or software. Software can be divided into systems software, which controls the operation of the machine and provides for development of other software, and applications software, which performs the actual task required by the user.

Two principal modes of computer operation are in common use: batch processing and real-time processing. Batch processing corresponds closely to the classical posting cycle. It may or may not involve interactive entry of data through on-line terminals. Real-time processing immediately updates master files when transactions are entered. Each mode has its own advantages and disadvantages and is an almost imperative choice in certain types of applications but may be inappropriate in other types.

In some systems, virtually all the processing resources are concentrated at a single location, while in others there is almost complete decentralization of resources. The modern concept of distributed processing attempts to combine the best features of both. Distributed processing is being implemented not only on large computers but also on clustered microcomputer configurations.

In recent years there has been a major trend toward end-user computing. In this approach to information processing, the end-users—accountants, managers, and the like—assume responsibility for the input, processing, and output of data, operating desktop work stations or personal computers. End-user computing contrasts with more traditional approaches in which data processing was the responsibility of computer programmers and operators in a separate computer department. End-user computing has been stimulated by the availability of low-cost hardware and powerful user-friendly software.

Appendix 1 discussed numbering systems, including the binary, octal, and hexadecimal systems, which are fundamental to computer processing. Some methods were described for converting back and forth between these systems and the conventional decimal numbering system. Appendix 2 was a table of the two principal codes for representing numeric and alphanumeric data: the American Standard Code for Information Interchange (ASCII) and the Extended Binary Coded Decimal Interchange Code (EBCDIC), together with their equivalent binary, octal, decimal, and hexadecimal values.

BIBLIOGRAPHY

Bolb, Richard A. "Human Interfaces for Managers." *Computer World*, July 16, 1984, pp. ID/1–18.

Holsapple, C. W., and A. B. Whinston. *Business Expert Systems*. Homewood, Ill.: Irwin, 1987.

Horten, Forest W., Jr. "Software's Next Dimension." *Computer World*, June 25, 1984, pp. ID/7–11.

Huskey, Harry D. "The Development of Automatic Computing." In D. L. Van Tassel, ed. *The Compleat Computer*. Palo Alto, Calif.: Science Research Associates, 1975.

An Introduction to Microcomputers. Vol. 0, *The Beginner's Book*. Berkeley, Calif.: Adam Osborne and Associates, 1977.

Kloek, Christopher D. "Searching Out Business Computing Alternatives." *Small Business Computers Magazine*, March 1980, pp. 20–23.

Kroenke, David M., and Kathleen A. Dolan. *Business Computer Systems*. Santa Cruz, Calif.: Mitchell, 1987.

O'Leary, Daniel E. "Expert Systems in Accounting in a Personal Computer Environment." *Georgia Journal of Accounting*, Spring 1986, pp. 107–117.

Paul, Lois. "First Large-Scale Computer, ENIAC, Turns 35 Years Old." *Computer World*, March 2, 1981, p. 5.

Reid-Green, Keith S. "A Short History of Computing." *Byte*, July 1978, pp. 84–94.

Watson, Hugh J., and Archie B. Carroll. *Computers for Business: A Managerial Emphasis*. Dallas: Business Publications, 1976.

DISCUSSION QUESTIONS AND PROBLEMS

1. Define and discuss the following terms:

- Analog computer
- Arithmetic/logic unit
- Applications software
- Batch processing
- Binary arithmetic
- Central processor
- Communications device
- Control unit
- Digital computer
- End-user computing
- Hardware
- Input device
- Input prompt
- Interactive batch processing
- Interactive processing

- Main memory
- Multitasking
- On-line, off-line
- Output device
- Output spooling
- Peripheral device
- Processor chip
- Real-time processing
- Screen menu
- Secondary storage
- Software
- Switch settings
- Systems software
- Tertiary storage
- Time sharing
- Word length

2. Express the characters of the string "Accounting" in terms of their ASCII and EBCDIC equivalents, using the following numerical representations:

a. Octal

b. Hexadecimal

c. Binary

3. a. Express the number 144 in (i) pure binary, (ii) the binary equivalent of the ASCII code, and (iii) the binary equivalent of the EBCDIC code.

b. Show the switch settings and the pattern of electrical pulses by which each of the binary words in (a) would be represented in a digital logic device.

4. A punched card contains 80 columns and therefore presents a physical record of 80 bytes. Logical records of the following lengths are to be punched onto cards:

a. 20 bytes

b. 80 bytes

c. 150 bytes

d. 256 bytes

e. 1,024 bytes

Required

Determine how many cards will be required to hold each logical record and calculate the percentage of wasted storage capacity if each logical record is to start on a new card.

5. Perform the following operations using 8-bit binary arithmetic (show all carry digits where applicable):

a. Add 13 to 25

b. Subtract 15 from 42

c. Subtract 20 from 10

d. Multiply 24 by 4

e. Divide 48 by 8

6. A processing operation posts invoice data to an accounts receivable master file. The invoice records are stored on magnetic tape, and the master file is maintained on magnetic disk. What would be the likely content of main memory at any one time during the operation?

7. a. Many organizations use a computer for only one or two functions, such as customer billing or payroll. Why should organizations of that type bother with applications software when the computer could be hard-wired to perform the desired operations?

b. Why was there such a strong incentive to develop high-level programming langauges to supersede machine code programming?

8. Several types of processing activities are listed here. Indicate what processing mode—pure batch, interactive batch, or real-time—would be most suitable for each. State the reasons for your choice.

a. Processing statements to credit card subscribers

b. Maintaining a computerized appointment file for a group of physicians

c. Maintaining customer files in a computerized check validation system

d. Processing quarterly pledge statements to a church congregation

e. Maintaining a grocery product inventory file for use with an automated point-of-sale checkout system

f. Processing journal entries in a general ledger system used by a small business

g. Processing third-party billings in a hospital

h. Processing purchase requisitions in a large inventory system

i. Processing sales commissions in a large wholesale firm

j. Processing biweekly paychecks in a small manufacturing organization

9. Black Manufacturing, Inc., currently operates a standard job cost system using a pure batch-processing mode. The labor inputs are made from machine-readable time cards that are punched with the job numbers and the hours worked by the employee on a particular job. Materials inputs are encoded onto magnetic tape from the store's requisition forms. Factory overhead is applied weekly as a burden on standard direct labor hours. The work-in-process master file is maintained on a magnetic disk cartridge that is checked out of the data library and is mounted in readiness for processing.

Required

a. What would be the advantages and disadvantages of converting from the present batch-processing mode to a real-time mode?
b. Could a strong case be made for adopting an interactive batch system?
c. What additional information would you need to make a strong argument in either (a) or (b)?

10. Compare the effectiveness of the interactive batch mode and the real-time mode for use in a sales order-processing system that is integrated with accounts receivable and inventory control.
a. Design a screen menu to be used in conjunction with a payroll system intended for use by small businesses.
b. Design a set of input prompts for entering time-card data in the payroll system in (a).

11. Three tasks are to be executed on a large computer. When they are run separately, each task places intermittent demands on the central processor. There are regularly recurring periods of central processor activity, followed by periods of dormancy during which the tasks are communicating with peripheral devices. The following data are available:

Task	Duration of C.P. Activity	Frequency of C.P Activity
A	100 milliseconds	2 per second
B	200 milliseconds	2 per second
C	500 milliseconds	1 per 2 seconds

Thus, every second task A requires two periods of central processor activity, each lasting for 100 milliseconds

(= 0.1 second). Every 2 seconds, task C requires one period of activity, lasting for 500 milliseconds.

Required

a. What is the average utilization of central-processor resources when the three tasks are executed separately?
b. What is the average utilization when the three tasks are executed concurrently in multitasking mode?
c. What is the percentage increase in execution time when the three tasks are run concurrently?
d. What would be the impact on the answers to (b) and (c) of introducing 0.2-second time slicing?

12. Fox Brothers Dairy bought a minicomputer two years ago to run its routine billings and payables activities and also to operate a sophisticated milk route accounting system. The milk route system requires a large number of daily transactions to be keyed into the machine via six on-line terminals. Processing is done in an interactive batch mode. Transaction entry to the milk route system is complicated, but comprehensive menus and input prompts are provided by the programs, and the data entry clerks have adapted well to the system without extensive training and without needing to refer constantly to operating manuals.

The machine is adequate for the batch-processing activities, but data entry has become inefficient because of the slow system response at the terminals. Delays of up to 20 seconds are common before the prompt appears on the screen permitting entry of each data element in a transaction.

The computer manufacturer has proposed that Fox should change to off-line data preparation, using magnetic tape as the input medium. It is estimated that the work load could be handled by four off-line devices, because the clerks could enter data continuously without having to wait for input prompts to be displayed. The cost of the four new devices required would be less than that of a larger computer necessary to reduce response time on input prompts to an acceptable level of about 5 seconds.

The tapes produced in the data preparation process would be read into the computer, and edit listings would be printed. Some errors could be corrected without producing a new tape, but more extensive changes would require some rekeying of input data.

Required

Discuss the proposed solution to Fox's problems. Is the solution workable, and would you recommend that Fox change to off-line data preparation? What additional problems would arise, and how could they be solved?

13. A distribution company maintains a fleet of 100 trucks for making deliveries throughout a five-state territory. Each truck can carry a maximum of 20 pallets containing the company's product. Sometimes all 20 pallets are to be delivered to the same customer, but more frequently each customer is to receive only 2 or 3.

The scheduler has the job of trying to ensure that trucks do not leave only partly full, but because of tight delivery schedules, trucks are not permitted to wait more than half a day for a full load. Impending shipments are identified between 48 and 72 hours before they are ready to leave.

The company wishes to install a computer system to help with scheduling shipments, but management realizes that the task cannot be fully automated because human judgment is necessary.

Required

Identify areas where the computer could help in the scheduling problem and the areas where the judgment and experience of a human scheduler would be required.

PROBLEMS BASED ON APPENDIX 1

A1. Convert the following to decimal numbers:

a. 111_2
b. 10110.011_2
c. 777_8
d. 1567.32_8
e. FFF_{16}
f. $3AC4.E_{16}$

A2. Convert the following decimal numbers to the numbering system indicated:
a. 100 to binary
b. 1000 to octal
c. 10,000 to hexadecimal
d. 37.5 to binary
e. 286.09 to octal
f. 791.34 to hexadecimal

A3. Convert the following:
a. 11011101_2 to octal
b. 10010110_2 to hexadecimal
c. 200_8 to binary
d. FO_{16} to binary
e. $65,536_{10}$ to binary, octal, and hexadecimal

7

Computer Hardware

CHAPTER OUTLINE

LEARNING OBJECTIVES

After you have studied this chapter you should be able to

- Identify the principal types of off-line and on-line input devices.
- Evaluate the performance characteristics of a range of input devices.
- Identify the principal types of soft-copy and hard-copy output devices.
- Evaluate the performance characteristics of a range of output devices.
- Identify the principal types of processor devices.
- Evaluate the performance characteristics of representative processor devices.
- Identify the principal types of external storage devices, including magnetic tape and magnetic disk.
- Evaluate the performance characteristics of the major types of external storage devices.

INPUT DEVICES

The input device forms the first interface between the computer and the users or operators. Its purpose is to accept input data in readiness for processing, encoding the data where necessary into machine-readable form. Input devices can be divided into off-line data preparation devices and on-line input terminal devices.

Data Preparation Devices

Data preparation devices are used in pure batch-processing systems. They are self-contained devices whose purpose is to transcribe input data into machine-readable form and to write the data to an intermediate storage medium. The first devices of this kind were *keypunch* machines and paper-tape punches, which produced punched cards and punched paper tape, respectively. These devices are now considered obsolete, because paper intermediate media are bulky, slow to read, and hold few data, and they have been replaced

by devices producing magnetic media. The most common data preparation devices in use today are *key-to-tape* machines, which produce magnetic tape, and *key-to-disk* machines which write to a magnetic disk—frequently a floppy diskette.

Data preparation devices are off line in the sense that their operation is not under the computer's control. The intermediate medium is subsequently read into the computer via an on-line input device. The use of data preparation devices has advantages, particularly in large batch-processing systems, because several keypunch operators can work continuously, punching input data onto the intermediate medium. Processing can then be done at regular intervals according to a routine schedule. The "traditional" off-line input devices, keypunch and paper-tape machines, had no provision for displaying menus or input prompts to help the operator; operators had to key "blind." But most modern key-to-tape and key-to-disk devices have small processor and display devices incorporated to provide such "user-friendly" features as menus and prompts. With this development, the distinction between data preparation devices, on the one

FIGURE 7.1   Video display terminal: The TeleVideo model 9920.
(Courtesy of TeleVideo, Inc.)

hand, and terminal devices and personal computers, on the other, is becoming blurred.

On-Line Terminal Devices

Terminal devices, often referred to as *work stations*, permit users to enter data into the computer under the control of a host processor device. Several terminal devices might be connected to a central processor in a time-sharing system. The data are normally written to an on-line file, such as a transaction file or scratch file, for subsequent processing; alternatively the data may be processed immediately in real time. Terminals are normally interactive and provide for the display of menus and input prompts. The first terminal devices were printer terminals, or "teletype" machines. These consisted of a keyboard connected to a small printer, and they generated a hard-copy printout of the data entered. Printer terminals are now rarely used, having been superseded by video display terminals (VDTs). These latter consist of a keyboard and a video monitor, or CRT.[1] A typical video display terminal is shown in Figure 7.1.

Video display terminals have several advantages over printer terminals. They can present more sophisticated input forms (screens have random access capability, whereas most printers are sequential devices). They are quieter, and they help reduce operating costs by not requiring a continuous supply of paper. However, if a hard copy of the input data is required, most modern display devices can copy the content of the screen onto a printer device.

The monitor associated with a video display terminal may be attached to the keyboard, may be freestanding, or may be built into the computer. This last configuration is popular in the design of microcomputers. In the fol-

[1] CRT stands for "cathode ray tube," but the acronym is now more familiar than the original name of the device.

lowing discussion, *video display terminal* is used to designate all combinations of a keyboard and a video monitor, regardless of the precise physical configuration.

Video display terminals normally display several kinds of material, including screen forms, the "echo" of the data entered through the keyboard, and small amounts of output. Screen forms were discussed in Chapter 4. Almost all terminals provide a screen echo of keyboard entries; but the echo can usually be suppressed if the data are confidential, as in the case of a password. Screen output might consist of the name of an account displayed in response to the entry of an account number. Such interaction serves as an aid to accuracy—the operator may be alerted to an erroneous entry—and so is an important control measure.

In addition to accepting data entered through the keyboard, some terminals provide for auxiliary modes of input. One example is an optical wand, or "light pen," which generates a signal from contact with the screen and can be used to select a data element, or a menu choice, from a displayed list. Another is a "mouse" which generates a signal from movement on a surface, such as a desktop, and usually produces sympathetic movement of a cursor on the screen.

Video display terminals can be classified according to their level of processing (logic) capability and data storage capacity. Three familiar types are *passive* (or *dumb*), *smart*, and *intelligent*. Passive terminals have minimal storage, sufficient to store about one line of data, and only the rudimentary circuitry required to display characters on the screen and to accept input from the keyboard. Smart terminals often have enough capacity to store a whole screenful (or page) of data and the logic capability to perform preliminary editing tasks on the data before transmitting them to the host processor.

Intelligent terminals are essentially microcomputers and have significant storage capacity—in the form of main memory and possibly also secondary storage—and significant processing capability. They can function, optionally, as stand-alone computers or as terminals communicating with a larger host computer. The main advantage of intelligent terminals lies in their superior response time, because user–machine dialogue can be controlled locally without having to wait for the attention of the central processor. The demands on central-processor resources are greatly reduced in this kind of sys-

tem. A smaller processor can be used for a given number of terminals, or more terminals can be connected to a given processor. As progressively more intelligence is invested in the terminals and correspondingly more reliance is placed on locally based processing, the central processor can eventually be eliminated. This is an important rationale behind a distributed processing system made up of networked microcomputers.

Other Input Devices

As noted, on-line input devices are needed in order to read the intermediate media generated by data preparation devices. The two most common devices for this purpose are the tape drive and the floppy disk drive, which will be discussed later.

Other types of input devices are designed to read documents coded with magnetic numerals and bar codes. Data written in magnetic ink are widely used on documents such as checks; the data can be read by magnetic sensing devices and entered directly into a computer. Optical wands or holographic readers, often seen in grocery stores, perform a similar function by reading the bar codes printed on product labels. The Universal Product Code (UPC) is a familiar example of an optical bar code (see Figure 7.2). This code, which appears on all grocery items sold in the United States, identifies both the manufacturer and the individual product.

Point-of-sale (POS) cash registers using a magnetic or optical wand, which can interface with on-line inventory

FIGURE 7.2 Universal Product Code (UPC) for a grocery item.

systems, are now commonly found in retail stores. Product numbers can be read from product labels, and prices, descriptions, and other data can be retrieved from product files for display on the cash register and to be printed on sales slips. Sales data can also be entered automatically into transaction files. On-line point-of-sale systems have brought the advantages of the perpetual inventory system within the reach of many retail establishments that could not have otherwise handled the bookkeeping effort involved.

Much research has been devoted to developing input devices that can read normal print, and devices with this capability are now routinely operating with acceptable reliability. Equivalent devices that can read handwritten material are under development but pose greater problems. Voice-recognition devices are now available, offering at least limited potential in situations in which other modes of data recording are unsuitable. One application would be for use by handicapped persons. Tuning such a device to a single person's voice—with its peculiar intonation and accent—is easier and more reliable than tuning one to recognize a range of different voices.

Electronic time clocks are available that automatically record the employee's badge number, the time at which the employee enters or leaves the plant, and in some cases the job number on which the employee is working. Such devices may eliminate the need for paper time cards. Electronic devices are also used to measure and automatically record other aspects of manufacturing processes such as the quantity of materials used. Devices of this type are particularly useful where materials are supplied continuously or where the process is not accessible to a human observer. An example would be the processing of radioactive material.

Various specialized input devices are becoming available to supplement the standard keyboard work station. In some cases, such devices are nothing but "toys," and their influence waxes and soon wanes. In other cases, new devices meet a real need and gain permanent acceptance. The objective should be to get the data into the computer as quickly, as efficiently, and as reliably as possible, but also to provide for those situations in which—because of the nature of the physical process or the nature of the operator—alternative means need to be employed.

Performance Characteristics of Input Devices

The performance of input devices depends heavily on the response time of the processor that serves the device. In this latter regard, as noted, intelligent terminals are normally faster than are passive terminals. Passive terminals, operated in a time-sharing mode, typically suffer from speed degradation under conditions of heavy usage, that is, at peak times during the workday. The efficiency of operation starts to decrease when the response time exceeds about 1 to 2 seconds and becomes intolerable when the response time exceeds 10 seconds. It should be remembered that the operator is held up by the response time at each screen prompt, and several screen prompts are normally required in order to enter a single transaction. Some overloaded time-sharing systems have response times of over 30 seconds.

Assuming a response time of one second or less, the performance of a work station depends primarily on the operator's efficiency. Given efficient operators—normally data entry clerks—the only way to increase the rate of input of data is to have more terminals. The number of work stations required is equal to the size of the work load and the number of transactions that can be entered in a standard workday. For example, if the work load is equivalent to 10,000 transactions per day and an average of 2,000 transactions can be entered through a single terminal each day, then a minimum of five terminals will be required. One or two additional terminals may be required to handle fluctuations of work load, to cope with variations of demand during the day, and to allow for terminal downtime. The number of transactions that can be entered through a terminal, of course, depends on the number of shifts worked per day.

There is little difference in efficiency between one brand of terminal and another, although there may be significant differences in the operator's level of fatigue. The layout and "feel" of the keyboard, the height of the screen, and the color and quality of the screen display all affect fatigue levels. The ergonomics of data entry work stations are now receiving more attention in this regard. Recently there have been suggestions that video display terminals emit harmful radiation and may pose a health hazard, particularly for pregnant women. So far the evidence seems to be inconclusive, but the issue is sufficiently important to warrant further study.

OUTPUT DEVICES

The output device forms the second interface, between the computer and the users, and serves the purpose of returning processed information to them. Most output is printed on paper media, but a significant amount is displayed on video monitors, and so devices of this latter type will be discussed first.

Video Monitors

Video monitors provide output in volatile form. The display vanishes as soon as the power is turned off or as soon as another display is brought up onto the screen; rarely is provision made to return to a previous display without repeating the associated processing operations. In some cases, particularly in interactive, end-user computing sessions in which the volume of output is small, this volatility is no hindrance to effective use. For instance, a user may wish to examine output from an electronic spreadsheet and to experiment with the input data or processing instructions before reducing the output to a more permanent form. Or the user may wish to browse through several displays, corresponding to different raw materials, before deciding on using substitute materials in a manufacturing process.

Output is often displayed on the same video monitor that forms part of the input device. Video display terminals are dual-purpose devices that can serve both the input and output functions. In other situations, a different screen may be needed, providing specialized screen characteristics that would make it inappropriate for a dual-purpose device. The standard video monitor has a screen measuring 80 columns by 25 rows and can display the usual ASCII characters: the numbers 0 through 9, uppercase and lowercase letters, and a few additional symbols. Monitors often offer character enhancement in the form of increased or decreased light intensity, reversed video in which dark characters appear on a light background, flashing characters, or audible "beeps." A monitor may display only a monochrome image or several colors. Characters can be enhanced, or colors can be changed, by means of the accompanying software, to highlight part of the image. Beeps can be used to alert the user to some situation such as the entry of invalid data.

Alternative video monitors may be bigger than the standard size or may provide for a wider range of screen images. Large-screen monitors, up to 80 columns by 66 rows, are available for displaying the equivalent of an $8\frac{1}{2} \times 11$ in. page of text, and even up to 132 columns by 66 rows for displaying whole pages of computer printout. Some of them can "zoom" in on a selected portion of the display and enlarge it to fill the screen. Not surprisingly, large screen monitors, particularly those with such innovative features, are substantially more expensive than are the standard ones.

Standard monochrome or color monitors are suitable for displaying numeric or alphanumeric data in tabular form or in a block format. However, they may not have the resolution to display high-quality graphics. Video monitors with graphics capability provide for output of more than just the ASCII characters. In the 1970s graphics monitors were available that could draw vectors, or oblique lines, on the screen by means of an internal scanning device. These have now largely been replaced by monitors that display small elements of light, or *pixels*, from which the required image can be constructed. The higher the resolution is, the smaller the pixels must be, and the more pixels per inch there must be. Presentation-quality graphics can now be produced on either monochrome or color monitors.

A fairly recent innovation is the split screen or *window*. This capability allows two or more output displays to be shown simultaneously in different regions of the screen. It provides an interesting way of "keeping track" of different aspects of the data being processed. For example, part of a spreadsheet may be shown in one window, a graph in another, and text in a third. Actually, the split screen is a capability of the output software rather than of the monitor itself; integrated end-user packages often offer this feature. Sometimes the displays overlap one another on the screen, and the user can change their apparent positions, similar to bringing a sheet of paper to the top of a pile of papers on a crowded desk.

Printers

Printers are the "workhorses" of the world of output devices, producing the large volumes of printout that typify modern computer systems. There are many types of printers, and they can be classified in different ways. One classification distinguishes among character printers, line printers, and page printers. A character printer (Figure 7.3) is one that prints one character at a time. The print head traverses the paper horizontally to produce a line of print, while the paper moves vertically through the device. In this respect, character printers resemble electric typewriters. They are usually much faster, however; a good typist can type at a rate of about 10 characters per second (c.p.s.), whereas modern character printers can print at speeds in excess of 300 c.p.s. Line printers (Figure 7.4) print a whole line at a time and so do not need a traversing print head. Line printers are typically faster than character printers; a typical line printer in a large computer installation has a speed of 2,000 lines per minute (l.p.m.), and some machines offer speeds of up to 20,000 l.p.m. At this speed, the King James Bible could be printed from cover to cover in less than five minutes. Page printers print a whole page at a time and have the useful characteristic that they behave as random, rather than serial, devices; data no longer need be sent to the printer one line at a time. A diagram can be sent, with the instruction that it be placed in the middle of the page; then a title can be transmitted, to be placed at the top of the page; and finally, a table of figures can be transmitted, to be placed elsewhere on the page. Special software is needed to exploit this kind of capability. Page printers range in speed from about five pages per minute (p.p.m.) to over 200 p.p.m.

Another classification addresses the manner in which the print is formed on the paper. One technology, now

FIGURE 7.3   Character printer with graphics capability: the NEC Pinwriter P2200.
(Courtesy of NEC Information Systems, Inc.)

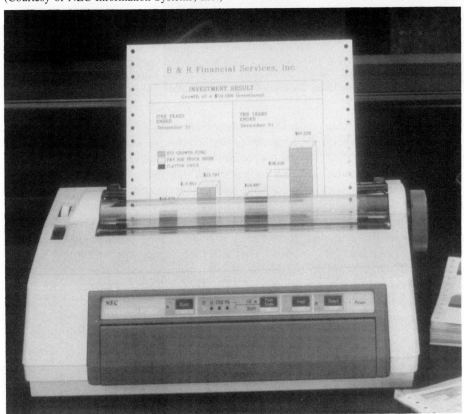

FIGURE 7.4 Large line printer. (Courtesy of Control Data Corporation)

virtually obsolete, has a heat-sensitive print head that "burns" the characters onto specially sensitized paper. Heat-sensitive printers were relatively cheap, but they were slow (on the order of 15 c.p.s.), and the paper was expensive and deteriorated rapidly, often turning brown after only a few weeks. The most common technology in use today is the impact printer. Hammers strike an inked ribbon laid over the paper, as they do in a typewriter. Impact printers can be made cheaply, are fast (up to about 3,000 l.p.m. in the case of line printers), are reliable, and can print multiple copies. This last feature has made possible the printing of multipart reports and documents which form one of the foundations of modern accounting systems.

Other types of printers include the "high-technology" electrostatic, xerographic printers, ink-jet printers, and laser printers. Page printers, and even some character and line printers, use one or other of these technologies. Electrostatic and xerographic printers combine the tech-

nology of the office copying machine with that of the computer printer. Even some small desktop printers now use the electrostatic technology. Ink-jet printers form the print by jets of ink directed onto the paper. They have made wide inroads into the market for color printers; jets of different colors can be turned on and off under software control. Laser printers, in which the characters are formed by a laser beam, have become popular in recent years. They offer the highest speeds together with the capability of printing graphics and even magazine-quality photographs. They also are much quieter than impact printers. Although laser printers cannot print multiple copies, at the high speeds at which they operate, additional copies can be produced by repeated printing of the same material. Laser printers are being used by some publishers to produce camera-ready originals as an alternative to conventional typesetting.

Yet another classification deals with the quality of print (Figure 7.5). The highest-quality print is produced

FIGURE 7.5   Quality of print from various types of printers.

Electric typewriter:

1234567890ABCDEFGHIJKLMNOPQRSTUVWXYZabcdefghijklmnopqrstuvwxyz

Dot-matrix printer:

ABCDEFGHIJKLMNOPQRSTUVWXYZ[\]^_`abcdefghijklmnopqrstuvwxyz
BCDEFGHIJKLMNOPQRSTUVWXYZ[\]^_`abcdefghijklmnopqrstuvwxyz{
CDEFGHIJKLMNOPQRSTUVWXYZ[\]^_`abcdefghijklmnopqrstuvwxyz{|

Dot-matrix printer with character enhancement:

ABCDEFGHIJKLMNOPQRSTUVWXYZ[\]^

Line printer

0123456789:;<=>?@ABCDEFGHIJKLMNOPQRSTUVWXYZ[\]^-`abcdefghijklmnopqrstuvwxyz
0123456789:;<=>?@ABCDEFGHIJKLMNOPQRSTUVWXYZ[\]^-`abcdefghijklmnopqrstuvwxyz
0123456789:;<=>?@ABCDEFGHIJKLMNOPQRSTUVWXYZ[\]^-`abcdefghijklmnopqrstuvwxyz

by printers referred to variously as "letter quality," "correspondence quality," or "typewriter quality." Impact printers of this type use hammers bearing fully formed characters, as does a typewriter. One of the most common letter-quality printers is the "daisywheel" printer in which the hammers are arranged around the periphery of a circle, resembling the petals of a daisy.

Many impact printers are based on the *dot-matrix* technology, in which each character is formed by wires that print a small rectangular array—or matrix—of dots on the paper. The dots are close enough together to produce readable character fonts, although under close inspection, the discrete dots are readily apparent. The print quality is sufficient for management reports and for most accounting documents, and dot-matrix printers allow various choices of font and character enhancements. Often, under software control, the font can be changed back and forth between, say, roman and italic or English and Japanese. Character enhancements include underscoring, boldface, condensed print, and expanded print in which the size of the characters may be increased for headings and the like. Word-processing software offers an increasing number of features to take advantage of improvements in the capability of dot-matrix printers. Dot-matrix printers also can print graphics materials.

A relatively recent innovation in dot-matrix printers is their ability to increase the density of the dots so as to approach the quality of letter-quality printers. Modern dot-matrix printers often have two operating modes, a high-speed, lower-quality mode suitable for printing drafts, and a lower-speed, "near-letter-quality" mode suitable for presentation material.

Other Output Devices

Dot-matrix and laser printers can produce acceptable monochrome graphics output, and ink-jet printers can produce color graphics. But for the highest-quality graphics, a plotter is recommended. Most plotters have a print head that traverses in two directions over a stationary sheet of paper, drawing continuous lines or curves and inserting legends consisting of discrete characters. Pens of different colors can often be interchanged at will by the accompanying software. Plotters are relatively slow but are available for a range of paper sizes up to several feet in each direction.

Microfilm printers produce output on microfilm instead of paper. The main application is printing large volumes of materials to be placed in archive storage. The combination of high density and human readability of microfilm media is an attractive feature for certain types of archive storage.

Voice synthesizers are available for producing audible data output. They are limited to small volumes of data but may be suitable for special purposes such as file query.

Performance of Output Devices

The many available printers enable the user to choose one whose speed is appropriate to the required output work load. The speed of printer devices is measured in characters per second, lines per minute, or pages per minute. Comparative calculations can be done by assuming a "standard" output task, such as printing a 100-page report. Suppose, for instance, that there were 50 lines per page and that on the average there were 90 characters per line. The time taken to print the report, using a 60 c.p.s. character printer, would be

$$\text{Time} = \frac{100 \times 50 \times 90}{60} = 7,500 \text{ seconds}$$

$$= 2 \text{ hours, } 5 \text{ minutes}$$

On the other hand, if a 1,000 l.p.m. line printer were used, the time would be

$$\text{Time} = \frac{100 \times 50}{1,000} = 5 \text{ minutes}$$

Or if a 200 p.p.m. page printer were used, the time would be

$$\text{Time} = \frac{100}{200} = 0.5 \text{ minutes}$$

$$= 30 \text{ seconds}$$

These calculations are obviously crude, and they ignore such factors as the time taken to perform a page shift. Also, with reference to character printers, the time necessary to execute a line feed may be fairly long compared with the time to print a character. Consequently, the results should be used with caution, but they provide a rough indication of the performance of printers of various types.

PROCESSOR DEVICES

Traditional computers consisted of single processor device, referred to appropriately as the *central processor unit (CPU)*, and a number of peripheral devices. For convenience, this discussion will emphasize the traditional, centralized computer configuration; but the reader should remember that such a configuration is only one of several commonly used. Today's computers may have several processing devices, sharing a common work load and servicing common peripherals, or the processing capability may be distributed throughout the system in the "peripheral" devices themselves.

Processor devices can be divided into three main components: the *control unit*, the *arithmetic/logic unit* (ALU), and *main memory*. Supporting components include a number of interface units associated with external devices—which may include other processors. The control unit controls the operation of the ALU and, indirectly, the operation of the computer system as a whole. It includes an internal clock that "paces" the system's processing activities. The arithmetic/logic unit provides the capability for performing the arithmetic operations of addition, subtraction, multiplication, and division, and the logical operation of comparison. The locations within the ALU, where the arithmetic and logical operations are actually performed, are referred to as *registers*. Small machines may have only small number of registers (perhaps six or eight), whereas large machines may have several hundred. The more registers a machine has, the fewer storage and retrieval operations there have to be between the ALU and main memory in order to complete a complex instruction. Main memory is a storage facility, providing fast, random access to its data content. The data links between the ALU and main memory are referred to as *buses*.

Virtually all processor devices currently in use are based on solid-state integrated circuits. The active electronic components are semiconductor *chips*, which consist of thin slices of silicon about the size of a fingernail on which the circuitry is etched photographically. "Processor" chips provide the functions of the control unit and the arithmetic/logic unit, and "memory" chips provide the main-memory capacity.

Operation of the Central Processor

The principal operations performed by the central processor are retrieving a data "word" from main memory, storing a word in main memory, comparing two words, and adding or subtracting two words.[2] A data word, which consists of a certain number of bits, is the data aggregate that the processor device treats as a unit. The buses must be "wide" enough (i.e., have enough parallel conductors) to transmit a whole word at a time, and each register must be long enough to hold a whole word. Usually the size of the bus and the size of the registers is the same, but some processors have registers that are twice as long as the width of the buses and that can hold two words end to end. Occasionally, some of the registers are longer than others.

Processor devices are often classified according to their word length; 8-, 16-, 32-, and 64-bit processors are in common use, and intermediate word lengths are also used. The first microprocessors used 8-bit words, but 16-bit word lengths are now the standard, and 32-bit processors are now used in the more powerful microcomputers (Figure 7.6). Departmental (mini-) computers typically use either 16-, 24-, or 32-bit processors; large mainframe computers designed for business applications typically use 32- or 48-bit words; and some large mainframes intended for scientific applications use 60- or 64-bit word lengths. A typical departmental computer is shown in Figure 7.7, and a mainframe computer is shown in Figure 7.8.

---

[2] The other arithmetic operations of multiplication and division can be reduced to successive additions and subtractions.

Main Memory

Main-memory devices have evolved substantially since the early days of electronic computing. The first memory technology to win wide acceptance was the magnetic drum, in which the data were recorded in the form of magnetic spots on the surface of a rotating cylinder. A read-write head moved along a generator of the cylinder, or a series of stationary heads were positioned along a generator, and could address any desired location on the surface, thereby providing random access. Magnetic drums gave way to magnetic core devices that had no moving parts. The data were stored in rows of small toroidal (doughnut-shaped) magnets activated by electric currents and were addressed by associated circuitry. Core memory provided substantially greater storage capacity and was more robust than magnetic drums were. Both types of magnetic storage device had the useful characteristic that the data remained in memory even when the computer was turned off.

But in the late 1970s, magnetic core memory was superseded by the present semiconductor memory devices. Semiconductor memory devices include *read-only memory* (ROM), in which the data are permanently "burned in," and *random access memory* (RAM) to which data can be written and read at will. Computers typically have a small amount of ROM, containing permanent data, often providing start-up, or "boot," instructions, and a much larger amount of RAM for general use. In general-purpose semiconductor memory, data are stored in the form of electric charges. The charge is volatile and must be refreshed by a continuous electric current. Consequently, they are sensitive to power failure unless battery backup is provided, and data are lost when the machine is turned off. However, semiconductor memory consumes less power than magnetic devices, is more compact, is considerably cheaper, and is becoming still cheaper as a result of mass production. The cost of memory devices per unit of capacity is now about 1 percent of what it was 10 or 15 years ago, and as the cost decreases, it is natural to buy more capacity. In the first generation of computers, 16 kilobytes (KB) of main memory were considered a lot. Today most business personal computers are sold with 640 KB of main memory, and some have capacities of several megabytes

FIGURE 7.6   Modern microcomputer: Compaq Deskpro 386. (Courtesy of Compaq Computer Corporation.)

(MB). Large computers may have tens of megabytes of main-memory capacity.

When a computer is turned on, main memory (except for the ROM portion) is empty. The first step is to boot the machine: The operating system (or at least part of it) is loaded into main memory, where it remains during the machine's subsequent operation. Some portion of main memory is also set aside to provide *buffer space*, which is used as a temporary place of residence for data in transit back or forth between secondary storage and the central processor. The operating system and buffer space may occupy anywhere from about 2 kilobytes (KB) to over 1 megabyte (MB) of storage space, depending on the type of processor and the complexity of the operating system.

The remaining capacity of main memory is available for loading applications software and is referred to as *user space*. It must be divided among all the jobs or tasks to be processed concurrently. In some older processors, main memory was partitioned into segments; tasks had to fit into a given partition, and unused space could not be allocated to another, larger task. This re-

FIGURE 7.7 Medium-sized departmental (mini-) computer: VAX8700. (Courtesy of Digital Equipment Corporation.)

sulted in an inefficient use of main memory. Most machines today permit a dynamic allocation of memory space, allowing user space to be allocated in any proportions, and even allowing space to be redistributed during the execution of the resident tasks.

When main-memory costs were much higher than they are today, it was natural to try to economize on capacity. As a result, there was a limit on the size of the task that could be run. And more important, the ability to run in a multitasking mode was limited (sometimes severely) by the number of tasks that could be accommodated in main memory. To alleviate these problems, the notion of *virtual memory* was devised. The idea was to leave the program software in secondary storage and to load into main memory only the particular "page" currently being executed. By this means, larger programs could be run, or a larger number of tasks could be run concurrently, than would be possible if all of each program had to be resident in main memory throughout the processing. The disadvantage of virtual memory processors was that their speed was reduced because of the need to load each page of the program (repeatedly, if that page formed part of a loop) from secondary storage. Virtual memory machines have declined in popularity now that much larger main-memory capacities can be installed. Interestingly, the opposite concept is now sometimes used, namely, the "virtual disk": Part of main memory is treated as though it were a secondary storage device, providing exceptionally fast access.

FIGURE 7.8 Large mainframe computer system: the Honeywell Bull DPS8000. (Courtesy of Honeywell Bull, Inc.)

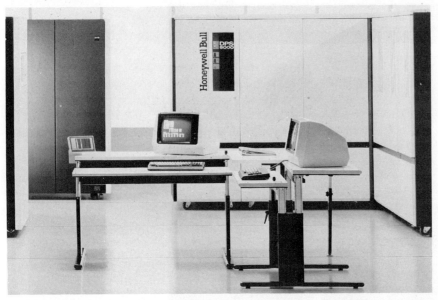

Performance of Processor Devices

The speed of the processor device depends on three factors: the cycle time, or frequency of the clock cycle; the number of clock cycles required for completion of an instruction; and the word length. The overall speed at which the computer executes programs depends on these factors and also on the efficiency of the software.

Most modern processors have cycle times of less than 1 microsecond, and the so-called supercomputers have cycle times of around 10 to 20 nanoseconds (a nanosecond is equal to 10^{-9} seconds). Microprocessors may require several clock cycles to perform a single instruction, whereas the more powerful mainframe processors are able to perform more than one instruction per cycle. The operating speed depends on the word length because two or more words may be required in order to represent a given number. For example, a number up to 65,535 ($2^{16}-1$) could be retrieved from main memory as a single unit and processed as a single unit by a machine with 16-bit buses and 16-bit registers. But a machine with 8-bit buses would have to retrieve it in two parts, and one with 8-bit registers would have to process it in two parts; subsequently the two parts would have to be re-

combined. The Intel 8086 processor, still used in several personal computers, has 16-bit registers, but only 8-bit buses.

The amount of internal memory capacity that should be installed depends on the required content of main memory. Typically, main memory must hold the operating system and must provide some buffer space for data en route to or from peripheral devices. In addition, it must provide space for the programs that are currently being executed (Figure 7.9). The required capacity therefore depends on the size of the programs that are to be run on it and, if the machine is intended to run in a multitasking mode, the number of programs that will be run concurrently. The number of programs can be assumed to be equal to the number of input devices that will be active at any one time. The size of programs has increased, by the addition of new features, to take advantage of the availability of cheap main memory capacity. For example, word-processing software, which used to require less than 64 KB of main memory, may now require over 256 KB. State-of-the-art spreadsheet software now needs over 512 KB. Accounting software, intended for operation on microcomputers, remains reasonably compact and is usually packaged in modules, each of which may occupy less than 256 KB. Accounting packages for use on larger machines typically include more programmed controls and may occupy much more main memory.

Suppose that eight programs are to be run on a computer in a multitasking mode and that they will make a combined total demand on main-memory user space of 1 MB. The operating system might occupy 128 KB, and buffer space might be 32 KB. The total memory capacity required would be 1,000 + 128 + 32 = 1,160 KB, or 1.16 MB:

Item		Size (KB)
Operating system		128
Buffer space		32
User space:		
Program A	64	
Program B	192	
...		
Program H	128	1,000
Total capacity required		1,160

The total main-memory capacity could be reduced by using virtual memory techniques, so long as the operating system provides for it. But as noted earlier, the processing speed would be reduced accordingly.

The first microcomputers which appeared in the mid-1970s had very little processing power. Their speed was low; they had little main-memory capacity; and they could handle only one job at a time. Moreover, their reliability was poor. Today's microcomputers have a great deal of power and rival the capability of much larger machines. They are fast, have substantially more memory capacity, and are reliable; and the larger microcomputers can handle limited multitasking operations or serve (that is, control) networks. *Departmental* (mini-) computers are designed for multitasking operations and, depending on their specific capability, can handle from about 6 to 60 passive terminals. Large mainframe computers are the fastest machines and can handle 100 or more passive terminals. The use of intelligent terminals reduces the demand on central processor resources, and a larger number of terminals can be connected to a given processor without suffering degradation of response time.

FIGURE 7.9 **Allocation of space within main memory.** All programs and data must fit within the available user space.

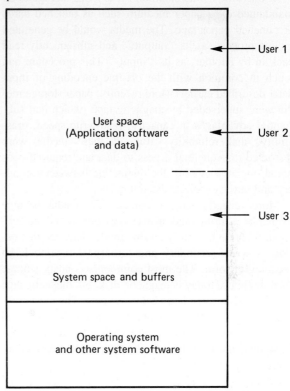

EXTERNAL STORAGE DEVICES AND MEDIA

External, or peripheral, storage provides for the permanent, nonvolatile storage of programs and data. External storage is customarily divided into secondary and tertiary storage (primary storage corresponds to main memory). Secondary storage is ordinarily on line in the sense that its content can be retrieved upon issuance of an instruction by a processor device, without the operator's intervention. The content of secondary storage is available to be loaded into main memory as needed for processing. Most secondary storage devices provide for random access to data. Tertiary storage is ordinarily off line and requires action by the operator to make the data available to the computer. Tertiary storage is used chiefly for archive or library storage of data and programs and for backing up secondary storage as a security measure.

At one time it was common for external storage to be maintained on a paper medium such as punched cards or punched paper tape. The media would be generated by one process, as its "output," and subsequently read back in by another, as its "input." This procedure had much in common with the off-line encoding of input data, described earlier. More recently, paper storage media were superseded by magnetic tape, which had substantial advantages in capacity, read-write speed, erasability, and reliability. But all these media were restricted to sequential access to data and required continual operator support; the distinction between secondary and tertiary storage did not exist.

More recently still, magnetic disk media became available, offering random access capability and the ability to function in a fully on-line mode. Thus the distinction between secondary and tertiary storage took on meaningful form. The most common secondary storage medium in use today is magnetic disk, but magnetic tape is still used in some large batch systems. The most common tertiary storage media are magnetic tape and "floppy" (flexible) disks. We shall now discuss magnetic disk and tape devices and their associated media.

Magnetic Disk

Magnetic disk devices consist of one or more disks, or *platters*, rotating on a common spindle. The data are stored in the form of sequences of magnetic spots lying along concentric *tracks* on the surface of the disks (Figure 7.10). Read-write heads provide for data storage and retrieval as the disks rotate. In some cases the read-write heads must be traversed radially to access the different tracks, in a manner similar to the tone arm of a record player. Alternatively, multiple heads are used, one over each track. In general, the access time depends on the disks' rate of rotation and on the search time, which is the time taken to reposition the read-write heads from one track to another. The search time is typically longer than the time taken for the disk to make a complete revolution. By eliminating the search time, the use of multiple heads produces faster access to the data; on the other hand, it increases the cost of the device. At a

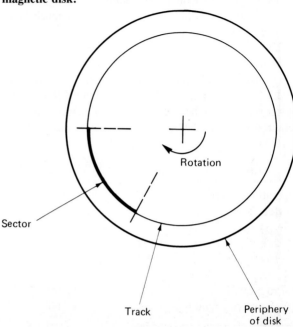

FIGURE 7.10 Arrangement of tracks and sectors on a magnetic disk.

minimum, there must be one read-write head for each disk surface. A popular, low-cost disk drive in widespread use today is the so-called Winchester drive, which has a single disk platter and a traversible read-write head.

Each track can be divided into *sectors*, which comprise the physical records. The set of tracks in a multiple-platter device, at a given radius from the spindle, form the geometry of a *cylinder*. The significance of a cylinder is that in a device with traversible read-write heads, all the data lying on a cylinder can be read without the need to reposition the heads. Systems software prepared with a particular type of disk drive in mind can exploit this feature in order to reduce access times.

The original magnetic disks were *hard* disks, in the sense that the disk platters were made from rigid sheet metal. Figure 7.11 shows a relatively large hard disk device, configured as a stand-alone unit. Figure 7.12 shows the popular "Winchester" disk drive with the cover removed.

Hard disk drives have capacities ranging from 2 MB up to about 100 MB per platter, or to about 1,000 MB

FIGURE 7.11 Magnetic disk drive for use with removable cartridges. (Courtesy of Control Data Corporation)

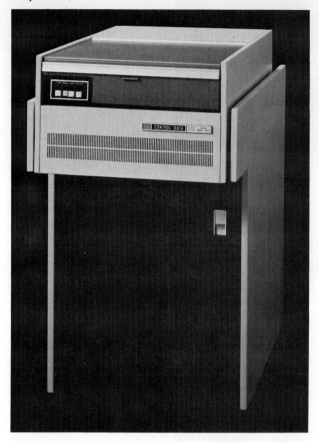

(1 gigabyte) for a multiple-platter drive. More recently the *floppy*, or flexible, diskette, was introduced (Figure 7.13). Diskettes, which come in three basic sizes—3.5 in., 5.25 in., and 8 in.—are made of thin plastic with a coating of magnetic material. Their capacity ranges from 100 KB to about 2 MB, depending on their size and recording density. Floppy diskettes are small and inexpensive and helped make possible the personal computer revolution, but they are not as reliable as hard disks are. Hard disk drives, particularly Winchester drives with capacities of 10 MB to 40 MB, have also become much smaller and cheaper, and they are now installed in many microcomputer systems.

A floppy diskette can be removed from the disk drive and replaced by another. In some hard disk drives, the disk platters are enclosed in removable cartridges (Figure 7.14). Although each diskette or cartridge may have limited storage capacity, a whole library of disks can be maintained, with unlimited total capacity. The appropriate disk can be inserted in the drive for each processing job. The concept of removable disk media marries the concepts of secondary and tertiary storage: The diskette or cartridge currently in the drive represents secondary storage, and those in the library or on the rack represent tertiary storage. Floppy disk drives are inexpensive, but hard disk cartridge drives are considerably more expensive than are their fixed, hard-disk counterparts. Nevertheless, without the capability to copy data to removable disks, which can be stored off line, the need for tertiary storage must be met by some other means.

Magnetic Tape

In magnetic tape media, the data are written in the form of parallel rows of magnetic spots arranged along the length of the tape (Figure 7.15). Seven- and nine-channel tapes are in common use, each channel corresponding to one longitudinal row of magnetic spots. The density of the data along the tape is expressed in bits per inch (b.p.i.) or characters per inch (c.p.i.), which are the same because the bits forming a single byte are arranged laterally. Tape drives are available for a variety of densities, but 800 b.p.i., 1,600 b.p.i., and 6,250 b.p.i. are the most common.

A standard reel of tape is 2,400 feet long and, at a density of 6,250 b.p.i., has a potential capacity of 2,400 × 12 × 6,250 = 180 MB. In practice, however, this potential is seldom realized because of the need to divide the length of the tape into physical records, or blocks, separated by interrecord gaps (typically 0.75 in. long) on which no data are written. The purpose of the gaps is to enable the tape drive to "find" the beginning and end of each physical record and to allow the tape to accelerate to maximum velocity and to decelerate to rest between the active records. A whole block is read or written as a unit in response to a command issued by a processor device. The interrecord gaps represent wasted capacity. To minimize the overall waste, several logical records are normally written in one physical record. The

FIGURE 7.12 Magnetic disk drive with the cover removed. (Courtesy of Control Data Corporation)

number of logical records per physical record is referred to as the *blocking factor*.

A typical magnetic tape drive is illustrated in Figure 7.16. Tape drives for handling reels of standard seven- or nine-track magnetic tape are expensive, largely because of the complexity of the mechanism needed to start and stop the tape between physical records. But for many archive and backup purposes, it may be acceptable simply to copy all of secondary storage to the tape, without the provision to read or write individual records. If so, there is a substantially cheaper option in the form of "streaming" tape drives, which accept tape cassettes resembling those used in home video or audio systems. Cassettes are available with capacities of up to 100 MB

and can be written to in less than five minutes. The cost of the drive is comparable to the cost of a floppy diskette drive. Streaming tape drives have become popular for use with the larger personal computers and may be used with some departmental (mini-) computer systems.

Other Storage Media

Several other types of external storage media have been proposed or used, including compact disks of the type used in home audio systems. A particularly attractive medium is the optical or video disk. Originally introduced as a means of recording television programs—and

FIGURE 7.13   Flexible "floppy" diskettes. (Courtesy of Memorex Corporation, Media Products Group)

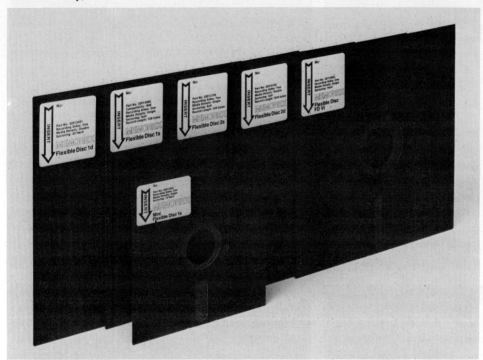

later superseded by the now-popular tape cassettes—the video disk offers advantages as a data storage medium because of its high storage density, together with random access capability. Capacities of up to 2,500 MB per platter have been achieved in the laboratory, and capacities of 1,000 MB per platter are possible under routine production conditions. The traditional disadvantage of optical disks has been that the data could not be erased, but industry commentators believe that this difficulty may soon be overcome. Meanwhile, its main uses are to store archive files and permanent material such as software or documentation.

Performance of External Storage Devices

Several decisions must be made in connection with external storage devices and media: How much capacity is required; how much must be in the form of on-line, random access storage; and what provision is to be made for backing up secondary storage? The total required

capacity can be related to the content of external storage: software and data. Provision must be made to accommodate all systems and applications software and to accommodate all data files, including scratch files and copies of other files resident in secondary storage during processing operations. The space required for temporary files is usually provided for by an allowance for "working space," which can often be equated with some percentage (20 to 100 percent) of the estimated capacity of the transaction and master files. However, it may not be necessary for all software and data to be on line at all times; part of this material could be maintained in tertiary storage.

Tertiary storage must be provided for archive and back-up purposes. If fixed disk drives are selected as the secondary storage media, some other medium such as magnetic tape or floppy diskettes must also be available. If the volume of on-line data were large, floppy diskettes would not be appropriate because of their limited capacity; the time and effort required to write the data to multiple diskettes would be prohibitive. Removable disk

FIGURE 7.14 Cartridge disk packs for use in magnetic disk drives. (Courtesy of Control Data Corporation)

cartridges offer a means of providing disk-based tertiary storage if the content of secondary storage can be copied onto the cartridges. This would not be possible, for instance, if only one disk drive were used and the cartridge contained all the platters. Experience has shown that magnetic tape offers the best medium for tertiary storage, and either standard reels of tape or streaming tape cassettes are suitable.

FIGURE 7.15 Format of data recorded on magnetic tape.

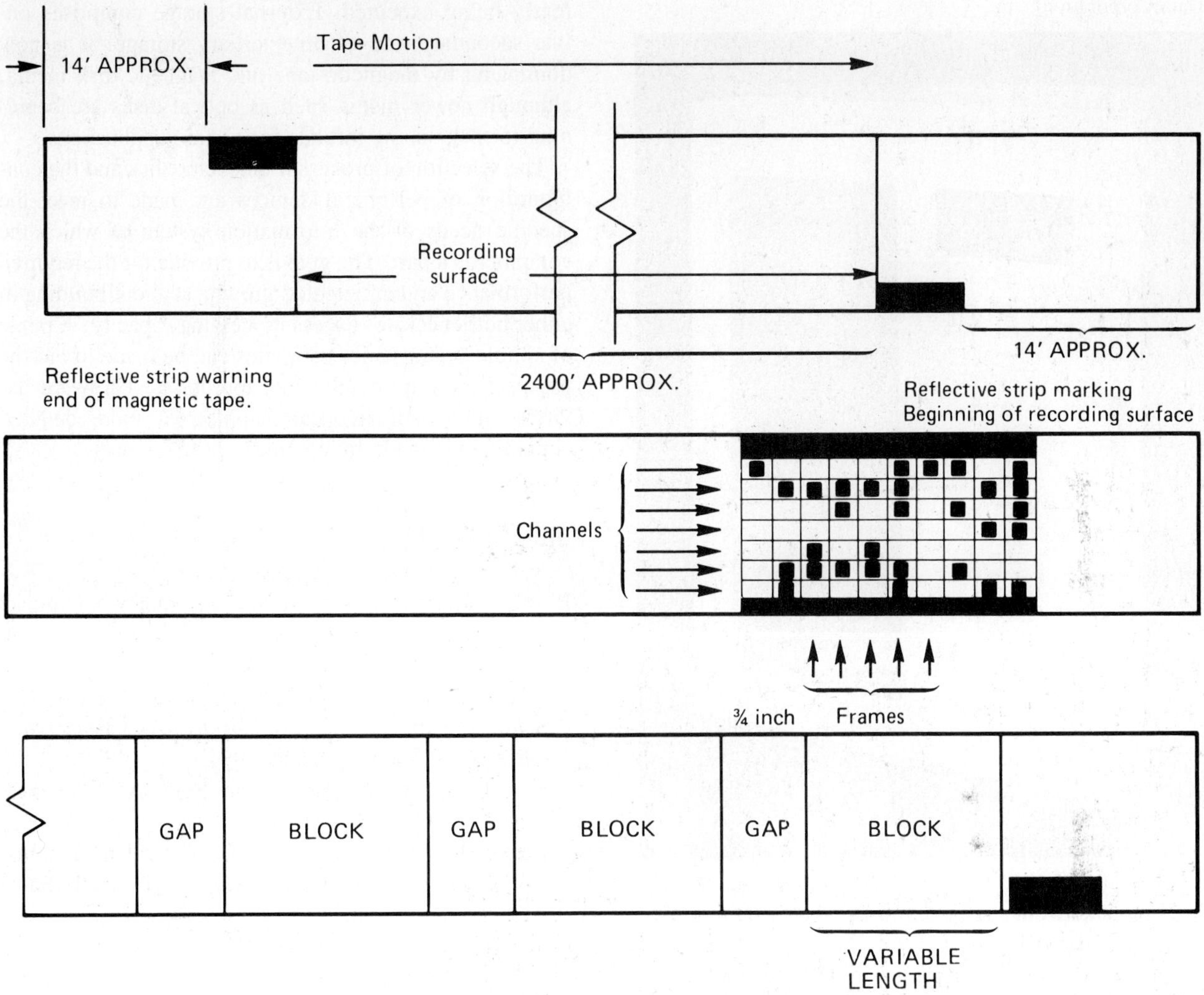

14' APPROX.

Tape Motion

Recording
surface

Reflective strip warning
end of magnetic tape.

2400' APPROX.

14' APPROX.

Reflective strip marking
Beginning of recording surface

Channels

¾ inch   Frames

GAP   BLOCK   GAP   BLOCK   GAP   BLOCK

VARIABLE
LENGTH

SUMMARY

The traditional computer consists of a central processor supporting a range of peripheral devices that provide for input, output, external storage, and communication of data.[3] The central processor unit (CPU) contains the control unit, the arithmetic/logic unit, and main (or pri-

[3] Telecommunications devices are discussed in Chapter 10.

mary) memory. It is the system's seat of intelligence or processing capability, on which the operation of the peripheral devices depends. Today, there is a marked trend toward distributing processing capability throughout the system into "smart" or "intelligent" peripherals. The work load, previously handled by the central processor alone, is now shared by a greater variety of devices which also perform specialized tasks, including input, storage, and output. The status of the central processor

FIGURE 7.16 Magnetic tape drive. (Courtesy of Control Data Corporation)

which must accommodate the program or programs currently being executed. External storage comprises on-line secondary and off-line tertiary storage. It is now dominated by magnetic tape and magnetic disk media, although newer media such as optical disks are beginning to make some inroads for certain applications.

The selection of processor characteristics and the configuration of peripheral devices are made to meet the specific needs of the information system of which the computer is a part. The goal is to provide for the required performance and anticipated growth, without building in either bottlenecks or excess processing capacity. A range of simple performance estimates can be made to aid the prospective user in selecting appropriate hardware devices. Such estimates can supplement more detailed computations made by computer professionals.

BIBLIOGRAPHY

Bittman, Mark. "Laser Printers and Other Nonimpact Page Printers." *CFO Magazine*, January 1987, pp. 33–40.

Christie, Linda, G., and L. John Christie. *The Encyclopedia of Microcomputer Terminology*. Englewood Cliffs, N.J.: Prentice-Hall, 1984.

"How Personal Computers Can Backfire." *Business Week*, July 12, 1982, pp. 56–59.

Kroenke, David M., and Kathleen A. Dolan. *Business Computer Systems: An Introduction*, 3rd ed. Santa Cruz, Calif.: Mitchell, 1987.

Miller, I. M. "Computer Graphic Applications." *Journal of Systems Management*, November 1980, pp. 22–35.

Moad, Jeff. "Pinning Hopes on a Vision of Storage." *Datamation*, February 1, 1987, pp. 17–19.

Nash, John F., and Vincent J. Giovinazzo. "Selecting Computer Hardware." *CPA Journal*, September 1982, pp. 57–63.

Osborne, Adam. *An Introduction to Microcomputers*. Berkeley, Calif.: Osborne & Associates, 1977.

Roberts, M. "Multiprocessing Networks vs. Mainframes." *Mini-Micro Systems*, November 1980, pp. 130–140.

Sehr, Barbara K. "High Noon for CD-Rom." *Datamation*, November 1, 1986, pp. 79–86.

is diminished, but the system as a whole is gaining efficiency and reliability.

Input devices can be divided into off-line data preparation devices and online terminal devices. Data preparation devices are used to encode data onto an intermediate storage medium for subsequent on-line input. The most popular terminal device in use today is the video display terminal, which consists of a keyboard and a video monitor. Video monitors are also used for small volumes of output, but by far the greater volume of output is generated on printers. A wide variety of printers is available, representing flexible choices in print quality, performance, technology, and cost.

Storage devices include both internal storage, or main memory, and external storage. Main memory contains the operating system, buffer space, and user space,

Sudan, L. K. "An Integrated Approach to Corporate Networks." *Mini-Micro System*, September 1980, pp. 120–126.

Thompson, Jacqueline, "Of Disks, Desks, and Data." *World*, Peat, Marwick, Mitchell & Co., January 1987, pp. 24–29.

Tomeski, Edward A. *Fundamentals of Computers in Business: A Systems Approach.* San Fransisco: Holden-Day, 1979.

Toong, Hoo-Min D., and Amar Gupta. "Personal Computers." *Scientific American*, December 1982, pp. 86–106.

Verity, John W. "Taming the DASD Monster." *Datamation*, December 1, 1986, pp. 77–80.

"The Videodisc Will Revolutionize Data Storage." *Business Week*, July 7, 1980, pp. 78–81.

White, R. M. "Disk Storage Technology." *Scientific American*, August 1980, pp. 138–148.

Wiener, Hesh. "The ABCs of Printing." *Datamation*, December 1, 1986, pp. 59–68.

DISCUSSION QUESTIONS AND PROBLEMS

1. Define and discuss the following terms:

- Blocking factor
- Character printer
- Daisy-wheel printer
- Disk cartridge
- Dot-matrix printer
- Fixed disk
- Floppy disk
- Hard-copy output
- Human readability
- Impact printer
- Keypunch machine
- Key-to-disk machine
- Key-to-tape machine
- Kilobyte, megabyte, gigabyte
- Large mainframe computer
- Laser printer
- Line printer
- Machine readability
- Magnetic disk drive
- Magnetic, optical wand
- Magnetic tape drive
- Microcomputer
- Microfilm printer
- Microprocessor
- Microsecond, nanosecond
- Minicomputer
- Operation code
- Page printer
- Paper-tape punch
- Plotter
- Point-of-sale device
- Printer terminal
- Register
- Removable disk
- Semiconductor memory
- Superminicomputer
- Video display terminal
- Winchester drive

2. What are the relative advantages and disadvantages of off-line data preparation using magnetic tape as the input medium and on-line data entry via an interactive video terminal?

3. A file containing 3,000 logical records, each of length 512 bytes, is to be encoded onto a machine-readable input medium in readiness for processing. The number of logical records written to one physical record is the blocking factor. Suppose the blocking factor is 5, the recording density is 800 bits per inch, and the inter-record gap is 0.75 inches. The five logical records can be written to a length of tape equal to $5 \times 512/800 = 3.2$ in., and the total length of the physical record is $3.2 + 0.75 = 3.95$ in. To contain the 3,000 logical records, or $3,000/5 = 600$ physical records, the required length of tape would be $3.95 \times 600 = 2,370$ in. $= 2,370/12 = 197.5$ feet.

Required

a. What length of magnetic tape would be needed, assuming a blocking factor of 1 and a recording density of 1,600 b.p.i.?

b. How much magnetic tape would be needed if the blocking factor were increased to 15 and the density to 6,250 b.p.i.?

4. A company intends to acquire a printer for printing internal management reports. The reports contain an average of 30 pages, with 55 lines per page and 100 characters per line. The company intends to run the printer for no more than seven hours per day, to allow time for preventive maintenance.

Required

Decide what printer speed (expressed in characters per second, lines per minute, and pages per minute) would be required if the company wanted to print

a. 1 report per day
b. 10 reports per day
c. 100 reports per day
d. 1,000 reports per day

What type of printer technology would be appropriate in each case?

5. A minicomputer, with a main-memory capacity of 2 MB, is to be used to support a number of interactive terminals. The operating system can be tailored to the precise number of terminals to be used, but the more terminals there are, the larger the operating system must be. For the particular system, the size of the operating system is given by

$$\text{Size (KB)} = 128 + 16 \times \text{number of terminals}$$

The amount of system buffer space provided also must increase with the number of terminals; approximately 8 KB per terminal is needed. Application programs, having an average size of 256 KB each, are to be run from individual terminals.

Required
a. What is the maximum number of terminals that can be supported if virtual memory capability is not available?
b. Suppose that virtual memory provisions allow for two programs to share the space otherwise required for one but that the size of the operating system has to be increased by 64 KB. What would be your revised answer to (a)?

6. For security reasons, Wise Corporation wishes to copy its entire data base once per day. Each copy is to be kept for five working days after which the storage medium can be recycled. The total capacity of the data

base is 30 MB, consisting of records whose average length is 300 bytes. Alternative backup schemes have been proposed, using floppy disks, removable disk cartridges, or magnetic tape.

The available floppy disks hold 1 MB each, cost $5, and have a useful life of 6 months. The floppy disk drive costs $500. It would take approximately 5 minutes to write a complete disk and 1 minute to change disks. The disk cartridges hold 5 MB each, cost $60, and have a life of at least 5 years. The associated disk drive costs $5,000. The whole disk can be written to in 15 minutes, and the time taken to change a disk cartridge is 5 minutes. The proposed magnetic tape drive costs $6,000, operates at a speed of 75 in. per second, and has a recording density of 800 b.p.i. A 2,400-ft reel of tape costs $10, and tapes typically last about 2 years.

Required

Advise management on the choice of backup medium and associated hardware.

7. An inventory system is to have its transaction and master files maintained on line to support an interactive processing mode. The file specifications are as follows:

File	Record (bytes)	No. of Records
Inventory master file	512	25,000
Receipts transaction file	128	5,000
Issuances transaction file	128	10,000
Backorder transaction file	256	8,000

Required
a. Determine the total required storage capacity, allowing for a contingency factor of 60 percent to cover scratch files and working space.
b. What type of disk device and medium would be most suitable to hold the files?

8. A company operates an accounting information system consisting of four stand-alone subsystems: payroll, job cost, purchasing, and general ledger. Payroll requires one input terminal and one printer. Job cost requires four input terminals and two printers. Purchasing requires three input terminals and two printers. The general ledger application requires one input terminal and one printer. If they could be combined, payroll and general ledger could share a common printer, and job cost and purchasing could share two of the input terminals.

Management is trying to decide whether to acquire four large microcomputers, two minicomputers, or a single superminicomputer. Some applicable price data, obtained from prospective vendors, are as follows:

Component	Price
Input terminal	$500
Printer	1,000
Large microcomputer	6,000
Minicomputer	25,000
Superminicomputer	80,000

Each machine requires its own secondary storage on magnetic disk. Each subsystem requires approximately 10 MB of capacity. Available disk drives cost $5,000 plus $100 per megabyte of capacity.

Required
a. Advise management on the most suitable configuration to meet the company's requirements, based on the data shown.
b. What other considerations should management be aware of before making a final decision?

9. First National Bank currently operates a central computer facility to serve its eight city-wide branches. The system is based on a large mainframe computer with 3 MB of main memory and 1,000 MB of on-line disk storage. Four 75 i.p.s. (inches per second) tape drives are used for data input and file backup. The principal input medium is magnetic tape. Each branch has a remote-job-entry (RJE) terminal consisting of a tape reader and a 300 l.p.m. printer; there is no interactive capability.

Management is considering replacing its existing system with a distributed processing system based on superminicomputers. Interactive terminals and optical character recognition (OCR) check-reading devices would be provided. Also, 24-hour automatic tellers would be installed at all branches. The proposed system would require four superminicomputers costing $250,000 each. Each would have 1 MB of main memory and 100 MB of local disk storage; in addition, the existing 1,000 MB disk capacity would be retained to support a central data base. Adaptation of the existing disk drives, installation of network equipment, and other conversion work would cost $75,000. New terminal equipment (including the automatic tellers) is priced at $450,000. A trade-in allowance of $100,000 has been offered for the existing mainframe machine.

Management has accepted the need for the new terminal facilities but is questioning the need to replace the existing mainframe with the four superminis. If the mainframe were retained, additional conversion costs of $100,000 would be incurred.

Required
a. What is the net cost of implementing the proposed distributed processing system?
b. How much would be saved by retaining the existing mainframe?
c. What would you recommend to management?

10. For three years, Sunshine Corporation has operated a minicomputer with eight passive terminals for data entry. With the growth in transaction volume, it has recently become harder and harder to keep up with the work load, and management is now considering buying six more terminals.

Additional passive terminals would cost $2,000 each, including the necessary interface hardware, and could be connected to the existing central processor. However, the system response, which is already slow, would deteriorate to an unacceptable level. The manufacturer has informed management that two solutions are available. One would be to enhance the central processor to the status of a superminicomputer at a cost of $25,000. Only minor changes to existing software would be necessary, costing about $3,000. The other option would be to replace the terminals with "intelligent" ones. These cost $6,500 each, but only 12 would be needed because each could handle a greater work load; intelligent terminals are more efficient and less dependent on central processor resources. On the other hand, substantial software modifications would be needed, costing at least $15,000. A $500 trade-in allowance could be arranged on each of the eight passive terminals. If management chose this second option, two fewer data entry clerks would be needed, enabling labor cost savings of $25,000 per year.

Required

a. Perform a detailed cost analysis of the two alternatives.

b. Advise management on the best course of action.

11. Blue State University is establishing a microcomputer laboratory for its business and computer science students. A total of 20 machines will be acquired for this purpose.

The microcomputers are sold with either one or two floppy diskette drives, which cost $300 each and can be connected to common external devices. The university administration is trying to decide whether to install the microcomputers as stand-alone units, in which case two floppy diskette drives would be required for each machine, or to connect all of them to a common fixed Winchester disk drive, in which case each machine would need only one floppy drive. The Winchester drive costs $10,000.

A further consideration affecting the decision is the acquisition of licensed program software for instructional use. If stand-alone units were operated, it would be necessary to buy a set of software for $3,000 and also to pay a royalty of $300 per copy to install the software in the other 19 machines. If the common Winchester drive is acquired, there is a good chance that only the single copy would be needed, and students could access it from the common storage device. The only uncertainty arises from a landmark lawsuit currently in progress that will decide whether software houses have the right to collect royalties on access to a single program from multiple terminals. The outcome of the case is not expected for at least nine months.

Required

a. Examine the cost, convenience, and reliability of the two alternatives.

b. What would you advise the university administration to do?

8

Computer Software

CHAPTER OUTLINE

THE NATURE OF SOFTWARE

Instructions
Programming Languages

SYSTEMS SOFTWARE

Operating System
Compilers and Interpreters
Editor
Systems Utilities

APPLICATIONS SOFTWARE

Accounting Software
Generalized Programs

END-USER SOFTWARE

Electronic Spreadsheets
Word Processing
Statistical and Modeling Packages
Graphics Packages
Data Management

DEVELOPMENT OF COMPUTER SOFTWARE

High-Level Languages
COBOL
Programming Techniques
Structured Programming

SUMMARY
BIBLIOGRAPHY
DISCUSSION QUESTIONS AND PROBLEMS

THE NATURE OF SOFTWARE

Instructions

Computer software consists of detailed instructions that direct the operation of the computer. Before software was introduced, "automatic" computers were programmed to execute a prescribed sequence of operations by means of the arrangement of electrical leads on a board resembling an old-fashioned telephone switchboard.

But virtually all general-purpose digital computers are now software driven. The sets of instructions are stored in a file encoded in an appropriate machine-readable medium and are read into the computer in the same way as are the data to be processed.

One important feature of software is the amount of detail it involves; the instructions must be spelled out precisely and completely. Instructions issued to a human being, say, in a procedure manual, can assume that the

person will exercise "common sense" or that the person will resolve any uncertainties in the light of previous experience. People can draw analogies with earlier situations and generalize from examples that they have been shown. In contrast, computers have no common sense; they have no capacity for conceptual thought; and they cannot exercise discretion at even the simplest level. One cannot show a computer an example and then tell it: "Process the next set of data in the same way." The computer has no means of abstracting the essential character of the process involved.[1] Instead, every detailed step in the program logic must be anticipated and provided for. This is not to say that computers cannot make decisions; they can, but the procedure to be adopted in choosing among the alternatives presented to it must be completely specified.

[1] Some interesting observations on the differences between the way in which people and machines "think" are given by D. R. Hofstader in "Metamagical Themas," *Scientific American*, September 1981, pp. 18–30.

210

The heart of the computer, the central processor, "understands" only machine code instructions. These instructions are presented to the control unit in binary form, and they consist of elementary commands, such as to load a data word from a specified address in main memory into one of the registers or to add two numbers together. The instructions contain an *operation code* and one or more *operands*. The operation code represents the command itself: load, add, subtract, compare, store, and so on. The operand tells the processor where to find the associated data, in a register or at a specified location in main memory. The repertoire of operation codes is called the *instruction set* for the particular processor. Simple processors, such as microprocessors, have a limited instruction set; large mainframe computers, at the other end of the spectrum, usually have an extensive one. If a desired operation code is not available on the machine being used, it must be replaced by a number of more basic ones, and the execution time will be correspondingly longer.

A machine code program consists of many instructions of the type just described. The program prescribes the instructions and the order in which they are to be executed. Normally, the processor executes the instructions in the order in which they are listed in the program. However, at a decision point, the order of the instructions may be modified according to some condition existing in the data. If two numbers are being compared, the subsequent course of the program may be different according to whether the first number is greater, less than, or equal to the second.

Although the program instructions have to be specified in minute detail, once the program is fully tested, the computer will carry out the instructions faithfully every time that the program is run. The user does not have to be concerned that the machine might suddenly decide to interpret the instructions in some other manner. This consistency is one of the great strengths of computer systems.

Programming Languages

The first computer programs were written directly in machine code. These machine code programs represented a major improvement over the hard wiring of the

computer for each job, but they still left a lot to be desired. A portion of such a program might look like the following:

```
0100101110001100110110101001110
1001101001110101011001101110001
1100110100110010110101100011000
0000000111001010111110110001010
```

It should be apparent that writing directly in machine code is tedious and that errors are easily made—but difficult to detect and correct. A great deal of effort was therefore directed toward developing easier methods of writing programs.

One of the first techniques to be developed was the use of *mnemonic codes* to represent the operation codes in the machine-level instructions. A mnemonic is something that assists the memory. Each mnemonic code corresponded to a machine code instruction and a simple translation program, called an *assembler,* was used to convert the mnemonic instructions into machine code. Some examples of mnemonic codes are as follows:

Instruction	Mnemonic	Binary Code
Load a register	LD	00001010
Add memory to register	ADD	11001010
Increment by one	INC	00110100
Compare memory locations	CMP	10101101
Subtract memory from register	SUB	10110010
Output to port	OUT	11010011
Halt	HALT	01110110

Programs using these mnemonic codes are said to be written in *symbolic* or *assembly*, language. Because of the close relationship between the codes and the machine instructions, assembly languages depend on the particular instruction set provided by the processor and its operating system. Assembly programs normally cannot be transported from one system to another. But assembly code can be highly efficient, and it is often used in the development of systems software. Most computers today are still furnished with assemblers for use in situations to which assembly programming is appropriate.

Most applications software is written in higher-level languages. These languages became available during the 1950s and 1960s, and new languages are still being developed at the present time. Most high-level languages are "procedure oriented" rather than "machine oriented." That is, they are directed to the solution of data-processing problems rather than to the operation of a given machine. Programs written in high-level languages are much easier to develop and maintain, and with minor modifications, they can be transported from one system to another.

An instruction in one of the most popular languages (COBOL) might look like the following:

```
ADD REG-HRS TO OT-HRS GIVING TOTAL-HRS
```

For the instruction to be executed by the central processor, it must first be translated into machine code. The code translation is performed by compilers and interpreters, which are discussed later. A single high-level instruction may translate into as many as 50 elementary machine code instructions. But the programmer does not have to be concerned with what the resulting machine code looks like, only that it will be executed when the program is run.

SYSTEMS SOFTWARE

Systems software consists of a set of programs that control the computer's operation, prepare application programs for execution, and supply certain generalized utility functions for the programmer. It provides an environment in which applications programs can be developed and used. Systems software is usually complex, and systems programming normally requires a higher level of expertise than does applications programming. It is written for a particular processor, and it is generally supplied by the manufacturer along with the hardware. Users rarely write systems software or even modify it. To some extent, they may be unaware of its existence; indeed, it might be said that good systems software should largely be invisible to the user—performing a necessary but unobtrusive function.

Operating System

The most important element of systems software is the operating system. The operating system schedules and controls the user's jobs, controls the internal operation of the central processor, and manages the data files and system library. Its specific functions are the following:

- To supervise the computer's overall operation.
- To load application programs and files for execution.
- To schedule the flow of tasks into and out of the central processor.
- To allocate processor and main-memory resources among the tasks being executed.
- To open and close files in secondary storage.
- To maintain communications with all peripheral devices.
- To diagnose errors and other problems and alert the human operator to their occurrence.

Operating systems help the human operator run the computer. In the earliest days of electronic computers, there were no operating systems, and the human operator had to sit at a console and manually perform all the necessary functions on banks of switches. The program would have to be loaded into specific locations in main memory; the machine would have to be instructed as to where the input data were coming from and where the output was to be directed; and the operator would monitor the execution of the job. The work was tedious and prone to errors, and, even with the relatively slow machines of that era, inefficiently used the system's resources. Today, with much faster machines and the complex modes of operation now used, it would be impossible for a human operator to control the system. To replace the manual operation of the earliest systems, simple supervisory programs were written to relieve the burden on the operator, and these supervisory programs have evolved into the operating systems of the present time.

Operating systems are designed to handle prescribed modes of processing. One designed for single-task, batch processing—in which one job is executed from start to finish without intervention by the user—has a relatively simple structure. It would load each task in turn, open the necessary files, make the assignments to the applicable peripheral devices, start the processing, and then monitor the execution until either the task was completed or a fatal error occurred that resulted in premature termination. When execution was completed, the files would be closed, and the peripheral devices were released in readiness for the next task to be executed. On the other hand, an operating system designed to handle multitask, interactive processing in real time would have to be much more complicated. In a multitasking environment, the operating system has to perform a number of crucial functions. It must load each task when appropriate system resources become available. It must assign main-memory space and ensure that each task writes to only its own portion of main memory. It must schedule the allotment of central processor time among the various tasks in accordance with priority assignments. It must "remember" which devices supply input to each task and where to route the output. It may have to supervise the temporary "roll-out" of tasks and their associated data to secondary storage when they can no longer be accommodated in main memory. It may have to supervise the continual exchange of data between main memory and secondary storage in a virtual memory system. It must monitor processing and diagnose errors for each task, while ensuring that a fatal error in one of them does not crash the whole system. And it must keep a log of the time and resources devoted to each task for accounting purposes. Modern operating systems require many person-years of development, and most of them are continually being revised to incorporate enhancements or to correct weaknesses that have come to light after going into service. Even though operating systems are normally subjected to extensive and rigorous testing, it is not uncommon for them still to have "bugs" after they are released to the user.

The operating system resides in main memory and may occupy anything from about 2 KB to 2 MB of storage. Sometimes portions of the operating system are "overlaid" and are read into main memory from secondary storage just when they are needed. Overlaid systems that reside on disk storage and whose components are loaded into main memory as needed are sometimes referred to as *disk operating systems*. Overlaying of the operating system reduces its demands on main-memory capacity but may substantially reduce execution speed.

Operating systems are usually developed for use by a particular processor, but the processor itself may be capable of supporting different peripheral devices. There must generally be a portion of the operating system assigned to handle the requirements of each type of device. Accordingly, the manufacturers often provide the operating system in modular form, allowing the user to configure the required form appropriate to the particular hardware configuration. By omitting modules that are not needed, the size of the operating systems can be kept to a minimum. The process of configuring the operating system in this manner is called *system generation,* or *SYSGEN*.

The first operating systems were written in machine code. Today, many operating systems are written in high-level languages (discussed later in this chapter) and subsequently are translated into object code in the same way as applications programs are prepared. In some cases, the system generation process involves code translation; in other cases, the required operating system is built up from object code modules.

Compilers and Interpreters

Compilers and interpreters are used to translate programs written in high-level languages into the low-level machine code instructions that are actually executed by the central processor. The original high-level program (as written by the programmer) is referred to as the *source program*, and the low-level machine code equivalent is called the *object program*. The difference between a compiler and an interpreter lies in the timing of the code translation relative to the execution of the resulting object code (see Figures 8.1 and 8.2).

An interpreter translates the source code, line by line, as the program is being executed. The code must be translated every time the program is run, which represents a poor use of central processor resources. Furthermore, both the high-level source code and the interpreter must reside in main memory during execution. This represents an inefficient use of main-memory capacity. Third, it represents a control weakness because the

FIGURE 8.1 Program code translation using an interpreter. The source code is translated line by line as the program is executed.

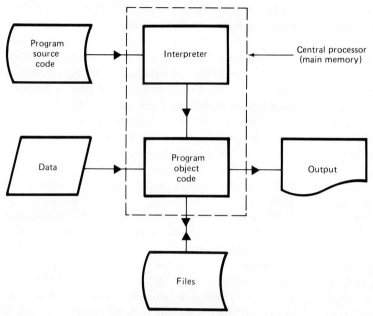

source code is accessible to the operator and thus is exposed to tampering.

Compilers translate the code only once, and production runs of the program use only the object code. Execution of compiled programs is almost always more efficient than is execution of interpreted programs, both from the point of view of main-memory utilization and in terms of processor speed. Moreover, the control weakness is avoided. It is virtually impossible to follow the logic sequence in compiled object code or to make program changes by modifying the code. Legitimate program changes can be made by modifying the source code and recompiling the program.

Interpreters are widely used on small micro- and minicomputers because of their inherent simplicity and because program development using an interpreter is usually much easier than it is with a compiler. With many interactive systems, it is possible to interrupt the execution of a job, make changes in the program, and then resume execution. Thus programs can be written and tested a few lines at a time. Also, the interpreter often tests the statements' syntax for validity as they are being entered. On small machines, particularly end-user ma-

chines, operating efficiency may not be a major objective, and the control problems probably are not important either. Finally, small machines may not have enough main-memory capacity to accommodate a compiler. Even though the combined size of the source code and the interpreter is usually greater than the size of the equivalent object code, it may be substantially less than the size of a compiler. If the only alternatives are to use an interpreter or to write programs in assembly language, most users are prepared to settle for using the interpreter.

On some small business systems, even though an interpreter is used, the source code is first translated into an *intermediate language*. This language is still at a higher level than machine code, but it is unintelligible to the user, and so program changes would be very difficult. By this means, the control weaknesses inherent in the use of an interpreter are greatly alleviated. Interpretation of the intermediate language may also be somewhat more efficient.

On large machines, interpreters are rarely used. Although ease of program development is a worthwhile objective, it is not nearly so important as efficiency of operation, particularly as the program will probably be

FIGURE 8.2   Program code translation using a compiler. The source code is compiled once and for all, producing the object code. The object code is then used in the program's subsequent execution.

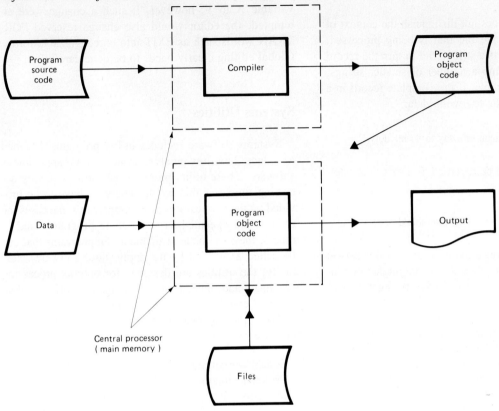

run a great number of times. Furthermore, the security characteristics offered by compiled programs are highly desirable.

Editor

Most systems software packages include an editor. The editor provides a means for retrieving, displaying, and modifying the content of a file and also a means of building certain types of files, such as program files, parameter files, and command files. New applications programs are often entered into an on-line device using the editor, and corrections and updates to the programs are made in the same way. Use of an editor to develop applications programs has almost entirely replaced the

older methods of off-line, manual editing of card decks or paper tapes.

Data files are sometimes edited, but only with considerable caution because of the obvious control implications. Safer methods of file maintenance are normally provided as part of the applications software, and fields to which data are posted as part of the routine processing of data should never be modified by direct intervention by the user. The availability of the editor to unauthorized persons could represent a major control weakness, and for this reason, it (along with most other components of systems software) should be confined to the systems development environment. The editor should never be made available to operating (and other) personnel who come in contact with ''live'' data.

The more sophisticated editors can be used for text

editing, or word-processing, purposes, but rarely do they provide the flexibility or ease of use of dedicated word-processing systems.

The editor usually does not distinguish the context of the data contained in the file that is being processed. Each record is treated as a string, and in turn the record can be broken down into a number of smaller strings, or substrings. For example, if the complete record in a certain file contained the following data:

"England expects every man this day to do his duty."

the whole record could be regarded as a string, or alternatively, the portions

"England", "expects every," "ry man this d", or "."

could equally well be regarded as strings, if this served the user's purpose. Of course, the record might not contain prose material, as in this example. It might contain only numeric data or characters that have no directly printable equivalent, such as the ASCII character "null." Editors often have special provisions made to display "unprintable" characters in some indirect manner.

The typical editor provides the following capabilities to the user:

• Add a record to the file.
• Delete a record from the file.
• Locate a specified string—either the next occurrence or all occurrences of the string.
• Change a specified string into a new specified string—again, either the next or all occurrences.
• Insert a specified new string into an existing record, displacing the "right-hand" portion of the record.
• Delete a specified string within an existing record.
• Insert part (or all) of another file within the file currently being processed.

The capability for changing all occurrences of a certain string to a different form is a very powerful (and potentially dangerous) capability. Referred to as *global editing*, it could be used (as one idealist has suggested) to change all occurrences of the word *hate* in a text file

to *love*. Applied to a file containing a FORTRAN program, it could be used to change all occurrences of the variable X to Y; however, if such a change were attempted, the editor would also change reserved FORTRAN words such as EXIT into unrecognizable forms. Global editing clearly needs to be done carefully.

Systems Utilities

Systems software includes utility programs designed to reduce the effort involved in developing applications software. These utility programs perform frequently occurring functions that would otherwise have to be provided by the applications programmer. In some cases the utilities are executed as stand-alone programs, and in others, they are made available as subprograms that can be called as needed by the applications software. Normally, the utilities are designed for optimal processing efficiency and, indeed, may be much more efficient than any that could be written by the average programmer.

The typical library of system utilities provided with business computer systems might include the following:

• Screen formatting
• Printer formatting
• File copying
• File sorting and merging
• Data management
• Telecommunications support
• Query languages
• Report generators
• Language extensions supporting compilers and interpreters

Modern screen-formatting utilities are quite sophisticated and have made it much easier to develop screen forms. Sometimes, several alternative forms can be stored and retrieved as needed to support particular interactive processes: file maintenance, transaction entry, and so forth. Many systems now provide the capability for accepting user-specified forms designed to match the corresponding paper documents such as invoices or accounts payable vouchers. Printer-formatting utilities have been developed to take advantage of the sophisticated technologies of modern printers. One popular software package, used in conjunction with dot-matrix printers, has the lines of print run down instead of across the page, which facilitates the output of wide spreadsheets. Other types of software, usually referred to as *page description languages*, provide for random access composition of output to page printers.

Utilities for copying, sorting, and merging files are frequently used in systems with conventional file structures. These are particularly useful because the associated functions are so important to business data processing. Data management utilities range in capability from very simple ones, which do little more than establish files with prescribed characteristics, to sophisticated data base management systems. Data base management systems are discussed in Chapter 9. Telecommmunications software controls the access to networks and the flow of data through the associated channels.

Query languages allow users to interrogate the data base, using ''plain English'' commands entered into an interactive terminal device. Report generators allow users to output the results of a data base query, or some other activity, in an effective, pleasing format. Headings, legends, and other textual material can be included as needed. Query languages and report generators are used in decision support systems. Language extensions supplement the repertoire of commands ordinarily provided by a compiler or interpreter and may extend the applicability of compilers or interpreters to areas where they were not originally designed to be used. An example is string-manipulation functions to support a FORTRAN compiler.

APPLICATIONS SOFTWARE

The applications software is the software most visible to the user. It performs the tasks in which the user is directly interested. In contrast, systems software operates ''behind the scenes,'' so to speak; and although informed users understand that it is necessary for the computer's operation, it does not appear to contribute to the actual processing of information.

Accounting Software

Accounting software is normally developed in the form of packages corresponding to the familiar accounting applications:

- General ledger
- Payroll
- Order processing
- Accounts receivable
- Purchasing
- Accounts payable
- Inventory management
- Fixed-asset management
- Sales analysis
- Budgeting
- Standard costing
- Job costing

In turn, each application is often divided into program modules. For example, the general ledger application might be divided into the following seven modules:

- Maintenance of the chart of accounts (entry of new account numbers, deletion of unwanted ones, and so forth)
- Journal entry
- Transaction posting
- Computation of net income
- Printing of journal and ledger listings
- Printing of financial statements
- End-of-period closing

These modules perform identifiable processing tasks and might correspond to the selections on the general ledger main menu.

The accounting applications and their component program modules are normally integrated with one another, reflecting the sharing of data and the flow of data from one to another. Because of this integration, the systems design must incorporate controls to ensure that the modules are run in the correct sequence, for example, to ensure that posting is performed before the financial statements are printed. Sometimes sequence controls of this type are built into the menu selection process. Additional controls must be in place in a multiuser system so as to avoid conflicts among several users who may be working concurrently with the same application. It is necessary, for instance, to prevent one user from posting transactions to the master file while another is carrying out file maintenance. On the other hand, the situation in which several users simultaneously enter transactions may not be a problem, and indeed this is a common situation.

Generalized Programs

Most applications software is written for a particular purpose such as the calculation of payroll deductions, input of general journal entries, and preparation of inventory reorder reports. When a program for a different purpose is needed, either completely new code is written or an earlier program is modified to adapt it to the new requirements. But the development of new progams— or even their modification—can be time-consuming and expensive. Generalized software offers the possibility of reducing this development time and cost.

Some generalized programs perform the desired processing tasks themselves, thereby taking the place of dedicated applications software. Tables of instructions residing in parameter files tailor the programs to the particular sets of requirements. Table-driven programs are relatively simple but inefficient because of their processing "overhead." Such programs are suitable for situations requiring maximum flexibility but have only limited use. Their most important applications are to design prototyping and auditing. Prototypes allow users to experiment with application designs before they are "cast in stone." And auditors are increasingly using generalized audit software to tap into clients' accounting systems. Record and file formats, as well as processing idiosyncrasies, can be emulated by the software, enabling the auditors to access data and verify samples of a client's processing activities.

Other types of generalized programs produce the program source code, taking the place of the human programmer. Such programs are often referred to as *software generators* or *code generators*. They produce the source code in response to sets of specifications, but once the code is generated, it is compiled and executed in the same way as is code written by a human programmer. Machine-generated programs are much more efficient than are table-driven programs because they do not have the processing overhead, and sometimes their operating efficiency is even higher than can be achieved with conventionally written programs.

The objective of generalized programs is to provide error-free programs in the shortest possible time and with the least expenditure of effort. The additional objective of code generators is to provide highly efficient programs that can compete with the products of human programming. Code generators are expensive to acquire or to develop, but the high initial investment can be amortized over a potentially large number of subsequent uses; and the incremental cost of producing a given application is very low. As the labor costs of human programming continue to rise relative to other costs of computerized information processing, the use of these types of generalized programs is likely to increase substantially.

END-USER SOFTWARE

End users who operate interactive terminals or personal computers sometimes write their own software. But usually they buy canned packages developed and marketed with the end user in mind. An impressive array of canned packages is now in common use, including

- Electronic spreadsheets
- Word processing packages
- Statistical and modeling packages
- Graphics packages
- Data base management packages

"Integrated packages" are also popular, in which several functions are combined. The various functions can be performed in turn on the same data, and sometimes the results of two or more can be displayed simultaneously on the screen or combined for output to a printer.

End-user software lies somewhere between the extremes of systems and applications software. Like applications software, it is normally dependent for its execution on the environment of an operating system. On the other hand, usually it does not perform an actual user-oriented task but simply provides a framework into which the user can enter instructions to perform the desired task. In this latter respect, end-user software resembles programming languages and language translators, albeit ones tailored to specific classes of user-related tasks. It also has some of the characterisitics of table-driven generalized software. The popularity of these packages demonstrates that the average business professional—including the accountant—is not averse to programming, but demands a kind of programming that is more user-friendly than are the conventional programming languages.

End-user software is developing so rapidly and is becoming so sophisticated that many people question the continued relevance of more traditional applications software. End-user software can be deployed quickly and effectively to solve simple information-processing problems, without the traditional dependence on computer professionals. A whole accounting system could be built using the more comprehensive packages available today. However, the effort in doing so would be substantial, and the system's operation would be much less efficient than that of comparable programs written in a conventional high-level language. End-user software, like other kinds of generalized software, requires considerable processing overhead. It is not intended for high-volume production operation, and attempts to use it for that purpose are rarely successful. End-user packages are designed for exploratory situations requiring flexibility but using low volumes of data; that is the role that they should play, and production data processing should be left to conventional applications software.

Electronic Spreadsheets

Electronic spreadsheets were first made available for microcomputers in the late 1970s, and in a few years became one of the most popular types of end-user software. To date, over a million copies of spreadsheet programs have been sold, and new uses for them are being discovered almost daily.

The electronic spreadsheet provides the machine-readable analog of the tabular paper worksheet. In its simplest form it consists of a matrix of cells in which data can be written and manipulated (Figure 8.3). The row and column coordinates of individual cells are usually expressed as letter–number combinations, such as A10 or E5. Typically, the cells' contents can be numerical values, narrative data such as legends or headings, or formulas for performing arithmetical and/or logical operations on the values in other cells. When an operation is performed, the result is written in the cell where the formula appears. Spreadsheet formulas represent a simple kind of declarative programming, and the instructions or formulas are entered in a form reminiscent of statements in BASIC or FORTRAN, for example,

$$+E5-2*C2/H19+5.2$$

FIGURE 8.3   Electronic spreadsheet. Numbers, captions, and formulas can be entered into specified cells.

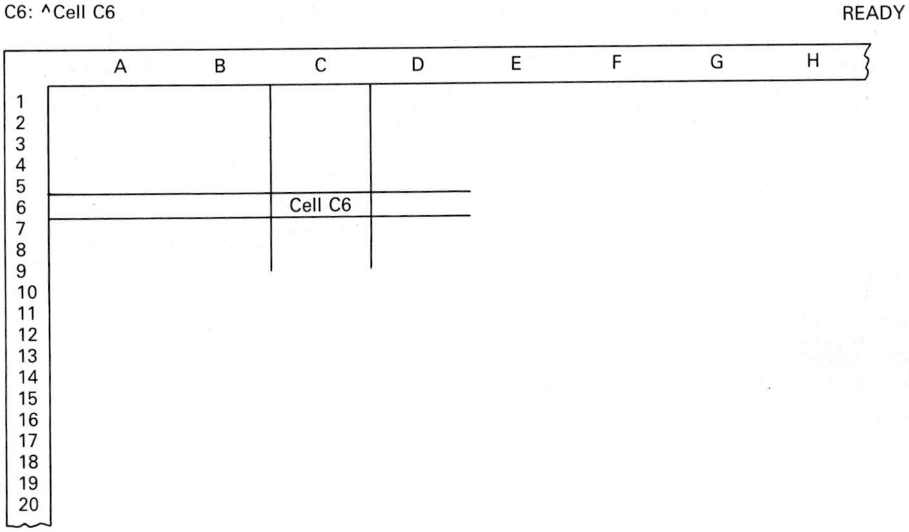

C6: ^Cell C6   READY

The number of mathematical functions available has increased dramatically since spreadsheets first came on the market. The leading products offer a range of statistical functions (including linear regression formulas), trigonometric functions, and compound-interest formulas. Other functions allow for the manipulation of data files included in the spreadsheet, including table look-up, sorting, and merging. Whole applications can be assembled using formulas and canned functions. And if multiple keystrokes are required to implement the applications, the instructions can be accumulated into a command file, or *macro*, and executed by a single keystroke.

One of the most common applications of electronic spreadsheets is to budgeting. Data for a base year can be entered, and then various assumptions concerning growth rates and other trends can be explored. Figures for gross margin, net income, return on investment, or earnings per share can easily be produced and are automatically adjusted when an input number or a mathematical function is changed. An example of the use of a spreadsheet for budgeting is shown in Figure 8.4. Figure 8.4(a) shows the worksheet itself, and Figure 8.4(b) lists the content of the cells, including the associated formulas.

Word Processing

Word processing is much older than personal computing; dedicated word processors date from the late 1960s. But the widespread availability of word-processing packages for microcomputers, and the subsequent development of similar software for use on systems involving interactive terminals has led to a revolution in the way that accountants and other professionals do their work. Whereas word processing was once regarded as a function to enhance the efficiency of office workers, it is now accepted as an essential tool for business people of all types and at all levels in the organization. Accountants in particular have found word processing to be a highly effective tool for creating engagement letters, correspondence, reports, proposals, quotations, and many other types of material. Material can be placed in secondary storage for later retrieval and further editing,

and successive drafts can be printed, each in clean-copy form. Although accountants may not be expert typists, their keyboard skills increase with experience, and working with a word processor avoids delays and communication problems in the typing pool.

Word-processing software permits the creation, editing, and printing of textual material. Full-screen editing allows the insertion, deletion, and alteration of individual words, as well as the formatting and manipulation of whole paragraphs or pages. Two main groups of word-processing software have emerged. One, typified by packages such as WordStar, are menu driven, and the commands are listed in menus and submenus that are displayed on the screen, in a "window" separate from the text. The other, typified by WordPerfect, are function-key driven; the commands are chosen from combinations of function keys and often are assisted by a cardboard or plastic template laid over the keyboard.

Special features usually permit text automatically to be underscored, printed in boldface, centered on the line, and right-justified. Other features are available in some packages, including drawing frames around portions of the text and changing from one character font to another—for example, from roman to italics, or from English to Arabic—or from one color to another. Such features have developed in parallel with advances in printer technology.

Standard "boiler plate" can be inserted into a document from secondary storage, and sometimes portions of the document being prepared and the boiler-plate file can be displayed in adjacent windows on the screen. Many software packages permit names, addresses, and salutations from a separate file of addressees to be inserted into form letters. If the letters are printed on a letter-quality printer, they look like individually prepared personal correspondence.

Some word-processing packages include a machine-readable English dictionary and the provision for verifying spelling in a text file. A further development of this capability is an on-line thesaurus that can display alternative words with the same general meaning. Packages are also available that can test for writing style and "readability." Some packages allow simple computations to be done on data in the text or columns of data to be sorted. Integrated software also permits portions

FIGURE 8.4 Simple example of spreadsheet usage. (Lotus 1-2-3; a product of Lotus Development Corporation.)

(a) Printout of the spreadsheet

```
                 ACCUMULATION OF MANUFACTURING COSTS

     Input Area:

     Purchases (net)                  $100,000.00
     Labor cost                        $45,000.00
     Overhead cost incurred            $39,000.00
     Application rate (% of labor)          80.0%
     Sales (net)                      $300,000.00
     Operating expense                 $90,000.00

     Inventories:                     Beg. balance End. balance
     Raw materials                     $30,000.00   $40,000.00
     Work in process                   $60,000.00   $50,000.00
     Finished goods                    $40,000.00   $50,000.00


     Output Area:

     STATEMENT OF COST OF GOODS MANUFACTURED

     Beginning work in process                      $60,000.00
     Direct materials:
        Beginning raw materials       $30,000.00
        Purchases                     100,000.00
                                    --------------
        Total                         130,000.00
        Ending raw materials           40,000.00     90,000.00
                                    --------------
     Direct labor                                    45,000.00
     Manufacturing overhead                          36,000.00
                                                  --------------
     Total                                          231,000.00
     Ending work in process                          50,000.00
                                                  --------------
     Cost of goods manufactured                    $181,000.00
                                                  ==============


     INCOME STATEMENT

     Sales                                          $300,000.00
     Cost of goods sold:
        Beginning finished goods      $40,000.00
        Cost of goods manufactured    181,000.00
                                    --------------
        Total                         221,000.00
        Ending finished goods          50,000.00
                                    --------------
        Unadjusted C.G.S.             171,000.00
        Under (over) applied overhead   3,000.00    174,000.00
                                                  --------------
     Gross margin                                   126,000.00
     Operating expense                               90,000.00
                                                  --------------
     Net income before tax                          $36,000.00
                                                  ==============


     Documentation:

     This template calculates cost of goods manufactured and
     net income.
     All materials and labor costs are considered to be direct.
     Overhead is applied on the basis of direct labor cost.
```

FIGURE 8.4 (continued)

(b) Printout of cell contents

```
A1:     '               ACCUMULATION OF MANUFACTURING COSTS
A3:     'Input Area:
A5:     'Purchases (net)
C5:     (C2) 100000
A6:     'Labor cost
C6:     (C2) 45000
A7:     'Overhead cost incurred
C7:     (C2) 39000
A8:     'Application rate (% of labor)
C8:     (P1) 0.8
A9:     'Sales (net)
C9:     (C2) 300000
A10:    'Operating expense
C10:    (C2) 90000
A12:    'Inventories:
C12:    (C2) 'Beg. balance
D12:    (C2) 'End. balance
A13:    'Raw materials
C13:    (C2) 30000
D13:    (C2) 40000
A14:    'Work in process
C14:    (C2) 60000
D14:    (C2) 50000
A15:    'Finished goods
C15:    (C2) 40000
D15:    (C2) 50000
A18:    'Output Area:
A20:    'STATEMENT OF COST OF GOODS MANUFACTURED
A22:    'Beginning work in process
D22:    (C2) +C14
A23:    'Direct materials:
A24:    '  Beginning raw materials
C24:    (C2) +C13
A25:    '  Purchases
A25:    +C5
C26:    \-
A27:    '  Total
C27:    @SUM(C24..C25)
A28:    '  Ending raw materials
C28:    +D13
D28:    +C27-C28
C29:    \-
A30:    'Direct labor
D30:    +C6
A31:    'Manufacturing overhead
D31:    +C6*C8
D32:    \-
A33:    'Total
D33:    @SUM(D22..D31)
A34:    'Ending work in process
D34:    +D14
D35:    \-
A36:    'Cost of goods manufactured
D36:    (C2) +D33-D34
D37:    \=
A39:    'INCOME STATEMENT
```

FIGURE 8.4 (continued)

```
   A41:  'Sales
   D41:  (C2) +C9
   A42:  'Cost of goods sold:
   A43:  '  Beginning finished goods
   C43:  (C2) +C15
   A44:  '  Cost of goods manufactured
   C44:  +D36
   C45:  \-
   A46:  '   Total
   C46:  @SUM(C43..C44)
   A47:  '  Ending finished goods
   C47:  +D15
   C48:  \-
   A49:  '  Unadjusted C.G.S.
   C49:  +C46-C47
   A50:  '  Under (over) applied
   C50:  +C7-D31
   D50:  +C49+C50
   C51:  \-
   D51:  \-
   A52:  'Gross margin
   D52:  +D41-D50
   A53:  'Operating expense
   D53:  +C10
   D54:  \-
   A55:  'Net income before tax
   D55:  (C2) +D52-D53
   D56:  \=
   A59:  'Documentation:
   A61:  'This template calculates cost of goods manufactured and net income.
   A62:  'All materials and labor costs are considered to be direct.
   A63:  'Overhead is applied on the basis of direct labor cost.
```

of spreadsheets, charts and graphs, and other material to be incorporated into text files and interspersed with interpretive commentary.

Statistical and Modeling Packages

Statistical packages provide for the computation of various statistical parameters from a body of input data. Sales analysis, market surveys, quality control, and audit testing all are typical applications of such computations. In some cases, the mean, standard deviation, skewness, and curtosis (flatness) of a given sample distribution are needed. In other cases, inferences of population parameters or forecasts of future values are required. Sometimes, regression models are used to determine the correlation among related sets of variables, such as costs and volume levels.

Modeling packages typically extend the range of applicability of spreadsheet and statistical packages. More extensive forecasting techniques may be incorporated, and simulations of realistic business situations may be possible.

Graphics Packages

Graphics packages are becoming popular as aids to the output and presentation of information. Such packages typically accept input data from a file or directly from a computation such as a statistical computation or a spreadsheet analysis and output the data as a graph, bar chart, or pie chart. The output may be displayed on a screen or printed on paper. Some software packages allow the graphics output to be animated. For example, they may show portions of a chart being built up step by step, sometimes synchronized with an accompanying audio commentary. Unfortunately (for obvious reasons), the output cannot be captured on paper. But an animated screen display, with or without audio, can have a dramatic impact on the viewing audience.

The quality of the output depends on the resolution of the screen or printers; low resolution devices produce graphs and charts that may have ''steps'' in them. The quality of printed legends and titles may also be poor on low resolution devices. Specialized graphics terminals or printers, or flat-bed plotters, offer the highest quality and are suitable for preparing ''presentation-quality'' graphics output. Color monitors and ink-jet printers permit graphics material to be output in a range of colors.

Some simple examples of computer-generated graphics material were presented in Chapter 4. Figure 8.5 shows some more ambitious examples.

Data Management

Data management packages allow the user to set up records and files and to use them to store and retrieve data. A businessperson might establish a client file, recording the name and address, date of contact, a summary of related background information, and even account balances. Simple ''programs'' can often be developed to perform posting and other tasks.

Data management packages can be classified into categories according to their degree of sophistication. ''File management'' packages usually are based on conventional files and may permit retrieval of data by only one key and in a single configuration. ''Data base'' packages

FIGURE 8.5 Examples of computer graphics output.

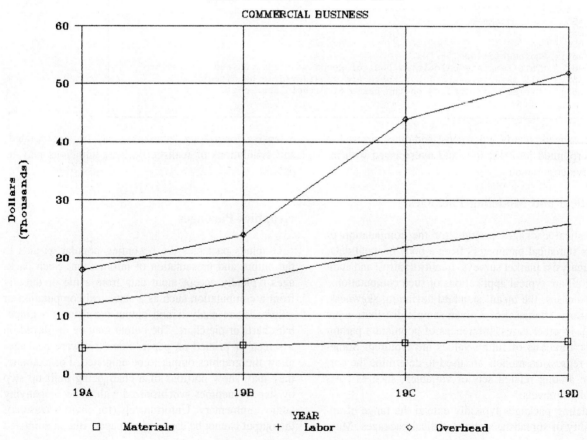

(unless, as is sometimes the case, they are misleadingly labeled) incorporate a data base management system (DBMS) of some level of capability, permitting retrieval by multiple keys and extraction of data elements in optional, user-defined configurations. A few packages are available based on relational data structures, allowing the user to "see" the data in various flexible tabular formats. Programmable data base packages store program "macros" for mathematically manipulating the data.

Data management packages often include built-in query languages and report generators. The query languages allow the user to interrogate the data base and retrieve information. Small amounts of data can be viewed on the screen, and larger volumes of data can be sent to the printer. Figure 8.6 shows a simple example of data query using a popular relational data base package.

Many packages provide for output of data—to the screen or printer—according to user-defined forms. Formatting information is supplied by the user, either before or at execution time, and formats can be written to secondary storage for subsequent use. Built-in report generators may allow a high degree of formatting flexibility, including report, page and column headings, pagination, footnotes, insertion of several levels of subtotals, and multiple table look-ups. A simple example was shown in Figure 4.17. Report generators are valuable in deci-

FIGURE 8.5 (continued)

TENNESSEE PLANT

TREND IN COST ELEMENTS

FIGURE 8.5 (continued)

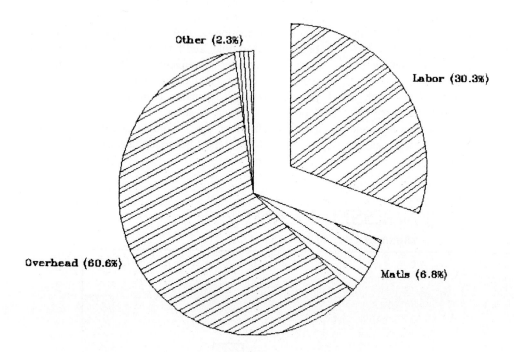

TENNESSEE PLANT

COST BREAKDOWN FOR 19D

sion support applications. Professional-looking reports can be generated quickly and on a custom basis; the particular report may never have been prepared before—and may never be needed again—but it can be prepared in a pleasing, effective format.

DEVELOPMENT OF COMPUTER SOFTWARE

High-Level Languages

Programming languages provide the framework, or format, in which applications software (and systems software) is written. Today, most applications software is written in "high-level" languages in which the instructions, or commands, are readily understood by the programmer. The earliest electronic computers were programmed in machine code, which was enormously tedious to write and almost impossible to modify after it had been written. High-level languages permit the source code to be developed in a form oriented to the problem to be solved, and the machine or object code to be produced automatically using a compiler or interpreter.

Some high-level langauages in common use are

BASIC
FORTRAN
COBOL
RPG
ALGOL
Ada
PL/1
Pascal
C Language

FIGURE 8.6 Data retrieval using the query capability of a data-base management system. (Rbase 5000; a product of Microrim Corporation.)

```
R>SELECT Employee Fstname MI Lstname Net=S FROM Master WHERE Dept eq 123
   Employee        Fstname          MI        Lstname           Net
  ------------   ---------------  ---------  ----------------  -----------------
   123456789     Ken              G          Black              $10,701.00
   345678901     Willy            B          Baker               $8,625.00
   567890123     Jake             J          Johnson            $12,430.00
   789012345     Thomas           G          Morgan              $8,245.00
   890123456     Jackie           C          Hickson             $7,790.00
  ------------   ---------------  ---------  ----------------  -----------------
                                                                $47,791.00
   R>
```

(a) Selection of specified columns from a table, using the WHERE clause, and insertion of totals. The query language provided in this package is utilitarian, and offers minimal formatting capability. Extensive formatting flexibility is provided in the report generator, as illustrated in Chapter 4.

```
R>SELECT Lstname MI Fstname Dept Rate FROM Master SORTED BY Lstname
   Lstname          MI        Fstname          Dept       Rate
  ---------------  --------  ---------------  ---------  -----------------
   Baker            B         Willy            123         $10.00
   Baxter           M         Lillian          678         $12.50
   Black            G         Ken              123         $12.50
   Hickson          C         Jackie           123          $9.50
   Johnson          J         Jake             123         $14.00
   Morgan           G         Thomas           123         $10.50
   Prince           W         Kirk             234         $14.00
   Robbins          O         Jill             234         $13.75
   Thomas           P         Susan            234         $11.50
   Williams         H         Gail             456          $9.00
   R>
```

(b) Selection of specified columns from a table and sorting of records.

In addition, numerous languages have been developed for special purposes or for use on particular hardware configurations. Of the languages listed, BASIC, COBOL, and RPG are the most familiar in business applications. FORTRAN and ALGOL are used extensively in scientific and engineering fields, but they have also been used in some business data-processing applications. Ada is a new scientical language and has been prescribed for use in all contracts administered by the Department of Defense. So far it has not been used for business purposes. PL/1 and Pascal are multipurpose languages. **C** language was originally developed for writing systems software, but more recently it has proved to be useful for business applications software. BASIC was originally developed as an interpretive language, although compiler versions are now available. All the other languages listed are compiler-oriented languages.

The characteristics of a programming language that business users need are

- Ability to accept both numeric and string variables
- Adequate precision of numeric representation and computation
- Flexibility in input, internal, and output formatting
- Use of mnemonic variable names

- A relatively high level of self-documentation
- Clarity of program logic
- Transportability from one machine to another

COBOL

COBOL, an acronym for "Common Business Oriented Language," was designed specifically for use as a business language, and it meets all of these requirements. COBOL handles numeric and string variables; in fact it treats *all* variables as though they are string variables. However, it provides "string arithmetic" routines to perform arithmetical manipulation of those designated as numeric. In string arithmetic, elementary functions such as multiplication are expanded into a series of manipulations performed on the decimal characters comprising the string. String arithmetic is computationally inefficient, but it is independent of the processor's word length; accordingly, high precision can be achieved even on a machine with a relatively short word length. Similarly, numbers can be represented in working storage to any desired degree of precision.

COBOL can represent not just the values of data elements but also their format. It does this by the use of "picture" clauses that can represent many punctuation styles. For example, the clause

```
PIC S9(5)V99
```

refers to a numeric data element with a total length of nine digits, five to the left of the decimal (which is an implied decimal in the corresponding file record). Leading zeros are to be eliminated, whereas the two digits to the right of the decimal are to be printed regardless of the number's value. If the value of the number is one thousand or more, a comma will be placed between the thousands and the hundreds. Almost any of these formatting requirements could be changed by modifying the picture clause. Furthermore, a dollar sign (either a fixed or a floating one) could be prefixed to the value, or the suffix DR or CR could be appended to the value.

COBOL accepts relatively long variable names, up to 30 characters in length, and thereby provides considerable flexibility for mnemonic representation. A "mnemonic" variable name is one that reminds the programmer what the variable stands for. An example is EXPENSE (as distinct, say, from just X). Compound variables can also be used, as long as they do not contain blanks, for example:

```
EMPLOYEE-NUMBER
YESTERDAYS-DATE
TOTAL-SALES
```

COBOL provides a high level of self-documentation; the commands resemble English descriptions of the processing operations. For example, the statement for performing a cost extension could be written as

```
MULTIPLY UNIT-COST BY
QUANTITY GIVING EXTENDED-COST.
```

Because of this self-documentation, the logic of COBOL programs is easily followed, and accompanying narrative documentation need not be as extensive as with most other programming languages. Figure 8.7 shows part of a COBOL program, illustrating the nature of the language.

An important feature of COBOL not found in other languages such as BASIC or FORTRAN is its structure. COBOL programs are divided into four sections, or "divisions":

- Identification division
- Environment division
- Data division
- Procedure division

The identification division shows the programmer's name and describes the circumstances of the program's development. The environment division shows the machine or hardware configuration on which the program is intended to be run. The data division lists the variable names and their attributes and allocates working space within main memory. The procedure division consists of the commands to be performed on the variables. The separation of the data and procedure divisions makes the COBOL programs clearer and makes subsequent program maintenance easier.

Finally, COBOL is one of the most transportable languages. The COBOL language was designed by a com-

FIGURE 8.7 Part of a COBOL program.

```
001 IDENTIFICATION DIVISION
002 PROGRAM-ID .....
003 AUTHOR .....
010 ENVIRONMENT DIVISION.
011 CONFIGURATION SECTION.
012 SOURCE-COMPUTER .....
013 OBJECT-COMPUTER .....
014 INPUT-OUTPUT SECTION.
015 FILE-CONTROL.
016     SELECT PAYROLL-FILE
017         ASSIGN TO .....
018     SELECT PRINT-FILE
019         ASSIGN TO .....

021 DATA DIVISION.
022 FILE SECTION.
023 FD  PAYROLL-FILE
024     RECORD CONTAINS 90 CHARACTERS
025     LABEL RECORDS ARE STANDARD
026     DATA-RECORD IS INPUT-OUTPUT.
027 01  INPUT-RECORD
028     02  FILLER
029 FD  PRINT-FILE
030     RECORD CONTAINS 132 CHARACTERS

061 01  TM-MARRIED-TAX-TABLE REDEFINES MARRIED-TAX-TABLE-VALUES.
062     02  TM-MARRIED-TAX-TABLE-ENTRY OCCURS 8 TIMES INDEXED BY TM-INDEX.
063         03  TM-LOW-VALUE              PIC S9(5).
064         03  TM-HIGH-VALUE             PIC S9(5).
065         03  TM-BASE-AMOUNT            PIC S9(4).
066         03  TM-PERCENTAGE             PIC SV99.
067 01  WS-FLAGS.
068     02  WS-EOF-FLAG                   PIC X(3).

124 01  DL-DETAIL-LINE.
125     02  DL-SOCIAL-SECURITY-NUMBER.
126         03  DL-SS-NO-1               PIC X(3).
127         03  FILLER                   PIC X(1)      VALUE "-".
128         03  DL-SS-NO-2               PIC X(2).
129         03  FILLER                   PIC X(1)      VALUE "-".
130         03  DL-SS-NO-3               PIC X(4).
131     02  FILLER                       PIC X(2)      VALUE SPACES.
132     02  DL-EMPLOYEE-NAME             PIC X(18).
133     02  FILLER                       PIC X(2)      VALUE SPACES.
134     02  DL-MARITAL-STATUS            PIC X(1).
135     02  FILLER                       PIC X(2)      VALUE SPACES.
136     02  DL-NUMBER-EXEMPTIONS         PIC 9(2).
137     02  FILLER                       PIC X(2)      VALUE SPACES.
138     02  DL-EARNINGS-THIS PERIOD      PIC ZZZ,ZZZ.99.
```

229

FIGURE 8.7 (continued)

```
149 PROCEDURE DIVISION.
150 000-PROCESS-PAYROLL-SECTION.
151     PERFORM 100-OPEN-FILES.
152     PERFORM 110-INITIALIZE-VARIABLES.
153     PERFORM 200-PROCESS-INPUT-RECORDS UNTIL END-OF-FILE.
154     PERFORM 370-WRITE-TRAILER-PAGE.
155     PERFORM 400-CLOSE-FILES.
156     STOP RUN.
157 100-OPEN-FILES.
158     OPEN INPUT PAYROLL-FILE OUTPUT PRINT-FILE.
159 110-INITIALIZE-VARIABLES.
160     MOVE "NO" TO WS-EOF-FLAG.
161     MOVE ZERO TO WS-PAGE-COUNT.
162     ADD 1 WS-LINES-PER-PAGE GIVING WS-LINES-USED.
163     MOVE "YES" TO WS-1ST-RECORD-FLAG.
164 200-PROCESS-INPUT-RECORDS.
165     IF WS-LINES-USED IS NOT LESS THAN WS-LINES-PER-PAGE
166         PERFORM 350-WRITE-HEADINGS.
167     PERFORM 300-READ-INPUT-RECORD.
168     MOVE INPUT-RECORD TO PR-PAYROLL-RECORD.
169     IF NOT END-OF-FILE
170         PERFORM 210-WRITE-DETAIL-LINES.
171     ELSE NEXT SENTENCE.
172 210-WRITE-DETAIL-LINES.
173     MOVE "NO" TO WS-1ST-RECORD-FLAG.
174     MOVE PR-SS-NO-1 TO DL-SS-NO-1.
175     MOVE PR-SS-NO-2 TO DL-SS-NO-1.

191 220-COMPUTE-FEDERAL-TAX.
192     MULTIPLY PR-EARNINGS-THIS-PERIOD BY WS-PAY-PERIODS-PER-YEAR
193         GIVING WS-ANNUALIZED-EARNINGS.
194     MULTIPLY PR-NUMBER-EXEMPTIONS BY WS-PERSONAL-EXEMPTION
195         GIVING WS-STANDARD-DEDUCTION.
196     SUBTRACT WS-STANDARD-DEDUCTION FROM WS-ANNUALIZED-EARNINGS
197         GIVING WS-TAXABLE-EARNINGS WS-ADJUSTED-EARNINGS.
198     IF SINGLE PERFORM 230-COMPUTE-SINGLE-TAX.
199     ELSE PERFORM 250-COMPUTE-MARRIED-TAX.
200     DIVIDE WS-FEDERAL-TAX-AMOUNT BY WS-PAY-PERIODS-PER-YEAR
201         GIVING WS-FEDERAL-TAX-AMOUNT ROUNDED.
202 230-COMPUTE-SINGLE-TAX.
203     MOVE "NO" TO WS-ENTRY-FOUND-FLAG.
204     PERFORM 240-LOOKUP-SINGLE-TABLE
205         VARYING TS-INDEX FROM 1 BY 1 UNTIL ENTRY-FOUND
206         OR TS-INDEX IS GREATER THAN WS-MAX-ENTRIES.

235 260-LOOKUP-MARRIED-TABLE.
236     IF WS-TAXABLE-EARNINGS IS GREATER THAN TM-LOW-VALUE(TM-INDEX)
237     AND WS-TAXABLE-EARNINGS IS NOT GREATER THAN TM-HIGH-VALUE (TM-INDEX)
238         MOVE "YES" TO WS-ENTRY-FOUND-FLAG.
```

FIGURE 8.7 **(continued)**

```
264 380-WRITE-REPORT-LINE.
265     WRITE PRINT-RECORD AFTER ADVANCING ONE PAGE.
266     ADD WS-LINE-SPACING TO WS-LINES-USED.
267 400-CLOSE-FILES.
268     CLOSE PAYROLL-FILE PRINT-FILE.
```

mittee of systems professionals, the Conference on Data Systems Languages, and it is subject to standards promulgated by the American National Standards Institute (ANSI). Compilers, designed for a wide variety of machines, conform to these standards, and consequently, programs can normally be transported from one machine to another with minimal or no modification. This feature provides confidence that once written and tested, programs can survive the enhancement or replacement of computer hardware, even replacement by hardware marketed by a different vendor.

One disadvantage of COBOL is the length of the programs. The program source code is typically long because of the ''wordiness'' of the language, and the object code is also typically longer than it would be if written in another language. A second disadvantage is that it is difficult or impossible to change the program at execution time. For example, COBOL would not permit a record field length to be changed in accordance with the value of an input variable, whereas this would be quite simple in FORTRAN. Generalized programs for business use, in which the field lengths are not known in advance, are better served by FORTRAN (and by certain other languages) than by COBOL. Another disadvantage is that COBOL, constrained as it is by the ANSI standards, has been slow to adapt to new technological advances in computer hardware. Consequently many people regard it as obsolete.

But despite these disadvantages, COBOL has become the dominant language for business use, accounting for roughly 80 percent of all business software. Not least because of the huge investment in COBOL programming, the business community has been largely unreceptive to the claims of newer, and perhaps superior, languages. So far COBOL has resisted the inroads of competing languages and seems likely to remain in widespread use for some time to come.

Programming Techniques

Some computer programs perform quite simple tasks, and others may perform very complicated ones. But regardless of the degree of complexity, the development of a program should be a four-step process:

- Development of specifications
- Coding of the program
- Testing and debugging
- Documentation

Program specifications form an interface between the programming phase and the overall systems design. The specifications identify the program's intent, inputs, processes, files, and outputs. Program specifications also usually describe the proposed program structure and logic. This description may be expressed as a program flowchart, and Figure 8.8 shows one for a program module designed to produce a file listing. But today more modern tools are available, one being the Nassi–Schneiderman diagram, illustrated in Figure 8.9 for the same example. Nassi–Schneiderman diagrams lend themselves well to programming in COBOL, and they have the advantage of being easy to prepare and modify. Other tools, including the popular HIPO method, are discussed in Chapter 13.

Coding converts the specifications into program source code. Sometimes a program will be written in assembly code or even directly in machine language. But more commonly a high-level language such as COBOL will be used. The high-level source code will subsequently be translated into machine, or object, code by means of an interpreter or compiler.

Debugging consists of correcting errors in the program. Errors are either syntax errors or errors in program logic. Syntax errors prevent the reliable translation of the program into object code and are usually caught by

FIGURE 8.8 Program flowchart for a file-listing program.

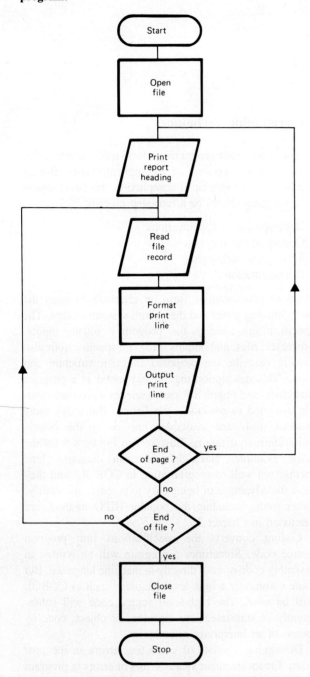

the interpreter or compiler. Errors in logic may survive the translation phase but emerge at run time, either causing premature termination of processing or resulting in erroneous output. Testing seeks to validate not just the coding logic but also the preceding design work. Testing should be systematic, using specially prepared test data simulating a broad spectrum of operating conditions. Invalid as well as valid data should be included to test the program's response to what will inevitably occur from time to time under production conditions. Along with the test data, the anticipated output should be identified for comparison with the actual output generated by the program. The program should be tested by someone other than the programmer. This separation of duties is necessary to maintain objectivity. Finally, the test results should be reviewed by a supervisor responsible for determining that the program meets the established specifications.

The program documentation normally is prepared in parallel with the other steps listed and provides a permanent record of the program's development. This documentation should include a copy of the specifications, flowcharts and other visual aids, listings, and copies of test results. Documentation is discussed in more detail in Chapter 13.

Structured Programming

Considerable attention has been given in recent years to "structured programming" techniques. Structured programming has two basic concepts. The first is a modular approach to software development. Applications are divided into program modules that in turn can be divided into smaller modules, or subprograms, that perform specific tasks or computational processes (Figure 8.10). The subprograms have various names—depending on the language used—such as subroutines, sections, or paragraphs. Finally, the subprograms consist of sets of program instructions.

For example, a general ledger application can be divided into program modules, one of which might provide for end-of-period closing. In turn, this program module might be broken down into several subprograms. One might set to zero the balances of all revenue and expense

FIGURE 8.9 Nassi–Schneiderman diagram for a file-listing program, corresponding to the program flowchart in Figure 8.8.

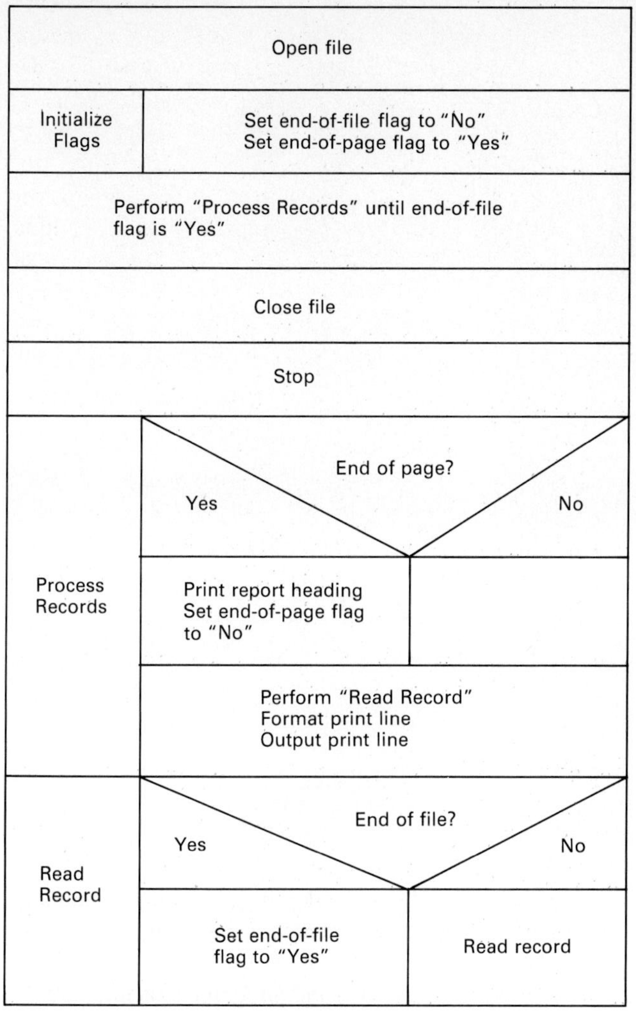

Open file

Initialize Flags	Set end-of-file flag to "No" Set end-of-page flag to "Yes"

Perform "Process Records" until end-of-file flag is "Yes"

Close file

Stop

Process Records

End of page?
Yes — No

Print report heading
Set end-of-page flag to "No"

Perform "Read Record"
Format print line
Output print line

Read Record

End of file?
Yes — No

Set end-of-file flag to "Yes" | Read record

accounts; another might set the new beginning balances of asset, liability, and equity accounts equal to the ending balances from the previous period; and a third might set to zero the activity fields in all the accounts. Each program and subprogram has its own inputs and outputs, which interface with other programs and/or subpro-

grams. The influence of the systems approach is clearly evident in this concept.

The second concept is that these modules should be linked together in a manner that expresses the processing logic as clearly as possible. The normal situation is for instructions to be executed in the order in which they

FIGURE 8.10 Hierarchical structure of applications software.

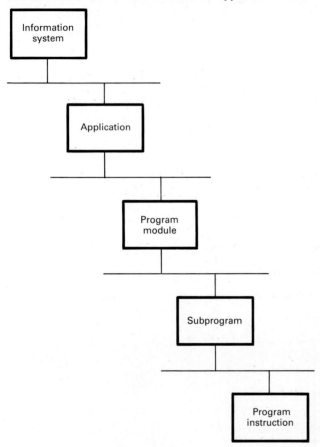

appear in the program; this is referred to as the *linear sequence structure*. But this sequence can be modified by program branching. Branching logic hinges on the use of two statements that can be expressed generically as

$$IF...THEN...ELSE$$

and

$$DO...WHILE \quad or \quad PERFORM...UNTIL$$

The first of these forms defines the program's *selection structure* and the second defines its *interation structure* (Figure 8.11). Theoretically, any required program logic structure can be represented using these three basic forms.

The advantages of good program structure are numerous. The logic pattern is likely to be more evident, to both the original programmers and others using the program at a later date. Coding is easier, and mistakes are fewer. Coding work can be divided up among several programmers working in parallel; each module can be developed and tested before the various modules are assembled, thereby enhancing the program's operating efficiency. And subsequent program maintenance may often be confined to particular segments of the program rather than to the whole program. Some programming languages lend themselves better to structured program-

FIGURE 8.11 Three basic logical forms used in structured programming.

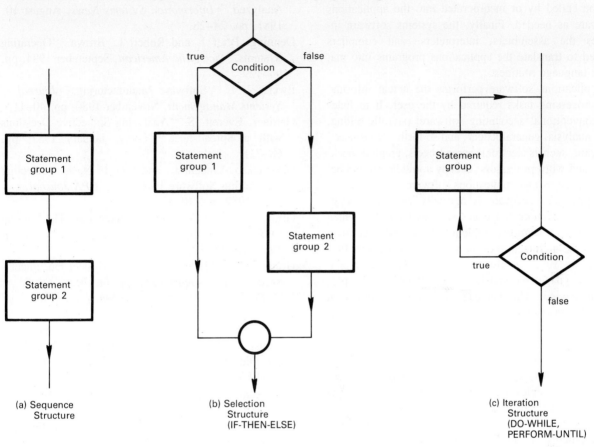

| (a) Sequence Structure | (b) Selection Structure (IF-THEN-ELSE) | (c) Iteration Structure (DO-WHILE, PERFORM-UNTIL) |

ming than do others. For example, well-structured programs can be written in COBOL, whereas this is quite difficult using BASIC.

SUMMARY

Computer software translates the potential of the computer hardware into a working system capable of processing information in accordance with user needs. Software consists of programmed instructions describing the processing operations to be executed by the processor devices. Software is to the computer what clerical procedures are to the accounting clerk.

Two major types of software are systems software and applications software. The systems software is machine oriented and provides an environment for the preparation, modification, and execution of the applications software. Its most important component is the operating system, which automatically supervises the computer's operation and helps the human operator run the machine. The use of operating systems enables a level of operating efficiency in the context of high speeds and complex modes of processing that could not be attained by a human operator alone. The systems software often includes a library of utility subprograms for carrying out frequently recurring processing operations. Such utility subprograms, for editing, screen formatting, data management, telecommunications, and report generation, can be called by or incorporated into the applications software as needed. Finally, the systems software includes the assemblers, interpreters, and compilers needed to translate the applications programs into machine language routines.

Applications software performs the actual information-processing tasks required by the user. It includes the conventional accounting software: payroll, billing, sales analysis, general ledger, and so forth. "End-user" software, such as electronic spreadsheets, graphics packages, and word processors, occupy a middle ground between systems and applications software.

Applications software is normally written in high-level programming languages such as COBOL, which are oriented toward the problem to be solved rather than toward the architecture of the particular processor. Programs are subsequently translated into low-level machine language that can be "understood" by the processor device. The language is translated either at execution time by an interpreter or in a separate process by a compiler.

The efficiency of new applications program development has been greatly improved. Structured techniques have been introduced to enable teams of programmers to develop modules that properly interface with one another and that can be assembled with a minimum of debugging into a working program. Along with these developments, generalized programs, including code generators, have emerged to eliminate coding effort almost entirely. But regardless of how programs are written, the secret behind successful operation is adequate testing and comprehensive program documentation.

BIBLIOGRAPHY

Baylin, Edward, N. "Criteria for Evaluating Programming Languages." *Interface*, Summer 1984, pp. 8–11.

Browning, Christine. *Guide to Effective Software Technical Writing*, Englewood Cliffs, N.J.: Prentice-Hall, 1984.

Celko, Joe. "Report Programs—Often Used, Seldom Analyzed." *Information Systems News*, August 10, 1981, pp. 24–28.

Denning, Peter J. and Robert L. Brown. "Operating Systems." *Scientific American*, September 1984, pp. 94–129.

Ewers, J. E. "Software Manufacturing." *Journal of Systems Management*, November 1980, pp. 40–41.

Gardner, Everett. S. "Analyzing Subjective Decisions with a Spreadsheet." *Lotus*, January 1987, pp. 68–71.

Giovinazzo, Vincent J., and John F. Nash. "Selecting Accounting Software Packages." *CPA Journal*, October 1982, pp. 40–45.

Grimm, S. G. "EDP User Documentation: The Missing Link." *Journal of Systems Management*, November 1980, pp. 15–19.

Grupe, Fritz. "Tips for Better Worksheet Documentation." *Lotus*, August 1985, pp. 68–70.

Hall, Donna A. "Microcomputer Spreadsheet Software: A Powerful Financial Planning Tool." *Georgia Journal of Accounting*, Spring 1986, pp. 159–169.

Higgins, D. A. "Structured Maintenance: New Tools for Old." *Computer World*, June 15, 1981, pp. 31–40.

Kay, Alan "Computer Software." *Scientific American*, September 1984, pp. 52–59.

Ledgard, H. F. *Programming Proverbs*. Rochelle Park, N.J.: Hayden, 1978.

Martin, James, and Carma McLure. *Diagramming Techniques for Analysts and Programmers*. Englewood Cliffs, N.J.: Prentice-Hall, 1984.

Miller, Steven E. "The Anatomy of a Spreadsheet." *Lotus*, July 1985, pp. 55–57.

"Missing Computer Software." *Business Week*, September 1, 1980, pp. 46–56.

Myers, Glenford J. *The Art of Software Testing*. New York: John Wiley, 1979.

Philippakis, Andreas S., and Leonard J. Kazmier. *Information Systems Through COBOL*. New York: McGraw-Hill, 1978.

Philippakis, Andreas S., and Leonard J. Kazmier. *Structured COBOL*. New York: McGraw-Hill, 1981.

Rice, J. G. "Build Program Technique: A Practical Approach for the Development of Automatic Software

Generation Systems.'' *Computer World*, May 3, 1981, pp. 47–56.

DISCUSSION QUESTIONS AND PROBLEMS

1. Define and discuss the following terms:

- Applications software
- Assembler
- Common Business Oriented Language (COBOL)
- Compiler
- Editor
- End-user software
- Fatal error
- Generalized program
- Global editing
- High-level languages
- Instruction
- Instruction set
- Interpreter
- Machine code
- Machine-generated code
- Mnemonic code
- Mnemonic variable name
- Nonfatal error
- Object code
- Operand
- Operating system
- Operation code
- Overlaying
- Program module
- Program package
- Program structure
- Program syntax
- Report generator
- Screen formatting
- Software package
- Source code
- Spreadsheet
- String, substring
- Supervisory program
- Symbolic, assembly code
- System documentation
- System generation (SYSGEN)
- Systems software
- System utilities
- Top-down programming
- User documentation
- Variable name
- Word processing

2. The following clerical procedure concerns the determination and payment of sales representatives' commissions:

Policy

Salespeople are entitled to a commission, payable monthly, equal to 5 percent of net sales. An additional bonus commission of 12 percent is payable on monthly net sales in excess of the established monthly quota.

Specific Instructions

a. Determine individual's gross sales for the current month.
b. Determine sales discounts, returns, and allowances.
c. Compute individual's net sales for the current month.
d. Check individual's current month sales quota.
e. Compute base commission.
f. Compute bonus commission, if any.
g. Prepare payment voucher, and submit to supervisor for authorization.
h. Route payment voucher to paymaster.

Required

a. Identify logical weaknesses and omissions in the procedures listed that would have to be resolved before a computer could carry them out.
b. Indicate how the procedures would need to be written (in English—or pseudocode—not in a programming language) if a machine were to be able to perform them successfully.

3. The following expression is to be evaluated using a small computer processor:

$$V = \frac{2X + 3Y + 1}{4Z}$$

The values of X, Y, and Z are initially in specified locations in main memory. Assume that the available operation codes are limited to the following:

Load data element from main memory into a register.
Add content of one register to that of another.
Divide content of one register by that of another.
Store data element from a register into main memory.

Assume also that there are only four registers available for holding data.

Required

a. Describe the steps necessary to calculate the value of the expression.

Item No.	Description	Quantity on Hand*	Reorder Point*	Unit Cost	Year-to-Date Usage*
100	1-in pipe	5,000	2,000	$2.00	12,500
101	2-in pipe	100	1,000	2.50	5,000
102	3-in pipe	1,000	500	3.50	6,500
103	4-in pipe	0	500	5.00	4,000
104	5-in pipe	250	500	7.50	3,500

* In feet.

b. Explain how the procedure could be simplified if an operation code were available to perform multiplication.

4. a. List and discuss the advantages of writing programs in high-level languages rather than in assembly language.
b. List and discuss the advantages and disadvantages of interpreters and compilers for translation of source code into object code.
c. What kind of irregularities could be perpetrated by an unscrupulous computer operator executing BASIC programs using an interpreter? What steps could be taken to minimize the threat of such an irregularity?

5. List some uses of the system editor in relation to the following files. Discuss the various uses, and identify any control problems that could arise:

a. A file containing an application source code in the course of development

b. A file containing an application source code after the object code version of the program has been released for use
c. A file containing an object code program
d. A parameter file containing screen locations used in conjunction with an interactive program providing menus and screen prompts
e. A master file containing employee name, address, and social security number
f. A transaction file containing employee time-card data
g. A text file containing a promotional letter to be sent to sales prospects

6. Data from the following file are to be printed using a report generator:

The report generator provides the following commands (in addition to one identifying the file to be accessed):

```
PRINT TEXT (X, Y, [string])
PRINT DATA LINE (X, Y, n)
```

The first command prints a specific string (enclosed in quotation marks, " ") starting at the coordinates X, Y on the page. The second prints a column of data corresponding to the nth field in the file, starting at the coordinates X, Y and continuing to the bottom of the page. X is measured horizontally from the left margin, and Y is measured vertically downward from the top of the page. X lies in the range 0 to 132, and Y lies in the range 1 to 66.

Required

a. Specify the commands required to produce the necessary report using all the fields contained in the file. An appropriate heading should be added, including the title "Inventory Status Report."

b. What changes would be needed to alter the order of the columns of data so that "Year-to-Date Usage" appeared immediately to the left of "Quantity on Hand"?

7. An accounts payable application consists of seven program modules:

- Enter voucher data from keyboard.
- Print open voucher report.
- Print accounts payable balances.
- Print cash requirements report.
- Select vouchers for payment.
- Write checks to printer.
- Perform end-of-month closing.

There are three data files: the vendor master file, a voucher transaction file, and a check transaction file. No formal posting process is involved; instead, voucher records remain in the voucher file until the end of the month following payment.

Required

a. Describe the functions likely to be performed by each program module.

b. Identify the files and input–output devices that must be accessed by each module.

c. Draw a program flowchart showing the operation of the check-printing module.

d. What controls would be needed to protect the files against inadvertent damage, assuming (i) only one user and (ii) multiple access by several users?

8. Discuss the uses of the following types of end-user software packages in developing accounting applications to be run on personal computers. In which kinds of applications would they be most suitable? What are the advantages and disadvantages of employing end-user packages instead of writing dedicated program code?

- Electronic spreadsheets
- Data base management packages
- Graphics packages

9. A generalized program is to be developed for posting transaction data to the master file. The fields in each file involved in the posting process are to be specified in an associated parameter file.

Required

a. Identify the operational steps to be performed by the program.

b. Design a parameter file containing the required information about the fields involved.

c. What are the major sources of operating inefficiency that would not be present in a dedicated program written for a particular application?

10. Identify the steps that would be taken to test and debug a program module designed to print invoices in an accounts receivable system. The module is required to access the shipment transaction file and the customer master file, format the invoice, and route it to the printer.

11. Arjuna Enterprises is a rapidly growing company whose accounting system is still in a state of flux. Considerable effort has been expended on determining stable system objectives so that the system design can be stabilized, but management's needs are just too volatile at this time.

Several business programs currently need to be written. Management recognizes that because of the volatility the programs will probably have to be modified substantially within the next few years, and it is searching for a solution to the problem of expensive software maintenance. You have been retained as a consultant to advise management on the best action to take.

One possibility would be to write the programs in COBOL and simply have the programs modified or rewritten when system requirements change. Another possibility would be to write table-driven generalized programs in FORTRAN or assembly language; then when requirements change, only the parameter files would need to be changed. A third possibility would be to use an electronic spreadsheet package and program the applications using macros.

Required

Identify and discuss the relative advantages and disadvantages of the three solutions, and recommend to management the best way to handle the problem.

12. You are a member of a study team sent by a major consulting firm to analyze the data-processing operations of a medium-sized service business. Your area of expertise is systems development, and you are particularly interested in the procedures adopted for testing newly written programs. During an interview with a programmer, you record the following comments:

Once I'm given a programming assignment, I am expected to see it through to the end. Together with the user, I help draw up specs for the program. Then I write the program and see that it's properly tested before release. You can't test just part of a complex, integrated program, so I wait until it's all finished and then test it as a whole. A few years ago, I took a couple of bookkeeping courses at an evening institute, so I know how to put together test transactions. You know, you have to get the debits and credits to balance! But there is never much wrong with my programs anyway, so a few tests are all that are needed. My boss usually asks me: "Does it look good, Jim?" I say, "Yeah," and he signs off the release form. He knows my programming is good, and he trusts me. You see, I have been with the firm since it started.

Required

Discuss the programmer's remarks and evaluate the effectiveness of this company's test procedures.

13. The payroll transaction file contains the employees' time card-entries for the week. Fields in this file contain the date, the employee number, and the employee's regular and overtime hours. Additional fields are provided for the employee's name and gross earnings, but these fields are initially empty. A computer program forming part of the payroll application is executed to write data to these two fields. The employee's name, wage rate, and payroll status (hourly or salaried) are retrieved from the employee master file. Gross earnings for hourly employees are determined by the following formula:

$$\text{Gross earnings} = (\text{regular hours} + 1.5 \times \text{overtime hours}) \times \text{wage rate}$$

Gross earnings for salaried employees are determined by multiplying the wage rate by 40.

Required

Analyze the required programming logic into the linear sequence structure and the two types of branching structure:

- Do … while
- If … then … else

Present your answer in the form of a program flowchart.

9

Data Base
Management Systems

LEARNING OBJECTIVES

After you have studied this chapter you should be able to

- Describe the principle of data base management systems.
- Discuss the potential of data base systems for real-time processing.
- Evaluate the advantages and disadvantages of the data base concept.
- Discuss the notion of logical data structure and schemas.
- Describe the purpose of the programming sublanguages associated with data base management systems.
- Evaluate the importance of the data dictionary.
- Discuss the notion of structural models and their three common forms.
- Analyze file specifications into efficient logical structures.

THE NATURE OF DATA BASE MANAGEMENT SYSTEMS

A data base management system (DBMS) is a combination of hardware and software providing a generalized and integrated data structure capable of supporting a number of independent user applications. The nature of such systems can best be understood by comparing and contrasting them with information systems using conventional file structures.

In a conventional file system, each application has its own set of data files: master files, transaction files, and others as needed (Figure 9.1). A data base system, however, has a single systemwide repository of data, and the storage needs of all applications are serviced from that one source (Figure 9.2). The data are regarded as a central resource to be managed and made available to all authorized users on a shared basis.

Conventional Versus Data Base Systems

A parable will help illustrate the implications of the differences between conventional and data base systems. Imagine a certain enterprise composed of several departments. Initially, each department has a storage room

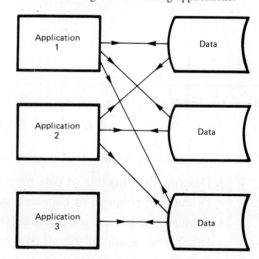

FIGURE 9.1   System using conventional files. Each application has its own data files, but system integration may result in sharing the data among applications.

in which its records are kept; later it is proposed to replace the storage rooms by a single room big enough to house the records of all the departments. There is some concern that there will be confusion among the different sets of records, but an exceptionally competent filing clerk is appointed to oversee the storage and retrieval of

FIGURE 9.2   Data base management system. The systemwide data base serves the needs of all applications.

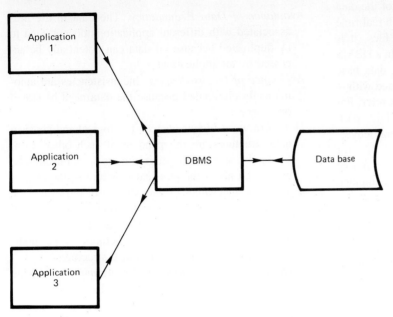

all material placed in the storage room. The users in the various departments soon lose their anxieties and become confident that their data are in good hands. As time goes by, the people actually realize that the new system is working to their advantage; they no longer have to worry about housekeeping in their individual storage rooms, and they are relieved of the task of hunting for material that they need. They really do not know how the filing clerk manages to keep everything straight in the storage room, but whenever they request some material from storage, it is promptly delivered to them.

The data base corresponds to the storage room, and the data base management system is the counterpart of the filing clerk. To distinguish between the "filing clerk" and the information system of which it is a part, the acronym DBMS will be used for the former and "data base system" for the overall system. The DBMS serves as a clearinghouse for data flowing into or out of the data base, and it processes all requests by the users for storage and retrieval of data items. As does the filing clerk in the parable, the DBMS assumes the responsibility for the data access strategies and also for "housekeeping" in the data base, thereby relieving the users

of a considerable burden that they have to bear in conventional systems.

Ownership of Data

In a data base system, the data are said to be "owned" by the system as a whole, whereas in a system based on conventional files, ownership of the data resides in the individual applications.

The concept of ownership of data applies not only to the data base as a whole but also to data aggregates. One data aggregate—for example, a record—can own one or more others. When one data aggregate owns another, the former is referred to as the *parent* and the latter as the *child*. Ownership is one type of relationship between sets of data aggregates. It implies the notion of hierarchy, a notion that is well established in data base theory. On the other hand, it is possible for a given data aggregate to be owned simultaneously by two or more parents. The existence of such relationships suggests that simple hierarchical structures may be limited in their applicability. This issue will be discussed more fully later in this chapter.

Real-Time Systems and Data Base

One of the most far-reaching applications of the data base concept is to real-time systems. Although real-time processing can be done using conventional files, it is much easier to do with the help of a DBMS. In a DBMS the transaction records can be stored in the data base with the instruction that they are to be associated with—or owned by—the master record to which they refer. For example, all general journal transactions involving cash may be owned by the cash record in the general ledger. Now suppose that at some given time, a user asks for the cash balance. The current cash balance need not be retrieved from a storage location but can be computed on demand. The system retrieves the subset of transaction records owned by the cash record and sums the contents of their ''amount'' fields, taking proper account of the debit and credit ''signs.'' The net total plus the cash balance at the beginning of the period is the current balance. Master file balances are sometimes said to reside in *virtual fields*, contrasting with the real fields in which they would be stored in a system using conventional files.

Associating transaction records with the master records that they affect not only provides a means of obtaining current balances; it also preserves the transaction history, showing how the balances came about, and eliminates the need for posting. On the other hand, on-demand retrieval of transaction records and computation of balances are less efficient than is classical posting and places considerable demands on the processor and disk access technology. Powerful system resources must be ''standing by'' ready to go into action to retrieve the necessary records and compute the balance, possibly while a user is waiting for the information at a terminal. If the information cannot be delivered quickly, the users will become frustrated, and the potential of the real-time system will remain unrealized.

Advantages and Disadvantages of Data Base Systems

Data base systems have both advantages and disadvantages as compared with conventional systems. The principal advantages, including the ones already noted, are

Avoidance of Data Redundancy. The data in the files associated with different applications do not need to be duplicated because all data can potentially be accessed by all applications.

Avoidance of Inconsistencies. Inconsistencies are automatically eliminated because the data need be stored only once.

Data Structural Independence. The logical and physical data structures are independent of each other. Consequently, application programmers do not need to be concerned about the physical structure of the files or about the mechanics of data storage or retrieval. Furthermore, the physical data structure can be changed if necessary without modifying the application programs. Similarly, the logical structures can be modified without affecting the physical structure.

Simplification of Application Programming. All file processing is handled by the DBMS, and access to the data is provided by standard ''calls'' that can easily be incorporated into the application code.

Possibility of Systemwide Controls. Because all access to the data is channeled through the DBMS, access and data integrity controls can be built into the DBMS. This capability further alleviates the burden of application programming.

Flexibility of Data Aggregates. Data elements can be combined in virtually limitless ways, providing the illusion of files of varying content and format. Different applications can perceive the same data in different configurations as needed. Similarly, a modification of the data aggregates used by one application need not interfere with the aggregates used by other applications.

Expansion Potential. The total storage capacity can be expanded as necessary without affecting the individual applications.

The advent of the DBMS has had a major influence on the development of applications software. The considerable burden of developing storage and retrieval algorithms, sorting and merging procedures, file integrity controls, and even posting routines has been lifted from the shoulders of the application programmer. In place of the subprograms needed in conventional systems for file handling, all that is needed in programs interfacing with a DBMS is a small number of call statements effecting access to the data base.

Set against these very substantial advantages are some significant disadvantages of the data base concept. The principal ones are

High Initial Investment. Data base systems are expensive to design and implement. Even if proven canned data base software can be acquired, its implementation in a real system can be a major undertaking.
Maintenance Effort. Maintenance of the data base requires the continued attention of highly trained personnel if the system is to operate successfully.
System Overhead. A significant portion of the central processor resources is devoted to operating the DBMS. The storage and retrieval of data usually require a complicated series of operations, even though this complication is not apparent to the user. Furthermore, a significant portion of the total storage capacity is occupied by physical access linkages (such as pointers and index files) that represent nonproductive use of disk space.
Error Contamination. The immediate availability of data to many different users prevents the easy isolation and correction of erroneous data. Careful screening and editing of data before release into the data base therefore are mandatory.
Vulnerability to System Failure. The data base concept puts all the data ''eggs'' into one basket. Elaborate measures, therefore, have to be taken to protect the data from a system crash or malfunction and to provide for speedy recovery if the data base is destroyed.
Access Controls. The potential availability of all data to all users poses severe control problems. Effective control measures are needed to prevent and/or detect attempts by unauthorized persons to access or modify the data base.
Elimination of Audit Trails. The movement of data from one file to another, familiar in conventional systems, is lost in data base systems—and with it the easy mapping of audit trails. Thus data base systems must be designed to preserve the auditability of transaction flows.

Data base systems place heavy demands on their organizational environment. They require the availability of highly trained professionals to establish and maintain the data base and the DBMS, and so the position of data base administrator has emerged in response to this need. Whereas relatively unsophisticated people can understand and work with conventional file structures, considerable technical expertise is required to exploit the potential of the DBMS—or even to keep the data base system operational. The external simplicity of the data base concept in the eyes of the users belies a great deal of inner complexity that someone in the organization must understand. Furthermore, the control implications of the data base system require careful planning and handling to protect the data and other resources of the organization.

Data base systems also require the use of powerful hardware configurations. The overhead associated with the complicated data structure consumes machine resources that are therefore not available for productive data processing. In large computer systems, this overhead may be relatively unimportant in terms of the total resources provided, but in small systems, it can substantially reduce the level of performance. For this reason, among others, the development of the DBMS for micro- and minicomputers has been slower than that for large mainframes. Even today, although most manufacturers of small computers claim to offer a DBMS as part of the systems software, few of these systems provide the kind of capability described in this chapter, the majority being little more than glorified file management systems.

Conference of Data Systems Languages (CODASYL)

The history of data base systems was influenced heavily by the Conference of Data Systems Languages (CODASYL). CODASYL was established in 1959 at a meeting of systems professionals in Washington, D.C., and is supported on a volunteer basis by a large number of computer specialists and government agencies. Their first task was to develop specifications for the COBOL language, and the conference has continued to support the development and improvement of this and other programming languages. But in the late 1960s, CODASYL was largely reorganized, and a major part of its work since that time has been devoted to stimulating research and development work on data base concepts and to establishing some degree of uniformity among the organizations concerned with data base systems. The Database Task Force and several other committees of CODASYL have produced a considerable volume of material over the last 20 years. Most observers acknowledge the contribution made by the conference, but its recommendations have not been free from controversy. Its recommendations also have been based primarily on the hierarchical and network models of data (discussed later in this chapter). These are widely used, but they are not the only relevant models. The relational model (also discussed later in this chapter) has proved increasingly successful and is currently being pursued by many designers and manufacturers. The relational model takes an essentially different approach to data base structure than has generally been proposed by the CODASYL task forces and committees.

DATA BASE SOFTWARE

A data base management system consists of a systems software package, used in conjunction with a random access secondary storage device, normally a magnetic disk drive. The arrangement of the data among the sectors, tracks, and/or cylinders of the disk drive comprises the physical data structure. The physical structure is of little interest to the applications programmer or the end user, but it is vital to the systems programmer developing the data base software because the physical structure may strongly influence data retrieval times. The DBMS handles the relationship, or *mapping*, between the logical and physical structures.

Data Base Sublanguages

The data base software consists of three languages or sublanguages:

• Data definition language
• Data manipulation language
• Query language

The data definition (or data description) language forms an interface between the systems software and the high-level "host" language, such as COBOL, in which the application is written. It forms a kind of language extension, or sublanguage, allowing the programming language to accept the logical structure of the data base. In a COBOL program the data definition language interfaces with the program's Data Division. The data definition language is invoked at compilation time and translates the logical structure into linkages among the data elements. The data manipulation sublanguage forms a second interface and translates "call statements" embedded in the applications program into executable instructions. In a COBOL program the data manipulation language interfaces with the Procedure Division. At run time, the object code equivalents of the call statements result in the storage or retrieval of data from the data base. The relationships among the data definition language, the data manipulation language, and the application program are illustrated in Figure 9.3(a).

A query language serves the same general purpose as does a data manipulation language, but it operates in real time in response to commands entered through a terminal device (Figure 9.3[b]). Query languages allow end users to interrogate the data base directly, without the need for an applications program. Query languages ordinarily operate as stand-alone languages, and not as sublanguages of a high-level programming language.

Storage and Retrieval of Data

Access to data elements in a data base takes one of two forms. By far the more common form of access, provided by the data manipulation language, is from applications software via call statements embedded in the programs. The precise forms of these call statements and the "verb" names assigned to them vary among the host programming languages and data manipulation languages. But the principal ones can be represented in generic form by

```
STORE
RETRIEVE
UPDATE
DELETE
```

FIGURE 9.3   Role of data base sublanguages.

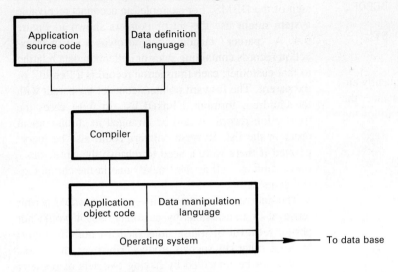

(a) Data base access from applications software

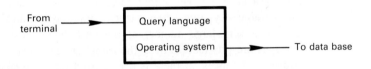

(b) Access from on-line terminal

The STORE command adds new records or data aggregates to the data base. A parameter list appended to the command may identify the content of the record and its placement in the logical data structure. The RETRIEVE command, as its name implies, retrieves an existing record from the data base: It could be a particular record specified by some attribute or content, or it could be the "next" or "previous" record in a sequence. The UPDATE command changes the content of a specified record, and the DELETE command causes a record to be made unavailable for subsequent retrieval. The RETRIEVE, UPDATE, and DELETE commands may also be appended by parameter lists.

The RETRIEVE command does not change the physical data structure, but the STORE and DELETE commands do change it. The UPDATE command may change the physical structure if the DBMS provides for retention of the former version of the record as a *before-*

image. (The new version is referred to as the *after-image*). The before-images and after-images correspond, at the level of the record, to the father and son versions of conventional files. The changes in the logical data structure may seem minor, but the necessary rearrangement of the physical structure—including its linkages—may be quite extensive. The user may not be aware of the extent of the "housekeeping" operations required by such changes. But they contribute to the processing overhead, which is manifested in the degradation of performance, characteristic of data base management systems.

The precise form of the commands available in query languages also varies from one language to another. But increasingly, query languages attempt to provide commands in "plain English," or at least in a kind of stilted, but still understandable, English. Some representative, generic examples are

```
DISPLAY THE SHIPMENT FILE
LIST THE SHIPMENT FILE FOR DATES BEFORE
  1/18/XX
DISPLAY THE SHIPMENT FILE SORTED BY
  PRODUCT
```

In modern interactive systems, a dialogue frequently ensues between the user and the system. For instance, the third example just shown might provoke the following question from the machine:

```
SORT BY PRODUCT NUMBER OR PRODUCT
  DESCRIPTION?
```

and then:

```
ALL PRODUCTS OR SPECIFIED ONES?
```

This kind of machine–user dialogue is common in decision support systems. In expert systems, the dialogue may become quite long, consisting of penetrating questions and finally resulting in, not just the output of data but also a recommendation of some course of action.

DATA STRUCTURE IN DATA BASE MANAGEMENT SYSTEMS

The concept of files made up of records, which in turn are made up of data elements or fields, loses its validity in a data base environment. Instead, records that are meaningful to a particular user may be assembled at retrieval time in response to a request submitted by that user. Another user, submitting a different request, may retrieve the same data elements and assemble them in some other way. Each user has a different view of the data, and the need to accommodate these different views results in the doctrine of structural independence. The description of the data base in terms of the data elements and the relationships among them is called the data base *schema*. Within the single schema, which relates to the data base as a whole, there may be multiple *subschemas* describing the data and relationships of interest to individual users.

The ability to retrieve data aggregates of various forms depends on the use of pointers, index files, and other structures (see Chapter 5) according to the particular design of the DBMS. For example, an accounts receivable system might use the set of pointers shown in Figure 9.4. A "parent" customer record owns a set of transaction records containing sales or collection data relating to that customer; each transaction record is a "child" of the parent. The forward pointers connect the parent with the children, forming a linked list. In most cases the transaction records would be arranged in chronological order in the list. Reverse pointers could also be incorporated if there were a need to retrieve the "previous" transaction as well as the "next" one in the chronological sequence.

The data structure shown in Figure 9.4 would permit retrieval of transactions by customer, but it would not permit retrieval of transactions (at least not efficiently) by some other key such as product. However, this weakness could be remedied by having two sets of pointers (Figure 9.5), one linking transactions to their customer parent and the other linking them to their product parent. Ideally a DBMS would allow retrieval of data by any conceivable key, but achievement of this ideal would require a very large number of linkages. In practice, linkages are provided to meet the users' anticipated retrieval preferences. If there is ever a need for retrieval by some new key, two options exist: Either a new set of linkages must be incorporated or the required data must be retrieved by some roundabout and probably time-consuming search process. In such a situation, the data base administrator would normally consult with the appropriate user groups and then decide how to proceed. In any case, the implementation of a DBMS—like any type of systems development—starts with users' needs.

Data Dictionary

The first step in defining the data base schema is to identify the data elements appearing in the system. Thus a *data dictionary* is prepared, in the form of a master list of data elements and their definitions. Although data dictionaries are used in most systems development activities, they are essential to data base systems because of the need for systemwide consistency. The preparation of data dictionaries is discussed more fully in Chapter 13.

FIGURE 9.4 Chain structure establishing "ownership" of the associated transaction records by a master record. Forward pointers are shown linking the records, but both forward and reverse pointers could be provided.

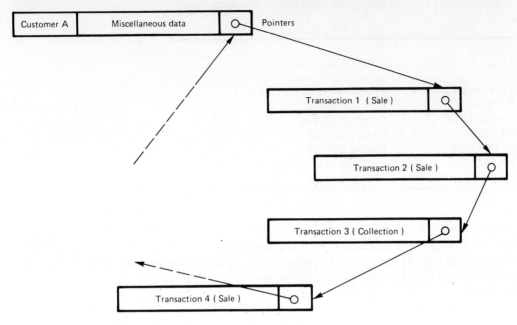

FIGURE 9.5 Complex chain structure establishing ownership of transaction records by two or more master records. Again, reverse pointers could be added if needed.

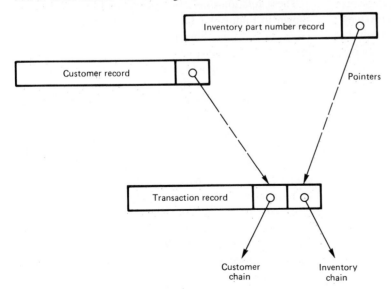

FIGURE 9.6 **Example of a simplified data dictionary for an order-processing system.** The variable names might be suitable if the host language were COBOL. In addition to the variable name and definition, the dictionary would normally specify other information such as the length of bytes and the data type.

Data Element	Variable Name	Definition	Other Data
1	CUST-NUMBER	Customer number	. . . . .
2	CUST-NAME	Customer name	. . . . .
3	CUST-ADDRESS	Customer address	. . . . .
4	INVOICE-NO	Invoice number	. . . . .
5	INVC-LINE-ITM	Invoice line item	. . . . .
6	INVT-PART-NO	Inventory part number	. . . . .
7	PART-DESCRIPT	Part description	. . . . .

At a minimum, the data dictionary should list each data element, its definition, its data type, and the length of the unformatted data element in bytes (Figure 9.6). Additional information might include the corresponding variable name in the programming language used and a reference to the subsystems or applications in which the data element appears.

Logical Data Structure

The second step in defining a schema is to identify the logical interrelationships among the data elements listed in the data dictionary. These relationships may exist because of the nature of the elements themselves, for example, the relationship between customer number and name. Or they may exist because of the need to retrieve information from the data base in some prescribed manner, for example, the relationship between customers and their associated invoices. It is necessary to identify both the direction of the relationship and its extent:

- No relationship
- One-to-one relationship
- One-to-many relationship
- Many-to-one relationship
- Many-to-many relationship

A one-to-one relationship exists between a customer number and the customer's name or address or between an inventory part number and the description of the item. A one-to-many relationship and a many-to-one relationship are the two views of a directed relationship between, say, a customer and an invoice or an invoice and the line items it contains. One customer may be sent many invoices, but each invoice refers to only one customer. Similarly, one invoice may contain many line items, but each line item is part of only one invoice. A many-to-many relationship exists between a customer and an inventory part. One customer may purchase many parts, and one part may be purchased by many customers.

These relationships can be expressed by a matrix, as shown in Figure 9.7 for the order-processing example. Frequently, as in this case, the matrix is symmetrical about its leading diagonal (with the appropriate reversal of the one-to-many and many-to-one linkages). But this is not always the case. In the example, there is a many-to-many relationship between customers and parts and between parts and customers. Assuming that this schema could be implemented, the user would be able to retrieve a list of all parts purchased by a given customer and also a list of all customers purchasing a given part. If it were decided that one of these types of retrieval would never be required, one of the linkages could be omitted.

An alternative method of presentation is the Bachman diagram, named after C. W. Bachman who first proposed this method. Figure 9.8 illustrates the diagram for the order-processing example. The convention dictates that one-to-one relationships are shown by a line joining

FIGURE 9.7   Relationship matrix showing the interrelationship among data elements in an order-processing system.

	Customer #	Name	Address	Invoice #	Line item	Part #	Description
Customer #	1 - 1	1 - 1	1 - 1	1 - M		M - M	
Name	1 - 1	1 - 1					
Address	1 - 1		1 - 1				
Invoice #	M - 1			1 - 1	1 - M		
Line item				M - 1	1 - 1		
Part #	M - M					1 - 1	1 - 1
Description						1 - 1	1 - 1

1 - 1 : one to one
1 - M : one to many
M - 1 : many to one
M - M : many to many

FIGURE 9.8   Bachman diagram showing interrelationships among data elements in an order-processing system. A line with no arrows designates a one-to-one relationship; a line with one arrow designates a one-to-many or a many-to-one relationship; and a line with two arrows designates a many-to-many relationship.

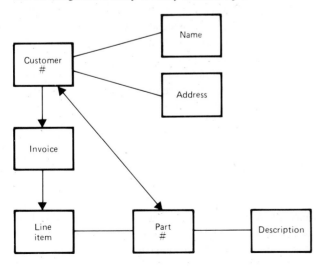

the two related data elements, with no arrows. A one-to-many or many-to-one relationship is shown by a line with one arrow, and a many-to-many relationship is shown by a line with two arrows.

Structural Models

Several models are used to describe the logical structures of data within the data base. The three most common at the present time are the

· Hierarchical model
· Network model
· Relational model

Hierarchical model. The hierarchical model is suitable for structures consisting of one-to-one and one-to-many relationships. The data elements are organized into an inverted tree structure in which each data element at a particular level "owns" the elements at the next lower level. All the elements are owned by the data element

FIGURE 9.9 Hierarchical model applied to invoices in an order-processing system. Each customer data element "owns" its associated invoice elements, and each invoice element owns its associated line-item elements.

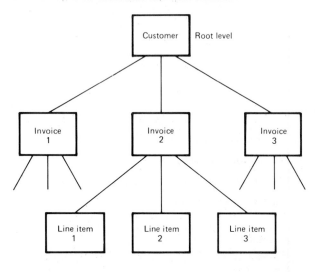

at the root of the inverted tree (i.e., at the top). Thus, in the order-processing example, a customer element owns its associated invoice elements, and each invoice element owns its associated line-item elements (Figure 9.9). No linkages are provided between the elements at the same level in the hierarchy, except the indirect linkages through their owner elements at higher levels. An analogy is with siblings who share a parent or cousins who share the same grandparent.

An important feature of the hierarchical model is that no data element is owned by more than one higher-level element. For this reason, the model cannot provide for many-to-many relationships,[1] such as the relationship between customers and inventory parts in the example. Accordingly, it would be difficult to retrieve a list of the inventory parts purchased by a given customer *and* a list of the customers who purchased a given part. Both these lists could be provided, but only at the expense of considerable effort in searching.

[1] One method that is sometimes used to remedy this deficiency is to duplicate data elements so that a many-to-many relationship is replaced by a number of one-to-many relationships. Such an approach naturally wastes storage capacity and may lead to inconsistencies.

The inability to handle many-to-many relationships is a major shortcoming of the hierarchical model. On the other hand, the model is simple to implement and is used by many data base schemas. Furthermore, retrieval of data elements occupying one-to-one or one-to-many relationships is highly efficient.

Network Model. A network model has no distinct hierarchy, but data elements can have several owners in addition to owning several other elements. The only restriction on the network is that it must be internally consistent; for example, a data element can own a "son" that in turn owns a "grandchild," but the grandchild cannot simultaneously own its grandparent.

Network models can in principle handle all types of relationship, including many-to-many relationships. Figure 9.10 shows a network application to the customers and inventory parts in the simplified order-processing system. It provides for the retrieval of the parts list for each customer as well as the customer list for each part number.

Network models are considerably more difficult to implement than are hierarchical ones because of the former's inherent complexity. In particular, there is no well-defined path through the network corresponding to the path from the root of the hierarchical tree through its branches. Many data base systems in use today do not provide full network capability.

Relational Model. In the relational model, the user is not concerned with the complexity of the relationships among data elements. Instead, data are perceived to be structured in the form of simple tables consisting of a key and associated fields. The tables present to each user the illusion of distinct files, although the same data may be viewed in terms of more than one table, according to the key that is selected. Figure 9.11 shows the data that appeared in the network model (Figure 9.10) in tabular form, as considered in the relational model. The left-hand table is keyed on customer, and the right-hand table is keyed on part number.

The relational model is an application of the mathematical framework of set theory, and it has emerged largely as the result of the work of E. F. Codd. It is supported by a powerful relational "calculus" by which the user defines, among other things, the retrieval keys

FIGURE 9.10 Network model applied to customers and inventory parts in an order-processing system. Each customer data element owns several part number elements, and each part number element is owned by several customer elements.

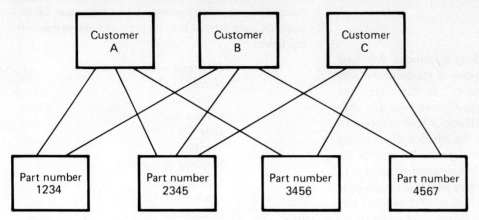

and the fields to be associated with those keys. The model can be used with relationships of all types, including many-to-many and many-to-one relationships.

The relational model has enormous potential, but its implementation is still at an early stage. None of the existing data base systems exploits its full potential, and some systems that claim to be based on the relational model are nothing more than network systems with a relational "front end." Relational data base systems relieve the applications programmer of much of the decision-making burden inherent in the other models. On the other hand, because of the internal "bookkeeping" re-

FIGURE 9.11 Relational model applied to the customers and inventory parts in the order-processing system. Regardless of the internal complexity, the user perceives the data in the form of tables and related fields.

Customer	Part No.	Other data
A	1234	......
	2345	......
	3456	......
B	1234	......
	2345	......
	4567	......
C	2345	......
	3456	......
	4567	......

Key = Customer

Part number	Customer	Other data
1234	A	......
	B	......
2345	A	......
	B	......
	C	......
3456	A	......
	C	......
4567	B	......
	C	......

Key = Part number

quired, relational data base systems tend to be slower than their earlier—and simpler—counterparts.

Logical Data Analysis

The logical schema describing a relational data base should be the optimal description of the particular data structure. Criteria of "optimality" in this context are simplicity and nonredundancy. Conventional file definitions frequently do not fulfill one or both of these criteria. A common violation of the criterion of simplicity is the need for variable-length records. An invoice file might need to accommodate an indeterminate number of invoice line items, or an inventory master file might need to accommodate an indeterminate number of LIFO layers. Variable-length logical records cannot easily be fitted into the fixed-length physical records of most types of storage media.

One example of redundancy is repeating the same group of data elements in different files; for example, the customer's name, address, and telephone number might be included in both the accounts receivable master file and the transaction file. Another example is the inclusion in a single file of two or more data elements that provide the same information; that is, an inventory master file might contain quantity, unit cost, and extended cost—the product of quantity and unit cost. Eliminating redundancy simplifies the data structure and reduces the necessary data base capacity and the number of data elements that must be processed and updated.

One of the designer's tasks may be to translate conventional file definitions, either from a preexisting information system or submitted by users, into the logical schema describing a relational data base. Any redundancy of data elements or repetition of fields should be eliminated. The objective is to derive the simplest, yet complete and internally consistent, set of specifications of the required data structure. The process of preparing such specifications is referred to as *normalization* and has been reduced to a straightforward, easy-to-follow procedure.

Three steps are needed. The first two are aimed at producing structural simplicity, and the third is aimed at eliminating redundancy. The first step is to place all repeated data elements into separate tables. An appro-

priate retrieval key also must be assigned to each table. A key may consist of the combination of two or more data elements; such keys are sometimes referred to as compound, or *concatenated*, keys. Consider, for example, a user-defined invoice file containing the following fields:

> Customer no.
> Name
> Telephone
> Invoice no.
> Date
> Terms
> Shipping instructions

Repeated fields

> Line item no.
> Product no.
> Description
> Unit of measure
> Unit price
> Quantity sold
> Extended price

This file would be partitioned into two separate tables, rather like the A and B subrecords described in Chapter 5. One would be keyed on the combination of customer number and invoice number, and the other would be keyed on the combination of invoice number and line item number:[2]

[Customer no.	[Invoice no.
Invoice no.]	Line item no.]
Name	Product no.
Telephone	Description
Date	Unit of measure
Terms	Unit price
Shipping instructions	Quantity sold
	Extended price

Note that the invoice and the line items occupy a one-to-many relationship. The two tables now are simpler than the original file and have fixed logical record lengths. This first step in the normalization process produces what is referred to as the *first normal form*.

The second step in the normalization process is to remove from each table any data elements (not them-

---

[2] Keys are denoted by the square brackets.

selves keys) that are fully specified by something other than the complete key assigned to that table. Data elements will be removed if they are fully specified by only part of a compound key. For example, "customer name" would be removed from a table keyed on the combination of customer number and invoice number because it is completely specified by customer number alone. The data elements that are removed are placed in separate tables.

The table appearing in the first normal form, which is keyed on the combination of customer number and invoice number,

[Customer no.
 Invoice no.]
 Name
 Telephone
 Date
 Terms
 Shipping instructions

is partitioned into three tables. One contains the date, terms, and shipping instructions specified on the invoice. Another contains the customer's name and telephone number. And interestingly, what is left of the original table is nothing more than the compound key relating the customer and invoice:

[Invoice no.]   [Customer no.]   [Customer no.
 Date   Name   Invoice no.]
 Terms   Telephone
 Shipping instructions

The end product of this second step is the *second normal form*.

The third step of the process is to eliminate redundancy. Any redundant data elements in a table are discarded. Thus the data element "extended price," appearing in the table keyed on the combination of invoice number and line-item number, is eliminated because it can be recovered as a virtual data element by multiplying unit price by quantity. The table in question thus is reduced to

[Invoice no.
 Line item no.]
 Product no.
 Description

Unit of measure
Unit price
Quantity sold

Finally, any redundant tables (i.e., any that are simply subsets of other tables) are eliminated. Thus the table keyed on customer number

[Customer no.]
 Name
 Telephone

could be eliminated if the same data were already contained in a customer "master" table. The result of the third step in the normalization process is called the *third normal form*.

The third normal form provides a description of the data that is easy to understand, easy to use, easy to implement, and easy to maintain. It consists of two kinds of structural entity. One is the table of data, such as the table in the example containing the invoice data, terms, and shipping instructions. Tables correspond to the data files in conventional systems. Tables may be accessible either by simple keys, such as invoice number, or by compound keys, such as the combination of invoice number and line-item number. Simple keys correspond to one-to-one relationships, whereas compound or concatenated keys correspond to one-to-many or many-to-many relationships. The other kind of structural entity is the relationships between keys, such as the relationship between customer number and invoice number in the previous example. The relationships have no actual data content; rather, they are in the form of directories and correspond to the index files in conventional systems.

A more comprehensive example of the normalization process, starting with the invoice file together with a customer master file and product master file, is shown in Exhibit 9.1. The resulting third normal form is shown diagramatically in Figure 9.12. This type of diagram, often referred to as a *data access diagram*, shows the sequence of operations by which the data would be accessed. The significance of each table and, relationship comprising the third normal form is further illustrated by Exhibit 9.2, which incorporates sample customer, product, and invoice data.

EXHIBIT 9.1. Illustration of the Normalization Process

Step 1: All repeated data elements are expanded into separate data structures or "tables," and appropriate keys are assigned. As before, retrieval keys are enclosed in square brackets [ ]:

User File Definition		First Normal Form	
Customer:	Customer no.	Customer:	[Customer no.]
	Name		Name
	Address		Address
	Telephone		Telephone
	Balance		Balance
Product:	Product no.	Product:	[Product no.]
	Description		Description
	Warehouse location		Warehouse location
	U/M		U/M
	Unit price		Unit price
	Quantity on hand		Quantity on hand
Invoice:	Customer no.	Invoice:	[Customer no.
	Name		Invoice no.]
	Telephone		Name
	Invoice no.		Telephone
	Date		Date
	Terms		Terms
	Shipping instructions		Shipping instructions
	Line item no.	Line Item:	[Invoice no.
	Product no.		Line item no.]
	Description		Product no.
Repeated	U/M		Description
fields	Unit price		U/M
	Quantity sold		Unit price
	Extended price		Quantity sold
			Extended price

SUMMARY

Data base management systems are complex systems software packages providing for centralized storage and retrieval of data. In such systems, the concept of the "file" loses its significance in favor of more general— and shared—data structures. The data base is regarded as a central resource to be accumulated, managed, and made available to all authorized users according to their needs. This concept contrasts with the notion of data management adopted in older types of systems in which files are "owned" by individual applications and are configured and formatted according to the requirements of those applications.

EXHIBIT 9.1 (continued)

Step 2: Any data elements (that are not themselves keys) will be put into separate tables if they are fully specified by something other than the complete key (e.g., if they are fully specified by only part of a compound key):

First Normal Form		*Second Normal Form*	
Customer:	[Customer no.] Name Address Telephone Balance	Customer:	[Customer no.] Name Address Telephone Balance
Product:	[Product no.] Description Warehouse location U/M Unit price Quantity on hand	Product:	[Product no.] Description Warehouse location U/M Unit price Quantity on hand
Invoice:	[Customer no. Invoice no.] Name Telephone Date Terms Shipping instructions	Invoice:	[Customer no. Invoice no.]
		Invoice Data:	[Invoice no.] Date Terms Shipping instructions
Line Item:	[Invoice no. Line item no.] Product no. Description U/M Unit price Quantity sold Extended price	Customer Data:	[Customer no.] Name Telephone
		Line Item:	[Invoice no. Line item no.] Product no. Quantity sold Extended price
		Product Data:	[Product no.] Description U/M Unit price

The data base concept is revolutionizing the way in which information systems are designed and used and offers numerous advantages to organizations that have the resources to exploit them. One of the principal advantages is the potential for implementing real-time processing. The posting process, required in conventional-file systems, is no longer necessary. Posting can be replaced by a process of associating transaction records with their "parent" master record. And balances can be determined, on demand, by retrieving and summarizing the appropriate subset of transaction records. The problem of noncurrency of data that plagues conventional batch systems is thereby automatically eliminated.

EXHIBIT 9.1 (continued)

Step 3(a): Any redundant data elements, within a given table, are eliminated:

Second Normal Form		*Preliminary Third Normal Form*	
Customer:	[Customer no.] Name Address Telephone Balance	Customer:	[Customer no.] Name Address Telephone Balance
Product:	[Product no.] Description Warehouse location U/M Unit price Quantity on hand	Product:	[Product no.] Description Warehouse location U/M Unit price Quantity on hand
Invoice:	[Customer no. Invoice no.]	Invoice:	[Customer no. Invoice no.]
Invoice Data:	[Invoice no.] Date Terms Shipping instructions	Invoice Data:	[Invoice no.] Date Terms Shipping instructions
Customer Data:	[Customer no.] Name Telephone	Customer Data:	[Customer no.] Name Telephone
Line Item:	[Invoice no. Line item no.] Product no. Quantity sold Extended price	Line Item:	[Invoice no. Line item no.] Product no. Quantity sold
Product Data:	[Product no.] Description U/M Unit price	Product Data:	[Product no.] Description U/M Unit price

However, data base management systems have some disadvantages relative to systems based on conventional files, and so the data base approach is not for everyone. In small, as well as some large systems, conventional files may still be the best choice.

In data base management systems, multiple users can perceive configurations of data that not only differ from one another but differ from the physical arrangement of the data in the storage medium. The logical structure, or schema, consists of the data elements and the relationships among them as viewed by the users. Three structural models have been proposed as a basis for dis-

EXHIBIT 9.1 (continued)

Step 3(b): Any redundant tables (i.e., any that are simply subsets of other tables) are eliminated:

Preliminary Third Normal Form   *Third Normal Form*

Customer: [Customer no.]   Customer: [Customer no.]
          Name   Name
          Address   Address
          Telephone   Telephone
          Balance   Balance

Product: [Product no.]   Product: [Product no.]
          Description   Description
          Warehouse location   Warehouse location
          U/M   U/M
          Unit price   Unit price
          Quantity on hand   Quantity on hand

Invoice: [Customer no.   Invoice: [Customer no.
          Invoice no.]   Invoice no.]

Invoice Data: [Invoice no.]   Invoice Data: [Invoice no.]
          Date   Date
          Terms   Terms
          Shipping Instructions   Shipping instructions

Customer Data: [Customer no.]   Line Item: [Invoice no.
          Name   Line item no.]
          Telephone   Product no.
                                          Quantity sold

Line Item: [Invoice no.
          Line item no.]
          Product no.
          Quantity sold

Product Data: [Product no.]
          Description
          U/M
          Unit price

cussing data base structure: the hierarchical, network, and relational models. Each has its strengths and weaknesses, but the relational model has emerged as the most versatile and the one that best accommodates the relationships in typical accounting and business applications.

Developing a relational data base schema requires considerable effort. A comprehensive data dictionary must be prepared, and the logical relationships among the data elements must be identified. These relationships are likely to be conceived initially in the form of equivalent "file" definitions. These file definitions can be

FIGURE 9.12   Data access diagram showing the third normal form for the example shown in Exhibit 9.1.

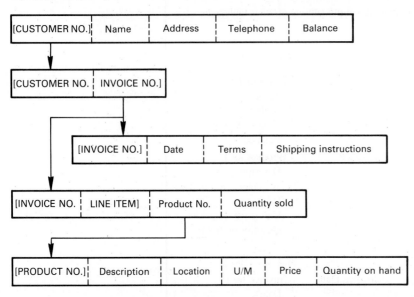

analyzed to produce a set of nonredundant tables—each with its own unique retrieval key—and an accompanying set of relationships among the keys. The process of analysis has been reduced to a set of "normalization" procedures, producing what are known as the first, second, and third normal forms of the data.

BIBLIOGRAPHY

Appleton, Daniel S. "The Modern Data Dictionary." *Datamation,* March 1, 1987, pp. 66–68.

Cardenas, Alphonso F. *Data Base Management Systems.* Boston: Allyn & Bacon, 1979.

Codd, E. F. "Recent Investigations in Relational Data Base Systems." *Information Processing 71.* Amsterdam: North Holland, 1974, pp. 1017–1021.

Date, C. J. "Debunking the Myth of Relational Systems." *Computer World,* March 30, 1987, p. 21.

Date, C. J. *An Introduction to Database Systems,* 3rd ed. Reading, Mass.: Addison-Wesley, 1981.

Lefkovits, Henry C. *Data Dictionary Systems.* Wellesley, Mass.: QED Information Systems, 1977.

McCarthy, William E. "The REA Model: A Generalized Framework for Accounting in a Shared Data Environment." *Accounting Review,* July 1982, pp. 554–578.

Meldman, M. J., D. J. McLeod, R. J. Pellicore, and M. Squire. *RISS: A Relational Data Base Management System for Mini-computers.* New York: Van Nostrand Reinhold, 1978.

Palmer, Ian. *Data Base Systems: A Practical Reference.* Wellesley, Mass.: QED Information Systems, 1975.

Powers, Michael J., David R. Adams, and Harlan D. Mills. *Computer Information Systems Development: Analysis and Design.* Cincinnati: South-Western, 1984.

Roberts, Martin B. *EDP Controls.* New York: Wiley, 1985.

Robichaux, Rory C. "The Database Approach." *Journal of Systems Management,* November 1980, pp. 6–14.

EXHIBIT 9.2.   Tables and Relationships Corresponding to the Third Normal Form for the Example in Exhibit 9.1

Cust. No.	Name	Address	Telephone	Balance
1234	Green	100 Oak St.	123–4567	$3,000
1235	Black	200 Ash St.	234–5678	$2,500
1236	Brown	300 Yew St.	345–6789	$1,500

Invoice No.	Date	Terms	Shipping Instructions
100	3/7/XX	net	UPS
107	3/12/XX	net	US Mail
123	4/10/XX	2/10,n/30	Truck
102	3/7/XX	net	Truck
118	3/31/XX	net	Air freight

Invoice No.	Line Item	Prod. No.	Qty. Sold
100	1	9876	24
	2	6666	9
	3	5567	15
102	1	6789	20
	2	2222	5
107	1	1033	36
	2	8765	108
118	1	9876	50
	2	3456	60
	3	6789	12
	4	5432	150
123	1	1928	10

Prod. No.	Description	Location	U/M	Unit Price	Quantity on Hand
1033	LH widget	Bin 26	Gl	$3.90	360
5567	RH widget	Bin 1	Dz	$6.50	27
6666	Short widget	Bin 5	Pr	$1.05	85
9876	Long widget	Bin 4	Ea	$4.75	120

Cust. No.	Invoice No.
1234	100
	107
	123
1235	102
	118
	154
1236	103
	115

Schroeder, Matthew T. "What's Wrong with DBMS." *Datamation*, December 15, 1986, pp. 67–70.

Schuster, Stewart A. "Relational Data Base Management for On-Line Transaction Processing." *Computer World*, June 15, 1981, pp. 19–30.

Wirth, Niklaus. "Data Structures and Algorithms." *Scientific American*, September 1984, pp. 60–69.

DISCUSSION QUESTIONS AND PROBLEMS

1. Define and discuss the following terms:

- Bachman diagram
- Data access diagram
- Data redundancy
- Data base administrator
- DBMS
- Data base system
- Error contamination
- Data definition language
- Hierarchical model
- Data dictionary
- Logical data structure
- Data inconsistency
- Many-to-many relationship
- Data manipulation language
- Network model
- Normalization
- One-to-one relationship
- One-to-many relationship
- Ownership of data
- Relationship matrix
- Retrieval key
- Physical data structure
- Relational model
- Query language
- Schema, subschema
- Structural independence
- System overhead

2. An integrated information system provides the functions of sales order processing, accounts receivable, and inventory management. Currently it is based on a conventional file structure. The principal files involved are

File	Record Length	No. of Records
Open order transaction file	100	10,000
Shipment transaction file	180	10,000
Open invoice file	250	3,500
Collections transaction file	120	2,500
Purchases transaction file	100	2,000
Customer master file	250	5,000
Inventory master file	250	20,000

It is estimated that there is a 25 percent duplication of data among the various files that could be eliminated by converting to a data base system. On the other hand, the DBMS would impose a system overhead equivalent to an additional 32 bytes for each existing record.

Required

a. Calculate the expected reduction in required storage capacity derived from eliminating the redundancy of data.

b. Estimate the additional capacity required to accommodate the system overhead of the DBMS.

c. Will the conversion to a data base system result in a net increase or decrease in the required storage capacity? By how much?

3. Three applications sharing a DBMS incorporate files whose logical structures are as follows:

Application	Data Elements
A	Employee number
	Name
	Date hired
	Marital status
	No. of dependents
B	Employee number
	Wage rate
	Total hours worked
	Gross earnings
C	Employee number
	Name
	Wage rate
	Date hired
	Date terminated

Required

a. Construct one possible physical data structure that could accommodate the needs of the three applications.

b. Assign representative lengths (in bytes) to the data elements. Determine the percentage saving in storage capacity from using a common data base rather than separate files in which data elements would be duplicated.

c. Identify the data elements for which there could be problems of data inconsistency if separate files were used.

4. Build a data dictionary, identifying the data elements and their lengths in bytes and data types, for a data base system providing for job cost and general ledger applications. The user is a construction company.

5. a. Identify the data elements required in a data base information system to be used in a school or college. The system is to store data on courses, instructors, students, classrooms, and textbooks.

b. Construct a relationship matrix, indicating all one-to-one, one-to-many, and many-to-many relationships among the elements identified in (a).

c. Draw a Bachman diagram showing the relationships defined in (b).

6. Three purchase orders selected from the records of Ajax Corporation contain the following data:

P/O No.
1001:

Vendor	Materials Ordered	Quantity
Bullen & Co.	Red widgets	10
	Green widgets	20
	Blue widgets	30

P/O No.
1002:

Vendor	Materials Ordered	Quantity
Caplan Corp.	Red widgets	100
	Blue widgets	50
	Yellow widgets	200

P/O No.
1003:

Vendor	Materials Ordered	Quantity
Bullen & Co.	Blue widgets	50
	Green widgets	100
	Yellow widgets	150

Required

a. Draw one or more diagrams, similar to that in Figure 9.9, establishing the hierarchical structure in which materials line-item records are owned by purchase order records and purchase order records are owned by vendor records. Label the purchase orders and materials involved.

b. Show the relationships instead as a network in which ownership of an entity by more than one ''parent'' is permitted. (Note that now there is no need to duplicate the materials records.)

7. Prepare tables similar to those in Figure 9.11 to illustrate the relational model using the data referred to in Problem 6. One table should identify the purchase orders and materials items associated with each vendor. Another should identify the purchase orders and vendors associated with each materials item. Construct any other useful tables that might be prepared from the same data.

8. The table on page 264 shows part of a simplified physical data base structure supporting an accounts payable application. The master records are accessed by means of an index file, and the transaction records owned by a given master file are connected in chronological order by forward pointers forming a ring or chain structure.

Required

a. Determine the balance due to Krypton Co. as of the last day of March.

b. The following transactions affecting Krypton took place during April, and they were entered at the record addresses indicated:

Date	Voucher Amount	Check Amount	Address
4/7	$ 550		48
4/10	130		603
4/15		$1,150	172
4/22	1,200		960

Incorporate these entries into the data base structure and establish all necessary pointers.

c. At the end of April, the March transaction records were archived and purged from the data base. Carry out the necessary maintenance on the data base structure, and set up a new beginning balance in the master record.

9. A DBMS has been installed by Brown Corporation to track work-in-process data through its manufacturing process. Management needs to be able to retrieve at will all transaction records relating to a specified job or all transactions relating to a specified department. On October 1, the data base contained the records shown in the table at the bottom of this page.

Data for Problem 8

Record Address	Record Type*	Vendor Name	Beginning Balance	Transaction Date	Voucher Amount	Check Amount	Forward Pointer
93	M	Krypton Co.	$2,400				168
115	T			3/15		$2,000	564
168	T			3/1	$1,000		302
302	T			3/7	250		115
564	T			3/24	900		781
781	T			3/31		1,400	93

* M = master record. T = transaction record.

Data for Problem 9

Record Address	Transaction Date	Job No.	Department No.	Cost Type*	Debit Amount	Credit Amount
52	8/15	308	14	M	$ 900	
71	9/2	311	14	L	250	
108	9/10	311	10	L	400	
112	8/19	309	14	M	1000	
133	8/31	311	01	O	765	
169	9/3	310	14	L	380	
181	9/20	311	12	M	800	
202	8/30	311	14	L	510	
219	9/14	312	14	L	350	
235	9/30	311	01			$3,700
237	9/30	311	01	O	975	

* M = materials, L = labor, O = overhead.

Required

a. Establish two sets of pointers identifying transactions (i) relating to job 311 and (ii) relating to department 14.

b. Job 311 was completed and transferred to finished goods inventory on 9/30. The relevant transaction records have now been archived and can be purged from the data base. Purge the records in question, and reestablish the pointers relating to department 14.

c. Suggest alternative ways in which the various transaction chains could be associated with master records relating to a given job or department.

10. The logical structure incorporated into the DBMS referred to in Problem 9 is based on the relational model. Prepare tables (similar to those in Figure 9.11) listing the transactions associated with job 311 and those associated with department 14, as of September 30. The transactions should be listed in chronological order, and running totals of materials, labor, and overhead costs should be included.

11. A project management information system is being developed to keep track of employee and task assignments. The decision has been made to base the system on a relational DBMS. As a first step toward establishing the data base schema, user-specified file definitions have been analyzed to produce the first normal form, and the result is given in the accompanying table.

Required

a. Continue the normalization process to provide the second and third normal forms and the final normalized form of the schema.

b. Draw the data access diagram corresponding to the final normalized form.

12. The purchasing cycle of Beltaine Company includes the purchasing, receiving, and accounts payable functions. Purchase requisitions are submitted by various user departments indicating the items to be purchased, the quantities needed, and the required delivery schedule. The purchasing department then issues the purchase orders to the respective suppliers and includes prices taken from vendor price lists. Upon delivery of the goods, the receiving department prepares a receiving

Data for Problem 11
Project Management System

1st Normal Form:

Employee:	[Employee no.] Employee name Date hired Specialty
Project:	[Project no.] Project description Date started Estimated total hours Actual total hours
Project task:	[Project no. Task no.] Project description Task description Estimated hours Actual hours
Employee assignment:	[Employee no. Project no.] Employee name Specialty Project description
Assigned task:	[Employee no. Project no. Task no.] Description Actual employee hours, this task

ticket listing the quantities of items received and their condition upon arrival. After receiving the vendor invoice, the accounts payable department prepares a disbursement voucher specifying the amount owed and the terms of payment.

Required

Construct a data dictionary for the purchasing cycle described here, listing the required data elements, their data type, the approximate length in bytes, and suggested variable names suitable for use in applications software written in COBOL.

13. The information services steering committee of a large automobile parts company is discussing plans for a data base management system to be implemented when a new centralized computer system is installed late next year. Alternative data base software packages will be available, providing for a hierarchical, network, or relational structural model. The first two types have been used for several years by other companies, whereas the relational type has only recently been announced by the manufacturer.

The information services manager is pressing for the relational model because of its conceptual superiority. But other members of the committee, including the controller (who has made it a point to stay abreast of developments in computer technology), are less sure. They feel that a network, or even a hierarchical model, would be adequate to meet the company's needs. Moreover, they are anxious about possible bugs in the relational model, as it has not yet been field tested. The information services manager countered this last argument by

expected that dual ownership of transaction records would ever be required.

Required

Evaluate the adequacy of the three structural models as a basis for meeting the needs of this user organization, and comment on the arguments for and against the use of the relational DBMS software. Take a position supporting either the information services manager or the controller.

14. The data access diagram for part of a job cost system and the partial data content of the corresponding tables are shown below and opposite. In the data access diagram, keys are shown in boldface.

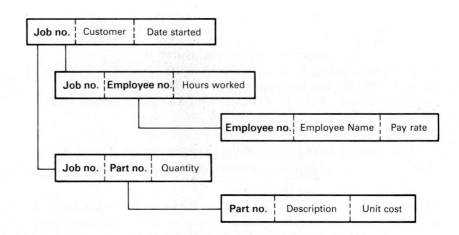

saying that even if there were bugs in the newly released relational package these would soon be fixed, and "If we buy one of the older models, we will be saddled with technology that is obsolete the day we install it."

The main purpose of the DBMS is to provide real-time processing of inventory transactions and on-line query of inventory balances. The system will establish the ownership of transaction records of inventory master records, and the primary retrieval key will be part number. There may be a need for occasional retrieval of inventory master records by other keys, but it is not

Required
a. Determine the prime cost (materials and labor cost) of each of the active jobs.
b. Comment on the mechanism of retrieving records from Tables 2 through 5.
c. Explore the possibility that Employee no. and Part no., in Tables 2 and 3, could be replaced by pointers.

15. At a meeting, representatives of the accounting department and the user services group drew up specifications for several files required in a new accounting application. One such file, an open purchase order file, was defined as follows:

Purchase order number (primary key)
Purchase requisition number
Vendor number
Vendor name
Date of issuance
Date of receipt
In-house part number*
Vendor catalog number*
Description*
Unit of measure*
Unit cost*
Quantity*

   *Repeated fields

The main objective is to provide the capability for personnel in inventory management and production to query the file in order to determine the status of an order and its content.

Several vendors may offer the same item. When an item is to be ordered, prices are compared in the most recent catalogs, and the order is sent to the vendor offering the most competitive price.

Required
a. Analyze the file specification into the first, second, and third normal forms to provide a set of data tables and relationships defining the schema of a relational data base.
b. Explain, by means of a data access diagram and a brief discussion, how the tables and relationships would be involved in the required query activity.

Data for Problem 14
TABLE 1

Job No.	Customer	Date Started
100	Red Company	1/1/99
101	Blue Company	2/2/99
102	Gray Company	3/3/99

TABLE 2

Job No.	Employee No.	Hours Worked
100	800	40
	801	40
	802	30
101	802	10
	803	40
102	804	40
	805	40

TABLE 3

Job No.	Part No.	Quantity
100	300	2
	301	5
	302	10
	303	6
101	300	4
	302	5
102	300	20
	303	1

TABLE 4

Employee No.	Employee Name	Pay Rate
800	M. Mercury	$8.50
801	V. Venus	$9.00
802	E. Earth	$7.00
803	M. Mars	$8.00
804	J. Jupiter	$10.00
805	S. Saturn	$9.00

TABLE 5

Part No.	Description	Unit Cost
300	10 in. widget	$100
301	12 in. widget	$120
302	14 in. widget	$140
303	16 in. widget	$160

10

Networks and Telecommunications

LEARNING OBJECTIVES

After you have studied this chapter you should be able to

- Evaluate the advantages and disadvantages of decentralizing computer facilities.
- Explain the concept and potential of distributed processing systems.
- Explain the concept of a telecommunications network.
- Identify and describe the most common network topologies.
- Discuss the problems of transmitting data over a distance and the ways to solve such problems.
- Identify the principal types of telecommunications media, and describe their characteristics.

CHAPTER OUTLINE

DECENTRALIZATION OF COMPUTER RESOURCES

Centralization Versus Decentralization

The first computers were centralized systems in two senses. A typical system consisted of a single central processor unit supporting passive peripheral devices. And the elements of the system were concentrated in one location; the hardware, data, and operators all were located in a single room. Organizations that had branches dispersed over a wide geographical area were forced to do one of two things. Either they could incur the (then very substantial) cost of duplicating computer resources at each branch, or they could send data by mail or courier to be processed at the central computer facility. Subsequent developments in computer technology during the mid-1960s alleviated this problem by allowing operators to access computers from remote terminals. Remote job entry and remote printing of output greatly reduced the problem of user–machine communications. However, the systems of that time could still be considered centralized because the heart of the com-

puter, the central processor, was still confined to a single location. Also, all of the files were usually stored at the main facility, and operators at the central site frequently had to load software and data files in response to requests made from users at the remote locations.

The advent of minicomputers in the early 1970s revolutionized user access to computing facilities by making it feasible to distribute processing capability throughout the organization. Minicomputers—and, later, powerful microcomputers—could be located at each branch, or even in each department, eliminating the need for a large central computer facility and the associated communications links. Thus the fully decentralized system, decentralized, that is, in terms of hardware, software, data, and operational control, came into being.

Today, designers can choose between centralized or decentralized computer facilities according to the needs of the organization and its users. The advantages and disadvantages of each are summarized in Exhibit 10.1. An important factor in this choice is the nature of the organization itself. Strong, centralized organizations are usually served best by a centralized information system, whereas decentralized organizations may be served better by a decentralized information system.

EXHIBIT 10.1 Advantages and Disadvantages of Centralized Versus Decentralized Systems

Centralized Systems

Advantages:
  Ability to install large, powerful resources available to all users
  Economies of scale
  Ability to assemble a team of specialists trained in various aspects of data processing
    and related technologies
  Large centralized data base
  Ready-made communications system for sharing information
  Effective central control over information resources

Disadvantages:
  Dependence on a single central processor, and the consequent impact of downtime
  Slow turnaround on batch jobs or degradation of interactional response time during
    peak operating periods (9:00 A.M. to 4:00 P.M.)
  Inflexibility to respond to different computing needs in different parts of the
    organization
  Possible emergence of an ''ivory tower'' syndrome among the specialists at the central
    facility

Decentralized Systems

Advantages:
  Flexibility to adapt to a variety of user needs
  Good reliability characteristics (not all the machines are likely to be down at the same
    time)

Disadvantages:
  Inadequate processing power to handle larger jobs
  Duplication of data bases or the possibility of not being able to access needed data
  No provision for sharing information
  Loss of central control over data-processing resources

Distributed Processing Systems

Developments during the late 1970s and early 1980s offered the possibility of a compromise between fully centralized and fully decentralized systems in the form of *distributed processing* systems. Distributed processing systems consist of multiple processors and appropriate peripherals connected by some form of network, permitting communication among the various elements and sharing of the common work load. The processor devices may be dispersed over a wide geographical area or may be confined to a single location. The first application of the distributed processing concept was to geographically dispersed information systems. Minicomputers located at the branches of an organization could either operate as stand-alone machines or, optionally, be connected to one another or to a larger central computer facility. In this way, the advantages of both centralization and decentralization could be realized, and users could have the best of both worlds.

In the early 1980s there was a strong move toward distributed processing systems, even in organizations that were not geographically dispersed. As processor devices became smaller and cheaper, hardware designers incorporated them in increasing numbers into peripheral devices. Thus emerged the "smart" and "intelligent" peripherals: terminals, disk drives, printers, and other devices. The processing capability incorporated into peripheral devices has removed much of the processing work load from the central processor. More peripheral devices can be connected to a processor of a given size, or a smaller processor can support a given number of peripherals.

The logical conclusion of this trend is to eliminate the central processor altogether, and this has been done in many types of modern systems. Such systems consist of nothing more than a number of intelligent "peripheral" devices connected by a communications network. Each user may have a self-contained desktop computer that can handle small jobs internally but that can share data or common peripheral devices or can call upon the resources of other machines when needed.

NETWORK SYSTEMS

Network Topology

Distributed processing systems depend on communications channels connecting the component devices. These channels usually consist of electrical conductors—wires or cables—through which data and other messages can be transmitted in the form of coded signals. Suitable hardware devices and software are provided to ensure that messages reach their intended destinations, without conflicting with other messages being transmitted simultaneously, and to prevent messages from reaching unintended or unauthorized destinations. The flow of messages through the communications system is like the flow of motor vehicles along highways and in fact is referred to as *traffic*.

The set of communications channels is referred to as a *network*. The computer devices that are connected together comprise the network's *nodes*. The hardware device that controls the flow of messages through the network is called a network *server*, and it normally comprises one of the nodes. The manner in which the nodes are connnected to one another is referred to as the network's *topology*. Topology is the study of spatial re-

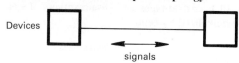

FIGURE 10.1   Point-to-point topology.

lationships without regard for the details of the relative physical placement of the nodes or the precise geometry of the interconnecting links. Some representative topologies are as follows:

Point to Point System. The simplest type of "network" consists of a single communications channel connecting two computer devices (Figure 10.1). Either of the two devices can act as the network server. The topology is represented by a straight connecting link between the two nodes. The actual physical arrangement may, of course, include a cable that winds around numerous obstacles from one device to the other, but the topology does not consider these complexities. The communications channel typically permits bidirectional transmission of signals, so that messages can be sent in either direction. No switching is required; the path of the signals through the system is clear; and the only possible problem of traffic congestion might be the collision of messages traveling in opposite directions.

Bus Network. In a bus network, each device is connected to a common conductor or *bus* that carries bidirectional signals from one device to another (Figure 10.2). This configuration is also referred to as a *multidrop* topology. One of the devices may act as the network server; or this function may be shared among all the component devices. In any case, each device must be able to discriminate among the various messages traveling along the bus and select those to be intercepted. There must also be some means of spac-

FIGURE 10.2   Bus topology.

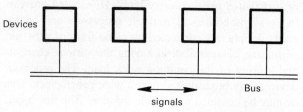

FIGURE 10.3 Ring topology.

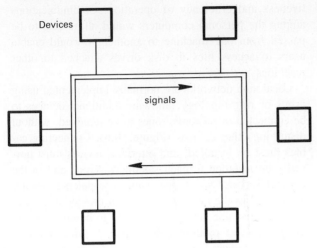

FIGURE 10.4 Star topology.

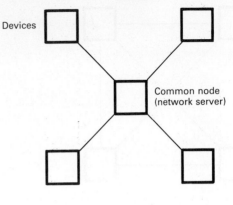

ing the messages traveling along the bus so as to avoid conflict. Bus topologies minimize the amount of cabling required, and much of the hardware can be bought off the shelf. But they are limited to bus lengths of about 1,000 feet.

Messages can be sent to a particular users, or messages can be "multicast" (to several users) or "broadcast" (to all users). However, protecting the privacy of messages intended for a single recipient may be difficult with this type of topology.

Ring Network. A ring network can be regarded as being equivalent to a bus topology whose two "ends" are connected together (Figure 10.3), although the electronic aspects of such a network are in fact more complex than this. Messages usually circulate around the ring in one direction only. One strategy for avoiding conflicts among different messages sharing the ring is to provide for passage of electrical "tokens" around the ring at specified intervals. Messages can be attached to "free" tokens as they pass transmitting nodes, in much the same way as travelers board vacant taxicabs. Such systems are referred to as *token ring systems*. Whatever strategy is adopted, messages in ring networks may be delayed when the traffic volume is high.

The same remarks made about bus topologies concerning multicast and broadcast messages and message privacy apply to ring networks.

Star Network. In a star network each device is connected to a common central node. On a small scale a central processor unit connected to its various peripheral devices represents a star network. In a star network supporting a distributed processing system, the central node is normally selected as the network server (Figure 10.4). Star networks are simple in concept, and the single control device can be used to monitor traffic within the network or to switch messages from one channel to another. The central node may be assigned certain centralized functions such as superior processing capability.

Radial transmission, back and forth from the central node to the satellite nodes, is fast and reliable. On the other hand, if messages need to be transmitted from one satellite node to another, switching facilities at the central node may become a vulnerable bottleneck. Reliability problems and traffic congestion may be the result.

Closely related to the star network is the tree topology. Tree networks have a "root" from which "branch" channels radiate to a number of nodes. From each of these nodes, several more "twig" channels radiate, and so forth.

Fully Connected Network. In a fully connected network, every device is connected to every other device (Figure 10.5). Any one of the devices can act as the network server, or the function can be shared. Messages can usually travel in both directions along each link. Traffic congestion is minimized in such a network, but control is difficult. Also, because there may be

FIGURE 10.5   Fully connected topology.

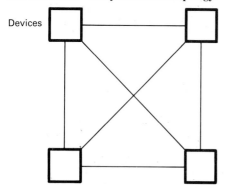

Devices

multiple routes for messages traveling from one node to another—it may be possible for messages to be relayed through an intermediate device—messages can inadvertently be duplicated.

From an economic standpoint, fully connected networks are inefficient because of the many communication channels necessary. The number of channels is related to the number of nodes, N, by the expression:

$$\text{Number of channels} = \frac{N(N-1)}{2}$$

Thus a network of 4 nodes requires 6 channels, one of 10 requires 45 channels, and a network of 100 nodes requires no less than 4,950 channels. There are more economical ways of networking large numbers of nodes, while still allowing them all to communicate with one another. The public telephone system provides an example, in which the millions of subscribers are connected by combinations of local star networks and point-to-point long lines. Private branch exchanges (PBXs), installed within an organization, also use star networks.

Representative Systems

Local area networks provide great flexibility to configure computer systems to meet specific user requirements. In many cases a number of personal computers are already in use, and the proposal to network them is made on the grounds of potential increases in the effectiveness and efficiency of operation. Communications among the personal computers would allow data to be passed from one machine to another or would enable users to access files in disk drives attached to other machines.

Local area networks are normally implemented using a bus or ring topology, allowing additional devices to be connected or unwanted ones to be removed, without disturbing other devices (Figure 10.6). Connecting cables must be installed, and interface devices must normally be installed in each satellite machine and in the network server. One of the personal computers is usually designated as the network server. To provide this function, the machine selected may need to be upgraded by the addition of main-memory capacity. Often the network server must have a more powerful processor than is needed for stand-alone operation. On the other hand, the "satellite" computers may also need to be upgraded; the network software occupies an appreciable amount of main memory, which is then not available for user programs and data.

Other advantages may be recognized later, and so the facilities may be enhanced to provide a broader range of capabilities. One enhancement may be the implementation of an inter-work-station, or interoffice, message system. This is usually handled simply by a software acquisition.

Another enhancement may be the addition of sharable peripherals such as large disk drives, tape drives, high-technology printers, plotters, and specialized monitors. In this way, facilities whose cost could not be justified for individual users can be made available to the group. In some cases, the devices can be attached directly to the network, while in other cases, a device server is needed to interface the network and the device. The purpose of the device server is to resolve potential conflicts among access messages coming from different points of origin.

A third enhancement may be access to the "outside world" via a gateway device. Access may be provided to a host computer, such as the organization's large mainframe computer, to a commercial data service, or to another network. Decentralized organizations may have local area networks (LANs) in each branch and also telecommunications capabilities between one LAN and

FIGURE 10.6 Typical local area network system.

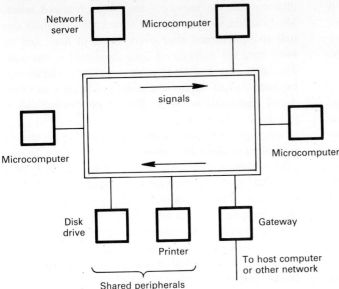

another. If communications are to extend over an appreciable distance, a modem may be necessary in addition to the gateway device.

Most wide area networks rely on communication channels provided by the public telephone utilities or "common carriers." The telephone companies provide ready-made networks that—as far as the user is concerned—correspond to either point-to-point or fully connected topologies. If traffic volume is low, ordinary dial-up telephone lines will suffice. As the volume increases, an organization's first option is to lease one or more higher-capacity lines from a telephone utility. Only if the lease costs of such an arrangement become prohibitive would an organization consider investing the huge sums necessary to build its own system of long-distance communications. Ordinarily the telephone utility companies can provide any kind of service that a user might need, and at a competitive price.

TELECOMMUNICATIONS TECHNOLOGY

The purpose of a telecommunications system is to enable data and associated control signals to be sent from a transmitting station to a receiving station. The communicating elements may be in the same room, or they may be separated by thousands of miles. It is often remarked that we live in an age of communications, and today much or most of the total volume of communications is transmitted electronically. The telephone, radio and television broadcasts, cable television, teleconferencing, electronic mail, and electronic funds transfer are familiar examples. Communications between computers and remote terminals or between two or more computers have long been a feature of many business information systems. Electronic data interchange, which has been gaining in popularity, allows direct communication among the computers of companies doing business with one another, so that, for instance, the electronic equivalent of a purchase order could be transmitted from the customer's computer to the vendor's computer. Other examples are interoffice message systems, facsimile transmission systems, data services such as those that provide up-to-the-minute stock prices, on-line library retrieval systems, electronic shopping systems, electronic bulletin boards, and security systems. The applications of data communications clearly extend beyond the boundaries of accounting and general business informations systems. But it is in the area of information systems that data communications have had a particularly important impact, and information systems would be very different from what they are today if technological advances in communications had not been so rapid or had taken a different path. Certainly, network systems, which have become so popular in recent years, would not exist as we know them.

Communications technology consists of the hardware and the supporting software necessary to send electronic signals over a distance. Technological considerations relate not only to the communications medium itself but also to the means of accessing the channel and, when necessary, conversion of the data into a form that can be transmitted through the particular medium. There are several different type of communications channels, and they can be evaluated and compared on the basis of capacity, reliability, and cost. Capacity determines the volume of data that can be transmitted in a given time and, consequently, the speed of transmission. Cost extends to the cost of installation, maintenance, and operation.

Modes of Transmission

The simplest kind of telecommunications channel, referred to as a *simplex* channel, permits transmission in only one direction. Cable television is a familiar example. A more complicated kind, referred to as a *half-duplex* channel, permits transmission in both directions, but in only one direction at a time. Thus, in a telephone system, only one person would be able to talk at a time; when that person stopped talking, the other person could start. Some intercontinental telephone services are of this type, as well as some mobile telephone systems, such as the older telephones carried in automobiles, and citizens-band (CB) radios. The most sophisticated kind of system, *full duplex*, permits concurrent bidirectional transmissions. Virtually all internal, land-based telephone systems are now of the full-duplex type.

The ability to handle bidirectional transmission may appear to be somewhat less important to data communication systems than to telephone systems. In some systems, data may need to be transmitted in only one direction, say, from a branch sales office to headquarters. But even in this type of system, bidirectional transmission is required in order to provide for acknowledgement

or confirmation signals from the receiving station, indicating that the messages have been received intact. Most modern systems provide for acknowledgement signals to be returned after every block of data, and no more data are transmitted until the signal is received. The return of acknowledgement signals could be accommodated in half-duplex channels, but at the cost of reduced transmission speed. This penalty is avoided in full-duplex channels.

The eight bits comprising a byte are transmitted in several ways along the communications channel. In *parallel communication*, which is used for distances of a few feet, the eight bits are transmitted along separate conductors. Parallel communication is used internally in most computer devices and may also used between the central processor and peripheral devices such as disk drives and printers. For greater distances it is customary to transmit the bits one at a time along the same conductor; this is referred to as *serial communication*.

The problem with serial communication is that the receiving station must be able to interpret the arriving string of bits as complete bytes, that is, be able to tell when one byte ends and another begins. Some systems, using what are referred to as *synchronous channels*, solve this problem by synchronizing the internal clocks in the transmitting and receiving stations. This is done by the transmitting a synchronizing signal at the beginning of the message. The arrival time of each subsequent byte can then be scheduled. But synchronization is usually feasible only for relatively short distances, and longer-distance channels are typically asynchronous. In this latter case, in order to delineate one byte from another at the receiving end, each byte is "encased" between *start* and *stop* bits. As will be seen later, the insertion of these additional bits slightly degrades the channel's capacity.

Capacity of a Channel

The capacity of a communications channel is measured in either bandwidth or bits of data per second. The bandwidth, measured in Hertz or megaHertz (millions of Hertz), refers to the channel's frequency response. The greater the bandwidth is, the wider can be the frequency spectrum of a transmitted signal. For example, voice-grade telephone lines provides a bandwidth of 4,000 Hz, which is adequate for speech transmission, although it does not provide the audio fidelity of a home stereo system. Facsimile transmission requires a bandwidth of somewhere between 16,000 to 60,000 Hertz, while television signals require a bandwidth of 4 megaHertz, or 1,000 times that of a telephone.

To transmit digitized data, comprising numeric, alphanumeric, and other characters, the more directly applicable measure of capacity is the signal transmission speed in bits per second (b.p.s.). The theoretical maximum speed in b.p.s. is equal to twice the bandwidth in Hertz; thus a bandwidth of 4,000 Hz (corresponding to a voice-grade telephone line) could accommodate a transmission speed of 8,000 b.p.s. In practice, this potential maximum speed is rarely achieved, and somewhat lower transmission speeds must usually be accepted.

In turn, the transmission speed in bits per second must be related to the effective message transmission speed, of more direct interest to the user, which is measured in characters per second. This relationship depends on the mode of transmission. With parallel transmission, the capacity in bits per second is equal to the transmission speed in characters per second. Thus a capacity of 4,800 b.p.s. per channel would permit a message to be transmitted at a speed of 4,800 characters per second.

On the other hand, with synchronous serial transmission, in which the 8 bits are transmitted one after the other, the effective speed in characters per second is only one eighth of the capacity in bits per second. Thus a capacity of 4,800 b.p.s. translates into 4,800/8 = 600 characters per second. With asynchronous serial transmission the speed in characters per second is only one tenth of the capacity in bits per second because of the inclusion of the start and stop bits. Thus the 4,800 b.p.s. channel would permit a speed of only 4,800/10 = 480 characters per second (Figure 10.7).

An older term for measuring the speed of digital transmission is the *baud* rate, named after Emil Baudot, a pioneer in data communications. For some types of modulation (discussed later), the baud rate is equal to the capacity in bits per second, but in others the two measures are different. There is no consistent relationship between the baud rate and the number of characters per second. Measurement in bits per second avoids any ambiguity and this should be the standard of reference.

Modulation and Demodulation

Whereas modern computer hardware deals almost exclusively with pulsed electrical signals, representing digitized data, many telecommunications media require the transmitted signals to be in the form of analog, or continuous waveform, signals (Figure 10.8). The reason for this requirement is that the impedance (electrical inertia) of the lines would soon smooth out the sharp gradients of the electrical pulses and obliterate the data content of the signals. Unless the channel bandwidth is particularly high, the restrictions on the length of channel and transmission speed for digital signals are usually intolerable. Even when a high bandwidth is available, analog transmission may more efficiently use the channel capacity, thereby allowing more data to be transmitted. If digital signals are converted into continuous-waveform analog signals, the signals must be converted back into digital form, at the receiving station, for either immediate output or further processing by another computer device.

Typically the digitized signal representing the data is superimposed on an analog carrier wave. The carrier wave is a steady signal that "carries" the data in somewhat the same way as a conveyer belt carries products along an assembly line. The process of superimposing the analog signal on the carrier is called *modulation*. The corresponding process, performed at the receiving station, in which the digitized signal is recovered from the carrier, is called *demodulation*. The device that performs the modulation and demodulation is appropriately called a *modulator/demodulator*, or *modem*. Modems may be packaged as freestanding devices or as cards to be inserted in a computer processing device. Some modems incorporate an autodialing feature that enables them to call a telephone number under the control of the keyboard or software.

One common method of modulation, referred to as *amplitude modulation* (*A.M*), varies the amplitude of the carrier in sympathy with the information to be transmitted. Another method, *frequency modulation* (*F.M.*), varies the frequency of the carrier while keeping its amplitude constant. A third method, *phase modulation* (*P.M.*), varies the phase of the carrier while keeping constant both the amplitude and the frequency. All three methods are used to broadcast radio and television signals as well as to transmit data.

FIGURE 10.7   Transmission modes. The figure shows how the message A to Z would be transmitted according to three different transmission modes: parallel, synchronous serial, and asynchronous serial. Asynchronous transmission is slower than synchronous transmission because of the need for start and stop bits. The ASCII equivalent of the message is as follows:

A	(blank)	t	o	(blank)	Z
01000001	01000000	01110100	01101111	01000000	01011010

(a) Parallel transmission

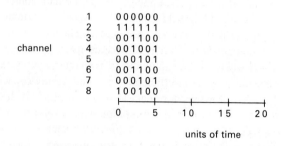

(b) Synchronous serial transmission

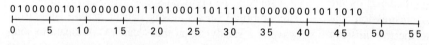

(c) Asynchronous serial transmission

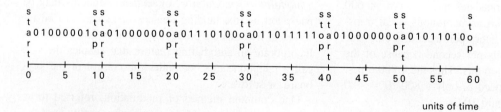

Multiplexing and Concentrating

Frequently a number of peripheral devices are in use in one location and must be connected to a host computer at another location. For example, a branch office may use several data entry terminals to input sales transaction data that will be processed at the corporate headquarters.

One arrangement is to have several communications channels, one for each remote device. However, such an arrangement might be highly inefficient because of unused channel capacity. A more efficient arrangement, referred to as *multiplexing*, is to share a single communications channel. Multiplexing transmitted signals is the analog of time sharing central processor resources.

FIGURE 10.8   Digital pulses and continuous waveform signals.

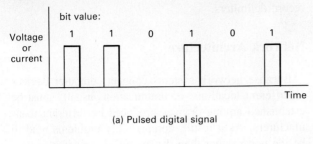

bit value:

Voltage or current

1   1   0   1   0   1

Time

(a) Pulsed digital signal

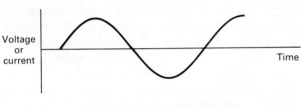

Voltage or current

Time

(b) Continuous waveform signal

A typical multiplexing arrangement is shown in Figure 10.9. The various devices are connected to a digital multiplexor, which combines the individual data signals into a single digital signal. In turn, the modem converts the digital signal into an analog signal for transmission.

Two common methods of multiplexing are frequency-division and time-division multiplexing. In frequency-division multiplexing, which is more applicable to analog signals, a certain portion of the available frequency bandwidth of the carrier is assigned to each signal. For instance, a signal with a bandwidth of 4,000 Hz might occupy the range from 2.00 to 2.04 MHz; a second signal might occupy the range from 2.04 to 2.08 MHz; and so forth. Time-division multiplexing is applicable to digital signals. The whole channel is dedicated to a single signal for a short interval of time, and then control is passed to the next signal. Time-division multiplexing is directly analogous to the time-slicing schemes used in central processor time sharing (see Chapter 6).

In a multiplexing arrangement, the capacity of the common channel must be adequate to provide for the combined bandwidth of the individual signals. Consider, for example, a situation in which eight devices are connected to a a multiplexor, each generating a signal with a bandwidth of 400 Hz (equivalent to about 80 characters per second, depending on the mode of transmission). The communications channel would need to provide a minimum bandwidth somewhat greater than 8 x 400 = 3,200 Hz. The required bandwidth is slightly greater than a simple multiple of the individual bandwidths because of the need to transmit "housekeeping" bits, analogous to the start and stop bits in serial transmission.

The required bandwidth of 3,200 Hz is within the capacity of a voice-grade telephone line. If more signals

FIGURE 10.9   Sharing of communications channels by means of a multiplexor or concentrator.

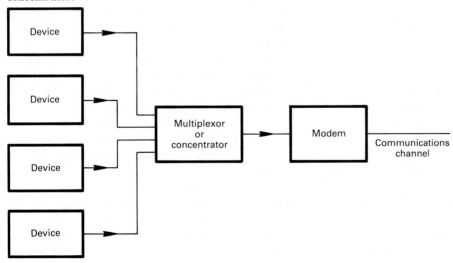

were multiplexed or if the bandwidth of the individual signals were greater, then the combined signal would exceed the capacity of the voice-grade line. However, even if a more expensive channel medium had to be used, the resulting cost might still be lower than the cost of separate telephone lines for each device.

Multiplexors usually allocated a certain fraction of the common channel capacity to each sharing channel, regardless of whether data are currently being transmitted. As as result, the total available capacity may not be used efficiently. A related device, referred to as a *concentrator*, allocates the capacity dynamically, according to the relative traffic volumes. It uses a form of time-division multiplexing called *statistical multiplexing*.

Communications Software

Software is important to telecommunications systems, both to control the flow of messages throughout the network as a whole and to control the interface between an individual device and the network. The control of the message traffic is roughly analogous to air traffic control in the air space around an airport and has similar objectives: to maximize efficiency of usage and to ensure arrival at the correct destination. Overall control is normally accomplished by systems software forming an extension of the operating system associated with the network server. The complexity of this kind of software varies with the complexity of the network.

Control over the interface between an individual device and the network is easier and may be accomplished by software executed by the local device or even by hardware alone. A simple example is the software that enables a personal computer to operate as a terminal and to communicate with a network. Such a software package usually programs a hardware interface that performs two main functions. It provides a temporary input–output port. And it converts the parallel digital signal from the central processor into a serial signal for output to the network, or it makes the reverse conversion for incoming signals. The hardware interface is a special-purpose logic device that must be programmed to ensure compatibility of "handshaking" protocols between the terminal and the network. Compatibility must be ensured with respect to tranmission speed, choice of

acknowledgement characters, type of message echoing used (if any), and the presence or absence of end-of-record delimiters.

Network Architecture

Because network systems connect computer devices in different locations, communications usually must be established among devices produced by different manufacturers. As a result, compatibility problems tend to be the norm rather than the exception. In order to help reduce these problems, the International Standards Organization has proposed a conceptual model of telecommunications systems that offers a common framework or terminology to be used to evaluate the modes of signal transmission and control used by the products of individual manufacturers. The model is referred to as the *Open Systems Interconnection (OSI) standard architecture*. To date, few of the packaged network systems offered by the leading manufacturers conform precisely to the standard, but the standard nevertheless provides an ideal toward which the manufacturers are striving.

The OSI standard architecture is hierarchical and consists of seven layers:

- *Application*. The message sent from one user to another.
- *Presentation*. The formatting, coding (e.g., ASCII, EBCDIC), digitizing, and possible encrypting of the message in readiness for transmission.
- *Session*. Management of the totality of the communication or dialogue between a particular sender and a particular receiver.
- *Transport*. The end-to-end flow of messages (including ackowledgement signals) from sender to receiver, and the possible division of the message into *packets* and the reassembly of packets that may have been sent at different times and by different routes.
- *Network*. The network hardware and communications software used to support and control the flow of messages.
- *Data link*. The devices, such as communications cards, multiplexors, concentrators, and modems, through which signals pass into the network.
- *Physical*. The nature of the physical transmission medium, such as a telephone line.

FIGURE 10.10 OSI standard network architecture.

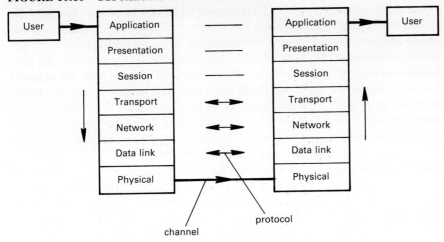

The lower levels of the model are specific to the particular hardware and software system provided. The upper layers, particularly the top two layers, are more general in nature and focus on the users' activities and concerns. However, the capabilities of the upper layers build on those of the lower layers. For example, the ability to implement a certain network topology extending over a certain geographical area (the network layer) depends on the capabilities of the transmission medium (the physical layer).

A user wishing to send a message through a telecommunications system interfaces with the applications layer. The message then travels "down" through successive layers to the physical layer, where it enters the physical transmission medium. At the receiving station, the message travels "up" through the layers, finally exiting from the applications layer (Figure 10.10). Except in the simplest situation of a point-to-point topology, the message is also likely to pass through intermediate nodes, such as switching devices, en route to the receiving station. At such intermediate nodes, the message travels up through some subset of the layers—typically as far as the network layer—and then down again before reentering the physical medium (Figure 10.11).

Any two nodes connected by a single channel must properly interface with each other; otherwise a message

FIGURE 10.11 Message transmission through intermediate nodes.

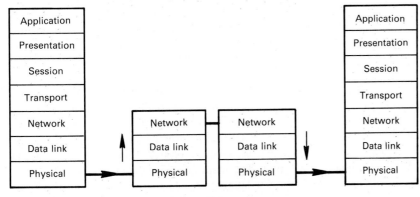

cannot be transmitted between them. And they must properly interface with each other on each of the several layers in the OSI model. Thus there must be compatibility of physical media, compatibility of modems and multiplexors, compatibility of mode of transmission (parallel, synchronous serial, asynchronous serial), and so forth. The rules of compatibility at any given layer are referred to as the communications *protocols* of that layer. Elements common to all protocols include error controls and message flow controls to ensure the integrity of messages from user to user.

But whereas there must be compatibility between any two nodes, there need not be compatibility all the way from the sending to the receiving stations. At an intermediate node, the medium might change from a telephone line to a microwave link; the type of modulation might be changed; and the mode of transmission might be changed, say, from serial to parallel. Such changes are made by protocol converters, which may be hardware devices, software, or a combination of both. The changes are important to the telecommunications specialists but are normally of no concern to the user, so long as end-to-end control of the message can be maintained.

The hierarchical structure of the OSI model allows for each layer's functional capabilities to be defined separately. It also allows complex problems relating to telecommunications systems to be divided into simpler problems that may be analyzed—and, if possible, solved—on one layer at a time. Among such problems are internal control problems, which are of particular concern to accountants.

TELECOMMUNICATIONS MEDIA

Telephone Lines

There are an estimated 100 million miles of telephone lines installed throughout the world, providing a ready-made system of data communications. Indeed, when the need for data communications first arose, people naturally turned to the existing telephone lines to meet their requirements. Where telephone lines were already in place, there was no additional installation cost, and the operating costs were relatively low even for long-distance communication. With regard to costs, a particularly attractive feature of dial-up lines was that the lines were available to be used at any time but incurred charges only when they were actually in use; fixed costs were thereby kept to a minimum. Even where special lines, such as Wide Area Telephone Service (WATS) lines, had to be installed for data communications, the cost was still acceptably low.

On the other hand, telephone lines, which usually consist of pairs of twisted copper wires, have relatively poor capacity characteristics. The familiar voice-grade, switched lines, which are laid into offices and homes, offer a bandwidth of 4,000 Hz and reliable transmission speeds of up to about 4,800 b.p.s. Leased voice-grade lines, which are dedicated to certain users and do not pass through switching equipment, have a higher signal-to-noise ratio and can accommodate speeds up to 9,600 b.p.s. *Broadband* telephone lines, which can also be leased from the telephone companies, offer speeds in excess of 10,000 b.p.s. But this speed is still low compared with that of some competing types of media.

Another problem with telephone lines is their vulnerability to eavesdropping or to unauthorized access to the facilities to which they are connected. Although various forms of controls help reduce this vulnerability, the underlying problem is a serious one.

Coaxial Cable

Coaxial cable is normally used for short-distance communications, such as within a building, but it is also used for intra- and intercity communications for distances of up to about 100 miles. Coaxial cable, in which an electrical conductor is surrounded by a magnetic and electric shield, offers a much higher capacity than does twisted copper wire. Standardized (T-1) coaxial data systems, which were first installed in 1962, carry data transmissions at a speed of 1.544 million b.p.s. (1.544 Mb.p.s). The main disadvantage of coaxial cable is its high installation cost, which can approach $100,000 per mile.

A major user of coaxial cable is the cable television (CATV) industry; a typical cable can carry between 34 and 54 simultaneous television transmissions. Some people have suggested that unused capacity in existing CATV installations be made available for data transmission. The concept is an interesting one, but the associated problems are substantial and have not yet been solved. One problem is that CATV systems do not have switching facilities. Another is that the cable drivers send signals in only one direction. A third problem is that the cables are normally concentrated in residential areas, away from the largest telecommunications users. And a fourth problem is the intense opposition from the telephone companies, which are seeking regulatory protection prohibiting CATV companies from offering such services.

Fiber Optic Cable

Fiber optic cable consists of thin filaments of glass, about 300 microns in diameter. Information is transmitted through the cable in the form of light waves, instead of electrical signals, as in other kinds of communications media. Specifically, lasers operating in the infrared range are used as sources of coherent light that can be interrupted millions of times per second to produce information-carrying pulses.

Fiber optic cable is cheap and offers signal-to-noise ratios that are far higher than with any competing type of medium. Furthermore, high bandwidths can be achieved—up to 50,000 MHz for unspliced cable less than one mile in length. Under practical conditions involving cable splicing, end-to-end bandwidths exceeding 1,000 MHz can readily be achieved. Because of the high bandwidth, signals can be transmitted in their original digital form without modulation. The associated access equipment is thereby simplified. Another attractive feature is that fiber optic cables are relatively tamper proof.

The first experimental fiber optic cable was used in Chicago in 1977, and since then they have rapidly become popular. Many office parks and even whole cities are now being "prewired," with fiber optic cable offering ready access to this type of medium. The long-distance telephone companies are are laying fiber optic cable between major cities in the United States. However, the installation of fiber optic cables is far from replacing the vast installed base of twisted-pair telephone wires.

Microwave Communications

Microwave communications rely on radio transmission between ground-based antennas. Their channel capacity is greater than that of coaxial cables, but not as high as fiber optic cables. Transmission speeds of up to 10 Mb.p.s. can be achieved. The disadvantage of microwave communications is the need for line-of-sight transmission from one antenna to another, and so antennas must be erected roughly every 20 miles across level ground and more closely in mountainous terrain. Installation costs are therefore high. Furthermore, microwave transmission may be interrupted by accumulated snow and ice on antennas and—at least in certain frequency bands—is also susceptible to interference from falling rain and snow. Finally, there are increasing concerns about the possible safety hazards of prolonged exposure to microwave radiation.

Satellite Communications

Satellite communications also rely on radio transmissions but, in this case, between a ground-based antenna and an antenna installed in a satellite in synchronous orbit above the earth. Signals are amplified by equipment in the satellite and are retransmitted to a terrestrial antenna at the receiving station. Radio frequencies of about 14,000 MHz are normally used. Satellite communications offer many advantages, including high capacity (comparable with microwaves), ability to function in mountainous regions, and independence of distance.

The first communications satellite—the Intelsat I—was placed in orbit in 1965. Since then many more satellites have been launched. By the early 1980s there was substantial excess capacity. But problems with launch vehicles during the mid-1980s have drawn attention to the potential problems of keeping enough active satellites in orbit to meet user demand. Now that the U.S. government has turned over the launching of communications satellites to the private sector, experience will tell whether these problems can be overcome.

SUMMARY

Computer-processing resources have been decentralized at two levels. On the one hand, geographically dispersed organizations have distributed processing capability throughout their divisions and branches. On the other, designers of computers have recognized the advantages of distributing processing logic throughout the computer system rather than concentrating it in a single central processor unit. This latter trend has resulted in the "distributed processing systems" in which smart or intelligent "peripheral devices" are connected, without the need for a separate processor, or at least without as powerful a central processor as would otherwise be needed.

The local area network has emerged as part of the end-user computer "revolution." Accountants, managers, and other business professionals who acquired personal computers for independent use later saw the need to connect them in clusters, so as to share both common resources and data. They also saw the need for connecting these clusters to larger host computers, in order to download and upload data.

The trend toward decentralization at both levels has produced networked computer systems. Network technology has advanced rapidly, producing both local area and wide area networks and also the capability of communicating between one network and another, or between a network and another computer. Several network configurations, or "topologies," have emerged to meet the needs of various types of networks. The most common of these, for local area networks, are the bus and ring topologies, in which component devices are connected along the length of a common communications channel. In wide-area networks, point-to-point and star topologies are more common.

The decentralization of computer resources has also highlighted the need for effective and efficient means of electronic data communications, or telecommunications. Telecommunications technology has also advanced rapidly, from its origins in the telephone and in radio and television broadcasting. Alternative communications media are available, including telephone lines, coaxial cables, fiber optics cables, microwaves, and satellite communications. These media offer a spectrum of capacity, cost, and control characteristics that can be matched to the needs of the particular network.

BIBLIOGRAPHY

Carson, Warren G. "Strategic Information Systems via a Micro-to-Mainframe Bridge." *Georgia Journal of Accounting* Spring 1986, pp. 171–189.

Charp, Sylvia, and I.J. Hines. "The Basic Principles of Networking." *Technological Horizons in Education Journal,* April 1988, pp. 94–98.

"An Electronic Pipeline That's Challenging the Way America Does Business." *Business Week*, August 3, 1987, pp. 80–82.

Gallegos, Frederick, Dana R. Richardson, and A. Faye Borthwick. *Audit and Control of Information Systems*, Cincinnati: South-Western, 1987.

Gross, Daniel, and Bruce Page. "Frontiers of Data Dispatch." *Computer World*, March 30, 1987 (supplement), pp. 1–6.

Hurst, Rebecca. "LANs: The Users' Report." *Computer World*, September 17, 1986 (Focus), pp. 14–17.

Pierce, John R. *Signals: The Telephone and Beyond*. San Francisco: Freeman, 1981.

Price Waterhouse. *Managing Microcomputers: A Guide for Financial Policymakers*. New York: National Association of Accountants, 1984.

Stallings, William. "Master Plan for LANs." *Datamation*, November 15, 1986, pp. 91–92.

Sundarrajan, Raj. "Fiber Optics and Data Communication." *Telephony*, August 17, 1987, pp. 58–64.

Teets, Charles G. "Avoiding Network Tie-Ups." *Computer World*, September 17, 1986 (Focus), pp. 23–30.

———"Standards: The New Fiber Diet." *Datamation*, March 15, 1987, pp. 60–64.

Titch, Steven. "Wide Area Nets: The Technology and the Word is Spreading." *Communications Week*, August 17, 1987, pp. C1–C7.

Winfield, Marc. "Fiber Optics for Maximum Security." *Telephony*, August 17, 1987, pp. 65–70.

DISCUSSION QUESTIONS AND PROBLEMS

1. Define and discuss the following terms:

- Asynchronous serial transmission
- Bus topology
- Coaxial cable
- Concentrator
- Distributed processing
- Fiber optic cable
- Fully connected topology
- Gateway
- Local area network (LAN)
- Microwave communications
- Modulation
- Modulator-demodulator (modem)
- Multiplexor
- Network
- Network architecture
- Network server
- Network topology
- Open Systems Interconnection model
- Parallel transmission
- Point-to-point topology
- Protocol
- Serial transmission
- Star topology
- Synchronous serial transmission
- Twisted-pair copper wire
- Wide area network (WAN)

2. A local area network connects eight personal computers, one of which operates as a network server. Each computer includes a keyboard and monitor and two floppy disk drives. Shared peripheral devices include a 32 MB hard disk drive, a 60 c.p.s. letter-quality character printer, and a 600 l.p.m. line printer. A gateway is incorporated, providing for communication with a large mainframe computer.

Required

Draw a diagram of the system assuming

a. a bus topology
b. a star topology

3. Suggest data communications media that would be appropriate to each of the following situations. Indicate also whether a modem would be required.

a. A remote data entry terminal is connected to a computer in another state. The terminal is used to enter branch sales transaction data and is operated for approximately one hour per day.

b. A remote printer in Maine is connected to a computer in New York State. The machine is a page printer, rated at 200 p.p.m. and is used for an average of five hours per day.

c. Two personal computers, located in the same room, are connected to pass data from one to the other.

d. The two computers in (c) are instead located 500 miles from each other.

e. Two mainframe computers, one in Texas and the other in California, share a common data base and a common work load.

f. A computer device communicates with another device in a neighboring major city. The user organization regards message security as of prime importance.

4. A computer in Michigan drives a remote printer at a regional distribution center in Kentucky. The typical output consists of reports containing product information. The average report is 100 pages long, and each page contains 66 lines, with 90 characters per line. What data transmission speed, in bits per second, would be required if a report must be printed in

a. 2 hours
b. 10 minutes
c. 1 minute
d. 10 seconds

5. a. Discuss the relative merits and demerits of coaxial cable, microwave links, and satellite links for high-speed data communications.

b. What special advantages does fiber optics cable have in competition with the media discussed in (a)?

6. The following organizations are dispersed over a large geographical area. Indicate whether a centralized, decentralized, or distributed processing mode would be most suitable, and defend your recommendation.

a. A conglomerate consisting of semiautomonous divisions operating in separate industries

b. An airline operating a reservation system through local offices in 50 cities

c. A distributor with local state offices staffed by two or three people

d. A financial institution with 30 branch banks

e. A service enterprise rule by an authoritarian founder-president

f. A chain of department stores in which accounts receivable, inventory, and payroll are serviced locally

g. A large state university with a campus at five separate locations

h. A government revenue agency with 16 regional offices throughout the United States

7. The data forming the content of the reports described in Problem 4 in Chapter 7 have to be transmitted over a distance of 4,000 miles, using some form of telecommunications channel.

Required

a. Determine the minimum transmission speed in bits per second necessary to support each of the four printer speeds identified.

b. What type of communications medium would be suitable in each case?

8. The message ''Today's sales = $250,000'' must be transmitted in ASCII over a telecommunications channel. Show the pattern of transmitted bits, assuming (a) a parallel, (b) a synchronous serial, and (c) an asynchronous serial mode of transmission.

9. The International Standards Organization has proposed a standard layered architecture for representing telecommunications systems. To which layer of the model could each of the following elements of a telecommunications system best be related?

a. An auto-dial modem

b. The bus network topology

c. A software package that programs a hardware interface between a microcomputer and a local area network

d. The systems software that controls the flow of messages throughout a local area network

e. Fiber optic cable

f. A branch office's requirement to send daily sales data to the corporate headquarters

g. The transmission of sales data, made by the branch office, September 12, 19XX

h. A hardware protocol converter that allows a parallel transmission channel to be interfaced to a serial channel

10. Ezekiel Manufacturing Company operates a central computer facility at its Memphis headquarters, linked to remote-job-entry (RJE) terminals at its ten branch plants. The system is used to process accounting and production data originating at the branches and to accumulate data for analysis and coordination by headquarters staff personnel. In particular, the weekly budget is tracked using data in the updated master files. Approximately one third of all processing resources are consumed by such headquarters activities.

Each terminal consists of a magnetic tape drive and a printer. Transaction data are submitted in daily batches together with a set of job control language (JCL) instructions that alert the operator at the central site to load the appropriate programs and data files. There is usually a sizable processing backlog, and often the output is not returned for printing until the next day. The slow turnaround is not a serious problem for regularly scheduled jobs such as the payroll, but it is causing major difficulties for production control and scheduling tasks for which decisions have to be made at short notice to ensure efficient operations.

A committee has been formed to advise top management on how to upgrade the system and provide improved services to the branches. One suggestion is to enhance the central facility by installing a more powerful computer, either with the present RJE structure or with a system of new interactive terminals at the branches. Another proposal is to install small stand-alone computers at the branches and to dispense with the costly communications links. A suggestion to install a network system has been examined but has been rejected because of its high cost.

Required

Evaluate the various proposals, indicating the advantages and disadvantages of each. Recommend the best solution to Ezekiel's problems, justifying your choice with suitable arguments regarding its effectiveness and cost.

11. A merchandising organization is planning to install a distributed processing computer system to support its sales order–processing and general accounting functions. The company's corporate headquarters is in Independence, Mo. There are three branches in the United States: in San Diego, Calif., Hartford, Conn., and West Palm Beach, Fla. A fourth branch has been set up in Shannon, Ireland, to handle trade with the European Economic Community.

An important consideration in these plans is the need to transmit appreciable volumes of data, on a daily basis, between the branch sales offices and corporate headquarters. Management is concerned about telecommunications costs and also about the security of its communications.

The company employs 30 accountants in Independence and an additional 18 accountants at the branch offices. A total of 20 individual work stations would be required at corporate headquarters. Three work stations would be required at the San Diego, Hartford, and Shannon branches, and 5 at the West Palm Beach Branch. Typical transaction volumes, storage capacities, and telecommunications traffic are estimated to be as follows:

12. Parsons Manufacturing Company, whose headquarters is in St. Louis, is planning a new computerized accounting information system. Of particular concern is the need for a telecommunications system linking the corporate headquarters and its three branches, located in Kansas City, Mo., Marietta, Ga., and Boca Raton, Fla.

Data traffic between St. Louis and Marietta is likely to be high, exceeding 40 MB per day, and will include real-time processing activities that require a transmission speed of at least 240,000 bits per second (b.p.s.). Traffic between St. Louis and the other two branches, and among the three branches, is unlikely to be greater than 4 MB per day, and so transmission speeds of 4,800 b.p.s. would be adequate.

Required

a. Prepare a block diagram depicting the network topology of the required telecommunications system.

b. List and briefly describe the telecommunications hardware that would be needed to implement the system.

Location	Transactions per Day	Storage Capacity (MB)	Transmissions (MB per Day)
Independence	20,000	5,000	—
San Diego	1,000	80	10
Hartford	2,000	90	10
West Palm Beach	5,000	100	30
Shannon	10,000	800	100

Required

a. Design an appropriate computer hardware configuration to meet the company's processing, storage, and telecommunications needs.

b. Draw a block diagram of your recommended hardware configuration. Be sure to identify all major devices required.

c. Suggest suitable telecommunications media for intracompany data channels.

c. Discuss the requirements for telecommunications channel media suitable for handling the stated traffic demands.

13. Most of the data traffic between St. Louis and Marietta, in Problem 12, consists of communications among four separate computer devices in St. Louis and three devices in Marietta.

Required

Discuss the problems of interfacing the seven computer devices with the network. What characteristics of the pattern of usage of each device should be considered?

If each device needed to transmit data for an average of ten minutes in each hour, how would that information affect the choice of telecommunications hardware?

PART THREE

THE LIFE CYCLE OF ACCOUNTING INFORMATION SYSTEMS

Part III covers the development of accounting information systems. Systems development can be divided into systems analysis, systems design, and systems implementation, which are discussed in Chapters 12 through 14, respectively. Chapter 11 describes the systems development project that is established in an organization and is responsible for developing the new information system. Chapter 11 also introduces some important techniques for managing the systems project.

11

Overview of Systems Development

LEARNING OBJECTIVES

After you have studied this chapter you should be able to

- Describe the purpose and scope of information systems development.
- Identify systems analysis, design, and implementation.
- Explain the systems development project.
- Describe how to budget for systems development.
- Describe how to assign responsibilities to the people in the systems project.
- Describe how to schedule systems development tasks.
- Describe how to track the project budget and schedule.

THE DIMENSIONS OF SYSTEMS DEVELOPMENT

Most business information systems are highly complex, covering many facets of the organization's activities, providing many different functions, and affecting the way in which many people do their jobs. An effective system enables the smooth running of the organization; an ineffective one may hinder operations to the point that the organization is doomed to an early death. An efficient system provides benefits to the organization far in excess of its costs; an inefficient one may become a serious drain on the organization's resources.

So pervasive is the information system's influence and so far-reaching are the consequences of its performance that it is not surprising that systems development is a highly visible activity in most organizations. Systems development must be carefully planned, tested, monitored, and evaluated at all stages to ensure that the end product lives up to its expectations.

Except in newly formed organizations, there is some kind of information system already in place. The system may be inadequate; it may largely be an informal system; but any ongoing organization has some means for providing operational data processing and decision support. Sometimes the existing system is manual, and the intention is to upgrade it to an automated one. In many cases, the system is already automated, but modification, upgrade, or replacement is needed. In a very few cases,

the system is already automated, but the intention is to downgrade it to a manual one. Automation is not necessarily a "must" for all organizations, and some highly effective and efficient manual systems are in use.

The process of developing an information system requires many types of expertise. Accountants, auditors, management consultants, systems analysts, programmers, computer professionals, and documentation specialists all may be required. Sometimes the organization can draw on its own resources to assemble a project team to do the work. More commonly, experts are called in from outside to work alongside in-house personnel. Sometimes, particularly in small organizations, the greater part of the work is done by outside people. Large public accounting firms usually have management advisory services departments that specialize in systems development and can put together teams with the necessary blend of experience. Consulting firms often provide the same kind of service. Computer manufacturers and dealers may also be able to assist in systems development, although they are not in a position to evaluate competing brands of equipment. But in any case, the acquisition of computer equipment is not the only, or even the dominant, task in the typical systems project.

Whether or not the outside specialist help is used in systems development, management must play a vital and continuing role. First, there are many decisions to be made along the way, including the decision to continue with the project in the light of information gathered up to that point. Second, the information system will be management's tool, and a great deal of input is required from management if the tool is to do the job that is needed. No project team can read management's mind and guess what kind of system it wants. In short, management cannot relinquish responsibility for the project and expect to obtain an effective system. Neither can management delegate responsibility too far down the chain of command. Top management must retain overall control of the project, even if day-to-day control is delegated to a project manager.

THE PHASES OF SYSTEMS DEVELOPMENT

The development of information systems can be broken down into three phases:

- Systems analysis
- Systems design
- Systems implementation

Systems Analysis

The key word in systems analysis is *consider*.

Systems analysis is evaluating an existing information system and its organizational environment in order to recommend improvement. This requires extensive data gathering to establish the system's objectives to determine the extent to which the existing system achieves those objectives, and to provide the broad outlines of an improved system. A number of specialized tools have been developed to help gather and analyze the data.

The recommendations for the improved information system are often expressed in a proposal to management setting out the kind of system that is envisioned and how it can be accomplished. Later, if management decides to proceed with the design phase, the proposal can provide the basis for a set of technical specifications on which the design will be based.

Systems analysis may include a preliminary survey to identify key problem areas in the existing information system or in the organization that it serves. The main systems analysis exercise will then build on the results of the preliminary survey. More detailed studies may also be performed with the objective of solving specific problems or determining whether solutions are workable.

Systems Design

The key word in systems design is *decide*.

Systems design is translating the recommendations made in the analysis phase into a form that can be implemented. It requires many decisions and considerable effort and expertise to produce a "paper model" of the proposed system. Systems design results in a complete description of the new information system, including its component subsystems; its inputs, files, and outputs; and its processing activities. Decisions—big and small—must be made about the structure of the system, about its information flows, about its mode of operation, about its required level of performance, and about the internal controls necessary to protect the system itself and the resources of its user organization. Documentation must be prepared describing how the system is designed and explaining how it is to be operated and used.

Systems design is commonly divided further into conceptual design and detailed design. Conceptual design deals with the overall features of the information system; the philosophy it reflects, the major subsystems that comprise its structure, and the technology that will support it. Conceptual design resolves the most important design decisions and establishes a framework in which detailed design can be carried out. Detailed design continues the design process to produce a complete model of the proposed information system and resolves the myriad minor decisions necessary to make it internally consistent and capable of doing the job for which it is intended. Modern structured design techniques may consider not just two layers, but several layers of design decisions.

Systems Implementation

The key word in systems implementation is *do*.

Systems implementation is the final phase of development in which a working information system is produced and set in motion in place of the old system. It requires a wide range of activities. Computer hardware may have to be acquired and the site prepared where it will be installed. Applications software may have to be acquired or developed. New business forms may be needed. The organization's data base may have to be converted into a new format or into a different storage medium for use with the new system. Extensive testing is necessary to verify that the new information system operates as it is supposed to. Personnel must be trained to operate and use the new system; additional personnel, perhaps with specific skills or experience, may have to be recruited, or existing positions eliminated and personnel displaced. This preparatory work may take much time and effort to "make it all happen."

Finally, the new information system must be put into operation. Conversion from the old to the new system is frequently carried out in stages—one or two subsystems at a time—to minimize the associated work load. Each subsystem should be run in parallel with the one that it is replacing until the reliability and accuracy of the new system have been demonstrated. This process, too, can take considerable time.

After conversion to the new system is complete, it is normally reviewed to evaluate the information system that has been installed and to evaluate the development project that produced it.

The Systems Development Project

The process of systems development is often organized into a formal project under the direction of a project manager. The systems project has its own sched-

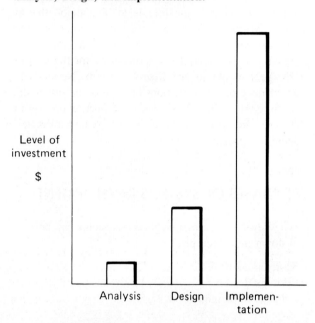

FIGURE 11.2 Relative levels of investment in systems analysis, design, and implementation.

ule, budget, organizational assignments, and management control mechanisms. It can be regarded as a separate organizational unit, comparable to a department, but it has a finite life and is dissolved once its job is completed.

Systems analysis, design, and implementation comprise the three phases of the project, and to a large extent they are self-contained. The points of transition—from analysis to design and from design to implementation—provide opportunities for top management's review and evaluation of the project (Figure 11.1). They also rep-

FIGURE 11.1 The three phases of systems implementation.

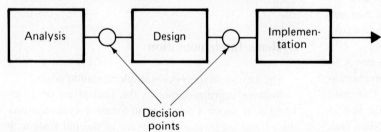

resent major decision points at which management must commit more and more money to the project. The systems design phase is usually much more costly than the analysis phase, and the implementation phase is more costly than either (Figure 11.2). At these points of major review, top management will want to evaluate the project and the progress to date. If there is any indication that the system end product will be less than satisfactory, the project can be redirected—or even aborted—to prevent the further waste of resources before the deficiencies can be remedied. The decision points between the analysis, design, and implementation phases are, of course, the major ones; management—including top management—should be involved with the project more or less continuously throughout its life. Decisions must be made during the whole course of the work and particularly during the design phase. Management needs to monitor these decisions and steer the project in a direction that will ensure its success.

Senior managers' thinking and judgment as they review the systems project are often invaluable; their broad viewpoints may see problem areas that the project team has missed. They have a better feel for what future operations will be, and they may be in a better position to evaluate the performance of the proposed system.

ILLUSTRATION OF THE DEVELOPMENT PROCESS

The three phases of systems development will become clearer if an example is considered.

Turquoise Products, Inc., is a medium-sized manufacturer of heating and ventilating equipment. It employs 900 people at three locations throughout the Southeast. Its payroll and billing functions are currently handled by a service bureau. The general ledger and tax reporting are maintained by a small local CPA firm that has served the company during the 15 years since it was founded. Accounts payable, inventory, cost accounting, and production control are done manually. Management believes that the present system is inadequate to meet its needs for planning and control information and also suspects that material improvements could be made in inventory and production control.

A consulting firm is called in to analyze the present situation and to make detailed recommendations for a new system. Three members of the consulting firm spend a week at the company's main plant and also make half-day visits to the other two locations. They talk to top management and other personnel; they study existing documentation and procedure manuals; and they flowchart the present information system. On the basis of the data gathered, they are able to determine the strengths and weaknesses of the present system and to make some preliminary recommendations. The recommendations are first discussed with top management, and some modifications are made at management's request; then a formal presentation is made to the board of directors. Finally, a written report is submitted documenting the consultants' findings and presenting their recommendations. Appropriate descriptive material and statistics are included to justify their conclusions. The consulting firm's fee for the initial engagement is $13,500.

Briefly, the consultants recommended the following:

- Acquisition of a large (super-) minicomputer to be installed at the main plant with remote terminals at the other two locations.
- Purchase of canned computer software to handle the functions of accounts receivable and payable, payroll, inventory control, cost accounting, and general ledger. (Production control has a large subjective element, and the consultants advised that the manual operation be retained.)
- Redesign of all operating procedures.
- Design of appropriate controls to provide for data integrity and to protect against irregularities.

After reviewing the consultant's report with selected members of middle management and with its CPA firm, top management asks the consulting firm to provide additional services. Specifically, the consultants are asked to prepare a request for proposal (RFP), soliciting bids for the computer hardware and software, and to assist the company's in-house personnel in the design of new procedures and controls. Thus, the analysis phase is completed, and the design phase is initiated.

A considerable amount of design work is necessary before the request for proposal can be written. The volume of data to be processed and the required file storage capacity must be determined. The reports that are to be generated and the data input necessary must be decided. The overall configurations of the system must be resolved as well as detailed matters pertaining to the flow of data from one part of the system to another.

The procedures and controls must cover the computer system and also other parts of the overall system that will remain manual operations. They involve organizational matters, transaction handling, paper flows, forms control, program and data library procedures, and a host of other considerations. Two additional members of the consulting firm are brought in to help with the design work, and a substantial number of in-house people, of all levels, are involved.

At the end of three months, the design work is complete, and the request for proposal is ready to be sent out to the prospective vendors. The total cost of the design phase, including the consulting firm's fees, amounts to $125,000. Management is satisfied with the progress of the work and decides to proceed with the implementation phase.

Six vendors respond to the request for proposal and submit their proposals for the computer hardware and software installation. One of the proposals is clearly unresponsive to the company's needs and is eliminated at once. The other five, with various minor variations in philosophy, appear to offer the needed system components. Their prices are as follows:

Bidder	Total Price
A	$135,000
B	168,000
C	157,000
D	196,000
E	156,000

Company A is the low bidder, but it is known to be a firm with little experience with systems of this size. Company D is the high bidder, and although its products have a very good reputation, the higher price cannot be justified. The other three bids are similar and seem to represent a consensus of the system's realistic cost. Of these three, Company E offers the lowest price, and its bid is accepted. Company E promises delivery of the system in 90 days.

A great deal of work has to be done during the three months preceding installation of the computer. It is recognized that a small data-processing department must be established to operate the system, and experienced personnel must be hired. One of the existing buildings must be enlarged to provide a computer room, and power and air conditioning equipment must be installed. New forms have to be ordered for invoices, checks, vouchers, picking slips, and so forth. A training program has to be established, and two members of the new data-processing department are sent for a week's training at the computer vendor's facility.

Delivery of the computer is delayed for a month because of a strike at the vendor's plant, but installation and shakedown finally begin. Various problems arise, and it is another month before the hardware and software are installed and ready for use. It has been decided to implement the system in stages and to bring up one subsystem every three weeks.

Management decides to bring up payroll first. Until the new system is fully tested and all bugs are eliminated, the old and the new systems will be operated in parallel. In that way, the output from the two systems can be compared and any differences investigated. Parallel operation is continued for two months for the most critical functions and for one month for the others. The schedule for implementation is not achieved, and a total of nine months elapses before all functions are running "live" and the old system is discontinued. The implementation phase has taken about one year to complete, at a total cost—including the price of the computer—of over $450,000.

As a final step, the consulting firm is called back to make a postimplementation review, to determine whether the system performs the functions for which it was intended, to see whether any weaknesses need to be remedied, and to evaluate the project from a cost and effectiveness standpoint. The consultants note several problem areas but report that overall the system is doing its job. The headaches encountered during installation were probably about average for a system of this size. The total cost of the system was 10 to 15 percent higher than their projections at the end of the design phase.

MANAGEMENT OF THE SYSTEMS PROJECT

Our example shows that systems development, even on a relatively small scale, can be complex and expensive. Many different people are involved; numerous tasks have to be accomplished over an extended period; and a substantial amount of money is spent or committed. If the project is not managed effectively, the end product may be unsatisfactory; schedules may not be met; and cost overruns will doubtless occur. For large projects, formal methods of project management may be essential, and even for small projects they are highly desirable. Project management requires planning, organization, and control. At the outset, the project is unlikely to be sufficiently well defined to permit detailed planning. Furthermore, the risk of cancellation cannot be ignored. But as the project progresses, it becomes easier to plan its future course, and the need to do so becomes increasingly urgent. Detailed planning can usually start toward the end of the analysis phase, and it should be completed well before implementation is due to commence. The plan can be refined at any stage, but its effectiveness as a control tool starts as soon as the plan begins to take shape.

The three areas to which careful management is most vital are the project schedule, the division of responsibilities among the parties involved, and the project budget. The remainder of this chapter will discuss these three areas and the tools available to support them.

Scheduling

The first step in the scheduling process is dividing the project into individual tasks, which should be essentially self-contained. The tasks ordinarily follow some kind of sequence, but two or more can be carried out concurrently. In regard to sequencing, the terms *predecessor* and *successor* are used to designate the previous and next tasks, respectively, relative to some reference task.

The work in each task should be examined so that the time necessary to complete it can be estimated. Also, to coordinate the scheduling exercise with the organizational and budgeting activities, it is helpful to identify who will carry out the particular task, and to estimate

its probable cost. Suppose that the applicable portion of a systems project can be divided into seven tasks and that the estimated time to complete each of them is as shown in the following table. In real life, the project would probably have to be broken down into more tasks if the scheduling and other planning activities are to be meaningful.

Task	Estimated Time (weeks)
A: Preparation of technical specifications	4
B: Conceptual design	8
C: Detailed design	12
D: Hardware acquisition	16
E: Software development	18
F: Site preparation	20
G: Installation and testing	6

It is assumed that once the conceptual design is completed, both detailed design and site preparation can commence at once. Hardware acquisition and software development can begin as soon as detailed design is completed. Installation and testing can start as soon as hardware acquisition, software development, and site preparation are completed.

The project schedule can be analyzed using the critical path method (CPM). A closely related method called PERT (program evaluation and review technique) provides interval estimates of the task completion times, whereas CPM permits only point estimates. Both CPM and PERT use a graphical representation of the project, as illustrated in Figure 11.3. The tasks are shown as the circles, and the lines connecting them (together with the arrows) represent the sequence of operations. The precise placement of the circles or the length of the lines are not important; these are purely a matter of graphical convenience.

The analysis tries to determine the start and finish dates of each task, relative to the initiation of the project, and also the completion time for the project. Because there may be a range of dates on which any given task may start (or be finished), both early and late dates are

FIGURE 11.3 Graphical representation of the system project and its component tasks.
A = preparation of specifications, B = conceptual design, C = detailed design, D = hardware acquisition, E = software development, F = site preparation, G = installation and testing.

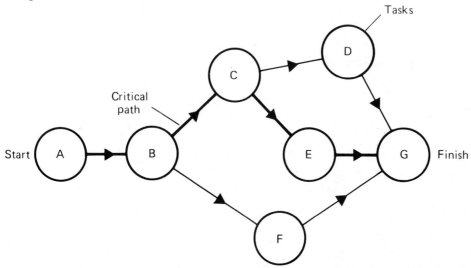

determined. For example, the early start date for a given task is the earliest date on which that task can be started, taking into account that all its predecessor tasks must already be completed. The late start date is the latest date on which the task can be started without holding up its successor tasks or delaying the project as a whole. Late start dates represent deadlines that must be met. Corresponding to each early start and late start date are an early finish and a late finish date. The determination of the various dates is illustrated in Figure 11.4.

The early start and early finish dates are calculated by working down the list of tasks, ensuring that all predecessor tasks are complete before the next task is allowed to start. For example, task G (installation and testing) cannot be allowed to start before tasks D, E, and F are complete. The early finish dates for these three tasks are 40, 42, and 32 weeks from go-ahead. Because all three must be complete, the earliest date on which task G can start is week 42. Task G requires 6 weeks, and so it could be completed by week 48. Because task G is the last task in the project, 48 weeks is also the completion time for the whole project.

The late start and late finish dates are determined by working *up* the list of tasks in Figure 11.4. The as-

sumption is that the overall completion time, in this case 48 weeks, must not be compromised. However, there is some flexibility in the dates on which two of the tasks can be started, and this flexibility is measured by the "slack," that is, the difference between the early and the late start dates. For example, task F (site preparation) is not required to be completed before the deadline, week 42, set by the late start date of its successor, task G. For task F to be completed by week 42, it could start as late as week 22. The early start date for task F is week 12, and so the slack in this task is 10 (22 − 12 = 10) weeks.

Note in Figure 11.4 that some of the tasks have slack, whereas others do not. If the path through the network (Figure 11.3) is plotted, joining all tasks for which there is no slack, the critical path will be obtained. It is shown by the thick line in the figure. The significance of the critical path is that it draws attention to the sequence of tasks whose prompt completion is critical to completing the overall project on schedule. Whereas task F (assuming that it was started on its early start date) could be delayed by as much as 10 weeks, without delaying completion of the project, if task C were not completed promptly, the project completion would be delayed. The

FIGURE 11.4 Determination of start and finish dates for the project tasks, using the CPM approach. The critical path is the path through the network (Figure 11.3) along which there is no slack. The slack is the difference between the early and late start dates, or between the early and late finish dates, for each task.

	Task	Estimated time	Early start*	Early finish*	Late start*	Late finish*	Slack
A:	Preparation of specs.	4 weeks	0	4	0	4	0
B:	Conceptual design	8	4	12	4	12	0
C:	Detailed design	12	12	24	12	24	0
D:	Hardware acquisition	16	24	40	26	42	2 weeks
E:	Software development	18	24	42	24	42	0
F:	Site preparation	20	12	32	22	42	10
G:	Installation and testing	6	42	48	42	48	0

* Weeks from go - ahead.

tasks on the critical path must be monitored more closely than the others, and if necessary, resources should be diverted from noncritical tasks to ensure that the critical ones are finished on schedule.

Organizational Assignments

Because there are many people involved in a systems project, some inside the organization and some outside, it is imperative that the responsibilities for carrying the various tasks be clearly spelled out. Otherwise, the responsibility for delays and omissions that become evident later may be difficult to pin down. In some cases, an individual, an in-house group, or an outside vendor may do all of a task; in other cases, the work may be shared. Shared tasks need more detailed treatment so that the people concerned fully understand, and are held responsible for, the part of the work that they are expected to do. Further subdivision of the tasks may be necessary if sharing responsibility is likely to pose a problem.

A common tool for analyzing and communicating the assignments is the responsibility matrix. A simple example of this tool is shown in Figure 11.5 for the illustration being followed in the text. The rows of the matrix correspond to the tasks to be performed, and the columns correspond to the various organizational groups involved. The X's in some of the cells designate the responsibilities that have been assigned. An obvious requirement is that all rows must have at least one X; on the other hand, if a column is empty, it simply means that the particular organizational group is not involved. Multiple X's in a row indicate shared responsibilities. In the simplified example, shown in Figure 11.5, it is evident that two or more groups are participating in all the identified tasks. Indeed, the level of sharing of responsibilities is far too great to permit effective project control. It has already been noted that further subdivision of the tasks would be necessary in real life. The high density of X's in Figure 11.5 emphasizes the need for doing so.

A further development of the responsibility matrix, which is sometimes used, replaces the X's by the number of person hours assigned to the particular task (or the appropriate portion of the task) or by the corresponding dollar budget. Provision of this additional information is helpful to the project managers for planning purposes. However, the budget data would normally be omitted from copies of the matrix made available for general distribution. There might be adverse responses if individual groups were able to compare their share of the budget with that allocated to other groups—particularly

FIGURE 11.5 Responsibility matrix showing assignment of task responsibilities among vendor and in-house groups for the example used in the text.

Project: Development of Accounting Information System	Responsibility:							
	Vendors				In - house			
Task:	Black & Black, Consultants	White Construction Co.	Red Electrics, Inc.	Blue Computer Company	Accounting	Data Processing	Management	Other
A: Preparation of specs.	X				X	X	X	
B: Conceptual design	X				X	X	X	
C: Detailed design	X				X	X	X	
D: Hardware acquisition				X		X	X	
E: Software development	X					X		
F: Site preparation		X	X	X		X	X	
G: Installation and testing			X	X		X	X	X

as some of the groups are part of the organization, whereas others are vendor firms. It may be preferable to communicate the individual budget figures in confidence to the groups to which they apply.

Management by Objectives

Among the approaches to management of systems projects, a particularly effective one is management by objectives (MBO). It is a useful adjunct to the assignment of responsibilities just described. The method emphasizes the need to specify the objectives of the project, and its purpose is to enhance the prospects that the project can be completed successfully within the constraints of the budget and schedule. The objectives, and their associated budget and schedule allowances, are mutually discussed and agreed to by the individual or group responsible for each task and the project manager (or an intermediate supervisor). Accordingly, the objectives of the project are adopted as the objectives of each member of the project team; as noted in Chapter 1, such a procedure is essential if suboptimal performance is to be avoided.

The first step is to define the objectives; the second step is to use them to measure and verify progress toward the achievement of those objectives. Care must be taken to establish and formalize objectives that will in fact produce the desired results. In this context, an objective has been defined as a commitment with the following characteristics:

- Its achievement can be verified.
- It is specific.
- The attainment of the objective is assigned a budget and a time frame for completion.[1]

In connection with each objective, a set of verifiable results is identified. For example, within the overall task of software development, a typical specific objective is "perform program testing." The corresponding verifiable results might then be (1) a comprehensive set of test transactions, (2) the documented test results, and (3) cross-referencing of the detailed test results to a previously defined test plan. The labor budget for carrying out the test program, as agreed by the personnel involved and the task supervisor, might be 100 hours. The objectives are documented, as are the steps taken to achieve each objective, the results attained, and the time taken. Subsequent review of the documented material gives management valuable data on the progress of the work and the performance of the individuals involved in it.

The use of management by objectives introduces the additional element of formality into the assignment of responsibilities and helps join the people on the project staff into a cohesive, committed team.

The Budget

For convenience, the budget can be structured to include the same tasks identified in the scheduling exercise. In this way, the schedule and budget can be closely related to each other. The cost of completing each component task is estimated, and then the sum of these costs, after any necessary revisions, is the total budget cost of

the project. For example, the cost estimates for the various tasks might be as follows:

Task	Estimated Cost
A: Preparation of specifications	$ 60,000
B: Conceptual design	120,000
C: Detailed design	216,000
D: Hardware acquisition	848,000
E: Software development	360,000
F: Site preparation	200,000
G: Installation and testing	150,000
Total estimated cost	$1,954,000

The estimated cost of equipment to be purchased is $800,000; the cost estimate for hardware acquisition includes $48,000 of labor and other costs.

After the total estimated cost for the project is determined, it is necessary to spread the budget over the total duration of the project so as to obtain the detailed rate of expenditure. This information is important to the related cash budgeting. The budget spread can readily be done once the schedule has been drawn up. The rate of cost incurred for the individual tasks must be calculated. Without information to the contrary, it can often be assumed that the cost will be incurred uniformly over time. For example, the cost of the specifications preparation, $60,000, can be assumed to be incurred at a rate of $15,000 per week over the four-week duration of that task.

The cost of the hardware should normally be treated separately because most organizations seek some form of financing or lease arrangement, and cash payments may not begin until some time after installation is complete. In any case, management of the project is usually more concerned with the other costs, which are largely labor costs and are the more likely candidates for cost overruns. Accordingly, for our example, the budget spread will be developed for the remaining costs, which total $1,154,000. These costs can be spread over the 48-week duration of the project, as shown in Figure 11.6[2]

[1] David Leigh, "Systems Management by Objectives," *Management Focus* (Peat, Marwick, Mitchell & Co.), May–June 1981, pp. 8–11.

[2] It is assumed in Figure 11.6 that all tasks start on their early start date, as determined from the CPM model. In practice, it might be beneficial to delay some of the noncritical tasks until closer to their late start dates.

FIGURE 11.6 Budget spread, by week, for the example described in the text.

Week	A	B	C	Task D	E	F	G	Weekly total	Cumulative total
1	15,000							15,000	$15,000
2	15,000							15,000	$30,000
3	15,000							15,000	$45,000
4	15,000							15,000	$60,000
5		15,000						15,000	$75,000
6		15,000						15,000	$90,000
.									
.									
11		15,000						15,000	$165,000
12		15,000						15,000	$180,000
13			18,000			10,000		28,000	$208,000
14			18,000			10,000		28,000	$236,000
.									
.									
23			18,000			10,000		28,000	$488,000
24			18,000			10,000		28,000	$516,000
25			3,000	20,000		10,000		33,000	$549,000
26			3,000	20,000		10,000		33,000	$582,000
.									
.									
31			3,000	20,000	10,000			33,000	$747,000
32			3,000	20,000	10,000			33,000	$780,000
33			3,000	20,000				23,000	$803,000
34			3,000	20,000				23,000	$826,000
.									
.									
39			3,000	20,000				23,000	$941,000
40			3,000	20,000				23,000	$964,000
41				20,000				20,000	$984,000
42				20,000				20,000	$1,004,000
43							25,000	25,000	$1,029,000
44							25,000	25,000	$1,054,000
45							25,000	25,000	$1,079,000
46							25,000	25,000	$1,104,000
47							25,000	25,000	$1,129,000
48							25,000	25,000	$1,154,000
	$60,000	$120,000	$216,000	$48,000	$360,000	$200,000	$150,000	$1,154,000	

Task A = Preparation of specs.
B = Conceptual Design
C = Detailed Design
D = Hardware Acquisition
E = Sofware Development
F = Site Preparation
G = Installation & Testing.

The table is a matrix in which the columns represent the component tasks and the rows represent the weeks of the project. Each cell of the matrix corresponds to the estimated cost of a given task in a given week. Addition of these amounts, along columns, recovers the total cost of each task. Addition along rows provides the total cost of the project to be incurred each week. The associated cumulative total cost reflects the total investment in the project since its inception.

Schedule and Budget Tracking

The schedule must be carefully tracked, particularly for tasks on the critical path, to discern advance warnings of any impending delay of project completion. Similarly, the budget must be tracked to help identify potential cost overruns.

A popular tool for schedule tracking is the Gantt chart, named after Henry Gantt who proposed its use during World War I. The Gantt chart is a horizontal bar chart (see Chapter 4) in which the bars represent the duration

of each task and the positions occupied in the project's overall time frame. Figure 11.7 shows a Gantt chart for the example project already used to illustrate the scheduling and budgeting processes. The horizontal scale represents the time from project inception or go-ahead, and there is a bar for each component task. In addition to showing the tasks, the chart may present other information such as the timing of significant milestones and decision points. Figure 11.7 shows the decision points at the end of the systems analysis and conceptual design phases, the date of shipment of the hardware from the manufacturer, and the expected date for the start of "live" operation of the new system. The Gantt chart is a helpful aid to schedule tracking because it shows at a glance what the project status should be at any given time during the course of the project.

In budget tracking, there is clearly some interest in determining whether the actual cost expended in any given week is equal to, less than, or greater than the budgeted amount. But most likely there will be fluctuations from week to week, and if an unfavorable variance in one week is followed by a favorable one the following

FIGURE 11.7 Gantt chart for the example described in the text.

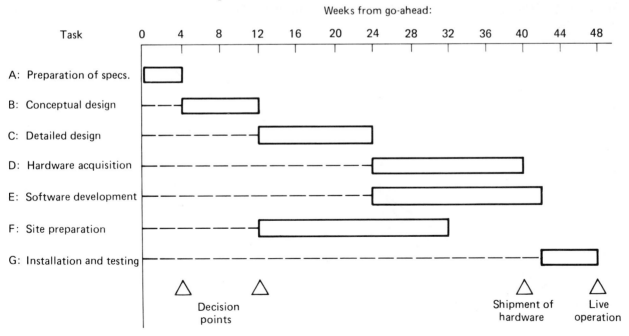

week, the fluctuations may be of little consequence. The more significant indicators of budget conformity are the cumulative cost for each task and the cumulative cost for the project as a whole. If the cumulative cost for a particular task already exceeds the budgeted amount for that task and if the task has still not been completed, then there will be a cost overrun unless an offsetting economy can be realized elsewhere in the project. Similarly, comparisons between the budgeted and actual expenditures for the whole project offer useful information on whether the costs are "getting out of line." Figure 11.8 shows such a budget comparison in graphical form. The budget line in the chart is given directly by the data in Figure 11.6.

The comparison of cumulative expenditures does not show a complete picture of the project unless information is also available about its conformity with the schedule. For instance, the information that the total costs are under budget is welcome, but it takes on a different complexion when coupled with the news that the project is behind schedule. A useful way of combining the schedule and budget tracking data is to present a Gantt chart and a budget comparison chart on the same sheet of paper or even to overlay them. Figure 11.9 shows the two charts, one above the other, with a vertical line representing the current point in time. As a further aid to clarifying the schedule status, a portion of the bars is shaded to represent the degree of completion. If all the tasks were exactly on schedule, the shading would extend precisely to the vertical line representing the current date. Any discrepancy between the extent of the shading and the position of the vertical line draws attention to a disparity between scheduled and actual progress. The combination of schedule and budget status gives the project management the kind of information needed for effective project control.

SUMMARY

The development of information systems is of prime importance to the organization because of the large investment of time, effort, and money involved and because the organization will have to live with the system for a long time. A poorly conceived information system can be an enormous burden to the organization it is supposed to serve. But a wisely conceived system can be a

FIGURE 11.8 **Comparison of budget and actual cumulative expenditures for the example described in the text.**

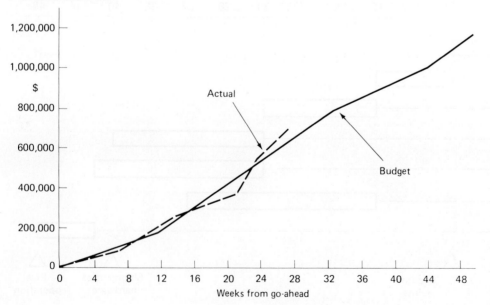

FIGURE 11.9 Combination of a Gantt chart and a budget comparison chart to provide project management information.

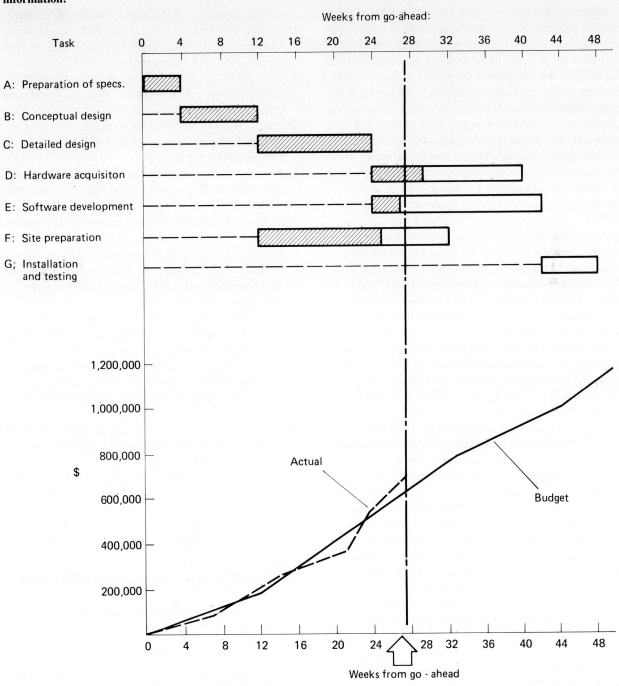

tool for effective and efficient operations far beyond the boundaries of immediate accounting concerns.

Systems development can be divided into three phases: analysis, design, and implementation. Systems analysis is an evaluation of the existing information system (if there is one), in the light of the organization's needs, and the formulation of plans for improvement. Systems design provides a complete paper model of the new or modified system. It requires many large decisions concerning the overall strategy of the design and also many small decisions regarding points of detail. Systems implementation includes the acquisition of the information-processing and organizational resources necessary to convert the design into a working system, as well as the actual operating transition from the old to the new system.

Not surprisingly, the systems development project is a high-visibility endeavor for the organization. Development of a successful information system clearly requires the involvement of the best professional and technical expertise available, but it also depends on management's ongoing involvement in and commitment to the development project.

The project must be appropriately staffed and closely managed to ensure that its objectives are achieved within applicable budget and schedule constraints. The project should engage a number of in-house individuals and groups, representing accounting, internal auditing, information services, and management. In most cases it also includes outside consultants, contractors, and vendors, including computer hardware and software suppliers. Assignments must be made clearly stating the responsibilities of each party.

A range of tools is available to support the management of the systems project, including specific tools for planning, organizing, and controlling the project. Project budgeting and scheduling are closely interrelated. Scheduling may require the use of formal methods, such as the critical path method (CPM), to dovetail the various development tasks to meet deadlines and minimize the project's total duration. Project control focuses on tracking the budget and schedule closely and on evaluating individual and group performance. Management by objectives (MBO) may be used to plan and control personnel responsibilities.

BIBLIOGRAPHY

American Institute of Certified Public Accountants. *AICPA Professional Standards*, Vol. 1, *Auditing, Management Advisory Services, Tax Practice*. New York: Commerce Clearing House, 1981.

Biggs, Charles L., G. Evans, and William Atkins. *Managing the Systems Development Process*. Englewood Cliffs, N.J.: Prentice-Hall, 1980.

Cleland, David I., and William R. King. *Systems Analysis and Project Management*, 2nd ed. New York: McGraw-Hill, 1975.

DeMarco, Thomas. *Structured Analysis and Systems Specification*. Englewood Cliffs, N.J.: Prentice-Hall, 1979.

Kirk, F. G. *Total System Development for Information Systems*. New York: Wiley, 1973.

Leigh, David. ''Systems Mangement by Objectives: An Effective Tool in Computer Systems Development.'' *Management Focus*. Peat, Marwick, Mitchell & Co., May–June 1981, pp. 8–11.

Martin, James, and Carma McLure. *Diagramming Techniques for Analysts and Programmers*. Englewood Cliffs, N.J.: Prentice-Hall, 1984.

McLean, Ephraim R., and John V. Soden. *Strategic Planning for MIS*. New York: Wiley, 1977.

Potter, Doug. ''Long-Range Systems Planning.'' *Datamation*, May 15, 1987, pp. 113–116.

Robertson, Leon H., and Tommy P. Hall. ''Network Analysis and Financial Planning.'' *Management Accounting*, April 1967, pp. 43–46.

Shelly, Gary B., and Thomas J. Cashman. *Business Systems Analysis and Design*. Anaheim, Calif.: Anaheim, 1975.

DISCUSSION QUESTIONS AND PROBLEMS

1. Define and discuss the following terms:

- Critical path method (CPM)
- Early start, early finish dates
- Gantt chart
- Late start, late finish dates

- Postimplementation review
- Predecessor, successor tasks
- Program evaluation and review technique (PERT)
- Project budget
- Project management
- Project schedule
- Request for proposal
- Responsibility matrix
- Slack
- Systems analysis
- Systems design
- Systems development
- Systems development project
- Systems implementation

2. Systems development can be divided into three phases: analysis, design, and implementation. Identify the analogous activities, corresponding to the three phases, in the following "projects":
a. Going to graduate school
b. Buying a home
c. Setting up a small consulting firm specializing in systems development

3. Identify the phase (analysis, design, or implementation) in which the following activities should be classified:
a. Defining system objectives
b. Evaluating procedures
c. Revising procedures
d. Reviewing documentation
e. Developing computer software
f. Recruiting data-processing personnel
g. Developing the systems proposal
h. Evaluating computer hardware bids
i. Preparing the request for proposal
j. Developing new forms
k. Ordering new forms
l. Training personnel
m. Testing the system

4. Discuss the value of help from consultants and independent auditors in the planning and implementation of new accounting information systems.

5. A design project consists of seven major tasks: preparation of block diagrams, development of the data dictionary, output design, processing design, file design, output design, and documentation. Development of the data dictionary can proceed concurrently with output design; processing can proceed concurrently with file design; and preparation of documentation can proceed concurrently with all tasks except preparation of block diagrams. Otherwise, all tasks must proceed in the order listed, and each must be completed before the next can start.

Initial planning for the project has provided the following estimates of the time required for each task:

Task	Time (days)
Preparation of block diagrams	15
Development of data dictionary	15
Output design	10
Processing design	30
File design	20
Input design	25
Documentation	30

Required
a. Using the CPM technique, estimate the minimum completion time for the design project.
b. Trace the critical path through the CPM network.
c. How much slack is there in each task that does not lie on the critical path?
d. How much time could be saved if development of the data dictionary could start five days from the beginning of the project, without waiting for completion of the block diagrams?

6. Each of the tasks listed in Problem 5 requires two people, except development of the data dictionary, which requires only one. All of these persons make a salary of $30,000 per year. In addition, the project is supervised by a project manager who makes $50,000 per year.

Required

Prepare a budget for the design project, including a breakdown of expenditures by week. Assume that all employees work a five-day week.

7. The implementation phase of a systems development project has been divided into 11 separate tasks. Their estimated duration and their sequencing relationships are as follows:

	Duration (weeks)	Task	Predecessor Activities	Successor Activities
A: Site preparation	16		None	C
B: Hardware acquisition	20		None	C
C: Hardware installation	2		A, B	E
D: Software development	20		None	E, F
E: Testing and debugging	8		C, D	I
F: Development of procedures	8		D	I
G: Personnel recruitment	6		None	H
H: Training	6		G	J
I: File conversion	3		E, F	J
J: Parallel operation	10		H, I	K
K: Acceptance testing and sign-off	2		J	None

Required

a. Using a CPM approach, determine the estimated completion time for the whole implementation phase.
b. Identify the tasks comprising the critical path.
c. Determine the slack in tasks that do not lie on the critical path.
d. What would be the impact of a delay of four weeks in software development?

8. Draw a Gantt chart using the results of Problem 7. Assume that all tasks begin on their late start dates. Add the following milestones to the chart:

Completion of site preparation
Delivery of the computer hardware
Beginning of parallel operation
Final sign-off

9. A systems study is to evaluate the effectiveness of the accounts payable and payroll applications in a certain organization. The study team is to be composed of the controller, the paymaster, a representative of the firm of external auditors, and two outside consultants. The tasks expected to be performed include the following:

Review of documentation
Observation of operating procedures
Flowcharting of operations
Analysis of exceptions over a three-month period
Interviews with support personnel
Evaluation of internal controls
Review of findings
Preparation of recommendations

Required

a. Make appropriate assignments of the various tasks to ensure that the study is completed satisfactorily. Draw up a responsibility matrix.
b. Analyze any shared assignments. Try to determine whether they would be beneficial from the standpoint of the combination of expertise and experience or whether they would be detrimental because of potential conflicts and buck passing.

10. The manager of a systems project is working on a budget for the extensive design phase. A number of component tasks have been identified, and their duration, start dates, and required level of effort have been estimated.

Required

a. Use appropriate means for analyzing the project's progress and presenting the results to top management.

Task	Duration (weeks)	Start Date*	Level of Effort[†]
Development of specifications	2	0	2
Design of major subsystems	6	2	3
Design of minor subsystems	13	5	4
File design	4	10	2
Forms design	6	12	2
Design of internal controls	6	14	2
Development of procedures and documentation	6	18	3

* Weeks from go-ahead
[†] Number of people per week

Required

a. Draw a Gantt chart using the data given.

b. The project team has an average effective salary rate (including allocated overhead) of $1,200 per week. Determine the total budget for the design project, and provide a budget spread by week.

c. Draw a graph showing the budgeted cumulative expenditure over the duration of the design project.

11. After 14 weeks, the design project in Problem 10 is the subject of a major review by top management. The following data are available:

b. Make reasoned projections of the likelihood that the project will be completed on schedule and on budget.

12. As an extension to Problems 10 and 11, make a detailed estimate of the costs to complete the project. Use the actual costs for tasks already completed, the current estimates for those in progress, and the budget figures for tasks that have not yet been started.

13. During the implementation phase of a large systems project, a meeting is called to try to find out why the project is six months behind schedule but is already

Task	Started*	Percent Complete	Expenditure To Date
Development of specifications	0	100	$ 3,450
Design of major subsystems	2	100	17,000
Design of minor subsystems	7	45	23,500
File design	9	75	5,350
Forms design			
Design of internal controls	Not yet		
Development of procedures and documentation	started		

* Weeks from go-ahead

over budget. The focus of attention is on converting from the old to the new system. Three groups are involved: accounting, data processing, and a firm of outside consultants. The project manager asks Sid Williams, the controller, to give his side of the story:

My people have done everything they were supposed to. Our original MBO item was spelled out in detail as "Provide assistance and monitor results." We have provided a lot of assistance, but so far we haven't seen any results. We have been submitting transactions now for months and have been waiting to get some comparative trial balances. But all that Deborah (the DP manager) keeps telling me is that there are problems. Her staff hasn't given us anything worth looking at.

Deborah Jenkins, the data-processing manager, now has her turn:

I have agreed all along that there are problems, but they are not our fault. Every time we show Sid some output, he glances at it, says it's wrong, and hands it back to us. We need more help in finding out where the errors are. I'm beginning to think that a lot of the errors are in the original data.

Williams reacts angrily to Jenkins's suggestions:

Don't give me that! Even if the transactions are wrong, they should still lead to the same output from the two systems. And debugging the new systems is not accounting's responsibility. We hired in these high-paid consultants to help D.P. get the new system working.

Required

a. What is the real problem here, and how should it be solved?
b. Evaluate the effectiveness of the project management on the basis of the evidence presented.

14. A three-month systems analysis exercise has been completed at Abra Melin Industries, Inc., and four members of the project team have just made a presentation to upper management to explain their findings. The formal proposal calls for a design effort expected to last eight months and to cost $750,000. There is considerable discussion over details of the proposal, but general agreement that the new system will meet the corporation's needs. And there is no substantial opposition to the estimated budget for the design phase.

At a meeting a few days later, the president tells the project manager that the design project has been approved:

You have your "green light." The executive committee accepted my recommendation that we proceed with the design. I have approved all but 10 percent of the funding you requested; unless third-quarter profits go up, we can't afford the whole $750,000. I have also arranged for the temporary reassignment of most of the people you asked to have your project team. You will need to find a substitute for Black because manufacturing can't spare him.

I have a lot of confidence in you and your people, which is just as well because what we don't know about computers and all that stuff would fill a book. Top management won't bother you unless you overrun your budget. Go to it, and we'll see you back in eight months!

Required

As the second in command of the project team, you are obviously happy that the design project has been approved, but you are somewhat anxious about the attitudes of upper management toward the project. Prepare a memorandum on behalf of the project manager to be sent to the president, stating the need for greater involvement by top management and suggesting that biweekly meetings be held to review progress on the design work.

12

Systems Analysis

LEARNING OBJECTIVES

After you have studied this chapter you should be able to

- Identify the objectives of the accounting information system in a given enterprise.
- Explain how to ascertain legitimate user needs and their priorities.
- Explain how to evaluate the existing accounting information system.
- Explain how to identify unavailable, but needed, and available, but unnecessary, applications.
- Explain how to identify and test candidate solutions to systems problems.
- Prepare a proposal for systems changes.
- Analyze critical success factors in order to learn important facts about an organization.
- Describe the chief methods for gathering data in a systems analysis exercise.
- Explain the chief methods of documenting the results of the systems analysis exercise.

CHAPTER OUTLINE

SCOPE OF SYSTEMS ANALYSIS

Systems analysis, as the term is used here, is the process of data gathering and evaluation, leading to the formulation of a proposal for improving the effectiveness and efficiency of an accounting information system. Its methods are broadly similar to those of the financial audit engagement, and still closer to the methods of operational auditing. Indeed, the objectives of systems analysis overlap those of operational auditing, the latter being directed toward the effectiveness and efficiency of the organization as a whole (or at least to some major part of it) rather than of just the accounting information system.

Some writers and other commentators take a broader view of systems analysis and include in it the initial aspects of systems design. Accordingly, there is confusion regarding the proper scope of systems analysis. Ultimately, of course, the drawing of boundaries is of little concern; the important objective is to develop improved accounting systems, and so how that process is divided up and what labels are attached to component activities are of relatively minor significance.

Here, following the precedent set by many other writers, the traditional assumption is made that "analysis" is a process of breaking down something into its component parts in order to study it. Systems analysis is therefore considered to include only the analytical processes leading up to and including the systems recommendations. "Design," in contrast, is the process of synthesis, in which a new system is built up from component subsystems. Systems design starts from the recommendations and extends to developing the complete specifications for a new information system.

OBJECTIVES OF THE ACCOUNTING INFORMATION SYSTEM

Defining the system objectives is the first step in systems planning. This phase of the work is sometimes referred to as *requirements analysis*. The end product of this part of the analysis should be a formal statement of objectives. The subsequent evaluation of the existing accounting information system and the recommendations for an improved system are based on these stated objectives.

To identify the objectives of the accounting system, analysts need to gather information about

- The nature and objectives of the organization
- The users' informational needs
- Information priorities
- Exceptions from standard procedures and processes
- Necessary controls
- Human factors

The Organizational Environment

Accounting information systems do not operate in a vacuum, but in the environment of a particular user organization. The systems analysts must understand the user organization and *its* objectives before considering more specific aspects of the system that is needed.

The organization is in a particular industry and geographical location; it is of a particular size; it is expected to grow at a particular rate; it is made up of a particular group of people with different levels of authority and responsibility; it has its own ways of doing business, special features, and idiosyncracies. These factors pertaining to the organization's survival, growth, and overall success are referred to as its *critical success factors*; they combine to make it unique. And the organization's uniqueness must be recognized before meaningful objectives can be set for the accounting system.

Clearly the objectives of an information system designed for a large manufacturing firm are different from those of a system designed for a government agency, a law practice, or a church. But on a more subtle level, the system objectives of a highly centralized organization are different from those of a decentralized conglomerate. In the former the primary information channels must radiate from the corporate headquarters, whereas in the latter, the primary channels may be confined to the operating divisions. The system objectives of a company with a progressive management team are likely to be different from those of a company whose managers

rely on time-honored, conservative modes of operation. Managers in the latter organization may not consider a decision support system important.

What kind of accounting system an organization should have depends on its size and growth plans. A system designed for a fast-growing start-up organization must be conceived differently from one intended for a more mature, static organization. The information system represents a long-term commitment and so must be able to accommodate projected increases in information throughput. Either spare capacity must be built in from the outset, or provision must be made to increase capacity as the need arises. Some parts of the system inherently have less flexibility to expand than others, and these must be identified and given careful attention at the planning stage. Planning for expansion is difficult, and there is a fine line between having too much capacity and not having enough.

Data should be gathered to measure the historical growth of the accounting system and to estimate its future growth. The parameters chosen to represent size should reflect the nature of the particular enterprise. Suitable parameters might include the numbers of employees, customers, and vendors; the number of inventory items; the numbers of purchases and sales; the total size of secondary storage; and the total number of transactions processed. These data could be documented for analysis, as shown in Figure 12.1.

The location of the organization is important. Support for high-technology systems—service support, spare parts, and highly trained personnel—may be readily available in one location but unavailable in others. This is particularly true of organizations involved in international business, but even North America is not homogeneous with respect to technological support. Similarly, if organizations operate in areas subject to natural disasters, social unrest, or political instability, there may be an understandable reluctance to make large investments in sophisticated equipment.

The organizational scenario presents a set of opportunities and constraints that must be taken into account in planning an accounting system. Special resources may exist that permit the organization to have an unusually sophisticated information system. Or there may be special constraints that severely limit what can realistically be expected. Unless the systems analysts appreciate the

FIGURE 12.1. The rate of growth of an accounting system.

Parameter	Actuals			Estimates	
	5 Years Ago	Last Year	Now	Next Year	5 Years from Now
Employees	200	350	400	400	500
Customers	1,000	1,500	1,600	1,700	3,000
Vendors	30	100	120	150	200
Inventory items	500	1,000	900	900	1,500
Secondary storage (MB)	20	100	150	200	800
Total reports prepared	10	40	42	50	60
Total transactions processed	9,500	15,000	19,500	22,000	30,000

organizational environment, the recommendations they make to management are likely to fall on deaf ears, or worse, an information system may be developed that does not "fit into" its user organization.

User Needs

The overall purpose of an accounting system is to meet statutory requirements for external reporting and to provide information to internal users in planning, control, performance evaluation, and decision making. External reporting is usually mandatory, but internal reporting is discretionary, and management is free to decide what information should be provided. In making this decision, management typically relies on the systems analysts to survey the system's users and to make appropriate recommendations, together with a formal or informal cost–benefit analysis.

Subject to upper management's final approval, the system should meet the users' legitimate needs for information, providing them with the outputs they need at the time they need them and in the form in which they want them. Consequently, an important component of systems analysis is soliciting users' opinions about which outputs are needed from the information system and the appropriate medium, information content, format, timing, and frequency of issuance.

Medium. The medium—documents, reports, or displays—should be appropriate to the information's use and distribution. Hard-copy output may be essential to one user but may be an embarrassment to another

who would prefer output to a screen. Sometimes information should be communicated in more than one medium; for example, summary information might be displayed on a screen, with the supporting details in a report.

Information Content. The choice of information content should aim at a middle ground between not providing enough information and providing too much. This choice should reflect the recipient's authority and responsibility; a good rule of thumb is that the higher the individual is in the organizational hierarchy, the less detail should be provided. Upper management ordinarily wants to see the "big picture," whereas a lower-level manager, such as a first-level supervisor, needs detailed information with a correspondingly narrow perspective. Managers at intermediate levels are best served, routinely, by summarized information but should have access to supporting detail upon demand.

When the systems analysts have surveyed the users regarding the information content of the outputs they have requested, the analysts may decide to draw up a comprehensive data dictionary for the system. A data dictionary, similar to those discussed in the context of data base management systems (see Chapter 9), provides a master list of the data elements and their definitions. The data dictionary is needed for the subsequent systems design and is drawn up either as part of the systems analysis exercise or early in the design phase.

Format. Information formats should reflect general principles of effective forms design (see Chapter 4) but otherwise whenever possible should be guided by personal preferences. Reports widely distributed within the organization may have to be standardized. But when the output is directed to only a few key individuals, individual preferences can be accommodated. Modern computer technology makes possible a degree of flexibility in formatting that did not exist in the days of manual reporting.

Timing and Frequency. The required timing and frequency of output depend on the nature of the information and on the urgency of decisions made by the recipients. Some types of information quickly lose their currency and, unless reported soon after the events to which they refer, are worthless. For example, data on last week's cash balances do not help in day-to-day cash management, any more than last week's commodities prices help a speculator. At the other extreme, data on land held for resale may still be valuable months after the appraisals were conducted. The required timing and frequency of reporting are often interrelated. If information about yesterday's or today's transactions is important, it probably needs to be reported every day. On the other hand, the frequency of reporting may simply be a matter of convenience. Customer statements are usually sent out once per month, even though fluctuations of the accounts receivable balance during the month are of interest to both the customer and the credit manager. The frequency of reporting may also interact with the choice of the output medium. The credit manager might be satisfied with receiving a monthly printed aging schedule of accounts receivable as long as he or she also has the capability of displaying selected customer balances on a screen.

Priorities

If users are simply asked to state their information needs, the result will usually be a "wish list." And if the system were to provide all of the desired outputs, it might become more expensive than the organization could afford, or at least it would have a poor cost–benefit ratio. However, not all the requested outputs are as important as others, and users must be asked to assign realistic priorities to their requests. Upper management should review these priorities and, if necessary, make

appropriate adjustments. Some systems analysts divide the requested outputs into three categories: essential, highly desirable, and marginal. The recommended new system then balances costs and priorities. In practical terms, this usually means providing all of the "essential" outputs, most or all of the "highly desirable" ones, and some of the "marginal ones," as long as those in the third category do not significantly increase the cost of the system.

Exceptions

Some types of information systems require rigidly standardized modes of processing, whereas others must accept numerous exceptions from standard procedures. For example, some payroll systems treat everyone in the factory as an hourly employee and assume that the whole work force is domiciled in a single state. Others may treat most as hourly employees but provide for job shoppers, contract workers, commissioned salespeople, and consultants and also provide for a multistate work force. Obviously, the latter payroll system must be substantially more complex than the former.

The degree of standardization and the nature of anticipated exceptions should be identified as early as possible and be documented so that they can be taken into account in systems planning. The discovery of exceptions at a later stage may result in the need for expensive changes in the design.

Controls

The objectives of the accounting information system extend to the internal controls incorporated into the system. The overall objectives of internal control are to preserve the integrity of the data, to safeguard the organizations resources, to encourage operating efficiency, and to enforce compliance with management's policies and procedures. But the specific degree of control depends on the system's vulnerability to threats of various kinds and on the consequences of failing to secure the system. For example, a dealer in gold coins faces a much greater risk of theft than does a dealer in concrete blocks. And a manufacturing organization that employs a large work force faces a different problem of enforcing management policies than does a small professional service organization. Companies that register with the Securities and Exchange Commission are now required by law to have a system of internal controls. But the nature of the controls and the level of assurance required from them remain largely a matter of management's judgment.

The systems analysts should identify the principal areas of vulnerability and determine the broad types of internal controls necessary to protect them. In this study, the analysts can be guided by standard lists of control principles and objectives, such as those discussed in Chapter 16.

Human Factors

The relationship between people and information systems is so strong that human factors cannot be ignored when formulating systems objectives. "People problems" must be identified as early as possible so that appropriate steps can be taken to deal with them. Employees may be unable or unwilling to learn new skills, and there may not be an alternative labor supply. The management team may not unanimously want a new information system. Certain managers may press for a new system that is not needed; others may feel threatened by the prospect of a new system and try to sabotage it. Organizational changes associated with the implementation of a new information system may affect the responsibilities and status of individuals, particularly in middle management.

The possibility of sabotage of a new information system must be considered. Groups of rank-and-file employees or individual managers who view a new system as a threat to their position can undermine a systems project. A manager can aggravate problems when they occur; he or she can become "concerned" about the adequacy of the new system, about the competence of the project team, or about any other area where anxiety can be engendered. Eventually, as these "concerns" spread, every problem becomes a crisis; and as crisis follows crisis, the new system becomes associated with failure, and the whole project is in jeopardy. Attempts at sabotage must be recognized and "nipped in the bud" at an early stage. Upper management must let it be

known that it is firmly committed to the project and that it has complete confidence in the project team. The one insurmountable problem is top management's unwillingness to give the project its full support.

On the other hand, the responsibility for dealing with people problems does not rest with top management alone. The attitudes of members of the project team can help alleviate anxieties or defuse potential trouble spots. Tact and diplomacy and a willingness to listen to people in a nonthreatening manner may make all the difference between success and failure.

Statement of Objectives

The information gathered concerning these issues should be reduced to a formal statement of objectives. The statement of objectives normally addresses the purpose of the system, the required outputs, and other relevant matters. The statement should be prepared and submitted to top management for approval. By approving the statement, management commits itself to the objectives and, at least tentatively, to the steps necessary to accomplish them. Once the statement has received the formal stamp of approval, it can be used as a basis for evaluating the existing system and for drawing up recommendations for improvement or replacement.

The information gathered may contain hard facts about the system and its environment and also more subjective material about potential problems. Upper management needs to be apprised of the perceptions of the project team concerning personnel problems, but these may be too sensitive to include in the formal document. In some cases, it may be more appropriate to communicate delicate matters to top management separately from the formal statement of objectives.

EVALUATION OF THE EXISTING SYSTEM

The existing accounting information system is evaluated in the light of the objectives established for the system in its particular organizational, geographical, and social environment. The system is evaluated from the standpoints of effectiveness and efficiency. The evaluation of effectiveness asks the question, ''Is the system doing its job?''; the evaluation of efficiency asks, ''How expensive (in terms of the consumption of resources of all types) is the system to operate?'' The system is evaluated to identify those areas where it is deficient and also areas where it may be performing adequately. The latter may tend to be overlooked in the atmosphere of concern for the deficiencies. But both strengths and weaknesses should be documented so that plans for an

improved or new system can build on existing strengths while seeking to remedy the weaknesses.

Walk-Through

A useful approach to the evaluation is for the systems analysts to ''walk through'' the processes comprising the information system. At each step the analysts should

FIGURE 12.2 Documentation of systems walk-through.

PROCESS: Approval of accounts payable vouchers.

Analyst: KJL   Date: 99/99/99   Process ref. no.:   999999

CHARACTERIZATION	DATA GATHERED
Objective	Approval of accounts payable vouchers.
Reason	To ensure that disbursements to vendors are made only for authorized, completed purchases and that disbursements are made in the correct amounts.
Methodology	An accounting clerk assembles vouchers and supporting documents: purchase requisitions, purchase orders, receiving documents, and invoices received from vendors. The vice-president reviews the documents and, if satisfied that all paperwork is in order, signs the vouchers. The vouchers are then returned to the treasurer's office where the checks are cut.
Personnel Involved	Accounting clerk. Vice-president for operations.
Timing	First and fifteenth of each month, or if one of those days falls on a weekend, on the following Monday.
Location	Front office, company headquarters.

Remarks and Recommendations:

gather and document facts relating to the objectives of this process, the reason it is performed, the manner in which it is performed, the personnel involved, and the timing and location of performance. These characterizations correspond to the six questions of the newspaper reporter: who, what, how, why, when, and where? From the answers to these questions and to further questions dealing with specific concerns that may arise from them, the analysts can form the necessary general understanding of the system and can identify areas warranting more detailed study.

To illustrate, suppose that a systems analyst is reviewing procedures for approval of accounts payable vouchers. The six characterizations might be documented as in Figure 12.2. The procedures appear to be effective insofar as they meet the objective of restricting payments to valid purchases and of verifying the amounts involved. They may also be effective insofar as there is no question that the vice-president for operations has the authority to approve the disbursements. On the other hand, unless this is a very small organization, the situation leaves a lot to be desired in regard to efficiency. The vice-president for operations has (or ought to have) more important things to do than routinely approving payables vouchers. The rigidly periodic approval cycle may result in lost discounts. Furthermore, the vice-president is rather far removed from the circumstances of the purchases and must rely on the paperwork to communicate all relevant details that might affect approval.

A good case could be made for delegating this responsibility to someone closer to the purchasing function, perhaps the immediate superior of the purchase agent. This individual could devote more frequent sessions to voucher approval, thereby enabling the organization to take advantage of discounts for prompt payment. Furthermore, the individual could more easily request additional information from purchasing or accounts payable if there was any doubt about a voucher.

Because authority in the organization appears to be rather heavily centralized, the final recommendation might compromise by calling for delegation of voucher approval responsibility up to a certain dollar ceiling. Approval of vouchers for disbursements exceeding that ceiling could remain the responsibility of the vice-president, who could accordingly spend more time reviewing them. But there should still be some procedure allowing for on-demand approval of a voucher when a discount is at stake. If the vice-president's other responsibilities do not permit such intrusion, the organization might find itself paying a substantial premium for its centralized management style.

Evaluation of Outputs

A major part of the evaluation with respect to effectiveness deals with the outputs provided by the existing information system. Evaluation of the outputs should consider the following questions:

- What outputs are produced from the existing system?
- To what extent do these outputs correspond to the desired outputs listed in the statement of objectives?
- Are outputs delivered on appropriate media?
- Is information assembled and "packaged" appropriately in terms of documents, reports, screen displays, and other media?
- Is reported information reliable and communicated at an appropriate level of precision?
- Is useful information buried in a mass of irrelevant data?
- Is information presented at the appropriate level of summarization?
- Are output formats adequate, and in what ways could they be improved?
- Are the timing and frequency of reporting adequate to meet user needs?
- Are outputs distributed, or otherwise made available, to the users who need them?
- Are internal controls adequate to protect data from unauthorized access?

Outputs from the existing system should be compared with the desired outputs listed in the statement of objectives. Figure 12.3 illustrates one method of documenting the comparison. Missing applications, output deficiencies in existing applications, and unwanted applications should be identified. Deficiencies may include missing documents, reports, and screen displays; incomplete information content; inadequate formats; inadequate timing and frequency of reporting; and inadequate distribution of reports. Comments on these and any other pertinent issues should be recorded as appropriate.

FIGURE 12.3 Comparison between existing and required accounting outputs.

PROJECT 9876
SYSTEMS ANALYSIS

Date: 1/15/99
Prepared by: VBP
Checked by: GFT

EXISTING APPLICATIONS

Application	Outputs	Frequency	Remarks
Accounts receivable	Invoices Invoice register	Weekly Weekly	Frequent errors
Payroll	Paychecks for hourly employees Check register	Weekly Weekly	Confusing format
Cost estimation	Estimated product cost based on specified parameters	On demand	Application developed but rarely used

REQUIRED APPLICATIONS

Application	Outputs	Frequency	Remarks
Accounts receivable	Invoices Invoice register Statements Schedule of aged receivables	Weekly Weekly Monthly Monthly	Required first of month
Payroll	Hourly paychecks Salaried paychecks Payroll journal W2 and 941A reports	Weekly Monthly Weekly Annually	Required by 1/31
Accounts Payable	Vouchers Voucher register Cash requirements forecast Checks Check register	On demand Weekly Weekly Semimonthly Semimonthly	Two-level authorization for amounts over $2,000 Required first and fifteenth of month
Inventory control	Stock status report Reorder report Stock query	Monthly Weekly On demand	Expedited items require special handling Terminals in sales and warehouse
Sales analysis	Breakdown by territory Breakdown by product	Weekly Monthly	

One common complaint is that although the information needed by a particular group of users is in fact reported, it is inappropriately "packaged"; the data are spread throughout a number of different reports, and the users must devote time and effort to assembling the data into the required form.

The right reports may be prepared, containing ostensibly the right kinds of information, but the data may be unreliable. A high incidence of errors undermines the users' confidence in the data, and users may turn elsewhere either for basic information or for confirmation of reported data. Reported data must be accurate, but it need not necessarily be communicated with a high degree of precision. Accuracy deals with the correspondence with the underlying economic facts; precision deals with the number of significant figures to which the data are expressed. Sometimes the issuance of reports is delayed because of excessive concern for precision—a level of precision that the users may not need.

Analysis of the movement of data from one location to another or from one organizational unit to another may help explain loss of data, processing delays, or bottlenecks. The transmittal medium—U.S. mail, private courier, or electronic communication, as the case may be—should be reviewed in terms of reliability, speed, and cost. Analysis of the movement of data within an organizational unit may reveal how information is handled and who is authorized to interact with it. Some individuals may have authority to initiate or modify information; others may have authority to receive it; still others may be denied access to the data. Study of the actual movement of data and comparison with management's stated policies may reveal control weaknesses or violations. If unauthorized persons have access to data, an assessment should be made as to whether this constitutes a threat to the information system or the organization's assets.

Controls may be effective but inefficient. Control measures should be evaluated as to their benefits and costs to the organization: The cost of a control includes out-of-pocket costs and also "hidden" costs associated with loss of operating performance. An example of an inefficient control is a cumbersome authorization procedure required before employees can use an office copying machine. Costs could probably be reduced by doing away with the authorization procedure, even though employees occasionally make copies for unauthorized purposes. The evaluation of internal controls will be discussed more fully in a later chapter.

RECOMMENDATIONS FOR IMPROVEMENT

Recommendations for improvement are made in the belief that the performance of the accounting information system can be brought closer to the ideal envisioned in the statement objectives.

Alternative Solutions

When the results from the evaluation of the existing system are studied, problems are identified, and the project team seeks solutions to them. In this search for solutions lies one of the most creative aspects of systems development. Alternative solutions should be sought to each major problem. Frequently there is more than one way to improve the system, and it is advantageous for the project team to explore these alternatives before making a final recommendation. Exploring a wider range of possibilities may result in the discovery of a better solution. It also helps avoid emotional attachment to the first solution that comes to mind, which might make the analysts inflexible toward alternatives that are forced on them later. The candidate solutions should be documented and presented to management during informal discussions. The importance of securing the involvement of upper management in systems planning cannot be stressed too much, and such discussions provide a good opportunity to tap the broad experience that top managers typically have. The final choice among the alternatives should be made after consideration by both the project team and management.

Proposed Changes in the System

Proposed system enhancements can typically be broken down into enhancements to outputs, processes, technology, and controls. Changing the outputs may be called for whenever a valid need is not being met. New applications may have to be added; existing applications may have to be modified to provide additional documents, reports, screen displays, or other items; formats may need to be improved; the distribution of reports or access to on-line screen displays may need to be changed; or the timing and frequency of reporting may have to be improved. Sometimes the necessary changes can be made without altering the basic structure of the information system, but in other cases the structure is entirely inadequate and must be replaced.

Changes to processing operations may mean revising clerical procedures or modifying or replacing computer programs. Such changes may consist of:

- Eliminating unnecessary processes
- Consolidating duplicate or redundant processes
- Simplifying processing methods
- Improving processing methods

Eliminating processes that are no longer needed, or consolidating two or more processes that perform essentially the same function, usually results in improved efficiency. On the other hand, consolidation should not be pressed to the point that desirable flexibility is lost or a bottleneck is created, causing intolerable delays. Furthermore, elimination of all redundancy may cause reliability problems. Modern information systems often build in intentional redundancy to improve performance and reliability; the distributed processing system is an important example.

Simplicity is a key word in new systems development. Simple processes often work better and more reliably than do complicated ones. But when an existing system is being modified, changes can rarely be justified on the basis of simplification alone. The advantages of simplifying the process are unlikely to be so great as to offset the cost and upheaval of making the changes, and furthermore, the risk of unanticipated side effects cannot be ignored. The same remarks apply to other improvements in processing operations. The old adage ''If it ain't broke, don't fix it'' is pertinent in this regard. Analysts should avoid the temptation to meddle with an otherwise satisfactory system just because they see a better way to do the job.

Changes in processing technology may be appropriate when the existing technology is inadequate to provide effective and efficient operation of the system. The changes may consist of enhancing the level or extent of automation, or they may take the form of adopting a new or superior technology. The appropriate type of computer support may change as the organization grows or undergoes other developments. Moreover, advances in computer technology and decreases in both hardware and software costs have brought sophisticated modes of processing within the reach of many organizations that could not have considered them earlier. In a very few situations, de-automation and a return to manual processing methods may be desirable.

The main issues to be resolved with respect to automation are

- What level of automation is appropriate?
- Is automation to be provided by in-house computer facilities or by an outside service bureau?
- If in-house facilities are recommended, what types of equipment will be required?
- What level of centralization of computer facilities is envisioned?
- How will the equipment be used?
- What major types of software will be required, such as data base management systems?
- How will the manual and automated parts of the system be interfaced?
- What are the organizational implications of the proposed system?
- What are the control implications of the proposed system?

Regardless of the degree of automation, some parts of the system are likely to remain manual; some tasks are better performed by people than by machines. Where automation is beneficial, it may be provided by an outside service bureau, an organization that sells computer-processing services on either a pure batch or an interactive basis. Service bureaus have become less popular over the last several years as a result of the availability of powerful computer hardware and software at relatively low cost. However, the ownership and operation of in-house computers result in additional responsibilities that the organization may be reluctant to bear.

In-house computer facilities may be centralized or dispersed throughout the organization, with or without interconnecting telecommunications channels. The advantages and disadvantages of decentralization were discussed in Chapter 10. Regardless of the degree of geographical decentralization, the facilities at any one location may consist of a single mainframe or departmental computer, or of clustered microcomputers providing equivalent total processing power—although less power available to any one job. The greater reliability offered by distributed processing systems may be the controlling consideration.

Data storage facilities may be incorporated in the form of conventional files owned by each application or by a shared data base management system. The advantages and disadvantages of the two approaches were explored in Chapter 9. The DMBS approach offers substantial advantages as long as the resulting complexity does not overstrain the available human and computer resources. The decision regarding the use of a DBMS is closely linked with the decision relating to real-time processing. Real-time processing can be implemented using a conventional file structure but is much easier to implement with a DBMS. But real-time processing may not be needed, and the control problems may be reduced by use of batch processing, with or without on-line data entry.

Enhancements in internal control may be appropriate if there is a significant control weakness and if the cost of incorporating and maintaining additional control measures is reasonable in relation to the associated risks. Alternatively, elimination of controls is appropriate when the cost of the controls is too high relative to the risks involved.

The desired level of controls depends in part on the nature of the organization and its particular vulnerabilities. Because of the type of business, the type of products, the location, and the type of people involved, some organizations require a higher level of control assurance than do others. Some organizations have greater responsibilities to outsiders and may face greater risks. The desired level of controls also depends on how much responsibility can be given to the people who will operate the system, compared with the responsibility that must be borne by the system designers. If people cannot be trusted to carry out written procedures, programmed controls may be needed that can be operated by computers. Systems can be designed with exceptionally high levels of controls; such systems are referred to (facetiously, but with some justification) as "gorilla proof." However, the control measures and procedures neces-

sary to accomplish this objective may carry a large penalty in initial cost and diminished operating efficiency.

Justifying the Changes

Any changes to the system must be justified in the same manner as are other business decisions. Three questions should be asked:

- Are the changes desirable?
- Are the changes cost effective?
- Are the changes feasible?

The justification for the recommendations must show that the changes will produce real benefits, which will more than compensate for the costs involved, and that the changes can be made in the environment of the organization. Cost effectiveness need not be interpreted in strict dollar terms. Any cost savings or improvements in revenue generation and collection will of course be desirable, but the intangible benefit of better information may persuade management that the costs are justified. On the other hand, the required investment must be justified not just in terms of the benefits to be derived but also on the grounds that the improvements in the information system will produce a return (tangible and intangible) that competes with alternative uses of the funds.

Major changes should be subjected to a feasibility study. Feasibility has more than one dimension. Technological feasibility can almost be taken for granted, but the practical feasibility of implementing the changes—in the particular environment of the organization, its location, its financial condition, and its people, and in a time frame relevant to the organization's needs—may not be so obvious. Any special resources or constraints are pertinent in this regard. The purpose of a feasibility study should be to convince management that the changes can be made in a reasonable time frame at a price that the organization can afford and without destroying the organization in the process.

Formal Recommendations

After reviewing the proposed changes to the system in the light of feasibility and other relevant considerations, the project manager may draw one of three conclusions regarding the information system as a whole:

- The existing system is as good as can be expected under the circumstances, and so no significant changes are warranted.
- The system is basically sound but should be modified, enhanced, or upgraded in specific areas in order to remedy identified weaknesses.
- A new system should be acquired or developed.

The first conclusion (which may require considerable courage on the part of the project manager) obviously requires little further action. The recommendation is communicated to management; the project team is disbanded; and operations continue as before. The latter two conclusions call for the preparation of a formal proposal setting out what should be done. Preparation of the proposal is required whether or not the systems analysis was conducted by outside consultants. Its purpose is to "sell" the recommended changes to the information system to upper management.

The systems proposal should summarize the results of the systems analysis up to that point and should present the final recommendations of the project team. Typically the proposal includes sections dealing with the following:

- Background scenario
- Major problems
- Alternative solutions
- Recommended system changes or new system
- Method of implementation
- Schedule of implementation
- Estimated cost
- Concluding remarks

The "background" section should provide a brief statement of the organizational environment as it affects the information system. "Major problems" should summarize the circumstances that led to the initiation of the systems project and should identify other major weaknesses in the existing system that came to light during the evaluation. The sections dealing with the alternative solutions and final recommendations should reference the statement of objectives (the statement could well be included as an appendix to the proposal). Finally, the justification for the final recommendations, including the results of applicable feasibility studies, should be summarized.

The section on implementation should outline the steps necessary to implement the proposed changes. It should identify in broad terms the level of computer technology, how it should be acquired, and the personnel requirements and organizational changes needed. The sections on schedule and cost can contain only broad generalizations because detailed planning in these two areas must await the design phase. However, management will appreciate receiving even rough-order-of-magnitude estimates to help them appraise the scope of the proposed work. The proposal should reference any schedule and budget projections already made at the commencement of the project, with suitable comments as to their continued relevance and attainability.

The "conclusions" section should briefly summarize the highlights of the earlier sections and document the overall conclusions. Acknowledgements are in order if certain individuals or groups have made notable contributions to the analysis. Finally, if the proposal was prepared by an outside consulting firm, some appropriate comments should be made that the firm appreciated the opportunity to serve the client organization.

In addition to the formal systems proposal, a set of technical specifications is often drawn up. The intent of the two documents is similar, to define the enhancements to the existing information system or the requirements for a new system. However, the technical specifications express the recommendations of the project team in precise technical language, whereas the systems proposal is expressed in language that management can understand. Upon approval of the systems proposal, the specifications—including whatever amendments or revisions are called for by management—form an interface between the analysis phase and the design phase of the systems development project. They represent the starting point for the design process.

TECHNIQUES IN SYSTEMS ANALYSIS

Systems analysis involves a considerable amount of data gathering, followed by analysis of the data, and then documentation and communication of the findings to management and other interested parties. The techniques of systems analysis are similar to those used in auditing: obervation, inquiry, examination, and review. The purpose of this section is to review a number of techniques in common use and to show how they contribute to systems analysis.

Analysis of Critical Success Factors

An examination of an organization's critical success factors (CSFs) provides considerable insight into the environment in which the information system has to function. Critical success factors, sometimes referred to as *key variables*, describe what it is about the organization—its products, policies, procedures, management style, employee attitudes, and so forth—that contributes to its success or on which its success depends. Some examples of critical success factors are employee loyalty, customer satisfaction, financial stability, professionalism, and social responsibility.

Critical success factors are often broken down into a hierarchy of subsidiary CSFs. For example, a primary CSF, "employee loyalty," may be considered to depend on three secondary CSFs: compensation, advancement opportunities, and good management. In turn, "compensation" may be divided further into three tertiary CSFs: salary, fringe benefits, and raise expectations. "Advancement opportunities" may include training programs, continuing education support, company growth, and a policy of "promoting from within." And "good management" may include participatory management, constructive feedback, respect for employees, and a willingness to listen.

Analysis of another critical success factor is shown in Table 12.1. Here the primary CSF: "customer satisfaction" is divided into three secondary CSFs: product quality, price, and availability. Each of these is subdivided into several tertiary factors.

Through an examination of critical success factors, the systems analyst can identify the components of each primary CSF and may be able to recognize the early warning signs of impending threats to the organization's well-being. The analyst can identify features of the existing accounting information system on which the or-

TABLE 12.1   Example of Analysis of Critical Success Factors

Primary CSF: Level 1	Subsidiary CSFs:	
	Level 2	Level 3
Customer satisfaction	Product quality	Product performance Reliability Appearance Brand image
	Price	List price Discounts Trade-in allowances Financing Lease arrangements
	Availability	Dealer location Demonstration models Delivery lead time Shipping arrangements

ganization may be particularly dependent, and which it would be reluctant to sacrifice. The analyst can also assess the impact of potential new features on the accounting system. Some new features can be expected to be beneficial and can be recommended without reservation. Other new features might have a negative impact and so should be avoided.

Review of Documentation

A good accounting system is well documented and is supported by comprehensive operating procedures covering all significant tasks. And the activities and responsibilities of all people in the system should be covered by detailed organization charts and job descriptions. Many of the data required by the systems analyst can, in principle, be obtained from an examination and review of this material. If the material exists, the amount of effort required by the systems analysis will be greatly reduced. Unfortunately, many systems are not documented, and operating procedures may never have been reduced to writing. Job responsibilities may have evolved over time, and job descriptions never drawn up. Documentation may originally have been prepared when the system was developed but was not kept current as the system evolved. Whatever the claims of management, the analyst should verify the currency of the documentation, and if the material is seriously out of date, the required information should be sought elsewhere.

Observation

Observation is a basic element in any systems analysis. By observing how people do their jobs, much can be learned about the underlying strengths and weaknesses of the information system. Comparisons can be made with documented procedures and job descriptions, and bottlenecks can be identified. A general impression can be gained of the level of cooperation and morale among the employees and of the quality of supervision.

Interviews

Much of the required information is normally acquired through interviews. These will be held with both management personnel and other key individuals. Certain types of information, such as the system and organizational objectives, will most likely come from interviews with top management. Other vital pieces of information, particularly concerning the workings of the existing system, may come from people at the operational level. In some situations, there are advantages in posing similar questions to both a manager and a subordinate; the similarities and differences between their answers may be enlightening.

Interviewing normally is a one-to-one encounter between an interviewer (the person conducting the interview) and an interviewee (the person being interviewed). Good methods of interviewing have been devised to make the encounter as productive as possible.

A major objective is to gather the greatest amount of reliable information while making minimal demands on the interviewee's time. Most business people, particularly top management, are busy, and their time is valu-

able. To achieve this objective, it is necessary to avoid irrelevancies and repetitions where at all possible.[1] Another objective may be to ensure the compatibility of the results of several interviews conducted with different individuals.

Structured interviewing has emerged in response to these objectives, and it has proved effective in improving the quality of the data gathered. The structured interview uses prescribed (and pretested) questions put to the interviewee in a prescribed order. The interviewer is given little, if any, discretion in modifying the format of the interview. In contrast, in an unstructured interview, the interviewer may modify or omit certain questions depending on the responses obtained to earlier ones.

Whether or not a structured approach is adopted, good interviewing practice requires attention to a number of important factors:

- Schedule interviews so as to minimize the impact on the person's normal work flow. Be ready to reschedule the interview if a conflict arises.
- Check with the supervisor before interviewing junior people.
- Have an organized plan for the interview, and prepare the questions in advance.
- Talk to the interviewee at his or her level. Do not ''play the expert.''
- Listen rather than talk. Do not prompt the person to give the answer you expect.
- Ask for help. Emphasize that the interviewee knows more about the work details than you do.
- Be uncritical and maintain an open mind. Listen (without agreeing or disagreeing) to complaints about the organization and its people.
- Answer questions about the purpose of the interview simply and honestly. Do not reveal confidential information, but do not be secretive.
- Treat the responses with confidence whenever possible. Serious revelations may need to be reported, but do not be a management ''spy'' on minor matters.

The interview should be conducted in an unthreatening manner so that the interviewer wins the trust of the in-

---

[1] Sometimes repetition is deliberately introduced in order to evaluate the consistency of the interviewee's responses.

dividual. When people in the lower levels of the organizational hierarchy are being interviewed, they may be suspicious that "something is going on" and may be afraid to give frank answers to the questions. An effort must be made to put the people at their ease. At the higher levels of the hierarchy, there may be other problems. Certain managers may want to "hold forth" on their private philosophies. Diplomacy is needed to work around such problems and still obtain the information needed.

The material obtained from each interview and from other sources will be combined to form an overall picture of the system and the way in which it operates. In the process of synthesis, additional questions are likely to arise. Follow-up interviews may need to be arranged to clear up any points of detail that are still unclear. Also, it is helpful for the analyst to get reactions from certain key individuals to the picture that has been built up to that point. In this way, misconceptions can be corrected before the final stages of the systems analysis are completed.

Questionnaires

Questionnaires can be addressed to a larger population than is usually convenient to interview individually. Questionnaires may be sent to a sample of employees, vendors, or customers. The quality of the information obtained in a single questionnaire may be lower than that acquired in an interview, but any reduction in quality may be offset by the advantage of multiple responses. Furthermore, questionnaires may be more appropriate than interviews when the responses to questions require research by the respondents.

The two most important aids to the successful use of questionnaires are to keep the questionnaires as short as possible and to make them easy to fill out. Long questionnaires evoke a negative reaction by the respondents and either are not returned at all or are completed in a hasty, careless manner. In any case, reminders may have to be sent if the questionnaires are not returned promptly. Questionnaires that are poorly designed, confusing, or difficult to complete often meet a similar fate to that of long ones. The techniques of good forms design, dis-

cussed earlier in this book, also are applicable to questionnaire design and should be reviewed.

A common use of questionnaires is to gather information on the internal controls; systems analysts and auditors frequently use this technique. Standard internal control questionnaires have been assembled by most of the large public accounting firms and also by some other institutions. They may include questions to be filled out by representatives of the client firm, but they consist largely of questions put to client personnel by the auditor; in effect, the questionnaires form the basis of structured interviews.

Job Station Analysis

Job station analysis is an in-depth study of the work performed at a particular work location, work station, or "job station" within the information system. The locations selected for this kind of analysis are usually those "nodes" in the system where several transaction paths converge and bottlenecks are likely to develop. An example is the input-output window in a data-processing department, where batches of transactions are submitted for processing and output is picked up by the users. Another example is the point at which disbursement vouchers are screened prior to approval.

In keeping with the systems approach, the job station can be treated as a subsystem with its own inputs, outputs, and processing activities; the inputs and outputs relate it to neighboring subsystems. A major objective of job station analysis is to identify and evaluate these inputs and outputs and the relevant processing activities, to assess the role played by the particular job station in the information system as a whole. The processing activities may use equipment, including computers, or they may be entirely manual. The responsibilities of the personnel involved can be evaluated in the light of their training, experience, general competence, and observations made about the effectiveness and efficiency of the job station subsystem. If the job station proves to be a bottleneck, additional equipment may be needed, or more employees may be required to operate the station. Alternatively, the work of the job station may need to be split up between two or more new stations.

FIGURE 12.4 Documentation of the results of job-station analysis.

Job stations	Approval of disbursement vouchers.
Personnel	Senior accounts payable clerks. Presently there are three senior clerks assigned to this job station.
Responsibilities	Review purchase orders, receiving reports, and vendor invoice for accuracy and consistency. Review and approve voucher for payment. Identify available discounts. Route to supervisor for signature.
Inputs	Purchase orders, receiving reports, vendor invoices, vouchers ready for signature.
Outputs	Validated vouchers ready for signature.
Equipment used	None.
Problems	1. There is a three-week backlog of vouchers awaiting approval.
	2. Discounts are being lost because of inability to process disbursements within discount period. Lost discounts are estimated to exceed $12,800 per year.
	3. Excessive overtime is being worked by senior clerks.
	4. Morale is deteriorating and turnover is increasing
Recommendation	1. Hire one additional senior clerk.
	2. Prescreen vouchers for available discount and expedite as appropriate.
Value	Increasing staff level will improve morale and help reduce employee turnover. Lost discounts can be reduced by at least 80 percent.

The results of the analysis of a particular job station can be summarized and documented in the form shown in Figure 12.4. The situation is described; the observed problems are noted; and preliminary recommendations are made for subsequent review by the project manager and by general management.

Flowcharting

Flowcharting is a most important tool in systems analysis. Flowcharts are normally prepared in parallel with the gathering of data by the methods described earlier. They provide a recording medium that assists in assembling the ''jigsaw puzzle'' of information; they also help in confronting apparent (or real) inconsistencies and revealing areas where vital details are still missing. Problems in a system—or potential solutions of the problems—often are more readily apparent from examination of a flowchart than from review of verbal descriptions. The problems may be operating ineffectiveness or inefficiencies or control weaknesses. Flowcharts represent a model of the information system and its component media—transaction flows, internal controls, and equipment—that can be used for both evaluating the existing system and planning an improved system.

Organization charts should be prepared early in the systems analysis. Information from these charts may help not only in understanding the nature of the organization but also in structuring the later stages of the work for maximum effectiveness. Block diagrams and data flow diagrams may be appropriate as a basis for identifying the major subsystems and the relationships and transaction flows among them. Systems flowcharts and/or document flowcharts will normally be used to show the detailed processing activities, transaction paths, audit trails, and internal controls in each subsystem, including the organizational responsibilities associated with the various activities. Figure 12.5 illustrates the use of systems flowcharting in systems analysis. Notes are frequently made on the flowcharts indicating problems to be solved or matters requiring further investigation. As more information is gathered, the analyst may add more comments, explanations, and suggestions for improvement.

FIGURE 12.5 Use of a systems flowchart in systems analysis.

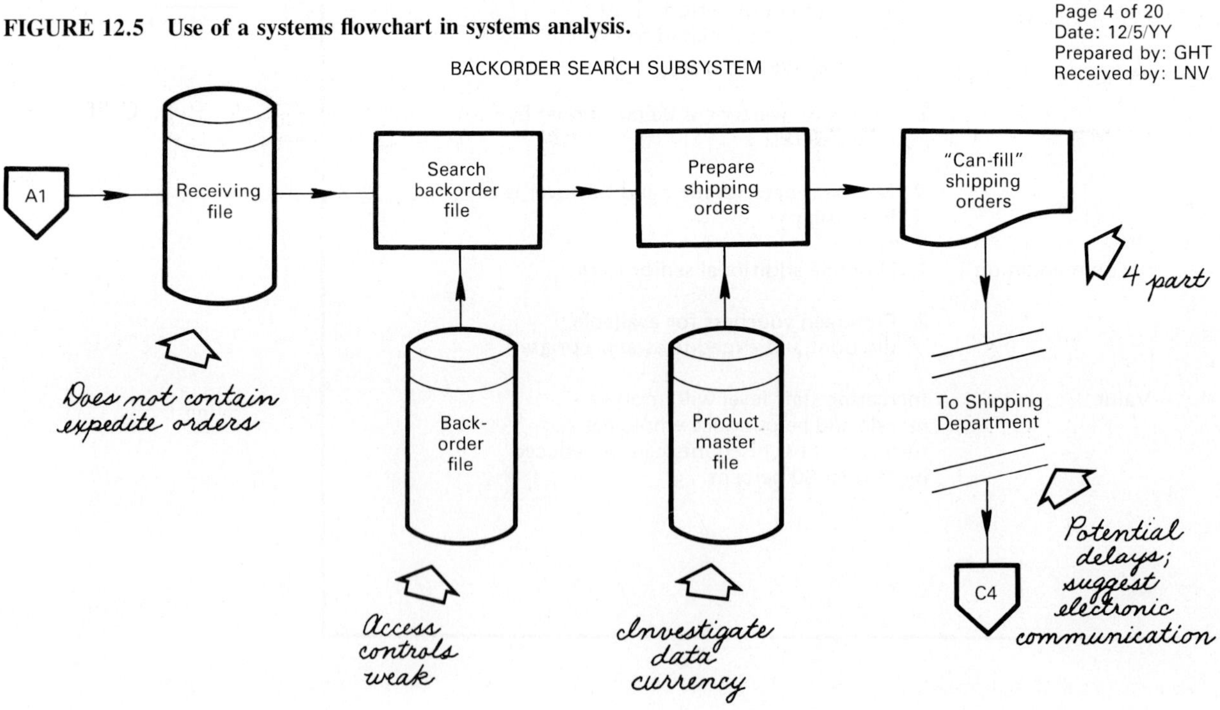

Page 4 of 20
Date: 12/5/YY
Prepared by: GHT
Received by: LNV

BACKORDER SEARCH SUBSYSTEM

SUMMARY

Systems analysis provides a basis for solving problems in information systems and for making recommendations for improving systems effectiveness and efficiency. It is a threefold process in which the objectives of the information system are defined, the existing system is evaluated, and recommendations are made for improvement or enhancement, or development of a new system. It is a process of fact finding, study, and consideration of the available alternatives.

The objectives of the accounting system have to be understood in the light of the organizational environment in which the system has to operate. Definition of these objectives entails gathering data on what type of system is needed, who is going to use the system, what the system is supposed to do, what level of technology is envisioned, what internal controls are appropriate, and how the system should interface with other facets of the organization's work. The statement of objectives that emerges from this process are subsequently used for two purposes: as a yardstick for measuring the adequacy of the present system and as a basis for planning a better one. The existing system is studied for the purposes of evaluating its operating effectiveness and efficiency and its internal controls.

Recommendations for improvement focus on what outputs are required from the system and how they should be provided, on the proper level of supporting technology, and on the nature and extent of the necessary controls. The changes may take the form of modification of the existing system or the development of a completely new system. Alternatively, when the existing system is perceived to be as good as can be expected under the circumstances, no changes may be recommended. The results of the systems analysis are normally presented to management as a formal proposal as well as being communicated through informal channels.

Systems analysis is largely a fact-finding mission. A range of techniques is available to assist in data gathering and analysis, including identification of critical success factors, review of documentation, interviewing, use of questionnaires, job station analysis, and flowcharting. This last is used both as an analytical and problem-solving tool and as one of the methods used to document the findings of the systems analysis.

BIBLIOGRAPHY

Awad, Elias M. *Systems Analysis and Design*. Homewood, Ill.: Irwin, 1979.

Canning, Richard G., ed. "Getting the Requirements Right." *EDP Analyzer*, July 1972, pp. 1–14.

Couger, J. Daniel, and Robert W. Knapp. *Systems Analysis Techniques*. New York: Wiley, 1974.

Davis, Gordon B. "Information Systems: To Buy, Build, or Customize?" *Accounting Horizons,* March 1988, pp. 101–103.

Gane, Chris, and Trish Sarson. *Structured Systems Analysis*. Englewood Cliffs, N.J.: Prentice-Hall, 1979.

Leeson, Marjorie. *Systems Analysis and Design*. Palo Alto, Calif.: Science Research Associates, 1981.

Munro, Malcolm C., and Gordon B. Davis. "Determining Management Information Needs: A Comparison of Methods." *Management Information Systems Quarterly*, June 1977, pp. 43–54.

Murdick, R. G., T. G. Fuller, J. E. Ross, and F. J. Winnermark. *Accounting Information Systems*. Englewood Cliffs, N.J.: Prentice-Hall, 1978.

Powers, Michael J., David R. Adams, and Harlan D. Mills. *Computer Information Systems Development: Analysis and Design*. Cincinnati: South-Western, 1984.

Shelly, Gary B., and Thomas J. Cashman. *Business Systems Analysis and Design*. Anaheim, Calif.: Anaheim, 1975.

Weinberg, Victor. *Structured Analysis*. Englewood Cliffs, N.J.: PrenticeHall, 1980.

DISCUSSION QUESTIONS AND PROBLEMS

1. Define and discuss the following terms:

- Feasibility study
- Interviewee
- Interviewer
- Job station
- Organizational environment
- Questionnaire
- Resources and constraints
- Statement of objectives

- Structured interviewing
- Systems effectiveness
- Systems efficiency
- Systems evaluation
- Systems proposal
- Systems requirements
- Timing and frequency of reporting

2. Identify features that would either help or hinder the development of an accounting information system intended for each of the following environments:
a. An individual acting as a neighborhood distributor for cleaning products, cosmetic items, and vitamin supplements
b. A nationwide retail mail-order chain
c. A family-owned furniture manufacturer operating in a small southern town
d. A regional wholesale trade association serving the plumbing industry
e. A state revenue authority
f. A manufacturer of small arms and munitions operating in a Middle Eastern country
g. A metropolitan Baptist church with 4,000 members

3. Estimate the necessary timing and frequency of management reports prepared in a large manufacturing firm on the following types of information:
a. Cash balance
b. Accounts receivable
c. Work in process
d. Raw materials inventory
e. Long-term investments supporting the pension fund
f. Fixed assets
g. Intangibles such as copyrights, patents, and trade secrets
h. Accounts payable
i. Long-term mortgage bonds
j. The stockholders' ledger
k. Product sales
l. Labor costs
m. Overhead costs
n. Utility expense

4. Identify any special resources or serious constraints likely to be important to the development of an accounting information system for the following types of organizations:

a. A charitable institution
b. A private technical school offering tuition in computer programming and systems analysis
c. A manufacturing firm headed by a man who started work at age 15 as a semiskilled lathe operator
d. A 100-bed hospital managed by a national health care syndicate
e. A textile mill dependent on a local semirural labor force
f. An internationally renowned manufacturer of computers and office machines

5. A system is being prepared for a small medical clinic staffed by four doctors and support personnel. The proposal calls for the installation of a computerized information system for handling all routine record keeping and patient billing functions. New forms and new operating procedures will be needed.

Required
Write the section of the proposal entitled "Method of Implementation."

6. Part of a systems analysis engagement consists of a study of the procedures for collecting employee's time cards from the various time-clock stations, verifying their data content, obtaining the necessary supervisor authorizations, and batching the cards for subsequent payroll processing.

Required
Identify the steps that would need to be carried out to support the study.

7. A structured interview is to be conducted among managers of different levels to gather information about the responsibility-accounting system used in a large service organization.

Required
Draw up a list of the questions to be included to determine the following:

What coding system is used
How the operating data are summarized as they flow up the organizational hierarchy from one reporting level to the next

Whether budget comparisons are included and in what form

What treatment (if any) is given to cost items that are not controllable at the particular reporting level

8. Design a questionnaire to be sent to customers of a large wholesale firm requesting feedback on the type of information to be included on the invoice forms. Currently, the main body of the invoice lists the product number, quantity, unit cost, percentage discount, and net extended cost. The upper part of the form contains the billing and shipping addresses, the invoice number, date, and the name of the sales representative responsible for taking the order.

9. Identify at least two major critical success factors associated with each of the following types of organizations, and analyze each factor into two or three levels of subsidiary CSFs, as appropriate:

a. A janitorial service
b. An interstate trucking company
c. A national public accounting firm
d. The Young Men's Christian Association (YMCA)
e. A regional vocational school

10. A systems analyst is trying to estimate the volume of data processing in a merchandising enterprise in five years' time. The analyst has gathered the following statistics for the most recent year:

Number of employees*	500
Number of customers	2,000
Number of vendors	300

* including 25 managers

Interviews with management have indicated that the average customer currently places five orders per year. Invoices are sent after every order, and statements are sent to all customers every month. Purchase orders are sent to vendors on an average of six times per year. Managers are paid once per month, and other employees are on a semimonthly pay cycle. Management has estimated that the number of customers will grow at a rate

of 10 percent per year and that their average order frequency is likely to increase to six orders per year in five years' time. The number of vendors will probably stay about the same, but because of bulk purchasing, the average number of purchase orders is likely to decrease to four orders per year. To accommodate the increased sales, a total of 50 more clerical, warehouse, and sales personnel will be required. Three more managers are likely to be hired. A proposal to put all employees on a monthly pay cycle has just been approved by management.

Required

Estimate the number of customer invoices and statements, vendor checks, and employee paychecks

a. Prepared in the most recent year.
b. Likely to be prepared in five years' time.

11. Ross Company, a distributor of light manufacturing parts, has been experiencing difficulties with the increasing size of its accounts receivable balances and slow payment by customers.

Presently all billing is done out of the home office in Chicago. Each week the 12 branch offices, which extend over a 20-state territory, submit details of shipments made to customers from their local distribution points. Invoices are prepared and mailed to customers after each sale, and bimonthly statements are sent to delinquent accounts. All sales are made on terms of 1/20, n/60.

Billings and collections are processed on a computer that has been in operation for about nine months. Eighteen clerks are employed in the accounts receivable department. The supervisor had frequently complained about the clerks' low morale, and there is increasing employee turnover, absenteeism, and tardiness in the department. There was resistance to the introduction of the computer, and management has more than once remarked that the company was better off under its old manual system.

Required

You, an MAS specialist with a national public accounting firm, have been called in as a consultant to advise the company. Draw up two separate solutions to the problems, to be submitted first to your own manager and then to the management of Ross Company.

12. Smith and Jones established a public accounting firm in a small town three years ago, after Smith obtained his CPA license and Jones retired from the army. Most of their clients are "mom and pop" companies, and the firm's activities consist almost entirely of write-up work. Smith and Jones do most of the work themselves.

Smith has ambitions to see the practice grow to serve larger client firms, to take on more interesting work, to hire additional staff, and to increase profits. However, because they are so heavily involved in the day-to-day activities, there is little chance of their devoting much time and effort to practice development.

Required

a. Suggest an "ideal solution" to the problem described.

b. Identify the constraints that would make it difficult to implement your solution in the "real-world" situation in which this organization operates.

c. What modifications to your ideal solution would make it more practicable?

13. As an analyst with a large public accounting firm, you are currently performing a systems study for the Southern Port Authority. Some information that you and your colleagues have gathered to date are presented in the data at the end of this section.

Required

a. Prepare a systems flowchart of the present purchasing procedures described.

b. Analyze the flowchart and prepare a list of potential improvements to the system.

14. As part of a systems analysis engagement that your consulting firm is undertaking for Peacock Brothers, a small wholesale company, you are presently conducting a job station analysis. The subject of your study is the billing group in the accounts receivable department. The group consists of a supervisor and four clerks. You have been warned that management is concerned about inefficiencies in the group, and you are aware that

there have been reports of careless work, tardiness, and excessive employee turnover.

The clerks process a total of 100 invoices per day, each consisting of a maximum of three to four product line items. Details of the transactions are taken from sales orders sent in by outside sales representatives. The clerks call the warehouse to verify that the product items are in stock and type up the invoices with prices extracted from standard price lists. All credit checking is done elsewhere, and all sales are made on standard terms of 2/10, n/30.

The group does its job in an old trailer parked behind the warehouse. No equipment is used aside from typewriters and a few mechanical adding machines. But you know that management is currently studying a proposal to automate the billing function, in which case the group would be disbanded. The results of your analysis will provide important input to management's decision.

Required

a. List the signal inputs, control inputs, and outputs of the job station, using the general systems approach discussed in Chapter 1.

b. Prepare questions that you want to ask (i) the supervisor and (ii) the billing clerks to help you understand the effectiveness and efficiency of this job station.

15. You are a systems analyst in charge of a small team engaged to evaluate a client's accounting system. Your present topic of attention is the credit department. The department, which is located at the corporate headquarters in Denver, performs centralized credit screening on behalf of sales branches throughout the United States. One of the concerns that led to the engagement was delays in the processing of credit applications.

Your investigation has revealed that prospective customers (mainly small to medium-sized companies) complete a credit application questionnaire, listing the name of their bank and three credit references. Applicants also submit copies of their most recent financial statements, including a balance sheet and income statement.

Clerks in the credit department screen the applications and check the references. Form letters are sent to the references, asking for a recommendation for the applicant company. Frequently the clerks have to follow up by telephone in order to secure the necessary information. While the references are being processed, junior accountants compute a series of financial and operating ratios from the applicants' financial statements. In some cases the information on the statements is incomplete, and so the accountants must call the applicants in order to obtain additional data. A scoring system is used in which points are awarded according to the strength of the computed ratios. All processing is done manually.

When the screening process is complete, the credit manager reviews the findings and decides whether to extend credit or to withhold it. The credit manager has other duties to perform but sets aside every Tuesday to making credit decisions.

You have been told by upper management that the present credit-screening system works well except for the delays involved: At best the credit department takes about two weeks to process an application, and sometimes it takes more than five or six weeks. Considerable ill will is being generated because of the delays, and some customers buy elsewhere before their applications are approved. Most of the customers do place orders but are subsequently attracted to other suppliers because of lower prices or other inducements. Customer loyalty is typically low throughout the industry. Order sizes range all the way from a few dollars to tens of thousands of dollars.

Required
a. Analyze this information to identify the objective and reason for the process, the methodology employed, the personnel involved, and the timing and location of the process.
b. Make brief recommendations as to how the processing of credit applications could be improved.

Data for Problem 13
SOME FACTS

The main activities at the port are the loading and unloading of ships. Exporters bring their goods to the port, clear customs, and store their goods temporarily in one of a number of large warehouses until their ship is ready to load. Incoming goods are also stored temporarily until the importer can pick them up.

The port employs 216 people in the following categories:

Loading and unloading operations	150
Maintenance of vehicles and equipment	45
Office and clerical	21
	216

The purchasing department processes an average of 22 purchase orders per day. These purchases are for both low-priced and expensive items. Office supplies and maintenance parts and supplies make up the bulk of the purchases. Occasionally, several times a year, a truck, a forklift, or some other expensive machine is needed that costs thousands of dollars. Very little inventory of parts and supplies is maintained. The maintenance shop keeps on hand some fan belts, oil, spark plugs, and a few other routine maintenance items. When a machine breaks down, especially if it is a crane or some other ship-loading equipment, it may stop the loading and thereby create an emergency purchase. This happens about four or five times per year.

This particular port authority is a quasi-governmental agency. The director reports to a state board and the authority receives a budget from the state. The port's operating policy is to set its fees so that the income from loading and unloading ships and other services just matches its costs. The director is cost conscious, like a profit-making manager, because his port is in competition with several other ports nearby. Speed of loading and unloading the ships, however, is more important to the ships' captains than is the amount of the fees. While a ship is in port it is unproductive, and except for fuel, most of the costs are fixed.

PURCHASING PROCEDURES
a. Purchase requisitions originate in various departments and are submitted to the director of operations (the chief executive officer).
b. The director of operations either approves or rejects the requisition. If approved, the requisition is for-

warded to the purchasing department for action. If rejected, the request is returned to the originating department.

c. **1.** For items under $25, the purchasing agent contacts an appropriate vendor and records the vendor's name and address on the requisition form.

 2. For items over $25, a request for quotation is sent to three potential vendors. Bids come back, and the lowest is accepted consistent with overall quality considerations. The names and addresses of all vendors are recorded on the purchase requisition form in the space provided.

d. The requisitions are then sent to the accounting department where they are coded as to the account to be charged (asset or expense) and a department responsibility code.

e. The requisitions are then returned to purchasing where prenumbered purchase orders are prepared with distribution as follows:

 1. Original—to vendor

 2. Copy 1—to current vendor file along with purchase requisition to await the material-received report (alphabetically by vendor)

 3. Copy 2—to originating department

 4. Copy 3—to purchasing department permanent file (by purchase order number)

f. Upon receipt of the vendor invoice from the vendor and the material-received report from the storeroom, these items are filed in the current file mentioned in (2) until both forms are received. Upon receipt of both the vendor's invoices and the material-received report, all items in the current file are pulled and attached together to form a vendor set (copy 1 of purchase order, purchase requisition, vendor invoice, and material received report).

g. All items are audited in purchasing with the following operations performed:

 1. Vendor prices and quantities are checked against invoice, material-received report, and the purchase orders.

 2. Extensions and footings on vendor invoices are checked. If an error is found in the vendor invoice, the vendor will be notified and the set will again be placed in the current file to await corrected invoice or credit memo.

h. Upon completion of the preceding audit step, the vendor set is noted in a vendor set log with purchase order number, vendor name, invoice number, and total amount recorded. This list is used to prove that this set has left the purchasing department.

i. The vendor set is sent to the accounts payable department.

j. After payment by accounts payable, the original vendor set is returned to purchasing.

k. The vendor set is noted as completed by purchasing in the vendor set log. This also shows that the vendor set was returned by accounts payable.

l. The vendor set is filed in a permanent file alphabetically by the vendor name.

13

Systems Design

CHAPTER OUTLINE

THE INGREDIENTS OF SUCCESSFUL SYSTEMS DESIGN

STRUCTURED DESIGN TECHNIQUES

Design Strategies
HIPO
Data Dictionary

DETAILED DESIGN

Output Design
Input Design
Design of Input and Output Screens
File or Data Base Design
Processing Design

PROTOTYPING

DOCUMENTATION

Technical Systems Documentation
User Documentation
Documentation Standards

SUMMARY
BIBLIOGRAPHY
DISCUSSION QUESTIONS AND PROBLEMS

THE INGREDIENTS OF SUCCESSFUL SYSTEMS DESIGN

Successful systems design can be treated as a critical success factor (CSF) and analyzed into five secondary CSFs:

- Economy
- Flexibility
- Simplicity
- Reliability
- Acceptability

Each of these can be analyzed further, as shown in Table 13.1.

The design of an accounting system must recognize the same economic constraints as any other business venture. The system must do its job, but it must also be cost effective. The initial costs of developing the system and the ongoing costs of operating and maintaining the system must be kept to a minimum. However there may be trade-offs between the initial and ongoing costs such that a greater investment in initial costs may pay off in terms of lower ongoing costs. Conversely, there may be situations in which higher initial costs cannot be justified because any reduction in ongoing costs would be marginal. Care must be taken in evaluating potential system features that carry a high price tag but that offer little other than "image." For instance, expensive computer equipment should not be bought when a simple manual system would do the job.

The organization is not a static entity, and accordingly the accounting system should be capable of adapting to changing conditions, growth of the organization, or demands for new kinds of information. Clearly, changes cannot always be anticipated. And to install a much larger processing capability than is initially needed would not be cost effective. But flexibility in the design may save major redesign or replacement of major pieces of equipment at a later date.

The system should be as simple as possible while still accomplishing the job for which it is intended. An accounting system has no intrinsic value; its value lies solely in the service it offers its users. Accordingly, the choice between any two alternatives, otherwise promising the same performance, should always be resolved in favor of the simpler one. Any temptation to complicate the design so as to impress the users, the auditors, other systems designers, or anyone else should be

336

TABLE 13.1   Critical-Success-Factor Analysis of Successful Systems Design

Level 1	Level 2	Level 3
Successful systems design	Economy	Low initial cost Low operating costs Low maintenance costs
	Flexibility	Growth potential Ability to accomodate changing requirements
	Simplicity	Conceptually simple Easy to operate Easy to service Provides clear audit trail
	Reliability	Low incidence of downtime Produces trustworthy information
	Acceptability	Compatible with organizational environment Satisfies users' needs Makes users' jobs easier Meets safety standards

avoided. In fact, mature, professional people are more likely to be impressed by functional simplicity than by needless complexity.

The users of the accounting system must be confident that the system will operate reliably and will provide trustworthy data. A system that suffers from excessive downtime is a liability rather than an asset. Similarly, a system than produces erroneous, invalid, or incomplete data is likely to be very costly to the organization. Accountants who are particularly concerned about the quality of the accounting data must be alert to features in the design that threaten the system's reliability. Often problems of unreliability can be traced to unwarranted complication in the design; in contrast, simplicity and reliability are usually close allies.

For an accounting system to be successful, it must win the acceptance of its users. Sabotage of a new information system by uncooperative users is a possibility, although fortunately is a rare occurrence. Most people are open-minded toward a new accounting system or a major system modification. But the developers of the system should ensure that the system makes the users' job easier, not more difficult. An information system that impedes people's work or impairs motivation in the organization can scarcely be regarded as worthwhile.

STRUCTURED DESIGN TECHNIQUES

One of the most important recent advances in systems development is the concept of structured design. Structured design follows a modular approach in which the system is divided, for design purposes, into a hierarchy of subsystems, extending from the highest, conceptual, levels to the lowest, detailed, levels (Figure 13.1). The conceptual levels define the "big picture," and the detailed levels correspond to the "nuts and bolts" of the system. In keeping with the concepts of general systems theory, each subsystem is defined in terms of its internal activities and its interactions with its environment of neighboring subsystems.

For convenience, the first-level subsystems are usually identified with the transaction cycles, the second level with the applications, and the third level with the major application modules, such as the billing function in the accounts receivable application. At a relatively low level in the hierarchical structure, immediately below the level of the application modules or possibly two levels lower are the functional subsystems, including the inputs, processes, and outputs. The precise number of levels considered in the analysis is a matter of judgment to be made in the light of the system's complexity.

FIGURE 13.1   **The accounting information system as a hierarchy of subsystems.**

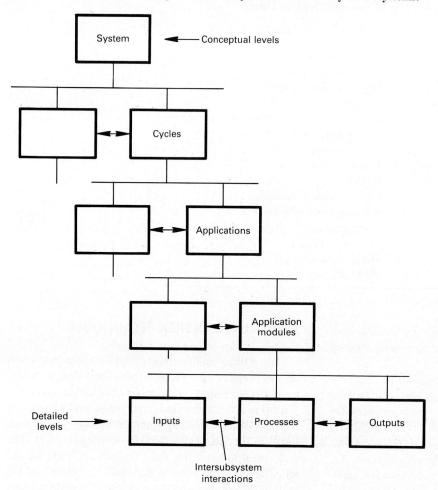

The project design team is normally divided into a coordinating group, a number of design subteams, and administrative support (Figure 13.2). Each subteam designs one or more subsystems. The coordinating group, which supports the technical work of the project manager and may be headed by an assistant project manager, maintains contact among the subteams and with the project as a whole. The coordinating group often operates a "control room" in which material of interest to the whole team can be displayed.

The subsystem designs prepared by the various subteams must eventually "fit together" to produce the total system. The interfaces between adjacent subsystems must be treated with special care; the output from one subsystem may form an input to another, and assumptions about data content and format, as well as about timing and frequency of communication, must be mutually consistent. The coordinating group has the prime responsibility for ensuring that this degree of consistency is achieved. Regular meetings are held, attended by the

FIGURE 13.2   Organization of the design team.

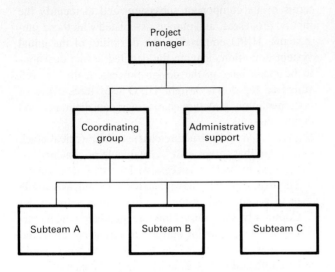

coordinating group and representatives from each subteam, at which mutual concerns are discussed and resolved.

Design Strategies

The modular approach requires that for design purposes, the system be divided into subsystems, and the hierarchical model guides the way in which it should be divided up. But the question remains as to the order in which the subsystems should be designed. This sequence is important because decisions pertaining to one subsystem may depend on those made in other subsystems. For example, the design of an input form cannot be completed until decisions have been made relating to the length and type of the data elements involved; in turn, these decisions may depend on the design of a file or an output item. The ideal strategy would be one that gave each subteam all the information necessary to complete its current task and that avoided the need for redesign to correct inconsistencies or oversights. Inconsistencies can arise between the designs prepared by two or more subteams or between a subteam's design and the objectives of the overall system. Unfortunately, this ideal is unat-

tainable; design subteams invariably have to work with incomplete information about neighboring parts of the system, and the need for redesign invariably arises.

The sequencing of the design concerns both the "vertical sequence" with respect to the level of subsystems in the hierarchical structure and also the "horizontal" sequencing among subsystems at the same level. With regard to horizontal sequencing, the design should start with output subsystems and work backward toward the input subsystems. The reason is that the outputs are determined by user requirements, whereas the inputs—and the processes and files—are determined solely by the need to support those outputs. The question asked by the designer is not "What shall we do with these time cards?" but "What must we do to provide paychecks, W-2 forms, and a payroll register?"

With regard to vertical sequencing, the issue is less clear. Two contrasting strategies have been proposed: *top-down* design and *bottom-up* design. The proponents of top-down design assert that the subsystems at the conceptual levels should be designed first and that the design should work downward to lower levels. The big picture should be decided on first, and the details should be filled in later. The proponents of bottom-up design argue that the detailed subsystems should be designed first and then assembled to produce the higher levels in the hierarchy. The top-down designer would start with a conceptual definition of the purchasing cycle and finally design a time card; the bottom-up designer would start by designing a time card and finally assemble it and all the other detailed components into a system providing for procurement of material and human resources.

The two strategies can be evaluated according to the likely amount of necessary redesign. In principle, top-down design is superior in this respect because there are fewer subsystems near the top of the design "pyramid" than at the bottom; consequently there are fewer subsystems that could need to be redesigned. On the other hand, the theoretical superiority of top-down design is not always realized in practice. In many cases it proves difficult to define the high-level subsystems adequately to permit unambiguous decisions to be made at the lower levels. The bottom-up designer has the practical advantage of being able to start with familiar items (like the time card) that are well understood and "standard" from one accounting system to another. Unfortunately, the assumed degree of standardization may not always be sufficient to enable the detailed designs to fit together into a coherent overall system. Bottom-up design is sufficiently successful to enable it to compete for acceptance, but it is less favored than top-down design.

Compromise strategies, which attempt to combine the best features of top-down and bottom-up design, are used by some design teams. In the last analysis, any rational strategy is preferable to an *ad hoc* approach in which the design proceeds haphazardly without an overall game plan.

HIPO

Several techniques exploit the notion of structured design, and top-down design in particular. One that has won wide acceptance is the documentation tool called *Hierarchy plus Input, Processing, Output*, or *HIPO*. Its

objectives are to define the structure of the system in terms of its component subsystem and to identify the inputs, processes, and outputs associated with those subsystems. HIPO emphasizes the flexibility of the initial system definition, leaving the detailed design decisions to be made later in the design process; it thus is well suited to top-down design. HIPO uses three types of documentation: structure charts, overview diagrams, and detail diagrams.

Structure Chart. A structure chart is a hierarchical block diagram that serves as a "visual table of contents" of the system and its successive levels of subsystems. The structure chart may relate to the system as a whole or to a major subsystem, such as the revenue cycle. Commonly the subsystems are numbered in hierarchical form; a major subsystem might be numbered 4.0, and its "progeny," at the next lower level, would be numbered 4.1, 4.2, and so forth. An example of a structure chart is shown in Figure 13.3.

The structure chart is particularly useful for the co-

FIGURE 13.3   Example of a structure chart or hierarchical block diagram, used in the HIPO technique.

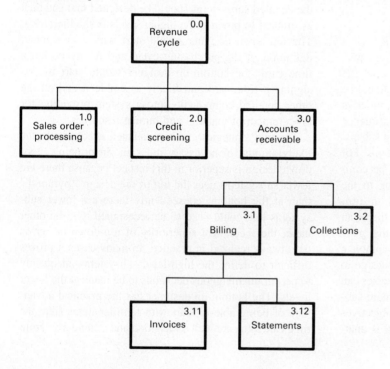

ordinating group, whose responsibilities are to assign tasks to the design subteams, to track the progress of the design effort, and to "fit all the pieces together."

Overview Diagram. Overview diagrams are block diagrams arranged in a three-column format, the columns corresponding to inputs, processes, and outputs. Typically they are prepared for subsystems, at the application or application module level, and thus further describe those aspects of the system corresponding to the upper portions of the structure chart. Several overview diagrams are usually drawn for a system, although there may be only one structure chart.

An overview diagram identifies the processing activities in each subsystem, together with their inputs and outputs (Figure 13.4). The overview diagram does not identify files as a separate entity but treats them as either inputs or outputs, according to whether they are read by or written to by the processing activity in question. Typical inputs might be "sales order,"

"picking ticket," and "customer master file." Typical outputs might be "invoice," "monthly statement," and "customer master file" again, if the process both reads and writes to that file.

In accordance with the notion of top-down design, the overview diagram defines the subsystems in broad terms, focusing on their interactions with other subsystems. But no attempt is made at this stage to describe the inner workings of the processing activities or to specify the relationships among the inputs, processes, and outputs. Note that no flow lines are drawn on the overview diagram linking these entities.

Detail Diagrams. Detail diagrams extend the description of the system to the lower levels of the structure chart. The whole of a detail diagram may correspond to one processing block on an overview diagram. Accordingly, it is usually necessary to prepare many detail diagrams. Detail diagrams (Figure 13.5) have the same three-column format as do overview diagrams.

FIGURE 13.4 Example of a HIPO overview diagram.

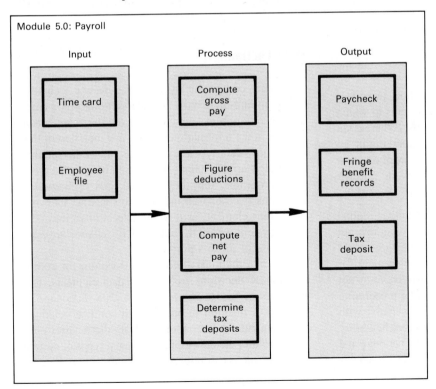

FIGURE 13.5 Example of a HIPO detail diagram.

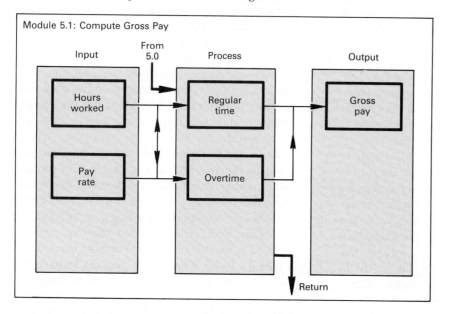

However, flow lines are drawn in detail diagrams to link processing activities with their inputs and outputs. Arrows may also be drawn (as illustrated in Figure 13.5) to show the relationship between a processing subsystem and its ''parent'' and ''progeny'' in the system hierarchy.

Detail diagrams, as their name implies, provide a more detailed description of the subsystems to which they relate than do overview diagrams. Whereas an input identified on an overview diagram might be ''sales order,'' an input identified on a detail diagram is more likely to be ''customer number'' or ''freight charge.''

HIPO is the successor of an earlier technique, called *IPO*, which involved overview and detail diagrams but did not include the structure chart. Some designers treat the overview and detail diagrams as a replacement for systems flowcharts. However, their objectives are not the same, and systems flowcharts should be prepared to supplement the HIPO documentation. Flowcharts, with their greater variety of symbols, provide more flexibility to describe the system. Furthermore, the national and international flowcharting standards provide for unam-

biguous interpretation of systems flowcharts by a broadly based audience.

Data Dictionary

Another component of structured-design documentation is a data dictionary. A data dictionary is a master list, or system-wide directory, of the data elements appearing in the information system, and their descriptions: definitions, data types and lengths, and other pertinent material. Variable names, to be used in associated computer programs, may be included; and formatting descriptions may also be included to illustrate the format of the data element, as it would appear at various points in the system. COBOL ''PICTURE'' clauses are particularly useful for this purpose.

The data dictionary provides a medium for communication of decisions, relating to data elements, to all members of the design team. The data dictionary also provides a medium through which conflicts relating to data elements can be resolved. Data dictionaries play a useful role in the development of most types of systems, but their role is essential in the development of data base systems because of the greatly increased potential for the sharing of data among the various applications. Responsibility for compiling and maintaining the data dictionary normally lies with the coordinating group.

Typically, systems analysts and designers work together with representatives of user groups to assemble lists of data elements used in the various applications. These lists, together with tentative descriptions, form the basis of the data dictionary. As the design proceeds, new data elements, usually submitted by the design subteams, are added to the dictionary. Other members of the project team can refer to the directory to obtain this information to incorporate into their design tasks.

Particularly during the early stages of compiling the data dictionary, analysis of the entries often reveals conflicts among the data elements. These conflicts can be classified as synonyms, alternative definitions, and close definitions. Synonyms are alternative names for the same data element; for example, one group in the organization may use the term *supplier*, whereas another may use *vendor*; or one group may use *gross margin* and another, *gross profit*. Alternative definitions involve two or more distinct data elements, all of which are referred to by the same name. Perhaps the best example is *total cost*. Close definitions arise when two or more data elements have almost the same meaning, for example, *total sales* and *total revenue*. Such semantic problems must be resolved so as to produce systemwide uniformity of definitions. Resolving the problems may take considerable effort and negotiation, and it must be done with care so that the future users of the system can understand the definitions that are adopted. Wherever possible, the names already understood by the users should be incorporated.

When a conflict over a data element arises, the problem can be resolved by those concerned. If the description is changed, some redesign may be required by the subteams that have already used the original description.

DETAILED DESIGN

Detailed design refers to the design of outputs, files, processes, and inputs in the lower levels of the design pyramid. As already noted, the outputs are designed first, then the processes and files, and finally the inputs (Figure 13.6).

Output Design

The output from an accounting information system may be quite extensive, consisting of a large number of output documents, reports, screen displays, and other items. Each item of output must be identified and specified in terms of its

- application
- purpose
- medium
- frequency and/or timing of issuance
- distribution or availability

as well as its data content and format. To illustrate, the output from an order-tracking and production control system might be five reports: open job order report, labor and materials usage report, machine utilization report, waste and scrap report, and closed job report. In addi-

FIGURE 13.6 "Horizontal" sequencing of subsystem design.

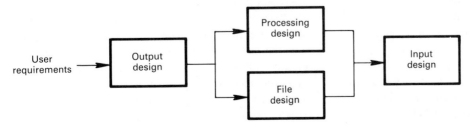

FIGURE 13.7   List of outputs required in a job-tracking and production control system.

OUTPUT DESIGN				
Application:	Job tracking and Production Control		Prepared by: Checked by:	
Project no:	463-7		Date:	
		Issuance:		
Item	Medium	Frequency	Timing	Distribution, etc.
Open job report	4-part paper	Weekly	8.30 Mon.	Production control Sales Accounting Plant manager
Material and labor usage report	4-part paper	Weekly	12.00 Mon.	Production control Stores Accounting Plant manager
Machine utiliza-tion report	4-part paper	Weekly	12.00 Mon.	Production control Scheduling Maintenance Plant manager
Waste and scrap report	3-part paper	Semi monthly	5th and 20th of month	Production control Stores Accounting
Closed job report	3-part paper	Semi monthly	5th and 20th of month	Production control Sales Accounting
Materials availa-bility query	Screen display	On demand	On demand	Production control Stores
Job query	Screen display	On demand	On demand	Production control Accounting

tion, two screen displays might be required, providing on-line query of materials availability and job status. The list of required items in this application could be documented as in Figure 13.7. Additional pertinent information could be included as necessary.

The data content and associated forms design must be documented for each output item. The lengths and data types of the data elements should conform to definitions in the data dictionary. Preparation of the forms should reflect the guidelines laid down in Chapter 4. Documentation of report form designs should include cover pages,

report headings, page headings, stub and column headings, stub and column data fields, page footings, report footings, and trailer pages. The various levels of subtotals and totals and their associated break points should also be defined. Comments and explanations should be added to enhance the value of the documentation but must be distinguished from the actual printed material. Figure 13.8 shows a possible layout for one of the reports provided by the production control and job-tracking system. The design of output screens is discussed later in this chapter.

Input Design

Input design also involves identifying all input data elements and designing appropriate means of capturing the input data. Appropriate input media must be selected, and document and screen input forms must be designed. In identifying input data elements, the objective is to confine the inputs to the fewest data elements necessary to support the required system outputs. If one or more necessary input data elements are missing, the system will not be able to provide the required outputs, and the entry of *unnecessary* data elements into the system will result in wasted keyboard effort and inefficiency.

A useful tool for testing the mutual consistency of the inputs and outputs is an input–output matrix. Figure 13.9 shows a simplified input–output matrix for a payroll system. The rows of the matrix correspond to the input data elements, grouped according to the type of input: time-card entry, file maintenance, and entry of tax tables. The columns correspond to the output data elements grouped by destination: paychecks, W-2 forms, and elements common to both. An X in one of the cells of the matrix indicates a relationship between the corresponding input and output; the particular input data element may form or contribute to the particular output element. For example, the number of dependents affects the federal and state withholdings (current and year-to-date) and net pay. If a column in the input-output matrix is empty, it means that the particular output is not supported by an input. If a row is empty, it means that the input is unnecessary and can be eliminated.

Input–output matrices are useful aids to input design. Companion aids, with much the same purpose, are input–file and file–output matrices. However, all of these types of matrices tend to be large and unwieldy. An input–output matrix for a complete accounting system may extend to several thousand rows and columns. Even one for a single application may have several hundred rows and columns, and its validity may be undermined because of data transferred to or from another application. The manual preparation of large input–output and similar matrices is tedious, and some designers now partially automate the process using electronic spreadsheets or other specialized software packages.

Input data consist primarily of transaction entries and file maintenance changes. In traditional systems, transaction data are captured on source documents, and forms must be designed for these documents. Data from source documents are keyed into an input device and encoded for processing. In some modern systems, transaction data are captured electronically, thereby eliminating the need for keying. File maintenance changes are normally supported by a written authorization, and the data are keyed into an input device in much the same way as are transactions data. Figure 13.10 shows a simple file maintenance authorization document.

Modern input devices normally provide for the display of screen forms to facilitate data entry. Often screen forms are designed to reproduce—as far as size and proportion constraints permit—the layout of the paper source document. Modern end-user software sometimes allows the users themselves to adapt the screen forms to any desired layout.

Design of Input and Output Screens

Screen displays may be used for both input and output purposes. Even screens intended for the input of transaction or file maintenance data often display incidental outputs, confirming that input codes or account numbers are valid. Documentation of screen form designs may therefore have to include system prompts, the "echo" of keyboard input, as well as system output. A problem that arises when documenting screen forms is the need to distinguish among these three types of material and also to distinguish them from designers' comments. Comments and explanations should normally be placed to the side of the area denoting the screen. Both output and input fields are normally shown by strings of 9s and Xs, according to whether the data elements are numeric or alphanumeric. Some designers place a frame around output fields or show the fields in boldface to distinguish them from input fields. Figure 13.11(a) shows a layout for one of the screen displays in the production control and job-tracking system, referred to earlier.

The software that generates interactive screens may include branch points, causing the screen form to change according to the outcome of a condition (IF) statement.

FIGURE 13.8 Design of an open job report forming part of a job-tracking and production control system.

```
                        XYZ COMPANY
                     OPEN JOB REPORT
                     REPORT # 9999

                      As of 99/99/99

          Distribution: X---------( )---------X
                        X---------( )---------X
                        X---------( )---------X
                        X---------( )---------X
                        X---------( )---------X
```

```
                              OPEN JOB REPORT                              Page 999
                              As of 99/99/99

  Prodn.   Date     Engin. specs   Quantity  ----------------- Cost to date -----------------   Percent
  order    started  reference      ordered   Materials     Labor         Overhead      Total    complete
-------------------------------------------------------------------------------------------------------
Department # 999:

99999999  99/99/99  X---(12)---X    99,999    999,999.99   999,999.99    999,999.99  9,999,999.99  999.9
                                              -----------  -----------   -----------  ------------
          Departmental subtotal            9,999,999.99  9,999,999.99  9,999,999.99  99,999,999.99
                                              -----------  -----------   -----------  ------------
          Grand total                      9,999,999.99  9,999,999.99  9,999,999.99  99,999,999.99
                                              ===========  ===========   ===========  ============

  Report # 9999.  Effective date: 99/99/99
```

```
  Report # 9999
  Open Job Report

  Total pages:            999
  Total departments:      999
  Total lines:         99,999
```

Header page with banner heading

Report heading

Page heading

Subheading (block heading). Break point is department.

Detail line

Subtotal (block total)

Total

Footnote

Trailer page

For example, in the screen design shown in Figure 13.11(a), entry of an invalid job number would result not in output of the materials and labor figures and other data but in the display of a diagnostic message. The output design is incomplete if it does not define the screen form under each of such conditions. Figure 13.11(b) shows the alternative form of the screen in the example system.

Representatives of user groups should be asked to review output design documentation to obtain feedback on the acceptability of the designs. Prototypes may also be developed, giving users a better "feel" for the outputs than could be obtained simply from paper documentation. Prototyping is discussed later in this chapter. In any case, after users have reviewed the output designs, they should be requested to record their approval in writing. Requiring users to sign off on components of the design forces them to review the material in more detail than they might otherwise do and often reduces the number of requests for changes at a later stage in the development process. If the users insist on later changes, the written approval will pin down responsibility for the additional—and possibly substantial—costs involved.

File or Data Base Design

In manual accounting systems, files are often maintained in the form of paper journals and ledgers. Subsidiary ledgers may also be established for individual customer or vendor accounts, or for employee, inventory, or fixed-asset records. Because of their volatility, subsidiary ledger records are usually maintained on cards. A form design for a simple inventory card is illustrated in Figure 13.12.

Automated systems may use either conventional files or a data base management system. As noted in Chapter 5, file design involves several factors, including the purpose of the file, its activity ratio and volatility, the medium on which it is stored, its organization, the required mode of access (sequential or random), the field and record layout, the maximum capacity of the file, and applicable controls. Clearly, the design decisions made in connection with these factors are not all independent of one another; for instance, a file residing on magnetic

FIGURE 13.9 Input–output matrix showing the relationship between inputs and outputs for a simple payroll system.

		Common			Paycheck					W-2 Form				
Date: June 21, 19XX Application: Payroll Prepared by: JFN Approved by: KKS		Employee #	Employee name	Address	Gross earnings	Fed. withholding	State withholding	FICA	Net pay	YTD gross earnings	YTD Fed. withholding	YTD state withholding	FICA earnings	YTD FICA
Time-card input	Employee #	X	X	X										
	Regular hours				X	X	X	X	X	X	X	X	X	X
	Overtime hours				X	X	X	X	X	X	X	X	X	X
File maintenance	Employee name		X											
	Address			X										
	Marital status					X	X		X		X	X		
	No. dependents					X	X		X		X	X		
	Wage rate				X	X	X	X	X	X	X	X	X	X
Tax tables	Federal tax tables					X		X	X		X		X	X
	State tax tables						X					X		

tape could not support random access. Field lengths and data types must be consistent with entries in the data dictionary. File controls are discussed in Chapter 17. Figure 13.13 shows a convenient way of documenting the design, specifically the design of a computerized inventory master file that would take the place of the manual inventory cards illustrated in Figure 13.12.

Design of the logical structure of a data base uses the contents of the data dictionary and also the relationships to be established among the data elements. These relationships can be documented by means of a relationship matrix, a set of Bachman diagrams, or the lists of tables and keys required for a relational data base. The storage medium is invariably magnetic disk, and random access is required. "File" organization and field and record layout do not need to be considered by the applications designer or programmer. Data base design was discussed at length in Chapter 9.

Processing Design

Processes must be designed to provide the required outputs, using as "raw material" the input data and the accumulated data base. Processing operations include the capture and verification of the input data, record and

FIGURE 13.10   **File maintenance authorization form.**

FILE MAINTENANCE AUTHORIZATION

File name: **Employee master file** _____   File No. **65-A39** _____

Record ID: **Empl. no. 106** _____

Changes: **Pay rate to $10.75**_____

Record ID: **Empl. no. 144** _____

Changes: **Dept. no. to 78** _____

Record ID: **Empl. no. 218** _____

Changes: **Marital status to D** _____

Record ID: _____

Changes: _____

Approved By: **KJH** _____   Entered by: **PTG** _____

Department: **Paymaster** _____   Date: **3/20/XX** _____

Form No. DP6677

file manipulation, file update (routine and nonroutine), various computations and analyses, and the preparation and formatting of output. In manual systems, information is processed as it flows from source documents to journals to ledgers to output documents and reports. Clerical procedures and forms are the basic building blocks of the processing operations. In automated systems—or more precisely, in the automated portions of such systems—the various items of paperwork are replaced by machine-readable files, and the clerical procedures are replaced by computer programs. In either case, processing design must consider the movement of data through the system and the tasks—manual or computerized—to be performed en route. And in either case, a clear audit trail must be maintained, permitting the

tracing of data back to an input or forward to an output. The audit trail may be in human- or machine-readable form.

Lower-level subsystems must be identified, and the nature of the processing tasks must be defined. Processing design is documented by HIPO detail diagrams and systems flowcharts. In addition, narrative task descriptions should be prepared, which can form the starting point for the development of either clerical procedures or computer programs. Task descriptions should list the inputs and the outputs, including files accessed, either passively in a read mode or actively in a write mode. Often the processing steps are described using some form of pseudocode. Pseudocode consists of concise statements resembling, but not necessarily conforming

FIGURE 13.11 Design of a screen form for on-line job query.
(a) Basic screen design.

```
                    JOB STATUS QUERY

Enter job #:        99999       Production order #:  99999999
Quantity ordered:   9,999       Product #:           XXXXXX
Date started:       99/99/99    Eng. specs ref.:     XXXXXXX
Percent complete:   999.99%

                                            Cost
Materials:  Est. total to complete          _____
            Usage to date                   $99,999.99
            Usage to date                   $99,999.99

            Remaining                       $99,999.99±
                                            =========

                                  Hours
Labor:      Est. total to complete          _____
            Usage to date            9,999.9 $99,999.99
            Usage to date            9,999.9 $99,999.99

            Remaining                9,999.9 $99,999.99±
                                     ======= =========

Enter continuation option (N, M, Q, Help):  X
```

NOTES

<———— Operator input

Input of job number results in retrieval and
display of quantity ordered, date started,
production order #, product #, engineering
specs reference, and percent complete.

Estimated total to complete, usage to date
and remaining materials dollars are displayed.
Estimated total to complete, usage to date
and remaining labor hours and dollars are
displayed.

<———— Operator selection. N = next job #, M = return
       to menu, Q = quit. H = help, displays help menu.

(b) Alternate screen design, assuming input of invalid data.

```
+--------------------------------------------------+
|                                                  |
|              JOB STATUS QUERY                    |
|                                                  |
|   Enter job #:  99999                            |
|                     Invalid job number, reenter  |
|                     or press <Escape> to quit.   |
|                                                  |
+--------------------------------------------------+
```

NOTES

<---- Operator input

Input of invalid job number results in display
of diagnostic message.
Possible causes of invalid number:
   Non-numeric character detected
   Field too short
   Field too long
   Job number not on file.

351

FIGURE 13.12 Subsidiary ledger card for a manual perpetual inventory system.

INVENTORY LEDGER CARD

Part number : 123456

Bin number : E · 29

Description : Grade A widget

Shipping weight : 4 lbs.

	RECEIVED				ISSUED				ON HAND		
Date	Ref.	Quant.	Unit Cost	Ext. Cost	Ref.	Quant.	Unit Cost	Ext. Cost	Quant.	Unit Cost	Ext. Cost
Jan. 1									90	1.20	108.00
5	A145	100	1.40	140.00					190	1.31	248.00
6					781G	40	1.20	48.00	150	1.33	200.00
15					803D	20	1.20	24.00	130	1.35	176.00
28					869P	40	1.25	50.00	90	1.40	126.00
Feb. 3	A263.	100	1.40	140.00					190	1.40	266.00
6					902J	30	1.40	42.00	160	1.40	224.00

to, the syntax rules of a high-level programming language. An example of a narrative task description is shown in Figure 13.14.

Another tool that may be useful is a decision table. Decision tables are used to define sets of rules used in a programmed decision, one in which the necessary course of action is completely determined by the given input conditions. They help ensure that appropriate actions are specified for all possible combinations of conditions. Decision tables may be prepared for either manual or automated processes and should be referenced in narrative descriptions and other relevant documentation.

A typical decision table is shown in Figure 13.15. It refers to the approval of accounts payable vouchers and provides a general authorization specifying what action a clerk is to take under various conditions. The decision table is in two parts: the upper, "condition," portion and the lower, "action," portion. According to the rules indicated by the decision table in Figure 13.15, if an invoice is received from a vendor, a voucher will be prepared, and the original purchase order will be retrieved from the files, along with the receiving document verifying that the goods have arrived. If the purchase order is missing, then the paperwork will be returned to the purchasing department for clarification. If the paperwork is complete, it will be examined to check that the quantity received is the same as the quantity ordered and that the quantity and price are correctly stated on the invoice. If the figures do not agree, the invoice will be returned to the vendor. If they do agree, check-cutting procedures will be initiated. Any other conditions prompt the clerk to set aside the voucher for further investigation.

FIGURE 13.13 Documentation of file design for a computerized system. The example relates to an inventory management system.

```
                              FILE DESIGN

   Project no.:      K88-143
   File no.:         143-1              File name:       Inventory master file

   Activity ratio:   35% per week       Prepared by:     PUJ
   Volatility:       10% per week       Checked by:      HTG
                                        Date:            7/16/99
   Access mode:      Random             Data dictionary reference:  1279/D
   Medium:           Magnetic disk
   Organization:     Ordered
   Primary key:      Part number
   Secondary key:    Part description


   Controls:         Daily backup and off-site storage
                     File maintenance requires Level-3 password
```

Field no.	Description	Type	Length (decimals)	Comments
1	Part number	N	15(0)	
2	Part description	A/N	30	
3	Location	A/N	5	
4	Unit of measure	A/N	2	
5	Shipping weight	N	5(1)	
6	Quantity on hand	N	5(0)	
7	Quantity on order	N	5(0)	
8	Quantity on reserve	N	5(0)	
9	Unit cost	N	7(4)	
10	Extended cost	N	8(2)	

```
   Form no. G2384, Rev. 3    Record length        87
   Effective date 3/1/99     Maximum records    5,000
                             Required capacity    435 KB
```

PROTOTYPING

User needs are carefully researched and evaluated during the systems analysis phase, and systems design responds by producing an information system that, to the extent possible, meets those needs. However, despite these efforts, users are often disappointed when—at implementation time—they finally see the finished system and start interacting with it. Users may have reviewed design documentation relating to input or output forms, operating procedures, or other aspects of the system.

They may have been invited to submit comments and suggestions for improvement and have subsequently signified their formal approval. But they may still be disappointed with the final article.

A major reason for such disappointment is that users have difficulty forming a mental image of what the system will look like and how it will operate. Design documentation may convey an accurate picture of the system to systems professionals, but it often fails to convey an adequate picture to the layperson. A partial solution to this troublesome problem lies in the use of prototyping.

FIGURE 13.14   Example of a narrative task description.

TASK DESCRIPTION

Task: no. 5.27
Computation of net income
Technology: Automated
References: None

Prepared by: KLP
Checked by: YTF
Date: 12/4/XX

Inputs	Documents Screens Files Other	Menu no. 5.271 General ledger master file
Outputs	Documents Screens Reports Files Other	Screen form no. 5.272 General ledger master file

Description

1. Processing is initiated by menu selection.

2. Retrieve asset, liability, and equity accounts from general ledger master file. Form total of asset "ending balance" fields. Form total of liability and equity "ending balance" fields.

3. Retrieve revenue and expense accounts from general ledger master file. Form total of revenue "ending balance" fields. Form total of expense "ending balance" fields.

4. Subtract total liabilities and equity from total assets. Subtract total expenses from total revenue.

5. If the two net amounts from step 4 are unequal, display diagnostic message: "Imbalance in trial balance. Net income cannot be determined." and terminate processing.

6. If the two net amounts from step 4 are equal, write net amount to "ending balance" of net income record. Display message: "Computation completed," pause for 10 seconds, and return to menu.

FIGURE 13.15 Decision table for preparation of accounts payable vouchers and vendor checks.

Condition :	Rule number						
	1	2	3	4	5	6	7
Invoice received	Y	Y	Y	N	Y	Y	
Purchase order on hand		Y	N	Y	Y	Y	
Receiving report on hand		N	Y	Y	Y	Y	
Figures agree					N	Y	
All other conditions							Y

Action :	Rule number						
	1	2	3	4	5	6	7
Hold in Accounting		X		X			
Return to Purchasing			X				
Return to Vendor					X		
Prepare voucher	X						
Cut check						X	
Investigate							X

A prototype is a working model of some part of the information system, reproducing selected characteristics of the real system. The prototype can be used to demonstrate a particular part of the system and allows users to interact with it and possibly to experiment with it. The users' reactions to the prototype can then be taken into account before the design of the production system is finalized.

Several different kinds of prototypes are in common use. Very simple, static prototypes may consist of nothing more than a sample input document or a report containing typical figures. More sophisticated, dynamic prototypes may involve interaction with a computer terminal or personal computer. A prototype may display an input form on a video screen and allow users to key in transaction data subject to point-of-entry controls. Some prototypes link the input and output functions, permitting users to enter data and then print out a related report. Others focus on the retrieval of data from a data base in response to user queries.

Development of prototypes should aim at representing aspects of the real system that will provoke the desired kind of feedback from users; other aspects can be sacrificed in the interests of simplicity and flexibility of use. In a prototype portraying the transaction entry function, for example, the input prompts and associated system responses should be correctly represented. For instance, if on entry of an employee number, the system is supposed to respond with the name of the employee—or with a diagnostic message in the case of an invalid number—then these responses should be represented by the prototype. On the other hand, the prototype need incorporate only a few employees, and extensive control checks may be simulated by a few IF statements in the associated software.

The prototypes' operating performance is usually not crucial. The response time of interactive prototypes should be approximately correct, as significant differences are likely to provoke negative user reaction, particularly if the real system turns out to be much slower than the prototype. However, the time taken to format and print a report may be less important than the flexibility to experiment with different report layouts to optimize user acceptance. Economy in the effort, time, and cost of developing the prototype is clearly a major objective. Spreadsheets, user-oriented data base packages, and other types of generalized software are often used for this purpose. Although such software might be unsuitable for use in production systems, because of poor operating performance under high-volume conditions, it may be ideal for prototyping because of programming ease and flexibility. In this context the usual arguments justifying investment in development costs in order to maximize operating performance or to minimize operating costs do not apply.

Prototypes can elicit important feedback from users at a time when the design is still flexible and changes can still be made easily and cheaply. Their use encourages user interaction in the design and can avoid costly mistakes or costly system modification during the implementation phase. Critics argue that prototyping distracts from the main task of designing the production system and question whether the value of the feedback obtained from prototypes justifies the development costs incurred. On the other hand, the increasing use of prototyping and the interest shown in this topic in the technical literature point to a widespread and growing recognition of its usefulness and cost effectiveness.

DOCUMENTATION

Documentation is an essential element in any accounting system. It addresses the users and other interested parties and explains what the system is and how it works. Documentation is the key to the system's successful operation, use, maintenance, evaluation, and future enhancement. Without it, the system is nothing but a "black box" with mysterious inner workings and relationships between inputs and outputs, which in themselves may be only partially understood.

Technical Systems Documentation

The documentation of an information system can be divided into two parts: the first addressed to technical personnel involved with the system and the second addressed to the users of the system. The former is appropriately referred to as *technical systems documentation* and is prepared for the benefit of programmers, systems analysts, auditors, and other systems professionals. It is written in precise technical language and offers an "inside" view of the system. Technical systems documentation typically includes the following:

- Overall narrative description of the system, its objectives, structure, and principal features
- HIPO charts
- Data dictionary
- Detailed systems flowcharts showing applications, transaction paths, and other lines of information flow through the system and also specifically showing audit trails
- Input definitions, including formatting and data preparation instructions for each application
- Narrative descriptions of major and minor subsystems

- Computer program descriptions, with source listings and lists of inputs, outputs, and files
- Decision tables and other supporting materials, where appropriate
- File definitions, by application, or logical data base schema
- Output definitions and formats, by application
- Internal controls, by application
- Summary of test procedures, including formal test plan, expected results, and comparisons with actual results
- Performance estimates

Much of the technical systems documentation is accumulated during systems development. Subsequently, as the system evolves, the systems documentation should be maintained by updates, additions, or deletions to keep it current. Each item of documentation should bear the name of the person who prepared it, so that when possible, future questions can be directed to the individual most familiar with that part of the system. Each item should also bear the date of the most recent revision of the material. Finally, all significant items of documentation should bear an appropriate authorization. This is necessary not only for the original system but also for subsequent modifications; the system should be modified only in response to a written authorization from a cognizant manager.

User Documentation

User documentation describes the system "from the outside, looking in." There are several different classes of users, who may have different capabilities and needs. Accordingly, several different types of user documentation are necessary. Clerical procedures are needed that pertain to the system's manual components. Instructions in interpretation may be required by users who simply receive output from the system. Operating procedures are required for professional computer operators. And instructions must be provided for laypersons who interact with the computer, including data entry clerks and end users.

Clerical procedures are addressed principally to clerical workers engaged in manual tasks such as preparing

FIGURE 13.16 Clerical procedure for preparation of accounts payable vouchers.

Procedure No: 1234 Departments Affected : Accounting Effective Date : 1 / 1 / 19XX Authorization : Controller	Subject : Preparation of Accounts Payable Vouchers Personnel : Accounts Payable Clerk
Company Policy	Vouchers are to be prepared in readiness for payment of vendor invoices. Vouchers must be supported by the Invoice, the associated Purchase Order, and (where applicable) the Receiving Report.
Instructions	1. Enter the Vendor Number and Name on line # 4, Form # 9876. 2. Enter the Invoice # and Due Date on line # 6. 3. Enter the Amount Due on line #9. 4. Enter any avaliable Discount on line #10. 5. Attach the Invoice and enter an "X" in column # 12, line # 12. 6. Attach the Purchase Order and enter an "X" in column # 3, line # 12. 7. If the Purchase Order is for Goods, attach the Receiving Report, and enter an "X" in column #4, line # 12. 8. If the Purchase Order is for Services, enter an "X" in column # 5 , line # 12.
Timing	On receipt of all vendor invoices.

inputs, filing, and preparing and distributing outputs. Clerical procedures are commonly associated with particular documents or reports: preparing payables vouchers or processing expense claims, materials requisitions, sales orders, or cash receipts. Occasionally they involve computation or analysis, such as computing payroll deductions or sales commissions, or reconciling bank statements. Written procedures spell out what the task entails, who is supposed to perform it, and how it is to be accomplished. Additional data may be included specifying the timing and frequency of the task, and a brief statement of applicable company policy may provide the background to the procedure. An example of a clerical procedure is shown in Figure 13.16.

Instructions to the recipients of accounting output should focus on what processing activities are involved, how the data should be interpreted, and what indicators might suggest possible processing errors or similar problems. Users of accounting reports need to have at least a general notion of the processing operations required to prepare the report content and of the inputs to the processes. Narrative descriptions and summary flowcharts or block diagrams usually suffice to provide this background information. Although the preparers of the output bear the major responsibility for preventing and detecting errors, users who have substantial experience in their specialties are in a good position to help and should be encouraged to identify suspected problems.

Documentation addressed to trained computer operators emphasizes the system's operation and provides instructions for executing the various programs and for handling data. Typically, it includes the following:

- Brief narrative description, covering the purposes of the system, the overall mode of operation, and the structure of the major applications
- Summary flowcharts (possibly just block diagrams) showing interapplication information flows
- List of programs with operating instructions
- List of principal files accessed by programs, and instructions for mounting tapes, disk packs, and the like
- Sample input illustrating what is required by each program
- Sample output showing what is produced by each program, and instructions for loading preprinted forms, and the like
- Control procedures
- Error-recovery procedures
- Crash-recovery procedures, including a disaster plan

The importance of recovery procedures cannot be overestimated. Even the best-designed systems fail occasionally as the result of faulty input, human error, equipment failure, or forces including sabotage, fire, and natural disasters. When such problems arise, the operators must know what to do to limit damage to files, software, and hardware and how to return to normal operating conditions promptly and in an orderly manner. Even in the relatively minor situation of the premature termination of a program, the operators need to know what files may have been contaminated and whether the program can simply be rerun. In the event of a major problem, there must be procedures for retrieving files, software, and documentation from off-site storage locations and possibly moving temporarily to alternative processing facilities. Response to large-scale problems require a carefully designed and tested disaster plan.

Preparation of end-user operator instructions faces a dual challenge. On the one hand, there is the need to document the operation of terminals, personal computers, and other equipment and associated software packages. In this regard, their requirements are similar to those of trained computer operators. On the other hand, there is the need to communicate effectively with laypersons whose knowledge of computer technology may be limited. Also, a wide range of general educational backgrounds may be needed. Data entry clerks, for example, may have reached only a relatively low level of general education. However, many end users may be highly trained professionals—in accounting, management, or other fields—who simply do not know a great deal about computers. In either case, many end users are nervous about computers and may require continual reassurance that they are performing the correct operator procedures, as well as simple remedies for recovering from incorrect procedures.

Considerable advances have been made in the development of user manuals for both hardware and software systems. Much of this is provided by manufacturers, who recognize that good end-user documentation is an essential part of the total product; some otherwise successful software packages, in particular, have failed in the marketplace because the manuals provided with them were too difficult to understand. The need for user-friendly documentation runs parallel with the need for user-friendly hardware and software. The main objective is to provide clear operating instructions and factual information, while protecting users from needless technical jargon. Commonly, user manuals contain representations of screen displays produced at each stage of processing. An example is shown in Figure 13.17.

FIGURE 13.17   Example of user documentation for a modern computer software package.

```
           AMERICAN COMPANY
        ACCOUNTS PAYABLE MENU
   PROGRAM SELECTION:

       1 ENTER VOUCHER DATA

       2 PRINT VOUCHER REGISTER

       3 PRINT CASH REQUIREMENTS REPORT

       4 SELECT VOUCHERS FOR PAYMENT

       5 PRINT CHECK REGISTER

       6 STOP

   ENTER SELECTION NUMBER
```

To select vouchers for payment, enter "4" on the keyboard and then turn to page 52 for further instructions.

Documentation Standards

Good documentation is not generated by accident; rather, it is produced as a result of careful planning and implementation by an organization that takes seriously the need for documentation. The preparation of documentation should be governed by appropriate standards established by the organization. Documentation standards are written policies that determine

- Who should prepare the various types of documentation
- What should be included (and what should be omitted)
- How the material should be presented
- What authorizations are required for each type of documentation
- How the documentation should be prepared
- How the documentation should be distributed
- How the documentation should be used
- What procedures are appropriate to review and maintain the various types of documentation.

The technical personnel who designed the system—accountants, systems analysts, consultants, programmers, and so forth—are usually the best people to prepare technical systems documentation. But such personnel should not prepare end-user documentation. Documentation targeted at laypersons should be prepared by individuals who are closer in attitudes and level of understanding to those who will need to read it. Documentation specialists are trained to interface between technical experts and laypersons. Documentation specialists do not need extensive technical qualifications, but they must be able to read technical specifications and translate them into plain English. They must be able to see the system through the eyes of the user.

Standardized writing styles may be out of place in many situations, but they are essential to the development of good documentation. The style should be as simple as possible, and the vocabulary should intentionally be limited. Different words for the same thing should not be used for the sake of variety; rather, the same word should be used throughout to avoid confusion. Many authorities recommend using a direct style in issuing instructions. For example, in a clerical procedure, "Take the stores requisition to the foreman and ask him or her to sign it" has more impact and is less likely to be misunderstood than is "A foreman's signature is required to authorize a stores requisition."

Reproduction and distribution methods for documentation should reflect both the need for economy and the environment in which it is to be used. A manual to be used on the shop floor needs to be reproduced on a more rugged material than one used in the accounting office. Ring binders may facilitate the update of documentation; individual pages can be replaced as necessary; however, there is a greater likelihood that pages will be lost or be removed by unauthorized persons.

Documentation should be distributed on a "need to know" basis. The purpose of documentation is to inform and instruct authorized persons about the system the way it operates, but it should not become the means by which unauthorized individuals gain information that they could exploit. Clearly, all personnel who are expected to comply with written procedures need to have access to those procedures. And computer operators, end users, and others need to have access to applicable user documentation. But technical systems documentation does not need to be widely distributed; indeed, its distribution should be restricted to ensure that it does not fall into unauthorized hands. If operating employees or outsiders have access to material of this kind, they might obtain insights into the workings of control techniques—or into the weakness of particular controls—that could be translated into irregularities.

SUMMARY

Systems design is the process in which plans for the information system are translated into a set of specifications, or a "paper model," describing the system and how it will operate. Systems design is a creative process of synthesis, in which large numbers of detailed components are assembled to form an integrated whole; it is also a decision-making process in which decisions—large and small—are made about each of those components and about how they should interact with one another. Management at all levels should participate in this decision-making process to ensure that the resulting information system truly meets the needs of its users. The task of the project team is to translate these decisions into appropriate design features.

Modern structured design methods emphasize the need to divide the overall system into a hierarchy of modular subsystems, extending from the conceptual levels down to the most detailed levels. But there are conflicting opinions as to the superiority of top-down and bottom-up design. In top-down design the conceptual levels are designed first, and the more detailed levels at a later stage. Bottom-up design takes the opposite approach; the design process starts with the detailed levels and works upward. Each approach has its strengths and weaknesses, but the objective in both cases is to minimize the amount of redesign made necessary by conflicts or inconsistencies.

Detailed design starts with user requirements and works backward through the system, from the outputs necessary to meet those requirements, to the processes and files, and finally to the inputs. Processing design pertains to both the manual and the automated parts of the system. Exceptions from standard procedures must be identified and accounted for in processing design. File design may relate to conventional files or to the schema of a data base management system. Care must be taken to ensure that the set of data elements contained in the inputs and files is consistent with those required to support the system outputs.

Prototyping is a tool of growing importance in systems design. Prototypes allow the user to gain a "feel" for what a new system component will be like and possibly permit users to experiment with the design before the final design decisions are made. Users should be aware that design changes may be relatively easy to make at the design stage but may be difficult and expensive to make later in the project.

A vital part of successful systems design is the preparation of documentation. Several types of documentation are required in order to meet the needs of different groups, including technical systems documentation, user documentation, and clerical procedures. Technical systems documentation provides a permanent record of the design process and explains how the system is intended to operate. User documentation and clerical procedures provide the basis for user training and help ensure that the system is used effectively and efficiently by those whom it is intended to serve. Documentation standards provide for effective preparation, use, and maintenance of documentation.

BIBLIOGRAPHY

Ameiss, Albert P., and Nicholas A. Kargas. *Accountants' Desk Handbook*. Englewood Cliffs, N.J.: Prentice-Hall, 1977.

Appleton, Daniel S. "The Modern Data Dictionary," *Datamation*, March 1, 1987, pp. 66–68.

Arens, Alvin A., and D. D. Ward. *System Understanding for Auditing*. Haslett, Mich.: Systems Publications, 1981.

Awad, Elias M. *Systems Analysis and Design*. Homewood, Ill.: Irwin, 1979.

Bohl, Marilyn. *Tools for Structured Design*. Palo Alto, Calif.: Science Research Associates, 1978.

Burch, John G., Jr., Felix R. Strater, and Gary Grudnitski. *Information Systems: Theory and Practice*, 2nd ed. New York: Wiley, 1979.

Crimm, Susan J. "EDP User Documentation: The Missing Link." *Journal of Systems Management*, November 1980, pp. 15–19.

Hussain, Donna, and K. M. Hussain. *Information Processing Systems for Management*. Homewood, Ill.: Irwin, 1981.

Orr, Kenneth. *Structured Systems Development*. New York: Yourdon Press, 1977.

Wilkinson, Joseph W. *Accounting and Information Systems*. New York: Wiley, 1982.

Yourdon, Edward, and Larry L. Constantine. *Structured Design*. Englewood Cliffs, N.J.: Prentice-Hall, 1979.

DISCUSSION QUESTIONS AND PROBLEMS

1. Define and discuss the following terms:

• Bottom-up design
• Clerical procedure
• Conceptual design
• Data dictionary

- Detail diagram
- Detailed design
- Decision table
- Documentation
- Documentation standards
- Error recovery
- File-output matrix
- HIPO techniques
- Input-file matrix
- Modular approach
- Narrative description
- Output specifications
- Overview diagram
- Procedures
- Programmed decision
- Structure chart
- Structured design
- Technical systems documentation
- Top-down design
- User documentation

2. a. Draw up a list of output items for an accounts receivable system.

b. Prepare a set of output specifications for the system, similar to that in Figure 13.7.

3. Mary Jackson, a practicing CPA, is concerned that her time and that of her two assistants be allocated properly to the various client engagements on which they work each week. Accordingly, she has asked you to design a timekeeping system that will give her a weekly report showing the breakdown of labor hours by client and the amount to be billed to each client based on prescribed hourly rates for herself and her two assistants, John Blair and Molly Wood.

Required

a. Identify the required inputs and outputs for the timekeeping system.

b. Construct a detailed input–output matrix relating the input and output data elements.

4. Design a subsidiary ledger card for use in a manual fixed-asset system. The fixed assets are delivery trucks, and the data entries should reflect the acquisition, maintenance, and depreciation of the trucks as well as record the departments to which they are currently assigned.

5. Construct a decision table for a credit approval subsystem. Company policy is that credit is to be approved automatically for orders of less than $50. For orders of $50 or more, credit is to be approved up to the previously assigned limit for the particular customer, as long as that customer's outstanding balance is less than $5,000. If the order is for more than $1,000, the credit manager is to be consulted if the order would otherwise be rejected.

6. A clerical procedure is to be established to calculate volume discounts in the billing subsystem. Company policy provides for a 10 percent discount if year-to-date purchases by the particular customer exceed $50,000 and a 20 percent discount if they exceed $200,000. The discounts are to be recorded in the sales journal and also entered on the invoices, which are prepared manually.

Required

Formulate the clerical procedure using a layout similar to that shown in Figure 13.16.

7. a. Analyze a computerized general ledger system into a hierarchy of component subsystems, down to the level of program modules, presenting your analysis in the form of a structure chart. Special journals and subsidiary ledgers are to be incorporated. The system is to operate in an interactive batch mode but is to provide for account query via a video terminal.

b. Assume that the system in (a) is to be designed using a top-down approach. Write a narrative description of the nature and operation of the system as a whole in a form that could provide a starting point for the definition and design of the lower-level subsystems.

c. Assume, instead, that the system is to be designed using a bottom-up approach. Write a narrative description of two of the program modules to provide a starting point for the integration of these subsystem modules into a coherent whole system.

8. Prepare a structure chart for the purchasing cycle, showing subsystems at least one level below that of the associated accounting applications. Include an appropriate numbering system for the subsystems at the various levels.

9. a. Prepare an overview diagram for the accounts receivable application.

b. Prepare detail diagrams for (i) preparing invoices and (ii) preparing a schedule of aged accounts receivable.

10. Prepare formal task descriptions for the two processes referred to in Problem 9.

11. Jupiter Company operates an accounts payable system in which a voucher transaction file is used to accumulate data from incoming vendor invoices. A separate check file records the subsequent payments. Both files are maintained on magnetic tape. The vendor master file to which voucher and check data are posted is maintained on magnetic disk. A father–son system is used in which the father version of the master file is preserved until the posting operation is verified as being complete and correct. Verification is done manually by scanning a printout that lists each vendor account, its change in balance, and the supporting transaction data. Upon successful verification, the son version is released for subsequent use. After posting has been completed, the transaction data are archived to a paper file.

Required
a. Prepare a systems flowchart depicting the posting operation described here.
b. Prepare a formal task description of the posting operation.

12. Gabriel Manufacturing Company uses an automated job order costing system in which separate transaction files for materials costs and overhead costs are maintained on magnetic disk storage. The data from these files are posted to the job order master file, which also resides on disk. A father–son system is used, and after posting, all transaction data are written to a single magnetic tape archive file.

New jobs are entered into the master file via a file maintenance program using a video terminal for input, and a printout is automatically generated showing all changes that have been entered.

The main output from the system consists of a weekly report showing the status of all jobs currently in process in the factory. This is prepared from the job order master file and is printed in three parts for distribution to the factory superintendent, the vice-president of manufacturing, and the supervisor of the production control department.

Required
Prepare a systems flowchart showing the posting scheme and related processes comprising Gabriel's system, and include footnotes explaining each step in the flow of transactions.

13. Develop a set of documentation standards for the preparation of clerical procedures for a manual accounting system. The standards should prescribe the form of the procedures and how they should be prepared, catalogued, filed, distributed, and maintained.

14. Ajax Corporation is an import–export company with suppliers and customers in North and South America, Europe, and the Pacific Basin. The company intends to prepare a performance report in which current-month and year-to-date revenues and costs are to be compared (in U.S. dollars) with budget projections. Revenues should be broken down by territory, and costs should be broken down by account category (salaries, shipping costs, administrative costs, and so on). Aggregate gains and losses on foreign currency translation should be reported in the calculation of net operating profit.

Required
Design a report form to meet these requirements. Show all variable fields (accounts, dollar amounts, dates, and so forth) in generic form using 9s and Xs. Be sure to define the precise lengths of each field, the punctuation to be included, and the spacing between adjacent columns. The report is to be printed on an 80-column printer. There is no need to design header and trailer pages.

15. During development of a new accounting system, the designers gave prospective users a prototype of the schedule of aged accounts receivable. The prototype was implemented using an electronic spreadsheet package. It allowed users to become familiar with the proposed layout of the report and to experiment with alternative layouts before the design was finalized.

Required
a. Discuss the objectives of prototyping.
b. To what extent would this example achieve those objectives?
c. Describe other methods of implementing prototypes, indicating their respective strengths and weaknesses.

16. As an accounting consultant you have been asked to assist in the design of a new computerized payroll system for a small custom manufacturing company. Specifically, your expertise is needed to design interactive screen forms for entry of weekly time-card data. The client organization employs 30 hourly workers and typically has six jobs in progress at any one time. Approximately 20 percent of the labor force turns over in any given year. The average job is completed in the factory in about one week. To avoid confusion, employee numbers and job numbers must not be recycled within a period of less than 10 years.

Data from time cards are to be entered, including employee number, regular and overtime hours worked, and a breakdown of total hours by job. When the employee number is entered, the system should respond with the employee's name or should display a diagnostic message if the number is invalid. Similarly, when the job number is entered, the system should respond with a 30-character alphanumeric job description or should display a diagnostic if the job number is invalid. After the user has completed the entry for each employee, the system should compare the total regular and overtime hours with the sum of the hours allocated to the various jobs. In the event of a discrepancy, the system should transfer to an edit mode, allowing the user to correct the data entered for that employee. The continuation option, based on the use of keyboard function keys, should provide for editing the transaction entry (even if the preceding comparison indicates no discrepancy), aborting the entry, accepting the entry and prompting for the next transaction, or returning to the main payroll menu.

Required

Design a set of screen forms to accomplish the transaction entry process. Be sure to provide for all contingent screens corresponding to the entry of invalid data. There is no need to design associated screen menus.

17. Prepare a design for the transaction file needed in the payroll system described in Problem 16. Estimate the file activity ratio and volatility ratio for inclusion in your file specifications. Also estimate the total file capacity required. File controls do not need to be designed.

14

Systems Implementation

LEARNING OBJECTIVES

After you have studied this chapter you should be able to

- Identify the principal steps in systems implementation.
- Discuss the issues in procuring computer hardware.
- Discuss the issues in purchasing or developing computer software.
- Describe the organization of the modern information services department, and discuss its objectives.
- Discuss the problems in systems conversion and how they can be solved.
- Identify the costs of operating a computerized information system.
- Explain why costs of computerized systems often increase over time and how to minimize those increases.

CHAPTER OUTLINE

OVERVIEW OF SYSTEMS IMPLEMENTATION

The implementation of information systems costs more, can take longer, and often causes more problems than do the two earlier phases of systems development combined. Translating the paper model produced in the design phase into a working system is a major undertaking that frequently taxes to the limit the patience and capabilities of the organization. Systems implementation consists of acquiring the resources specified in the design and putting those resources into operation in place of the old system. The resources may include computer hardware and software, other equipment, supplies, buildings, people, and skills.

The principal steps in systems implementation are

- Acquisition of computer hardware
- Acquisition of computer software
- Site preparation
- Installation of hardware and software
- Testing
- Changes of management responsibility
- Personnel recruitment and layoff
- Training
- Acquisition of new supplies
- Conversion
- Live operation and final sign-off
- Postimplementation review

Acquisition and Installation of Computer Facilities

Computer hardware and software are acquired to support the requirements defined in the systems design. Sets of specifications should be drawn up to facilitate the procurement process. Hardware and software products can be purchased from local computer stores, from mail-order stores, from dealers, or directly from the manufacturers. Software can be bought in the form of canned programs or can be custom developed. In the latter case, management can decide whether to use in-house programmers or to contract the development to an outside software house.

The scope of necessary site preparation depends on the nature and demands of the equipment to be installed. A small personal computer may fit on one end of a desktop or even be carried in a brief case. A large mainframe computer may require the construction of a computer room (Figure 14.1)—or even a new building—and may require installation of a special power supply and climate control: heating, ventilation, air conditioning, and humidity control. A raised floor may have to be installed to cover electric wiring and to provide a safe working environment for the operators. Distributed or networked systems may require installation of wiring throughout the building or beyond.

Installation of hardware means unpacking and assembling the various units of the computer: terminals, disk and tape drives, central processor units, and other components. Software installation may require configuring applications programs and drivers to operate in the particular environment of the processor and peripheral devices. Software may also need to be configured specially to operate in the environment of the systems software to be used.

Systems Testing

Testing of the new system normally proceeds in stages. Individual software packages may be tested else-

FIGURE 14.1 Photograph of a computer room. The photograph shows the VAX8700 computer system. (Courtesy of Digital Equipment Corporation.)

where on another machine; some of the issues involved in software testing were discussed in Chapter 8. Initial, or "shakedown testing" is usually carried out at the time of hardware installation: It includes a range of tests intended to verify that the hardware is fully operational. Shakedown testing is normally followed by much more comprehensive testing of the complete system. Systems testing must be carried out under conditions simulating real-life operations, in order to make sure that the system will perform the job for which it was designed.

A formal test plan should be developed in which simulated transaction and master file data are identified that explore the full range of operating conditions. Both valid and invalid transaction data should be included, and deliberate attempts should be made to "break" the new system. Anticipated outputs should be identified and documented before transaction data are entered into the system. Comparison between the anticipated and actual output should be documented, and any discrepancies identified for investigation. Final approval and release of the system for operational use should come after a careful review of the test results and the system specifications.

Organizational Changes and Training

The information system is so closely integrated into the work of the organization that a number of organizational and administrative changes may be necessary to accommodate the new system. Personnel responsibilities may change; new positions may be created; and old ones may be eliminated. New employees with particular skills may need to be recruited to fill positions opened up by the new system. Some individuals displaced by the changes may be retrained for other jobs; others may have to be laid off. Care must be taken to minimize the negative impact on people's lives as well as to minimize any loss of morale in the company.

Training must be provided for people directly affected by the new system, such as computer operators, and also for the much larger number of people whose work will be affected indirectly. This latter group will include everybody who prepares data for processing, receives output from the system, or otherwise interacts with the system. For some, training will consist of nothing more than a short briefing on the use of new forms or new procedures. For others, extensive training may be required to prepare people for radical changes in the ways they do their jobs.

Included in the training for all groups should be explanations as to why the new system was needed and how it will benefit the organization. Management should try to convey its enthusiasm for the new system, so as to allay any anxieties and create a positive attitude to the system. Any criticisms of the new system—justified or otherwise—should be addressed to the project team and should not be allowed to undermine the rank-and file users' confidence in the system.

Conversion

Conversion is the actual process of bringing the new system into operation and terminating the operation of the old system. Conversion is the most critical part of the whole development project, and care must be taken to minimize the impact of the transition on the user organization. Careful planning is the most effective means of smoothing the transition. Nevertheless, things can still go wrong, and developers must be careful not to transfer the whole burden of operation to the new system until its credibility and reliability have been demonstrated under conditions of live operation.

Computer supplies, such as disk packs, tapes, paper, and printer ribbons, must be purchased in readiness for conversion, and new preprinted forms may be required. The lead time to get the new forms is normally several weeks, and so they must be ordered in plenty of time. During conversion, forms inventories should be controlled carefully so that supplies of the old forms are available until no longer needed, but efforts also should be made to avoid being left with large stocks of obsolete forms on hand.

Once the new system is in routine production operation, outstanding contracts with suppliers, consultants, and other outside vendors can be terminated. The systems project is now approaching its completion, and the project team can soon be disbanded. A postimplementation review should be performed before this occurs.

The review provides an opportunity to evaluate the project itself and also the new system, to determine what went right and what went wrong.

When the project team is disbanded, some of the in-house members of the team will return to the departments from which they were originally recruited. Others may be absorbed into the systems group of the information services department to provide continuing support in the form of hand holding and troubleshooting and to form the nucleus of a future project team. Information systems are not static, and further changes and enhancements are likely to be required sooner or later. In large organizations, systems development is a more-or-less continuous process, and a permanent systems group is maintained to respond to needs as they occur.

ACQUISITION OF COMPUTER HARDWARE

Hardware Specifications

Computer devices must be selected to meet the input, processing, secondary storage, output, and telecommunication requirements specified in the design. Then the devices must be configured into a working system. The following is a summary of the principal decisions that must be made relating to hardware devices in each of the five areas:

1. INPUT DEVICES
   Video display terminals
   Mode of operation: passive, smart, intelligent
   Screen characteristics: size, monochrome or color, resolution
   Keyboard design: number pad, function keys
   Special features: light pen, mouse, etc.
   Ergonomics
   Other input devices
2. PROCESSOR DEVICES
   Control unit
   Speed: cycle time (nanoseconds), processing speed (instructions per second)
   Multitasking or multiprocessing capability
   Maximum number of peripherals supported

Arithmetic/logic unit
Word length (bits): registers, buses
Number of registers
Instruction set
Main memory
Capacity (megabytes)
Memory allocation: static, dynamic
Virtual memory capability
3. SECONDARY AND TERTIARY STORAGE DEVICES
   Magnetic disk
   Type: floppy diskette, fixed disk, cartridge disk
   Capacity (megabytes)
   Speed: access time (milliseconds), data transfer rate (megabytes per second)
   Magnetic tape
   Type: reel-to-reel tape, streaming tape
   Tape speed (inches per second)
   Recording density (bits per inch)
   Other storage devices
4. OUTPUT DEVICES
   Printers
   Type: character, line, page printer
   Speed (characters per second, lines, pages per minute)
   Print quality (draft, near letter quality, full letter quality)
   Multiple-copy capability
   Technology: dot matrix, daisy wheel, laser, etc.
   Video monitors
   Screen characteristics: size (rows, columns), monochrome or color, resolution (pixels per inch)
   Graphics capability
   Special features: zoom capability, etc.
   Plotters
   Bed size (inches)
   Number of pens: color capability
   Speed (inches per second)
   Other output devices
5. TELECOMMUNICATIONS DEVICES
   Network
   Georgraphic extent (LAN, WAN)
   Topology (ring, bus, etc.)
   Required network servers
   Channels
   Type: dial-up telephone lines, leased lines, company-owned channels, etc.
   Medium: twisted-pair copper wire, coaxial cable, fiber optics, etc.

Capacity: bandwidth (Hz), transmission speed (bits per second)
Modems
Type: half duplex, full duplex
Speed: bits per second
Special features: autodial
Multiplexors, concentrators
Other communications devices

Hardware requirements should be translated into formal specifications that list the types and quantities of the required items of equipment, together with associated performance criteria, and form the basis for the pro-

curement process. Because not all manufacturers offer equipment with the same capabilities, *minimum* performance requirements should be stated, allowing vendors to propose products that exceed these minima, as long as the total price is still competitive. A typical set of hardware specifications is shown in Figure 14.2.

Selection Criteria

A wide range of computer hardware products is offered for sale, with different capabilities, different brand

FIGURE 14.2   Computer hardware specifications.

Item	Minimum Requirements	Quantity
Central processor	16-bit word length on registers and buses. 100 nsec cycle time. 1 MB main memory, with dynamic memory allocation. Multitasking option. Peripheral interfaces and network (LAN) server.	1
Video display terminal	Monochrome. 80 col. x 24 row screen. Keyboard with function keys and number pad. Full-screen editing in block mode.	8
Magnetic disk drive	60 MB fixed and 20 MB removable cartridge.	2
Magnetic tape drive	Reel to reel. 6,250 b.p.i. density. 75 i.p.s. tape speed.	1
Character printer	Dual mode dot-matrix printer: 80 c.p.s. near letter quality, 150 c.p.s. draft mode. Software selectable fonts. Graphics capability. Color option.	3
Line printer	600 l.p.m., solid character, impact printer	1
Plotter	Flat-bed plotter. 6 colors. 4 i.p.s. plotting speed.	
Modem	2,400 b.p.s., full duplex, smart modem.	

names, and different costs. Even at any given level of capability, equipment marketed by different manufacturers may vary significantly in price. Accordingly, shopping for hardware products can be bewildering.

The main selection criteria for computer hardware are performance, compatibility, operation, availability and vendor support, economics, and brand image. These criteria can be analyzed into critical success factors as follows:

1. Performance
   Minimum initial configuration
   Expansion potential
2. Compatibility
   Compatibility with other hardware
   Ability to run required software
3. Operation
   Ease of use
   Maintainability
   Reliability (downtime as percentage of total)
   Environmental demands
4. Availability and Vendor Support
   Delivery lead time
   Location of manufacturer
   Service support (on-site, "normal working hours" coverage, 24-hour coverage)
   Service call response time
   Location of spares inventory
   Location of backup machine
5. Brand Name
   Reputation of manufacturer
   Stability of manufacturer
6. Economics
   Invoice cost
   Trade-in allowance
   Freight costs and other incidentals
   Future resale value
   Cost of service support
   Availability of financing or lease arrangements
   Maintenance costs
   Operating costs
   Tax effects

The objective should be to select equipment that represents a middle ground between under- and overcapacity. A difficult question with respect to performance centers on the optimal amount of spare capacity that should be incorporated to handle expected growth. Most organizations are expected to grow over time, and in fact computers themselves stimulate growth, in much the same way as the construction of new highways stimulates automobile and truck traffic. Either spare capacity must be built in at the outset, or there must be provision to upgrade the system at a later date without the need for a major redesign. Different considerations apply to the processor device, on the one hand, and to storage capacity and peripheral devices, on the other. Both main-memory and secondary storage capacities can usually be expanded within broad limits. And the number of peripheral devices can be increased as necessary.

But as additional peripheral devices are connected to the processor, terminal response times are likely to increase, possibly to an intolerable level. The speed of the processor device may block further expansion. Accordingly, it is a good strategy to build in substantially more processing capacity than is required at the outset, to allow for growth. Failure to do so may necessitate less satisfactory alternatives. Replacement of the processor device by a larger, more powerful one may necessitate major changes in other parts of the system, including peripherals and software. Adding a second processor may be possible in only certain types of systems. Large mainframe processors can sometimes be run in parallel, with a shared data base and shared peripherals, but small processors usually can be operated only singly. If the existing processor becomes inadequate, the only option may be to arrange them as stand-alone systems, each with its own peripheral devices.

Two questions often arise with regard to compatibility: "Can I connect my existing equipment—tape drive, disk drive, printer, and so on—to the new computer?" and "Can I buy cheaper components and plug them into my brand-name computer?" The answer to both questions may be yes or no, and the computer industry has not been consistent in its determination or even its willingness to let users "mix and match" components. Major manufacturers often try to discourage users from acquiring "foreign" components (that is, components made by competitors), whereas many small manufacturers market products that are intended to be used with brand-name equipment. Many "plug-compatible" devices can indeed simply be plugged in. But sometimes, special interface units must be acquired, or software drivers developed, before the pieces of equipment can "talk to each other." When plug-compatible devices are being considered, it is wise to insist that the vendor organization take responsibility for seeing that the equipment operates satisfactorily. It is also wise to check that the incorporation of foreign components does not invalidate warranties or service contracts.

The most important issue with respect to the relationship between hardware and software is whether the hardware will run the software necessary to perform the required processing operations. This may not be a problem if custom software is to be developed. But if canned programs are to be used or if particular types of end-user software have been proposed, it is necessary to confirm that those software packages will run on the proposed processor device. Compatibility with existing software is another problem. Programs written in COBOL are generally transportable, without modification, from one mainframe computer to another, although they may have to be recompiled. However, they may not be directly transportable among smaller machines whose compilers may not conform to the ANSI standards. Similarly, programs written in other languages not subject to national standards may require modification. Software sold in object code form, such as end-user packages, will normally run only on machines using the same operating system.

Ease of operation is a concern with all computer equipment, but principally with terminals and personal computers intended to be run by laypersons, and much has been done in recent years to simplify operating procedures. Much has also been done to improve the reliability of computer equipment and to reduce the amount and frequency of necessary maintenance. The downtime of modern computers should typically be less than 1 percent of total operating time, as long as routine maintenance schedules are faithfully followed.

Small personal computers can often be bought "off the shelf" at computer retail stores or even obtained from mail-order stores. But large machines usually must be ordered from the manufacturer. Delivery lead times are typically 60 to 90 days, but some major computer manufacturers traditionally have large backlogs and accept orders for delivery in two to four years. Prospective users must evaluate the impact of long lead times and

may need to make interim arrangements while awaiting delivery.

The location of the manufacturer is of no immediate concern, as long as service support can be obtained locally and spare parts are inventoried locally. Some computer manufacturers headquartered outside the United States have extensive facilities throughout the country and offer a level of support superior to that offered by their domestic competitors.

The reputation and stability of the manufacturer are major concerns of prospective buyers. Some manufacturers have consistent track records of supplying and supporting good products. Others have less favorable track records or have a reputation for frequently changing product lines and failing to support equipment (or software) sold only one or two years earlier. Many computer firms have gone out of business, and the industry has a history of volatility, with "shakeouts" every two to three years.

The Procurement Process

Organizations can choose to approach a single manufacturer or dealer, but there are advantages in inviting competitive bids from a number of sources. A "request for quotation" (RFQ), consisting of a copy of the hardware specifications and a cover letter, is submitted to several vendors. Although some vendors will not respond to requests for open-bid quotations, most will, particularly on large jobs. And the final cost to the procuring organization is likely to be lower; vendors will shave prices in order to be competitive.

If the hardware specifications are still fluid, a request for proposal (RFP) may be issued. Vendors will then submit proposals on how the company's needs can best be met. Different types of hardware may be suggested by different vendors. Evaluation of the responses is usually more difficult than when vendors are simply bidding on specific hardware items. On the other hand, vendors may be able to propose new products of which the developers were unaware or solutions that the developers had not considered.

In either case, vendors may be requested to complete a questionnaire soliciting information about the qualifications and experience of the vendor organization and about the financial and technical stability of the manufacturer (if different from the vendor). The questionnaire may also solicit more information about the proposed products than is typically included in sales brochures. The questionnaire forces vendors to answer specific questions that might not otherwise be addressed. Finally, the questionnaire may request the names of other companies that have bought similar systems and that can attest to the quality of the equipment and the service provided. The responses to the questionnaire help eliminate unsuitable vendors and/or manufacturers. They may also help improve the comparability of the bids and avoid an ''apples and oranges'' problem.

When the responses to the solicitation have been received, the formal selection process can begin. Vendor proposals commonly fall into three categories: those that are simply not responsive to the organization's needs, those that are responsive but are ''out of line'' with the others in terms of price, and then a middle ground from which the real choice will be made. The most important issue is whether the proposed hardware system will meet the needs of the user organization. Price is also impor-

tant, but it may not be the overriding factor. As in any business decision, both tangible and intangible factors should be considered.

Many user organizations retain consultants to help them in the bid process and to help evaluate the responses. The consultants can provide expertise relating to new products and new technologies. Having the request for proposal prepared by an outside firm may add stature to the organization's solicitation and may protect management from vendors' high-pressure sales tactics. On the other hand, the consultants' experience and reputation should be investigated. Because of familiarity, consultants may be biased toward certain types of equipment and certain manufacturers; they may therefore overlook the qualities of alternative products. Furthermore, biases sometimes result from a lack of complete independence; cases arise in which consultants (and even large consulting firms) have hidden relationships with dealers or manufacturers. At some time in the future, licensing of computer consultants may protect the public from such abuses, but at present, the integrity of consultants is a matter of individual reputation.

FIGURE 14.3   Logical computer hardware configuration.

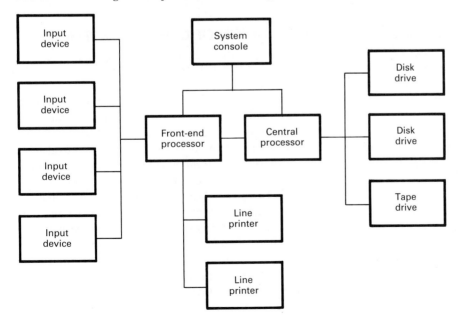

FIGURE 14.4 **Physical computer hardware configuration. Layout of computer room.**

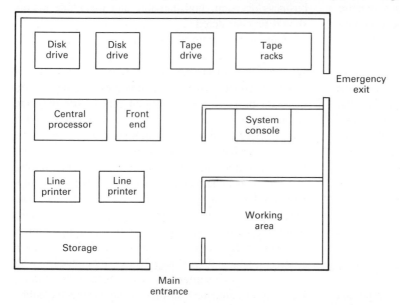

Hardware Configuration

The hardware configuration deals with the way in which the various devices are connected to one another and with their physical placement within the user organization's facilities. The interrelationships among the devices is described by the logical hardware configuration. It provides a ''map'' of the hardware system to help the technicians install the connecting wiring. Block diagrams are often used to depict the logical hardware configuration, and an example is shown in Figure 14.3. This example illustrates a large mainframe computer supported by a front-end processor handling input and output and acting as a peripheral interface.

The physical placement of devices in the computer room and elsewhere is described by the physical hardware configuration. The design of computer rooms must consider lighting requirements, location of power supplies, climate control facilities, electrical outlets, storage facilities, and other equipment. It must also consider operator traffic patterns, access to work areas, and location of emergency exits. An example of a computer-room layout is shown in Figure 14.4. It is for the computer system referred to in Figure 14.3; input terminals are assumed to be in another area.

Physical hardware configurations may also show the layout of devices in end-user work areas. Such plans are important if local area networks are to be installed and may show the location of outlets for electrical, telephone, and coaxial cable facilities.

ACQUISITION OF COMPUTER SOFTWARE

Systems and End-User Software

A discussion of the acquisition of computer software must consider the three types of software: systems software, end-user software, and applications software. Until recently, systems software was normally provided by the hardware manufacturer and was ''bundled'' into the price of the hardware. But increasingly, systems software is being priced separately and is being offered for sale by independent software houses. The main selection criteria are effectiveness in supporting the operation of applications programs, efficiency of operation, and cost. Efficiency is a major consideration, and the throughput of a computer can be affected dramatically by the efficiency of the operating system.

Most end-user software is acquired from independent

software houses. The procurement of such packages has much in common with the procurement of computer hardware, already discussed. Performance, ease of use, good documentation, compatibility with existing hardware, and cost are the principal selection criteria. Technical journals often present in-depth comparisons of competing end-user packages, and these comparisons can help prospective buyers.

Although most people speak of ''buying'' systems software and end-user packages, such software is usually acquired under a license agreement. Licenses, which require users to pay either a one-time or an ongoing fee, give users the right to operate the software. Typically they commit the supplier to correct and, in some cases, upgrade the software when needed. But licenses withhold many of the privileges of outright ownership. In particular, license terms usually prohibit the user from making copies of the software—although *site licenses* may be available that permit copying for use at a specified location. Frequently software firms also incorporate controls in their products in an attempt to frustrate would-be pirates. Although software piracy is widespread, some software firms have a reputation for taking prompt legal action against violators.

Applications Software

Applications software can be acquired ''off the shelf'' in the form of canned packages, or it can be developed to users' individual specifications. The main advantages of canned programs are

- They are fully operational and usually are fully ''debugged.''
- They can be demonstrated to the users before a purchase commitment is made.
- They can be implemented immediately.
- They usually are well documented.
- They are substantially cheaper than custom programs.

On the other hand, these advantages must be set against the disadvantages of canned programs, primarily in terms of flexibility. Canned software is targeted at a hypothetical set of general requirements, and every user is therefore forced into the same ''mold.'' Some degree of flexibility is normally provided—such as the choice

of account numbers and names in a chart of accounts. But flexibility to accommodate alternative screen forms or report layouts may be more limited. What compromises must be made to fit the mold will depend on individual circumstances. But the pressure to adapt to canned programs, particularly in the accounting area in which so many programs are available, is nevertheless strong.

Custom software obviously can be designed to fit virtually any set of individual requirements and can reflect any degree of personal or corporate idiosyncrasy. On the other hand, the disadvantages are

- High cost
- Long development lead time
- Risk that it will never work correctly
- Risk that it will never be adequately documented
- Risk that ongoing support will be unavailable

Good software is not written from one day to the next; the average applications programmer produces fewer than 20 lines of usable code per day. It requires careful design, effective coding, meticulous testing, and good documentation. The lead times for software development are long, and the cost is high. The cost of custom software is many times greater than it is for canned software. Moreover, development lead times are usually longer, and costs are higher than initial estimates, whether or not the additional costs are passed on to the buyer.

Custom software can be developed by in-house programmers or can be contracted out to software houses. Large organizations normally have a systems group, including applications programmers, who are responsible for new software development as well as maintenance programming. But smaller organizations may be unable to bear the overhead costs of a systems group and must turn to outside vendors. If software development is contracted to a small software house—and most software houses are small—the user faces the risk that the job may never be completed. The software industry is notoriously unstable, and the ''half-life'' of the smallest software houses is less than one year; the vendor may go out of business before the software is delivered. On the other hand, the prices charged by larger firms, which can offer stability and commitment, may be even higher. When code generators are in more common use, prices may come down. But at the moment, custom software is often too expensive an option for all but relatively large systems.

The procurement of applications software requires a set of specifications, including detailed task descriptions, and also a set of conditions to which the software house will commit itself. These conditions pertain to the development, testing, documentation, and installation of the software and to the provision of ongoing support after implementation has been completed. Problems with the software may not become apparent for some time after installation, and users need to have someone to turn to when problems do arise.

PERSONNEL IN COMPUTERIZED INFORMATION SYSTEMS

Small computer systems are sometimes installed in one-person businesses and are operated by the same individual who performs every other functional role. Also, an increasing number of accountants, managers, and other professional people are using terminals or personal computers. In small businesses, computers may be operated by bookkeepers or secretaries whose main function lies elsewhere. But as organizations of increasing sizes are considered, we find more formal functional groups emerging, until finally the fully fledged information-processing department, information services department, or information center, takes shape. The older term "data-processing department" is now falling into disuse as the responsibilities of this group become broader and more comprehensive. Whereas the data-processing department was responsible for the narrow function of data processing, the information center is responsible for the total information function within the organization.

The information function, whether or not it is organizationally separated from other functional roles in the organization, is as specialized as are the legal or accounting functions. The information profession has its own associations, its own professional designations, and a growing awareness of its identity and place in contemporary society. And over time, as user needs develop and technology advances, the role of these professionals is being redefined. Their role is changing from that of

narrowly defined data processors to that of information providers in a broader context of end-user computing, decision support, administrative support, and consulting.

Various types of skills comprise the information function, and it will be of interest to examine what kinds of people are involved and what they do. The following discussion is presented from the viewpoint of the large information services department because there the various roles are most clearly defined. In smaller organizations, some of the activities may be shared or not carried out at all.

The Information Services Department

The large information services department is headed by a manager usually referred to as the head of information services, head of data processing, or—where out-of-date titles persist—head of EDP. The precise title somewhat reflects the thinking of top management and others regarding the scope of the information function in the organization. This individual typically reports to a vice-president with the responsibilities of a chief information officer. The head of information services occupies a staff relationship to the rest of the organization, but exercises line authority within the department itself. The head of information services is often a member of an information services, or data-processing, steering committee that oversees all information-processing, decision support, and related activities in the organization.

Two main groups report to the head of information services. These two groups, which should be separated for internal control reasons, are the systems group and the operations group (Figure 14.5). Other groups or individual positions are included as needed.

The Systems Group

The systems group is responsible for systems development, including the enhancement and replacement of major computer hardware. It handles the design, programming, testing, and documentation of applications software. Liaison with user groups and consulting services may also be provided. The systems group typically is staffed by systems analysts, computer special-

FIGURE 14.5   Organization chart for an information services department.

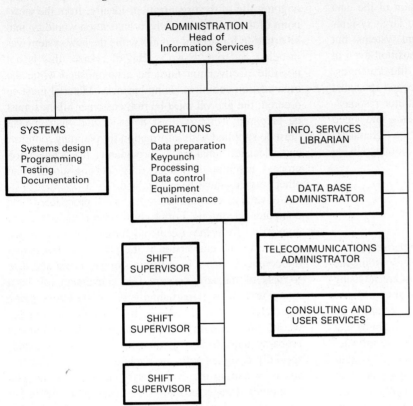

ists, programmers, and documentation specialists. It may be structured into teams responsible for systems analysis, new program development, maintenance programming, documentation, and user services.

The Operations Group

The operations group is responsible for preparing input, operating the computer, delivering output, and exercising applicable controls. The group has overall responsibility for maintaining the computer hardware, with appropriate support from outside service and maintenance vendors. Personnel staffing in the operations group typically include data entry clerks, computer operators, technicians, and input–output control personnel. The operations group may be structured on these functional roles; alternatively, if the department works more

than one shift, it may be structured into teams responsible for operations throughout each shift.

In traditional batch-processing operations, the information services librarian serves as the custodian of disk packs, floppy diskettes, tapes, and documentation relating to programs and data. These materials are released to computer operators and other authorized persons as needed. Sometimes the library function—consisting of one or more individuals as appropriate—is attached to the operations group, but commonly it is given separate status in the department.

The data base administrator, supported by a small specialist staff, is responsible for overseeing the maintenance and security of the data base and monitoring the storage and retrieval of data. An additional responsibility may be to assist in meeting new user needs for data storage and retrieval as they arise. The data base administrator typically oversees and advises on the use of query languages by accountants, managers, and others in decision support activities. The position of the data base administrator is almost essential to large systems involving complex data base management systems, but there may be a need for an equivalent position even in smaller systems based on conventional file structures. Some organizations are now adding a second specialist position of telecommunications administrator responsible for the growing volume of audio, data, and video messages transmitted over communications channels, both within the organization and to and from the outside world.

Consulting Services

Increasingly, information services departments are providing consulting services to end users within the organization. In-house consulting groups are advising users on the acquisition and use of personal computers. In some large organizations, specialists in certain types of software are available to demonstrate programs and to help in training and troubleshooting after the software has been acquired. Technicians may be retained to repair personal computers, and inventories of spare parts or occasionally needed peripherals may be maintained. Libraries of software packages are also sometimes kept for loan to personnel throughout the organization.

As the need for professional computer operators and programmers declines, the strength of information services departments is being maintained by increases in user services.

CONVERSION

The Conversion Process

Conversion is the process in which the burden of providing information-processing services to the organization passes from the old information system to the new one. "Live" production operation of the new system begins, and the old system is retired. Conversion is sometimes referred to as *cutover*. The main objective of conversion is to bring the new system to the point of full

production operation while minimizing disruption of the ongoing life of the organization. Ideally, from the viewpoint of the project team, the organization would go into hibernation for several months while the new system was installed and put to work. But of course, this is not possible. Conversion must be accomplished while the organization continues doing business: Material must be ordered; the payroll must be run; customer billings must be prepared; vendors must be paid; and management must be supplied with information for planning, control, and decision making. Throughout the conversion process, essential data processing, decision support, and other services must be maintained.

Conversion extends to forms, files, procedures, and computer operations. Forms conversion is the process of converting from the use of old forms to the use of the new ones. File conversion is the process of translating the company's data base to the storage media and data formats of the new system. File conversion can be a major undertaking, particularly if the system is being automated for the first time. In that case, keying the whole data base into a machine-readable medium is probably unavoidable. If the old system is automated, specially designed software may be obtained to perform any reformatting that is necessary and to write the data to another storage medium. One of the problems in file conversion is that the data base will not "stand still" during the process; business goes on and the file content continues to be changed. Often it is necessary to load the files in stages, entering the less volatile material first, and then updating them to add more volatile data so that the files are current at the time that live operation commences.

Although the new system is expected to be thoroughly tested by the time that live operation begins, the old and new systems should be operated in parallel for some period of time. The objective of parallel operation is to provide additional assurance that the new system works correctly and reliably under actual operating conditions. Output from the old and new systems should be compared to make sure that ostensibly equivalent data are in fact the same; for example, the two sets of invoices produced by the two billing systems should be compared to verify that they do contain the same data. The period of parallel operation should extend over at least two cycles of the principal applications: two billing periods, two pay periods, and so forth. Two months is a commonly adopted period in practical cases. Parallel operation places a considerable burden on the organization to handle the work load, and so temporary help may have to be hired during this period. On the other hand, simply to turn the old system off on a Friday and to turn on the new one Monday is to invite major disaster as a result of unforeseen problems.

When the new information system has multiple applications, "phased conversion," in which one application is converted at a time, offers distinct advantages. The process is illustrated by a Gantt chart in Figure 14.6. Phased conversion minimizes the additional work load by spreading it over a longer period. If a problem arises with one of the applications, attention can be concentrated on solving it before converting another application. Phased conversion works well when the applications are essentially independent of one another, or when there is a mutual flow of information in only one direction. But difficulties can be encountered in integrated systems because of more complex sharing and movement of data among the various applications. In highly integrated systems the problems of interfacing applications—some of which are on the new system while others are still on the old one—may be insurmountable. Simultaneous conversion of two or more applications may be the only available course of action.

Conversion Headaches

System conversion is an anxious time for any organization and any project team. The demands on people's time and energy are at a premium, and many individuals are probably working long hours and are subject to unusual stresses. Problems and delays are commonplace and naturally cause frustration. Tempers are short, and scapegoats may be sought to take the blame for the things that have gone wrong. The scenario is familiar to anyone who has lived through the final stages of systems development.

The problems of conversion are real, and they are likely to occur to some degree in even the best-managed projects. But they can be minimized by careful attention to details at the systems analysis and design stages. Most problems—particularly those that attract wide attention—result from errors, omissions, or inconsistencies in the systems design. Difficulties can also be minimized

FIGURE 14.6 Phased conversion. One application is converted at a time. In this case each new application is run in parallel with its old counterpart for two months.

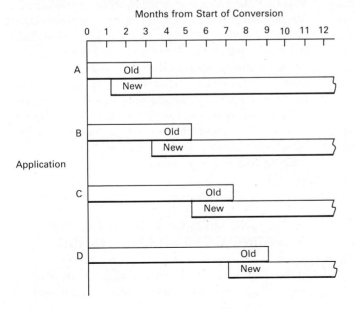

by careful planning of the conversion process itself. As already noted, phased conversion, when feasible, helps keep potential problems within manageable proportions. But whether or not it can be used, conversion must be planned so that all system components—hardware, software, forms, documentation, trained people, and data— are available as and when they are needed. Many conversions have been held up because of missing supplies or documentation or because file conversion took longer than anticipated.

Fortunately, the potential difficulties are now well recognized, and most systems professionals have acquired valuable experience regarding the implementation process and its pitfalls. As they become more experienced, the time should come when most system conversions proceed with substantially fewer headaches than in the past. Considerable progress in this direction has already been made.

POSTIMPLEMENTATION REVIEW

After system conversion has been completed and the new system is operating ''live,'' it is appropriate to carry out a postimplementation review. The objective of the review is to evaluate the development project to see what can be learned from it and to evaluate the new system. Some aspects of the review can commence as soon as conversion is complete, or even during the conversion process itself, but the bulk of the work is best started after the immediate pressures have abated and life in the organization has returned to normal.

As with any other lengthy and expensive project, the systems development project should be reviewed to establish what went right and what went wrong. By the time that the system has gone into operation, the consequences of many of the design decisions will have become apparent, and their wisdom can be evaluated. Personnel can be evaluated also, to identify those who performed well and those who did less well. Similarly, if an outside consulting firm or accounting firm was involved, its contribution can be evaluated as a basis for recommending the firm to other organizations that need help in the systems area.

Expenditures made during the systems project should

be compared with the budget figures. One purpose of the comparisons is to evaluate the effectiveness of cost control; another is to improve the cost estimates made in future systems projects. The costs of operating the new system should be evaluated too, to determine whether they are in line with the projections made at the time of systems analysis and design. If the operating costs are substantially higher than the original projections, the validity of major design decisions may be in question. For example, it may have been decided to acquire an in-house computer because the operating costs were believed to be lower than the costs of an outside service bureau. With the benefit of hindsight a different decision might have been made.

A major part of the review should be addressed to the performance of the new system. A study should be made to determine whether the system is doing the job expected of it and whether it is helping the people who depend on it. The actual capabilities of the system should be compared with the statement of objectives and the technical specifications prepared earlier. Variances from the specifications should be noted and evaluated; they may be minor and of no real consequence, or they may be so serious as to undermine the usefulness of the system.

The postimplementation review should also seek to determine whether the system objectives changed over the life of the project. In a highly volatile environment, it is possible that the objectives changed so dramatically that the system is irrelevant by the time it is installed, and major revisions may be necessary. Even in less extreme situations, some modifications may be called for to maintain the system's effectiveness. The need for system maintenance is ongoing, and to this extent, the postimplementation review lasts indefinitely. Some mechanism must be provided by the organization to gather information about changing conditions and needs that point the way to further modification of the system.

THE ECONOMICS OF ACQUIRING AND OPERATING COMPUTERIZED SYSTEMS

The acquisition, maintenance, and operation of computerized systems incur various costs. A useful way of classifying these costs is as the initial costs of acquisition and implementation and the ongoing costs of maintenance and operation. Ongoing costs can be divided further into fixed and variable components as a basis for studying their behavior over a range of processing volume, or *throughput*.

Initial Costs

Initial costs are associated with systems implementation. The principal costs in this category—aside from the indirect ones associated with systems analysis and design and with organizational changes—correspond to major steps in implementation: hardware and software acquisition, site preparation, installation, testing, training, and conversion.

Hardware aquisition costs include the labor costs expended during vendor and equipment selection and the net cost of the equipment itself. The net equipment cost is the invoice cost plus incidentals—freight charges, insurance, and sales tax—and less applicable discounts, trade-in allowances, and other offsets such as the investment tax credit. Software acquisition costs may be for the purchase of canned packages or the development of custom software; in the latter situation, an initial payment may have to be made at the time the contract is signed, and progress payments may have to be made during the development work. Software costs can be expected to be between 20 percent and 200 percent of the cost of the hardware, and even higher percentages are not uncommon.

Site-preparation costs include costs of any necessary construction or remodeling, installation of climate-control equipment, and installation of cables for power and data transmission. The costs of installing hardware and software are mostly labor costs, but when the installation is done by suppliers, only a part of these costs may be passed on to the user organization. Testing costs also will probably be split between vendors and the organization; suppliers should test individual components of the system, but they are not normally in a position to test the whole system. The organization cannot rely on suppliers to conduct all the necessary testing. Similarly, suppliers may provide some "free" training for the organization's employees, but a large portion of these costs is likely to be born by the organization. Training is not only an initial cost but extends over the life of the system because of employee turnover and transfers.

System conversion costs include the costs of procuring new forms and supplies but consist largely of labor costs. Conversion costs may extend over an appreciable period of time, and its associated costs are difficult to estimate reliably; much depends on how smoothly the work proceeds. Abnormal labor demands are not uncommon, and as already noted temporary help may be needed to handle the work load.

It is tempting to add one more cost item, which could be labeled *surprises*. There are numerous instances of costs that do not come to light until during or after systems implementation. Sometimes a major redesign is found to be necessary; in other cases, additional hardware or software must be bought to make the system work. The costs may vary from what might be considered "normal contingencies" all the way to amounts that are comparable with or are more than the original estimates for the complete system. In many cases, the unanticipated costs result from cutting corners at the planning stages. The greater the care taken in the design of information systems, the smaller the chance will be of encountering expensive surprises at the implementation stage.

In principle, the initial costs should be capitalized and amortized over the useful life of the system. But in practice, some of the cost items, particularly labor costs, may be absorbed into current expenses. It may prove difficult, for instance, to distribute the labor costs of salaried personnel between the new system development and their other responsibilities. Part of the system's initial costs may be financed by borrowing. Similarly, the costs of hardware and software acquisition may be converted into ongoing lease costs. Interest expense on the outstanding debt represents an additional ongoing cost. Interest and lease costs and software license fees must be added to the cost of maintaining and operating the system.

Ongoing Costs

Aside from interest expense, lease costs, and license fees, the principal ongoing costs are associated with the system's maintenance and operation. Maintenance includes both routine preventive maintenance and emergency repairs on the computer hardware. It can be provided by in-house technicians, the hardware manufacturer, or a third party. In either of the two latter cases, maintenance can be paid for on a "time-and-materials" basis, or it can be covered by a service contract. Service contracts provide maintenance services for a monthly fee. Such contracts ordinarily cover both parts and labor, but otherwise the extent of the service can vary according to the terms (and cost) of the agreement.

A minimal level of coverage provides repairs to equipment transported to the service vendor's facility. A high level of coverage provides for the vendor's technicians to be on site, 24 hours per day, seven days per week, ready to respond to any eventuality. Between these extremes lies a popular type of on-site service referred to as "normal business hours" coverage. For a monthly fee equal to about 1 percent of the list price of the hardware, technicians from a service depot provide regular scheduled maintenance and respond to emergency calls at the user's site, as needed. The response to emergency repair calls depends on the distance from the service depot and on the technicians' current work load; it may vary from less than 2 hours to several days. Until the technicians arrive and correct the problem—which may mean obtaining a spare part, such as a disk drive, from the nearest spares inventory—the user organization may be without information-processing facilities. If uninterrupted processing is essential to the organization, on-site technician support must be provided, and duplicate processing facilities may also be needed.

Operating costs pertain to utilities, supplies, communications, and labor. Utility costs cover the electric power needed to run the computer equipment and also the power consumed by climate-control equipment installed in the computer room. Supplies costs cover paper stock, printed forms, printer ribbons, replaceable storage media (reels of tape, floppy diskettes, disk cartridges, and so on), and any incidental items. Communications costs include the costs of telephone lines or other communications media. The cost of dial-up or leased telephone lines may be appreciable, but the costs of operating and maintaining other media, such as microwave or satellite links may be much higher.

Labor costs usually represent the largest component of operating costs. They include the wages and salaries of all personnel directly or indirectly involved in operating the system: data entry clerks, computer operators, technicians, systems analysts, programmers, and information-processing specialists.

Another, potentially high-cost item pertains to security and controls. Security and control measures range from procedures for backing up files, to physical and electronic measures controlling access to the computer, to separation of organizational responsibilities. The cost of these measures must not be overlooked, but it is difficult to distinguish between the portion of these costs that should be related to the computer system from the remainder for more general internal-control concerns throughout the organization. Substantial costs are incurred to provide control measures even in a manual information system.

Cost Behavior

The behavior of system-related costs to changes in operating volume, or throughput, can be understood by examining the behavior of individual cost items. Individual items may be fixed costs, purely variable costs, or semivariable costs (which include both a fixed and a variable component). The following table shows such an analysis:

Cost item	Fixed	Variable
Amortization of initial costs	All	
Maintenance costs	Mostly	
Utilities	Mostly	
Supplies		All
Communications	Some	Some
Labor	Mostly	
Security and controls	Mostly	

Labor costs in the systems area are mainly discretionary fixed costs, because most of the personnel are salaried. The shortage of information-processing personnel has forced organizations to treat their computer operators, programmers, and other systems specialists as a long-term human resource. Such personnel cannot easily be rehired, and so they are usually retained even during

SYSTEMS IMPLEMENTATION **383**

slack periods. Accordingly, the variability normally associated with labor costs is lost.

The only cost item with strong variability is the supplies cost. But this is ordinarily a very small component compared with the total. The overall behavior of systems costs with respect to throughput is dominated to a great degree by the fixed costs (Figure 14.7). A good approximation to overall cost behavior is obtained by neglecting the variable component entirely. The only changes are likely to result from system enhancement, which increases the level of fixed costs.

Charging Users for Information Services

The information-processing facilities are resources used by various user departments. If these departments are responsibility centers, some form of charge-back or transfer-pricing arrangement may be desirable to bill users for the services provided. Charge-back arrangements seek to allocate the costs equitably among users and also place a dollar value on the services, which may help motivate more efficient utilization. Furthermore, the charges generate ''revenue'' for the information services department, which can then be evaluated as either a profit center or—perhaps more appropriately— a break-even center.

Charges for systems work—systems analysis, programming, and consulting—are relatively easy. A rate per hour can be established for each labor grade, permitting user departments to be charged for the time spent in providing support services to those departments. The rate should be based on the average full-cost labor rate of the particular class of employees.

There are greater difficulties in charging for use of centralized processing facilities. The ideal way to bill users for computer use would be to measure the usage and multiply the result by an appropriate unit cost. Thus, if a given department incurred 1,000 units of usage and if the unit cost were $10.00 per unit, that department would be charged 1,000 × $10.00 = $10,000 for the period. Unfortunately, such an ideal is undermined by two important factors:

- Computers are complex resources whose utilization is not effectively described by a single measure. Processor time, terminal connect time, main-memory demands, input–output volume, and external storage capacity all are defensible measures of usage, but they are not generally proportional to one another.
- Computer costs are mainly fixed, and so a representative unit cost is difficult to determine. Identifying a billing rate presents a similar problem to determining a prescribed application rate for fixed overhead.

FIGURE 14.7   Behavior of information system costs with respect to throughput.

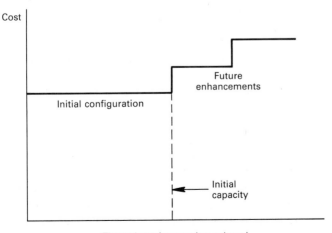

If the charge-back arrangement is to be equitable, the various determinants of computer usage will have to be billed separately, and this will result in a complicated billing formula. Processor time, main-memory capacity, secondary (and tertiary) storage capacity, and input–output volume must be billed separately. Whether they can be billed on the basis of a cost per unit of usage depends greatly on the ability to forecast accurately both total costs and total usage.

If total usage cannot be estimated reliably, billings should be based on a share of estimated fixed costs. In other words, departments would share the cost of the installed capacity, regardless of how much each one actually used the facilities. Deciding what share each should bear is another problem. One solution is to base the shares on estimates of usage that are submitted by each department, with a premium charge levied on departments that exceed their estimates. To illustrate, suppose that three user departments submitted estimates of processor time:

Department	Processor Time (hours)	Fraction of Total
A	1,000	1/3
B	500	1/6
C	1,500	1/2
Total	3,000	

If the total cost of "processing" (as distinct from storage, input, output, and so on) were determined to be $30,000 per year, then Department A would be charged $10,000, Department B, $5,000, and Department C, $15,000 for processing. Similar calculations would be made for storage capacity and other applicable measures of total resource consumption. The premium charge would "keep departments honest" in their estimates. For example, if Department B (which initially benefits from its low estimate) actually used 1,000 hours of processor time, it might be charged a premium of $12 per hour of usage over and above its estimate of 500 hours. The total premium would be $(1,000 - 500) \times \$12 = \$6,000$, and its total bill would be $11,000. This figure is intentionally greater than the $8,571 that the department would have had to pay if it had submitted an original estimate of 1,000 hours.

Cost Effectiveness of Computerized Systems

Operating and other system-related costs are usually evaluated during the postimplementation review. At that time, the level of these costs may be compared with estimates made during the design stage, and frequently, the actual costs are found to be higher than the estimates. Also, after a computerized system has been in operation for some time, costs are often found to be still higher. Because variable costs are considered to be small or insignificant, these increases cannot be attributed solely to increases of throughput. Sometimes the increase in costs can be traced to specific enhancements that have been requested by users, but in many cases the cost growth just seems to have a momentum of its own. And unless positive steps are taken to contain the increases, such costs are likely to continue rising.

The most productive areas in which to seek cost reductions include

- Elimination or consolidation of functions
- Downgrade of facilities
- Vigilance in utilization of secondary storage capacity
- Careful evaluation of enhancement proposals
- Vigilance in preventing abuse of facilities

User requirements change over time, and so the system must be flexible to adapt to changing realities. System functions that are used less than they were earlier, or less than was anticipated at the design stage, should be eliminated or combined with other functions. Although the corresponding development costs cannot be recovered, cost reductions may be possible through reduced lease costs and license fees, and cash inflows may be generated through the disposal of surplus equipment. Similarly, if usage has declined or anticipated growth in usage has not been realized, processor devices and/or peripheral devices can be retired or traded for less expensive ones. Similarly, staffing levels can possibly be reduced.

A major source of inefficiency often lies in the utilization of on-line storage devices. Most systems are periodically enhanced by the acquisition of additional disk storage capacity. Sometimes the enhancement is justified by legitimate increases in demand for file space. On the other hand, an apparent increase in demand may simply reflect lack of vigilance in purging "dead" files or transferring little-used programs and data from relatively expensive on-line storage to cheaper media. Material should not be retained in secondary storage just because it "might be useful." The number and size of data files tend to grow indefinitely unless there is an established policy of capacity management. Record retention policies should be reviewed to determine whether retention periods for certain classes of data can be reduced. And specific persons should be assigned the responsibility of enforcing the policies.

Proposed system enhancements of any kind should be scrutinized to determine whether the need is genuine. Demands for additional terminals or personal computers may be met by reassigning underutilized existing units instead of purchasing new ones. Processing turnaround can possibly be improved by running low-priority jobs at night, thereby reducing peak demand during the day.

Abuse of resources can take a number of forms. One form is running jobs on the computer that could easily and more efficiently be done by hand, or running jobs more times than is necessary. Adjustment of charge-back rates may help discourage such abuse. Another form is using computer facilities for unauthorized purposes. Managament should make it clear that no unauthorized use will be tolerated and that firm disciplinary action will result from violation of the policy.

SUMMARY

Implementation, the third major phase of information systems development, brings the systems development project to completion. The long process of planning is finally over as the components of the new system are assembled and put to work. Systems implementation typically includes the acquisition, installation, and testing of computer hardware and software, followed by conversion, in which the new information system starts to run "live." Conversion can cause headaches, but most of the problems can be avoided by careful planning. The computer hardware may be acquired on the basis of competitive bids by a number of vendors. Software may be acquired in the form of canned packages or may have to be developed from the ground up. In the latter case the cost is likely to be much higher, and there are significant risks.

System testing is a vital step and should be based on an established test plan covering the full range of anticipated system operations. The submission of invalid, erroneous, and unauthorized transactions should be part of the test plan to verify the system's ability to react accordingly.

The implementation of new systems often necessitates organizational changes. New employees may need to be hired, and existing employees whose services are no longer required may need to be transferred or laid off. Departmental boundaries may be altered, and managers' responsibilities may increase or decrease accordingly. In the information services area, new positions are being opened up as a result of technological advances and the need for individuals with special skills and expertise. In particular, the data base administrator and telecommunications administrator occupy key positions in the modern organization.

The culmination of the implementation phase is conversion from the operation of the old system to the operation of the new one. Essential processing must continue during the systems transition. Conversion can be a time of considerable frustration for the people involved, but the number and severity of the headaches encountered can be minimized by careful planning. A phased conversion of applications and the provision for parallel operation until the satisfactory operation of each new application is demonstrated help ensure a smooth transition to the new system.

The systems development project concludes with the postimplementation review. The review provides an opportunity to reflect on the success of the project, to evaluate the performance of the people involved, and to evaluate the effectiveness and efficiency of the information system that has been produced. The results of the postimplementation review are of immediate interest and also serve as a point of departure in future systems projects.

The new system's performance and economy are of particular interest in the postimplementation review and throughout the life of the system. Many information systems fail to meet the cost estimates set during the design phase, but most systems experience increases of cost after implementation. Such cost increases are worrisome to management and should be investigated to determine their causes. Once the causes have been identified, steps can be taken to eliminate them or reduce their effect.

BIBLIOGRAPHY

Anderson, Anker V. *Budgeting for Data Processing.* New York: National Association of Accountants, 1983.

Cerullo, M. J. "Information Systems Success Factors." *Journal of Systems Management*, December 1980, pp. 10–11.

Giovinazzo, Vincent J., and John F. Nash. "Selecting Accounting Software Packages." *CPA Journal*, October 1982, pp. 40–45.

"How to Buy Enough Computers." *Business Week*, December 3, 1980, pp, 83–84.

Joslin, Edward O. *Computer Selection: Augmented Edition.* New York: Technology Press, 1977.

Kleinberger, Herbert, J. "Ten Stumbling Blocks to Successful Software Package Installations." *Price Waterhouse Review*, no. 1, 1987, pp. 48–51.

Kloek, Christopher D. "Searching Out Business Computer Alternatives." *Small Business Computers Magazine*, March 1980, pp. 20–23.

Krass, Peter. "The Computer Room: Putting the Pieces Together." *Datamation*, July 15, 1987, pp. 54–63.

"Missing Computer Software." *Business Week*, September 1, 1980, pp. 45–46.

Morris, Michael F., and Paul F. Roth. "Focus on EDP Cost Effectiveness." *Management Focus.* Peat, Marwick, Mitchell & Co., January–February 1981, pp. 8–31.

Muggridge, J. L. "An Accountant's Guide to Computers." *The Accountant's Magazine*, March 1980, pp. 114–116.

Nash, John F., and Vincent J. Giovinazzo. "Selecting Computer Hardware." *CPA Journal*, September 1982, pp. 57–63.

Polston, Morris V. "Staffing Your 24-Hour Computer Center." *Datamation*, July 15, 1987, pp. 75–76.

Price Waterhouse. *Managing Microcomputers*, New York: National Association of Accountants, 1984.

Roxburg, K. "Feasibility Studies—Advice for First-Time Computer Users." *The Accountant's Magazine*, May 1980, pp. 204–206.

Scannell, T. "Invasion of the Mainframe Snatchers: Starring Mini and Superminis." *ComputerWorld*, July 27, 1981 (special report), pp. 1–26.

Stamps, David. "A New Climate for Leasing." *Datamation*, December 1, 1986, pp. 85–88.

"Telecommunications: Everybody's Favorite Growth Business." *Business Week*, October 11, 1982, pp. 60–70.

Toong Hoo-min D., and Amar Gupta. "Personal Computers." *Scientific American*, December 1982, pp. 86–107.

DISCUSSION QUESTIONS AND PROBLEMS

1. Define and discuss the following terms:

- Canned programs
- Conversion
- Custom software
- Data base administrator
- Discretionary cost
- Downtime
- Information services librarian
- Fixed-cost component
- Hardware key
- Information services department
- Initial costs
- Ongoing costs
- Logical hardware configuration
- Phased conversion
- Physical hardware configuration
- Plug-compatible equipment
- Service contract
- Shakedown
- Site preparation
- Software transportability
- Speed degradation
- Systems group
- Telecommunications administrator
- Throughput
- Variable-cost component
- User services

2. List the principal concerns of each of the following types of organization in selecting (i) computer hardware and (ii) applications software for the implementation of an automated business information system:

a. A small retail store converting from a manual system
b. A medium-sized accounting firm doing extensive client write-up work
c. A large aerospace company upgrading its network computer system
d. A large state bank with a centralized data base system
e. A presidential campaign national headquarters
f. A Methodist church with 1,500 members

3. You are about to acquire a departmental (mini-) computer for your local insurance agency and had planned to deal directly with an internationally recognized manufacturer of business machines. However, a friend at the Rotary Club suggests that you should issue a request for proposal and open the procurement to competitive bids.

Required

What are the advantages and disadvantages of sole-source procurement versus a competitive-bid process for the type of system envisaged?

4. As a systems consultant, you have been retained to prepare a vendor questionnaire to be sent to several manufacturers who are submitting bids on a large computer system. List the types of questions that should be included in the questionnaire.

5. Pacific Company operates a computerized information system providing the applications of purchasing, inventory control, and order processing. An analysis of data-processing costs over a 12-month period has produced the following data:

Cost Item	Average Monthly Cost
Amortization of initial costs	$ 8,000
Service and maintenance	2,500
Utilities	400
Labor	12,000
Supplies	300

Management has now decided to add payroll and billing to the system, which will increase throughput by 40 percent.

Required

a. Estimate the average monthly cost of the data-processing function, assuming that labor is a purely variable cost item.
b. Some time after the new applications have been implemented, an extended strike takes place at Pacific's plant. As a result, data-processing throughput is reduced to 90 percent of its original level. Determine the monthly cost of the system, assuming that the labor force is maintained at the level to which it had been built up in (a).
c. Determine the monthly cost, assuming the same facts as in (b), except that some employees are laid off, allowing the labor cost to decrease by 20 percent from its maximum level.

6. Consultants to Jacobs Company are designing a new computerized accounting system that will provide real-time processing in its main building and telecommunications facilities between this building and a warehouse located several miles away. A central data base is to be maintained, with a single 300 MB. hard disk drive and a tape drive for backup. Output requirements call for a 300 l.p.m. line printer and two 80 c.p.s. character printers in the main building and two similar character printers at the warehouse. An analysis of input requirements indicates that the following work stations will be needed:

Location	Department	Number of Work Stations
Main building	General accounting	5
	Accounts receivable	3
	Accounts payable	1
	Payroll	2
Warehouse	Inventory control	1
	Shipping	2
	Total	14

Required

a. Prepare a set of computer hardware specifications and a sketch of the logical hardware configuration, assuming that the requirements are met by a departmental computer with interactive terminals.

b. Repeat part (a), assuming that a network system is to be used with desktop microcomputers. Briefly justify the network topology you are recommending.

7. Baxter Corporation is preparing to solicit bids on a new computer system. A distributed processing system is planned, consisting of 16 microcomputers connected by a local area network with a bus topology. Fifteen of the microcomputers are to be equipped with 640 KB of main memory and two floppy diskette drives. Two of these machines are to be equipped with color monitors, while the others are to have monochrome monitors. The sixteenth machine, which will act as the network server, is to have 1 MB of main memory, a 10 MB hard disk drive, and a color monitor. In addition, the network is to share two 40 MB disk drives, a 6,250 i.p.s. tape drive, two 200 c.p.s. character printers, a 600 l.p.m. line printer, and a three-color flatbed plotter.

Required

a. Prepare a block diagram defining the logical hardware configuration.

b. Prepare a specification sheet similar to Figure 14.2, listing the hardware components required.

8. A schedule is being drawn up for the conversion stage of a systems development project and also for the postimplementation review. Four application subsystems are to be converted: cost estimation, raw materials inventory, payroll, and accounts receivable. There is minimal integration of the subsystems, and phased conversion would be feasible if management decided to proceed in that manner. The required tasks and the projected work load are as follows:

Task	Estimated Duration (weeks)	Level of Effort (people)
Recruitment and training	6	4
Forms procurement	6	1
File conversion	1*	4*
System testing	4*	4*
Parallel operation	8*	6*
Postimplementation review	3	3

* Per application

The tasks are to be performed in the order shown. Regardless of whether phased conversion is to be used, the postimplementation review is not to start until all applications have been fully converted and are fully operational.

The total work load is 311 person weeks, and the minimum time necessary to complete all the tasks is 28 weeks. However, management is concerned about the peak level of effort that would be required and is trying to decide whether to adopt a phased-conversion procedure to reduce the peak effort, even though the final completion date would be delayed substantially.

Required

a. Prepare a schedule showing the level of effort required per week if the four applications were to be converted concurrently.

b. Prepare a modified schedule showing the level of effort required if a phased conversion were adopted. Assume that file conversion for the next application can commence four weeks before the expected completion of parallel operation of the current application. Compare the peak level of effort obtained with the value given in (a).

c. Construct a Gantt chart depicting the schedule developed in (b).

d. Management decides to adopt a phased-conversion approach, as described in (b). However, some unexpected problems developed while testing the second application (raw materials inventory), and it was estimated at the time that parallel operations would have to be extended to 12 weeks on that application. On the other hand, management is reluctant to delay completion of the whole project and insists that conversion of the remaining two applications begin on schedule. Determine the impact on the peak level of effort resulting from the additional time necessary to complete the implementation of the inventory subsystem.

9. The information services department of Sunshine Company consists of six people. The manager and assistant manager of the department currently do all the systems development work and supervise the other four employees. The latter group prepares the data and operates the computer.

With the expansion of the information services activities and the acquisition of a new computer, approval has been given for the addition of four new positions. At least one of the new positions must be for an additional computer operator, but the information services manager can choose the personnel to fill the other three positions.

Required

a. What types of personnel would you recommend be recruited?

b. What organizational changes would you recommend to take advantage of the department's expansion?

10. A centralized computer facility operates a charge-back system to allocate costs to user departments within the organization. The rate scale used considered four different measures of computer usage:

Connect time:	$10 per hour
CPU time:	$2 per minute
Input–output volume:	$0.10 per thousand characters
File storage:	$10/MB per month

The monthly charge is equal to the total of the four individual charges, with a contractual minimum of $350 per month.

One of the user departments, cost accounting, incurred charges over a six-month period based on the following usage:

Month	Connect Time (hours)	CPU Time (minutes)	I/O Volume*	On-line Storage (MB)
May	20	50	600	2
June	15	40	600	2
July	8	30	400	3
August	20	45	800	4
September	40	70	1,200	6
October	30	80	1,500	9

* Thousands of characters.

Required

a. Compute the charge for time-sharing services for each of the six months.

b. An outside commercial time-sharing company charges $20 per hour of connect time, regardless of the amount of CPU usage and input–output volume, with a minimum monthly charge of $500. This minimum charge includes up to 10 MB of on-line storage; for larger amounts of storage, there is a charge of $12 per megabyte. If allowed to do so by upper management, should the cost accounting department switch to the outside time-sharing company?

11. Smith and Jones Associates, a small CPA firm, currently uses a commercial service bureau to handle the data processing for its client write-up work and is paying an average of $1,800 per month. Jones is now looking into leasing a minicomputer so that all data processing can be done in house.

Typical monthly lease rates for computer hardware (assuming a 60-month straight lease) are 2.5 percent of the manufacturer's list price for the equipment. Service maintenance contracts are available for 1 percent of list price. The required applications software can be obtained under a license agreement for $200 per month, and all program revisions and enhancements are provided at no extra charge. Other costs of operating the computer are estimated to be about $150 per month.

Required

How expensive a computer can Smith and Jones Associates afford without increasing its monthly expenditure on data processing?

12. Uriel Corporation issued a request for proposal to several vendors for bids on a large superminicomputer. The system specifications included 30 on-line terminals, three printers, and both disk and tape storage. Custom software was to be developed for all accounting applications. The vendors were specifically asked to state how routine and emergency service support were to be provided. The three bids received offered the following proposals:

Bid 1

This bid was received from a well-known minicomputer firm. The central processor was one of the largest and most powerful sold by that firm. All peripherals were manufactured in house by the firm. Software was to be subcontracted to a reputable local software house, but the bidder was to retain overall responsibility for the whole system. Service and maintenance would be provided by the manufacturer's local franchised dealer.

Bid 2

This bid was received from a medium-sized firm that specializes in custom software and acts as a dealer for several computer hardware manufacturers. The proposed hardware configuration would consist of well-matched components manufactured by three different companies and include a central processor near the middle of the particular manufacturer's product line. Service support would be provided by a nationwide third-party service organization whose nearest depot was in a neighboring city.

Bid 3

This bid was received from a large computer manufacturer with an international reputation. It proposed a central processor near the lower end of its product line (in size, not in quality), together with peripherals, some of which were imported from an Asian country and sold under license. All the components would be serviced by the company's own technicians operating from a local depot. This bidder does not sell software, but a list of local software houses was attached to the proposal, with the recommendation that Uriel negotiate a separate contract with one of them.

Required

a. As a consultant to Uriel Corporation, advise the company on the strengths and weaknesses of each vendor's bid.

b. The three bids were as follows: Bid 1, $205,000; Bid 2, $185,000; and Bid 3, $230,000 (including a reasonable estimate of the software cost). Which proposal would you recommend?

13. You are a member of a study team conducting a postimplementation review at Perdurabo Associates, a large professional service company. The recently installed information system provides for the routine accounting functions and also for budgeting, decision support, and professional timekeeping. This last function is to be used for client billing, comparative performance evaluation, and practice development.

The system is based on a large departmental computer with interactive terminals located throughout the building. It is anticipated that professionals at all levels will use extensively the interactive capability in their work. Several weeks of in-house training have already been provided, and complete user documentation is available to support the interactive processing mode.

Required

List the activities you would wish to investigate as part of your review, and indicate the steps you would take to obtain the needed information.

14. Foster Corporation is implementing a new computerized information system that will support the accounting function and other information-processing needs throughout the organization. As part of the associated reorganization, a new information services department is being established. The continuing (and growing) demand for end-user computing has been recognized, and one of the functions of the new department will be to provide consulting services to in-house users. However, all other information-processing services are to be centralized in the interests of economy of scale and the ability to offer adequate processing "horsepower" to handle the largest jobs. Both batch and interactive computing services will be provided, and a large centralized data base will be established. Telecommunications services will be provided for integrated voice, data, and facsimile transmission. Some new systems work and maintenance programming will be performed.

Required

a. Draw an organization chart for the new information services department.
b. Briefly describe the role of the various organizational units in the department.
c. Indicate the level to which the head of the department should report. What other managers would probably report to the same level?

15. At a meeting of the information-processing steering committee, the chairman questioned the costs of the information-processing function in the company. Over the five years since the present system was installed, costs have nearly tripled, although user requirements and demand have increased by no more than 50 percent. The effects of inflation on labor costs, repairs and maintenance, and utilities have been high, but not nearly high enough to explain the large increase in costs.

During the ensuing discussion, several suggestions were made, but nobody seemed able to pinpoint the real cause of the problem. It was decided, therefore, to conduct a study to make recommendations for dealing with the problem.

Two weeks later, the study team held its first meeting.

The team consisted of the assistant controller, the assistant director of internal auditing, the assistant head of information processing, and two members of the company's external auditors. The team was charged with investigating the problem and making an interim report within 45 days.

Some initial fact finding by the study team discovered the following:

Repairs and maintenance, which had initially been handled by an external firm, were now performed by in-house technicians. The size of the information-processing department has increased substantially in recent years. The number of computer operators has increased from 8 to 13 and the number of programmers from 5 to 8. A data base administrator was also hired 18 months ago. Despite the claim that user demand had increased by less than 10 percent per year, on-line monitoring devices indicated a rate of increase of over 20 percent. The number of interactive terminals increased from 35 to 60 over the five-year period. Secondary storage capacity increased from 300 MB to 750 MB. Response time at the on-line terminals rose from an average of one second to more than four seconds.

Required

You are the assistant director of internal audit. List questions to which you would like to seek answers over the next few days of the study.

PART FOUR

CONTROL OF ACCOUNTING INFORMATION SYSTEMS

Part Four discusses the important subject of control and audit of accounting information systems. Chapter 15 introduces the basic concepts of internal control and reviews the major professional and legal pronouncements that have molded the internal control system as we know it. Chapter 16 describes the twelve fundamental control principles and the extensive hierarchy of control objectives that stem from them. Chapter 17 discusses the control environment within the organization and the control measures and techniques that can operate under the umbrella of a satisfactory control environment. Chapter 18 provides a brief overview of the external audit engagement, including the evaluation of internal controls and the use of computers as audit procedural tools.

15

Introduction to Control of Accounting Systems

LEARNING OBJECTIVES

After studying this chapter you should be able to

- Discuss the nature and purposes of internal control.
- Identify the relationship between internal control and risk.
- Describe the impact of both people and computers on risk.
- Describe the historical development of internal control from the standpoint of professional pronouncements.
- Identify the broad classifications of internal controls.
- Discuss the auditor's role in evaluating internal controls and detecting fraud.
- Discuss recent legal developments relating to internal control.

THE NATURE OF INTERNAL CONTROL

Business Controls

Accounting systems are subject to controls of various kinds. Some of these originate outside the enterprise and are referred to as *external controls*; others originate inside the enterprise and are referred to as *internal controls* (Figure 15.1).

External controls stem from the legal, regulatory, professional, and societal environment in which the enterprise operates. Examples of external controls are legal requirements for the incorporation of certain checks and balances within the accounting system, requirements of taxation authorities and government regulatory agencies for the same, requirements imposed on the structure of the system by the accounting profession (and enforced by the need to obtain an unqualified opinion on the financial statements by the external auditors), requirements imposed by securities exchanges, and societal pressure on every organization to "keep its house in order."

Internal controls form part of the broader group of controls known as *management controls*. Management control covers the whole of the organization's activities and ensures that management's wishes are carried out. Other examples of management controls include budget tracking, quality control, and enforcement of safety standards. Internal controls correspond to those aspects of management control relating to the accounting function. Internal control has four main objectives:

- Safeguarding the organization's assets
- Preserving the accuracy and reliability of the accounting data
- Promoting operational efficiency
- Encouraging compliance with management policy

Internal controls have traditionally been divided into *accounting controls*, which relate principally to the first and second objectives, and *administrative controls*, which relate primarily to the third and fourth objectives. Examples of accounting controls are credit-checking procedures, use of prenumbered documents, separation of incompatible duties, and access controls relating to the computer facilities. Examples of administrative controls are personnel policies, formal job descriptions, the

FIGURE 15.1   Hierarchy of business controls.

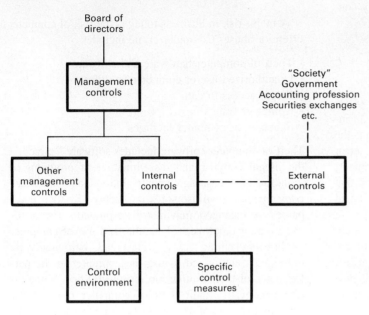

internal audit function, and physical security. The division of internal controls into these two groups was well intentioned, but it has led to uncertainties about the correct classification of individual control measures and, in some cases, has distracted attention from the real issue, which is to choose the proper combination of controls—the *control system*—so as to meet the necessary control objectives. For this reason, emphasis is now placed less on the attempt to classify controls and more on the design of effective control systems.

Internal controls have also been classified according to whether they related to manual processing operations or to automated processes. The latter were often referred to as *EDP* (electronic data-processing) *controls* and were further subdivided into *general controls*, which were systemwide in their operation, and *application controls*, whose operation was confined within a particular application such as payroll processing. These distinctions were important when many accounting systems were still based entirely on manual processing, whereupon the designers needed to be concerned only with manual controls. They also were important at a time when computerized systems were less highly integrated than they are now. However, today virtually all accounting systems

are automated to some degree, and many are highly integrated around data base management systems and other systemwide processing tools. Consequently, designers must be concerned with a much broader range of controls. Some specific control measures relate more closely to manual processes, which may be embedded even in largely automated accounting systems, and some to automated processes themselves. But again, present concern is directed more to establishing effective control over the accounting system as a whole than to classifying controls on the basis of somewhat artificial distinctions.

On the other hand, a meaningful distinction can still be made between those control measures that create an overall environment of control within the organization and those that address specific needs. Without an effective control environment, the more specific control measures are unlikely to be effective. For example, a password control aimed at preventing unauthorized access to computer facilities can be successful only if the computer facilities are afforded adequate physical security and if procedures have been established for dealing with the unauthorized disclosure of passwords. In the design of effective internal control systems, the synergistic relationship between specific control measures and the control environment—and also among the various specific control measures—must be carefully considered and understood.

Internal Controls and Risk

Internal controls are implemented in order to offset various types of risk, in much the same way as do insurance policies. There are ever-present risks that the organization could be harmed by either human error or intentional irregularities, including embezzlement, fraud, and sabotage. Irregularities include actions that are prohibited by company policy and also illegal activities.

The first two objectives of internal control—safeguarding the assets and preserving the integrity of the accounting data—remind us that there is significant risk in these two areas. The organization's assets are protected in the first instance by physical security measures, for instance, by locking the warehouse. But effective protection must also consider that the assets could be misappropriated by penetration of the accounting system and that the inventory could be stolen by falsifying shipping records. Thus, it is necessary to protect the accounting system by an effective system of internal controls in order to achieve an acceptable degree of control over the company's assets. And although they do not appear on the balance sheet, other resources must also be protected against deliberate attempts at sabotage as well as against damage or loss through negligence. One example of such resources is the accounting data base; many organizations can be hurt more by the destruction of their data bases than by the destruction of their inventory or fixed assets.

Preserving the accuracy and reliability of the accounting data is a matter of serious concern for both external and internal users of the data. The most pervasive threat to the data is from human errors in manual processing, in data entry to computer systems, and in the development of computer programs. Other threats are associated with equipment malfunction and with deliberate irregularities. The objectives of internal control in this area are, first, to discourage errors and irregularities and, second, to provide procedures for the effective detection of errors and irregularities.

Computer Crime

A major risk in business today is the risk of computer crime or abuse. Computer crime includes

- Theft of computer hardware and software
- Unauthorized use of computer facilities
- Illegal access to data
- Computer fraud
- Sabotage of computer facilities

Theft of computer software includes software "piracy," the illegal copying and dissemination of programs in violation of license agreements. Individuals sometimes copy for their own use software licensed by their companies, or managers may distribute pirated software for use by their employees. Unauthorized use of computer facilities by employees is widespread, particularly by individuals authorized to use the computer in the performance of their routine job responsibilities. Some individuals justify their theft of computer time on the grounds that the variable cost of computer usage is low; however, this reasoning ignores the large capital investment represented by the fixed costs. Unauthorized usage detracts from the capacity of the system to accommodate authorized processing tasks.

Illegal access to data may involve people either inside or outside the organization. Networked systems using telephone lines as communications media are particularly vulnerable to this kind of activity. Perpetrators eavesdrop on messages or access data files from remote terminals, for a variety of reasons. Among the most common reasons are industrial espionage, gaining "insider information" for investment purposes, or gathering information for blackmail or extortion.

Computer fraud involves changing programs or data for illegal financial gain or other unfair advantage. The stakes in computer fraud are high, reportedly averaging more than $1 million per incident, compared with $10,000 for a bank robbery, in which the chances of detection are much greater. Sabotage against computer facilities can be the action of disgruntled employees (or ex-employees), commercial rivals, extremist groups, or terrorists. Fortunately, the incidence of sabotage by this last group has so far been small in the United States. But sabotage by individuals with grudges against management or particular companies is a major problem.

Perpetrators may smash computer equipment or may destroy data or programs.

Computer crime is an attractive option to unscrupulous individuals because of the potentially high stakes, low detection rates, and even lower conviction rates. In an American Bar Association survey, nearly 150 major corporations admitted that they had lost several million dollars as a result of computer crime. But the Federal Bureau of Investigation estimates that few computer crimes are ever reported and that only 1 in 20,000 computer criminals ever goes to jail. One reason often cited for the failure to report most computer crimes is that companies wish to avoid the embarrassment—and the risk—of admitting that their controls were inadequate.

A major problem in securing convictions is that society largely condones the crimes. Juries tend to identify with computer criminals, who are typically white, well educated, and socially respectable and do not have criminal backgrounds. Another problem, at least until recently, is that state and federal laws have been lax and slow to respond to changing technology. The extension of legal concepts, such as simple trespass, to penetration of computer systems, and theft, to copying of machine-readable data, has caused difficulty in both the legislatures and the courts. Fortunately, the situation is now changing, and some recently enacted laws are described later in this chapter.

But managers cannot and should not rely on legal remedies to combat computer crime. The main line of defense must be the organization's internal control system. Often managers fail to take advantage of available control devices, even relatively cheap ones, until a major crime has been committed. Organizations must take computer crime much more seriously.

INTERNAL CONTROLS AND THE ACCOUNTING SYSTEM

Internal Control Principles and Objectives

The accounting profession has identified certain control principles, which are broad statements concerning the need for a control environment and specific control measures to combat related types of risk. Although there is virtually universal acceptance of the concepts underlying these principles, their formulation has not been standardized. Nevertheless, there is substantial support for a set of 12 control principles, dealing with

- The control environment
- Authorizations
- Incompatible duties and responsibilities
- Classification of information
- Transaction processing
- Accuracy of data
- Error correction
- Systems security
- Security of data
- Systems development
- Documentation
- Physical safeguarding of assets

These control principles are general and apply to a wide range of organizational types. In turn, each control principle can be expanded into a set of more specific control objectives that relate to given types of organizations and given types of information systems. For example, under the control principle dealing with system access and usage, a control objective might deal with access to a computerized system via a data communications network. In turn, again, each control objective must be addressed by the incorporation of one or more control measures into the information system. Depending on the success of the control measures, the control objective will or will not be achieved.

Aside from providing a conceptual framework for understanding controls, the 12 control principles, together with representative sets of control objectives, serve as a model for both systems designers and auditors concerned with the adequacy of control measures in any particular accounting system. Control principles and objectives will be discussed in more detail in the next chapter.

Internal Controls and Automation

The question is often asked whether computerization of the accounting information system improves or worsens the control situation. And the answer is not immediately clear. Manual processing is subject to random errors and inconsistency; regardless of their competence, clerks occasionally make mistakes, and the transactions in question will be processed differently than they should be and differently than similar ones are. Automated processing avoids such inconsistencies. If the software has been properly tested and if the computer runs at all, all the transactions will be processed correctly. On the other hand, if there is a ''bug'' in the software or if there is an equipment malfunction, all the transactions will be processed incorrectly, and the results will be correspondingly more serious. Large amounts of data may be contaminated, and recovery and correction of the errors may be more difficult.

Transactions commonly are created by computerized systems. Purchase orders may be generated automatically by an inventory management system. Paychecks are produced routinely by a payroll system, or vendor checks by an accounts payable system. Because of the typically large volumes, the review of such transactions may not be as careful as it should be. Some internally created transactions, such as automatic adjusting entries, do not even generate a document that can be intercepted, and review is at best only an after-the-fact process. In a manual system, in which every transaction is created by a human being, errors or unusual circumstances are more likely to be detected and investigated before the damage can spread.

Another problem with computerized systems is that stored data are invisible and can be destroyed easily and quickly. Machine-readable records can be erased, duplicated, or destroyed, in many cases without leaving any trace as to what happened or who was responsible. Moreover, in networked systems, the records can be illegally accessed or tampered with from a distance, even from thousands of miles away.

Large volumes of data may be stored in a single location and in a single storage device. And this concentration exposes the data to a variety of risks. Equipment malfunction, natural disasters, operator error, or deliberate sabotage can destroy large amounts of data much more readily than would be possible in a manual system. In manual systems, data are normally stored on paper media, which are more durable than magnetic records. Moreover, the stored data are normally distributed among many filing cabinets, possibly in several different offices. Conversely, at least in traditional, centralized data-processing facilities, all transaction paths converge on the computer room. A small number of computer operators have access to data from all parts of the organization and access to the programs used to process the data. A control problem in the computer room accordingly can place all transactions—and master files—at risk. In a manual system, transaction processing is distributed among many people and may be distributed over a wider area.

Considerations of this type demonstrate that automation changes the control picture and that additional controls are required to deal with new types of risk that did not arise in manual systems. But in spite of the additional risks, when adequate controls are established, computerized systems can provide more accurate and reliable information than was possible with the manual systems that they superseded.

Internal Controls and Human Factors

Regardless of the degree of automation, internal control objectives are ultimately achieved through people. People recognize the risks, or they fail to do so until a major problem arises. People choose to incorporate internal controls or do not. People design the controls, adequately or poorly. People carry out control procedures or, through negligence or otherwise, do not carry them out. People depend on the controls and feel secure, or they feel ill at ease. And sometimes people intentionally evade the controls and perpetrate irregularities. There is a danger, when discussing internal controls, to overemphasize the technical aspects at the expense of the human behavioral ones. Although the technical aspects are clearly important, it should be remembered that the success of the internal control system depends on the performance of the people involved.

Some organizations take internal controls more seriously than do others. Although virtually all managers pay lip service to the need for internal controls, in some organizations managers are lax in their enforcement of the controls and communicate by their attitudes that the controls are unimportant. In turn, the rank-and-file employees respond by ignoring the control procedures. Most organizations require that employees who travel in the course of their jobs submit airline ticket stubs to support their expense claims. But if an employee loses his or her stub and still is reimbursed for travel expenses—without a reprimand or formal recording of the incident—that employee and others are likely to be less careful to retain their ticket stubs on future trips.

Passwords may be issued for access to the computer, but data entry clerks may write their passwords on the side of the terminals. Unless the supervisor takes prompt action against violators, employees will soon come to ignore the control importance of the password system. Furthermore, unless the internal or external auditors take action against the supervisor, more damage will be done. An organization may have a procedure manual outlining programming and documentation standards to be followed by systems development personnel. But when work is rushed, the standards are ignored. Soon the programmers and others understand that production is more important than the controls and that the standards are a luxury to be observed only when they have plenty of time.

A chief executive may stress to his or her subordinates that everyone should take a full two-week vacation every year but personally never take more than two or three days at a time. Soon the lower-level managers get the message that forgoing the full two weeks, rather than violating company policy, actually is a sign of importance in the organization. Eventually the policy falls into disuse, and as a result, unscrupulous individuals may conceal irregularities by declining to take vacations during which others would perform their jobs.

In order to avoid problems such as these, upper management must give the internal control system its full support. Management should publicize control procedures among those to whom they apply and should make it clear that violations will be dealt with promptly and impersonally. Top managers should demonstrate that they feel as bound by the control procedures as does the most junior employee in the organization. Internal controls are not intended to be repressive. On the contrary, most employees accept the need for controls and, assuming that the controls are reasonable, are willing to abide by them as long as they know that everyone else will do likewise.

This set of attitudes relating to the internal controls in the organization is referred to as the *control consciousness*. A favorable control consciousness provides the human backdrop against which other, tangible components of the control environment and specific control measures have a chance of being successful.

PROFESSIONAL PRONOUNCEMENTS ON INTERNAL CONTROL

Much of the professional and legal literature on internal controls has been written from the standpoint of the audit function. It focuses largely on the auditor's responsibilities for evaluating the internal controls and reporting on the results. In particular, the various pronouncements of the American Institute of Certified Public Accountants (AICPA) in this area have taken the form of audit statements or guidelines. However, this material is also relevant to the systems designer. By studying the related audit requirements, the designer can gain valuable insight into the extent of the controls that would be deemed adequate, in different situations, to reduce applicable risks to an acceptable level.

Definition and Classification of Internal Controls

In 1949, the AICPA proposed a definition of internal controls that has essentially stood the test of time:

Internal control comprises the plan of organization and all of the coordinated methods and measures adopted within a business to: safeguard its assets, check the accuracy and reliability of its accounting data, promote operational efficiency, and encourage adherence to prescribed managerial policies.[1]

Herein originated the four broad objectives of internal control, which have already been mentioned. The AICPA added, by way of explanation: "This definition is broader than the meaning sometimes attributed to the term. It recognizes that a 'system' of internal controls extends beyond those matters which relate directly to the functions of the accounting and financial departments."

[1] Committee on Auditing Procedures, *Internal Control: Elements of a Coordinated System and Its Importance to Management and the Independent Public Accountant* (New York: AICPA, 1949).

The reference to the internal control system was an important one—particularly at the time, when the word *system* was not used as widely as it is today—and emphasized the need for a coordinated set of control measures working together to achieve the control objectives.

Subsequent literature interpreted the 1949 definition by introducing the notion of accounting controls and administrative controls. The former were assumed to address the need to safeguard the assets and check the accuracy and reliability of the accounting data. They were intended to include the systems of transaction authorization and approval, organizational controls providing for separation of duties, physical control over assets, internal auditing, and the processing controls that maintain the accuracy and security of the accounting records. The latter were assumed to address the need to promote operational efficiency and encourage adherence to managerial policies. They were only indirectly related to the financial records but nevertheless helped provide a favorable environment in which the accounting controls could operate.

Accounting controls have the most bearing on the financial statements and thus are the ones of most concern to external auditors. However, managers—and their agents, the internal accountants (including the internal auditors) —are concerned about accounting controls and administrative controls. Accounting controls are sometimes referred to as *preventive controls* and administrative controls as *feedback controls*. But the latter do not have a monopoly on the feedback mechanism inherent in all control systems.

In 1972, the definitions of accounting and administrative controls were restated as follows:

Administrative control includes, but is not limited to, the plan of organization and the procedures and records that are concerned with the decision processes leading to management's authorization of transactions. Such authorization is a management function directly associated with the responsibility for achieving the objectives of the organization and is the starting point for establishing accounting control of transactions. . . .

Accounting control comprises the plan of organization and the procedures and records that are concerned with the safeguarding of assets and the reliability of financial records and con-

sequently are designed to provide reasonable assurance that:
(a) Transactions are executed in accordance with management's general or specific authorization.
(b) Transactions are recorded as necessary (1) to permit preparation of financial statements in accordance with generally accepted accounting principles or other criteria applicable to such statements and (2) to maintain accountability for assets.
(c) Access to assets is permitted only in accordance with management's authorization.
(d) The recorded accountability for assets is compared with existing assets at reasonable intervals and appropriate action is taken with respect to any differences.[2]

The phrase "includes, but is not limited to" in the definition of administrative controls may imply that the earlier objectives pertaining to operational efficiency and managerial policies were assumed to remain in effect. But the definition is broadened to include at least part of the procedure for authorizing transactions.

The definitions of accounting and administrative controls were expressed as objectives and were intended to be independent of the method of information processing in use. Consequently, they applied equally to manual, semiautomated, and automated systems. But additional insight was provided in 1974 into the nature of controls in computerized information systems, or what at that time was referred to as "EDP controls." Statement on Auditing Standards (SAS) No. 3 defined *general controls* and *application controls*:

Some EDP control procedures relate to all EDP activities (general controls) and some relate to a specific accounting task such as preparation of account listings or payrolls (application controls).

General controls comprise (a) the plan of organization and operation of the EDP activity, (b) the procedures for documenting, reviewing, testing, and approving systems or programs and changes thereto, (c) controls built into the equipment by the manufacturer (commonly referred to as "hardware controls"), (d) controls over access to equipment and data files, and (e) other data and procedural controls affecting overall EDP operations. . . .

Application controls relate to specific tasks performed by

[2] *AICPA Professional Standards* (New York: Commerce Clearing House, 1981), vol. 1, AU sec. 320.27.

EDP. Their function is to provide reasonable assurance that the recording, processing, and reporting are properly performed. . . . Application controls are categorized as "input controls," "processing controls," and "output controls."[3]

General controls are systemwide controls that—if effective—provide a favorable environment in which the more specific application controls can function effectively. On the other hand if the general controls are inadequate, the resulting weakness may undermine the effectiveness of the application controls. The relationship between the two types of controls is in some ways analogous to the relationship between administrative controls and accounting controls.

The attempts to classify controls into administrative and accounting controls and later into general controls and application controls provided insight but they also caused problems. The various areas of controls are not necessarily mutually exclusive. Some of the procedures and records normally considered in accounting control may also be involved in administrative control. For example, sales and cost records may be used for accounting control purposes and also for setting prices and other management decision processes. Similarly, certain controls in computerized systems may span the boundaries between general and application controls. An example is an access control that is incorporated into application software and that also uses some feature of the operating system or computer hardware.

Statement on Auditing Standards No. 48, which was issued in 1984, reviewed the material contained in SAS No. 3 in the light of recent technological and other changes. Two important recommendations were made. The first was that automated systems were now so widespread that they must be considered the norm. Accordingly, internal controls should normally be discussed in the context of computer-based accounting systems. The second was that the distinction between general controls and application was now regarded as of less significance than it once was and that the more important concern was to design controls that were effective for the ultimate objectives of internal control. Specifically, SAS No. 48 stated:

[3] Ibid, AU sec. 321.06-8.

Whether the control procedures are classified . . . into general and application controls, the objective of the system of internal accounting control remains the same: to provide reasonable, but not absolute, assurance that assets are safeguarded from unauthorized use or disposition and that financial records are reliable to permit the preparation of financial statements.[4]

The distinction between accounting and administrative controls is still being made. Whether this distinction will also be dropped at some time in the future remains to be seen. Classification problems tended to distract attention from the primary concern that the particular control should effectively and efficiently contribute to the achievement of the overall control objectives. The main criterion from the accountant's (and more particularly the auditor's) viewpoint is the bearing that particular controls have on the reliability of accounting data, regardless of their formal classification as accounting or administrative controls.

Auditor's Review of Internal Controls

The professional standards for auditors have for many years required a review of the client's internal controls prior to making an examination of the financial records. The Second Standard of Field Work states:

There is to be a proper study and evaluation of the existing internal controls as a basis for reliance thereon and for the determination of the resultant extent of the tests to which auditing procedures are to be restricted.[5]

SAS No. 3 extended the auditor's responsibilities to include the evaluation of general and application controls in computerized information systems. It described this portion of the evaluation as being "an integral part of the auditor's evaluation of the system." Another AICPA publication, entitled *The Auditor's Study and Evaluation of Internal Control in EDP Systems*, provided detailed

[4] Statement on Auditing Standards No. 48, "The Effects of Computer Processing on the Examination of Financial Statements." (New York: American Institute of Certified Public Accountants, 1984).
[5] American Institute of Certified Public Accountants, *Statement on Auditing Standards No. 1* (New York, AICPA, 1958).

step-by-step procedures for studying internal controls in computerized information systems. It also contained a list of 19 control objectives for general controls and 12 for application controls, together with recommendations for documenting computerized systems. The coverage of application controls was limited to batch-oriented systems, but the guide stated that "many of the control objectives, techniques, and compliance testing procedures . . . are applicable to advanced systems." "Advanced systems" were defined as on-line or real-time systems that use random access processing techniques.

Statement on Auditing Standards No. 20, which was issued in 1977, required auditors to communicate to senior management and the board of directors (or the audit committee) any material weaknesses in internal accounting controls that are discovered. A material weakness is described as:

A condition in which the specific control procedures or the degree of compliance with them do not reduce to a relatively low level the risk that errors or irregularities in amounts that would be material in relation to financial statements being audited may occur and not be detected within a timely period by employees in the normal course of performing their assigned functions.[6]

The risk referred to here is *audit risk* and not the type of risk about which managers are most concerned. Audit risk focuses on the possibility that the financial statements might be misstated and not be detected. Management is concerned with a broader range of risks, including safeguarding assets, promoting efficiency, and encouraging compliance with its policies.

Statement on Auditing Standards No. 30 dealt with reporting on internal controls, either in connection with the annual financial audit or separately. The statement described four types of report that may be issued in that context. The auditor may

(a) Express an opinion on the entity's system of internal accounting control in effect as of a specific date.
(b) Report on the entity's system, for the restricted use of management, specified regulatory agencies, or other specified third parties, based solely on a study

and evaluation of internal accounting control made as part of an audit of the entity's financial statements that is not sufficient for expressing an opinion on the system itself.
(c) Report on all or part of an entity's system, for the restricted use of management or specified regulatory agencies, based on regulatory agencies' pre-established criteria.
(d) Issue other special-purpose reports on all or part of an entity's control system for the restricted use of management, specified regulatory agencies, or other specified third parties.

The Auditor's Responsibility for Detecting Fraud

There is considerable confusion regarding the scope of audit liability with respect to fraud. *Fraud* is deliberate deception practiced to secure unfair or unlawful gain. Fraud may be perpetrated by lower-level employees or management. Management fraud is considered particularly serious and is defined in the professional literature as "deliberate fraud committed by management that injures investors and creditors through materially misleading financial statements."[7]

Fraud is one of several types of activity collectively referred to as *irregularities*. Irregularities are defined as

intentional distortions of financial statements, such as deliberate misrepresentations by management, sometimes referred to as management fraud, or misappropriations of assets, sometimes referred to as defalcations. Irregularities in financial statements may result from misrepresentations or omission of the effects of events or transactions, manipulation, falsification, or alteration of records or documents, recording of transactions without substance, intentional misappropriation of assets for the benefit of management, employees, or third parties.[8]

The traditional position of auditors in the United States, supported by pronouncements of the AICPA, has been that auditors are required to report instances of illegal

[6] *AICPA Professional Standards* Vol. 1. AU sec. 320.08 (New York: Commerce Clearing House, 1981).

[7] *AICPA Professional Standards* vol. 1, AU sec. 327.03 (New York: Commerce Clearing House, 1981).
[8] Ibid.

acts, including fraud, to personnel at a sufficiently high level to ensure that appropriate action will be taken. But auditors also insist that they are not required to extend their examinations specifically to search for such acts. This position is in contrast with the situation in some other countries where auditors are expressly directed to look for fraud. The applicable professional standards for U.S. auditors state that "the auditor is not an insurer or guarantor; if his examination was made in accordance with generally accepted auditing standards, he has fulfilled his professional responsibility."[9] The auditor considers that his or her primary responsibility is to attest to the financial statements. The auditor should plan and conduct the engagement with an attitude of professional skepticism, recognizing that the audit procedures may uncover errors or irregularities, and should exercise due skill and care in searching for any kind of problem that could have a material effect on the financial statements. The client's own internal controls, together with the independent audit, provide reasonable assurance that the financial statements are not misstated. The client's controls include the monitoring of employees' activities by management and management's activities by the board of directors, the internal audit function, the audit committee, and the internal accounting control procedures. These controls should be sufficient to prevent or detect fraud, at least as long as it is not perpetrated by top management itself. If fraud were perpetrated by upper management, evidence could be concealed more easily and the auditors would have little chance of detecting it, no matter what procedures they adopted.

Auditors point out that to audit specifically for fraud would make engagements substantially more expensive and that the costs would not be reasonable in relation to the benefits to either the client or society at large. The inference is that fraud is not sufficiently widespread to warrant extraordinary measures by the auditor to uncover it.

But society has not necessarily endorsed this detached attitude. The Cohen Commission, chaired by Manual F. Cohen, which made an independent study of auditors' responsibilities, concluded: "All segments of the public—including the most knowledgeable users of financial statements—appear to consider the detection of fraud as a necessary and important objective of an audit."[10] The subject of auditors' responsibility is likely to be debated for a long time. At some time in the future, a legal solution of the problem may be sought, but at present, differing opinions and some degree of confusion persist.

LEGAL ASPECTS OF INTERNAL CONTROL

Until comparatively recently, the law distanced itself from matters of internal control, reflecting society's belief that the internal affairs of business enterprises should not be the subject of government regulation. However, in the late 1970s, growing public distaste for the ways in which some segments of big business conducted themselves finally resulted in limited legal intervention, in the form of the Foreign Corrupt Practices Act (FCPA). Still more recently, both federal and state governments have taken action to stem the tide of computer crime, and these actions have an important bearing on internal controls.

The Foreign Corrupt Practices Act

The Foreign Corrupt Practices Act of 1977 resulted primarily from allegations of corporate wrongdoing made during the Watergate investigations that preceded and followed the resignation of President Richard M. Nixon. From the testimony of corporate executives, the Securities and Exchange Commission (SEC) learned of money "laundering"—often involving foreign banks—in order to make illegal domestic political contributions and also to pay bribes to foreign officials to secure export sales. The fact that bribery was common in the countries in which U.S. companies were competing for business was not accepted as justification for the practice. Evidence in congressional hearings indicated that the money laundering and bribery were often concealed by circumventing the companies' internal accounting controls.

The FCPA established criminal liability for acts in-

[9] *AICPA Professional Standards* vol. 1, AU sec. 327.13 (New York: Commerce Clearing House, 1981).

[10] Commission on Auditors' Responsibilities, *Report, Conclusions and Recommendations* (New York, CAR, 1978), p. 2.

volving bribery of foreign officials, a provision that applies to all U.S. companies. It also contains accounting provisions for record keeping and internal control. These latter provisions apply only to SEC registrant companies. The accounting provisions, which form an amendment to Section 13(b)(2) of the Securities Exchange Act of 1934, read as follows:

Every issuer which has a class of securities registered pursuant to Section 12 of this title and every issuer which is required to file reports pursuant to Section 15(d) of this title shall:
(a) make and keep books, records, and accounts, which, in reasonable detail, accurately and fairly reflect the transactions and dispositions of the assets of the issuer; and
(b) devise and maintain a system of internal accounting control sufficient to provide reasonable assurance that
   (i) transactions are executed in accordance with management's general or specific authorization.
   (ii) transactions are recorded as necessary (1) to permit preparation of financial statements in accordance with generally accepted accounting principles or other criteria applicable to such statements and (2) to maintain accountability for assets.
   (iii) access to assets is permitted only in accordance with management's authorization.
   (iv) the recorded accountability for assets is compared with existing assets at reasonable intervals and appropriate action is taken with respect to any differences.

The language of this section of the FCPA is almost identical to that of the 1972 definition of accounting controls proposed by the AICPA.

With the passage of the FCPA, the law required for the first time the establishment of internal controls in accounting information systems. On the other hand, it does not indicate how managers or auditors are to respond. The act itself requires management to install appropriate internal controls, but the only reference to the required degree of control is the phrase "reasonable assurance." The term usually refers to the situation in which the cost of the controls is not expected to exceed the benefits to be derived from them, but this is a professional rather than a legal interpretation. The FCPA does not prescribe additional actions on the part of external auditors. Following the passage of the FCPA, the

AICPA expressly recommended that its members not try to provide assurances regarding clients' compliance with the act.

In a proposal issued in 1979, the SEC indicated its intention to require managers to make a formal statement on their compliance with the FCPA and to require external auditors to report on the accuracy and reasonableness of management's statement. The proposal met with stiff opposition from managers, who had no explicit guidance on what constituted compliance, and from auditors, who feared the legal liability that might result from the expanded attest function. In 1980 the SEC withdrew its proposal, partly under pressure, but ostensibly to allow more time for private-sector initiatives to improve standards of internal control and associated reporting. One such initiative was SAS No. 30, which has already been mentioned. Other initiatives came from the American Bar Association, which prepared a guide on management responsibility under the FCPA, and the Institute of Internal Auditors, which in 1978 issued the *Standards for the Professional Practice of Internal Auditing*. Issuance of these standards was regarded as a major step toward upgrading the profession.

To date there have been no new major legal developments dealing with internal control. The provisions of the FCPA remain on the statute book, but no companies have been brought to trial for failing to comply with the act. Public concerns, which led to passage of the FCPA, have abated, and interest in internal controls is now once again primarily confined to managers, systems designers, accountants, and internal and external auditors.

Computer Crime and the Law

Neither the federal nor the state branches of government moved fast to counter the growing threat of computer crime. Various statutes were invoked on a piecemeal basis to prosecute computer and computer-related crimes, including the Trade Secrets Act, the Espionage Act, the Electronic Funds Transfer Act, the Fair Credit Reporting Act, the Privacy Act of 1974, the Right to Financial Privacy Act (1978), and the Internal Revenue Code.

Several attempts were made to extend copyright protection to computer programs and data, so as to protect them from piracy. The Copyright Law (1976) did not refer specifically to programs or data, but the Congressional Record refers to programs and data bases as copyrightable "writings." Later, the Computer Software Copyright Act (1980) was passed to give formal, exclusive rights to the developers or owners of computer programs. Some protection against piracy is also provided by the Trade Secrets Act.

The first attempt to introduce comprehensive legislation to combat computer crime was made in 1977 in the form of the Federal Computer Systems Protection Act. It was finally signed into law in 1984 and made all unauthorized use of federal government computers a punishable crime. The act did not extend protection to the private sector, but it provided important legal precedents that opened the way for further legislation.

In 1984, the Congress added two sections to Title 18 of the U.S. Code: Section 1029, "Fraud and Related Activity in Connection with Access Devices," and Section 1030, "Fraud and Related Activity in Connection with Computers." Section 1029 makes it a crime to produce or use a counterfeit access device. Section 1030 prohibits access to a computer without authorization with the intent of obtaining restricted information or modifying or destroying data in a computer operated by, or on behalf of, the federal government. In addition, the Congress passed the Small Business Computer Crime Prevention Act, which provided for the formation of a task force to study the impact of computer crime on small businesses.

The Computer Fraud and Abuse Act of 1986 expanded federal jurisdiction to cover interstate computer crime in the private sector. The act makes it a federal crime to alter data stored in a computer located in another state used by the federal government or operated by federally insured financial institutions. Unauthorized access to a "federal interest" computer with intent to perpetrate theft or fraud becomes a felony under the act if either the victim suffers a loss of at least $1,000 or the files accessed contain medical records. Jail terms of up to five years are prescribed for first offenders and ten years for a second offense. Trafficking in stolen passwords and all other forms of trespassing in a computer to obtain data with intent to defraud become misdemeanors. The wording of the Computer Fraud and Abuse Act avoids conflict with state laws. But because most computer crime is interstate, the impact of the act should be far-reaching. Moreover, this and other recent legislation helps make clear that the intangibles of data and programs are protectable resources in the eyes of the law.

The Electronic Communications Privacy Act of 1986 makes it a felony to intercept electronic communications and a misdemeanor to break into electronic-mail storage facilities. The act permits persons or corporations whose communications have been intercepted the right to sue for damages, whether or not any financial loss resulted from the interception. Prior to passage of the act, other federal and state laws gave victims recourse against penetration of data bases, but interception of communications was perfectly legal.

In addition to these federal laws, laws have been enacted in most of the states to combat intrastate computer crime. But these laws are far from uniform in their provisions, with the result that an action that is illegal in one state may be legal in another. Furthermore, some of the laws are formulated in such broad terms that there is confusion as regards their true intent. In one state, for instance, the law fails to distinguish adequately between a computer and a television receiver or video cassette recorder.

At the time of writing, there are no international laws relating to computer crime. Some discussions have taken place among groups from different countries, mostly with the objective of reaching agreements to protect individual privacy. In 1980, the Organization for Economic Cooperation and Development (OECD) issued guidelines encouraging voluntary compliance with national privacy laws in the area of international data transfer.

Aside from improvements in legal remedies to combat computer crime, computer users are under increasing pressure to accept more responsibility for their own security measures. Unless they do so, there are already indications that government regulation may step in and mandate minimum levels of computer security. Most observers regard such government intervention as undesirable and believe that computer security—backed up by enforceable law—should remain in the hands of management and the computer professionals.

SUMMARY

Accounting information systems are controlled by agencies outside the organization—the government, the accounting rule-making bodies, the external auditors, and others—as well as by the internal agency of management. Internal controls traditionally were regarded simply as management's response to the presence of various types of risk. But today the incorporation of internal controls into the accounting system is legally mandated, at least for companies that report to the Securities and Exchange Commission. Nevertheless, what controls to incorporate and how they should be implemented are still determined largely on the basis of reasoned response to risks.

Much of the professional literature on internal controls has been written from the viewpoint of the external auditor. The auditor's primary concern in this regard is to determine the extent to which the controls can be relied upon to help substantiate the fairness of the financial statements. An extensive body of literature has defined and classified the many internal controls and provides guidance on what kinds of controls are appropriate to different situations. The fundamental aims of internal controls are to safeguard the organization's assets, to maintain the integrity of the accounting data, to promote operational efficiency, and to encourage compliance with management policies. Such definitions, together with the practical guidance, are beneficial not just to auditors seeking to evaluate the controls but also to accountants and managers responsible for developing internal controls.

The professional literature has also defined the auditor's responsibilities for evaluating internal controls and also restricted his or her responsibilities with respect to fraud. In the United States, the external auditor must report fraud if it is discovered but does not bear the primary responsibility for detecting it.

The growing problem of computer crime and abuse is of concern to managers and auditors alike. One of the most serious problems is society's ambivalent attitude toward this type of "white-collar" crime. The law has been slow to move against computer crime, but recently both federal and state governments have enacted laws that promise to facilitate more effective legal action against computer criminals than has hitherto been possible.

BIBLIOGRAPHY

American Institute of Certified Public Accountants. *AICPA Professional Standards.* Vol. 3, *Accounting.* New York: Commerce Clearing House, 1981.

American Institute of Certified Public Accountants. *The Auditor's Study and Evaluation of Internal Control in EDP Systems,* Audit and Accounting Guide. New York: AICPA, 1977.

American Institute of Certified Public Accountants. *Management, Control and Audit of Advanced EDP Systems,* Computer Services Guidelines. New York: AICPA, 1977.

Arthur Andersen & Co. *A Guide for Studying and Evaluating Internal Accounting Controls,* AA Pub. no. 2880, Item I. Chicago: Arthur Andersen & Co., 1978.

Diebold, John. "Computer Security: An Issue of Survival." *Datamation,* October 1, 1986 (supplement), p. 1.

Horner, Larry D. "What Every CEO Needs to Know and Do—About Computer Security." *Datamation,* October 1, 1986 (supplement), p. 2.

Mautz, Robert K. et al. *Internal Control in U.S. Corporations: The State of the Art.* Research Study and Report prepared for the Financial Executives Research Foundation, New York, 1980.

Parker, Donn B. *Crime by Computer.* New York: Scribner's, 1976.

Roberts, Martin B. *EDP Controls.* New York: Wiley, 1985.

Study Group on Computer Control and Audit Guidelines. *Computer Control Guidelines.* Ottawa: Canadian Institute of Chartered Accountants, 1970.

DISCUSSION QUESTIONS AND PROBLEMS

1. Define and discuss the following terms:

- Accounting controls
- Administrative controls

- Application controls
- Computer crime
- Control environment
- External control
- General authorization
- General controls
- Incompatible duties
- Management control
- Manual controls
- Material control weakness
- Specific authorization

2. A company policy requires computer operators to show an ID card and sign for all tapes and disk cartridges checked out of the data-processing library for batch-processing runs. The policy is strictly enforced during the day shift, but there is no librarian on duty at night. At 5:30 P.M. the librarian leaves on a table outside the secured library area all files required for scheduled runs during the night shifts.

Required
Comment on the different messages conveyed by official company policy and by the actual situation that is allowed to exist. What risks is the company exposed to as a result of this control weakness?

3. The business environment is recognized to have an important influence on the control system within the information system.

Required
Discuss the effect that the key factor in each of the following situations would have on the control system:

- Black Co. is a one-person business.
- Blue Co. is a dealer in gold coins.
- Green Co. is a government defense contractor.
- Purple Co. operates in a Middle East country.
- Red Co. is a regulated utility company.
- White Co. is a manufacturer of automobile parts.
- Yellow Co. operates a technical school teaching computer programming and computer science.

4. In a well-known case, the top management of an insurance holding company conspired to create phony insurance policies that were subsequently sold to rein-

surers. Out of total reported assets of $143 million at the time the scandal was exposed, over $27 million represented fraudulent policies.

Required
Discuss the role of internal controls in helping prevent and/or detect management frauds of this type. Can society rely on the external auditors to expose major management fraud of this type?

5. A computer crime that has been perpetrated at several banks and financial institutions is referred to as the *salami* technique. All calculated interest amounts are rounded down, and the fraction of a cent "sliced" from each computation is then transferred to an account opened by the perpetrator (or an accomplice) who is usually a programmer in the information services department.

Imagine that the following account balances form a representative sample of one tenth of 1 percent of the population of accounts at the Third National Bank:

Account	Balance
1	$ 35.04
2	191.66
3	273.50
4	301.81
5	397.15
6	412.02
7	688.25
8	1,517.09
9	3,242.34
10	10,083.10

Required
a. Calculate the total amount stolen over the course of one year if the bank pays 5.5 percent annual interest, compounded monthly. For simplicity, assume that no additional deposits were made to the accounts listed and that there were no withdrawals of interest or principal.

b. What changes to the facts stated here would result in larger profits to the perpetrator of the irregularity? Does the size of the account balances influence the profitability of the scheme?

6. You are a member of a study team charged with developing a computerized information system for an interstate trucking company. The company's headquarters is in Mobile, Alabama, and it has truck terminals in seven states. The company's fleet consists of 25 tractor-trailers and 70 large vans.

Two major factors have affected profitability in recent years. One is increased competition resulting from the deregulation of the trucking industry. The other is the continuing increase in fuel costs. Management is particularly interested in efficiently using its fleet of trucks and in minimizing the number of long-haul trips with less than full loads. Incentives are offered to customers if they accept a flexible schedule to enable the company to combine small loads to be shipped to distant locations. But even with these incentives, customers are reluctant to wait for more than a few days. In the case of perishable loads, customers normally insist on overnight delivery.

A sophisticated truck-scheduling package, marketed by a national software firm, is to be incorporated in the information system along with custom programs providing the standard accounting functions. The system is to be on line, with interactive computer terminals located at each of the seven truck terminals. Output is to include monthly management reports presenting a detailed breakdown of operating costs and productivity per truck-mile.

Required
a. Your area of specialty is internal controls. From this description, identify the environment factors that could be expected to influence the design of the controls, and explain the nature of that influence. What other information would you need to complete your definition of the system control environment?
b. Your consulting firm is concerned about the incidence of computer crime and is interested in identifying areas of vulnerability in each of the systems it designs. What sensitive areas (if any) are there in the trucking information system described here?

7. Zebra Company has an information services department that services the processing needs of accounting, marketing, and production scheduling. Phil Sanders, the controller, called Patricia Cook, a programmer in the systems group, and asked her to develop a program for analyzing accounts receivable records and providing a monthly report. She agreed to do so and began work. After several weeks, she called Sanders and told him that the program was finished. The following day, Sanders received the first report generated by the new program. He noticed at once that the format was inadequate for his purposes, and a few days later, an assistant pointed out that the analysis was performed incorrectly.

Sanders pointed out the problems to Cook, who reluctantly agreed to try to correct the program. Three months went by, and Sanders was still receiving monthly reports with the wrong format and incorrect analysis. After complaining to the manager of the information services department, Sanders learned that Cook was no longer with the company. It emerged later that although the object-coded programs were available and a procedure had been established for running the monthly reports, no source listing could be found.

Required
Identify and discuss the control weaknesses that permitted the situation described here to develop.

8. A small company operated a two-year-old interactive computer system to support its inventory control and general accounting functions. A terminal operator was responsible for data entry of inventory transactions. If she entered an inventory issuance transaction in an amount that exceeded the previous balance on hand, a message would be displayed on her screen indicating a negative inventory balance. A negative inventory level is impossible, of course, but that was what the computer indicated.

The operator's instructions required that a negative inventory report be prepared for the stock manager whenever such a negative-balance message was displayed. The data entry clerk did this, but the stock manager ignored the reports. He did not know what to do with the information, and nobody was complaining about stock outages.

At year-end, an audit revealed that approximately 3

percent of all inventory items had negative balances and that there were, in fact, significant shortages of some items. But no one could be sure because the records were unreliable.

Required

Discuss this situation from the standpoint of management's concern for good control. What modifications would you suggest to the system (including its people, procedures, and other system components) to ensure that similar problems could never occur?

9. Networked systems are vulnerable to wire tapping. Discuss the possible crimes that may be associated with the interception of messages being transmitted over communications channels.

10. Some computer criminals plant "logic bombs" in computer programs. These are unauthorized sections of code that trigger some action—either advantageous to the criminal or detrimental to the organization—based on the entry of a transaction or file maintenance change that conforms to some criterion preselected by the perpetrator.

Required

List and explain some possible actions that a computer criminal might wish to provoke using such a technique.

11. During the 1970s the AICPA sought to clarify the purpose of various internal controls by proposing an elaborate system of classification. Now, as illustrated by Statement on Auditing Standards No. 48, the trend appears to be away from further attempts to classify internal controls.

Required

Discuss the reasons for this apparent shift of emphasis. In your discussion, explore the possibility that larger concerns might be occupying the attention of the professional bodies in the area of internal controls.

12. Concerns about computer privacy cover a wide spectrum. At one end of the spectrum, many members of the general population are concerned about the establishment of national data bases from which personal data could be accessed at will by government and commercial organizations. At the other end, the SEC and the New York Stock Exchange are concerned that securities traders and corporate raiders are gaining access to insider information—some of it from accounting data bases.

Required

Discuss the issue of computer privacy, and identify possible measures that may be taken to protect both accounting data and the public interest.

13. Progress has been slow in the development of adequate legal protection against computer crime. The failure of state and federal legislatures to enact appropriate laws before the 1980s is attributed partly to public indifference to the problem of computer crime and partly to legal issues that are only now being addressed and solved.

Required

a. Discuss the development of federal computer-crime legislation and the legal issues that have been at least partially resolved to date.
b. Comment on public attitudes toward computer crime. Are these attitudes still an obstacle to effective legal protection?

16

Control Principles and Objectives

LEARNING OBJECTIVES

After studying this chapter you should be able to

- Discuss the meaning of internal control principles and objectives.
- Describe the broad types of risk in accounting information systems.
- Identify the 12 basic internal control principles.
- Identify some specific internal control objectives stemming from each control principle.

INTRODUCTION TO CONTROL PRINCIPLES AND OBJECTIVES

Internal Control Principles

The primary objectives of internal accounting controls are to protect the resources of the enterprise and integrity of the accounting data. The complementary objectives of administrative controls are to encourage operational efficiency and compliance with management policies and procedures. These primary objectives form the backdrop against which the organizations's internal controls operate, and they must be understood as a prerequisite to the intelligent design and evaluation of internal control measures and techniques.

But within the framework of these broad objectives are more specific ones associated with the particular organizational environment, the form of the information system, its technology, its structure of component subsystems, and the existence of any special threats or areas of vulnerability that the system may face.

Identifying the applicable set of specific objectives serves two main purposes. The first is to assist the planning and design of appropriate controls to be incorporated in the accounting system. The second is to provide a basis for evaluating the internal controls as part of the external audit or for some other purpose. Establishing the controls is management's responsibility, and evaluating them is the auditor's responsibility. An example of a specific control objective is that the acceptance of customer orders is contingent on the favorable outcome of a credit check; if this objective is not achieved, bad debts may increase. Another is that wages and salaries are paid only for work duly authorized and actually performed; if this objective is not achieved, labor costs may be higher than they need be. A third objective is that effective separation of duties be maintained between the data-processing personnel and the users of the information system. This objective reflects the special problems of the computerized information system with its concentration of transaction paths. In each case, the control objective is related to a corresponding area of risk.

414

Control objectives can be classified in a number of ways. One convenient mode of classification is into administrative and accounting control objectives or, in the case of an automated system, into general control and application control objectives. Another method of classification is into two major groups: (1) financial planning and control objectives and (2) systems control objectives, with the latter divided further into five minor groups.[1] The application control objectives and some of the manual accounting control objectives can be classified further based on their place in the information system: Control objectives relating to the accounts receivable subsystem are distinguished from those relating to inventory control, or objectives relating to the purchasing cycle from those relating to the revenue cycle. The cycle approach has proved to be useful because it helps produce a coherent picture among organizations in widely different types of businesses.

The classification scheme used in this text starts by identifying a number of broad control principles related to certain areas of risk. Each principle can subsequently be extended into a list of control objectives. This approach provides a logical structure that helps explain the origin of each control objective and also helps detect any omissions that might exist in the set of objectives established for a particular information system.

The relationship of risk, control principles, control objectives, and control measures is shown in Figure 16.1. Risk is the underlying problem; control principles and objectives reflect what needs to be done to solve that problem. Control measures represent what *can* (or *has*) been done.

Standardization of Control Objectives

Although the control objectives relate to particular characteristics of the system and its organizational environment, all systems have similarities. Obviously, a professional service organization would not be interested in control objectives pertaining to inventories, and a retail store that makes only cash sales would not be directly

[1] Arthur Andersen & Co., *A Guide for Studying and Evaluating Internal Accounting Controls,* Pub. no. AA 2880 (New York: Arthur Andersen & Co., January 1978).

FIGURE 16.1 **Relationship of control principles and objectives and application of control objectives.**

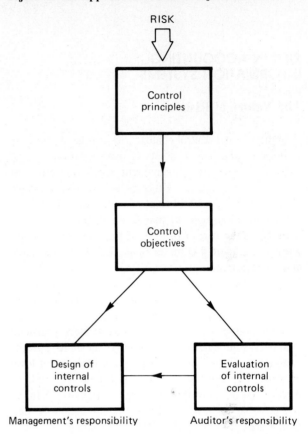

interested in control objectives dealing with credit arrangements. But virtually all organizations have a payroll system and some form of payables system and, as a result, may face similar problems arising from them.

This degree of commonality has made it possible for standard lists of control objectives to be drawn up. The primary motivation for the establishment of lists of objectives has been to provide checklists for auditors evaluating internal controls; on the other hand, the lists also provide a starting point in the selection of appropriate control techniques for design purposes. Most large accounting firms have prepared such lists, and other organizations offer lists of control objectives[2] to smaller

[2] See, for example, Martin B. Roberts, *EDP Controls* (New York: Wiley, 1985).

accounting firms that do not wish to prepare their own or that might not have the resources to do so.

RISK IN ACCOUNTING INFORMATION SYSTEMS

The Nature of Risk

In the internal control context, risk is related primarily to the potential loss of assets or damage to the organization associated with inadvertent accounting errors or deliberate irregularities. Other aspects of risk are associated with the possibilities of adverse external audit reports, embarrassment to management, and even legal liability on the part of officers of the company if major wrongdoing should come to light. Risk is an inevitable and ever-present ingredient of all business activities: People can make mistakes; machines can malfunction; and unscrupulous individuals can take advantage of opportunities to perpetrate irregularities.

Some authorities use the term *risk* to mean a general and pervasive quality and *threat* to mean its specific counterpart. From this perspective, at the general level there is the risk of loss of assets, and at the specific level there is the threat of theft from the warehouse. A threat is a possible event or activity that could exploit the particular area of vulnerability. The composite of all related threats add up to a given type of risk.

Internal control objectives stem from the overall situation of risk or from specific threats. In the same manner, some control techniques are aimed at reducing the overall risk, whereas others are aimed at reducing the severity of specific threats, that is, either preventing the events in question or reducing the damage that the events could cause. The primary goal is to reduce the associated risk to an acceptable level. Where this level is set will depend on the needs of the organization and on the price that management is prepared to pay (Figure 16.2). Controls are expensive and must be justified by the benefits to be derived: the reduction of losses from errors or irregularities. Prudent managers seek a level of "reasonable assurance" at which the costs are properly balanced against the expected losses. Absolute assurance would be prohibitively expensive, and so managers will

FIGURE 16.2   Trade-off between risk and cost of internal controls.

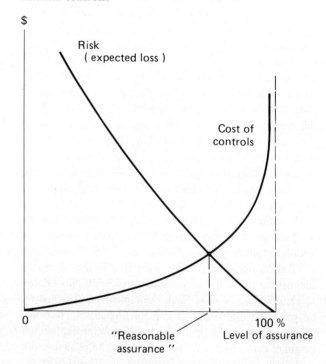

be satisfied if they can establish controls that, though not 100 percent "watertight," are judged to be adequate in the particular circumstances.

The assessment of risk involves two considerations: the estimated probable loss associated with each threat and the expected frequency of occurrence. An infrequent but large loss and a frequently occurring small loss might be regarded as being equally serious. The most serious risk is associated with losses that potentially are both large and frequent. Precisely the same considerations go into the determination of premiums by insurance companies. In addition to the size of the potential loss and the likely frequency of occurrence, the analysis of risk examines the type of resource exposed to the threat, the vulnerability to loss or damage, and the seriousness of the threat. Some parts of the system are likely to be more vulnerable than others are. When data are transcribed from one document to another or are encoded onto machine-readable media, there is a substantial risk of errors. When cash is handled, there is a substantial risk of theft.

Identification of areas of varying degrees of risk within a given information system allows the designer to establish control priorities. Because control dollars are limited, it is sensible to spend them in the most profitable manner, that is, where the risk of loss from errors or irregularities is greatest.

The professional literature distinguishes between two kinds of risk in accounting information systems: *inherent risk* and *control risk*.[3] Inherent risk depends on the nature of the asset, class of data, or system feature in question. For example, cash is much more likely to be stolen than are concrete blocks or used automobile tires. Large volumes of complex transactions, or the account balances derived from them, can be expected to contain more errors than do a few simple transactions. And machine-readable data bases are more easily destroyed—by human error, equipment failure, or sabotage—than are paper records stored in filing cabinets.

Control risk refers to the possibility that the internal controls will fail to protect the asset, class of data, or system feature that is subject to the particular degree of inherent risk. For example, cash may be stolen despite its being locked in a safe; error-checking controls may be inadequate to protect even a few simple transactions from careless mistakes; and a filing cabinet may remain unlocked because security procedures are ignored. On the other hand, effective controls can be developed to protect cash, prevent or detect errors, and secure stored data. Whereas systems design can do little to reduce inherent risk, control risk can be reduced substantially, and therein lies one of the most important goals of good design.

Before the applicable set of internal control objectives can be established, the designer must identify the main types of risks, including inherent and control risks, in the particular system. A good point of departure for this identification process is an analysis of the organization's critical success factors (see Chapter 12). The critical success factors are those on which the organization's success depends. These are the factors that management is most concerned with preserving, thus a threat to one of the critical success factors is a direct threat to the or-

ganization's well-being. Accordingly, control objectives relating to such threats acquire a higher priority than do others. For example, if effective fixed-asset management is a critical success factor for a company that leases heavy equipment, an important control objective for that company would be keeping detailed service and maintenance records. Or, if a critical success factor of a financial institution is the ability to provide round-the-clock credit-card verification to retailers, a corresponding control objective would be the avoidance of computer downtime.

Risk in Manual Information Systems

There are numerous risks in manual systems or in the manual portions of automated systems. Some of these risks are associated with human errors or with the failure of individuals to abide by company policies, procedures, and authorizations—or management's inability to enforce them. Other risks have to do with possible damage to or misuse of facilities and with temptation on the part of unscrupulous individuals to divert company assets to unauthorized use. Representative examples include

- Inadequate training and supervision of personnel
- Absence of written procedures
- Inadequate authorization of transactions
- Failure to comply with company policies and procedures
- Inconsistency of processing procedures
- Undetected errors in transaction recording and processing
- Improper disposition of output
- Loss or damage to physical assets
- Theft of cash, securities, inventory, or other assets
- Unauthorized purchase of goods or services
- Unauthorized initiation of production activities

Risk in Computerized Systems

Some aspects of automation help reduce risk, whereas many others serve to increase it. The threat of random errors, inherent in manual operations, is normally reduced: Machines have a much higher degree of consis-

[3] Statement on Auditing Standards No. 47. "Audit Risk and Materiality in Conducting an Audit:" (New York: American Institute of Certified Public Accountants, 1983).

tency than do human operators. On the other hand, machines are incapable of exercising judgment and may process large numbers of transactions incorrectly, quite unaware that the results are incorrect or even nonsensical. Furthermore, as seen in the previous chapter, the use of automation opens up the potential for computer crime in the form of theft, embezzlement, extortion, espionage, and sabotage.

Some types of risk that are peculiar to computerized systems are

- Inadequate procedures for systems development and program changes
- Acquisition of computer hardware and software that fails to meet user needs
- Inadequate systems and user documentation
- Undetected hardware or software malfunctions
- Unauthorized access to computer facilities, programs, and/or data
- Penetration of the accounting system through telecommunications channels
- Use of the computer to perpetrate irregularities or illegal activities
- Unreliability of processing capability owing to equipment downtime
- Catastrophic loss of processing capability
- Inadequate management review of processed output, particularly negotiable or action documents
- Loss or contamination of data during transmittal from the users to data processing
- Loss or contamination of data during encoding into machine-readable media
- Inadequate editing and/or correction of data subsequent to encoding
- Undetected errors in file or data base update
- Loss or contamination of the accounting data base
- Loss or contamination of data during transmittal over telecommunications channels
- Unauthorized access to or modification of data during transmittal over telecommunications channels
- Loss or contamination of data during return of output to users
- Excessive computer hardware and software acquisition costs
- Inefficient use of computer resources
- Excessive operating and maintenance costs

Some of these risks are aggravated because of the concentration of data and the convergence of transaction paths in the data-processing area. Whereas in manual systems, transaction processing and file storage are usually dispersed through numerous work stations or departments, in automated systems they may be concentrated in a single information services department. Any weaknesses in the data-processing function can therefore expose a large number of accounting processes to possible errors or irregularities.

Today's business organizations are highly dependent on their computer processing resources. In consequence, these risks are potentially serious, and management must take positive steps to reduce the organization's exposure. However, the end result can be an accounting information system that not only out-performs any comparable manual system but offers superior internal control effectiveness and efficiency.

INTERNAL CONTROL PRINCIPLES

The internal control principles address the risks just identified and spell out management's primary responsibilities for establishing and maintaining an adequate set of internal controls. The internal control system is intended to safeguard the organization's resources and ensure the accuracy and reliability of the accounting data—the province of accounting controls. And it is also intended to promote operational efficiency and encourage compliance with management policy—the province of administrative controls. The accounting literature contains a wealth of material on *accounting control principles* but comparatively little on *administrative control principles*. The reason for this imbalance is that auditors—to whom most of the literature is addressed—are primarily concerned with accounting controls.

A list of definitive accounting control principles has emerged that reflects the prevailing philosophy of the accounting profession.[4] These principles include the

---

[4] The 12 accounting control principles discussed here form a composite of principles listed in publications of the major accounting firms and the auditing and accounting guide, *The Auditor's Study and Evaluation of Internal Control in EDP Systems* (New York: American Institute of Certified Public Accountants, 1977).

need to provide an organizational environment conducive to control; the need to establish formal procedures for transaction processing; and the need to provide adequate security of the data base, the accounting system, and the physical assets. The accounting control principles are 12 in number and can be expressed as follows:

1. *Control environment.* Management by its policies, procedures, and actions should maintain an organizational environment that provides for effective supervision and that is conducive to system control.
2. *Authorizations.* Management should establish the authorizations and criteria for the creation and execution of transactions and communicate these requirements to the personnel concerned.
3. *Incompatible duties and responsibilities.* The organization of duties and responsibilities should be arranged so as to minimize opportunities for any person both to perpetrate and to conceal errors or irregularities in the normal course of duty.
4. *Classification of information.* Management should establish a plan for the classification of information that serves the needs of the organization and that conforms with Generally Accepted Accounting Principles.
5. *Transaction processing.* Management should establish and maintain procedures for recording and processing transactions and should communicate these requirements to the personnel concerned.
6. *Accuracy of data.* The operating procedures should periodically verify the accuracy of the stored data and reports that are produced from the data.
7. *Error correction.* The system should have adequate procedures for identifying and correcting errors that might be created by people or by the system's equipment and facilities.
8. *Systems security.* Management should have an adequate plan and implementation procedures to control access to and use of systems resources and to ensure the reliability of the information-processing function.
9. *Security of data.* The system should provide adequate protection of data during input, storage, processing, transmission, and output.
10. *Systems development.* Accounting information systems should be developed and maintained in accordance with the organization's goals and objectives.
11. *Documentation.* An adequate plan and implementation procedures should exist for providing and controlling systems specifications and documentation.
12. *Physical safeguarding of resources.* The organization's financial, information-processing, and other resources should be afforded adequate physical security.

There is as yet no corresponding, widely accepted list of administrative control principles. Some possible topics that could be the subject of such principles are

- Effective capacity planning to match the performance of computer facilities to the present and expected needs of the organization
- Acquisition of batch-processing facilities providing adequate turnaround time in relation to the needs of information users
- Acquisition of interactive computing facilities providing adequate response time in relation to the needs of data entry, data base query, and management decision support
- Design of user–machine and machine–user interfaces to promote the effectiveness and efficiency of user personnel
- Effective budget planning and control of the costs of acquiring, operating, and maintaining information resources
- Control of system usage to ensure efficiency and discourage waste of resources

INTERNAL CONTROL OBJECTIVES

Internal control objectives are the specific expression and extension of the control principles to individual activities, organizational units, or situations within the organization. Whereas the control principles may apply to all types of organizations or accounting information systems, the set of applicable control objectives should be tailored to the needs of a particular organization and system. Thus the following accounting control objectives are simply a sample of what might be needed in any given situation.

Furthermore, in presenting these control objectives, we shall emphasize the objectives dealing with the computerized elements of the accounting information system. Additional objectives relating more directly to functional controls in the planning/control, reporting, purchasing, production, and revenue cycles are covered in Chapters 19 through 22. Note that there are a few areas of overlap in which a given objective may appear under more than one control principle.

Principle No. 1: Control Environment

Management by its policies, procedures, and actions should maintain an organizational environment that provides for effective supervision and that is conducive to system control.

The first internal control principle addresses the risk that despite the existence of specific control measures in the information system, the organizational climate might be such as to make them ineffective. The fault may lie in inadequate company policies, in poor supervision and management attitudes, or in a negative organizational culture.

Six specific internal control objectives fall into this category:

• Responsibility for establishing and maintaining a proper control environment should be accepted at the highest levels in the organization.
• Management should establish personnel policies and procedures for recruiting, training, evaluating, and terminating employees that take into account the risks inherent in each person's responsibilities.
• Management should establish policies dealing with employee conduct to discourage activities that might undermine the effectiveness of internal control.
• All personnel should be kept aware of the importance of internal control and the need for strict compliance with control procedures.
• Well-defined procedures should exist for handling control violations.

• Managers should be allowed adequate time for supervision.

Internal accounting controls can be effective only in a favorable organizational and administrative environment. Such an environment promotes "control consciousness" among managers and employees alike. Overall responsibility for the control environment must be accepted by top management and the board of directors. This makes good business sense and also protects the corporate officers. Individuals at these levels can face civil or criminal charges for illegal acts perpetrated within the organization.

Good management is one of the best controls for the prevention of errors and irregularities. A good manager sees that the employees are well trained in the proper procedures, that the work load is equitably balanced among employees, and that each person receives proper rewards for performance. High standards are expected and maintained for quality and quantity of work. All employees understand that errors must be corrected immediately and that a control violation is a serious matter. Procedures should be established for dealing promptly and effectively with significant violations of company policy and procedures. Personnel policies should state management's thinking regarding the seriousness of a record of errors, excessive absenteeism, and other matters that are alien to good working habits. Time and effort should be continually devoted to maintaining employees' awareness of company policies and procedures.

Job descriptions should help identify the risks associated with different positions. Effective recruiting methods are obviously important to ensure that job applicants are properly screened and that good people are hired. But carefully controlled termination policies are also essential. Steps must be taken to ensure an orderly transition of responsibility to successor personnel and to avoid the very real danger of recriminatory actions.

Control consciousness includes a willingness to enforce disciplinary measures where necessary, but it should not be regarded as negative and repressive. Responsible employees should benefit from the system and should be encouraged to see it in a positive light. Contented employees who view their conditions as fair and equitable are normally motivated to abide by control regulations; in contrast, disgruntled employees are prone to make mistakes, ignore control procedures, and even sabotage the systems with which they are involved.

Principle No. 2: Authorizations

Management should establish the authorizations and criteria for the creation and execution of transactions and communicate these requirements to the personnel concerned.

The second principle arises from the risk that company employees may initiate unauthorized transactions either through negligence or as part of deliberate attempts to circumvent controls or perpetrate irregularities.

Six control objectives that fall under the heading of this principle are the following:

- The amounts, timing, and conditions of all transactions should be authorized in accordance with management's wishes.
- Acquisition and disposition of assets should be authorized in accordance with management's wishes.
- Provision should be made, under the general authorization of transactions, prohibiting the data-processing department from initiating or authorizing transactions.
- Access to processing areas or computer facilities should be limited to authorized individuals, acting in accordance with management's wishes.
- A written manual of systems and procedures should be prepared for all computer operations and should provide management's general and specific authorizations to process transactions.
- Only properly authorized input, prepared in accordance with management's general or specific authorization, should be accepted for processing.

All transaction activity, whether relating to the acquisition or disposition of assets, or otherwise, should be controlled under management's general or specific authorizations. General authorizations pertain to whole classes of transactions and represent the norm; specific authorizations pertain to individual transactions. An example of a general authorization is a standard inventory reorder policy, and an example of a specific authorization is approval of a travel request.

Written policies and procedures for processing transactions are indications of management's recognition and acceptance of its internal control responsibilities. The procedures document the methods of processing that management has authorized for the transactions in question. Without these written statements employees may never know precisely what the authorized procedures should be, and in turn, the auditors may have problems in identifying whether or not employees are adhering to management's authorizations.

The acquisition and disposition of assets and the initiation of adjustment transactions clearly may have a large impact on the company's resources and its financial statements. Written general or specific authorizations indicating the personnel who are assigned to handle the transactions and the procedures for doing so should govern the creation and treatment of all such transactions.

Several of the foregoing objectives relate specifically to the data-processing function in automated systems. There is, moreover, some overlap between some of them and the objectives listed under Principle No. 3, dealing with incompatible duties, which is considered next.

Principle No. 3: Incompatible Duties and Responsibilities

The organization of duties and responsibilities should be arranged so as to minimize opportunities for any person both to perpetrate and to conceal errors or irregularities in the normal course of duty.

The third principle acknowledges the fundamental need to separate the functions of operations and custodianship of resources from the functions of recording and maintaining accounting data. Incompatible duties or responsibilities circumvent an essential check and balance in the control system. They may result in errors being made and concealed or, more seriously, may expose the organization to undetected defalcations or other irregularities. In addition to the traditional ones pertaining to information systems of all types, certain other combinations of incompatible functions arise solely in computerized data processing.

Four control objectives fall under the heading of this principle:

- Effective separation of duties should be maintained between the individuals who authorize transactions and those who record the transactions.
- Effective separation of duties should be maintained between the individuals charged with the custody of organizational resources and those responsible for the maintenance of related accounting records.
- Effective separation of duties should be maintained between the data-processing function and the user functions.
- Effective separation of duties should be maintained between the personnel responsible for systems development and the personnel assigned to the routine processing of data.

Organizational assignments should be made so that at least two individuals (or sometimes departments) are involved in every transaction. Anyone who can initiate transactions or who has access to assets and simultaneously is responsible for making accounting entries is in a position to commit and conceal errors or perpetrate and conceal irregularities. For example, handling cash and keeping cash records are incompatible duties. Similarly, purchasing and receiving merchandise, hiring and servicing the payroll, inventory custody and sales, and accounts receivable and collections all would be considered incompatible duties. Obviously, collusion or conspiracy could take place between two individuals, but this is comparatively rare. For practical purposes, separation of duties can be used to reduce substantially the incidence of undetected errors or irregularities.

In automated systems, the separation of responsibilities has to include separation between the systems and operations functions, within the data-processing department, and between the data-processing department and the users. The systems development function and the operations function should be separated to discourage programming irregularities involving fraudulent processing of live data. New systems or system components should be developed and tested using simulated data; live data should be processed only using completed systems that have been properly authorized and released for production use.

The data-processing function should be separated from its users partly as an extension of the objective relating to separation of the functions of transaction origination and processing and partly to compensate for the concentration of transaction flows into the data processing area. Initiation of transactions is the responsibility of the user groups; processing of the transactions is the responsibility of the data-processing personnel.

A major problem exists with incompatible responsibilities in small organizations that have simply too few employees to achieve effective separation of duties. If a particular control objective cannot be achieved, a weakness will exist unless compensating controls can be established to restore the necessary control environment.

Principle No. 4: Classification of Information

Management should establish a plan for the classification of information that best serves the needs of the organization and that conforms with generally accepted accounting principles.

The fourth principle recognizes the risk that without a proper framework for the classification of transaction data, the accumulation and processing of accounting records may not conform with generally accepted accounting principles or other applicable standards. As a result, the external financial statements may be misstated, and internal reports may provide unreliable or incomplete information for management decision making.

Two control objectives can be identified within this principle:

- Management should establish criteria for the classification of information via the chart of accounts or otherwise.
- Transactions should be classified in a manner that permits the preparation of reports in accordance with generally accepted accounting principles and management's wishes.

An adequate framework should exist to support the accurate, timely recording and proper recognition of economic events. Such a framework is based on the classification and summarization of transaction data. Classification depends on the use of a suitable coding system (see Chapter 2), which may be modeled on the chart of accounts or have some other suitable basis. The coding system provides a basis for tracing the audit trail and should identify the origin of the transaction, its essential characteristics, and the purposes for which it is to be processed. Summarization is aimed at the different needs of financial accounting, operational control, government regulations, and tax responsibilities. The process of summarization must be consistent with generally accepted accounting principles and with any other applicable recording and reporting requirements.

Principle No. 5: Transaction Processing

Management should establish and maintain procedures for recording and processing transactions and should communicate these requirements to the personnel concerned.

The fifth principle arises from the risk that transaction recording and processing may be incorrect or incomplete and, consequently, may undermine the reliability and usefulness of the accounting data. There is also the risk that even though appropriate procedures may have been established, they may not have been adequately communicated to operational personnel or may not be properly enforced.

Six control objectives fall into this category:

- Transaction-processing procedures should be established in accordance with management's wishes and should be put in writing.
- Procedures should be established for reporting significant economic events.
- Procedures should be established for the recognition, classification, and summarization of individual transactions.
- Procedures should be established to ensure that all authorized transactions are processed once and only once.
- Procedures should be established for the proper and timely maintenance of accounts in the general ledger, subsidiary ledgers, and other master files.
- Reports should be prepared accurately, promptly, and

consistently and should fairly present the information to which they relate.

There should be strict control over transaction execution, recording, and processing. The need for written procedures for handling input, processing activities (manual or computerized), and output has already been mentioned. Without written guidelines, the processing procedures may vary depending on the individuals involved, and the lack of processing uniformity may contribute to erratic errors and unreliability of financial statements, management reports, and other system outputs.

The preceding objectives for transaction processing and transaction authorization can be expanded into a large number of control objectives pertaining to individual applications or transaction cycles. For example, the objective relating to the reporting of economic events translates into more detailed objectives pertaining to transactions involving the handling of equities and investments, procurement of goods and services, employment of labor, production, extension of credit, shipment of goods and rendering of services, and collections from customers. Some of these objectives are listed in Chapters 19 through 22. The same remarks regarding the expansion into large numbers of detailed objectives can be made about the objective relating to the recognition of individual transactions.

It is necessary to ensure that all transactions are processed and that no transactions are processed more than once. Completeness is essential, but undetected duplication can be as serious as incomplete processing. The objective relating to maintenance of accounts applies to both routine posting and nonroutine file maintenance. Achievement of these objectives helps achieve the final one dealing with the reporting of transaction activity.

Principle No. 6: Accuracy of Data

The operating procedures should periodically verify the accuracy of the stored data and the reports that are produced from the data.

The sixth principle recognizes that financial records are worthless if they do not correspond to economic reality.

Although care must obviously go into maintaining the accuracy of data capture and processing, the added safeguard of direct verification is essential.

Five control objectives fall under this heading:

- On a continuing basis, internal auditors or some other independent group within the organization should review and test computer-processing activities.
- Output control totals should be reconciled with input and processing controls.
- Output should be examined and tested by comparison with original source documents.
- Recorded account balances should be periodically substantiated and evaluated.
- The system should contain clearly defined audit trails indicating the processing steps performed, their timing, the individuals responsible for processing, and the results of each significant processing operation.

Continual vigilance must be exercised to maintain the validity of the data. Physical asset values should be periodically compared with the corresponding recorded balances to verify the accuracy of the accounting data. If the records do not agree with the actual asset counts, then there is evidence that errors have been made or that assets have been added or removed without authorization. On the other hand, the converse is not necessarily true; correlation between the actual and the recorded amounts does not prove that errors or irregularities have not occurred. Assets may have been stolen before they were recorded or the records illegally amended to reflect the removal or theft of assets.

The frequency of comparison between the physical assets and the records will depend on the vulnerability of the particular asset. For example, cash on hand will often be counted daily, whereas inventory may be counted only once a year. The cost of the control must be reasonable in terms of the risk of loss that the control is intended to eliminate.

Along with the validation of the accounting records against the physical assets, several control objectives pertain to the internal consistency of the data. These include the comparison of processed data in summarized form, such as control totals, or in detail with the corresponding data in the original source documents. To be able to do this, clear audit trails must be preserved through the processing operations.

Principle No. 7: Error Correction

The system should have adequate procedures for identifying and correcting errors that might be created by people or by the system's equipment and facilities.

The seventh principle recognizes that errors are inevitable no matter how "tight" the controls measures are: The most conscientious and trusted employee can make a mistake, and the most reliable piece of equipment can sometimes fail. If errors go undetected, the value of the accounting records and reports may be in serious question.

Eleven control objectives fall in this category:

- The control features inherent in the computer operating system and other support software should be utilized to the maximum possible extent to provide control over operations and to detect and report hardware or software malfunctions.
- The data validation problems in the complete description of the data elements used by a data base management system should be controlled.
- The data consistency problems in the data base should be controlled.
- A designated individual or group should be responsible for receiving all data to be processed, for ensuring that all data are recorded, for following up on errors detected during processing to see that they are corrected and resubmitted by the proper party, and for verifying the proper distribution of output.
- The system should verify all significant codes and account references used to record transaction data.
- Conversion of data into machine-readable form should be controlled.
- Movements of data between one processing step and another, or between departments, should be controlled.
- The correction and resubmission of all errors detected by the application system should be reviewed and controlled.
- Controls should prevent processing the wrong file, detect errors in manipulation, and highlight operator-caused errors.
- Limit and reasonableness checks should be incorpo-

rated in programs to identify unusual transactions for further scrutiny.

- Run-to-run controls should be incorporated to check the consistency of successive processing operations.

Appropriate measures must be taken to provide for early detection and prompt, systematic correction of errors, regardless of their source. No information system can be entirely free from errors; the cost of preventing or detecting all errors would be prohibitive. Instead, the goal of error control is to reduce the incidence of errors to an acceptable level, with ''acceptable'' depending on management policy and the nature of the data being processed. Errors in cash receipts or disbursements may be pursued until every cent is accounted for, whereas small discrepancies in the weight of nontoxic industrial waste would not normally be treated so seriously.

The incidence of errors is likely to vary considerably from one part of the system to another. Data capture has traditionally been a highly vulnerable area. In automated systems, another vulnerable area includes those points of interface at which data are communicated to the data-processing department or where data are transcribed from human-readable form into machine-readable form. Within the computerized data-processing function, there is a need to compensate for the invisibility of both the data and the processing operations. In general, responsibility for detecting errors should be shared between the designers of the system and the people operating it. But wherever possible, programmed controls should be utilized to test automatically and routinely for error conditions.

Principle No. 8: Systems Security

Management should have an adequate plan and implementation procedures to control access to and use of systems resources and to ensure the reliability of the information-processing function.

The eighth control principle reflects the need to avoid abuse of information-processing resources, including unauthorized use, theft, damage, or destruction of hardware, software, documentation, or data. It also recognizes the high level of dependency of most organizations on their computerized information systems and the seriousness of loss of processing capability, even for short periods of time.

Eight control objectives fall into this category:

- Access to accounting information systems should be limited to those persons who require it in the performance of their authorized duties.
- Access controls should extend to electronic as well as physical access to computer facilities.
- Access to computer programs and program documentation should be limited to those persons who require it in the performance of their authorized duties.
- Access to critical forms should be limited to those individuals authorized to process or maintain particular applications and acting in accordance with management's wishes.
- Access to systems resources by auditors should be unrestricted.
- Positive steps should be taken to ensure the reliability of computer resources.
- Provisions must be made to continue essential data-processing activities in the event of temporary inoperability of computer facilities.
- Logs of computer activity should be maintained for review by managers, auditors, or computer operators.

Access to and usage of the system—including facilities, programs, documentation—should be restricted to persons who require such access in the conduct of their authorized duties. Access should be denied to persons who might damage facilities or who are suspected of intent to perpetrate irregularities. Access to facilities may involve physical contact or, in computerized systems, electronic access via remote terminals or communications channels. Emphasis should be on controlling access to systems that interface with public telephone lines because of the high risk of penetration.

Steps must be taken to ensure that information systems provide an acceptable level of reliability. But total reliability—of either human or computer elements—is impossible to attain, and the organization must acquire the means for continued processing of essential data even during periods when the primary facilities may be out of action. The time taken to diagnose computer hardware or software problems and rectify them may be much longer than the maximum tolerable delay in information-processing activities. The payroll must be processed on schedule, and billings must go out to customers to ensure needed cash flow. The more dependent the organization is on the computer facilities, the more urgent it is for prompt emergency repairs to be performed or alternative data processing facilities to be made available.

Organizations should also develop disaster plans for dealing with large-scale destruction of computer facilities and/or stored data as a result of equipment failure, natural disasters, human error, vandalism, sabotage, civil disturbance, terrorist action, or war.

The last objective relates to the need for system logs to provide a permanent record of both normal and abnormal processing activities. Run logs acquire considerable importance to compensate for the invisibility of data processing within the computer. They also provide an important means by which error conditions, operating irregularities, and unauthorized access to data can be detected and investigated.

Principle No. 9: Security of Data

The system should provide adequate protection of data during input, storage, processing, transmission, and output.

The ninth principle recognizes the risk of damage to or destruction of the accounting data base and the impact that such an event could have on the continued operations of the enterprise. Data must be protected before, during, and after processing and during transmission from one location to another.

Eight control principles fall under this category:

- Access to data files should be limited to those individuals authorized to process or maintain particular applications and acting in accordance with management's wishes.
- Stored data should be properly safeguarded against unauthorized modification, destruction, or loss.
- Update of master files and transaction files should be controlled to prevent unauthorized changes and to ensure accurate and complete results.
- The system should contain provisions to prevent user conflicts and processing errors when data are shared among multiple users.

- System output should be distributed only to authorized users.
- Applicable security controls should extend to data stored at off-site locations and data stored or processed on computers operated by end users.
- Data transmitted through telecommunications systems should be protected against distortion, interruption, loss, diversion, or unauthorized access.
- Specific system controls should be established and maintained to permit reconstruction of events and recovery of data in the event of damage or loss.

The organization's data base is a valuable resource to be protected with the same vigilance and vigor as are its other resources. Many organizations that have experienced catastrophes have learned that the loss of tangible assets can be less serious than the loss of their accounting records. Data files must be protected against misuse and, in the event of destruction or loss, must be capable of being reconstructed promptly to allow ongoing business activities to continue and to meet statutory requirements. Messages transmitted through telecommunications systems must be protected to ensure their integrity and their arrival at the intended destination. Such data must also be protected against eavesdropping or unauthorized modification during transmission. Shared access to data even by authorized persons can cause conflicts and loss of data, and programmed controls should be incorporated wherever feasible to protect the integrity of the data.

Principle No. 10: Systems Development

Accounting information systems should be developed and maintained in accordance with the organization's goals and objectives.

The tenth principle stems from the risk that lack of planning and control in the systems development area can result in the implementation of systems that do not meet the needs of the organization. Costly mistakes can be made—and the organization may have to live with these errors for many years. The negative impact on the operations of the business can be substantial.

Ten control principles can be classified under this heading:

- The procedures for systems design, including the selection of software packages, should require the active participation by representatives of the users and, as appropriate, the accounting department and internal auditors.
- All systems projects should be adequately planned and controlled from initiation to completion.
- Each system should have written specifications that are reviewed and approved by an appropriate level of management and user departments.
- Systems testing should be a joint responsibility of users and information-processing personnel and should include tests covering the whole range of operating conditions.
- All systems changes or enhancements should be approved before implementation to determine that they have been authorized, tested, and documented.
- Final approval should be obtained prior to placing new systems into operation.
- Systems and end-user software should be subjected to the same control procedures as those applied to installation of and changes to applications programs.
- Internal auditors or some other independent group within the organization should review and evaluate proposed systems at critical stages of development.
- Management should provide training for systems personnel in both the technical and managerial aspects of new systems so that they can maintain those systems in accordance with organizational goals and objectives.
- Standards and procedures should be established guiding the acquisition and operation of personal computers by end-user departments.

The development of new systems or applications must be controlled to ensure that the end product meets the requirements for which it was intended. Participation in the development project by user groups, including accounting and internal auditing, is almost essential, and management should also exercise close and continuous supervision. Systems development should not simply be delegated to information-processing professionals. Systems enhancements must be subjected to similar authorization and testing procedures as are completely new

systems. Training programs are normally required to help users and others to use information-processing facilities effectively and efficiently.

Standards for the acquisition and use of personal computers by end users are desirable to avoid unwarranted duplication of resources, incompatibility of hardware and software, maintenance problems, and inability to process information in accordance with the organization's needs.

Principle No. 11: Documentation

An adequate plan and implementation procedures should exist for providing and controlling systems specifications and documentation.

The eleventh principle recognizes that an undocumented system is a liability rather than an asset to the organization. Failure to provide adequate documentation is an unwise economy and can result in improper or inefficient utilization of systems resources, expensive studies when changes or enhancements are required, and substantial increases in the cost of audit engagements.

Four control objectives arise from this principle:

- Each system should have written specifications that are reviewed and approved by an appropriate level of management and applicable user departments.
- Management should require several levels of documentation and establish formal procedures to define the system at appropriate levels of detail.
- Procedures should be established for the proper maintenance of documentation.
- Adequate controls should be exercised to protect the integrity of documentation and to limit access to documentation to authorized persons.

Good documentation is the key to successful information systems, and documentation must be controlled to ensure that it is complete and current. Documentation is required at different levels of detail and must be written in a form that can be understood and properly used by its intended audience. Maintenance of documentation is an ongoing requirement to stay abreast of the continual enhancement of information systems typical of most organizations. Obsolete documentation may be of archeological interest, but is of little help to users, systems professionals, or auditors.

Proper custody of technical systems and other documentation is also essential to prevent loss, damage, or misuse by persons interested in perpetrating irregularities. Access to details of control measures could help unscrupulous persons devise ways of circumventing the internal controls. Access to documentation should be strictly on a "need-to-know" basis.

Principle No. 12: Physical Safeguarding of Resources

The organization's financial, information-processing, and other resources should be afforded adequate physical security.

The twelfth principle acknowledges that physical security is fundamental to protecting the investment made in the resources of the enterprise. Lax security exposes the resources to accidental but avoidable damage, to acts of violence, and to misappropriation.

Four control objectives arise from this principle:

• Computer resources and other equipment should be protected against accidental damage, abuse, loss, or theft.
• Special security should be provided for parts of the system in which passwords, identification codes, authorization codes, or encryption keys are entered and stored.
• Physical security must extend to remote input, processing, and output facilities; to computing resources operated by end users; and to off-site storage facilities.
• Adequate insurance coverage should be maintained to compensate for the damage or loss of physical resources.

The resources of the organization must clearly be protected. In this regard, emphasis must be on protecting accounting records and data; computer hardware and software components that have theft value; processing facilities that may be the target of unauthorized use; and all types of electronic equipment that are easily dam-

aged. Care must be adopted in selecting physical security measures, assigning custodianship responsibilities, establishing and enforcing procedures for disposing of assets. Access to and disposition of the resources by way of negotiable and action documents must also be controlled.

Some physical security measures are necessary in order to guarantee the effectiveness of other internal control measures. For example, unless access to the computer room is restricted, the integrity of internal controls such as passwords and encryption keys entered through the system console are undermined. Similarly, unless access to administrative areas is restricted, the effectiveness of authorization controls and separation of duties may be impaired. In this way, physical security can be regarded more as an environmental factor, influencing the effectiveness of many other types of controls, than as a specific control measure.

The final control objective recognizes the need to maintain adequate insurance coverage to help the organization survive the damage to or loss of physical—or in some cases even intangible—resources. In an extreme situation, failure to maintain adequate coverage could undermine the going-concern principle in the eyes of an external auditor.

SUMMARY

The purpose of internal controls is to reduce risk. There is risk in both the manual and the automated portions of the accounting information system, although it may take specific forms that depend on the processing technology. Risk in manual systems centers on human error. Risk in computerized systems may involve equipment failure, but it also reflects human error in programming, testing, and verifying input data. Furthermore, the power of computerized systems makes them vulnerable to accidental and/or deliberate abuse.

The 12 basic accounting control principles articulate management's primary responsibilities in the face of the prevailing risks. They are a series of general statements addressing broad types of risk, and they apply to virtually every type of organization. The 12 control principles address the need for

- A favorable control environment
- A proper system of authorizations
- Avoidance of incompatible duties and responsibilities
- Proper classification of information
- Effective procedures for transaction processing
- Verification of the accuracy of accounting data
- Procedures for prompt error correction
- Security of information-processing facilities
- Effective security of accounting data
- Orderly procedures for system development and maintenance
- Comprehensive documentation of the system
- Provision of adequate physical security

Each control principle gives rise to a number of more specific control objectives that must be achieved, in any particular enterprise and information system, in order to reduce the associated risks to an acceptable level. Applicable sets of control objectives, in turn, form the starting point either for the design of effective control measures and techniques or for the review of controls by an external auditor.

BIBLIOGRAPHY

American Institute of Certified Public Accountants. *AICPA Professional Standards.* Vol. 3, *Accounting.* New York: Commerce Clearing House, 1981.

American Institute of Certified Public Accountants. *The Auditor's Study and Evaluation of Internal Control in EDP Systems*, Audit and Accounting Guide. New York: AICPA, 1977.

American Institute of Certified Public Accountants. *Management, Control and Audit of Advanced EDP Systems*, Computer Services Guidelines. New York: AICPA, 1977.

Arthur Andersen & Co. *A Guide for Studying and Evaluating Internal Accounting Controls*, AA Pub. no. 2880, Item I. Chicago: Arthur Andersen & Co., 1978.

Burrows, James H. "Future Directions for Computer Security: The Role of Standards." *Datamation*, October 1, 1986 (supplement), p. 5.

Cangemi, Michael. "The Internal Auditor's Role in Computer Security." *Datamation*, October 1, 1986 (supplement), p. 6.

Halper, Stanley, D., Glenn C. Davis, P. J. O'Neill-Dunne, and Pamela R. Pfau. *Handbook of EDP Auditing.* Boston: Warren, Gorham & Lamont, 1985.

Roberts, Martin B. *EDP Controls.* New York: Wiley, 1985.

DISCUSSION QUESTIONS AND PROBLEMS

1. Define and discuss the following terms:

- Control environment
- Control objective
- Control principle
- General authorization
- Incompatible duties
- Material control weakness
- Reasonable assurance
- Risk
- Specific authorization
- Threat

2. Identify and discuss the main areas of risk faced by

- A small beauty shop
- A hospital
- A bank
- A manufacturing company
- A charity
- A local government agency

3. Identify and discuss the main areas of risk faced by the following types of organizations in the data-processing function:

- A professional person keeping business records on a personal computer
- A small business with ten employees, one of whom is a bookkeeper who processes the payroll on a personal computer
- A medium-sized business in which all computer operations are performed by the accounting department

• A large organization operating a distributed network system based on dial-up telephone lines

4. On April 15, Joe Delano, a programmer employed by Reed Co., was given two weeks' notice following some trouble in the data-processing department. During those two weeks, Delano managed to modify the payroll programs so that after entry of a processing date after May 1, no deductions would be made from employee paychecks. He also modified the billing programs to destroy the format of all invoices printed by the computer. He deleted master file records corresponding to a number of the firm's largest customers and purged the backup copies of the files so that the records could not be reconstructed. Delano then destroyed the source listings of most of the programs he had written and stole magnetic tape files containing several expensive software packages.

Not satisfied with his "work," Delano went back to the company one night early in May, damaged several pieces of computer hardware, and stole two portable terminals.

A police investigation, conducted some time later, revealed that Delano had two previous convictions for employment-related crimes.

Required

List and discuss the control weaknesses that could allow an employee to carry out the acts described.

5. The top management of Onyx Corporation became aware of frequent errors in both internal accounting reports and customer billings and other output documents. The internal auditors were requested to investigate the situation in the accounting department.

It emerged that all the offending operations were manual ones. There had been excessive absenteeism, tardiness, and employee turnover of clerical personnel in the department. The auditor interviewed two clerks who handled the billing operations and received two different versions of how the invoices were to be prepared. Both clerks said that they had learned the procedures from their predecessors on the job. One of the clerks added, "It doesn't matter whether we make mistakes or not; Mrs. Foley (the supervisor) still screams at us."

Required

Discuss the control environment and practices at Onyx that led to the situation described here.

6. One of the control objectives, listed under Principle No. 5, reads: "Procedures should be established for the recognition of significant economic events."

Required

List the significant economic events that would occur in each of the following accounting activities:

• Purchasing
• Accounts payable
• Sales
• Accounts receivable
• Inventory management
• Payroll

7. Suggest the appropriate frequency with which accounting records in the following areas should be independently verified. Also indicate the best means of verification, and identify the risks that could occur from failing to carry out the proper verification.

• Cash in the checkout register in a retail store
• Cash in a petty cash drawer
• Accounts receivable in a mail-order business
• Merchandise in a department store
• Inventory in a building supplies company
• Small tools in a manufacturing shop
• Typewriters in a government agency
• Investments in a pension fund portfolio
• Heavy machinery in a construction company
• Parcels of land held by a developer

8. List the errors that could be made in the capture, processing, and reporting of accounts payable transactions in a computerized accounting system. The transactions are originated upon receipt of a vendor invoice and notification from the receiving department that the goods have arrived. Transactions are encoded onto magnetic tape and are processed semimonthly. Checks are produced to be mailed to vendors, and a report is prepared for management listing all the outstanding payables vouchers remaining to be paid.

9. Mr. White serves as financial secretary and treasurer of the First Baptist Church in a small town.

His responsibilities include maintaining all accounting records, receiving pledge income and plate collections, and making disbursements for all church expenses.

Mr. White, who is 71 years old, is a lifelong member of the church and is highly respected in the community. He took over the unpaid job 15 years ago after retiring from the military and after his predecessor passed away. The church officers have always been full of praise for the manner in which Mr. White performed, but lately there has been some concern because of his failing health. No one has been found to help Mr. White with the work.

Required

Discuss the risks inherent in Mr. White's position in the church.

10. Review the list of control objectives presented in this chapter, and identify those that are most directly applicable to
a. Purely manual processing
b. Automated batch processing, using magnetic tape as the input medium
c. Automated real-time processing, supported by a data base management system

11. You are a member of a team developing a system of internal controls for Pentacle Prosperity, Inc., a regional investment brokerage firm.

The client firm employs 65 account executives at 12 branches throughout the Midwest. A sophisticated interactive computer system is used to provide up-to-the-minute prices of stocks and commodities and also to accept transaction input by the account executives. Transactions include purchases and sales of securities, speculations in commodities and interest rate futures, option puts and calls, and investments in tax shelters.

Your assignment consists of designing internal controls in the area of transaction authorization. As a starting point, you have obtained from the audit department a checklist of control objectives. (Assume that this checklist contains the control objectives listed in this chapter.) But you are concerned that some of the objectives on the checklist may not be applicable to the particular client and that other relevant control objectives may have to be added.

Required
a. Review the control objectives listed in the chapter relating to transaction authorization. Identify those that you believe are relevant to the client firm's situation.
b. Suggest other objectives that you wish to consider in the design of the internal control system.

12. One of the control objectives, listed under Control Principle No. 6, states: "The system should contain clearly designed audit trails indicating the processing steps performed, their timing, the individuals responsible for processing, and the results of each significant processing operation."

Required

List the problems that could occur (i.e., the risks faced) in a modern accounting system if this control objective were not achieved.

13. One of the control objectives, listed under Control Principle No. 10, states: "All system changes or enhancements should be approved before implementation to determine that they have been authorized, tested, and documented."

Required

List the risks faced in a large organization if this control objective is not achieved.

14. Hengist and Horsa, Inc., is a wholesale food broker ("middle man") dealing in groceries, meat, fresh produce, and other items. H&H buys from farmers, canning plants, meat producers, and mills, and sells to small- to medium-sized supermarkets and convenience stores. To the extent possible, H&H arranges for food products to be shipped direct from suppliers to retail stores. But the company does inventory some products at six distribution centers for subsequent shipment to retailers. H&H aims at a "just in time" inventory policy, partly because of potential deterioration of the goods, but also to minimize on storage capacity, much of which has to be refrigerated storage. In addition to the regional warehouses, H&H operates three sales offices and has a fleet of delivery trucks.

H&H has operated successfully for many years and

has now reached a sales volume of over $200 million per year. Its strategy has always been to satisfy the customer. High product quality and guaranteed, on-schedule delivery have been the hallmarks of its way of doing business. And this strategy has paid off in terms of strong customer loyalty and ability to survive and grow in this increasingly competitive industry. Competition comes not only from other food brokers but also from vertically integrated supermarket chains.

H&H strives to keep customers fully informed of the status of their orders, and this has led to the present development of a comprehensive computerized information system for handling purchase and sales order processing as well as the other traditional accounting functions. Specifically, the following applications are to be implemented:

- Purchase order processing
- Inventory management
- Sales order processing
- Accounts payable
- Accounts receivable
- Payroll
- Fixed asset management
- General ledger
- Budgeting

Of primary concern is the need for a fully integrated system, allowing on-line tracking of order status from the time orders are called in by customers—and from the time that orders are placed with suppliers—to the time that products are delivered to retail stores. In order to provide this level of integration, a state-of-the-art relational data-base management system is to be installed.

Required

a. Prepare an analysis of the client's critical success factors.

b. Using these critical success factors as a guide to the organization's control concerns, develop a list of applicable control objectives. Assign a priority (high, moderate, low) to each control objective.

15. Propose a list of *administrative control principles*, corresponding to the *accounting control principles* listed in the chapter. The administrative control principles should address the need for operational efficiency and compliance with management policies and procedures. Of how much interest would these principles be to (a) managers, (b) internal auditors, and (c) external auditors?

17

Control Measures and Techniques

LEARNING OBJECTIVES

After studying this chapter you should be able to

- Discuss the importance of the control environment in the organization.
- Identify the chief tangible and intangible factors in the control environment.
- Explain the relationship between the control environment and specific control measures.
- Discuss the major organizational controls, including separation of duties.
- Describe the purposes of systems development and systems controls.
- Discuss the authorization and control of data input.
- Identify the major issues in control of transaction processing.
- Describe effective control of file and data base content.
- Describe the issues in telecommunications controls.
- Discuss the major controls over systems output.
- Explain the need for confirmation controls.

CHAPTER OUTLINE

THE CONTROL ENVIRONMENT

The importance of the control environment has already been mentioned. It addresses the requirements of Control Principle No. 1, as described in Chapter 16. By the control mechanisms they establish and by their regard for the importance of controls, the top managers in an organization create an attitude toward controls that permeates the thinking of everyone in that organization. This atmosphere forms the environment in which the formal control system must operate.

In a report issued in 1979, a special advisory committee of the AICPA made the following statement regarding the internal control environment in an organization:

The Committee has found the term *internal control environment* to be a convenient way to describe these factors. Some are clearly visible, like a formal corporate conduct policy statement or an internal audit function. Some are intangible, like the competence and integrity of personnel. Some, like organizational structure and the way in which management communicates, enforces, and reinforces policy, vary so widely among companies that they can be contrasted more easily than they can be compared.[1]

The committee made the important point that the control environment has both tangible and intangible aspects.

The tangible factors in the control environment pertain to the formal control structure that management establishes in the organization. They can be grouped, for convenience, into five broad categories, the first four of which take the form of management policies:

1. Organizational policies
2. Policies relating to employee conduct
3. Personnel policies and procedures
4. Accounting and information services policies
5. Physical security

We shall describe each of these so as to identify those visible controls that contribute to a satisfactory control environment.

The intangible factors reflect the attitudes and day-to-day actions of top management that either encourage or discourage the development of effective controls and compliance with control procedures. For an organization to have an adequate system of internal controls, it must have a satisfactory control "consciousness" among its people. Our discussion of the control environment will conclude with an exploration of the control consciousness and the ways in which it can be fostered in the organization.

A "road map" of the factors comprising the internal control environment is presented in Figure 17.1.

Organizational Policies

A company's organizational structure should be designed to carry out the operations of the business in the most effective manner and should be adjusted periodically to meet the ever-changing demands of the business. The characteristics of the organizational structure establish the framework for the control system. An organi-

[1] American Institute of Certified Public Accountants, *Internal Accounting Control—Report of the Special Advisory Committee* (New York: AICPA, 1979), p. 12.

FIGURE 17.1 Map of internal control environment.

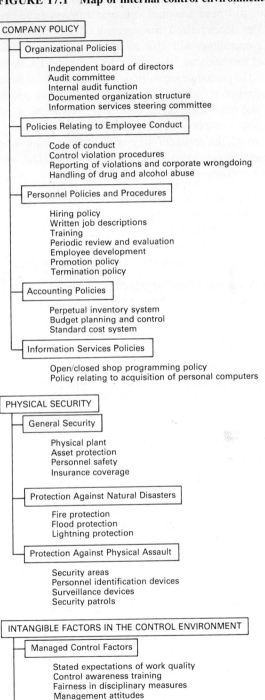

zation operating with centralized management, for example, will need a control structure different from one that has decentralized management. The size of the firm's operations will also affect the need for certain control mechanisms. The larger the company, the more formal the procedures usually need to be, because senior management is further removed from the daily operations and relies more on the reporting of company activities than managers in small companies do.

Although the details of the control structure vary from company to company, there are several organizational control concepts that are widely applicable:

• Independent board of directors
• Audit committee
• Internal audit function
• Documented organization structure
• High-level information services steering committee

An independent board of directors is one in which a significant number, preferably a majority, of the members are neither current nor former employees of the corporation. Board members who are also corporate managers or who are financially dependent on management's decisions may not be as objective in evaluating management's activities as are those who are not. But in any case, a truly independent board member is one who is independent in spirit as well as in financial relationships.

Boards of directors have the legal power as elected representatives of the stockholders to govern the corporation, but normally the board delegates this authority to management. Board members, however, still are responsible for overseeing corporate operations, evaluating management's performance, and assuring themselves that the corporation is in compliance with applicable laws and regulations. To meet these broad obligations, board members need adequate information about corporate activities. Moreover, they must study this information so that they understand company operations and the economic and competitive climate in which they occur. The size and complexity of the company and its operations will affect the amount of study required.

An audit committee is a standing committee of the board of directors. It forms one of the three essential

FIGURE 17.2 The three components of the audit function.

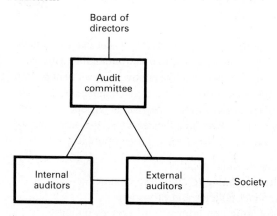

components of the audit function, the others being the internal and external audit activities (Figure 17.2). Collectively these three bear overall responsibility for internal control in the organization. Normally, the audit committee is responsible for making recommendations to the full board regarding the selection of the external auditors, reviewing significant financial information, seeing that an effective internal control system is maintained, conducting or directing any investigations of possible fraud or management irregularities, and generally serving as a communications link between both the internal and external auditors and the board of directors. Audit committees composed of independent board members can ensure that its decisions are free from mangagement's influence. For many years, the SEC and the AICPA stressed the desirability of independent audit committees, and in June 1978 the existence of such a committee became a requirement for listing on the New York Stock Exchange.

The internal audit function may be performed by one person or by a whole department, depending on the size of the company. Internal auditors review and evaluate the data-gathering system for accuracy and reliability, check the adequacy of internal controls and compliance with established policies and procedures, and participate in systems development projects. Some internal auditors have expertise in information-processing technology, and increasingly they are being assigned the responsibility for approving the controls in new systems prior to implementation. The internal auditors should report at a high level in the organization to ensure proper independence. In many organizations, they report functionally (although not organizationally) to the audit committee of the board of directors and, through their reports, increase the flow of information necessary for the committee to do its job. In addition to its routine studies, the internal audit group may also act as the investigative arm of the audit committee when a possible fraud or irregularity is suspected. A technically competent internal audit function for investigating the company's systems and performing in-depth control reviews is a major factor in establishing and maintaining a satisfactory control environment.

A documented organization structure requires an organization chart showing the separation of functions and responsibilities to provide for proper checks and balances. The larger and more complex the organization, the more formal the documentation needs to be. Written job descriptions detailing the duties, authorities, and responsibilities of each key employee provide for formal channels of authority and provide documented evidence of separation of duties. The written job descriptions, which should be required reading for all new employees and kept readily available for reference, form the communications vehicle for informing all concerned parties of this control structure.

An information services steering committee establishes or approves information-processing policies and operating standards, approves systems projects, sets priorities for implementing systems, evaluates the effectiveness of processing operations, and generally monitors and evaluates processing activities. Such a committee used to be known as the data-processing steering committee, but its name—and charge—has evolved as the responsibilities of the information function in the organization have expanded.

In many companies, the information services steering committee is chaired by a senior member of management and has representatives from each of the user groups and at least one information-processing specialist to provide technical expertise. The committee exercises a control function to ensure that the company's investment in systems facilities is utilized effectively and that the systems effort is coordinated with other operating functions and management policies.

In small companies, these committee duties may be handled by the executive committee or the chief executive officer. Many small companies have no in-house professional information services staff and have to rely on outside consultants, external auditors, or computer vendors as their source of advice. All computer users, regardless of size, need a source of information-processing experience on which they can depend for objective assistance in defining the alternatives when relevant management decisions must be made. This assistance will also alert them to difficulties in obtaining and using computer hardware and software and to the controls necessary to ensure satisfactory operations from their computerized systems.

Policies Relating to Employee Conduct

Written policies are management's formal method of communicating to all employees its thinking about how various business matters should be handled in the organization. Employee policies should be designed to influence and determine operating decisions and help to establish the required control environment. The policies should state the philosophy and ethics that are to govern company activities, but the policy alone will not be effective unless it is supported by disciplined management enforcement. For the policy to have meaning, the decisions and actions of all employees must comply with the spirit and content of the policy statement.

The following policies can be expected to influence the control environment:

- Policy setting forth an expected code of conduct and business ethics for all employees in their dealings with customers, vendors, fellow employees, and others.
- Policy stating the importance of controlling operations and the seriousness of control violations.
- Policy listing the penalties for various control violations and the procedures for dealing with violators.
- Policy on the reporting of suspected fraud or other irregularities.

The achievement of satisfactory internal control depends heavily on how employees and managers conduct themselves in their work. Organizations should establish codes of ethics or rules of conduct to guide individuals tempted to engage in activities that could threaten the internal control environment. An example of such an activity is acceptance by a purchase agent of bribes or loans from a supplier. Another example is employees' acceptance of part-time jobs with customers, vendors, or competitors of the company.

Management should have written policies stating the importance of adhering to control procedures and listing the penalties that will automatically be imposed on violators for various offenses. Penalties can range from a reprimand to firing and possibly prosecution. In addition, all violations should be recorded for future reference. Second and subsequent offenses may carry a heavier penalty than first offenses do. When there has been a violation, written control-violation procedures can be invoked impartially, without regard for personality factors. The need for such impartiality is most important when the violator is a member of the management team or is a relative of a manager.

With regard to the reporting of fraud or other illegal activities, many organizations have installed "hot lines" that employees can use anonymously to report suspected wrongdoing. All reports should be brought to the attention of top management and should be followed up, by either the internal auditors or the audit committee, as appropriate.

Personnel Policies and Procedures

The professional accounting literature stresses the importance of personnel in control matters:

The internal accounting control environment and the control procedures themselves are highly dependent on the competency and integrity of the company's personnel. . . . Dishonest or incompetent employees can make most control procedures inoperative. For example, misunderstanding of instructions, mistakes of judgment, carelessness, or other personal factors related to competence and integrity can result in errors in the performance of control procedures. Collusion between employees can circumvent certain control procedures. Similarly,

management personnel may often be in a position to circumvent or override control procedures intentionally. Accordingly, management should consider whether the company policies and procedures with respect to hiring, evaluation, compensation, promotion, training, and so forth, are conducive to the employment of competent, honest personnel.[2]

The hiring of honest, competent employees requires a thorough checking of the applicants' qualifications and work history. And the specifications of the job opening must be matched to the applicant's training and experience. After a person is hired, follow-up procedures should ascertain that the new employee is settled in the right job. Trial work periods, transfer policies, and the new employee orientation sessions are a few of the techniques that help achieve satisfactory employee placement.

Similar considerations apply to the company's policies and procedures with regard to performance evaluations, compensation, promotions, training, and other relevant matters. A summary of the personnel matters that may have a significant bearing on the control environment are the following:

- The hiring process and associated policies and procedures that demonstrate appropriate efforts to recruit and maintain an honest and competent staff.
- Performance review and evaluation procedures that focus on helping the employees improve performance or on providing documentation for personnel actions.
- Promotion, transfer, retirement, and termination policies that employees perceive as fair and equitable.
- Training programs for both management and nonmanagement personnel designed to keep employees professionally competent in their fields.
- Individuals addicted to alcohol or drugs, or those with other potentially harmful personal habits, should be given the opportunity to enter rehabilitation programs. Continued employment in sensitive areas should be contingent on the success of the programs.

The importance of training as a control measure cannot

---

[2] American Institute of Certified Public Accountants, *Report of the Special Advisory Committee on Internal Control* (New York: AICPA, 1979), p. 14.

be underestimated. In one study, a sample of auditors and systems personnel ranked training second in importance only to file and program access controls in a list of 59 necessary internal controls for small computerized systems.[3]

With regard to alcohol and drug abuse, there has been considerable debate in recent years on employees' constitutional rights to refuse to submit to drug testing. At the time of this writing, no definitive legal position has been taken. Nevertheless, it should be recognized that individuals who engage in substance abuse are a threat to the control environment in a number of ways. They are more likely to make mistakes, possibly serious ones, in their work; their judgment may be impaired; they may neglect their responsibilities; they may steal to support their habit; and they may be susceptible to blackmail.

Accounting and Information Services Policies

Overall policies relating to the accounting function can have an important impact on the achievement of a satisfactory control environment. Some examples include

- Double-entry bookkeeping
- Perpetual inventory system
- Formal budget process
- Standard cost system

All of these provide for some kind of comparison—between total debits and credits, between inventory records and the physical count, and between budget or standard figures and actuals—which can help detect errors or irregularities. The first of these is taken for granted in virtually all profit-seeking organizations but, unfortunately, is not adopted in all small not-for-profit organizations. A budget is a most important item in the control environment. It enforces a discipline, first, in the articulation of management's plans and the preparation of the budget and, subsequently, in the tracking of the budget, the review of variances, and possible corrective action.

[3] Bonnie P. Stivers, "Control and Auditability Features of Selected Small Business Computer Accounting Systems," Ph.D. diss., Georgia State University, 1983.

The budget forms a vital link between internal control and the broader function of management planning and control.

Policies relating to other functions within the organization may also have important internal control implications. An example is policies relating to the information services function. Serious control problems pertaining to the use of microcomputers can often be avoided by management policies regulating the acquisition of microcomputer hardware and software, as well as by policies establishing training and consulting support for end-user computer operation. Management attitudes that ignore the need for—or the inevitability of—end-user computing contribute greatly to control risks in this area.

Physical Security

Many specific control measures would be ineffective if the organization did not maintain a satisfactory level of overall physical security. Physical security, which addresses Control Principles Nos. 8, 9, and 12, applies to hazards such as fire, flood, storm, and earthquake damage and also to threats of unauthorized entry to facilities, theft, and sabotage.

Physical security is achieved through the suitable placement of facilities as well as through the use of more specific protective measures. Facilities that are sensitive to flood damage, such as computers and archive record vaults, should be located on high ground. Facilities subject to theft, such as warehouses and stores, and other facilities housing sensitive equipment or records should be located away from public access routes.

Facilities should be protected with fences and locked gates and should be well lit. Fire, flood, and burglar alarms and surveillance cameras should be located at strategic points around the facilities. Security guards should be placed at points of entry and exit, and should patrol facilities on a scheduled and an unscheduled basis. Employees entering and leaving the facilities, or moving about within the facilities, should be prepared to identify themselves and should submit to search upon reasonable suspicion of concealing unauthorized materials. Entry to areas of high sensitivity should be restricted further.

Intangible Factors in the Control Environment

The intangible aspects of a control environment mainly reflect top management's attitudes toward controls and its commitment to creating a corporate atmosphere conducive to the achievement of the control objectives. Through a variety of nonverbal media, upper management communicates its beliefs about internal control to middle management and to the employees at large. In turn, the lower echelons of management and the rank-and-file employees take their cues from top management and think and behave accordingly. These intangible factors create the working climate in which the controls function and in large part determine the effectiveness of the formal control procedures.

The intangible factors in the control environment contribute to the culture of the organization. They influence the perception among operating personnel as to whether top management takes controls seriously. They influence the way in which employees view control procedures: how seriously a control violation is treated in that organization, whether timely corrective action is taken when control weaknesses are reported, and what type of discipline is likely to be administered if anyone deliberately overrides the control system.

The intangible factors in the control environment may reside largely in the minds and attitudes of the employees, but they cannot be left to chance. Rather, they should be deliberately fostered through top management's actions and attitudes, in much the same way as upper management should "manage" the corporate culture. Some examples of management actions that promote a favorable control environment are the following:

- Expectations of quality work and good performance shared by the employees themselves
- Ongoing efforts to maintain employees' awareness and understanding of control procedures
- Timely corrective action when a control weakness is reported by internal or external auditors
- Fair but effective application of disciplinary measures that persuade employees that controls are not to be circumvented

The end product of these efforts is the degree of control "consciousness" in the organization. A high degree of control consciousness does not reflect repressive management and a cowering work force. Rather, it reflects a contented work force that understands its responsibilities and is prepared to act in a mature, cooperative manner.

SPECIFIC CONTROL MEASURES

Under the umbrella of a favorable control environment, specific internal control measures, techniques, and procedures can be implemented with some degree of assurance that they can be effective. Whereas the control environment seeks to reduce overall risk, these specific control measures address specific risks and threats. Control measures should be incorporated into the accounting system at design time, although new controls may have to be added if weaknesses are detected at a later time.

The present treatment of control measures divides the extensive range of controls into eight broad categories:

- Organizational controls
- System development and security controls
- Input controls
- Processing controls
- File and data base controls
- Telecommunications controls
- Output controls
- Confirmation controls

The control measures in these categories include controls pertaining to manual as well as computerized portions of the system. They include controls that could, if desired, be classified as administrative or accounting controls, as general controls or application controls. The categories intentionally cut across the boundaries between those classifications so as to provide a more coherent and integrated picture of the controls and the control objectives to which they relate.

One question that auditors often ask is "Where does the control reside?" In general, internal controls can reside in

- Management policies and procedures
- Job descriptions

- Operating procedures
- Computer software
- Computer hardware
- Physical security measures

Sometimes a given control measure will depend on elements residing in more than one of these areas. For example, a computer access control may depend on a feature of the computer software as well as a related operating procedure and possibly a management policy. Frequently, two or more control measures, residing in different parts of the system, will jointly contribute to the achievement of a control objective. As already noted, the intent is not to relate individual control measures to individual control objectives on a one-to-one basis. Rather, the intent is to achieve all applicable control objectives using the totality of internal controls.

An overview of representative control measures and techniques, broken down into the eight categories, is presented in Figure 17.3. The nature and function of these controls will now be discussed in detail.

ORGANIZATIONAL CONTROLS

Control objectives are ultimately achieved through people, and so it is not surprising that certain important controls apply to organizational matters. Organizational control measures run parallel to the organizational factors in the control environment and in fact stem directly from them.

Separation of Duties

First and foremost are controls that separate incompatible duties. These stem directly from Control Principle No. 3. The two classical examples of incompatible duties are between the creation or authorization of transactions and the recording of those transactions, and between the custody of assets and the maintenance of the related accounting records. For instance, credit approval should be separated from servicing of accounts receivable, and custody of cash should be separated from maintenance of cash records. In the area of purchasing, approval of purchase requisitions should be separated from issuance of purchase orders, purchasing itself should be separated from receiving, and disbursement approval should be separated from preparation of checks for signature.

Other examples of incompatible duties can be found in computerized data processing. Centralized data processing should be separated from the user functions. This control measure is intended to maintain independence between the originators of transaction data (the users) and the processors of the data (computer operators, and the like). It can be accomplished organizationally by arranging for the head of information services, the controller, and the heads of other user departments to report to the same individual—often the vice-president for information services or the vice-president for finance. This individual, preferably advised by the information services steering committee, exercises the necessary control functions and ensures proper independence. The head of information services should not report to the controller, or vice versa.

The data-processing function was separated from the user functions largely to compensate for the concentration of data storage and processing in the computer area. This was a serious problem when batch processing was the norm. Among other things, the rule extended to procedures for correcting errors in transaction data. Errors made by data-processing personnel, such as keypunch operators, should be corrected by those personnel, whereas errors in batches of source documents should be returned to the originating department for correction. The problem of concentration of data and processing in the computer room is somewhat alleviated in interactive systems, particularly those oriented toward end-user processing. In these modern systems, responsibility for data custody and processing is distributed throughout the organization. Consequently, although there is little possibility of separating the user and the data-processing functions, the need for such separation is also reduced.

The duties of the system group and the computer operators who perform routine processing should also be separated. Systems analysts and programmers developing new systems should not have access to "live" data. Instead, program development and testing should be

FIGURE 17.3 Map of internal control measures and techniques.

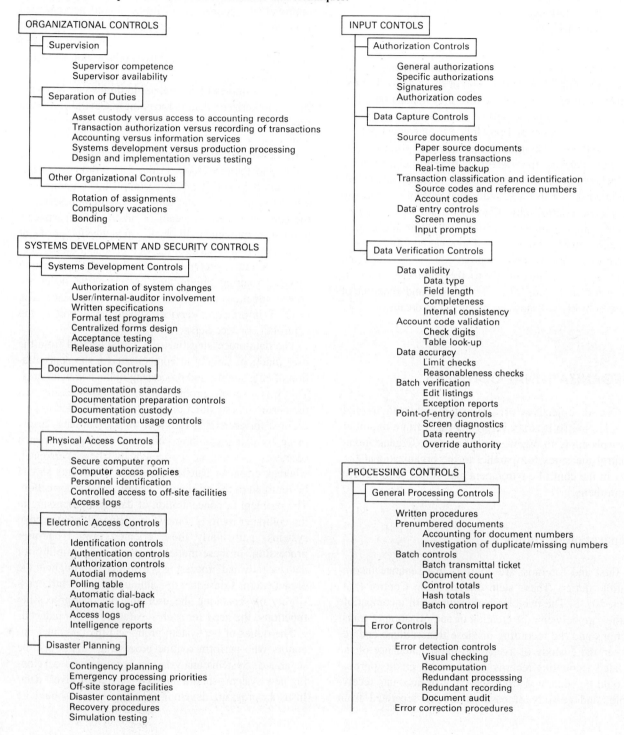

ORGANIZATIONAL CONTROLS

Supervision

  Supervisor competence
  Supervisor availability

Separation of Duties

  Asset custody versus access to accounting records
  Transaction authorization versus recording of transactions
  Accounting versus information services
  Systems development versus production processing
  Design and implementation versus testing

Other Organizational Controls

  Rotation of assignments
  Compulsory vacations
  Bonding

SYSTEMS DEVELOPMENT AND SECURITY CONTROLS

Systems Development Controls

  Authorization of system changes
  User/internal-auditor involvement
  Written specifications
  Formal test programs
  Centralized forms design
  Acceptance testing
  Release authorization

Documentation Controls

  Documentation standards
  Documentation preparation controls
  Documentation custody
  Documentation usage controls

Physical Access Controls

  Secure computer room
  Computer access policies
  Personnel identification
  Controlled access to off-site facilities
  Access logs

Electronic Access Controls

  Identification controls
  Authentication controls
  Authorization controls
  Autodial modems
  Polling table
  Automatic dial-back
  Automatic log-off
  Access logs
  Intelligence reports

Disaster Planning

  Contingency planning
  Emergency processing priorities
  Off-site storage facilities
  Disaster containment
  Recovery procedures
  Simulation testing

INPUT CONTOLS

Authorization Controls

  General authorizations
  Specific authorizations
  Signatures
  Authorization codes

Data Capture Controls

  Source documents
    Paper source documents
    Paperless transactions
    Real-time backup
  Transaction classification and identification
    Source codes and reference numbers
    Account codes
  Data entry controls
    Screen menus
    Input prompts

Data Verification Controls

  Data validity
    Data type
    Field length
    Completeness
    Internal consistency
  Account code validation
    Check digits
    Table look-up
  Data accuracy
    Limit checks
    Reasonableness checks
  Batch verification
    Edit listings
    Exception reports
  Point-of-entry controls
    Screen diagnostics
    Data reentry
    Override authority

PROCESSING CONTROLS

General Processing Controls

  Written procedures
  Prenumbered documents
    Accounting for document numbers
    Investigation of duplicate/missing numbers
  Batch controls
    Batch transmittal ticket
    Document count
    Control totals
    Hash totals
    Batch control report

Error Controls

  Error detection controls
    Visual checking
    Recomputation
    Redundant processsing
    Redundant recording
    Document audit
  Error correction procedures

FIGURE 17.3 (continued)

Computer Operating Controls

    Uninterruptible power supplies
    Scheduled equipment maintenance
    Scheduled batch-processing operations
    Console log

Recovery Controls

    Recovery from errors
    Recovery from premature termination
    Crash recovery
    Emergency repair provisions

FILE AND DATA BASE CONTROLS

File Security Controls

    Secure file library
        Protection from loss or theft
        Protection from improper usage
        Protection from physical damage
        Protection from magnetic contamination
        Sign-out procedures
    File/record retention policies
    File backup procedures
        Backup schedules
        Off-site storage
        Recovery procedures
    File access logs
    Data base integrity routines

File-processing Controls

    File identification controls
        Tape labels
        Disk directories
        Data dictionary
    File protection controls
        Read/write protection
        File passwords
        Father/son protection of master files
        Before/after image controls
        Record lockout
        Intent-to-update flags

File Maintenance Controls

    File maintenance authorizations
    Change listings
    Unalterable change logs

TELECOMMUNICATIONS CONTROLS

Message Integrity Controls

    Message headers
    Message routing
    Acknowledgement signals
    Echo verification
    Completeness checks
    End-to-end error controls
    Message logs

Message Security Controls

    Hard-wired networks
    Tamper-proof channel media
    Encryption

System Penetration Controls

    (Overlap with electronic access controls)

OUTPUT CONTROLS

Output Integrity Controls

    Report trailer pages
    Visual checking

Output Security Controls

    Custody of preprinted forms
    Authorized distribution lists
    Minimum number of copies
    Custody of output
        Transfer of responsibility
        Dual custody of sensitive output
    Disposal of spoiled output
    Security of output displays
        Terminal privacy
        Suppression of keyboard echo

CONFIRMATION CONTOLS

Asset Confirmation

    Cash count
    Confirmation of accounts receivable
    Inventory count
    Review of inventory values
    Fixed-asset audit

Other Confirmation Controls

    Bank reconciliation
    Internal audit examinations
    Miscellaneous confirmations

done only with simulated data. Conversely, operators responsible for processing live data should not have access to programs except in tamper-proof form. This latter requirement can be met by making only object code versions of programs available to the operators. Failure to observe either of these control requirements invites programming fraud. The separation of duties between the systems and the operations groups is now becoming less crucial, as less applications programming work is being undertaken. Most organizations now acquire canned accounting software rather than develop it in house. The main responsibility of the systems group, where it still exists, has shifted to areas other than applications programming. Consequently, the problem is largely disappearing. This development is particularly helpful for small businesses that do not have enough personnel to maintain effective separation of duties.

A third area requiring separation of duties within the information-processing function is in systems development itself. Development of applications programs should be separated from program testing, to ensure that testing is objective. Once again, the need for such separation is declining with the increasing dependence on canned software packages that have already been rigorously tested by the time that they are offered for sale.

Rotation of Assignments

Rotation of assignments within an operational group extends the protection afforded by separation of duties. The intention is that no one individual should always perform the same task, lest he or she be able to conceal a long-standing pattern of errors or irregularities. Enforced vacations serve the same purpose. However, in no case should rotation of assignments or enforced vacations conflict with the requirements for proper separation of duties. Borrowing employees from other departments to help out during vacation periods can be a dangerous procedure.

Bonding

Employees in sensitive positions, such as those in which they handle cash, should be bonded. Bonding increases the formality of the responsibilities in question

and protects the organization by discouraging defalcations. Also, bonding arrangements provide for independently discharged procedures for dealing with violations of trust, should they ever occur. In small companies and institutions, bonding can help compensate for the infeasibility of maintaining effective separation of duties.

SYSTEMS DEVELOPMENT AND SECURITY CONTROLS

The accounting system and its associated computer facilities represent a major long-term resource of the enterprise. Therefore, steps should be taken to ensure that the resource is developed in accordance with management's wishes and that subsequently it is used in the manner for which it was intended.

Systems Development Controls

In accordance with Control Principle No. 10, adequate controls should be exercised to ensure that the system properly meets the needs of the organization. Systems development controls ensure that new systems and system changes reflect the needs of the users and are properly authorized, tested, and approved for release. Specifications should be drawn up jointly by users and data-processing personnel. Representatives of user departments, particularly from accounting and internal control, should participate in the development effort and also be involved in the selection of computer software packages. Newly developed systems or purchased software should be tested in accordance with a planned test program and the results reviewed in the light of the system specifications before approval and release for use.

Documentation Controls

Accounting systems should be adequately documented to provide a basis for effective operation, use, audit, and possible future systems enhancement. Documentation also provides a basis for reconstruction of the system in the event of damage or destruction. Documentation should be prepared, approved, maintained, and disseminated in accordance with established documentation standards. The existence of and adherence to a set of documentation standards provides good evidence that management takes seriously the need for adequate documentation.

Computer Security Controls

Computer hardware, systems software, applications software, and documentation should be protected from accidental damage, theft, or misuse. These controls address the requirements of Control Principles Nos. 8 and 12. Physical security measures are needed to secure the hardware and software against theft, fire, flood, lightning, earthquakes, sabotage, or other perils. These measures run parallel to similar physical security controls intended to protect cash, inventory, securities, and fixed assets. They should be based on a vulnerability analysis of that system.

The computer center should be located in a secure area and be provided with smoke and water detectors, fire suppression devices, burglar alarms, surveillance cameras, and other suitable protective devices. Peripheral equipment such as terminals or personal computers that are located outside the secure area should be individually locked, and security personnel should be assigned to patrol all areas where information-processing facilities are used. Procedures should be developed for dealing with suspected computer crime in whatever form it might emerge.

Proper custody should be provided for computer software and documentation. Software packages are easy to steal, and there is a ready market for pirated copies of proprietary software. Similarly, documentation, though it does not necessarily have economic value in itself, may have theft value in its potential for circumventing controls and subsequent irregularities. Software and documentation should be deposited in a secure location such as an information services library and should be released to authorized users only upon identification. Library personnel should have access to schedules of routine computer operations so as to be able to verify the authenticity of requests for software packages. Items should be logged into and out of the library, evidencing responsibility for safe custody, and items not returned should be promptly followed up and accounted for.

An important class of controls deals with recovery from equipment failure and, more importantly, recovery from disasters that may put the computer facilities out of action for an extended period. Provision should be made for recovery from large-scale damage to the system resulting from natural disasters, accidents, or sabotage. The key to timely recovery from a disaster situation is careful contingency planning. Various scenarios should be envisioned, including escalation situations in which the damage increases after the initial disaster. Those critical resources and services that would receive the highest priority in an emergency should be identified. In most cases, only about one third of all information-processing qualifies as "essential processing" in this context; this normally includes payroll processing, customer billing, and statutory reporting.

Alternative processing facilities should be located, and copies of all essential programs, files, and documentation should be stored at a secure off-site location. A team of key individuals under the direction of a disaster coordinator should be specially trained in recovery situations, and all procedures for dealing with such contingencies should be tested in simulation exercises.

Access Controls

Access controls are an extension of the computer hardware and software controls and pertain specifically to access to computer facilities. They provide for selective use of computer resources in accordance with management's wishes. Access controls can be divided into two groups: physical access controls and electronic access controls. Physical access controls depend on the physical security measures already listed but include policies restricting personnel entry into secured computer areas. Such policies reflect the vulnerability of equipment, software, and data to theft or damage and also the need to control the temperature, humidity, and dust level in the computer room. All personnel entering the computer room should have clear identification such as a badge. In addition, the following are typical policies pertaining to representative personnel groups:

Personnel Group	Policy on Access to Computer Room
Computer operators	Unlimited access subject to job schedules and proper identification.
Repair and maintenance technicians	Access during scheduled maintenance periods or during emergency downtime
Programmers	Access at specified times when live data are not being processed. Programmer access is better provided via remote terminals.
Outside consultants	Access if escorted by authorized employees.
Managers	Access in accordance with job responsibilities.
External auditors	Access if escorted by authorized employees.
Internal auditors	Unlimited access subject to identification.
Visitors (public)	Supervised access during "open house" sessions when programs and data have been removed. Otherwise, a viewing area may be provided with a window overlooking the computer room.

Physical access controls should extend to off-site storage locations and vaults used for archive storage.

Electronic access pertains to the use of computer facilities from remote terminals located either in the vicinity of the host computer or at geographically distant points requiring use of electronic communications links. The objective of electronic access controls is to reduce the risk of illegal penetration of the computer facilities. Hard-wired systems, in which all terminals are close to the host computer, offer greater security than do geographically dispersed systems that rely on long-distance communications channels.

Access to a computer from a remote terminal should always require authentication of the prospective user. Users should be required to submit a valid identification code and password before being granted access. Codes and passwords should be at least five characters in length. They should be changed periodically, say, once per month, and automatic disciplinary action should be taken against any individual communicating a password to an unauthorized person. Password files should themselves be read protected. Password systems can be configured to limit access to specified programs or files. Many organizations have a three-level password system in which the first level permits routine data entry, the second level permits routine processing, and the third level permits nonroutine activities such as file maintenance. Also the password systems can be configured to limit access from specified terminals.

Automatic dial-back devices are easy to install and provide additional user authentication for systems dependent on telephone lines. As soon as a caller logs into the computer system, the device terminates the telephone session and automatically dials the telephone number listed as belonging to the identification code of the caller; on-line contact between the terminal and the computer is then reestablished. Dial-back devices reduce the risk of unauthorized penetration of the system and also may alert an authorized user of an attempted impersonation.

Access to computers from remote terminals should be capable of being monitored. An unalterable log should be maintained of all actual or attempted access to the system. Logs should record who accessed the system and from what terminal, using what password, and what file retrieval or processing activities were performed. Repeated attempts to access the system with invalid passwords should be automatically monitored and reported for investigation. Reponsibility for reviewing the content of access logs should be assigned to specific individuals. Access logs provide only an "after the facts" control, but they permit investigation of suspicious access activities, and their existence may discourage prospective irregularities.

All electronic access controls should periodically be subjected to penetration tests. Conducting such tests is a useful function of the internal auditors, although consultant advice may often be required. Intelligence reports may also provide a useful guide to the success of the access controls. Conversations overheard at public user groups and messages displayed on "hacker" electronic bulletin boards may reveal details of attempts—successful or unsuccessful—to penetrate the system in question.

INPUT CONTROLS

Input controls refer to the authorization, capture, classification, entry, and verification of input data. Input data include transactions and file maintenance changes.

Authorizations

Only authorized transactions should be accepted for processing. Authority to create a transaction is delegated by upper management by means of a general authorization or a specific authorization. A general authorization applies to a whole class of transactions and is communicated via a job description, a clerical procedure, an approved payroll wage and salary list, an approved price list, an approved list of customers to whom credit has been extended, and so forth. General authorizations can also be built into computer programs that are approved for use in creating classes of transactions such as routine adjusting entries in a general ledger system. Automatically created transactions should routinely be subjected to management review and exceptions identified for investigation.

A specific authorization applies to one and only one transaction and is granted on a case-by-case basis. Examples of specific authorizations arise in connection with the extension of credit to a new customer, the approval of a payables voucher, the approval of a wage raise, a promotion, the signing of a contract, or the write-down of obsolete inventory. Specific authorizations often approve departures from the provisions of a general authorization. Specific authorizations are usually recorded by a signature but can be indicated by the entry of an authorization code into an on-line terminal.

Source Documents

Traditionally, transactions have initially been captured on paper source documents. Source documents provide a nonvolatile medium with favorable control characteristics. Data can be recovered from source documents in the event that subsequent, processed versions of the data are lost, damaged, or destroyed. Source documents also provide a starting-point for verification: Account numbers, amounts, authorizations, identification numbers, and other data can be checked visually and unusual data queried. Source documents provide useful evidence in a subsequent audit of the financial statements, and they can be retained to satisfy statutory record retention requirements. However, many systems now bypass source documents in favor of direct electronic data capture. The data may be captured by means of a magnetic or optical wand, by an on-line time clock, or by direct entry via a keyboard. For example, telephone orders may be keyed directly into a sales order–processing system. Direct electronic entry saves time and may help reduce transcription errors. On the other hand, the data may be lost if the system goes down soon after entry or if a secondary storage device malfunctions before the records can be backed up. To compensate for this risk, redundant storage devices may be needed. Alternatively, a paper document can be printed in real time as the data are being entered electronically.

Transaction Classification and Identification

Transactions should be given a unique identifier that can help trace an audit trail. The identifier commonly is a combination of a source code and a reference number. The source code classifies the transaction according to its point of origin—accounts receivable, cash disbursement, payroll, or whatever. The reference number may correspond to a source document; for instance, that used in a cash disbursement system may correspond to the voucher number or the check number. Alternatively the reference number may be assigned at the time the transaction is keyed into the computer; many input programs simply assign reference numbers in order of entry. Examples of transaction identifiers in a hypothetical system might be: AR/1234, CD/4456, PA/9876, GL/7721.

Data Entry Controls

Keyboard entry of transaction and other data should be made in response to screen prompts. ''Blind'' keying of data, as in electromechanical keypunch machines, is prone to transcription errors. Input prompts not only reduce errors but they also assist in the training process and serve as a ready reminder, even to experienced data entry personnel, as to the order, format, and other characteristics of the required input. Menus provide similar assistance, reminding users of the available programs and their correct operating sequence.

Data Verification Controls

Transaction entry is particularly vulnerable to error contamination. Transcription of source documents into machine-readable form invites a variety of errors which must be detected and corrected before processing can continue. Most automated systems provide for some form of programmed editing or error checking; such editing can be done on a batch or point-of-entry basis. In either case the input data are subjected to a number of edit checks so as to isolate possible errors. Some commonly used edit checks are

- Valid data type
- Valid field length
- Valid account number or code
- Valid combination of fields
- Logical relationships
- Reasonableness of numeric amounts
- Completeness of data
- Sequence of transaction, document, or batch numbers

Tests for valid data type (numeric, alphanumeric, and so on) and field length can easily be provided to distinguish a date from somebody's name or to reject a three-digit zip code. Acceptable combinations of fields and logical relationships can also be tested; in a particular application, it may be necessary to test that the value of one field is greater (or less) than the value of another. The dollar amount of a single line item on a sales order must be no greater than the total gross value of the sale. Tests for missing data are readily provided. The edit program can isolate missing or duplicate transaction numbers or transaction numbers that are not in ascending sequence. Similar controls to isolate missing, duplicate, or otherwise invalid documents or batches can also be provided, supplementing other forms of batch controls.

Account numbers or codes can be validated by reference to a master file or a table of permissible codes.

In many interactive systems, input of a customer number, for example, results in the display of the customer's name and address on the screen or, if the number is not validated, in the display of a diagnostic message. The display of additional information about the account entity permits visual cross-referencing to the data on the source documents.

If numeric codes are used, they can be partially validated by the use of self-checking digits appended to the account number itself. The appended check digit or digits are related to the body of the account number by some arithmetic algorithm. An account number/check digit combination that does not satisfy the algorithm indicates an invalid entry. The algorithm is chosen to minimize the risk that an invalid code—particularly one containing a common mistake such as the transposition of two digits—would be accepted by the system; that is, the algorithm is chosen to minimize the so-called Type II error. The Type I error, rejecting a valid code, usually does not arise. One common type of algorithm forms the sum of the numeric digits weighted by their own positional values (1,2,3, and so on, starting from the right). The resulting sum is then converted into a one- or two-digit number by some other simple operation. To illustrate, the initial computation for the account number 4683 produces a total of 53:

$$\begin{array}{cccc} 4 & 6 & 8 & 3 \\ \times & \times & \times & \times \\ 4 & 3 & 2 & 1 \\ \hline 16 & + \; 18 & + \; 16 & + \; 3 \end{array} = 53$$

The total can be converted into a single digit by subtracting it from the next highest multiple of 11 (in this case, 55), yielding

$$\text{Check digit} = 55 - 53 = 2$$

The resulting composite account number is 4683.2. Check digits provide less security than do master file or table look-up but may save retrieval time and may be more economical when many account numbers or codes are in use.

Limit or reasonableness checks are usually performed on amount fields to verify that the data conform to expected characteristics of magnitude or sign. An example is a check that the number of hours appearing on a weekly time card is a positive number lying between 0.1 and 60; the implication is that other values are unusual and warrant further scrutiny. More complicated reasonableness checks may refer to allowable limits contained in a master file or table. For example, in a purchasing system, a request for typewriters might be queried if the quantity exceeded 10, whereas as request for screws might not be queried until the quantity exceeded 100,000.

In a batch system it is customary for the edit program to be run after the input data are keypunched onto a scratch file. The edit program outputs an edit listing that is examined manually to determine why the offending transactions have been rejected. Procedures should be established for prompt review of the edit listing and either correction of erroneous or invalid transactions or determination that they are in fact correct. A time card claiming an unusually large (or small) number of hours may simply reflect an unusual situation in the workplace. Processing of such unusual, but nevertheless valid, transactions should require supervisory approval in the form of a signature or initials on the edit listing or entry of an authorization code into the machine. Positive controls are necessary to ensure that all corrections and resubmittals of input data are handled in a timely manner.

Batch edit-checking programs are of two types (Figure 17.4). Often the whole batch is held up until all transactions have ''passed'' the edit checks. But in other systems, the ''good'' transactions are allowed to continue for further processing while the rejected ones are being investigated. In this latter case the edit listing may take the form of an exception report listing only the rejected transactions. The choice between the alternative forms of verification requires a trade-off between delaying the processing of the accepted transactions and destroying the integrity of the batch, which may be critical to the success of other controls.

Interactive systems, and particularly real-time systems, usually involve edit checking in the form of *point-of-entry controls*. These perform the same type of edit checks as do batch systems (with the possible exception of those controls relating to batch structure) but are incorporated into the data entry programs instead of into

separate programs run after keying is completed. Transactions, or individual fields, which trigger one of the edit checks, are rejected immediately upon entry, and a diagnostic message is displayed on the screen. Diagnostics such as ''Invalid date,'' ''Alphanumeric character in numeric field,'' and ''Transaction does not balance'' are familiar in interactive systems.

Provision must be made to override the point-of-entry controls when the transaction data are exceptional but valid. Otherwise the transaction would be rejected repeatedly. Usually this contingency is handled by entering an authorization code. Such authorization codes must be closely monitored to prevent abuse.

PROCESSING CONTROLS

The overall objective in transaction processing is that every transaction be processed promptly, that no transaction be processed more than once, and that all processing should be accurate and complete. Similar objectives apply to processing of other kinds of data such as file maintenance changes. Various control measures are available to help achieve these objectives.

Written Procedures

The use of written procedures relates directly to Control Objective No. 5. Written procedures guide employees and help ensure uniform, effective, and efficient processing of data; they also communicate management's authorizations and provide a standard for verification of compliance. Procedures should be prepared for each step in every manual operation, including those involving interaction with computer facilities. All procedures should be dated and approved by an appropriate manager. Responsibility for maintaining the currency of operating procedures should be assigned to specific individuals. Procedures manuals should be made available to all relevant personnel and should be ''required reading'' for all new employees. Master copies of all procedures should be kept by the controller and collectively comprise the controller's manual.

FIGURE 17.4 Transaction verification in batch systems.

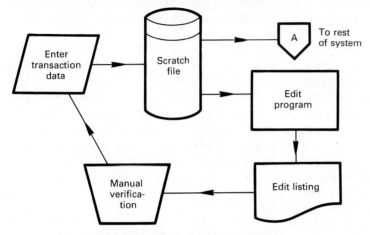

(a) The whole batch of transactions is retained in a scratch file
until corrections are made. After correction,
the batch is released for further processing.

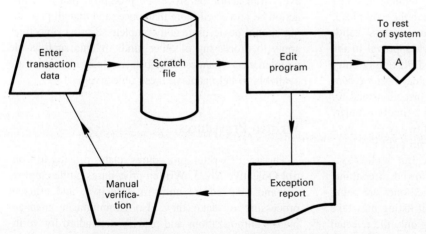

(b) Only those transactions rejected by the edit program are held back for
correction. "Good" transactions are allowed to continue.

Prenumbered Documents

Prenumbered documents are used extensively to keep track of transactions and to ensure that all transactions are accounted for. This technique pertains to Control Principle No. 5 and helps ensure that all transactions are processed once and only once; missing or duplicate transactions can readily be identified. Prenumbered documents, along with proper forms control, help reduce the risk of insertion of unauthorized transactions. Frequently, transaction journals or registers are maintained in order of the numbers on their supporting documents, thereby providing a check on the integrity of the numerical sequence.

Batch Controls

Batch controls pertain to Control Principles Nos. 5 and 7 and are used in both manual systems and automated batch-processing systems. A batch consists of a set of related transactions or records or other types accumulated for processing at the same time. Batch controls are designed to ensure that as it progresses through the various processing stages, the batch contains the same set of records, that none have been lost, and that none has been added. Typical batch controls include

- Record count
- Control totals
- Hash totals
- Batch transmittal ticket
- Batch control report

A record count can be made at different points in the system and, if it remains the same, indicates that the same number of records are in the batch. It helps guard against the accidental loss of records. However, by itself it does not necessarily confirm that the same records are present; one could have been removed and another substituted. A control total is a total of some amount or quantity field contained in the transactions; an example is the total of all the net amounts due in a batch of invoices. A hash total is the total formed from data elements, such as customer numbers, which would not normally be the subject of arithmetic operations; the hash total has no economic, accounting, or arithmetic significance. But it should remain the same throughout processing. A change in a control total, or hash total, from one job station to another is evidence that records have been lost or duplicated or that unauthorized ones have been substituted. To illustrate the use of batch controls, assume that the following transactions comprise a batch:

Employee #	Hours Worked	Gross Pay
531	40	$240.00
532	45	247.50
534	40	280.00
545	30	225.00
548	50	262.50

Figure 17.5. Batch transmittal ticket.

BATCH TRANSMITTAL TICKET

Date: 99/99/99   Batch #:   99999999999
Point of origin: Sales
Destination: Accounts receivable
Transaction type: Sales orders
Document count: 100
Document numbers (range):   13,667–13,766
Control total: Gross sales = $48,331
Hash total: Customer numbers =   590,475

Authorized by: _____
Received by: _____
Processed by: _____
Date/time: 99/99/99, 99.99

Form #918273

The record count is 5; a hash total of employee numbers yields 2,690; and the control totals of hours worked and gross pay are 205 and $1,255, respectively.

A further control measure for control totals formed from transaction amount fields compares the control total with the difference between the related account balance before and after posting. Any discrepancy provides evidence of incorrect or incomplete posting (see Chapter 5).

A batch transmittal ticket is illustrated in Figure 17.5. It consists of a paper document attached to a batch of source documents in transit from one job station to another. It serves as a kind of "shipping document" for the batch. In a manual process, the originating and destination job stations may correspond to successive processing steps in the accounting department, or in a centralized computerized system, one of them may be the data-processing department. The transmittal ticket records the origin and destination of the batch, the number of documents included, and other information such as control and hash totals. It may also serve as a "receipt" to be signed and returned to the sender department upon arrival at its destination. Batch tickets are often prenumbered as a precaution against the loss of whole batches of records or the insertion of unauthorized ones. The preparation of batch transmittal tickets and the calculation of control and hash totals should be performed independently of the recording and processing of the transactions and the subsequent balancing operations.

Batch control reports are often prepared in computerized systems and supplement the function of batch transmittal tickets. A batch control report usually records the actual record numbers as well as reconciling all control and hash totals. It may analyze control totals and compare them with totals formed earlier in the processing sequence or even with totals formed on previous occasions. "Run-to-run" controls involving previously derived totals may be used to confirm the update of master files.

Error Controls

Error controls pertain to Control Principle No. 7, and their purpose is to detect errors in input data that may have evaded the verification controls as well as errors that may have occurred after input. In manual systems and in automated systems in which intermediate output is obtained, visual checking is appropriate. Experienced people often have a talent for spotting data that "look wrong." Document audits verify all the data contained in a document set. For example, a document audit of a disbursement voucher reconciles the quantities and dollar amounts with those on the original purchase requisition, purchase order, receiving ticket, and vendor invoice. Prices, extensions, and other details of the document may also be verified. Document audits are normally conducted on a sample basis because of the great amount of effort required.

Processing and storage redundancy are important aids to error control and can be used in all types of systems. For example, in a manual system, dual processing or balancing is often used when cash is received. Amounts on remittance slips are verified against check amounts, and then the remittance slips are separated from the checks. Each stack of documents is totaled and balanced with the other before processing; similar balancing can be performed after processing. In both manual and automated systems, recomputation of the same quantity, dollar amount, extension, or total at different stages in the process ensures that the initial computation was cor-

rect and that the data were not altered during processing. Although computerized systems that have been thoroughly tested normally offer consistent and accurate processing, data can be contaminated for a variety of reasons, including perpetration of irregularities. Processing redundancy may also be advantageous in real-time systems in which the cost of loss of data owing to system malfunction is particularly high, for example, an electronic funds transfer (EFT) system.

An example of redundant recording of data is the inclusion of both the account number and name in a transaction record. Normally, in the interests of conserving file space, only the account number is included. However, the presence of both allows a comparison to be made at any time, possibly drawing attention to contamination of the data or to fraudulent alteration of the records after initial data capture. Another example, combining redundant recording and redundant processing, is the recording of a quantity, a unit cost, and the corresponding extended cost. Normally, only two of these three data elements are recorded, and the third can be calculated as required. But all three might be recorded as a control measure to allow recomputation and verification of the extended cost. The emergence of an inconsistency at some point during processing would indicate the contamination of the records after their initial capture in the input program.

Computer-Operating Controls

Computer-operating controls seek to ensure that computer facilities are available for information processing as and when needed and that processing is in accordance with management's authorizations. Maintenance schedules should be established for all hardware items, both inside and outside the computer room, including mainframes, departmental computers, microcomputers, and peripheral devices. Conformity with these schedules should routinely be checked.

Batch-processing operations are amenable to routine scheduling and therein lies an important control measure. Internal auditors, or others charged with control responsibilities, can challenge computer operators performing operations other than those scheduled on the particular day. Also, as noted later, operating schedules assist in file library control.

Computerized systems should incorporate some means of monitoring all processing activity and providing a permanent log of that activity. Departmental and large mainframe computers normally include a system console through which commands are entered for operating the system. The console device should be a printer terminal or should have a small printer attached to provide a printout of all commands entered through the console. The same device, or a second one, should record a summary of all jobs initiated from remote terminals. The printout can be retained as a permanent record of operations. Greater protection is provided by a sealed magnetic tape or disk device that is resistant to tampering.

The record of activity should include the date and time, the identification number and password of the user, the terminal from which the run was initiated, the programs run and files accessed, the duration of the run, and the amount of main memory used. Review of the console log can provide useful clues in the event of suspected unauthorized use of the computer, and the existence of the log may deter would-be perpetrators from risking detection.

Microcomputers, even clustered microcomputers providing processing power equivalent to that of a mainframe computer, rarely incorporate a system console or other logging device, which constitutes one of the most serious control weaknesses of such systems.

Recovery Controls

Modern computer facilities properly installed, tested, and routinely serviced are resistant to malfunction. On the other hand, no set of processing controls is complete without provision for an occasional system failure and downtime and also for a catastrophic failure of the system. Provision must be made for prompt recovery from premature or abnormal termination of a computer run or from a system crash. Normally, programs cannot simply be restarted unless associated records and files are returned to their original condition, which is why father and son versions of master files and before- and after-

images of data base records are important. Recovery provisions must include procedures for reinstating files, rerunning programs, and recalling contaminated output.

Uninterruptible power supplies, based on batteries or generators, are needed if processing is to continue during periods of power failure. Provision must be made for running high-priority programs on alternative processing facilities in the event of extended downtime caused by hardware failure. Provision must also be made for emergency repairs, so as to minimize nonproductive downtime. But the repair of hardware systems may take several days and occasionally take several weeks. Provisions for recovery from hardware malfunction must interface with large-scale disaster planning.

FILE AND DATA BASE CONTROLS

File controls are intended to protect file data from loss, damage, contamination, unauthorized access, illegal modification, or improper processing. Data base controls are the analog in data base management systems.

File Custody

Paper files should be stored in a dry location, free from fire and flood hazard and secure against theft or unauthorized access. Record retention policies should reflect legal mandates as well as the continued economic usefulness of various types of file materials. Custody and maintenance of files should be assigned to specific individuals, who should also be responsible for purging records in accordance with the retention policies. Procedures should be developed for properly destroying file records when their usefulness or mandated retention period has expired; sensitive paper records should be shredded.

When not in use, magnetic media should be stored in a secure location that is also free from stray magnetic radiation. It should be remembered that electric motors, such as those used in vacuum cleaners and office copying machines, emit strong magnetic fields. Library custody of file media has already been mentioned.

File-processing Controls

Controls are required to ensure that the correct file is used in processing operations and that it is used in the correct manner. In the case of magnetic tape files, internal and external labeling serves this purpose. An external label is a human-readable label on the outside of the reel, describing the file or citing a reference number (descriptions are sometimes avoided so that file content is not revealed to unauthorized users). An internal label is a machine-readable descriptor which can be compared with a target code contained in the associated software package. Magnetic tape media also have a physical control device, in the form of a plastic ring, which protects against loss of data owing to inadvertent use in a write mode. If the ring is omitted, a write-protect mechanism will be activated in the tape drive. The ring must be inserted to disable this mechanism for legitimate unprotected operation.

Magnetic disk cartridges should bear an external label for easy reference. Virtually all magnetic disk media have a machine-readable directory that lists the names and code numbers of files contained on the disk and that provides access to those files. In some cases, the directory references to sensitive files can themselves be read protected. Directories may contain read or write protection or password protection for specified files. Directories should contain a log indicating the date and time of the most recent access to each file.

File-processing activity should be subject to appropriate access controls. Particularly sensitive operations, such as file maintenance, should be subject to more stringent access controls than other processes are. File maintenance should be permitted only by specially designated persons and only in response to written authorizations. An unalterable log should be maintained of all file maintenance activity, and a responsible individual—not otherwise involved in file maintenance activities—should be assigned to review the log routinely and compare all recorded changes with documented authorizations.

"Father" versions of master files should be opened only in a "read" mode during posting operations, and the "son" versions should be released only following verification. In data base systems, before-images of all updated records should be maintained until verification is completed. Files in real-time environments should be protected by file or record lockout controls. These controls should be activated during file maintenance activities and also selectively activated during routine posting operations to prevent simultaneous update from two different terminals. Record locks are normally provided in most data base management systems. Closely related controls, incorporated in data base management systems, are "intent to update" flags. They are used to alert users that a particular record has been identified as the target of update as a result of a transaction entry. Users viewing the record in a query mode would thus be warned of the impending change and could defer a related decision until the flag is removed. And while the flag is set, other users attempting to update the record would find it write protected. In systems with complicated data structures, utility programs should be run routinely to verify the integrity of index files, pointers, and other linkages.

File Backup

All machine-readable file media should routinely be backed up, and the backup copies should be stored in a secure, off-site location. The backup medium should provide the appropriate readability characteristics and minimize cost. Magnetic tape is the most popular machine-readable backup medium because of its low variable cost; however, the cost of the tape drive must also be considered. Reel-to-reel tape drives are typically used in large systems, and tape cassette drives, which are less expensive, are available for use in microcomputer systems. Floppy disks provide an even cheaper alternative when the volume of data is small. Paper or microfilm may be used if machine readability is not important. The frequency of backup operations should be related to the volatility of the files in question and to the effort in reloading data in the event of data loss or damage. Virtually all transaction files should be backed up at least once per day, and master files in batch systems involving a classical posting cycle should be backed up once per posting period. Files in real-time systems may need to be backed up more often than once per day.

TELECOMMUNICATIONS CONTROLS

Telecommunications controls seek to protect communications channels and networks from a variety of threats, including

- loss or distortion of data
- routing of messages to the wrong receiving station
- wiretapping, eavesdropping, or unauthorized monitoring of messages
- introduction of unauthorized messages
- penetration of associated computer facilities via open channels

Errors in data transmission are commonly caused by line noise or faulty switching equipment. Most errors can be detected by the incorporation of a parity bit into each byte, enabling the receiving station to perform automated byte-by-byte error checks. Error detection codes may also be incorporated into message trailers (Figure 17.6). These codes contain control totals resembling those used in batch-processing controls. Upon detecting an error, a negative acknowledgement signal is returned to the sender, allowing retransmittal of the invalid part of the message. Messages are frequently broken up into units, blocks, or "frames" to facilitate both transmission and verification. In some cases, acknowledgement signals cannot be returned, for instance, in a half-duplex channel, or provision for retransmittal may be impracticable, for example, when messages are generated by real-time processing. In such cases, error-correcting codes may be used, enabling errors to be both detected and corrected at the receiving station. However, error-correcting codes are successful only if there is a fairly high degree of message redundancy.

Headers containing coded destination information are normally incorporated into transmitted messages (Figure 17.6). The headers are broadly similar to those written to magnetic tape files. Headers can verify the access authority of the receiving station, and a suitable acknowledgement signal can be returned to the sender indicating that the destination is valid and is open to receive data. Because a message may pass through several communications devices, including one or more local area networks, telephone lines, and other media, full end-to-end controls must be in place to ensure that the message arrives at the intended receiving station and that it is accurate and complete.

Alternative channels should be identified for use during main channel downtime. For example, dial-up telephone lines can be used if leased lines are temporarily inoperative—as long as they provide adequate capacity for a minimum level of essential communications.

Penetration of communications channels is a potential weakness of all distributed systems. Wide area networks are particularly vulnerable because of the extent of their exposure, but these risks can be reduced by using fiber optic channels which are resistant to tampering. Networks relying on public voice-grade telephone lines offer the least security of all.

To prevent eavesdropping on messages communicated over insecure networks, some form of *encryption* is needed. Encryption is also referred to as *encipherment* or *scrambling*. Encryption devices typically involve a mathematical encryption algorithm and a numeric key (Figure 17.7). The algorithm provides a general strategy by which the message can be scrambled, usually by altering the binary digits comprising the message. The algorithm can and often is made public. But the key, which is confidential, determines the precise pattern in which the bits are altered, and it also determines how

FIGURE 17.6 **Format of telecommunications messages.**

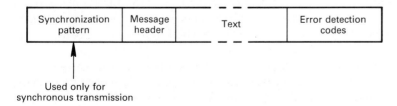

FIGURE 17.7 Encryption of messages in telecommunications systems.

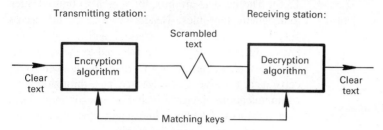

the message can be decrypted at the receiving station. In principle, the encryption key can be broken by a trial-and-error process; however, the number of permutations is so large—keys ordinarily consist of 64-digit binary numbers—that such a process would take too long to be practical. From a technical standpoint, encryption schemes are virtually secure, but keys are sometimes not treated with proper confidentiality, which is the one significant weakness of such systems. Control awareness training and clearly stated disciplinary measures for violations help reduce the residual risks. As with passwords, encryption keys should routinely be changed and old keys destroyed.

OUTPUT CONTROLS

Output controls are intended to ensure that output from the accounting system is complete, accurate, and appropriately utilized. The nature of the output produced by each program—target output device, type of display, type of stock paper or preprinted forms, expected volume of output, required number of copies, and distribution of the output—should be described in user or operator documentation. As a reminder to a computer operator, the same information can usefully be displayed on the system console.

Printed output produced by a computer should bear header and trailer pages. The header page should indicate the date of processing, the run number, the batch number (if appropriate), the identification of the originating department and responsible individual, and the proper disposition of the output. The trailer page com-

municates the message "This is the end." The trailer page can also be used to record the number of pages of output and summary figures such as the number of transactions or accounts processed. The appearance of the trailer page tells the computer operator that printing is complete and that the output device can be used for the next job or turned off, whereas a pause in printing may not mean that printing is complete. In the case of output displayed on a screen, trailer screen forms can achieve the same objective; in addition to summary statistics, they typically contain a continuation option to return to a main menu.

Whenever possible, only the required number of copies of printed output should be produced. If additional copies have to be produced, they should be disposed of in accordance with authorized procedures; sensitive material should be shredded. Spare or spoiled printout should never be thrown away in a trash can or dumpster except with supervisory approval.

Preprinted document forms, particularly "action document" forms such as checks, sales orders, credit memos, purchase orders, and production orders should be afforded appropriate custody and issued, as needed, only for authorized use. A log should be kept for each type of preprinted form, indicating the serial numbers of all documents issued and voided, and spoiled forms should be properly accounted for. Ranges of document numbers used should be reconciled with internally generated transaction numbers, record counts, control totals, and hash totals.

Disposition of printed output should be regulated in accordance with written documentation. Output material, even of low-level sensitivity, should be kept in the custody of computer operators until signed for by its authorized recipient; printout should never simply be stacked on a table for anyone to pick up. Responsibility for conveying sensitive material to its proper destination should be assigned to specific individuals, and dual custody should be required when moving negotiable documents to and from safe storage.

Display of output on video terminals should be restricted to designated terminals. Display of sensitive material should be permitted only on terminals afforded suitable privacy. Passwords entered into computer devices should not result in visible echo on the screen.

CONFIRMATION CONTROLS

Confirmation controls address Control Principle No. 6 and are intended to verify that the accounting records correspond to economic reality. One of the most common controls in this category is counting cash on hand. Because of the liquidity of cash, this should obviously be done at frequent intervals, for instance, daily.

Reconciliation of the bank statement can be classified as a confirmation control. In order to avoid incompatible responsibilities, the bank reconciliation should be performed by an individual who does not process cash receipts or disbursements. In very small organizations, where other controls may be inadequate or nonexistent, the bank reconciliation may be one of the few effective internal controls and can provide a measure of protection against errors or irregularities that otherwise would be lacking. The reconciliation should never be neglected.

Another important confirmation control is the physical inventory count, which is a direct means of validating the perpetual inventory records. The perpetual inventory system itself provides an essential control function. The frequency with which the physical inventory count is taken depends on the nature of the inventory items and the effort and cost of completing the count. Sensitive items can be counted more frequently than the whole inventory is. Individual inventory items should routinely be reviewed to ensure that values are not misstated because of errors or as a result of deterioration, obsolescence, or decline of market value. Standard costs, or even rough estimates of manufacturing costs, provide additional control over errors in individual valuation.

Confirmation of accounts receivable validates the receivables balance. The allowance for bad debts should be reviewed and, when necessary, adjusted to ensure that net receivables are properly valued. Verification of other asset categories would include routine reviews of investment portfolios and regular internal audits of fixed assets. Responsibility for custody of items such as tools, test equipment, office equipment, calculators, and personal computers should be confirmed, and the condition and location of the items verified. Fixed-asset valuations for expensive equipment should be reviewed in the light of maintenance records and depreciation schedules.

SUMMARY

Internal control measures are designed to operate effectively and efficiently in a particular organization and information system. The first requirement is to establish through various tangible and intangible methods a favorable control environment in the organization. The tangible aspects of the control environment include a number of policy matters, together with an appropriate level of physical security. The control environment is important because it contributes to "control consciousness" which is an intangible but necessary element without which the more detailed control measures would largely be ineffective.

Specific control measures can be divided into the eight categories of organizational controls, systems development and security controls, input controls, processing controls, file and data base controls, telecommunications controls, output controls, and confirmation controls. These categories cut across boundaries between administrative controls and accounting controls, between manual and computer-oriented controls, and between general and application controls.

Organizational controls, which include the need for separation of duties, form a bridge between the organizational elements of the control environment and corresponding specific control measures. Systems development and security controls relate to the systems development project and the security of the accounting system during its operational life. They include recovery plans that could be implemented in the event of large-scale damage to the system resulting from natural or other causes. The information system is the lifeline of the organization, and loss of processing capability, even for a short time, could seriously threaten the survival of the organization.

The extensive catalogue of input controls, processing controls, file and data base controls, telecommunication controls, and output controls combine to ensure that transactions are processed to provide complete, accurate, and meaningful information to the users. They also recognize that much of the information is privileged and must be protected from unauthorized persons. Confirmation controls recognize that the accounting data are meaningful only to the extent that they correspond to economic reality.

Effective control in any given area normally depends not just on the effectiveness of a single control measure but also on the effective interaction among a number of control measures and the interaction of all of them with the environmental factors. The goal should be to construct a system of internal controls that mutually serve to reduce risks to an acceptable level.

BIBLIOGRAPHY

Armstrong, James R. "Maintenance Seen Key to Preventing Data Loss." *Computer World*, November 28, 1983, pp. 5–6.

Burch, John G., Jr., and Joseph L. Sardinas, Jr. *Computer Control and Audit: A Total Systems Approach*. New York: Wiley, 1978.

Campbell, Robert P. "Locking Up the Mainframe." *Computer World*, pt. 1, October 10, 1983; pt. 2, October 17, 1983.

Chandler, John S. "A Microcomputer Is Not Just a Small Computer: An Internal Control Perspective." *Georgia Journal of Accounting*, spring 1985, pp. 119–129.

"Computer Security: What Can be Done." *Business Week*, September 26, 1983, pp. 126–130.

"Disaster Cases Show Need for Recovery Plans." *Computer World*, November 28, 1983, pp. 19–21.

Gallegos, Frederick, Dana R. Richardson, and A. Faye Borthwick. *Audit and Control of Information Systems*. Cincinnati: South-Western, 1987.

Halper, Stanley D., Glenn C. Davis, P. J. O'Neill-Dunne, and Pamela R. Pfeu. *Handbook of EDP Auditing*. Boston: Warren, Gorham & Lamont, 1985.

Institute for Computer Sciences and Technology. *Computer Science and Technology: Audit and Evaluation of Computer Security*. Washington, D.C.: National Bureau of Standards, October 1977.

Neu, Clyde W. "Small EDP Shop Risks." *Journal of Systems Management*, June 1976, pp. 36–39.

Lobel, Jerome. "The Manufacturer's Responsibility for Computer Security." *Datamation*, October 1, 1986 (supplement), p. 8.

Roberts, Martin B. *EDP Controls*. New York: Wiley, 1985.

Stamps, David. "Disaster Recovery: Who's Worried?" *Datamation*, February 1, 1987, pp. 60–64.

Tyran, Michael R. *Computerized Accounting Methods and Controls*, 2nd ed. Englewood Cliffs, N.J.: Prentice-Hall, 1978.

Westin, Alan F. "New Eyes on Privacy." *Computer World*, November 28, 1983, p. 21–24.

DISCUSSION QUESTIONS AND PROBLEMS

1. Define and discuss the following terms:

- Access controls
- Audit committee
- Batch controls
- Confirmation controls
- Confirmation of accounts receivable
- Console log
- Control consciousness
- Data entry controls
- Information services steering committee
- Disbursement voucher
- Documentation controls
- Edit checks
- Edit listing
- Error controls
- File maintenance controls

- Forms control
- Hardware and systems software controls
- Intangible factors in the control environment
- Internal auditors
- Management policies
- Organizational controls
- Output controls
- Personnel policies and procedures
- Prenumbered documents
- Processing controls
- Reconciliation of the bank statement
- Record retention
- Separation of duties
- Systems development controls
- Tangible factors in the control environment
- Transaction log
- Transaction origination controls

2. Discuss the respective roles of internal auditors, the audit committee, and the external auditors in achieving the overall control objectives.

3. List as many examples as you can of situations requiring specific management authorizations. Assume that the setting is a small manufacturing firm that normally makes standard parts but that occasionally takes on custom fabrication jobs.

4. During processing, a batch of transactions was rejected by a programmed batch-balancing control. An examination of the transaction log revealed the following contents in the batch:

Document #	Date	Account Code	Amount
253	3/1/XX	3158	$14,370
254	3/2/XX	2096	20,500
255	3/2/XX	2437	2,945
255	3/2/XX	2437	2,945
257	3/3/XX	0972	8,320
258	3/2/XX	3660	6,095
259	3/5/XX	1491	17,380
260	3/5/XX	1491	17,380

The batch control ticket that accompanied the original documents provided the following information:

Document count = 8
Hash total (formed from account codes) = 17301
Control total (of amounts) = $103,090

Required
What information that might explain the rejection of the batch and the underlying causes can be gleaned from these data?

5. A well-known formula for determining economic order quantities in an inventory control situation is

$$Q^2 = \frac{2DK}{C}$$

where Q is the reorder quantity, D is the demand, K is the cost of reordering, and C is the unit carrying cost or storage cost. The corresponding formula for the cost of maintaining a given inventory policy is

$$T = \frac{KD}{Q} + \frac{QC}{2}$$

Required
a. Apply these formulas to determine the appropriate order quantity and maintenance cost for an inventory of invoice forms. On average, 400 invoices are written per month; printing setup costs are $100 per batch printed; and storage costs are $5 per month per thousand forms.
b. If management decides to restrict order quantities to no more than three months' supply for fear of obsolescence, what impact would such a policy have on the order quantity and cost of maintaining the inventory of invoice forms?

6. What deficiencies must have existed in the overall control environment for the following situations to have been able to occur?
a. The company president was implicated in a case of high-level fraud, but the matter was successfully hushed up.

b. A new computer system was implemented, but several user groups complained that they had not been consulted at the development stage and that the new system did not meet their requirements.

c. Auditors overlooked the fact that an employee performed incompatible duties over an extended period because the employee's job responsibilities were not documented.

d. An internal auditor suspected that an irregularity was being perpetrated by the assistant controller. But she could not follow up on her suspicion because the individual involved was her supervisor.

e. An employee expected to be fired on account of a control violation, but six months later he was still on the job. Management was currently distracted by the possibility of a hostile takeover.

f. After a new computer operator had been on the job for three weeks, it was discovered that she had no qualifications or experience.

g. When the internal auditors conducted an inquiry into the high incidence of errors in the accounting department, it emerged that three clerks had recently been transferred there from other departments. Although they had some accounting experience, none of them was acquainted with the company's accounting procedures.

h. A customer complained about being overcharged on an invoice, and it turned out that the error was deliberate. The billing clerk, who had not benefited personally in any way, defended herself as follows: "I thought you would appreciate my trying to bring more money into the company."

i. A password to the company's computer system was found written on a piece of paper in the drawer beneath an input terminal.

j. A colleague explained to a new employee: "It doesn't matter what you do here; just don't get caught."

k. After an employee was given notice of dismissal for poor work, he systematically destroyed all the company's accounts receivable records.

l. When it was discovered that a large batch of paychecks was issued, all containing errors, a manager shouted angrily: "I don't care what caused this, but some heads are going to roll!"

7. The president of a small company boasted to associates at the Rotary Club: "Fortunately we don't need internal controls. You see, we are a family business, and we are not going to steal from one another."

Required
Discuss the views of this individual.

8. Propose control measures to deal with the risks identified in Problems 12 and 13 in Chapter 16.

9. A password system is being designed to limit access to on-line data files and program files to designated, authorized persons. A partial list of the files is as follows:

Data Files	Program Files
Customer master file	Purchasing
Vendor master file	Accounts payable
Employee master file	Sales order processing
Production specs file	General ledger posting
Standard cost file	Payroll processing
Budget master file	Accounts receivable
General ledger file	Production control
Sales transaction file	Cost variance analysis
Purchasing transaction file	Employee fringe benefits

Required
Indicate which of these data files and programs should be accessible to individuals in each of the following departments:

a. Sales
b. Purchasing
c. Paymaster's office
d. Factory superintendent
e. Warehouse
f. Accounting

10. A company accepts sales orders over the telephone and immediately keys the data into an interactive terminal. The sales data are accumulated in a transaction file and are processed once per month to print customer statements and update master files. At that time, a sales register is also prepared listing all sales transactions closed during the preceding month.

Required

What programmed controls would you recommend be incorporated into the system to prevent and/or detect errors in transaction data?

11. First National Bank installed on-line terminals for its tellers at eight local branches. The terminals, which are connected to a central computer at the bank's main facility, are used for verifying customer balances and recording all deposits and withdrawals. Real-time processing is performed to ensure currency of data in customer files.

Required

List the controls you would expect to find in a system of this type. Give particular attention to controls that would be advisable as a result of the on-line, real-time mode of processing that is used.

12. An algorithm used for implementing a control digit scheme multiplies each successive digit in the account number by the numbers 1, 2, 3, and so on, and sums the resulting products. For example, the computation for the account number 394 is

$$
\begin{array}{ccc}
3 & 9 & 4 \\
\times & \times & \times \\
3 & 2 & 1 \\
\hline
9 + & 18 + & 4 = 31
\end{array}
$$

The "units" digit in the result (i.e., the 1 in 31) is selected as the control digit and is appended to the account number to produce the composite number 394.1.

Required

Test the following account numbers for integrity, and identify any invalid ones:

a. 009.9
b. 061.3
c. 117.4
d. 255.1
e. 306.7
f. 448.2
g. 593.6

Verify that this algorithm is effective in detecting most transposition errors (e.g., entry of account number 726.1 erroneously as 762.1).

13. A simple encryption algorithm (real-life algorithms are much more complicated than this) consists of changing the values of the first and seventh bit of each seven-bit binary word in the ASCII code. Thus, if the first bit is a zero, it will be changed to a one, and vice versa; the seventh bit is changed in like manner. For example, the binary word corresponding to the letter T: **1**010100, would be changed to **0**010101, which corresponds to the NAK or "negative acknowledgment" symbol. Similarly, the number 2 (**0**110010) would be changed to the letter s (**1**110011).

Required

Using this algorithm, encrypt the message "Send money" for transmittal over an insecure telecommunications channel. (Be sure to insert leading zeros where necessary to make each binary word seven digits long, and do not forget to scramble the "space" symbol [ASCII symbol 32] between the two words in the message.)

14. It is often stated that control is achieved through people. And personnel policies certainly make an important contribution to an organization's internal control environment.

Required

Identify and discuss the main aspects of personnel policy from an internal control standpoint. Present your answer in the context of a large service organization such as an insurance company.

15. A small business bought a departmental computer with four terminals for use in its accounting department. Canned software packages were acquired for transaction input, posting, and report preparation. All master files reside on magnetic disk storage, and file maintenance is performed by direct access to these files. A program is provided for displaying the contents of a record and incorporating any desired changes. Both narrative and balance fields in the master records can be updated in this manner, and the documentation supplied with the software suggests that errors in account balances can conveniently be corrected by means of the file maintenance program. No listing or other hard-copy log is provided of file maintenance activity.

The file maintenance program can be called up from any of the four terminals, but normally only the supervisor makes changes in the master files. The other employees say that they are ''scared to touch'' these files.

Required

Discuss the control implications of the file maintenance procedure just described, and suggest ways of reducing the risks involved.

16. A computer operator in the data-processing department was negligent in carrying out operating procedures and inadvertently mounted a reel of magnetic tape containing the inventory master file instead of a blank tape to be used to store scratch files during payroll processing. The inventory tape had been checked out from the file library in readiness for processing the following day.

The operator realized that control violations were treated seriously at the company and was anxious to avoid trouble. He waited until later that day, when a temporary worker was in charge of the file library, and managed to obtain a backup copy of the master file tape. He used this tape for the next day's inventory processing and threw away the damaged reel of tape in a trash can. Seeing that the header record of the ill-fated tape appeared on the system console log, the operator also destroyed the printout, telling his supervisor that the paper had become jammed in the printer.

Required

What control weaknesses allowed the operator to make the mistake and then conceal it? Comment on the overall concern for controls in the data-processing department.

17. Therion Company had installed a large interactive computer system to handle its accounting and other information-processing functions. One day, a data entry clerk in the accounting department inadvertently entered an erroneous command into an on-line terminal and was surprised to see a display of the central password file. It contained a complete list of all current passwords, the names and ID numbers of the individuals to whom the

passwords were issued, and the tasks or files to which they gave access. The information extended over several screen ''pages,'' with continuation commands allowing the viewer to study each screen in turn. The clerk recognized the potential value of the information and spent the next hour copying it down. Shortly after this incident she quit her job and sold the information to MacGregor, Inc., a major competitor of the company.

Over the next two years, personnel at MacGregor routinely accessed Therion's files over the telephone lines. The rival firm retrieved sensitive data on production and sales targets. It also made subtle changes to data that misled managers into making faulty decisions on a number of occasions. The penetration went unnoticed until an employee of MacGregor finally placed an anonymous call to Therion's manager of information processing.

Upon receipt of the call, all passwords were changed, but fearing adverse publicity and disciplinary action, the manager decided that the matter would be better hushed up. The assistant manager, the only other person to ''get wind'' of the affair, was given a sizable raise to keep quiet. As a result, neither upper management nor the directors of the company ever learned of the problem.

Required

Discuss the situation described here, and identify the control measures that should have been taken (a) to prevent the disclosure of the passwords, (b) to prevent the exploitation of the disclosure, and (c) to ensure that the affair could never have been concealed.

18. Desktop microcomputers, operated by users, are considered more vulnerable than are large mainframe computers located in a secure computer room.

Required

a. Describe controls that could be implemented in a large accounting office: (i) to protect microcomputers from unauthorized access and (ii) to protect file data stored on microcomputers.

b. To what other major risks are microcomputers—operated either in a stand-alone mode or as part of a local area network—particularly vulnerable, and what controls can be implemented to reduce those risks?

18

Auditing of Accounting Systems

LEARNING OBJECTIVES

After studying this chapter you should be able to

- Discuss the nature of audit risk.
- Explain the principal steps in the audit engagement.
- Describe the auditor's need to evaluate internal control.
- Identify the objectives and the broad features of the internal control questionnaire.
- Discuss the purposes of compliance testing and substantive testing.
- Describe the use of the computer as an audit tool.
- Describe the most important computer audit techniques.
- Explain the purposes of generalized audit software.

CHAPTER OUTLINE

AUDIT RISK

The financial statements present management's assertions as to the financial position and results of operations of the enterprise. Implicit in these statements are further assertions concerning ownership rights, valuations, and allocations and the completeness of the data they contain. The purpose of the external audit is to examine and test these assertions and to express an opinion about them.

The auditor is asked to issue an opinion on the basis of a limited program of observation, examination, testing, and other procedures. In no case can the auditor observe all the client's significant activities, examine all the financial records, or test all the internal controls for effectiveness. Auditing is based on the notion of selection of procedures and sampling of accounting records, followed by inference as to the fairness of the statements. The inference rests on the auditor's judgment

after gathering an amount of evidence that is deemed to be sufficient given the circumstances.

The possibility that the inferences made could nevertheless be incorrect is referred to as *audit risk*. The professional literature contains the following comments:

The ultimate risk against which the auditor and those who rely on his opinion require reasonable protection is a combination of two separate risks. The first of these is that material errors will occur in the accounting process by which the financial statements are developed. The second is that material errors will not be detected by the auditor's examination.

The auditor relies on internal control to reduce the first risk, and on his tests of details and his other auditing procedures to reduce the second.[1]

[1] American Institute of Certified Public Accounts, *Statement on Auditing Procedures, No. 33* (New York: AICPA, December 1973).

This statement explains the so-called risk of incorrect acceptance. It is the risk that the financial statements may result from accounting processes that contain material errors or may otherwise be misstated, despite the auditor's belief on the basis of available evidence that they are fair. This is the global equivalent of the "beta risk" considered in statistical sampling tests of an individual account balance. In parallel with the risk of incorrect acceptance is the "risk of incorrect rejection"—the equivalent of the "alpha risk"—which refers to the possibility that the financial statements could be *fair* despite the auditor's belief that they are misstated.

The foregoing statement by the AICPA also mentions the two methods adopted by the auditor to reduce the risk. The evaluation of internal controls is intended to provide a means of assessing the reliability of the accounting process and the likely correctness of the financial records. The other audit procedures, including substantive testing, are designed to reduce the risk that the auditor may draw the wrong inferences from examination of the accounting records.

Audit risk is an accepted element in any audit engagement and is understood (at least by informed people) in the interpretation of the auditor's opinion. The auditor seeks "reasonable assurance"—not absolute assurance—that the financial statements are not misstated, in the same way as management seeks reasonable assurance that major losses will not occur because of errors or irregularities. The auditor's professional and legal obligations are met when the audit engagement is conducted according to Generally Accepted Auditing Standards. This is not to say that the auditor does not take these obligations seriously or does not strive to minimize audit risk; quite the contrary. But no matter how conscientious and thorough the audit procedures are, the fundamental element of risk remains and must be accepted.

THE AUDIT ENGAGEMENT

Audit engagements clearly have to be flexible to adapt to individual circumstances. However, the overall pattern is well established, involving three phases: planning of the engagement, gathering and examination of evidence, and communication of the results of the audit.

In more detail, the following major steps can be identified:

• Organizational planning of the engagement
• Determination of audit objectives
• Initial selection of procedures
• Review of internal controls
• Compliance testing
• Substantive testing
• Additional procedures
• Documentation of the audit
• Preparation of the opinion and recommendations

Organizational planning consists of assigning responsibilities to members of the audit team, determining the intended scope of the engagement, drawing up a work plan, and preparing a schedule and budget for the engagement. The planning phase includes these activities and identification of the audit objectives and tentative selection of appropriate audit procedures. The review of internal control, the performance of compliance and substantive testing, and the conduct of any necessary additional procedures make up the data-gathering and examination phase. The preparation of audit documentation, issuance of the opinion, and development of recommendations constitute the communication phase.

Audit Objectives

The main objectives of the typical audit engagement are (1) to evaluate the effectiveness of the internal controls; (2) to determine whether the organization's resources are being used effectively and in conformity with management's general or specific authorizations; (3) to review the integrity, reliability, and efficiency of the information system; and (4) to assess the fairness (or otherwise) of the external financial statements and prepare a formal opinion. In addition, the auditor usually has more specific objectives arising from particular concerns. These concerns, which relate to the general risks and specific threats expected to be faced by the organization, include many that are common to all types of clients and others that may apply to a particular client. They may stem from prior knowledge of the organization, its environment, and the type of information system that supports it. An auditor performing a repeat audit will often have concerns relating to weaknesses that were identified in the prior year's working papers and that may not yet have been remedied. In all cases, the scope of the audit and the detailed procedures selected will reflect the general and specific concerns of the auditor.

Audit Procedures and Techniques

Audit procedures are performed on all major activities comprising the accounting system: accounts receivable, payroll, inventory control, and so forth. The procedures use five basic audit techniques:

- Observation
- Inquiry
- Examination and inspection
- Confirmation
- Testing

Observation is watching the various accounting and data-processing activities as they are performed. Inquiry consists of asking questions of appropriate client personnel. Examination and inspection relate to both the physical assets of the organization and the records and documentation that describe them. Confirmation is securing of written audit evidence from outside parties, as in the confirmation of accounts receivable. Testing includes a variety of techniques designed to help the auditor assess the quality of the data and the reliability of the information system.

The procedures are designed to achieve the audit objectives as efficiently as possible and, in particular, to provide a high probability that any material errors or irregularities will be exposed. Individual procedures that can accomplish more than one objective are preferred over those that can accomplish only a single objective.

Review of Internal Controls

The evaluation of internal controls has for a long time been an important part of the audit engagement because its outcome influences the reliance that the auditor can place on the internal controls to support information gathered in other phases of the engagement. But passage of the Foreign Corrupt Practices Act, and more specifi-

cally the SEC proposal for auditor attestation to an internal control statement by management (see Chapter 15), have given the evaluation new significance. Furthermore, auditors are increasingly being asked to evaluate internal controls apart from the requirements of formal audit engagements.

The evaluation of internal controls has several steps that are described in more detail later in this chapter. It includes an initial review of the controls and subsequent testing to determine their effectiveness. The review identifies the appropriate control objectives and then, within the information system, the control measures and techniques that accomplish those objectives. Details of the control devices incorporated in the system are gathered from various sources, including the review of documentation and interviews with company personnel. Standard questionnaires and checklists are used for assembling and analyzing the data being gathered.

Audit Testing

Two types of testing are utilized in auditing: compliance testing and substantive testing. Compliance testing is concerned with assessing the effectiveness of the controls and forms part of the evaluation of internal control. It is carried out on the information system, rather than on the associated data, but it is intended to help assess the system's potential for providing high-quality data. Compliance tests are performed for both the manual and the computer controls. An example of compliance testing is the testing of a control designed to prevent unauthorized access to the computer facilities or testing of a control intended to prevent unauthorized extension of credit to a customer.

Substantive testing is concerned with the quality and reliability of the accounting data and is carried out directly on the data. Examples of substantive testing are the physical inventory count and confirmation of accounts receivable. Another example is the recalculation of payroll deductions or sales commissions. Substantive testing includes tests on details of transactions and account balances and also analysis of ratios, variances, trends, and fluctuations of accounting data. Statistical methods often play an important role in this kind of analysis.

FIGURE 18.1 Reduction of the scope of substantive testing made possible by reliance on internal controls.

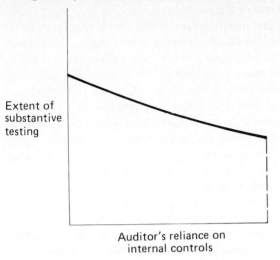

The scope and nature of audit testing depend substantially on the outcome of the evaluation of internal controls. If the outcome of the preliminary review is favorable, compliance testing will be undertaken to verify the effectiveness of the controls and to determine how much audit reliance can be placed on them. If the outcome is unfavorable—or if subsequent compliance testing fails to confirm the effectiveness of the controls—an extended program of substantive testing will be required (see Figure 18.1). In general, the greater the strength of the internal controls, and the greater the reliance that can be placed on them, the less is the need for extensive substantive testing. But regardless of the status of the internal controls, some substantive testing must always be performed to support the audit opinion.

Additional Procedures

Additional procedures may be called for if the results of the other techniques are considered inadequate to express an audit opinion. Procedures of this type are often needed as part of the initial audit engagement performed for a client. The results of the procedures are then available for the benefit of audits conducted in subsequent years.

Documentation of the Audit

All aspects of the audit procedures should be documented as they are carried out, to provide for review of the engagement by a manager or partner, to support the opinion should it ever be challenged, and to provide background information to assist future audits of the same client. The audit documentation takes the form of working papers, which consist of material relating solely to the current engagement and also material of more lasting value. A summary of the schedule and budget for the engagement, a list of principal audit objectives, copies of completed questionnaires, checklists, flowcharts, organization charts, a summary of the conclusions, and miscellaneous notes all are included in the working papers.

The working papers should provide[2]

- Evidence that the engagement was properly planned, conducted, and reviewed
- Evidence that the client's internal control system was properly evaluated
- Data demonstrating that the financial statements are consistent with the client's records
- Evidence that the opinion was properly supported by evidential material
- Resolution of any exceptions or unusual matters
- Conclusions reached by the auditor concerning the engagement

The preparation of working papers by the auditor should be governed by appropriate documentation standards in much the same way as is the preparation of documentation by the client company (see Chapter 13).

Auditor's Opinion and Recommendations

The culmination of the audit engagement is the preparation of the auditor's report or opinion to be published with the client's financial statements. The typical "short-form" report consists of a scope paragraph and the opinion paragraph. The scope paragraph indicates what type of examination the auditor made; the opinion paragraph

---

[2] American Institute of Certified Public Accountants, *Statement on Auditing Standards, No. 1.*, sec. 338.05 (New York: AICPA, 1973).

indicates the auditor's formal conclusions resulting from the engagement. The opinion can be unqualified, qualified, or adverse; alternatively, a disclaimer can state in effect that no opinion can be expressed. Except in the most favorable situation, in which an unqualified opinion is expressed, the auditor must state in the report what circumstances prevented the issuance of an unqualified opinion.

In addition to the formal opinion, the auditor may communicate a variety of recommendations to management. These may further explain the meaning of the opinion or identify problems that, though not material enough to compromise the financial statements, nevertheless call for management's attention. Also, the auditor may wish to report weaknesses in the internal controls or suggest ways of improving efficiency. In contrast with the opinion that is intended for publication and that carries the auditor's full professional and legal responsibility, the recommendations to management are confidential and can be more informal.

EVALUATION OF INTERNAL CONTROL

The evaluation of internal control includes both a review of the controls and compliance tests to determine whether the controls are effective. In detail, the typical evaluation consists of the following steps:

- Review of the controls
- Identification of relevant control objectives
- Identification of system attributes, in the form of control measures or techniques, that either achieve or fail to achieve those objectives
- Determination of the extent of reliance that can be placed on the internal controls
- Tests of compliance to verify the effectiveness of the control measures

Internal Control Review

The need to understand the business environment as a basis for understanding the controls was mentioned in Chapter 15. The internal control review includes a study of the environment for this purpose. The review then

expands into a study of the accounting system, the major transaction flows, the extent of automation, and the basic structure of the internal controls.

A preliminary review is often made to gain an initial "feel" for the effectiveness of the controls. On the basis of this preliminary review, the auditor can tentatively assess the significance of the controls and determine whether continuation of the evaluation is worthwhile.[3] In one case, the auditor may conclude that the control structure is so inadequate that it would be a waste of effort to pursue the review further or to plan for subsequent compliance testing. In another case, the initial conclusions might be sufficiently favorable to warrant continuation of the review, but negative factors might subsequently come to light that would cause the auditor to abandon the review at a later stage. In a third case, the review might be completed favorably, but subsequent compliance testing might fail to demonstrate the effectiveness of the controls. In a fourth case, both the extended review and subsequent compliance testing might prove successful, indicating that significant reliance can be placed on the internal controls. The decision process leading to a conclusion regarding the internal controls is divided into several steps, as shown in Figure 18.2.[4]

Control Objectives

Identification of the relevant control objectives has been made much easier with the publication by large accounting firms and others of standardized lists of objectives (see Chapter 16). These lists are often drawn up in the form of questionnaires or checklists that the auditor can use while gathering the required information about the control measures provided in the information system. Some of the objectives may not be applicable to the particular client, but the standardized lists at least help draw attention to controls that might otherwise be

---

[3] American Institute of Certified Public Accountants, *Statement on Auditing Standards, No. 3,* para. 25 (New York: AICPA, December 1974).

[4] A more sophisticated and complete version of such a diagram appeared in the Auditing and Accounting Guide, *The Auditor's Study and Evaluation of Internal Controls in EDP Systems* (New York: AICPA, 1977), pp. 21–24.

FIGURE 18.2 Auditor's decision process in evaluating internal controls.

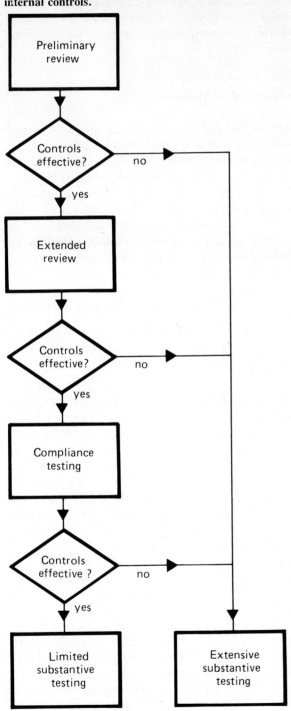

overlooked. The auditor must identify a subset of the standard list of applicable objectives and possibly add other required objectives. Ultimately, the auditor's professional judgment must be brought to bear in "interpreting, adapting, or expanding such generalized material as appropriate in particular situations."[5]

Internal Control Questionnaire

Typical internal control questionnaires are laid out in sections dealing with the major components of the information system. A major part usually deals with the computerized elements of the system. One widely used questionnaire for computer controls is divided into sections according to Systems Control Principles similar to those listed in Chapter 16.[6] Under each principle is a number of control objectives together with specific questions that help determine whether the objective is achieved in the system under review. For example, under the principle dealing with the control environment (corresponding to Principle No. 1 in Chapter 16), there are three control objectives listed:

(A) On a continuing basis, internal auditors or some other independent group within the organization should review and test computer processing activities.
(B) Management should establish personnel policies and procedures for selecting and evaluating systems personnel that take into account the risks inherent in each person's job.
(C) Management by their policies, procedures, and actions should allow systems managers adequate time for supervision.

Under the first objective, two specific questions are included:

1. Is there a management committee or group outside the EDP organization that oversees the EDP operators, monitors performance, and in general, guides the activities of the EDP personnel?

---

[5] American Institute of Certified Public Accountants, *Professional Standards*, AU 320.66, vol. 1 (New York: Commerce Clearing House, 1981).
[6] Martin B. Roberts, *Internal Control in EDP Systems* (Atlanta: Administrative Systems Design, 1980).

2. Do the internal auditors or some other independent group review and test EDP activities and report periodically to the control committee established by management?

The questions are arranged so that a "yes" answer indicates a favorable outcome, and a "no" answer indicates a negative outcome for the particular control objective. Space is provided in the questionnaire for explaining any "no" answers. Space is also provided for designating an identification number to the particular control, for cross-referencing other material in the working papers, for referencing the source of the information, and for indicating the significance of the control in question. An illustration of pages from the control questionnaire is presented in Figure 18.3.

Identification of Control Measures

After the applicable set of control objectives has been defined, the information system is examined to determine what control measures are provided to achieve each of the stated objectives. Given that a certain level of assurance is required, the evaluation must determine where audit reliance can be placed. An important question in the mind of the auditor is "What would happen— or, more specifically, what could go wrong—if the objective were not achieved? What accounts would be affected, and what would be the likely problems?" In short, the auditor is concerned about the risks to which the particular control objective is related.

The actual identification of the controls starts with a determination as to what controls are supposed to be incorporated in the system. This determination is made from a review of system and other documentation, from interviews with key company personnel, and from observations of the data-processing activities as they are performed. The auditor is seeking to build a picture of the internal control system from information obtained from various sources. Flowcharts of portions of the information system are often prepared to provide insight into the processing activities and the way in which the controls fit into the overall picture. As relevant information is gathered, the answers to questions contained in the questionnaire can be completed. If adequate documentation is not available, the auditor will be forced to reconstruct much of it during the engagement to provide a basis for analysis. This greatly increases the effort required and correspondingly increases the cost of the audit.

Assessment of Reliance

On the basis of the results of the review of internal controls, the auditor reaches certain preliminary conclusions regarding the adequacy of the controls. As previously noted, if the conclusions are favorable, the effectiveness of the controls will be evaluated further by means of compliance testing. On the other hand, if the results are unfavorable, the auditor may conclude that no significant degree of reliance can be placed on the internal control system and that compliance testing would therefore be pointless. In this latter situation, or if compliance testing is later abandoned because of negative results, the whole burden of the audit examination must fall on substantive testing.

Compliance Testing

The second part of the evaluation consists of tests of compliance to determine whether the internal controls are being applied and operating as they are intended to. Compliance testing is sometimes referred to simply as "risk analysis" or "risk assessment." Typically, the auditor selects several transactions in each functional area (accounts receivable, payroll, and so forth) and traces them through the entire system. The transactions may be actual ones that have already been processed by the client, or they may be test transactions designed for the purpose. In the former case, and particularly with manual systems, transactions initiated at different times during the year are included to test the consistency with which control procedures have been applied. If the system is automated, greater consistency can normally be expected, but it still cannot be taken for granted. In all cases, the operation of each control is observed and documented as the transactions flow through the system.

In general it would be prohibitively expensive to test all the controls. Instead, compliance testing is usually concentrated on the areas of internal control that the auditor considers most critical and that must be verified to achieve the desired level of assurance. This is an example of the principle of cost effectiveness that must pervade all areas of the audit engagement.

Results of the Evaluation

The conclusions reached from the evaluation consist of a set of explicit statements regarding the strengths and weaknesses of the internal control system. The conclusions form the basis of any recommendations for improvements that are to be made to management. Auditors are responsible for informing management when weaknesses are exposed and for offering assistance in remedying the weaknesses. In the case of serious weaknesses, substantial redesign of the information system may be required to accommodate the needed controls.

SUBSTANTIVE TESTING

Substantive testing is carried out in two forms: verification of classes of transactions and verification of the correctness of individual account balances. The aim in both cases is to substantiate dollar balances or to detect monetary errors.

The tests of transactions frequently are performed on classes of high-volume transactions such as purchases, billings, and payroll transactions that mainly affect the income statement. The transactions should be selected from the whole accounting period under examination. The objectives are to determine that the information system is functioning properly and that the transactions are correctly recorded and classified. The tests of account balances are concerned primarily with year-end amounts appearing on the balance sheet. Complete or sample tests may be performed as the auditor sees fit. A complete count of cash would normally be made because of the high risk of control problems.

Substantive testing also includes an analytical review that is basically a search for exceptions or unusual items. Comparisons may be made with previous year's financial statements, with budgets or standard cost allowances, with industry figures, or with any other appropriate reference. Ratios, trends, and statistical relationships (provided by regression analysis or otherwise) may be scrutinized to help identify abnormal amounts, changes, fluctuations, or patterns. These phenomena can provide clues to underlying problems that are then investigated to obtain satisfactory explanations.

Sometimes procedures are used that combine the functions of compliance and substantive testing. These are usually referred to as *dual-purpose* tests which verify both the controls and the account balances. Use of dual-purpose tests can improve the efficiency of the audit.

APPROACHES TO EDP AUDITING

Auditing Around the Computer

When automated information systems first appeared, auditors were confronted by the dilemma of a "black box" that they did not understand but that obviously held the key to much of the processing of the data with which they were concerned. Their response was a sensible one in the circumstances: They audited "around the computer." The auditor observed and checked the input and then "walked around to the other side" and observed the output. Input and output were examined for mutual consistency, but little regard was given to the detailed processing steps in between. Files were examined only if hard-copy printed listings were available. To adopt the perspectives of general systems theory (Chapter 1), the workings of the black box were not ascertained, except possibly to some limited degree by a process of experimentation.

In some cases, auditing around the computer may allow the auditor achieve the audit objectives. However, the approach can be inefficient; much more testing and experimentation are often required than would be necessary if the auditor had access to the internal operations of the system. And perhaps more seriously, the auditor may be severely hampered in the evaluation of the internal accounting controls provided in the system. It may not be possible to trace the audit trail through the auto-

FIGURE 18.3 **Pages from questionnaire used in the review of internal controls in EDP systems.** The original questionnaire extends to 23 pages.

QUESTIONNAIRE FOR GENERAL REVIEW OF EDP INTERNAL CONTROLS

SYSTEMS CONTROL PRINCIPLE NO. 1: **MANAGEMENT SHOULD ESTABLISH THE AUTHORIZATIONS AND CRITERIA FOR THE CREATION AND EXECUTION OF TRANSACTIONS AND COMMUNICATE THESE REQUIREMENTS TO THOSE PERSONS PERFORMING THESE FUNCTIONS.**

A. Control Objective: Provision for general authorization over the execution of transactions (prohibiting the EDP department from initiating or authorizing transactions [G-2]).*

NOTE: *Answers to all the questions should be "yes." The EDP department is basically a service organization to the users, however, controls are joint responsibilities for both the users and EDP. Because of different circumstances controls will vary among installations but any "no' answers should be explained.*

1. Are the EDP department personnel prohibited from:
   (a) initiating or authorizing transactions?
   (b) performing initial data preparation?
   (c) originating master file changes?
   (d) having custody over non-EDP assets?
   (e) performing duties in non-EDP operating areas of the organization?

2. Is there a control, independent of the EDP department, over the transactions submitted to EDP for processing?

3. Are prenumbered forms used for source documents when practical?

4. Are all computer-generated transactions and the criteria that authorized the transactions printed for subsequent review by authorized personnel?

5. Are transactions that change a master file approved by an authorized person outside the EDP organization prior to submission to EDP?

6. Is a record made of the "before" and "after" status of all master file changes for critical fields and approved by a person authorized to make these changes?

7. Where transactions are input from terminals, do these users maintain an independent control over the accuracy of the input transactions and the data in their files?

8. For DBMS installations — are all file structure maintenance activities involving data bases logged on hard copy and these logs reviewed by the Data Base Administrator?

B. Control Objective: Access to computer hardware should be limited to authorized individuals (G-15).

NOTE: *A vital axiom of security is to restrict computer hardware access to those persons who are authorized to operate these devices. Physical protection, location of terminals, location of printers and other traffic-creating machines, floor arrangements, and operating procedures should be designed with a security orientation. Answers to all questions should be "yes," explain any "no" answers.*

1. Is all computer processing for production preplanned and the operations run according to a published schedule? Explain any exceptions.

2. Is access to computer hardware restricted to authorized persons by locks, badges, or other physical devices? Are these devices changed periodically? Explain.

3. Are programmers and systems personnel denied access to the computer room and especially to the operator's console?

4. Are machine utilization records and console logs prepared for all computer operations and checked periodically to scheduled processing to detect unauthorized operations?

5. Do all terminals have locks? Is their use limited to authorized operators?

*GENERAL CONTROL NO. 2 from *The Auditor's Study and Evaluation of Internal Control in EDP Systems*, AICPA Audit and Accounting Guide, 1977. Other control objectives from this source are similarly coded with G for general controls and A for application controls.

FIGURE 18.3 (continued)

Number of Control	Is This Control Present	Source of Data on Control	Data Verified By	Significance of Control in This Organization			Reference To Working	Action and Comments Regarding Achievement of Control Objective, Deficient Controls, Compensating Controls, and Other Pertinent Control Matters.
				Very	Average	Not Very		

	198	198	198
Prepared By			
Data			
Received by			

FIGURE 18.3 (continued)

QUESTIONNAIRE FOR GENERAL REVIEW OF EDP INTERNAL CONTROLS

4. Are periodic reports submitted routinely to management regarding the status of all projects in progress?

5. Does the system manager know what each of his people is working on currently and the status of this work?

SYSTEM CONTROL PRINCIPLE NO. 5: **THE OPERATING PROCEDURES SHOULD MAKE PROVISION FOR VERIFYING PERIODICALLY THE ACCURACY OF THE STORED DATA AND THE REPORTS THAT ARE PRODUCED FROM THIS DATA.**

A. Control Objective: On a continuing basis internal auditors or some other independent group within an organization should review and test computer processing activities (G-19).

NOTE: *Periodic matching of recorded data to the physical assets, or in some cases to source documents, is a verification of the system's accuracy. These and other tests should be made periodically by an independent group. Answers to all questions should be "yes," explain any "no" answers.*

1. Do the internal auditors or some other independent group make periodic reviews and tests of the accuracy of stored data and the reports generated from these data? Do these tests include:
   (a) accuracy of period cutoffs?
   (b) accuracy of transaction coding?
   (c) completeness of data?
   (d) tests of the error correction and re-submission procedures?
   (e) comparisons of recorded data to physical assets or source documents?

2. Do the internal auditors or some other independent group make periodic reviews and tests of the control procedures and techniques used in EDP processing? Do these tests include:
   (a) comparison of written instruction with actual operations?
   (b) tests of program controls?
   (c) tests of run-to-run processing controls?

B. Control Objective: Output control totals should be reconciled with input and processing controls (A-10).

NOTE: *An important feature of good control is control continuity from the initiation of the input to the delivery of the system's output. This requires the balancing of output controls to input controls. Many systems have this check designed so that the balancing is performed automatically with the results of the comparison printed on a report. All answers should be "yes," explain any "no." These questions should be answered for each significant EDP application.*

1. Do users, an independent control group, or the computer program balance output control totals to input and processing controls? Explain how this is done.

2. Are there written instructions as to how these checks are to be made?

3. Does the system produce control totals that facilitates the balancing of processing controls to input controls to ensure that all authorized transactions are processed, that no unauthorized transactions are processed, and that the processing is accurate?

4. For terminal input — are remote batching procedures, including normal batch control methods, used when practical?

C. Control Objective: Output should be scanned and tested by comparison to original source documents (A-11).

NOTE: *Certain non-numeric data may be critical from the standpoint of accuracy. Shipping instructions, customers' names and addresses, and terms of purchase are examples of such data. Special procedures have to be set up to verify this type of data. Answers should be "yes," explain any "no" answers. These questions should be answered for each significant EDP application.*

1. Is critical non-numeric data that cannot be controlled by balancing, such as master file name and address changes, given an item-by-item comparison of the revised file to the source input document?

FIGURE 18.3 (continued)

Number of Control	Is This Control Present	Source of Data on Control	Data Verified By	Significance of Control in This Organization			Reference To Working	Action and Comments Regarding Achievement of Control Objective, Deficient Controls, Compensating Controls, and Other Pertinent Control Matters.
				Very	Average	Not Very		

	198	198	198
Prepared By			
Data			
Received by			

mated parts of the information system. Unless intermediate printed output is routinely provided, an informed judgment about the transaction paths may be difficult to make.

Generally Accepted Auditing Standards require that the auditor understand the flow of transactions through the information system and the basic structure of accounting controls. Sometimes, auditing around the computer provides an adequate basis for satisfying the standards and is intentionally chosen as the most effective and efficient audit strategy. In other cases, reliance on auditing around the computer undermines the auditor's ability to satisfy this standard. When an application has a material effect on the financial statements, auditing around the computer may not be an acceptable strategy. As the limitations of auditing around the computer have become more widely recognized, auditors have increasingly turned to auditing "through the computer."

Auditing Through the Computer

Auditing through the computer requires the ability to trace transaction paths from input to output: through the automated as well as the manual parts of the system. The flow of data is verified at each stage of the process as well as at its starting point and destination, and the content of machine-readable files is examined directly. Internal controls can be examined directly and tested as they operate on data at the particular points in the process at which they are placed. Auditing through the computer demystifies the black box by detailed examination and testing of the programs and data and attempts to discover its mechanisms by direct inspection.

The terms *auditing around* and *through* the computer have been challenged as implying too simplistic a picture and implying a value judgment that may in some cases be faulty.[7] In their place, the terms *auditing with* and *auditing without* the computer were proposed. Other authors reserve the expression *auditing with the computer* for the use of the computer as a primary audit tool. This latter convention will be adopted in the present work.

[7] Geoff Horwitz, "Needed: A Computer Audit Philosophy, *Journal of Accountancy*, April 1976, pp. 69–72.

Computer-Assisted Auditing

The trend toward greater audit sophistication in the environment of automated information systems did not stop at auditing through the computer. The next step was to use the computer itself as an audit tool. It was recognized that the computer provided an excellent means of examining the data underlying the financial statements—that is, a means of gathering audit evidence. The ability to access data files, particularly on-line files, retrieve records at will, extract statistical samples from the client's data base, and perform test calculations on the data opened up new avenues of audit procedures. Computer-assisted auditing offered enormous advantages over the comparable manual procedures and, indeed, made feasible a number of procedures that would otherwise have been clerically impractical. In some cases the client's computer is used. In other cases the auditor brings a portable computer for use in audit testing.

Necessary Audit Skills

A major problem posed by auditing through the computer, and still more by the use of the computer as an audit tool, is the need for auditors to have a working knowledge of computer systems. Most people now entering the accounting profession have had some formal training in computers and computer programming, and the accepted proficiency standards for auditors (as measured by the content of the Uniform CPA Examination) now require understanding of automated systems. However, many older CPAs have never received such training. And even CPAs who have had one or two courses in computer topics in college and have taken advantage of relevant continuing education courses find it hard to stay abreast of the rapid developments in computer technology or to understand the highly complex systems that many of their clients operate. The problem is typically solved in one of two ways.

One approach is for CPAs to acquire and maintain the technical skills necessary to understand and work with each new generation of computers used by their clients. This approach places a considerable burden on continuing education—formal or informal—but the CPA is able to conduct personally any or all parts of the audit engagement. Also, the auditor is able to understand the systems being examined.

The other approach is to delegate those parts of the audit that deal directly with the computer to an audit specialist. This individual should preferably be a trained auditor, but one who has acquired expertise in the field of automated systems beyond what is typically required of the general audit staff member. The auditor in charge maintains overall responsibility for the audit and continues to supervise all aspects of the work; there must be no question of abdicating responsibilities. But the supervising auditor nevertheless relies on the advice of the specialist on matters directly related to the computer and its detailed operation.

Each of these two approaches to the problem of the required technical expertise can be effective, but each has its disadvantages. In the one case, the auditor must acquire and maintain skills beyond the normal proficiency requirement and in a highly volatile field essentially distinct from accounting. Furthermore, despite all reasonable attempts to stay current, the auditor may still be unfamiliar with a particular feature of a client's system. In the other, the supervising auditor inevitably sacrifices some measure of control over the engagement. Moreover, there is always the possibility of differences of opinion among members of the audit team that the accountant in charge is ill equipped to resolve. There has been considerable debate within the profession as to which of the two approaches is better; even the major accounting firms in this country do not agree on which approach to take. Furthermore, some smaller firms, and many individual CPAs, have not adopted either approach and basically still take the route of auditing around the computer—not as a reasoned choice but because of the lack of appropriate computer literacy.

COMPUTER AUDIT TECHNIQUES

Computer audit–testing techniques can be divided into the following categories according to whether the

client's application software, data, or both are used in the test and according to the type of testing performed:

- Observation of routine processing with the client's programs and data
- Reprocessing of the client's transaction data using audit software
- Testing of the client's data files using audit software
- Testing of the client's system using data supplied by the auditor

The four techniques are illustrated in Figure 18.4 and are explained next.

Observation of Routine Processing

The objective of observing routine processing is generally to observe the input, processing, and output of data as the routine data-processing function is actually performed (Figure 18.4a). Observations of processing during the engagement can supplement information gathered by the auditor relating to processing operations during the rest of the year. In some cases, much can be learned from this procedure; as noted earlier, compliance testing often includes the observation of routine processing. But the auditor may have concerns that cannot be resolved by direct observation. It is difficult to test the proper functioning of controls that might not be triggered by the particular set of data currently being processed. For example, a control ostensibly provided to segregate time-card records reporting more than 20 hours of overtime in any given week, and list them on an exception report, could not be tested if no time cards submitted during that pay period happened to claim more than 20 hours.

The effectiveness of observing routine processing is considerably enhanced by using modern computer audit techniques that enable the auditor to monitor the processing of transactions as they flow through the system; additional output is generated at strategic points along the transaction path producing a more complete audit trail and allowing the auditor to study individual steps in the process. These techniques are sometimes collectively referred to as *tagging and tracing*. Audit software to monitor transaction processing in this way must interface

FIGURE 18.4   The four computer audit techniques.

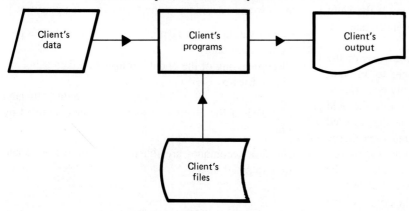

(a) Observation of client's routine data-processing activities.

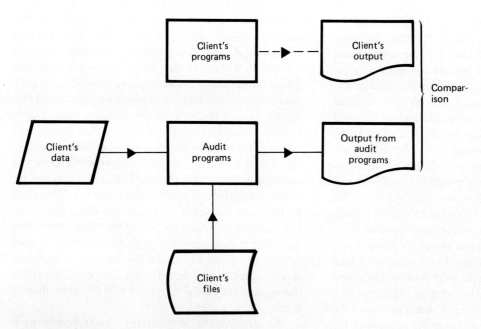

(b) Use of audit software to reprocess client's data. The client's output is compared with output from audit programs.

with the client's applications software; often it resides permanently as a module within the applications software. The module may be activated just during the audit engagement to produce detailed data about the processing being observed, or it may be used to accumulate summary data on an ongoing basis. If the module is permanently installed, tests must be conducted to ensure that it has not been tampered with.

Even without specialized software, the auditor can use capabilties routinely provided by the operating systems of most large computers. Run logs typically capture a wealth of useful information on the date and time of each run, the job number, the identification number and password of the user, the duration of the run, the amount of main memory used, and other details of execution. These logs should be reviewed and compared with op-

FIGURE 18.4 (continued)

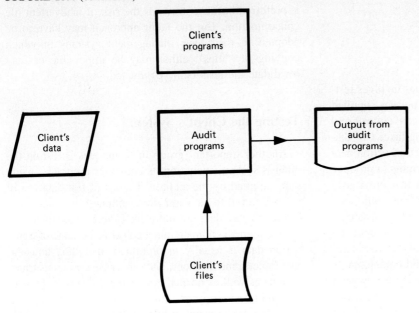

(c) Use of audit software to analyze client's data files.

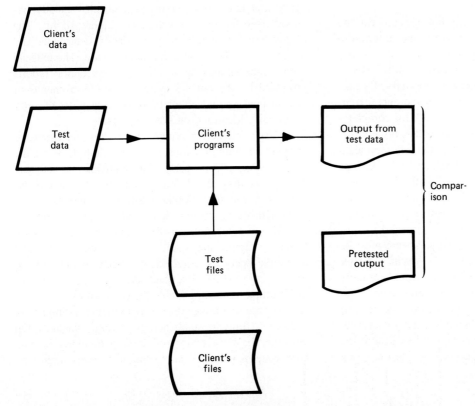

(d) Use of test data in conjunction with client's program. The
output is compared with pretested output supplied by auditor.

erator documentation and with schedules of routine processing.

Testing the Client's Data

An important group of audit techniques involves testing the client's data using computer programs supplied by the auditor. Such programs are collectively referred to as *audit software*. This kind of testing takes two distinct forms. In the one case, the client's transaction data are reprocessed using the auditor's programs to produce output that should be comparable with that previously generated by the client (Figure 18.4b). The audit software is pretested and contains relevant control measures. Any discrepancies between the two sets of output are identified for investigation. The major objectives of reprocessing are to assess the accuracy and completeness of the client's routine processing, to verify the account balances reported in the financial statements, and to evaluate the operation of controls supposedly incorporated in the client's programs. Reprocessing of client's data is often referred to as *simulation*.

In the other case, the intent is not to reprocess the data but to examine the client's records and files and to perform various types of tests to determine the quality of the information they contain (Figure 18.4c). Tests of this type form a major component of substantive testing. Such tests might include verification of footings, extensions, and totals; examination of records for completeness and correctness; comparison of ostensibly equivalent data in different files; calculation of significant ratios; and regression analysis of selected relationships within the data. The tests are aimed partly at assessing the accuracy of processing but also, and more important, at identifying unusual items that might provide clues to underlying problems or irregularities.

When using either of these techniques, care must be exercised to avoid contaminating the client's master files: reprocessing of the transaction data would normally result in double posting. The usual procedure is to process the actual transaction data with a *copy* of the master file data, rather than with the original. Otherwise, a specially written program can be used to restore the master file records to their status before the test program

is run. The former approach is more commonly used and is preferred because it avoids the risk of inadvertent file contamination. But the latter approach may have to be adopted in data base management systems in which copying of "files" either may be impossible or may invalidate the tests being conducted.

Testing the Client's System

Another important group of techniques is testing the client's system, including its computer programs, using data supplied by the auditor. The set of test data is still often referred to as a *test deck,* although in today's environment the data are more likely to be maintained on magnetic media than on punched cards. A range of transaction data is usually incorporated, including unusual, incomplete, inconsistent, and otherwise erroneous transactions as well as normal, valid ones. The objectives of the audit test data are similar to those of test data designed to debug newly written software (see Chapter 8). The expected results of the test data are known in advance and are compared with the results actually obtained from the client's programs (Figure 18.4d). The response of the client's programs can be determined and the effectiveness of the controls evaluated. The unusual transactions should be identified on exception reports produced by the client's system, and the erroneous or invalid ones should either be rejected at point of entry or properly identified on error reports.

In large interactive computer systems, an extensive array of records and files may be required to test the client's programs properly. The equivalent of the test deck under these conditions is sometimes called an *integrated test facility.* Sometimes test transactions are entered and are processed along with the client's routine transaction data, with artificial master records established to capture the resulting posting summaries. The technique becomes a hybrid of aspects of three of the four testing schemes described here. The main advantage of simultaneous testing is that the behavior of the system can be observed under normal operating conditions and without disrupting established processing schedules. On the other hand, a major problem, particularly in data base systems in which the technique is most frequently used, is that the test transactions may have unsuspected side effects on account balances—on net income, production summaries, employee benefits, and elsewhere—that the auditor may overlook. The client's records may still be contaminated even after reversing or correction entries have been made with the intention of restoring the files to their proper condition.

Several audit techniques are used for testing the client's system by means other than processing data. One is reviewing the client's applications software source code. This technique extends the normal review of documentation and can be highly effective in determining whether the software conforms with applicable programming standards, whether it is consistent with related items of documentation, whether it contains necessary programmed controls, and whether it is free from programming irregularities. Improper accounting practices may come to light more readily than by using other techniques. Typically, the source code is reviewed manually, but specialized software—for analyzing program structure, cross-referencing variable names, automatically preparing program flowcharts, and other purposes—is available for assisting the auditor in the task.

Authenticity of Files and Programs Tested

Certain precautions need to be taken to ensure that transaction and master files and application programs provided to the auditor for testing are indeed the ones actually used by the client for routine processing. Otherwise, the conclusions reached from the audit tests are worthless. Different files or programs are sometimes provided simply as a result of negligence by the client, but files or programs may be substituted with the intent to deceive the auditor. The complexity of modern computer systems and the ''invisibility'' of file content make it difficult to detect differences. Standard utility software can be used to verify that a file is a true copy of a given original, but the authenticity of the file purported to be the original may remain in doubt.

In the case of conventional batch systems, program and data files are generally checked out of a file library in the form of card decks, reels of tape, or disk cartridges. The auditor can request these on a surprise basis,

to make it more difficult for ''doctored'' files to be prepared and substituted for the real ones. Alternatively, the auditor can conduct the tests immediately after the client's routine processing has been performed, while the files are still loaded on the machine. Program files can also be compared with copies secured at an earlier time. If no changes have been documented during the intervening period, the program files should be identical. Utility software can be used to determine the equivalence of program files even if they are in object code form. If any differences are detected, the client will have to explain them, either as undocumented system modifications or as file substitution.

If on-line systems are in use, the data files and program files may already be loaded on secondary storage and can be accessed directly from a terminal. Standard systems software normally includes routines for listing the entire contents of the disk directory or all the header records on a given reel of magnetic tape; this may have to be done from the system console so as to circumvent normal access controls. The file directory listings should be scrutinized, preferably after appropriate sorting, to determine whether there are alternate versions of the same program or data file (both father and son versions of master files are often stored on magnetic disk storage). The client should be asked to identify files that are not listed in available documentation and that could be surrogate versions of active files. Data on record lengths and record counts, retained in most file directories, often provide clues to similarities among files listed under different names. Two files, each with a specified record length of 256 bytes, one containing 1,200 records and the other 1,205 records, may be different versions of a master file; the extra 5 records in the second may be part of an irregularity. Examination of file directories is useful for other purposes, too, for instance, to assess the efficiency of storage capacity utilization and to detect the presence of ''dead'' files.

GENERALIZED AUDIT SOFTWARE

Auditors use programs that carry out essentially the same processing tasks as the client's own applications software: to perform reprocessing or simulation tests. In some cases, these programs are written by personnel within the accounting firm; in other cases, they are acquired from systems houses. Auditors also use systems software utilities, provided by the manufacturer, for sorting, copying, or comparing files and may use spreadsheets or other end-user packages for specific purposes. In addition, generalized audit software packages that perform a much wider range of analytical tasks on the client's data or on the system itself are being used more often.

Generalized audit software is one form or application of the generalized software concept discussed in Chapter 8. Its purpose is to permit the auditor to perform a variety of audit-related tests on site at the client's computer facility. The problems of operating inefficiency that plague many types of generalized software are relatively unimportant to audit software that is not intended for production use but that is needed for maximum flexibility.

Functions of Generalized Audit Software

Most generalized audit software is intended to analyze the client's data files. Some of the more common functions provided are the following[8]:

- Scanning of files to retrieve records of audit significance.
- Selection of random or stratified record samples and analysis, including the calculation of inferred population statistics.
- Performance of basic arithmetic operations on record content for such purposes as verifying extensions.
- Identification of records whose contents satisfy prescribed criteria (in which, for example, a particular data element exceeds a given threshold or one data element exceeds another). This capability is useful in selecting exception items.
- Extraction of subtotals, control totals, record counts, and hash totals.
- Summarization of files by aggregation of prescribed groups of records.

[8] John G. Burch, Jr., and Joseph L. Sarduras, Jr., *Computer Control and Audit* (New York: Wiley, 1978), pp. 363–365.

- Record-by-record comparison of one file and another to identify differences.
- Sorting of files according to prescribed keys.
- Copying of selected records or fields from one file to another.
- Printout or display of calculated results in flexible user-determined formats.

The particular task to be performed by the audit software is selected by input of coded instructions, laid out initially on specification sheets. The specification sheets list the files to be accessed, the records and fields to be retrieved, and the processes to be performed on them. Predetermined functions are usually provided for analysis, output, and other purposes and can be selected without the need for detailed coding in the sense of the typical computer program. Sometimes the specification sheets are reduced to checklists on which the auditor selects functions to be performed by means of "yes" or "no" responses. Some examples of the specification sheets used in one generalized audit software package are presented in the appendix to this chapter.

The data on the specification sheets are entered through an interactive terminal or are read in after being encoded onto a machine-readable medium such as magnetic tape. The audit software usually must be compiled on the client's system before it can be run, although some available packages are structured in the form of interpreters ready for immediate use. Alternatively, recompilation is not required if the software is run on the auditor's computer. A few audit software packages are flexible enough to accept small insertions of program code at execution time, to allow them to perform tasks not provided for in the basic design.

Acquisition of Generalized Audit Software

Most audit software has been developed by the major accounting firms, although some software houses specialize in this kind of programming. Sometimes standard utility programs or end-user packages can be adapted for use as audit software, but more typically the best products are those that have been developed specifically for the intended usage. Considerable care and ingenuity are required in the design of generalized packages. A major design objective is to make the packages easy to operate—partly to make them appealing to auditors with only moderate degrees of computer literacy and partly to enhance audit independence by allowing auditors to operate the packages with minimal assistance from the client's data-processing personnel.

A range of generalized audit software packages is now offered for sale. But good audit software is expensive, and the auditor must carefully evaluate a candidate package before making the required sizable investment. The most important selection criteria are

- Capability and flexibility of the programs
- Transportability to a variety of machines
- Adaptability to a variety of storage media
- Ability to interface with available data base management systems and other systems software
- Ease of use
- Adequacy of documentation
- Vendor support (initial and ongoing)
- Cost

Transportability to a variety of different computers is the most important, except in the situation in which an accounting firm has only a small number of clients, all with the same type of hardware, or in which the auditor's own computer is used. This objective has largely been achieved in the case of mainframe computers, in which generalized audit software has been used most extensively but there are still significant problems of transportability among smaller machines.

It is important to verify that the audit software does not make excessive demands on machine resources, which would place it outside the range of typical systems. Considerable strides have been made in this direction, and packages are now available that can be operated on microcomputers. The software should be capable of interfacing with different secondary storage media (magnetic disk, tape, punched cards, and so on). The ability to interface with standard data base systems is becoming increasingly necessary; with many modern systems, the only way in which to access the data files is via the data base management system. Ease of use and comprehensive, understandable documentation are

vital if the audit software is to be used by personnel other than computer specialists. Support should be available from the software vendor (or from some other source) for initial implementation and training, and also for ongoing hand holding and resolution of problems as they arise.

APPENDIX: SPECIFICATION SHEETS FOR GENERALIZED AUDIT SOFTWARE PACKAGES

The following seven pages show samples of specification sheets used with the AUDITPAK II system developed by Coopers and Lybrand. The exhibits are reproduced here by courtesy of the firm. The complete set comprising the AUDITPAK II system provides more extensive capability than is illustrated. The specification sheets are a series of questionnaires in which the auditor designs the tests to be conducted on the client's files. The results of the tests are printed in report form or are written to a file for further analysis.

The specification sheets included here solicit the following information:

1. Environmental Definition Parameters
   a. *Environment specifications,* in which the user specifies the hardware configuration and other details of the system on which the package is to be used and the files that are to be accessed
   b. *Field descriptions,* in which the user identifies the fields to be processed, their location within the file record, and formatting requirements for the resulting output
2. Job-processing Parameters
   a. *Options,* in which the user enters a narrative description of the audit test to be performed and appropriate report headings
   b. *Selection criteria,* in which the user specifies criteria for selection of records of audit interest
   c. *Simple calculations,* in which the user can request arithmetic operations of addition, subtraction, multiplication, or division on specified fields
   d. *Output file specifications,* in which the user can

Environment Definition Parameters

ENVIRONMENTAL SPECIFICATIONS (Required)

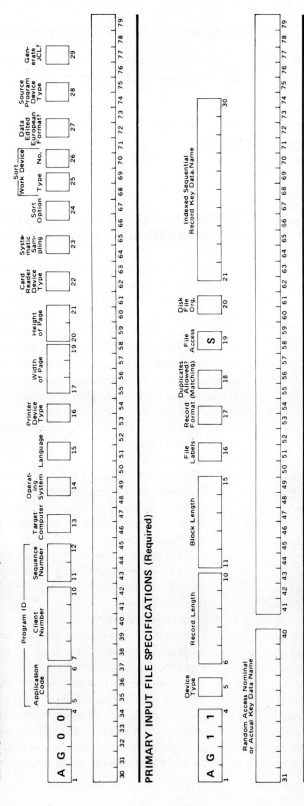
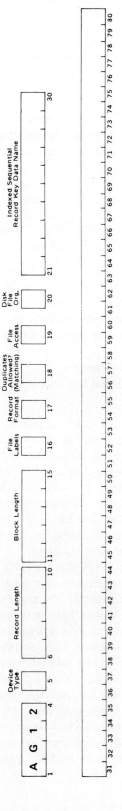

PRIMARY INPUT FILE SPECIFICATIONS (Required)

SECONDARY INPUT FILE SPECIFICATIONS (Optional)

AUDITPAK II QUESTIONNAIRE — CG 201, 202 and 203 (10/80) — These forms apply to **Release 3.0** and above of Auditpak.

Environment Definition Parameters

FIELD DESCRIPTIONS (Required)

A	G	2	0
1			4

REPORT SPECIFICATIONS

REPORT COLUMN HEADINGS

CONTROL SEQUENCE

	INPUT DATA NAME	STARTING POSITION IN RECORD	LENGTH	DATA TYPE ALPHA	NO. OF DECIMAL POS.	MATCH FIELDS OR MAJOR/MINOR SEQUENCE	JOB 1	JOB 2	JOB 3	JOB 4	JOB 5	JOB 6	JOB 7	JOB 8	JOB 9	LINE ONE	LINE TWO

SOURCE

5 | 6 7 8 9 10 11 12 13 14 15 | 16 17 18 19 20 | 21 22 23 24 | 25 | 26 | 27 | 28 29 30 | 31 32 33 | 34 35 36 | 37 38 39 | 40 41 42 | 43 44 45 | 46 47 48 | 49 50 51 | 52 53 54 | 55 56 57 58 59 60 61 62 63 64 | 65 66 67 68 69 70 71 72 73 74

JOB 1: SORT / PRINT / TOTAL
JOB 2: SORT / PRINT / TOTAL
JOB 3: SORT / PRINT / TOTAL
JOB 4: SORT / PRINT / TOTAL
JOB 5: SORT / PRINT / TOTAL
JOB 6: SORT / PRINT / TOTAL
JOB 7: SORT / PRINT / TOTAL
JOB 8: SORT / PRINT / TOTAL
JOB 9: SORT / PRINT / TOTAL

AUDITPAK II QUESTIONNAIRE — CG 204 (10/80) — These forms apply to Release 3.0 and above of Auditpak.

C&L

Job Processing Parameters

OPTIONS

	COBOL Code Supression	Last Field No. on Line 1	Last Field No. on Line 2	Detail Report Vertical Spacing	Add'l Digits for Total Size	Total Description	ID Print Option	Reinitialize Calculation Fields	Match Function
Job No.									

A G 2 3
1 4 5 6 7 8 9 10 11 12 13 14

15 16 17 18 19 20 21 22 23 24 25 26 27 28

29 30 31 32 33 34 35 36 37 38 39 40 41 42 43 44 45 46 47 48 49 50 51 52 53 54 55 56 57 58 59 60 61 62 63 64 65 66 67 68 69 70 71 72 73 74 75 76 77 78 79 80

DESCRIPTION OF AUDIT OBJECTIVE

A G 2 5   Job No.
1 4   5

line	TEXT
6 7	55
1	
2	
3	
4	
5	

6 – 9 and A – Z may be used for further lines of comments.

REPORT HEADINGS

A G 2 6   Job No.
1 4   5

line	TEXT
6 7	55
1	
2	
3	

AUDITPAK II QUESTIONNAIRE — CG 205, 206, and 207 (10/80) — These forms apply to Release 3.0 and above of Auditpak.

C&L

Job Processing Parameters

SELECTION CRITERIA

A	G		Job No.		
1		4			5

TEST NO.	IF									IS		COMPARED TO																															ACTION IF CONDITION IS:						

DATA NAME

RELA-TION-SHIP

CONSTANT

DATA NAME, VALUE, STRING OF VALUES OR RESERVED NAMES

RANGE COMPARISON

LOWER LIMIT

UPPER LIMIT

CONJ. AND/OR

TRUE / FALSE

CODE / NO. / ID

Column numbers: 6 7 8 9 10 11 12 13 14 15 16 17 | 18 19 | 20 | 21 22 23 24 25 26 27 28 29 30 31 32 33 34 35 36 37 38 39 40 41 42 43 44 45 46 47 48 49 50 | 51 | 52 53 54 | 55 56 57

AUDITPAK II QUESTIONNAIRE — CG 208 (10/80) — These forms apply to Release 3.0 and above of Auditpak.

C&L

Job Processing Parameters

SIMPLE CALCULATIONS

A G 1   Job No. ☐

CALCULATION OPERANDS

CALC NO.	ITEM ID	A DATA NAME OR VALUE	+ − * /	B DATA NAME OR VALUE	RESULT DATA NAME	SIZE	DECIMAL ALIGNS	PRINT LEVEL SUPPRESS	TOTAL	EDIT FORMAT	RESULTS — REPORT COLUMN HEADINGS LINE ONE	LINE TWO

6 7 | 8 9 | 10 11 12 13 14 15 16 17 18 19 | 20 | 21 22 23 24 25 26 27 28 29 30 | 31 32 33 34 35 36 37 38 39 40 | 41 42 | 43 | 44 45 | 46 | 47 | 48 | 49 50 51 52 53 54 55 56 57 58 | 59 60 61 62 63 64 65 66 67 68

C&L   AUDITPAK II QUESTIONNAIRE — CG 209 (10/80) — These forms apply to Release 3.0 and above of Auditpak.

488

Job Processing Parameters

OUTPUT FILE SPECIFICATIONS

	Job No.	Record Code	Level	Include/Exclude Record	Item ID	Record Length	Block Length	Device Type		

A G 7 0

(1 ... 4) 5 6 7 8 9 10 11 ... 15 16 ... 20 21 22 ... 41

OUTPUT FIELD DESCRIPTIONS

A G 7 1

	Job No.	Record Code	FIELD NO.	ITEM ID	FIELD LENGTH	C O N S T A N T	D A T A T Y P E	RECORD FIELDS
								DATA NAME / VALUE

(1 ... 4) 5 6 7 8 9 10 11 12 13 14 15 16 17 18 19 20 21 22 23 24 25 26 27 28 29 30 31 32 33 34 35

AUDITPAK II QUESTIONNAIRE — CG 212 and 213 (10/80) — These forms apply to Release 3.0 and above of Auditpak.

C&L

489

Job Processing Parameters

END OF JOB STATISTICS

A G 9 0	Job No.	
1 — 4		5

ITEM ID	TYP.	DATA NAME	ITEM ID	TYP.	DATA NAME	ITEM ID	TYP.	DATA NAME	ITEM ID	TYP.	DATA NAME
6 7	8	9 18	19 20	21	22 31	32 33	34	35 44	45 46	47	48 57
ITEM ID	TYP.	DATA NAME	ITEM ID	TYP.	DATA NAME	ITEM ID	TYP.	DATA NAME	ITEM ID	TYP.	DATA NAME
6 7	8	9 18	19 20	21	22 31	32 33	34	35 44	45 46	47	48 57
ITEM ID	TYP.	DATA NAME	ITEM ID	TYP.	DATA NAME	ITEM ID	TYP.	DATA NAME	ITEM ID	TYP.	DATA NAME
6 7	8	9 18	19 20	21	22 31	32 33	34	35 44	45 46	47	48 57
ITEM ID	TYP.	DATA NAME	ITEM ID	TYP.	DATA NAME	ITEM ID	TYP.	DATA NAME	ITEM ID	TYP.	DATA NAME
6 7	8	9 18	19 20	21	22 31	32 33	34	35 44	45 46	47	48 57
ITEM ID	TYP.	DATA NAME	ITEM ID	TYP.	DATA NAME	ITEM ID	TYP.	DATA NAME	ITEM ID	TYP.	DATA NAME
6 7	8	9 18	19 20	21	22 31	32 33	34	35 44	45 46	47	48 57
ITEM ID	TYP.	DATA NAME	ITEM ID	TYP.	DATA NAME	ITEM ID	TYP.	DATA NAME	ITEM ID	TYP.	DATA NAME
6 7	8	9 18	19 20	21	22 31	32 33	34	35 44	45 46	47	48 57
ITEM ID	TYP.	DATA NAME	ITEM ID	TYP.	DATA NAME	ITEM ID	TYP.	DATA NAME	ITEM ID	TYP.	DATA NAME
6 7	8	9 18	19 20	21	22 31	32 33	34	35 44	45 46	47	48 57

C&L **AUDITPAK II QUESTIONNAIRE** CG 214 (10/80) — These forms apply to Release 3.0 and above of Auditpak.

arrange for results of the tests to be written to a file for further analysis

e. *End-of-job statistics,* in which the user can request totals or summary statistics

SUMMARY

The audit engagement is undertaken to provide a basis for the opinion, expressed by the auditor, about the client's financial statements. The typical audit engagement, which shares several characteristics with systems analysis, consists of the selection of audit objectives and procedures, an evaluation of the internal controls, substantive testing, and the preparation of the opinion. Substantive testing is aimed at substantiating the data contained in the financial statements. The evaluation of internal controls, which consists of an initial review of the controls, followed by compliance testing, determines the necessary extent of other procedures, including substantive testing.

Auditing involves risk. Audit risk is associated with the possibility that (1) material errors might have been made in the accounting process and that (2) the financial statements might be misstated but not be detected by the auditor's examination. Risk of this second type arises principally because all audit examinations are based on a process of sampling, followed by inference and interpretation of the results, rather than on complete examination. But even if a complete examination were practicable, 100 percent reliance would still not be possible. The auditor seeks to reduce the first type of risk by compliance testing of the internal control system and seeks to reduce the second type by an adequate level of substantive testing.

The audit examination of computerized information systems typically requires various types of compliance and substantive testing, directed toward both the client's accounting system and the client's data. Three main approaches to auditing computerized information systems are auditing around the computer, auditing through the computer, and auditing with the computer. The first of these has now largely been rejected because of its inadequacy. Today, there is a strong trend toward the third

of these approaches, and computers—either the client's or the auditor's—are now important audit tools. The use of computers, together with generalized audit software, provide a flexible basis for designing appropriate examinations of the client's data base.

BIBLIOGRAPHY

American Institute of Certified Public Accountants. *Management, Control and Audit of Advanced EDP Systems.* Computer Services Guidelines. New York: AICPA, 1977.

American Institute of Certified Public Accountants. "Audit Risk and Materiality in Conducting an Audit." Statement on Auditing Standards No. 47. New York: AICPA, December 1983.

Burch, John G., Jr., and Joseph L. Sardinas, Jr. *Computer Control and Audit: A Total Systems Approach.* New York: Wiley, 1978.

Cash, James I., Jr., Andrew D. Bailey, Jr., and Andrew B. Whinston. "A Survey of Techniques for Auditing EDP-Based Accounting Information Systems." *Accounting Review*, October 1977, pp. 813–829.

Cooke, John W., and Gary M. Winkle. *Auditing: Philosophy and Technique*, 2nd ed. Boston: Houghton Mifflin, 1980.

Halper, Stanley D., Glenn C. Davis, P. J. O'Neill-Dunne, and Pamela R. Pfeu. *Handbook of EDP Auditing.* Boston: Warren, Gorham & Lamont, 1985.

Hubbard, Thomas D., Johnny R. Johnson, and Ann B. Pushkin, eds. *Auditing: Concepts, Standards, Procedures*, 2nd ed. Houston: Dame, 1986.

Perry, William E. *Identifying Audit Risks in a Computerized Business Environment.* New York: American Institute of Certified Public Accountants, Continuing Professional Education Division, 1981.

Porter, W. Thomas, and William E. Perry. *EDP Controls and Auditing*, 3rd ed. Boston: Kent, 1981.

Sardinas, Joseph L., ed. *EDP Audit Symposium 1979/80.* Amherst: University of Massachusetts, School of Business Administration, 1980.

Scott, Richard, John Page, and Paul Hooper. *Auditing: A Systems Approach.* Reston, Va.: Reston, 1982.

DISCUSSION QUESTIONS AND PROBLEMS

1. Define and discuss the following terms:

- Analytical review
- Audit objectives
- Audit procedures
- Audit reliance
- Audit report and opinion
- Audit risk
- Audit software
- Audit techniques
- Audit testing
- Compliance testing
- Generalized audit software
- Integrated test facility
- Internal control questionnaire
- Review of internal control
- Risk of incorrect acceptance
- Risk of incorrect rejection
- Simulation
- Substantive testing
- Test desk
- Working papers

2. One of the control objectives listed in Chapter 16 reads as follows:

Access to data files and programs shall be limited to those individuals authorized to process or maintain particular systems, and in accordance with management's wishes.

Required

Suggest a number of questions that could be incorporated in an internal control questionnaire to determine whether the objective is achieved in a system under review.

3. An auditor is evaluating the internal controls in a small business in which all data-processing operations are performed by a staff of three people, assisted on occasion by a clerk from the accounting department who had previous keypunch experience. Although the level of application controls appears to be satisfactory, the auditor is concerned about the achievement of the control objectives relating to incompatible responsibilities.

Required

Discuss the potential for small businesses of this type to achieve the objective of separation of duties in the data-processing area. Also comment on the advisability of placing any audit reliance on application controls when there is a pervasive weakness in the area of general controls.

4. Discuss the terms *auditing around, through,* and *with* the computer, and explore the implications of each with regard to the need to satisfy the auditing standard of understanding the flow of transactions through the accounting information system.

5. Discuss the advisability of using computer specialists to audit modern automated information systems. Include in your discussion some comments about large computer facilities and also micro- or minicomputer systems.

6. What are the main objectives of examining a client's application software source code? Are the benefits likely to outweigh the costs if the latter must reflect not only the effort in tracing the program logic but also the need for the auditor to be familiar with programming languages and techniques?

7. Discuss the problems arising from the possible contamination of client master files caused by improper audit-testing techniques. What are the auditor's responsibilities for correcting data so contaminated? What can be done to minimize the risk of damage to files caused in this way?

8. Discuss the auditor's concerns regarding the authenticity of data and program files provided by the client for conducting audit tests. Evaluate the effectiveness of the measures commonly taken to reduce the risk of either inadvertent provision of wrong versions of the files or deliberate substitution of "doctored" files.

9. During an audit engagement, the auditor recognizes the need for a computer program to analyze the client's work-in-process records. The computer is not one of the most common brands, and the auditor is not familiar with the programming language it employs. Management offers to have the necessary program written in-house and agrees to cooperate in any tests that the auditor might want to make to verify that the program is written according to the auditor's specifications.

Required

Discuss the problems of relying on an audit program written by an employee of the client firm, and suggest ways in which any risks could be minimized.

10. An auditor was examining the run log maintained by a large mainframe computer. One page of the log, relating to processing performed during the night shift of December 1, revealed the following:

Problem 10

Date	Time	Operator ID	Job No.	Duration (secs.)	Memory (KB)
XX1201	03:05:11	783	2269	186	203
XX1201	03:16:24	096	3042	237	14
XX1201	03:23:07	817	0668	55	85
XX1201	03:37:22	096	0901	14	563
XX1201	03:45:46	817	0333	346	90
XX1201	03:58:10	783	3043	9	406
XX1201	04:01:07	817	2269	186	203
XX1201	04:11:53	126	1670	208	173
XX1201	04:25:19	817	0512	56	91
XX1201	04:45:00	783	3043	297	406

Other information gathered by the auditor was as follows:

a. Operators 96, 506, 783, and 817 were scheduled to work that shift.

b. Job numbers between 0 and 999 relate to production control, those between 1000 and 1999 to payroll processing, those between 2000 and 2999 to accounts payable, and those between 3000 and 3999 to accounts receivable; job numbers above 4000 relate to unscheduled, miscellaneous jobs.

c. Payroll processing is scheduled to be run on the fourteenth and the last day of the calendar month.

d. According to available documentation, production control programs are small, requiring less than 100 KB of main memory and less than 100 seconds of execution time.

e. According to the same source, accounts receivable and payable programs are large and require more than 100 KB of main memory and 2 to 6 minutes of execution time.

Required

Analyze the data presented here and draw up a list of questions requiring further investigation.

11. Shiva, Inc., operates an interactive batch system based on a minicomputer, in which all files are maintained on magnetic disk storage. You are an audit staff member conducting tests on the client's program and data files and are suspicious about file authenticity. You decide to list out the directory of one of the disk volumes from your system console. The listing contains this information:

Problem 11

Date: XX0626
Volume: B

File ID	Record Length	Record Count	Access Priv.	Date Estab.	Date Last Access
COLLECT .OBJ	256	408	RO	790324	XX0622
CUSTMER.DAT	203	2046	RW	790916	XX0624
CUSTMER.BAK	203	1983	WO	XX0624	XX0624
DICK .CBL	256	2073	RW	740109	750810
DISBURS .DAT	160	1289	RW	XX0620	XX0621
INVOICE .OBJ	256	326	RO	790406	XX0624
INVOICE .CBL	128	1072	RW	811123	XX0319

(continued on next page)

Problem 11 (continued)

Date: XX0626
Volume: B

File ID	Record Length	Record Count	Access Priv.	Date Estab.	Date Last Access
OPNINVC .DAT	187	1135	RW	791035	XX0620
OPNVCHR.DAT	206	953	RW	810711	XX0530
OPNVCHR.SCR	206	1	WO	XX0530	XX0530
PAYMENT.OBJ	256	509	RW	XX0620	XX0630
RESERCH .OBJ	256	510	RO	810720	XX0520
SALSANL .OBJ	256	326	RO	XX0620	XX0620
STATMNT.OBJ	256	495	RO	790318	XX0110
VENDOR .DAT	237	1506	RW	XX0622	XX0622
X123456 .DAT	160	34	RW	XX0621	XX0621

Accompanying documentation explained that the file name extensions indicated the type of file: DAT = data, CBL = COBOL source, OBJ = compiled object code, SCR = scratch file, BAK = backup file. The access privilege could also take these values: RW = read-write, RO = read only, WO = write only.

Required

a. Identify files that have suspicious characteristics that you wish to examine further.
b. What tests might you consider for determining whether certain files have the same or similar content?
c. What recommendations would you make to management even if your suspicions concerning file authenticity are allayed?

12. Lunar Corporation operates a large computer with a data base management system. A complete log of transaction activity is maintained on magnetic tape for audit purposes and to provide a backup for rebuilding the data base in the event of a system crash.

As part of an audit examination, you are testing a set of these tapes relating to operations during the month of August. Most of the data appear to be quite routine, but you are puzzled by the large volume of transactions leading to payables disbursements. None of the individual transactions is for an abnormally large amount, but collectively the cash disbursements are heavier than expected—particularly because purchases are normally light during the summer.

Required

a. List reasons that could explain the high volume of disbursement transactions.

b. What additional examinations or tests could be performed to determine whether the high volume indicates an irregularity?

13. During an audit engagement you decide to perform an analytical review of a small client's accounts receivable records for the month of January. The client has provided you with the following printouts of the customer master file and the single transaction file used:

Problem 13
Master File

Customer Number	Credit Limit	Balance: 1/1/99	1/31/99
103	5,000.00	1,125.00	0.00
105	3,000.00	2,394.80	2,394.80
108	2,000.00	591.50	244.50
111	2,000.00	60.00	60.00
119	10,000.00	351.25	(100.00)
121	2,000.00	1,450.00	2,175.00
126	10,000.00	7,493.15	5,493.15
127	3,000.00	1,899.00	1,899.00
131	30,000.00	0.00	108,866.00
137	2,000.00	580.00	1,205.00
140	7,000.00	3,327.10	
146	2,000.00	236.90	854.30
147	12,000.00	1,055.00	0.00
152		330.00	(412.50)
153	20,000.00	18,984.25	20,633.65
161	4,000.00	2,300.00	3,399.75
166	4,000.00	1,900.00	1,900.00
170	2,000.00	554.70	574.70
172	3,000.00	1,080.80	880.00
179	2,000.00	120.00	0.00
		$45,519.29	$150,067.35

Transaction File

Transaction Date	Customer Number	Amount: Debit	Credit	Explanation
01/01/99	121	1,090.35		
01/02/99	153	742.50		
01/03/99	103		1,125.00	
01/06/99	161	59.75		
01/06/99	127		200.00	
01/07/99	121		95.50	Merchandise return
01/08/99	108		743.00	
01/09/99	153	906.90		
01/10/99	131	96,500.00		
01/13/99	119		500.00	
01/14/99	121	715.00		
01/15/99	146		682.60	
01/16/99	161	1,040.00		
01/16/99	105	268.00		
01/17/99	137	625.00		
01/19/99	188		1,267.00	
01/20/99	119	437.50		
01/21/99	152		742.50	
01/22/99	121		984.85	
01/23/99	131	12,366.00		
01/24/99	147		1,055.00	
01/27/99	179		120.00	
01/27/99	119			
01/28/99	146	1,300.00		
01/29/99	119	48.75		
01/30/99	108	396.00		
01/31/99	119		437.50	
		$116,495.75	$116,495.75	

Required

a. List the errors, questionable data elements, and unusual transactions or account balances in the two files.

b. Prepare questions that you wish to ask the client in order to clarify concerns that you have regarding the data.

c. Discuss the methods you would use if the files contained a much larger volume of data—perhaps hundreds of thousands of records.

PART FIVE

ACCOUNTING
APPLICATIONS

Part Five examines the more common applications comprising the accounting information system. The material is organized into four chapters covering the planning/control and reporting cycles and the three operating cycles: the purchasing cycle, the production cycle, and the revenue cycle. The structure of the four chapters is the same. The broad features of the particular transaction cycle and its component applications are first reviewed, and then the pertinent inputs, files, outputs, and processing activities are examined. The most common decision support activities relating to each cycle and the use of routine reports in management decision making are explained. The content of the principal documents and files is described, providing a guide for systems designers, and a few representative management reports are selected for discussion and illustration. Relevant internal control objectives are reviewed, and suitable control techniques are proposed for achieving those objectives.

19

The Planning/Control Cycle and the Reporting Cycle

CHAPTER OUTLINE

OVERVIEW OF THE PLANNING/CONTROL CYCLE AND THE REPORTING CYCLE

Budget Preparation
Preparation of Expense Budgets
Establishment of Manufacturing Cost Standards
Cost Estimating
Budgeting in Professional Service Organizations
Budget Tracking and Responsibility Accounting
Management Reporting
External Reporting
Accounting Transactions

DECISION SUPPORT AREAS

Long-Range Planning
Sales Forecasting

STRUCTURE OF THE PLANNING/CONTROL CYCLE AND THE REPORTING CYCLE

Inputs, Files, and Outputs
Processes
Key Documents
Principal Files
Selected Reports

INTERNAL CONTROLS IN THE PLANNING/CONTROL CYCLE AND THE REPORTING CYCLE

Control Objectives and Risks
Control Measures

SUMMARY
BIBLIOGRAPHY
DISCUSSION QUESTIONS AND PROBLEMS

OVERVIEW OF THE PLANNNING/CONTROL CYCLE AND THE REPORTING CYCLE

The planning and control cycle refers to long- and short-range management planning and the necessary control processes to ensure effective and efficient implementation of those plans. The accounting information system supports both types of planning. Long-range planning requires examining alternative courses of action in the light of engineering, purchasing, production, marketing, financial, and personnel considerations and overall company goals and objectives. Such an examination requires the analysis of historical data and forecasting of future trends and usually requires a synthesis of quantitative and qualitative decision inputs. In long-range planning, management relies on the accounting information system, particularly in its decision support role.

But the area of short-run planning is where the impact of the accounting information system is felt most strongly. The process of budget preparation, through which management articulates its short-term goals, depends on outputs from the accounting system in both its decision support and its operational data-processing roles. Budget preparation involves projections of both revenues and costs for the coming period, which are based largely on historical accounting data. Other features are the establishment of manufacturing cost standards and the preparation of estimates and quotations for custom goods and services, which also are based largely on accounting data.

The control functions of budget tracking and standard cost tracking—including the analysis of standard cost variances—depend for their effectiveness almost totally on the accounting system in its routine operational data-processing role. These control functions form important interfaces between the planning/control cycle and the reporting cycle. The heart of the reporting cycle is the general ledger application together with external and internal reporting. Internal reporting often is based on some form of responsibility accounting system.

Budget Preparation

The budget is upper management's own statement of what it wants the organization to achieve during the coming year and what it believes can be achieved. The budget represents both a target—for revenues, expenses, and financial resources—and a commitment by upper management to the attainment of that target. Once the budget has been approved by top management, it becomes the target for the organization as a whole.

Although top management always approves the budget, alternative styles of budgeting assign different roles to middle and lower management with respect to other aspects of preparation. In the authoritarian style of budgeting, little or no input is either solicited or accepted from middle and lower management, and the budget is prepared and approved by top management alone. In contrast, in participatory budgeting, which has gained popularity over the last decades, budget guidelines are issued by top management, but input is solicited from lower levels of management or even from operating personnel. The guidelines communicate upper management's goals for growth, but the inputs from lower levels reflect the "grass-roots" response to these goals. Sales people may be asked to predict how much they think they can sell and at what prices; production people may be asked to estimate how much they can produce and at what costs; and managers throughout the organization may be asked to submit budget requests for departmental expenses. Upper management reviews these inputs and usually modifies them in the light of its own future plans and its assessment of what is feasible in order to produce the master budget. But the influence of the inputs should still be recognizable to them when the final budget is disseminated. Participatory budgeting is believed to result in improved morale and better performance because it gives lower-level managers a sense of involvement. They feel that they have contributed to the budget decision process, even though they know that their proposals are not likely to be honored in full.

The master budget, which relates to the organization as a whole, consists of a number of more detailed budgets relating to component segments and activities within the organization. Examples of such component budgets are the sales budget, the purchasing budget, and the overhead budget. The component budgets must properly interface with one another and each must contribute to the overall master budget. If the master budget is regarded as a system, the component budgets comprise its subsystems.

The starting point in the budgeting process, at least for profit-seeking organizations, is the sales budget, and like the budget as a whole, it combines a forecast of what can be sold with a commitment to reach that level of sales. The sales budget sets the scale for the whole organization's activities. It determines the levels of production, purchasing, staffing, and all the associated expenses and financing requirements. It provides major input to decisions relating to necessary inventory levels. The effect of the sales budget percolates through the other component budgets in a direction opposite to the physical flow of goods or services.

At any point in the budget preparation process, a conflict may arise. It may turn out, for instance, that production cannot meet the projected sales demand, that raw materials cannot be purchased in the necessary quantities, or that skilled labor cannot be recruited in the required numbers to support the budgeted level of production. Or it may turn out that the company cannot finance the desired level of activity. If such conflicts cannot be resolved by other means, the sales budget may have to be revised downward. Budget preparation is an iterative process, and many "passes" through the component budgets may have to be made before a consistent master budget is achieved.

After the master budget is approved by top management, it becomes the organization's official plan for the coming year. It is normally broken down into shorter-term budgets covering each quarter, each month, and even each week during the year. The breakdown may simply be proportional or may reflect anticipated seasonal variations.

Not-for-profit organizations may have no "sales" as such, and their budgeting process may start from the anticipated revenues from donations, fund raising, tax assessments, or government appropriations, as the case may be. The other components of the budget must then be arranged to fit the revenue constraints so that the organization does not overspend. Budgeting for not-for-profit organizations often is a process of assigning budget priorities to the various component programs so as to best accomplish its intended mission.

Preparation of Expense Budgets

Some types of expenses fall into the category of engineered costs which vary in a well-defined manner with volume or level of activity. Examples of engineered costs are direct materials, direct labor, and sales commissions. The budgeting of engineered costs is normally straightforward once the sales and production budgets have been formulated. Other costs are discretionary and are budgeted on the basis of management's priorities and the organization's ability to obtain the necessary resources. Examples of discretionary costs are advertising and research and development costs. Most administrative expenses are discretionary.

There are several approaches to the budgeting of discretionary items:

• Previous expenditure levels
• Industry averages
• Zero-based budgeting

The first approach is based on the assumption that what was spent in the past was appropriate and, possibly with minor adjustments, can provide the basis for what should be spent in the future. The adjustments can take account of inflation and also can provide for any necessary changes in real dollar terms:

Next year's budget

$$= \text{Last year's budget}$$
$$+ \text{ inflation}$$
$$\pm \text{ real-dollar increase or decrease}$$

Organizations without a previous track record may turn to industry figures as a guide to the appropriate level of expenditures in different areas. Figures may be available, for instance, that indicate average levels of administrative costs in organizations of various sizes or average levels of promotional expenses for different levels of sales. Even organizations with a track record may find industry averages useful to see whether their own costs are in line with their competitors'.

Zero-based budgeting (ZBB) is an alternative to using previous budgets as a basis for future ones. It warns against setting budget amounts on the basis of past experience because the earlier amounts may have been too high or too low or because individual items might not represent worthwhile expenditures at any level. Accordingly, ZBB recommends that all expenditures be justified as though they were new ones and that no budget items be allowed to acquire momentum and continue to absorb funding without review. Furthermore, according to ZBB, the budget amounts should be set each year at a level that reflects the relative priorities that the items have at that time. ZBB was first introduced in government agencies but has spread to many organizations in the private sector.

Establishment of Manufacturing Cost Standards

Standard cost allowances, when used, must be integrated with the master budget. Standard costs pertain to individual tasks and single units of product, whereas the budget relates to whole organizational segments and functions. Industrial engineering methods, including time-and-motion studies, provide one way of setting quantity standards. Previous experience is another. In labor-intensive operations, the learning curve helps take account of improvements in productivity over the course of long production runs. These improvements should be reflected in progressively tighter labor-hour allowances.

Standard overhead rates should be consistent with the budgeted amounts of overhead items. The rates can be either departmental or plantwide. Departmental rates can pay closer attention to differences in the mix of overhead costs from one department to another but depend on precise allocation of common cost items, including service department costs. Difficulties and uncertainties in allocation may negate any advantages to be gained. Many companies settle for plantwide rates, even though some anomalies in product costs are known to result from using them. On the other hand, some companies appreciate the improvement in product costing and use departmental or even subdepartmental rates.

Whether or not a standard cost system is in use, manufacturing organizations must choose a suitable base on which to apply factory overhead to the product. In traditional labor-intensive production operations, overhead has usually been applied on the basis of labor hours or labor cost. But with increasing levels of automation, labor costs often form a much smaller fraction of total product costs than they used to. In highly automated plants, overhead should be applied on the basis of a more representative measure of value, such as machine time.

Cost Estimating

Organizations that offer custom goods or services for sale often face the problem of pricing for competitive bidding. Prices need to be determined with care to steer a narrow course between prices that are too high and those that are too low. The former will fail to win contracts and lose market share, and the latter will reduce profits on contracts that are won.

The strategy most often adopted is to estimate costs—either direct or full costs—and then to add a markup to cover additional costs, contingencies, and profit. Cost estimating is normally based on prior experience, and firms often accumulate historical cost data specifically for this purpose. Extrapolation of cost data to the prospective new products may be judgmental or may involve the use of estimating models. In either case, adjustment for inflation and other changes may be appropriate.

Estimating models typically attempt to describe the product in terms of quantitative attributes, such as size, materials and labor requirements, and machine time. Then appropriate unit costs are attached to these attributes. For example, suppose that the repair of a piece of equipment is estimated to require 20 hours of semiskilled labor and 10 hours of skilled labor and that replacement parts are required costing $150. If the labor rates for semiskilled and skilled labor are $10.00 per hour and $15.00 per hour, respectively, the estimated direct cost of the job will be

$$\text{Direct cost} = 20 \times 10.00 + 10 \times 15.00 + 150 = \$500$$

Overhead costs might be applied on the basis of total cost or, more likely, on the basis of labor hours or labor cost.

Some unit-cost parameters used in estimating models are similar to manufacturing cost standards, and the two are sometimes combined. But estimating models may contain attributes other than materials and labor quan-

tities, such as the dimensions of a container or the color of a label.

Budgeting in Professional Service Organizations

Professional people working in business organizations often resent having their work regulated by cost standards; they typically feel that the nature of their work and their particular type of skills places them above the level where cost controls are appropriate. Such people include medical practitioners, lawyers, accountants, advertising copy writers, scientists, and engineers. Their feelings deserve consideration, but without standards of any type, budgeting becomes almost impossible, and there is little basis for individual performance evaluation. Some type of tactfully handled education may be needed to encourage acceptance of management controls while emphasizing recognition of the need for professional and creative freedom.

The best performance standards for professional people are standards that they themselves have helped establish. Participatory budgeting is almost essential in this area if the standards are to be effective. Standards can be set at budget preparation time for recurring tasks and at the start of an engagement for one-of-a-kind tasks. Management by objectives (MBO) is applicable, in which standards are mutually agreed to by individuals and their supervisors. MBO was discussed earlier in connection with systems project planning. Once the standards are accepted, they provide a basis for the subsequent tracking of labor hours and other costs, and for performance evaluation.

Budget Tracking and Responsibility Accounting

Many organizations—in manufacturing or service industries and even in the not-for-profit area—operate a responsibility accounting system. In such a system the budget figures for costs and revenues are broken down among a number of responsibility centers. These centers, normally related closely to segments of the organization chart, identify areas of management authority and responsibility. Budget tracking focuses on the same responsibility centers to provide a basis for evaluating both individual and collective performance.

The budget provides the normative standard or benchmark against which actual performance can be evaluated. Both individuals and groups are likely to be evaluated largely on the degree to which they have achieved or conformed to their respective budget targets. Variances from budget are normally defined as

$$\text{Variance} = \text{Actual} - \text{Budget}$$

and the variances are typically labeled *favorable* or *unfavorable* according to whether they contribute to higher or lower short-run profits. Thus a cost overrun is reckoned to be an unfavorable variance, but revenue in excess of budget is regarded as a favorable one. These labels provide a convenient shorthand for the "sign" of the variance, but they should not be misinterpreted. "Cutting corners" on some cost items may temporarily increase profits but may have adverse consequences over the longer term.

Many management reports include comparisons with budget and associated variances; both revenue and cost data are typically reported in this manner when applicable. Often variances are highlighted when they exceed some prescribed threshold in dollars or percentage. The intention is to draw attention to those items in which the variance is material enough to warrant management concern and corrective action and to de-emphasize items in which the activities conform with top management's plans. The underlying concept here is "management by exception."

Responsibility accounting concepts prescribe that the content of management reports be tailored to the responsibilities and authority of their recipients. Typically a hierarchical system of reporting is adopted, running parallel to the lines of authority in the organizational hierarchy. Each line item on a report relates to an activity for which the recipient manager has responsibility. If the recipient is a first-level manager in a manufacturing firm, the line items may relate to materials, labor, and overhead costs. If the recipient is a member of middle management, the line items may relate to the activities of whole departments for which he or she has responsibility. In turn, the summary of that manager's total area of responsibility forms a single line item on the report of

FIGURE 19.1   Hierarchical reporting in a responsibility accounting system.

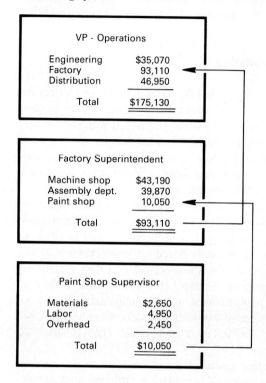

the next higher manager in the organizational hierarchy (Figure 19.1).

Another prescription of the responsibility accounting concept is that only controllable items should be included on a management report. Items that cannot be controlled at that level in the organization or over a reasonable time frame presumably do not affect any decisions that the particular manager might take. Conceivably they could also distract attention from more relevant information. Furthermore, the presence on a responsibility report of noncontrollable items might mislead a supervisor making a performance evaluation.

Management Reporting

Responsibility accounting provides a systemwide framework for reporting routine operational data, including budget comparisons. The responsibility accounting system forms part of the reporting cycle. In addition, many management reports can be treated more conveniently as outputs from the three operating cycles: the purchasing cycle, the production cycle, and the revenue cycle, which will be discussed in the next three chapters.

Traditionally, internal reporting has meant the preparation of paper reports. But recently there has been a trend toward "paperless" reporting, in which data are made available to managers in machine-readable form. "Reports" can be distributed on floppy diskettes or can be retrieved from a data base of processed data using networked personal computers or interactive terminals. This newer strategy reduces the volume of paper—and the volume of data—distributed to managers, much of it of little direct interest. Instead, managers can extract just those items that are of interest to them. But more important, it provides the data in a form that managers can access, using spreadsheets or other types of end-user software. Additional processing or experimentation can be performed as needed. In the future, we can anticipate considerably greater use of this mode of communication, resulting in much more efficient transfer of information from the accountant providers to the managerial users.

External Reporting

External reporting includes preparation of the external financial statements, tax reports, and a variety of applicable government regulatory reports. Most external reporting is nondiscretionary, being required by law. As such, cost–benefit considerations, to which internally consumed output from the accounting information system is supposed to conform, do not apply. Correspondingly, the format of external reporting is dictated by either pronouncements of the professional rule-making bodies or government directive. To that extent, the organization is relieved of designing effective output forms and modes of delivery. Recently, provisions have been made to communicate electronically some forms of external reporting, including reporting to the Securities and Exchange Commission and the Internal Revenue Service. In this way, the information can be made available more quickly to its external users, and computer analysis for research and other purposes can be performed without the very substantial effort involved in

keying data from printed reports. There are likely to be more opportunities or demands for electronic delivery of external financial data in the future.

Accounting Transactions

There are no transactions in the planning and control cycle, because this cycle's activities lie outside the boundaries of the traditional journal-ledger processes. On the other hand, there are numerous transactions in the reporting cycle. Although most routine transactions are transferred to the general ledger application from other subsystems, such as accounts receivable, accounts payable, and payroll, many transactions are entered directly into the general journal which forms part of the general ledger application (Figure 19.2). Figure 19.3 shows a screen menu used in a widely used general ledger software package, which provides for direct entry of various types of transactions.

All adjusting entries and reversing entries are normally entered directly into the general ledger application. Such entries that remain the same from one period to another may be generated automatically. Also, many nonroutine journal entries, such as those recording a stock or bond issue, are entered through the general ledger application.

DECISION SUPPORT AREAS

Several of the activities already discussed, including budgeting and estimating, overlap the boundaries between operational data processing and decision support. In addition, there are other activities in the planning and control cycle that can be characterized more as decision support activities. Among these are long-range planning and sales forecasting.

Long Range Planning

Long-range planning is commonly based, at least in part, on historical accounting data. Historical transaction data may be combined with purely qualitative parame-

FIGURE 19.2   Entry of transaction data into the general ledger application.

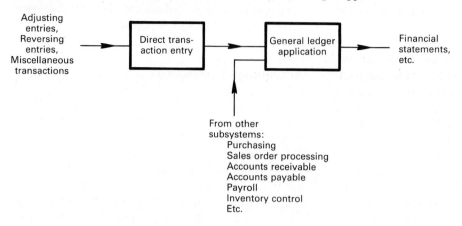

From other
subsystems:
    Purchasing
    Sales order processing
    Accounts receivable
    Accounts payable
    Payroll
    Inventory control
    Etc.

FIGURE 19.3   Screen menu for direct entry of transactions into the general ledger application. (Courtesy of BPI Systems, Inc.)

```
                            BPI Systems, Inc.
                    General Accounting - Version 1.10
                         Menu 1 - Data Entry

    1 Run Queue                    2 Erase Queue
    3 Change/Exit BPI System       4 Enter Company Code and Dates
    5 Change Menu                  6 Print on  Screen /Printer

   11 Enter Cash Disbursements    21 Print Cash Disbursements
   12 Enter Cash Receipts         22 Print Cash Receipts
   13 Enter Invoice Register      23 Print Invoice Register
   14 Enter Merchandise Purchased 24 Print Merchandise Purchased
   15 Enter Cash Register         25 Print Cash Register
   16 Enter General Journal       26 Print General Journal
   17 Enter Standard Entries      27 Print Mdse Purchased (Due Date)
   18 Enter External Entries

    Data Drive:   B
    Company Code: XXXXXX
    Password    : XXXXXX        As-Of   Date: MM/DD/YY
                                Today's Date: MM/DD/YY

   Command Queue: Empty

   Enter Command Number ==>
```

ters, representing management's strategic goals and objectives, to produce long-run forecasts and targets. Managers typically perform large numbers of "what if" calculations before reaching even tentative proposals to be discussed with other high-level managers.

Today calculations of this kind are frequently performed using electronic spreadsheets. Figure 19.4 illustrates the use of a spreadsheet for examining the impact on profits of different assumptions relating to sales and cost trends.

Sales Forecasting

Because the sales budget establishes the volume level for all other components of the budget, much care must be taken to obtain a reliable sales forecast. There are a number of methods of sales forecasting, some judgmental and some quantitative. No single method can be considered completely reliable and most organizations try to minimize their risks by employing a combination of methods.

FIGURE 19.4   Electronic spreadsheets used for budget projections. The parameters labeled "Ratio" are the ratios of cost of sales and operating expense to sales. "Trend" is the percentage change in these items from one year to the next. Changes in the parameters relative to base year are highlighted. The spreadsheets were prepared using LOTUS 1-2-3, a product of Lotus Development Corporation.

```
                        XYZ COMPANY
                FOUR YEAR BUDGET PROJECTION

     Item         Base Year      Year +1      Year +2      Year +3

Sales            $100,000.00   $110,000.00   $121,000.00   $133,100.00
Cost of Sales    $ 60,000.00   $ 66,000.00   $ 72,600.00   $ 79,860.00
  Gross Margin   $ 40,000.00   $ 44,000.00   $ 48,400.00   $ 53,240.00
Op. Expense      $ 30,000.00   $ 33,000.00   $ 36,300.00   $ 39,930.00
  Net Income     $ 10,000.00   $ 11,000.00   $ 12,100.00   $ 13,310.00

Parameters:

     Item          Ratio         Trend

Sales            100.0%         10.0%
Cost of Sales     60.0%         10.0%
Op. Expense       30.0%         10.0%
```

(a) Base-line computation

```
                        XYZ COMPANY
                FOUR YEAR BUDGET PROJECTION

     Item         Base Year      Year +1      Year +2      Year +3

Sales            $100,000.00   $110,000.00   $121,000.00   $133,100.00
Cost of Sales    $ 60,000.00   $ 66,000.00   $ 72,600.00   $ 79,860.00
  Gross Margin   $ 40,000.00   $ 44,000.00   $ 48,400.00   $ 53,240.00
Op. Expense      $ 30,000.00   $ 31,500.00   $ 33,075.00   $ 34,728.75
  Net Income     $ 10,000.00   $ 12,500.00   $ 15,325.00   $ 18,511.25

Parameters:

     Item          Ratio         Trend

Sales            100.0%         10.0%
Cost of Sales     60.0%         10.0%
Op. Expense       30.0%          5.0%
```

(b) Effect of a reduction in operating expense trend

FIGURE 19.4 *(continued)*

XYZ COMPANY
FOUR YEAR BUDGET PROJECTION

Item	Base Year	Year +1	Year +2	Year +3
Sales	$100,000.00	$110,000.00	$121,000.00	$133,100.00
Cost of Sales	$ 60,000.00	$ 72,000.00	$ 86,400.00	$103,680.00
Gross Margin	$ 40,000.00	$ 38,000.00	$ 34,600.00	$ 29,420.00
Op. Expense	$ 30,000.00	$ 31,500.00	$ 33,075.00	$ 34,728.75
Net Income	$ 10,000.00	$ 6,500.00	$ 1,525.00	($5,308.75)

Parameters:

Item	Ratio	Trend
Sales	100.0%	10.0%
Cost of Sales	60.0%	20.0%
Op. Expense	30.0%	5.0%

(c) Effect of an increase in cost of sales trend

XYZ COMPANY
FOUR YEAR BUDGET PROJECTION

Item	Base Year	Year +1	Year +2	Year +3
Sales	$100,000.00	$105,000.00	$110,250.00	$115,762.50
Cost of Sales	$ 60,000.00	$ 66,000.00	$ 72,600.00	$ 79,860.00
Gross Margin	$ 40,000.00	$ 39,000.00	$ 37,650.00	$ 35,902.50
Op. Expense	$ 30,000.00	$ 33,000.00	$ 36,300.00	$ 39,930.00
Net Income	$ 10,000.00	$ 6,000.00	$ 1,350.00	($4,027.50)

Parameters:

Item	Ratio	Trend
Sales	100.0%	5.0%
Cost of Sales	60.0%	10.0%
Op. Expense	30.0%	10.0%

(d) Effect of a decrease in sales trend

One approach is to solicit input from the sales representatives and the sales manager. The individual representatives have closer relationships with the customers and may know their buying intentions. The sales manager can be expected to have more "feel" for the overall market conditions and the standing of the company's products versus competing products. Another approach is to carry out market surveys among existing and potential customers. This method has been found to be useful when assessing the degree of acceptance of new products. On the other hand, people's *intentions* to buy may never translate into firm orders.

A third approach is to try to forecast sales on a statistical basis using historical sales as input. Several methods of time-series analysis are available that extrapolate the historical sales trend to the coming period or periods. Two of the most common statistical forecasting techniques are linear regression and exponential smoothing. For details of such methods, the reader should refer to any standard text on statistics.

STRUCTURE OF THE PLANNING/CONTROL CYCLE AND THE REPORTING CYCLE

Inputs, Files, and Outputs

A summary of the inputs, files, and outputs associated with the planning and reporting cycles is shown in Table 19.1. In a nonparticipatory budgeting system, inputs to the budget preparation process may be solicited from only upper management. In a participatory system, formal inputs are normally solicited from each organizational segment and key manager; these inputs then take the form of departmental, divisional, and other segment budget requests. Inputs to the budget-tracking and reporting applications include data that have not been entered into the system via other transaction cycles; most of the data normally reach the reporting cycle applications through supporting subsystems such as payroll and purchasing. What remains may include accounting adjusting and closing entries and other quantitative and nonquantitative data required for particular reports.

The only files peculiar to the planning/control and reporting cycles are the budget master file and the master and transaction files relating to the general ledger application. However, virtually all other master and transaction files in the business information system may be accessed to produce either internal or external reports.

Aside from various reports that document and communicate the budget decisions made by upper management, the main outputs are the annual report to the stockholders; tax returns to federal, state and local revenue authorities; 10K reports filed with the Securities and Exchange Commission (SEC); government regulatory reports; and the host of internal reports addressed to managers at all levels in the organization. In this book, most of the detailed internal reports will be discussed in the context of the three operating cycles which form the subject of the next three chapters. In this chapter, we

TABLE 19.1   Summary of Inputs, Files, and Outputs Associated with the Planning/Control Cycle and Reporting Cycle

Application	Inputs	Files	Outputs
Budget preparation	Departmental budget requests	Buget master file Standard cost file	Budget schedules and listings Standard cost allowances
Budget tracking	Sales figures, time cards, materials requisitions, purchases, overhead allocations	Budget master file Standard cost file All transaction and master files	Budget tracking reports Standard cost variance reports Responsibility accounting reports
External reporting	Adjusting and closing entries, nonaccounting and other miscellaneous data	General ledger transaction file General ledger master file All other transaction and master files	Annual report Tax returns 10K report Government regulatory reports
Internal reporting	Nonaccounting and other miscellaneous data	All transaction and master files	Miscellaneous internal reports

shall describe only those reports that have general application.

Processes

A systems flowchart of the major accounting activities in the planning/control cycle and the reporting cycle is shown in Figure 19.5. Approved budget figures are entered into the budget master file in what amounts to a file maintenance operation. Appropriate listings of the budget figures are made for verification, documentation of the budget, and communication to managers within the organization. Data in the budget master file are then available for comparison with actual amounts in the general ledger master file and other relevant master and transaction files as appropriate. Budget-tracking reports, responsibility accounting reports, and other internal reports may reference the budget master file and such other files as are needed.

Direct accounting entries may be made into the general journal transaction file and periodically posted to the general ledger master file. Figure 19.5 shows the typical father–son system in which the existing master file is protected until posting has been completed and verified. Data from other subsystems may be written to the general journal transaction file but are more commonly retained in separate transaction files and transferred to the general ledger system in summary form. These summary data may or may not appear in the general journal file or its associated listings. The external financial statements—the income statement, balance sheet, statement of retained earnings, and other supporting statements—are prepared from data in the general ledger master file. This file contains both income statement and balance sheet accounts. The general ledger master file is normally the source of most of the data required to be reported on tax returns, 10K reports, and other government regulatory reports.

Principal Files

Budget Master File. The budget master file is normally structured on the basis of the chart of accounts and provides for a one-to-one record comparison with the general ledger master file. This arrangement greatly facilitates comparisons between budget and actual amounts. The budget master file should provide for random access for query purposes and for the preparation of management reports. In a manual system, a card file is suitable; in an automated system, magnetic disk storage is most appropriate.

The file typically contains the following data elements:

- Account number
- Account name
- Supporting schedule reference number
- January budget
- February budget
- March budget
- April budget
- May budget
- June budget
- July budget
- August budget
- September budget
- October budget
- November budget
- December budget

The budget spread by month allows seasonal variations to be represented in detail. A spread by quarter provides less detail but may be adequate for some purposes. The file is normally sorted by account number, and the account number is the primary retrieval key.

General Ledger Master File. The general ledger master file is the heart of the accounting system and also forms the repository for large amounts of data used for performance evaluation. Like the budget master file, it should support random access. The file usually contains data elements such as the following:

- Account number
- Account name
- Account type
- Beginning-of-year balance
- First quarter balance
- Second quarter balance
- Third quarter balance
- Fourth quarter balance
- Beginning-of-month balance

FIGURE 19.5 Systems flowchart of the budgeting and reporting processes.

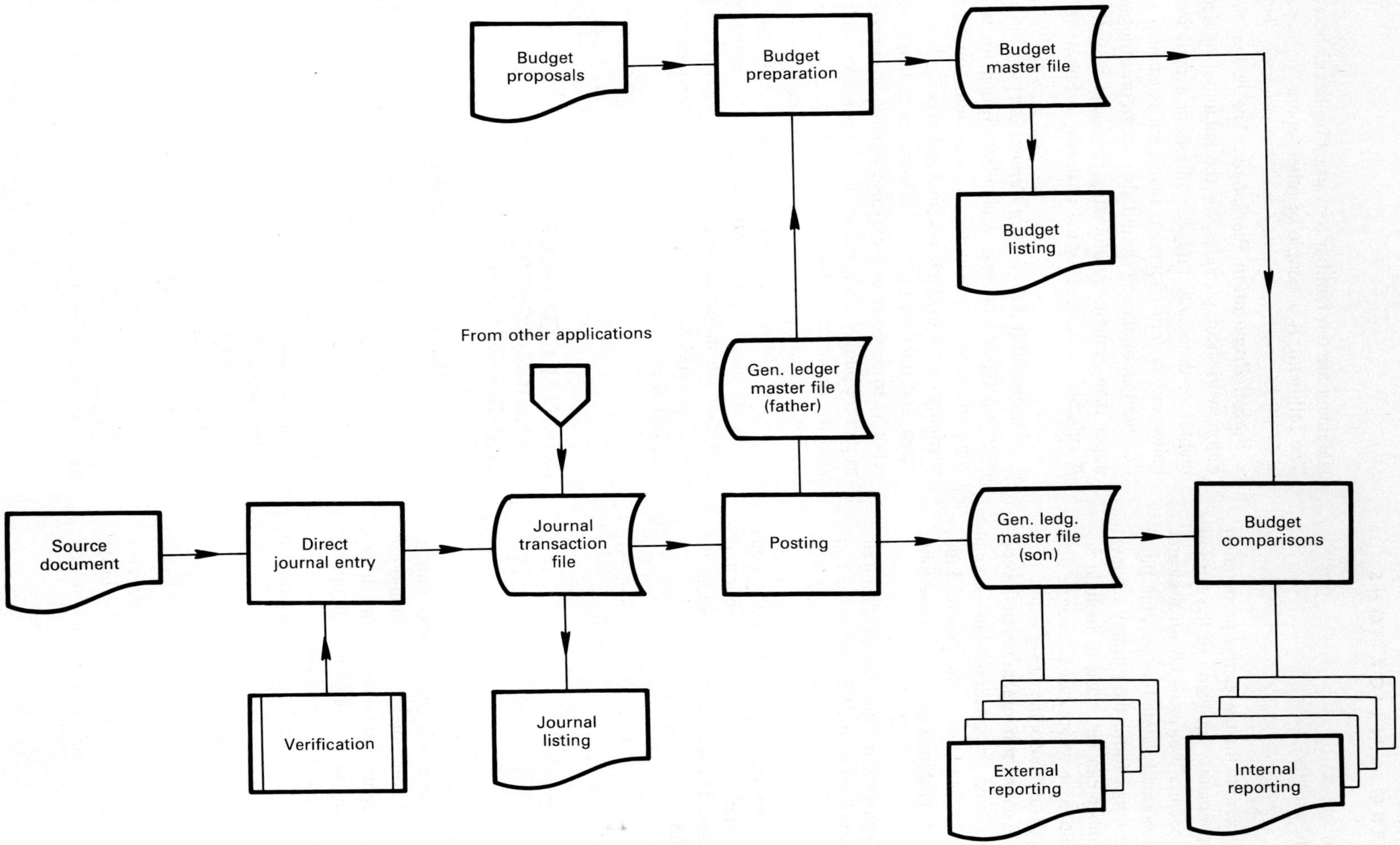

• Current month debit activity
• Current month credit activity
• Ending balance

The quarterly balance permits the retroactive preparation of interim financial statements. Inclusion of the current activity fields is not essential but provides for a clearer audit trail. The file is normally sorted by account number, and the account number forms the primary retrieval key. The account number can be coded to include account type or classification (in which case a separate field would not be required) and also the designation of a responsibility center. In a nonprofit organization the coding could extend to a fund designation; thus account number 1010.1 might denote cash in the general fund, and 1010.2 might denote cash in a special-purpose fund.

General Journal Transaction File. The general journal transaction file provides for the direct entry of general journal entries and also may serve as an interface file between other subsystems and general ledger application. The general journal transaction file usually needs to support only sequential access, and so magnetic tape is a satisfactory medium. The file typically includes the following data elements:

• Transaction date
• Source code/reference
• Explanation
• Account number*
• Amount*
• Debit/credit flag*

---

* Repeated fields.

Sometimes there is need for a reference number among the repeated items, but the common identifier should not be omitted, as it relates components of the same transaction. The debit/credit flag can be omitted if an appropriate sign convention is adopted for amounts. A common convention is that positive amounts correspond to debits and negative amounts to credits.

Selected Reports

Many of the reports produced by the planning/control and reporting cycles have been illustrated earlier in the book, and the conventional balance sheet and income statement are too familiar to warrant further elaboration. The following is a sample of other reports.

Budget Preparation Worksheet. The budget preparation worksheet provides for the submittal of departmental or divisional budget requests in a participatory budgeting system. Segment managers must justify the line-item amounts and should also assign priorities to aid upper management in allocating necessary budget cuts. A suitable worksheet format is shown in Figure 19.6.

Responsibility Accounting Report. Responsibility accounting reports provide a standard format for budget comparisons throughout the organization. Emphasis is normally on controllable revenue and expense items, but assets and liabilities may be featured in certain types of reports. In revenue and expense reports, it is common to present budget comparisons for the current month and also for the year to date. The year-to-date comparison shows a clearer picture of the effect of cumulative variances and of the likelihood of an end-of-year cost overrun or revenue shortfall. An example of a responsibility report for an industrial organization is shown in Figure 19.7, and the equivalent report for a public-sector organization is shown in Figure 19.8.

INTERNAL CONTROLS IN THE PLANNING/CONTROL CYCLE AND THE REPORTING CYCLE

Control Objectives and Risks

The principal control objectives relating to the planning and reporting cycles are[1]

• The objectives of the organization and the strategies for achieving those objectives should be defined and communicated to concerned individuals and groups.
• Management's plans and the performance of the enterprise should be reported regularly to concerned individuals and groups.

---

[1] See, for example, Arthur Andersen & Co., *A Guide for Studying and Evaluating Internal Accounting Controls*, Pub AA2880, Item 1 (Chicago: Arthur Andersen & Co., 1978).

FIGURE 19.6 **Budget preparation worksheet.**

```
                        ROCKFORT FINANCIAL SERVICES, INC.
                          DEPARTMENTAL BUDGET ESTIMATE
                          For Fiscal Year Ending 9/30/99

Department: Estate Planning                Prepared by: A.B. Head
                                           Date: 6/1/99

                                       Last year's    Real
                      Priority                Budget +     Increase    Recommended
                        Code    Last year:   Inflation   <Decrease>     Budget
     Item                     Budget   Actual
-----------------------------------------------------------------------------------
Salaries (Class A)       1    246,000  253,500    270,600      50,000      320,600
Salaries (Class B)       2    105,200  104,900    115,720       7,500      123,220
Transportation           1      9,460   10,030     10,406       1,000       11,406
Travel                   2     29,150   28,840     32,065     <1,000>       31,065
Supplies                 2     14,080   13,470     15,488        -0-        15,488
Publications             3      3,700    3,600      4,070        -0-         4,070
Legal services           1     39,100   44,380     43,010       4,000       47,010
                              --------  --------   --------    --------     --------
                             $446,690  $458,720   $491,359     $61,500     $552,859
                              ========  ========   ========    ========     ========
```

FIGURE 19.7 **Budget tracking report for an industrial organization.**

```
                              AJAX CORPORATION                           Page 1
                        MONTHLY BUDGET TRACKING REPORT
                           Month of November 19XX

Responsibility center # 94              Export Sales Division, Palo Alto, CA
Status: Revenue center                  Manager: Mary Beth Manson
        Account:             This month:                 Year-to-date:
 Number    Name          Actual    Budget    Variance     Actual      Budget     Variance
 ------  --------------  ---------  ---------  --------   ----------  ----------  ----------
  4100  Sales—Europe      4,330,000  4,000,000   330,000   46,593,000  44,000,000   2,593,000
  4200  Sales—S. America  9,758,500 10,000,000 <241,500>  103,798,000 110,000,000 <6,202,000>
  4300  Sales—S.E. Asia   7,643,500  7,000,000   643,500   68,124,000  66,000,000   2,124,000
  4400  Sales—Japan       2,657,000  3,000,000 <343,000>   30,789,000  33,000,000 <2,211,000>
  4500  Sales—S. Africa     939,000  1,000,000  <61,000>   11,678,000  11,000,000     678,000
  4900  Currency gains<losses> 46,500      -0-    46,500    <137,000>        -0-     <137,000>
                         ----------  ----------  --------   ----------  ----------  ----------
        Subtotal         25,374,500 25,000,000   374,500  260,845,000 264,000,000 <3,155,000>
                         ==========  ==========  ======   ==========  ==========  =========

        Account:             This month:                 Year-to-date:
 Number    Name          Actual    Budget    Variance     Actual      Budget     Variance
 ------  --------------  ---------  ---------  --------   ----------  ----------  ----------
  5100  Wages and Salaries  229,000    200,000    29,000   2,749,000   2,500,000     249,000
  5200  Advertising       1,513,000  1,500,000    13,000  17,567,000  16,000,000   1,567,000
  5300  Travel              694,000    700,000   <6,000>   7,723,000   8,000,000   <277,000>
  5400  Supplies             47,600     50,000   <2,400>     391,000     400,000     <9,000>
  5500  Miscellaneous        77,500     75,000     2,500     988,000   1,000,000    <12,000>
                          ---------  ---------   ------   ----------  ----------  ----------
        Subtotal          2,561,100  2,525,000    36,100  29,418,000  27,900,000   1,518,000
                          =========  =========   ======   ==========  ==========  =========
```

FIGURE 19.8 Budget-tracking report for a not-for-profit organization.

```
                         CITY OF RED RIVER                    Page 1
             STATEMENT OF EXPENDITURES, TRANSFERS AND ENCUMBRANCES
                      Fiscal Period Ending 12/31/1999

   Expenditures
   & Transfers       Appropriation      Actual     Encumbrances    Variance*

General Government      480,000        483,200                      (3,200)
Schools                 610,000        528,700       50,000         31,300
Police                  375,000        381,000                      (6,000)
Fire Department         180,000        179,100                         900
Parks & Recreation       90,000         87,500                      (2,500)
Transfer to Debt         60,000         60,000                        -0-
Service
Miscellaneous            49,000         24,600       14,000         10,400
                     $1,844,000     $1,744,100      $64,000        $35,900

* (Excess) deficiency of actuals and encumbrances relative to appropriations
```

• Reporting procedures should be established and maintained in accordance with management's wishes.

• Reporting practices, along with performance evaluation procedures and incentive programs, should motivate decisions in accordance with management's plans.

• Access to budget, accounting and financial data, and to the budget process, should be permitted only in accordance with management's wishes.

• Budget and transaction authority should be established in accordance with management's wishes and communicated to concerned individuals and groups.

• Transactions should be authorized, recorded and processed accurately and promptly in accordance with management's wishes.

• Recorded account balance should periodically be reviewed and substantiated.

These objectives stem from concern about various errors and irregularities at both the planning and reporting stages. Short-term plans and plans relating to individual company segments may fail to contribute to long-term and companywide goals or conflict with other short-term or segment plans. Plans may be unrealistic in terms of the organization's resources, opportunities, and threats. Opportunities may arise that the organization is unable to exploit, or resources may be wasted on irrelevant programs. Funds may be committed to projects that upper management has decided to reject. Individuals may inadvertently be motivated to make decisions contrary to the best interest of the organization.

Penalties may be imposed for the late filing of, or the failure to file, government tax or regulatory reports. Penalties may also be imposed for failing to include reports or disclosure of particular activities.

Published reports may not reflect transaction activity or may attribute it to the wrong accounting period. Transactions may be approved or created by unauthorized persons, in unauthorized amounts, or at unauthorized times. Transactions may be recorded and/or processed incorrectly or not recorded and processed at all. Fictitious transactions may be recorded so as to misstate reports or conceal irregularities. Adjusting entries may be made that misrepresent the underlying economics.

The flow of information may be faulty or may be intentionally obstructed, thereby withholding necessary information from authorized decision makers. Critical decisions may therefore be made on incomplete or erroneous information. Imperfections or irregularities in data processing may expose assets to unauthorized use, loss, or misappropriation. Such imperfections and irregularities may also undermine the performance evaluation of individuals and company segments. Similarly, improper intracompany allocations of revenues and costs may distort responsibility reports.

Reported account balances may not reflect historical costs or actual economic conditions. Market values of investments, inventory, and other items may have fallen below book values. Fixed assets may have fallen in value as a result of neglect or abuse.

Control Measures

Authorization controls figure heavily in the planning and reporting cycles. The budget is upper management's principal vehicle for short-term planning and serves to delegate authority to middle and lower management. A travel budget amount, for example, implies authority to a manager to spend up to that amount without having to obtain separate approval for each trip. The budget must be properly authorized—both as a whole and in line-item detail—in order to assign responsibilities down the chain of command. The budget must also dovetail with other authorization documents such as job descriptions. The procedures for preparing the budget must be authorized.

Communication of authority and qualifying criteria such as dollar ceilings above which approval is required from higher-level management should be explicit and put in writing. An unwritten delegation of authority is likely to make lower-level managers uneasy and also to cause concern to upper management when that authority is exercised in unintended ways.

Similarly, performance evaluation criteria should be spelled out so that lower-level managers understand how their handling of responsibilities will be judged.

Procedures must be established and authorized for tracking the budget and preparing responsibility reports. Care must be taken to distribute direct revenues and costs properly and to allocate indirect costs fairly. Where difficult allocation problems arise, possibly the items themselves cannot be controlled and should be omitted from the reports or labeled *noncontrollable*. Reports should be prepared according to authorized schedules.

The chart of accounts and associated coding schemes should be properly authorized, and a method of uniquely identifying transactions should be established. General and specific authorizations should be defined for recording, processing, and reporting transactions. These authorizations should extend to procedures for handling adjusting and closing entries and for end-of-period cutoff. Similar authorizations are required for access to the information system and for such sensitive activities as file maintenance.

Internal audit procedures should be established to verify that budget preparation and tracking and transaction authorization, recording, and processing are being handled in accordance with management's written policy and procedure manuals. Provision should be made for independent confirmation, on an appropriate sample basis, of data appearing in management reports. All computer-created transactions should be subject to management review. The utility of internal management reports should routinely be reviewed.

External reports, including the annual financial statements, tax returns, and government regulatory reports, should be independently reviewed for content, format, and compliance with statutory regulations before issuance or filing. Ratio analysis and analysis of trends and variances provide some assurance that reported amounts are correct. Checklists should be used to verify compliance with filing deadlines.

SUMMARY

The planning and control cycle pertains to management's planning activities and to the associated steps that management takes to ensure that its plans are duly carried out. The planning component refers to both long-term and short-term planning, the latter including budget preparation. Modern approaches to budgeting hinge on the desirability of involving managers at all levels in the organization in the budget process. In order to provide for such a participatory style of budgeting, worksheets must be provided to gather the budget proposals from individual managers and from organizational segments. Budget proposals should take account of inflation as well as reflect proposals for real growth or contraction. The budget process may extend to establishing manufacturing cost standards.

Budget tracking is one of the principal tools of management control, and the interpretation of variances from the budget provides a basis for informed corrective action. Responsibility accounting is based on the principle that information given to managers should be tailored to their responsibilities and authority. Noncontrollable items (at the particular level in the organization or over the reporting time frame) either should be carefully segregated from controllable items or should be excluded from the reports.

The budget process should be protected by controls to ensure that the budget properly reflects the wishes of top management. Authorization controls play a major role because of the close relationship between budget allocations and management responsibility.

The planning/control cycle also includes activities such as project planning and management by objectives (MBO), in which the activities of managers, accountants, and other professionals are planned. The control component includes budget tracking, analysis of standard cost variances, and performance evaluation of individuals and groups throughout the organization. It also embraces the control environment and systemwide internal controls, other than those identified with other transaction cycles, as well as more specific controls dealing with budget preparation and tracking.

The reporting cycle includes the general ledger application, which forms the heart of the accounting system. The general ledger system receives informational inputs from most of the other subsystems in the business information system and is the source of most of the external reports issued by the organization, including external financial statements and tax and regulatory reporting. It also is the source of many systemwide internal management reports.

Internal controls in the reporting cycle focus on protecting the accounting data base and the reliability of data in internal and external reporting. Particular care must be taken to ensure that external reports are accurate and complete and are issued in a timely manner. In the case of tax and other types of government reporting, penalties are frequently imposed for late submittal. User's confidence in the external reports is enhanced both by the organization's internal controls and also by external controls through the instrument of the auditor's opinion.

BIBLIOGRAPHY

Arens, Alvin A., and D. Dewey Ward. *Systems Understanding for Auditing.* Haslett, Mich.: Systems Publications, 1981.

Evaluating Internal Control: A Guide for Management and Directors. Publ. no. 39078. Cleveland: Ernst & Whinney, 1979.

Forms for the Key Operations of Business. Glenview, Ill.: Moore Business Forms, 1977.

Gelinas, Ulrie J. "Using an Illustration of a Conceptual Information System to Improve Pedagogy in MIS Courses." *MAS Communication*, vol. 5, no. 3, October 1981, pp. 17–27.

Pescoe, Jerome K. *Encyclopedia of Accounting Systems.* Englewood Cliffs, N.J.: Prentice-Hall, 1976.

DISCUSSION QUESTIONS AND PROBLEMS

1. Define and discuss the following terms:

- Budget preparation
- Budget tracking
- Discretionary cost
- Engineered cost
- Expense budget
- External reporting
- General ledger
- Internal reporting
- Long-range planning
- Management by objectives
- Manufacturing cost standards
- Master budget
- Planning and control cycle
- Reporting cycle
- Responsibility accounting
- Sales forecast
- Short-range planning
- Zero-based budgeting

2. Discuss the different information requirements of the planning/control and reporting cycles, and indicate how computer systems can contribute to meeting each requirement.

3. "The requirements of the planning/control cycle place a heavier emphasis on the decision support function than do the other transaction cycles."

Required

Evaluate the truth of this statement, and comment on the use of decision support technologies in the planning/control cycle and other cycles.

4. Foster Industries, Inc., is preparing the budget for 19B. Company policy is to base the budget on the previous year's budget, with appropriate adjustments for inflation and other factors. Budget and actual cost figures for the engineering department for 19A were as follows:

Item	Budget	Actual
Salaries	$ 750,000	$ 785,000
Wages	240,000	247,500
Materials & supplies	60,000	53,700
Testing	98,000	94,300
Subcontracts	126,500	143,800
Computer usage	44,500	51,900
Professional fees	1,200	1,200
Travel & transportation	5,400	5,350
Other direct costs	50,000	43,000
Overhead	594,000	594,000
	$1,969,600	$2,019,750

The variance in labor costs arose from salary and wage adjustments made midway through the year. The budget for the coming year should reflect the annualization of these increases and provide for an additional 8 percent raise at midyear. Materials and supplies expenditures and subcontracts are expected to remain at 19A budgeted levels. Computer usage is expected to increase by 15 percent over budgeted levels for 19A, but unit costs should remain the same. The remaining costs (other than overhead) are expected to increase at a 6 percent rate because of general inflation. Overhead is applied at the rate of 60 percent of total budgeted labor costs.

Required

a. Prepare the budget for the engineering department for 19B, using a worksheet similar to that shown in Figure 19.6. (Priorities need not be included.)

b. As a staff member on the budget committee, what questions would you want to ask the manager of the engineering department before drafting a final budget recommendation for the department?

5. Design a budget-tracking report form for a charitable organization headquartered in a large American city. The organization provides shelters for the homeless, disinstitutionalized mental patients, and runaway teenagers and also responds to pleas for disaster relief from areas in the United States and abroad.

Income comes from several sources, including United Way allocations, grants from nationwide relief agencies, direct fund raising, interest, and miscellaneous contributions. Expenditures should be broken down into appropriate administrative costs and program costs, and the latter should be broken down further into in-state, out-of-state, and foreign charity programs. Comparisons should be made for the current month and year to date and should include actuals from the previous year and budget and actual figures for the present year.

6. Prepare a series of graphics presentations illustrating the budget comparisons made in Figure 19.7. Show the breakdown of sales from the various regions and to show the breakdown of the total cost budget among the component functional areas.

7. Indicate the control weaknesses that allowed the following incidents to take place, and suggest control measures that would have reduced the likelihood of their occurrence:

• A member of middle management approved substantial expenditures for a budget item, unaware that the project had been canceled some time earlier.
• A first-level manager inadvertently exceeded her departmental equipment budget when she purchased a machine tool costing $35,000. The problem was not noticed until an internal auditor was examining paid vendor invoices.
• The budget for 19A was approved by top management, even though it was inconsistent with the official five-year plan drawn up two years earlier.

- A new supervisor in the service department was told to ignore the unfavorable variances on his budget-tracking report because they were due to seasonal factors. Someone explained, "The figures will probably all balance out by year-end."
- A research scientist, worried about exceeding her labor budget on a project, was told by the director of research to charge next month's hours to "lost time" "so that we don't look bad when the comparisons come out."
- A manager attended a three-day executive training program but, due to an oversight by the organizers of the program, never paid the $1,200 registration fee. When the manager submitted an expense claim for his travel expenses, he did not list the registration fee, and so did not benefit personally from the unexpected "windfall."
- A young branch manager was terminated for poor performance. It was later found that the manager's branch was actually profitable but the operating figures had been distorted by an error in allocating indirect costs.
- An external auditor discovered that computer-generated adjusting entries to the general ledger had been in error for the last ten months, ever since a new program was released.
- Management was seriously embarrassed when the balance sheet and the cash flow statement, published in the company's annual report, contained obvious inconsistencies. The problem was caused by an error in a computer program.
- Substantial penalties and interest had to be paid for the late deposit of taxes withheld from employees' wages.

8. Eastern Corrugated Products, Inc., manufactures cardboard boxes to customers' specifications. The company uses a quantitative model in which the price of a box is based on the number of square feet of cardboard required, multiplied by a unit price based on the type of material. The amount of cardboard used to make a box is approximately equal to

$$\text{Area} = 2\,(WH + DH) + 2.5\,WD$$

where W, H, and D are the width, height, and depth of the box, respectively (the extra area associated with the product of the width and depth is accounted for by the overlap of cardboard on the top and bottom of the box). The cost of cardboard stock is as follows:

Weight (lb.)	Price ($/1,000 sq. ft.)
40	40
60	50
80	60
100	65
120	70

Additional charges are made for cutting and folding, for printing labels on the boxes, and for multicolor labels. Applicable cost data are

Item	Charge ($ per thousand)
Cutting and folding	30
Label printing:	
one color	10
each extra color	5

A surcharge of $20 per order is made for producing small lots of fewer than 1,000 boxes.

Required

Estimate the total price of the following orders and the unit price per box:

a. 2,000 boxes of dimensions: W = 12″, H = 6″, D = 12″, made of 60 lb. material, with a two-color label

b. 3,000 boxes of dimensions: W = 24″, H = 18″, D = 6″, made of 40 lb. material, with a one-color label

c. 1,000 boxes of dimensions: W = 30″, H = 24″, D = 24″, made of 100 lb. material, with no label

d. 500 boxes with the same characteristics as in (c)

9. Analyze the following data to determine meaningful variances from budget. In each case, suggest possible reasons for the variance, and identify the lowest level of responsibility in the corporate hierarchy to which the variance could be charged.

Item	Budget	Actual
Materials costs	$146,000	$159,500
Factory labor costs*	$184,000	$188,250
Advertising expense	$ 55,000	$ 47,500
Research & development expenditures	$ 38,000	$ 56,000
Executive salaries†	$108,000	$ 97,200
Legal expenses	$ 15,000	$ 96,000
General & adminstrative expenses	$ 42,000	$ 39,000
Development costs of new information system‡	$100,000	$ 73,500

Notes:
* 5 percent of the labor force was laid off during the year.
† The company made a loss for the second straight year.
‡ The total cost of the system is estimated to be $250,000.

10. A large hotel in a major city reports internal operating data on the basis of responsibility centers that parallel the segments of the organization chart. Part of the organization chart relates to the promotion and operation of its lucrative convention business:

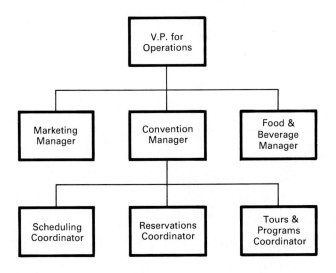

Operating costs accumulated during 19A included these figures:

Responsibility Center	Cost Item	Amount
V.P for operations	Salary	$95,000
	Admin. expenses	34,500
	Travel & transp.	23,700
Marketing manager	Salary	$60,000
	Other expenses	22,750
Convention manager	Salary	$55,000
	Other expenses	34,300
Food & beverage manager	Salaries	$66,000
	Other expenses	19,400
Scheduling coordinator	Salaries	$52,500
	Other expenses	3,700
Reservations coordinator	Salaries	$74,000
	Supplies	9,420
	Telephone	13,650
	Computer services	17,300
	Miscellaneous	6,270
Tours & programs coordinator	Salaries	$38,500
	Other expenses	12,900

Required

Prepare sample internal reports for 19A, for the reservations coordinator, the convention manager, and the vice-president for operations, to illustrate a hierarchical cost-reporting system.

11. a. Distinguish between the terms *forecast* and *budget*, and discuss their mutual relationship in a business environment.

b. Participatory budgeting is intended to engender a feeling of involvement in the budget process among managers at all levels in the organization. On the other hand, upper management often has to trim budget requests made by lower managers or even reject requests outright. Discuss the realism of the participatory budgeting concept and the likely behavioral advantages to be gained.

12. During the initial design process, the following specifications for the general ledger transaction file and master file were submitted by the assistant controller:

Transaction File	Master File
Date	Account number
Transaction ID	Account name
Account number*	Account type
Account name*	Beginning balance
Amount*	Debit activity
Debit or credit flag*	Credit activity
Explanation	Ending balance
Posting flag	

* Repeated fields

Master file records are to be retrieved primarily by account number, although the need for occasional retrieval by account name is anticipated.

Required

Analyze these file specifications to provide a normalized logical data structure defining the schema of a data base management system. Provide tables and relationships to describe your final normalized form, and draw a data access diagram showing how data elements would be retrieved.

13. a. Draw a HIPO overview diagram describing the budget-tracking process.
b. Draw a HIPO detail diagram describing the preparation of a budget-tracking report.

14. A pertinent internal control objective for the reporting cycle is

Transactions should be authorized, recorded and processed accurately and promptly in accordance with management's wishes.

Required
a. List the risks (the things that could go wrong) if this control objective were not achieved.
b. List applicable controls to reduce the risks referred to in (a).

20

The Purchasing Cycle

CHAPTER OUTLINE

OVERVIEW OF THE PURCHASING CYCLE

The purchasing cycle involves the ordering, receiving, and payment for goods and services required by the organization. "Goods" may be raw materials, merchandise, supplies, fixed assets, or certain intangibles such as patents or computer programs. "Services" may be the work of the organization's employees or the services of outside vendors, including contractors, catering firms, janitorial firms, towel services, consultants, and auditors.

The purchasing cycle usually includes purchasing, receiving, accounts payable, and payroll. Payroll is sometimes excluded so as to form a cycle of its own. But the differences between payroll and accounts payable are scarcely important enough to justify the further fragmentation of the cycles; rather, the similarities between them call for a unifying approach in which payroll is accepted as an integral part of this cycle. On the other hand, the payroll operations are somewhat simpler than is the procurement of goods and services from outside sources, and some of the steps in the latter have no counterparts in the payroll application.

The purchasing cycle, represented at this stage by the procurement of goods and services from vendors, consists of the following steps:

• Identification of a need
• Placement of an order
• Receipt of the goods or services
• Approval for payment
• Disbursement of cash
• Recording of the transactions involved

Identification of a Need

Goods or services may be needed in any of several different areas. Inventories may be routinely reviewed to identify items whose on-hand balance has fallen below a predetermined reorder point. Certain items may automatically be ordered at regular intervals unless a stop order is issued.

A stock clerk may have received a stores requisition that could not immediately be filled. Orders may have been received from customers that resulted in a back-order request. Long lead-time procurement of materials may have been initiated to support production of a weapons system. A purchasing agent may have learned of an attractive volume discount or, alternatively, may have learned of an impending strike at a major supplier's plant.

A contractor may be needed to relay the paving in the parking lot. A consultant may be needed to help in a systems analysis exercise. A software house may be needed to write a computer program or to modify an existing one.

The need for the acquisition of goods or services may have arisen from the initiative of an in-house person, from the closing of a sale by an outside broker or agent, or from the visit of a vendor's representative. The need may be a routine one, or it may be for a ''one-of-a-kind'' item or service.

Placing the Order

In some cases, the order for the goods or services is issued by the originating department. But more commonly there is a central purchasing, buying, or procurement department through which all orders are channeled. The originating department issues a purchase requisition, and the purchasing department prepares a purchase order that is sent to the particular vendor. This separation of duties is important from an internal control standpoint.

Goods that are routinely purchased are usually ordered from suppliers' catalogues or price lists. Upon receipt of the purchase order, the vendor typically responds with an acknowledgment or confirmation that the goods can be supplied at the stated price. Alternatively, the vendor may respond with the notification of a price increase or with an explanation of why the goods are unavailable. Sometimes substitutes are suggested, and the purchasing department (usually in consultation with the originating department) must ascertain whether substitutes are acceptable. Somewhat the same procedure is followed for the routine procurement of outside services.

If nonroutine purchases are involved, there may be no applicable price lists, and bids may be solicited from prospective vendors. The example of acquisition of computer hardware and software by competitive bid has already been mentioned (Chapter 14). A request for quotation (RFQ), or request for proposal (RFP), is prepared and sent to one or, more commonly, several vendors. The vendors may or may not choose to respond to the solicitation, according to their expectations of winning the competition and the estimated profitability. In turn, the purchasing department may decide not to accept any of the bids and to look elsewhere for the required goods or services. If the development of custom goods or the provision of complicated services is involved, a formal contract may be drawn up containing a set of specifications spelling out what the vendor is expected to provide or do. The contract then becomes a supplement to the purchase order. Contracts of this type frequently identify ''deliverable items,'' which may include manufactured products, subassemblies, computer programs, reports, or materials of other kinds.

Receiving

When the goods are received from the vendor, they are checked by the receiving department, possibly with the assistance of quality control, to verify that their identity, quantity, and quality conform to the expectations of the purchase order. A receiving report or ticket is prepared detailing this information and providing a basis for subsequent payment of the vendor invoice. If the goods do not conform with applicable specifications or if the goods were never ordered, they may be returned to the vendor. If there are some deficiencies but the goods are generally acceptable, the goods may be retained but an allowance claim submitted to the vendor requesting a reduction of the invoice amount to be paid.

Whereas goods are normally received at discrete points in time, services may be rendered over an extended period. A receiving report is therefore not applicable, but some formal statement must be made that the services have been duly provided. An acceptance report often serves this purpose, and one is usually signed off when a new computer system has been installed and testing completed. The acceptance report supports the vendor's claim for payment in the same way as the receiving report does.

Payment

If no credit arrangements have been reached between the vendor and the buyer organization, cash terms may be insisted upon, or payment may have to be made in advance. But when credit arrangements are in effect, the goods are usually delivered in anticipation of payment at some later date. Issuance of a valid purchase order is conventionally understood to imply a promise to pay, in accordance with the applicable terms, as long as the goods or services conform to the specifications. Even when credit has been extended, contracts for custom goods or services may require advance payments before work commences and progress payments during the course of the work. Commonly, the progress payments are scheduled to coincide with the passage of certain milestones in the work. In this way, the buyer organization has some assurance that the work is progressing at the rate claimed by the vendor.

Approval for payment is normally a formality as long as the goods or services have been provided as ordered and the quantities and prices are correct as stated on the invoice. If the invoice data are not correct, the invoice may be returned to the vendor for resubmittal. Also, as already mentioned, an allowance claim may be sent to the vendor requesting an adjustment of the invoice amount to reflect deficiencies in the goods or damage sustained during shipment. When any discrepancies or uncertainties regarding the invoice have been resolved, a voucher is prepared. Attached to the voucher are copies of the supporting documents: the purchase order, the receiving report (or acceptance report), and the vendor invoice. This package of documents then receives the approval for payment, and the disbursement activities commence.

Disbursement may be made immediately upon approval of the voucher, or it may be delayed until some time in the future. The payment schedule adopted will depend on the availability of any favorable discounts for prompt payment and on the organization's current cash position. Typically, the vouchers are placed in a file and await their turn for payment according to such priorities as management may establish. A cash requirements forecast may be prepared at regular intervals, such as once per week or twice per month, showing the amount of cash needed to pay certain categories of vouchers. Also, a schedule of aged accounts payable may be prepared, analogous to the more familiar schedule of aged receivables. After review of the cash requirements forecast and the aging schedule, management will select vouchers for payment and decide on a payment date. Many organizations have regular payment dates each month, such as the first and the fifteenth. On those dates, batches of checks are written and mailed out.

Payroll and the Purchasing Cycle

In the case of the payroll component of the purchasing cycle, there is no analog of the processes of identifying needs or placing orders for goods or services. Recruitment of personnel is considered to lie outside the province of the payroll application and in a separate area of personnel administration.

The analog of the accounts payable voucher (or perhaps that of the vendor invoice or receiving report) is the employee time card or time sheet. These documents detail the services provided by the individual employees and, upon authorization by the supervisor, initiate the payment process. Supplementary information may be submitted on a work report giving a more detailed breakdown of the tasks performed by the employees. Individuals who do not receive regular compensation submit vouchers stating the amounts of commission or other income that they have earned.

Approval of the time cards, time sheets, or commission vouchers is normally routine, and the obligation to pay the employees is guaranteed by the employment contract (actual or implied) and supported by law. An important difference between accounts payable and payroll is that payroll payments cannot be delayed to suit management's convenience. Except in the rarest of circumstances, wages and salaries must be paid according to the established schedule: weekly, biweekly, semimonthly, or monthly.

Issuance of the checks and preparation of a check register are directly analogous to the corresponding activities in accounts payable. An additional requirement of payroll processing, however, is the handling of deductions and tax withholdings. Regular returns and deposits have to be made to the federal and state revenue authorities. Also, detailed records must be kept both for employee information and to meet the legal requirements of making periodic reports to revenue authorities and issuing W-2 forms to employees at the end of the calendar year. Finally, provision must be made for handling group insurance premiums, credit union deposits, purchases of U.S. savings bonds, contributions to United Way, payment of union dues, and other payroll deduction plans.

Accounting Transactions

The purchasing cycle includes at least two formal accounting transactions: one related to the receipt of goods or services and the incurrence of the liability to pay for them and the other related to the subsequent disbursement of cash. These two transactions must be captured so as to be reflected in the general ledger and financial statements. Identifying the need to acquire goods or services, placing the order, and approving vouchers for payment are not considered to constitute formal transactions, but they have obvious importance to management and must be recorded for planning and control purposes.

With regard to payroll, the disbursement transaction is more complicated than that relating to accounts payable because of the need to recognize a number of accrued liabilities at, or close to, the time of payment. Some of these liabilities are contributions by the employees, for example, tax withholdings and credit union deposits; others represent expenses to the organization, such as vacation or sick leave fringe benefits. The transaction may be even more complicated if cash advances have been made previously to employees, and records need to be kept to show the residual balance owed by the individuals in question.

TABLE 20.1 Summary of the Inputs, Files, and Outputs Associated with the Purchasing Cycle

Application	Inputs	Files	Outputs
Purchasing	Purchase requisition	Open purchase order file Vendor master file	Purchase order Purchase register Open purchase order report Receiving report
Receiving	Shipping document (Purchase order)	Receiving file	Receiving report
Accounts payable	Vendor invoice Expense claim Voucher (Purchase order) (Receiving report)	Open voucher file Vendor master file Check file	Voucher register Open voucher report Schedule of aged accounts Cash requirements forecast Checks Check register
Payroll	Time card Salaried time sheet Work report Commission voucher	Payroll transaction file Employee master file Check file	Payroll register Deduction register Paychecks Check register Labor distribution report Federal and state returns W-2 forms and 941-A forms Employee earnings records

The cash disbursements journal is sometimes treated as part of the purchasing cycle; alternatively, it can be thought of as part of the general ledger application, which in turn belongs to the reporting cycle. In either case, it forms an important interface between the purchasing and the reporting cycles, recording the flow of vendor and employee payments entries into the general ledger. In some organizations, the check register services as a cash disbursements journal. This may be appropriate if all disbursements are made in the form of checks and as long as there is no confusion between disbursements made against accounts payable and those made for payroll purposes.

STRUCTURE OF THE PURCHASING CYCLE

Inputs, Files, and Outputs

A summary of the inputs, files, and outputs associated with the purchasing cycle is shown in Table 20.1. The input documents consist of purchase requisitions; vendor shipping documents; vendor invoices; accounts payable vouchers and other disbursement claims; and time cards, time sheets, and work reports for payroll purposes. In addition, there are some intermediate documents such as receiving reports that are outputs from one application and inputs to another; these are shown in parentheses in Table 20.1.

The principal files are the vendor and employee master files, the open purchase order file, and the open voucher file. A receiving file may be included to provide an interface with the inventory control application, and check files are sometimes prepared to accumulate check data prior to printing accounts payable or payroll checks. The open purchase order and open voucher files are hybrids, having some of the characteristics of both transaction and master files. They contain transactionlike records, but they may be the target of posting processes. A record is created when a purchase order or a voucher is prepared. And it is flagged "closed" when the goods or services are received or when the voucher is paid. The closed records are purged or archived at some convenient point in time, such as the end of the month or the end of the quarter.

The payroll transaction file is used to accumulate time-cards and other labor inputs prior to processing. Payroll processing has a strong inherent periodicity (stronger, indeed, than in almost any other application), and because of this, summary data are often posted to the employee master file (or payroll master file) at the same time that deductions and withholdings are calculated and paychecks prepared. If the input data are also entered only at the time that payroll processing is to be performed, then the transaction file has no lasting value, and it degenerates into a kind of scratch file. However, the transaction file does assume more importance when time-card data are entered more frequently than payroll processing, say, daily. In some situations, daily time-card data have to be accumulated for preparing state labor certificates, which are required for certain types of public works contract, particularly in the construction industry.

In the payroll application, an additional master file must be maintained to hold withholding tables. These tables, which are provided by federal, state, and sometimes local revenue authorities, specify the percentages that must be withheld from earnings in different wage brackets. Separate tables are usually provided for single, married, or other designated tax payers.

The principal output documents, appearing in the purchasing cycle, are purchase orders, checks, and tax forms such as W-2 forms. Management reports include the purchase register, the voucher register, the open purchase order report, the open voucher report, the cash requirements forecast, the schedule of aged accounts payable, the check register, and the various payroll registers. Payroll registers are frequently established to record the distribution of labor hours, the accrual of employee deductions and benefits, and the accumulation of withholding amounts.

Processes

Systems flowcharts of the major processing activities in the purchasing cycle are presented in Figures 20.1 through 20.4. Figure 20.1 illustrates the preparation of purchase orders for ordering goods and services. The vendor master file is accessed to retrieve the vendor address and other data, such as the name and telephone number of the contact person and the availability of credit terms. The purchase register provides a chrono-

FIGURE 20.1 The ordering of goods and services in response to a purchase requisition.

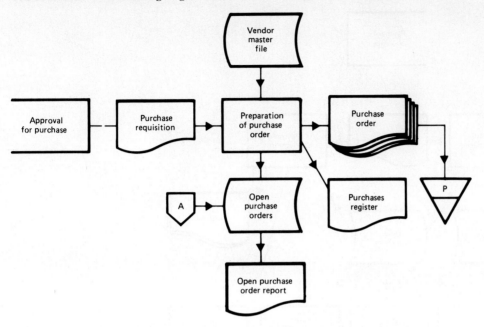

logical log of all purchase orders issued. The open purchase order file accumulates summary records of the purchase orders, and as noted, these records remain open until the goods or services have been received. The open purchase order report is a listing of this report; it may be presented in chronological order of the issuance of the open purchase orders, or it may be sorted by vendor.

The receipt of goods and the preparation of the receiving report are shown in Figure 20.2 The goods are checked against the original purchase order and the ven-

FIGURE 20.2 Receipt of ordered goods.

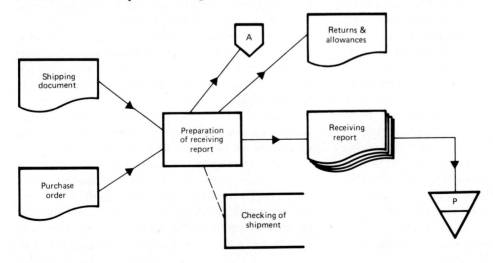

FIGURE 20.3 Payment for goods and services received.

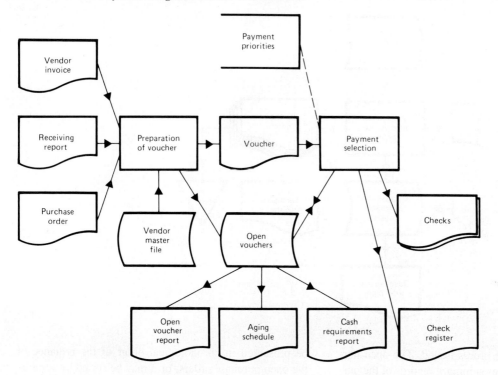

dor's shipping document. The goods will normally be returned if they were not ordered or if they are deficient. Action to prepare an allowance or insurance claim will be initiated if the goods are deficient or damaged but are to be accepted. If the shipment is complete and the goods are acceptable, the associated record in the open purchase order file is retrieved and flagged "closed." Partial shipments are recorded in some appropriate manner without closing the open purchase order record.

The preparation of accounts payable vouchers and payment of the vouchers are shown in Figure 20.3. Records are added to the open voucher file upon receipt and verification of the vendor invoices. The records remain open until payment is made. The open voucher report, the schedule of aged accounts payable, and the cash requirements forecast are usually prepared from the open voucher file, with appropriate analysis, summarization, and sorting. After approval of the vouchers and selection for payment, the checks are prepared together with the associated check register. As already men-

tioned, the checks may be printed and signed some time after the decision is made to proceed with payment.

The flow of paperwork associated with ordering, receiving, and paying for goods and services is depicted by a document flowchart arranged in columnar fashion (see Figure 20.4). This type of flowchart draws attention to the set of documents initiated and received by each organizational unit. It is particularly useful in determining whether a given department or unit has all the paperwork it needs to make a decision, such as the one to approve payment of a voucher.

Figure 20.5 shows the systems flowchart for the typical payroll process. The payroll calculation determines deductions and tax withholdings. Access is to a tax table file and to the employee master file that contains details of each employee's marital status and number of dependents. The payroll register, labor distribution report, deduction register, and withholding returns are normally prepared at that time. Preparation of the checks usually follows immediately, together with the preparation of

FIGURE 20.4   Document flowchart showing the movement of paperwork in the ordering, receiving, and payment for goods and services. The initiating department is indicated by the multipart document symbol, but no attempt is made to show the precise number of copies of each document.

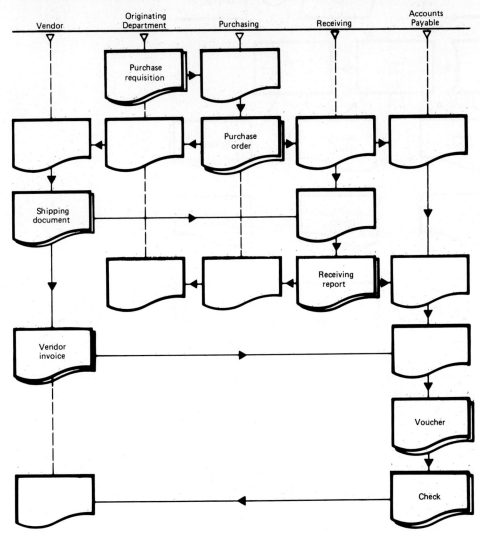

the check register. The employee master file is often updated as part of the same sequence of operations rather than as a separate posting operation. Quarter-to-date and year-to-date summary data must be maintained for each employee for tax and other purposes.

In addition to the processes already described, file maintenance provisions must be made for the addition, deletion, and update of records in the vendor master file, the employee master file, and the tax table file. In the case of the open purchase order and open voucher files, editing facilities should be provided only if suitable controls can be built in to prevent abuses. Errors in transaction files are better remedied by the entry and processing of reversing transactions. In this way, a record is

FIGURE 20.5 Payroll process.

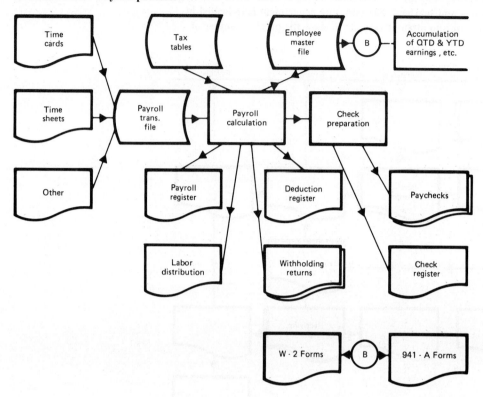

maintained the error and the means taken to correct it. Figure 20.6 shows a typical screen menu used to maintain the vendor master file in an accounts payable system.

Key Documents

Purchase Order. A purchase order is issued to a particular vendor to order goods or services and implies a commitment to make payment according to agreed terms and conditions. A single purchase order may request shipment of a number of separate line items. It should contain the following types of data (not all may be applicable in any given situation):

- Form number and description
- Name and address of initiating organization
- Name and address of vendor or supplier

- Vendor number
- Purchase order number
- Requisition number
- Authorization
- Date of issue
- Required delivery schedule
- Terms and conditions
- Shipping instructions
- Insurance required
- F.O.B. point
- Responsibility for damage
- Billing instructions

These data appear only once on the purchase order. In addition, there may be repeated line items:

- Item code or number
- Description
- Quantity ordered
- Unit of measure

FIGURE 20.6 **Screen form for vendor master file maintenance.** (Courtesy of Management Science America, Inc.)

```
DATE 06/07/81          VENDOR INQUIRY - SETUP INFORMATION   CURRENT: 26
L1/L2 ; CORP

VENDOR NUMBER    : 47915              STATUS     : ACTIVE
        NAME     : ACME DISTRIBUTION INC.   SHORT NAME : ACMEDISTRI
---TERMS/DISCOUNT----   ---DISTRIBUTION---   ------TAX INFORMATION-----
TERMS CODE     : 92     PROJECT OPT: YES     1099 CODE : 3
DISCOUNT PCT1  : 0010   --INDICATORS--       USE TAX   : 21
DISCOUNT DAY1  : 015    EXPENSE  : 3         TAX CODE  : SSN
DISCOUNT PCT2  : 0015   PAYABLES : 1         TAX ID/SSN: 863162110
DISCOUNT DAY2  : 020    CASH     : 3
FINAL PAY DAY  : 025    DISCOUNT : 4         ------MISCELLANEOUS-------
DISCOUNT DELAY : 005    SALES TAX: 2         CATEGORY CODE 1 : 101
PAYMENT DELAY  : 010    FREIGHT  : A         CATEGORY CODE 2 : 102
                                             CATEGORY CODE 3 : 103
------EMPLOYEE CREDIT CARDS------            SIC CODE        : 3266
CREDIT TYPE 1    : AX                        1 INVOICE/CHK   : ONE
CREDIT ACCOUNT 1 : 8961533341065             CHECK SEQUENCE  : 0000000001
CREDIT TYPE 2    : BA                        MAX INVOICE AMT :   500,000.00
CREDIT ACCOUNT 2 : 153688431911532           VENDOR ON HOLD  : ON HOLD
NEXT SCREEN : 27  NEW VENDOR:   47915
ACTION:----
```

- Unit price
- Extended price
- Line-item discount
- Net extended price

Purchase order forms should be prenumbered for control purposes. Purchase orders are normally prepared with multiple copies for distribution to the vendor, to the originating department, to the receiving department, to the warehouse or stockroom, and to accounting. One copy is retained for the purchasing department's records. The vendor may be sent two copies, a retention copy and an acknowledgment or confirmation copy to be returned to the purchasing department to indicate acceptance of the order. A typical purchase order is shown in Figure 20.7.

Receiving Report. The receiving report is sometimes referred to as a *receiving ticket* or *receiving document*.

It is issued for goods received as the result of a purchase or consignment or as part of an arrangement for the storage or deposit of goods owned by another party. It is also issued for goods returned by a dissatisfied customer. The receiving report typically contains

- Form number and description
- Name and address of vendor or supplier
- Vendor number
- Date received
- Shipped via
- Transportation charges
- Freight bill number and date
- Purchase order number
- Requisition number
- Department of destination
- Received by/checked by
- Accepted/rejected
- Partial or complete
- Comments

FIGURE 20.7 **Purchase order form.** (Courtesy of Winn-Dixie Stores, Inc.)

"WINN-DIXIE - THE SMART PLACE TO GO FOR GOOD THINGS TO EAT"

PURCHASE ORDER FROM

Winn-Dixie Stores, INC.

Shipping Address →

5050 EDGEWOOD COURT, WEST JACKSONVILLE, FLORIDA 32205

TO

PURCHASE ORDER No. J -

SHOW THIS NUMBER ON YOUR BILL OF LADING AND INVOICE

| DATE | | SHIP VIA |
| WEIGHT | | ARRIVAL DATE |

Mailing Address → DEPT. BOX B, JACKSONVILLE, FLORIDA 32203

Signature of Purchaser:

| TERMS | TRADE DISCOUNT |
| FOB | REPRESENTATIVE |

W/D CODE	QUANTITY ORDERED	RECEIVED	PRICE	DELIVERED COST	LOCATION NUMBER	CONV. FACT.	PALLET SIZE	PACK	SIZE	COMMODITY	MANUFACTURE NUMBER

SHIP AS ORDERED TO WEST JACKSONVILLE NO BACK ORDERS ACCEPTED

SHIPPER MUST CERTIFY ON BILL OF LADING THAT FREIGHT HAS BEEN SORTED OR SEGREGATED ACCORDING TO SIZES, BRANDS OR OTHER DISTINGUISHING CHARACTERISTICS AND SO TENDERED TO THE CARRIER.

Repeated line items:

- Item number
- Description
- Quantity received
- Unit of measure
- Condition

Receiving reports should be prenumbered. The distribution of the report should include the purchasing department, the warehouse or stockroom, the originating department, and accounting. An additional copy may be sent to quality control, and one copy is retained by the receiving department.

Accounts Payable Voucher. A voucher is prepared to initiate the disbursement to vendors and other payees for goods or services supplied or amounts owed. It should contain the following data:

- Form description and number
- Name and address of vendor or payee
- Vendor number
- Date of issue
- Vendor invoice number
- Invoice date
- Due date
- Terms

- Purchase order number
- Requisition number
- Purchase order and receiving report attached (Y/N)
- Account number
- Gross amount of purchases
- Net amount of purchases
- Freight and handling charges
- Sales tax (if applicable)
- Total amount due
- Discount
- Net amount due
- Authorization for payment

Accounts payable vouchers should be prenumbered. Vouchers are sometimes prepared as a single copy; in other cases, a second copy is made to support the check sent to the vendor.

Accounts Payable or Payroll Checks. Checks are written to disburse cash to vendors, employees, or other authorized payees. Accounts payable checks, supported by a copy of the voucher, may contain only the name and address of the payee, the net amount, and a reference to the voucher number. If a copy of the voucher is not attached, the voucher information must be summarized on the check stub. Payroll checks should contain the following data:

- Date of check
- Name and address of employee
- Employee number (badge number, clock number, and so on)
- Social security number
- Department or unit
- Occupation code
- State of domicile
- Pay period
- Regular hours
- Overtime hours
- Special hours (holiday, and so on)
- Pay rate
- Gross earnings
- Deductions (itemized)
- Withholdings (itemized by federal and state withholding and FICA)
- Other adjustments or allowances
- Net pay

Frequently, paychecks also contain data on year-to-date gross earnings, deductions, withholdings, and net earnings. Provision of this information relieves the organization of the legal responsibility to issue a W-2 form immediately upon the termination of an employee during the calendar year.

Principal Files

Vendor Master File. The vendor master file should provide for random access of records for interrogation and for retrieval of data in the preparation of purchase orders and accounts payable vouchers. In a manual system, a card file is suitable; in an automated system, magnetic disk storage is most appropriate. The file should typically contain the following data elements:

- Vendor number
- Vendor name and address
- Contact name and telephone number
- Product codes
- Credit terms
- Balance
- Year-to-date purchases
- Year-to-date payments
- Comments

The file is normally sorted by vendor number, and the vendor number is the primary retrieval key.

Open Purchase Order File. The open purchase order file can be accessed randomly or sequentially. In manual systems, the file is often made up of copies of the purchase orders themselves. In automated systems, summary records are usually maintained in a separate file on magnetic disk or tape storage; the copies of the purchase orders are retained as a hardcopy backup and to provide detailed information on the respective orders. The content of the file should be as follows:

- Date of purchase order
- Vendor number
- Purchase order number
- Requisition number
- Department code
- Gross dollar amount

- Date of receipt
- Partial/complete flag
- Open/closed flag
- Comments

The vendor name and address could be added to the file, but this would introduce redundancy, as the same information is retained in the vendor master file and can be retrieved upon specification of the vendor number. If the master file is capable of only sequential access, the inconvenience of retrieval may justify inclusion of the name and address in the open purchase order file, even at the expense of increased storage requirements. The file is normally sorted by purchase order number, but because purchase order numbers are usually assigned in numerical sequence, the file is automatically sorted chronologically.

Open Voucher File. The open voucher file should ideally be accessed randomly, but it could be accessed sequentially if this mode were more convenient. In a manual system, the file could be composed of copies of the vouchers themselves; in a computerized system, a separate summary file is appropriate. The main purpose of the file is for sorting and analysis in the preparation of the cash requirements forecast and other management reports. The typical content of the file is as follows:

- Date of voucher
- Vendor or payee number
- Voucher number
- Vendor invoice number
- Purchase order number
- Requisition number
- Receiving report number
- Account number
- Due date
- Discount date
- Gross amount due
- Discount
- Net amount due
- Date of payment
- Amount paid
- Partial/complete payment flag
- Open/closed flag

The vendor (or payee) name and address could be added (as before) at the cost of data redundancy. The file is normally sorted by voucher number, which will be the same as chronological order if the voucher numbers are assigned sequentially.

Employee Master File. The employee master file can be accessed sequentially because the activity ratio is normally low. Card storage, in a manual system, or magnetic tape storage, in an automated one, are appropriate. The typical content includes the following data:

- Employee number
- Employee name and address
- Telephone number
- Social security number
- Department code
- Date of hire
- Date of birth
- Date of termination
- State of domicile
- Marital status
- Number of dependents
- Pay rate
- Pay type (hourly, salaried, and so on)
- Pay period (weekly, monthly, and so on)
- Deduction basis (itemized)

Quarter-to-date data:

- Gross earnings
- Deductions (itemized)
- Federal withholding
- FICA
- State withholding

Year-to-date data:

- Gross earnings
- Deductions (itemized)
- Federal withholding
- FICA
- State withholding

The file is normally sorted by employee number, and records are retrieved by employee number. Note that records for ex-employees cannot be purged immediately upon termination because of the need to preserve tax information until the end of the calendar year. Entry of the termination date serves as a flag that payroll processing for the particular employee is to be discontinued.

Records for all terminated employees can be purged at year-end.

Selected Reports

Many of the reports in the purchasing cycle were illustrated earlier in the text. Here, a few key reports are described to provide further insight into the type of information presented in them.

Open Purchase Order Report. The open purchase order report is essentially a listing of the open purchase order file, except that master file data such as the vendor name and address may be inserted in each line item. The report may be sorted by purchase order number (i.e., chronologically) or by vendor. In the former case, there is little difference in format between this report and the purchase register. However, the purchase register lists all purchase orders that have been issued during the period, whereas the open purchase order report lists those that remain open at the end of the period: The open purchase order report is a status report, not an activity report. When the report is sorted by vendor, subtotals can be included showing the aggregate dollar amount of purchases outstanding to each vendor. A grand total of outstanding purchases can be presented, whichever mode of sorting is chosen.

Cash Requirements Forecast. The purpose of the cash requirements forecast, or report, is to show the total dollar amount of the outstanding vouchers and, therefore, the amount of cash that is required to pay them. The vouchers are usually broken down into suitable categories to assist management in deciding which vouchers to pay if the available cash resources are insufficient to cover all of them. The categories are sometimes associated with date ranges, in which case the report resembles the schedule of aged accounts payable; the emphasis is on the age of the vouchers and on the availability of discounts. Alternatively, the categories can be associated with vendors, whereupon the emphasis shifts to the amount owed to each one. Management may wish to pay certain vendors and to withhold payment to others. In both cases, some basis is provided for allocating the cash resources according to an appropriate system of priorities. An example of a cash requirements forecast is presented in Figure 20.8. The vouchers in this example are sorted by vendor and then by date. A cumulative total cash requirement is shown for each vendor and also an overall cumulative total.

Payroll Withholding Report. Federal and state returns have to be filed, along with the associated cash deposits, within a prescribed period of time after the issuance of the payroll checks. In addition, quarterly and annual summary reports must be prepared for federal and state revenue authorities. In some states, the 941-A form must be supported by a detailed statement of the earnings and withholdings of each employee. At year-end, similar information appears on the W-2 form.

An example of a quarterly report of earnings and withholdings is shown in Figure 20.9. It shows the withholdings of federal income tax, FICA contributions, and state income tax withholdings, together with applicable totals.

INTERNAL CONTROLS

Control Objectives and Risks

The principal control objectives pertaining to the purchasing cycle are the following:[1]

- Goods or services are purchased only with proper authorization.
- Goods or services received are correctly recorded as to account, amount, and accounting period.
- Salary, wage, and benefit expenses are incurred only for work authorized and actually performed.
- Salary, wages, and benefits are calculated using the proper rates.
- Salaries, wages, and benefits and related liabilities are correctly recorded as to account (department, activity, cost center, etc.), amount, and period.
- Cash disbursements are for goods or services authorized and received.

[1] Ernst and Whinney, *Evaluating Internal Control: A Guide for Management and Directors,* Publ. no. 39078 (Cleveland: Ernst & Whinney, 1979).

FIGURE 20.8   A cash requirements forecast with vendor categories.

page 1

ABC COMPANY

CASH REQUIREMENTS FORECAST

As of 4 / 30 / XX

Vendor number	Name	Voucher number	Due date	Amount	Cum. $ this vendor	Cum. $ overall
123	Aries Co.	3041	3/27/XX	$1,240	$1,240	$1,240
		3176	4/25/XX	570	1,810	1,810
		3204	5/03/XX	3,090	4,900	4,900
			Sub - total	$4,900		
234	Taurus Assoc.	3016	3/18/XX	980	$980	5,880
		3168	4/20/XX	2,330	3,310	8,210
				$3,310		
345	Gemini Bros.	3115	4/04/XX	1,960	$1,960	10,170
		3190	4/28/XX	2,500	4,460	12,670
		3206	5/04/XX	680	5,140	13,350
				$5,140		
			Grand total	$13,350		

Form # Z987, Rev. 2.

• Cash disbursements are recorded correctly as to account, amount and period.

These objectives stem from concerns about potential errors or irregularities. Unauthorized purchases might be made of goods or services that the organization does not need and that could lead to excessive inventories or excessive storage charges. Individuals might be able to acquire items for personal use and charge them to the organization. Purchases might be made at terms that are unfavorable to the organization but that facilitate ''side deals'' for the benefit of unscrupulous individuals.

Purchases might be recorded in the wrong amounts, not recorded at all, or charged to the wrong period—possibly as part of a deliberate attempt to manipulate income. Purchases might be intentionally misclassified or incorrectly recorded to conceal unauthorized acquisitions for personal use. Available discounts might be taken but not recorded and the amounts of the discounts misappropriated.

Payroll expenses might be incurred for work not authorized or work not performed. Corresponding to the errors in payroll expenses, there may be improper accruals of sick leave, vacation, pension, or other benefits. Time cards or work reports may be padded, or time cards may be submitted for fictitious employees. Wages and benefits might continue to be paid to an employee who had been terminated. Earnings may be incorrectly recorded (and paid) as the result of an erroneous wage rate or as the result of an error in the payroll calculations. Errors understating earnings or overstating withholdings and deductions are likely to provoke an immediate challenge from the employee involved, but errors of the opposite type are unlikely to be reported.

Payroll expenses may be wrongly classified or charged

FIGURE 20.9 A quarterly tax withholding report.

						Page 1
		XYZ CORPORATION				
		QUARTERLY WITHHOLDING REPORT				
		As of 9/30/XX				
Employee number	Name	S/S number	Gross earnings	Federal W/H	FICA	State W/H
501	Holden, D.	123 - 45 - 6789	$9,312.15	$1,396.82	$558.72	$744.92
502	Wiley, J	234 - 56 - 7890	7,051.09	1,057.66	493.58	564.09
503	Irwin, R.	345 - 67 - 8901	11,288.00	2,257.60	790.16	959.48
504	Macmillan, A.	456 - 78 - 9012	10,027.34	1,504.05	701.89	802.16
505	Prentice, H.	567 - 89 - 0123	6,990.50	1,048.50	419.40	489.30
506	West, B.	678 - 90 - 1234	7,534.05	1,130.10	452.04	527.38
507	Addison, W.	789 - 01 - 2345	8,118.75	1,317.70	568.26	568.26
508	Business, P.	890 - 12 - 3456	7,942.00	1,191.30	476.52	555.94
509	Grid, P.	901 - 23 - 4567	5,966.25	894.90	357.96	417.62
		Total	$74,230.14	$11,798.63	$4,818.53	$5,629.15

Form # A666 / T

to the wrong accounting period. Intentional overstatement of employee earnings may be related to a kickback arrangement between the employee and an individual in the paymaster's office. Payroll deductions or withholdings may be charged to the employee but not recorded and the amounts misappropriated.

Payments may be made for goods or services that have not been authorized or received. Duplicate payments may be made to a vendor. Payment may be made to the wrong vendor or the check sent to the wrong payee. Vendor invoices may be altered (and possibly photocopied to hide the changes) and the amounts misappropriated. Check signatures or endorsements can be forged, and "void" notations can be erased. Improper check requests may be submitted, or questionable or illegal payments made. Recall that illegal payments were a major target of the Foreign Corrupt Practices Act.

Cash disbursements may be incorrectly recorded or not recorded at all. The disbursement and distribution of the checks can be recorded in different accounting periods. Checks intended for approved vendors may be made out to other individuals, even though the correct payee is listed in the cash disbursements journal. The bank reconciliation may be manipulated to offset misappropriations against old outstanding checks.

Control Measures

Many of the internal control measures described in earlier chapters, particularly those in administrative or general controls, have systemwide relevance. They relate equally to the purchasing cycle, the production cycle, the revenue cycle, and any other transaction cycle that may be involved. The need for written policies and procedures, the insistence on proper authorization of transactions, the separation of duties between the custody of assets and the recording of transactions, independence of the data-processing function from the users, provision for file backup, physical security of the plant and computer facility, and access controls on interactive terminals all are global.

Of more direct interest here are those controls that are peculiar to or have some special relevance to the purchasing cycle and to the achievement of the control objectives listed earlier. The main emphasis is on the need for properly authorizing orders for goods and services and on controls for disbursing cash.

Separation of Duties

There must be adequate separation of duties among the purchasing function, the receiving of goods and services, and the preparation of accounts payable vouchers. This organizational control is intended to reduce the likelihood that goods or services could be diverted for unauthorized use. There must also be separation of duties between the authorization of vouchers and the signing of checks. Here the objective is to ensure that vouchers are properly prepared and supported by associated documentation and that they apply to goods or services validly acquired by the buyer organization.

In the payroll area, there must be separation of duties among the hiring of personnel, the setting of wage rates, the collection and approval of time cards, and the preparation of paychecks. Also, as before, there must be separation between the responsibilities of preparing checks and signing them. The objective of these controls is to ensure that paychecks are issued only to valid employees, for work actually performed under management authorization, and in the proper amounts.

Control of Documents

The need for prenumbered purchase order forms, receiving reports, and accounts payable vouchers has already been mentioned. The transactions for which they are the source documents should be entered in numerical sequence in the respective journals or registers. All documents numbers must be accounted for, including those that are spoiled or voided. Any gaps in the numerical sequence must be identified and explained, and any duplicate document numbers must be investigated and resolved. All deviations from the unbroken sequence of document numbers must be promptly identified in an exception report. Vouchers should be reconciled with purchase orders and receiving reports before payment is authorized.

All accounts payable and payroll checks should also be prenumbered and control maintained over all document numbers from the time of preparation of the checks through to the reconciliation of the bank statement and the return of the canceled checks.

The inventory of action documents, such as purchase orders and checks, should be carefully controlled, and only a few authorized people should be given access to them. Having boxes of unissued purchase order forms and check forms standing next to the printer in the computer room invites trouble.

Authorization of Transactions

Proper authorization must be given for ordering goods or services; for accepting vendor prices, terms, and conditions; for receiving goods or services; for collecting and approving time cards; and for disbursing cash.

The authority for ordering goods and services normally resides with the originating department manager. This individual may have the authority to sign purchase requisitions up to a prescribed dollar ceiling, whereas larger orders may require the approval of a higher-level manager. The authority to accept vendor prices and conditions is usually shared between the manager of the originating department and the purchasing department. The latter can be expected to have greater experience in securing favorable prices and terms and experience in understanding trade-offs between price and quality, or between price and ready availability. On the other hand, the purchase will ultimately be charged against the originating department's budget, and the manager of that department should normally have the last word on what constitutes acceptable quality or an acceptable delivery lead time. Sometimes there are established policies regarding the sources from which goods and services can be procured. When there are available sources within the organization or among its affiliates, managers may not be free to buy from outside vendors.

The authority to receive and check incoming shipments of goods lies with the receiving department and quality control. When services are being procured, and occasionally when specialized goods are involved, the judgment of the originating department manager may be necessary in deciding whether the vendor has met all necessary responsibilities.

The collection of employee time cards and the verification of their authenticity and content are normally the responsibility of the employee's immediate supervisor. The supervisor must verify that the employees actually worked the number of hours claimed and that the work was duly authorized. Particularly attention must be given to any claims for overtime or special-time rates. Wherever possible, time clocks should be installed to provide an objective basis for labor inputs; however, additional administrative controls may be necessary to prevent abuses such as the punching of one employee's time card by another individual.

The authority to prepare checks for signature lies with the accounts payable department in the case of vendor checks and with the paymaster in the case of payroll checks. In manual systems, the checks are signed by a representative of the treasurer's staff. This individual has the final responsibility for verifying that all supporting documents have been properly prepared and that the documents properly substantiate the claim for payment. Management policies should stipulate that a countersignature is required on all checks exceeding a specified amount. In computerized systems, the checks are normally printed automatically and may also be signed automatically using facsimile plates. Special controls are needed to prevent abuse of the automatic check-writing facilities. The check-signing machine and signature plates should be locked, and access to them should be restricted to a small number of authorized persons.

Other Input Controls

The need to ensure that all transactions are properly authorized can be met by having the responsible individual sign or initial all applicable documents. No paperwork should be processed further without that authorization.

In manual systems, it is not usually too difficult to limit access to activities in the purchasing cycle to authorized persons. But special care must be taken in computerized systems, particularly those permitting interactive processing from remote terminals. It would be inappropriate if payroll programs or files could be accessed from the warehouse, or accounts payable programs or files from the training school. Restriction of access is important throughout the information system, but it is particularly important to the purchasing cycle because of its sensitivity to irregularities. Controls must be built into interactive systems, to restrict operation of program, or access to files, to designated terminals in the departments that are authorized to service those applications. Passwords provide an additional safeguard, but they should not be relied on to carry the full burden of protection.

The processing of accounts payable vouchers and the processing of the payroll are normally batch processes, whether or not an interactive system is in use, and they lend themselves well to the incorporation of batch controls. Card counts, record counts, control totals, cross footings, and hash totals all should be employed to verify that batches of vouchers or time cards are complete and that duplicate processing cannot take place. The batch controls should extend throughout processing to the preparation, signing, and distribution of checks. When automatic check-signing equipment is being used, the meter readings on the machine provide a further batch total that should be reconciled with earlier totals.

File Controls

Care must be taken to verify that the correct master files and tax tables are used for accounts payable and payroll processing. All purchasing, receiving, accounts payable, and payroll files must be protected against unauthorized access or modification. File maintenance activities must be carefully controlled, particularly when wage rate fields are exposed to possible modification or update. Tax tables must be suitably modified to reflect changes in withholding amounts and associated wage brackets as they become effective.

Processing Controls

Reasonableness checks should be made to validate data entries for purchases, receipts, labor hours, and disbursements. Such controls are readily programmed into computerized systems, but they can also be developed as processing procedures for manual systems. All order quantities should be positive, and all quantities received should also be positive (unless returns are treated as negative receipts in the particular system). It may be feasible to compare the numerical values of the quantities appearing in accounts payable and payroll transactions with some predetermined standard. An order for 100,000 nuts and bolts may be valid, but one for 100,000 delivery trucks would most likely represent an error. All labor hours should be positive numbers and should bear a reasonable relationship to the standard 40-hour workweek. A claim for an unusually large number of hours should be treated as an exception for closer scrutiny. Similarly, a wage rate substantially greater than some reference, such as a negotiated union rate, should also be identified on an exception report. Routine independent checks should be made of all transaction data, and supervisory approval should be mandatory before exception items are processed further. The exceptions may be correct, but they may be the key to identifying inadequacies in the verification of input data or the key to uncovering an attempt to perpetrate a deliberate irregularity.

Output Controls

A check register must be prepared in parallel with the preparation and signing of checks, listing the check number, some appropriate reference such as a voucher number, the name of the payee, and the amount of the check. The number of checks written should be reconciled to the number of vouchers approved for payment or to the number of employees active for that pay period. As noted, all check forms must be accounted for, and any spoiled or voided checks retained for audit. At the time that the bank reconciliation is performed, the canceled checks should be compared with the entries made in the check register and the disbursements journal. The bank reconciliation should be carried out by an individual who is independent of the check preparation and signing.

Care must be taken to verify that all paychecks are properly distributed to employees and that all vendor checks are mailed.

Many organizations maintain a separate bank account for payroll. This account serves as an imprest fund; it is replenished shortly before the paychecks are distributed, and the balance is reduced to zero (or to some nominal amount) after the checks are cashed. No deposits are accepted by the bank except the ones for the periodic replenishment of funds, and only payroll checks are written on the accounts. Imprest funds of this type are also sometimes used for accounts payable or for the reimbursement of employee expenses. This practice is often used at branch offices, at which the number of people is too small to support the proper segregation of duties. The objective is to restrict the amounts that can be withdrawn from the account and also to monitor the disbursement activities. The bank statement would normally be mailed directly to the organization's headquarters for reconciliation with copies of vouchers furnished by the branch supervisor.

Some small organizations are sometimes tempted to make disbursements in the form of currency or to "net out" a receivable and a payable and write a check for the difference. Such practices are unwise because of the resulting confusion of the audit trails. Except for the very smallest amounts, for which a petty cash fund is appropriate, all disbursements should be made by check. Also—except in rare circumstances in which a final settlement is being made between disputing parties—receivables and payables should be separated.

SUMMARY

The purchasing cycle deals with the acquisition of productive resources—materials and labor—in preparation for conversion and distribution. It embraces the applications of purchasing, receiving, accounts payable, and payroll. The purchasing function relates to the acquisition of raw materials, supplies, services, and outside contracts. The acquisition of materials and the hiring of labor share common features, from an accounting viewpoint, except for the rather conspicuous feature of tax withholding and the legal requirement to maintain detailed employee records for tax and other purposes.

The principal documents in the purchasing cycle are purchase requisitions and purchase orders, receiving documents, vendor invoices, accounts payable vouchers, expense claims, time cards, and checks. The principal files are the vendor and employee master files, the receiving file, the open puchase order file, and the open voucher file. Major reports are the purchases journal, the open purchase order and open voucher reports, the cash requirements forecast, the check register, the labor distribution report, and the payroll-withholding report.

Internal controls in the purchasing cycle emphasize the need for proper authorization for purchases, the need to compare vendor invoices with the goods or services received, and the need to control carefully the disbursement of cash. In the payroll area, the main control emphasis is on the authorization of work to be performed, on paycheck preparation and distribution, and on the proper disposition of deduction and withholding amounts. In this last area, the organization acts as a temporary custodian of public funds.

BIBLIOGRAPHY

Arens, Alvin A., and D. Dewey Ward. *Systems Understanding for Auditing.* Haslett, Mich.: Systems Publications, 1981.

Ernst & Whinney. *Evaluating Internal Control: A Guide for Management and Directors*, Publ. no. 39078. Cleveland: Ernst & Whinney, 1979.

Forms for the Key Operations of Business. Glenview, Ill.: Moore Business Forms, 1977.

Gelinas, Ulrie J. "Using an Illustration of a Conceptual Information System to Improve Pedagogy in MIS Courses." *MAS Communication*, vol. 5, no. 3, October 1981, pp. 17–27.

Pescow, Jerome K., ed. *Encyclopedia of Accounting Systems.* Englewood Cliffs, N.J.: Prentice-Hall, 1976.

DISCUSSION QUESTIONS AND PROBLEMS

1. Define and discuss the following terms:

- Acceptance report
- Cash requirements forecast
- Deliverable items
- Employee master file
- Goods
- Open purchase order file
- Open purchase order report
- Open voucher file
- Open voucher report
- Payroll deductions
- Purchasing cycle
- Purchasing department
- Purchase order
- Purchase register
- Purchase requisition
- Receiving department
- Receiving report
- Request for proposal
- Request for quotation
- Services
- Tax tables
- Tax withholding
- Tax-withholding report
- Time card, time sheet
- Vendor master file
- Voucher

2. Describe the steps most likely to be taken to procure a custom computer program from an outside software house. Assume that the need for the new program was determined by the accounting department. Assume also that the organization has a data-processing department but that there are no in-house programmers with the required degree of experience to write the program.

3. A purchase order was issued to Z Corporation for the procurement of several items:

Description	Quantity	Price
Grade A widgets	100	$20
Grade B widgets	50	15
Grade C widgets	30	10
Grade D widgets	80	8

When the shipment arrived and was checked, a receiving report was prepared containing the following data:

Description	Quantity	Condition
Grade A widgets	80	OK
Grade B widgets	50	OK
Grade C widgets	80	damaged
Grade D widgets	200	OK

A few days later, an invoice was received from Z Corporation in the amount of $4,727.50. The invoice listed the items and quantities shipped, except that 100 units of Grade A widgets had been billed. Also, the price charged for Grade B widgets was 5 percent higher than that shown on Z Corporation's current price list.

Required

Discuss the actions to be taken with respect to (a) the shipment and (b) the invoice.

4. The transaction file and master file included in a simplified payroll application are shown in the table at the end of this section. Post the transaction data to the master file, being sure to update all appropriate fields in the master file.

5. Four employees of K Company submitted weekly time sheets containing the following data:

Employee	S/S #	Regular Hours	Overtime Hours
Apollo, A.	987–65–4321	40	0
Bacchus, B.	876–54–3210	36	0
Ceres, C.	765–43–2109	40	4
Demeter, D.	654–32–1098	40	8

All the employees earn $10 per hour except Ceres, who earns $12 per hour. Time and a half is paid for overtime (the overtime premium is 50 percent). A deduction of $15 per week is made from all employees as their contribution to a group insurance plan. In addition, Apollo and Demeter deposit 10 percent of their gross earnings in a credit union.

Federal income tax is withheld according to the following schedule:

Weekly Earnings	Withholding
0 to $200	10% of total earnings
$200 to $500	$20 + 20% of earnings over $200
$500 and over	$80 + 30% of earnings over $500

Social security (FICA) tax is withheld at a fixed rate of 7 percent on earnings up to a year-to-date total of $30,000; none of the employees has yet approached that

limit. State withholding tax is figured at one fifth of the federal income tax withholding.

Required

Determine for each employee and in total for all four employees:

a. Gross earnings for the week
b. Deductions
c. Federal income tax withholding
d. FICA withholding
e. State income tax withholding
f. Net pay

6. Design a payroll check suitable for K Company mentioned in Problem 5, and insert the data for Mrs. D. Demeter. This employee's year-to-date data (before inclusion of the current week's figures) are as follows:

Gross earnings	$10,320
Deductions:	
Group insurance	240
Credit union	1,032
Withholdings:	
Federal income tax	2,090
FICA	722
State income tax	418

7. a. Design the layout for an open purchase order report for Grand Manufacturing Company. The data to be included are

Purchase order number
Date of order
Requisition number
Name of originating department
Vendor number
Vendor name
Requested delivery date
Gross dollar amount
Number of items to be delivered

b. Redesign the purchase order to include a list of the items ordered, specifically, the following information:

Manufacturer's item number
In-house part number
Description

Quantity ordered
Unit of measure (each, pair, dozen, quart,
   feet, pounds, etc.)
Unit price
Extended price

8. Design the purchase order form to be used by Grand Manufacturing Company, as described in Problem 7. The company's address is Box 999, Oceanville, Kentucky 36070.

In addition to the data listed in Problem 7, the following information is to appear on the purchase order:

Vendor address
Shipping instructions (U.S. mail, truck,
   parcel service, etc.)
Insurance value
F.O.B. point
Terms

9. Draw a columnar document flowchart, similar to that in Figure 20.5, for the flow of paperwork in the ordering and payment for services provided by an outside contractor. The work consists of decorating the factory building, relocating certain pieces of machinery, and installing new electric wiring. The work is expected to take three months and to cost a total of $35,000. Monthly progress payments of $8,000 are to be made, and the balance of $11,000 is to be paid upon completion of the work.

10. The cash requirements report for Poor Company is shown in the table at the end of this section. At the date of the report, Poor Company had available cash resources of $6,500. A further $3,000 is expected to become available within another 15 days.

Required
a. Prepare a recommended payment schedule for the vouchers listed in the table, assuming that there are no special priorities to be observed.
b. Management is under pressure to pay Xenon Co.'s invoices in full so as to obtain an extension of badly needed credit. What revisions of the payment schedule would be necessary to accommodate management's wishes?

11. Slick Joe works on the loading bay of Ace Trucking Company. From overhearing a conversation in a bar,

Joe learns of a social indiscretion involving Mrs. White of the paymaster's office. Mrs. White is a very conservative person and a highly trusted employee; however, she is insecure about her social image, and she currently is in financial difficulties.

Under threat of blackmail from Joe, Mrs. White reluctantly agrees to falsify his earnings records to show more hours than he has actually worked and a substantially higher pay rate. In return, he promises her 10 percent of the additional amount appearing on his paychecks.

Required
What control weaknesses would have to exist for Slick Joe to be successful in perpetrating this irregularity?

12. In a computerized accounts payable system, a daily batch control report is prepared listing the documents contained in each batch of payables vouchers, their dollar amounts, and certain control totals. These data are subsequently compared with the data on the batch transmittal slips that accompany the transactions to data processing. The control report prepared for October 13 contained the information shown in the table at the end of this section.

The transmittal slip accompanying batch no. 12345 indicated a document count of 10, a batch total of $10,155, and a hash total of 4,490. The hash total is formed by summing the parts of the document numbers following the hyphen.

Required
Investigate the discrepancies between the data on the transmittal slip and those on the batch control report, and discuss your findings.

13. A local branch of Uranus Industries has been established to service the company's products in East Tennessee. Some large accounts are covered by service contracts and billed from the home office in Ohio. But many small repair and maintenance jobs are handled on a time-and-materials basis for cash. A small inventory of supply items and spare parts is maintained, and some cash sales are made to walk-in customers. The branch is operated by Buck James and his wife Sara, who works as Buck's secretary and bookkeeper. Four field service men are employed at the branch.

The branch has its own bank account into which cash receipts are deposited and on which checks are written for the payroll and to pay for incidental purchases of supplies. Most of the inventory is shipped in by truck from the home office.

As an internal auditor at the home office, you are concerned about the control of cash receipts and disbursements at the East Tennessee branch. There has been no problem so far, but you feel that more formal controls are desirable. Ideally, you would like to see all cash receipts and disbursements handled out of the home office, but this is infeasible because of the nature of the business. You also realize that an effective separation of duties is out of the question because of the small size of the branch staff.

Required

a. Propose a system for cash disbursements at the branch that would reduce the risk of defalcation.
b. How would your system interface with the cash receipts activities at the branch?
c. What additional controls would you suggest to improve the control environment at the branch?

14. During the initial design process, the following specifications were proposed for the purchases transaction file and the open purchase order file:

Purchases Transaction File	Open Purchase Order File
Date of issuance	Purchase order number
Purchase requisition number	Date of issuance
Purchase order number	Purchase requisition number
Originating department	Originating department
Vendor number	Vendor number
Vendor name	Vendor name
Vendor address	Vendor address
In-house item number*	In-house item number*
Vendor catalog number*	Vendor catalog number*
Description*	Description*
Unit of measure*	Unit of measure*
Quantity*	Quantity*
Unit cost*	Unit cost*

* Repeated fields

Transaction records are to be retrieved by date of issuance of the purchase order. Open purchase order records are to be retrieved by purchase order number.

Required

Analyze these file specifications to provide a normalized logical data structure defining the schema of a data base management system. Provide tables and relationships describing your final normalized form, and draw a data access diagram showing how data elements would be retrieved.

15. a. Draw a HIPO overview diagram describing raw materials procurement.
b. Draw a HIPO detail diagram describing the preparation of a receiving document.

16. A pertinent internal control objective for the purchasing cycle is

Wages and benefit expenses are to be incurred only for work authorized and actually performed.

Required

a. List the risks (the things that could go wrong) if this control objective were not achieved.
b. List applicable controls to reduce the risks referred to in (a).

Data for Problem 4
Payroll Journal (Transaction) File

Date	Employee No.	Regular Hours	Overtime Hours	Pay Rate	Gross Pay	Deductions
9/30	10	40	0	$7.00	$280.00	$ 56.00
9/30	11	40	5	6.00	285.00	71.25
9/30	12	36	0	8.00	288.00	86.40
9/30	13	40	0	7.50	300.00	90.00
9/30	14	40	10	6.50	357.50	143.00
9/30	15	0	0	7.25	0.00	0.00
9/30	16	40	2	7.00	301.00	105.35

Employee Master File

Employee No.	Name	Current Period Earnings Gross	Deductions	Net	Year-to-Date Earnings Gross	Deductions	Net
10	Dakota, S.	$280.00	$56.00	$224.00	$1,400.00	$280.00	$1,120.00
11	York, N.				1,425.00	356.25	1,068.75
12	Carolina, S.				1,152.00	345.60	806.40
13	Island, R.				1,500.00	450.00	1,050.00
14	Mexico, N.				0.00	0.00	0.00
15	Virginia, W.				290.00	72.50	217.50

Data for Problem 10
*Poor Company Cash Requirements Report
(as of May 15, 19A)*

Vendor	Voucher No.	Due Date	Gross Amount	Discount Date	Discount Percent	Cumulative Amount*
Helium Co.	332	5/03	$ 250	4/13	2%	$ 250
	346	5/10	1,300	4/20	2	1,550
	391	6/03	875	5/19	2	2,425
Neon Co.	318	4/20	700	4/01	1	700
	329	5/01	550	4/10	1	1,250
	358	5/15	2,400	4/25	1	3,650
	373	5/26	160	5/06	1	3,810
Xenon Co.	325	4/23	300	4/03	1.5	300
	347	5/10	1,900	4/20	1.5	2,200
	386	6/01	2,500	5/17	1.5	4,700

* Cumulative cash requirement, by vendor, excluding discount.

Data for Problem 12

Batch Number	Document Number	Transaction Date	Amount
12345	24-445	10/04/XX	560.00
	24-446	10/04/XX	275.00
	24-447	10/07/XX	1,360.00
	24-448	10/08/XX	945.00
	24-449	10/08/XX	1,920.00
	24-449	10/09/XX	1,075.00
	24-450	10/10/XX	450.00
	24-451	10/11/XX	2,100.00
	24-453	10/12/XX	880.00
	24-455	10/12/XX	880.00
		Batch total	$10,445.00
		Document count	10
		Hash total	4,491

21

The Production Cycle

LEARNING OBJECTIVES

After studying this chapter you should be able to

- Describe the major activities of the production cycle.
- Explain the principles of materials management and production control.
- Explain the principles of providing customer services.
- Discuss the accumulation of costs of production or of services provided.
- Identify the principal inputs, files, processes, and outputs in the production cycle.
- Identify the content of major documents, files, and reports in this cycle.
- Identify the main control issues in the production cycle.
- Discuss the main control measures in this cycle.

CHAPTER OUTLINE

OVERVIEW OF THE PRODUCTION CYCLE

Receipt of Raw Materials
Issuance to Production
Conversion into Finished Goods or Provision of Services
Disposition of Finished Goods
Management of Inventories
Accounting Transactions

STRUCTURE OF THE PRODUCTION CYCLE

Inputs, Files, and Outputs
Processes
Key Documents
Principal Files
Selected Reports

INTERNAL CONTROLS

Control Objectives and Risks
Control Measures
Separation of Duties
Control of Documents
Authorization of Transactions
Other Input Controls
File Controls
Processing and Output Controls

SUMMARY
BIBLIOGRAPHY
DISCUSSION QUESTIONS AND PROBLEMS

OVERVIEW OF THE PRODUCTION CYCLE

The production cycle is concerned with the conversion of raw materials into finished goods, with the provision of services to customers, and with the management of inventories. It is sometimes referred to as the *manufacturing cycle,* the *conversion cycle,* or the *inventory cycle*.

The production cycle is found in its most complete form in the manufacturing enterprise, with its production activities and inventories of raw materials, work in process, and finished goods. It is found in a similar form in the construction company, which maintains an inventory of materials and accumulates costs in a construction-in-progress account that is the direct analog of work in process. The production cycle is also significant in some types of service organizations, particularly those that provide customer services and bill customers according to the precise nature and volume of the services rendered.

An example is the repair and maintenance firm, in

which a job order costing system may be adopted for the accumulation of labor and material costs for billing purposes. Another example is the public accounting firm. The production cycle is more limited in form in the merchandising or distribution enterprise, which may have only a single inventory and only the vestige of a production activity. A production cycle may be identified, at least by analogy, in the extractive and agricultural industries and in the health care field. This chapter emphasizes the manufacturing organization, but many of the concepts apply more widely, and occasional reference will be made to applications in other types of organizations.

In the manufacturing organization, the production cycle embraces the applications of production control, cost accounting, and inventory management. This last should, more properly, be treated as two separate applications: one concerned with the management of raw materials and the other concerned with finished goods. The principle activities are as follows:

- Receipt of materials into raw materials inventory
- Issuance of materials to production
- Conversion of raw materials into finished goods
- Transfer of the product into finished goods inventory
- Management of inventory levels
- Recording of the accounting transactions

Related activities include the maintenance of quality control and the monitoring of inventory valuations and the possible write-down, or write-off, of valuation to reflect loss of economic value. Another important activity is the periodic physical count of inventory to verify the correctness of the accounting records or (in a periodic inventory system) actually to provide data for inventory values and cost of sales. Emphasis is on the perpetual inventory, rather than on the periodic inventory, approach, because of the greater role played in the former by accounting records as the repository of cost data and as the basis for inventory control.

Receipt of Raw Materials

"Raw materials" include sheet metal, rolled or extruded metal sections, lumber, sand, concrete, petroleum, plastic, cloth, and other basic materials. It also includes the purchased parts and subassemblies used in production. Silicon chips and printed circuits represent raw materials to the computer manufacturer, even though they are finished goods to a components supplier. Raw materials include such "indirect" materials as paint, lubricant, wire, thread, and screws.

The ordering and receiving of raw materials forms part of the purchasing cycle discussed in the previous chapter. In the case of commonly used materials, inventory levels are routinely monitored to identify those items requiring replenishment. In the case of new materials, or materials used only occasionally, requirements may be identified in anticipation of future production; sometimes the first orders for materials are placed more than one year before production is scheduled to commence.

After materials have arrived and have been checked, they are transferred to the warehouse or stores and are recorded in raw materials inventory. The movement of goods into the warehouse and any subsequent movement from one warehouse location to another should be ac-
companied by suitable paperwork. This is necessary to document the transfer of responsibility for the goods from one individual or group to the next. Upon arrival at the new location, a warehouse or stores acceptance report is issued, analogous to the receiving report prepared when the goods first arrived at the plant. Subsequently, the goods become part of the inventory at that location, and the inventory records show the identity and quantity of the goods in question.

Issuance to Production

The list of materials and their respective quantities required in the manufacture of a unit or batch of goods is called the *bill of materials*. It is usually prepared by the production control department from engineering specifications. If complex products are involved, the preparation of the bill of materials can be complicated, and computer programs are often used to "explode" the product, first into its component subassemblies and then into its basic materials and parts; sometimes a number of levels of subassemblies can be identified.

Some of the materials may be needed for production to start; other materials may not be needed until production has progressed to a later stage. Batches of materials are issued from the warehouse or stores in response to materials requisitions, or stores requisitions, initiated by the factory department in which the manufacturing operation is being carried out.

The amount of material issued is recorded for costing purposes and, of course, depletes the raw materials inventory. Quantities can be compared with the amounts listed on the bill of materials as a measure of the efficiency of materials usage. If materials are spoiled and new materials have to be issued in their place, a spoilage report should be prepared to record the incurrence of abnormal waste or scrap. The spoiled materials are either reworked or are returned to the stores for subsequent disposition. Even under normal conditions, a certain amount of scrap is usually generated, and records of the amounts should be maintained so that the scrap material can be accounted for properly. The scrap or waste material will be recycled, sold, or otherwise disposed of. Environmental considerations may demand that the waste be suitably treated before release from the plant or transferred to approved disposal sites; the problems of disposal of hazardous waste have received much publicity in recent years.

Conversion into Finished Goods or Provision of Services

The steps taken to convert raw materials into finished goods are usually laid down in the form of work orders prepared by the production control department. Work orders are also used to detail the work required in service and maintenance operations. The work orders identify the tasks to be performed, the labor grades to which they should be assigned, and often the standard allotment of labor hours to each task. Subsequently, as the work proceeds, time cards and labor tickets will be submitted as a basis for determining labor costs. In some cases, the time cards themselves indicate the work orders or jobs on which labor was expended; in others, the time cards specify only the total hours worked each day, and the breakdown of hours by job is shown on a separate labor ticket.

The three cost inputs to production are the costs of materials, labor, and factory overhead; this last reflects the costs of operating the production facility, and it is applied to the product via a process of allocation. The materials input is taken from the materials requisitions or stores requisitions, and the labor input is taken from the time cards or labor tickets. Overhead is applied according to some appropriate "base," such as direct labor hours or direct labor cost; in a machine-intensive operation, a more suitable base may be machine hours. Either plantwide or departmental overhead rates may be used.

In a job order cost system, the cost inputs are accumulated for individual units or batches of product. In a process costing system, the costs are accumulated and distributed to the product on an average basis, usually at the end of each month. Job order costing clearly provides more detailed product cost data and also better control. On the other hand, it is a more expensive system and can be justified only when there is a need for the higher-quality information. Job order costing is most suitable for low-volume, high-cost items and for custom goods or services in which detailed costs are required for billing purposes; process costing is suitable for low-cost, high-volume, mass-produced items. Both job order and process costing systems can be adapted to a standard cost environment. For further details on job order costing, process costing, and standard cost systems, the reader is referred to any introductory text on cost accounting.

As the manufacturing process continues, the product reaches one or more points at which it is inspected for quality. The inspection may include measuring, weighing, or testing the product to determine whether it conforms to specifications. It is carried out by the quality control, or quality assurance, department. Sometimes all goods are subject to inspection, but more commonly the production is sampled and only a small proportion inspected; the latter approach is essential if the inspection process results in the destruction of the item in question. If inspection sampling is used, the results must be interpreted on a statistical basis. Any units or batches of product that are rejected by inspection are returned for rework or are scrapped. Appropriate records must be kept of the inspection procedure and its outcome, and scrap or spoilage reports prepared as necessary.

Disposition of the Finished Goods

Upon completion of the conversion process, the goods may be transferred to finished goods inventory to await sale and shipment. Alternatively, they may be shipped directly to the customer without passing through inventory. This latter disposition is the normal case when the goods are produced to the specifications of a particular customer. The shipment of goods to customers represents part of the revenue cycle, which is discussed in Chapter 22.

Management of Inventories

Inventories are replenished by the receipt of purchased raw materials or by the completion of finished goods; they are depleted by issuance of materials to production or by the shipment of products to customers. These transactions must be processed so as to update the perpetual inventory records of the organization. Specifically, the transactions must be posted to one or more inventory master files. Normally, separate master files are maintained for raw materials and for finished goods; there is no essential difference between them, but they are usually separated as a matter of convenience.

In a manual system, the master files are typically maintained on inventory cards. Receipts and issuances of each item are recorded, and a running balance is determined for control purposes. In an automated system, the master files can be maintained on magnetic tape or magnetic disk. Disk media have the advantage of providing random access for query or interrogation of inventory levels. However, there may be serious problems of data currency unless posting is carried out at frequent intervals, say, daily; the data in the master file are current only immediately after posting has been completed. Real-time systems provide the only effective solution to data currency problems in fast-moving inventories.

In addition to providing for query of inventory levels, the master files form the basis for the preparation of at least two management reports. One is the inventory status, or stock status, report, which lists all items together with their on-hand balances and associated cost data. Separate status reports are usually prepared for raw materials and for finished goods. The inventories may be maintained at standard cost. Alternatively, the cost data may reflect any one of the cost flow models, such as FIFO, LIFO, weighted average, or specific identification. The structure of the master files is more complex if any model except weighted average is used because of the need to store multiple cost layers. If the weighted-average model is used or if standard costs are employed, there will be only one unit cost.

The other report is the reorder report, which identifies items whose on-hand balance has fallen below, or is in danger of soon falling below, a predetermined reorder point. The reorder point depends on the anticipated future usage or demand for the item and on the lead time for obtaining replenishment—either from the purchase of materials from suppliers or from the production of finished goods. Reorder points must be routinely reviewed to ensure that they reflect current information. Data on usage levels are often included in the inventory status report for this purpose. In some automated systems, the identification of items needing replenishment leads directly to the preparation of a purchase requisition or a production order. But more commonly the data on

the reorder report provides input to a discretionary decision by a stock clerk or inventory manager. Most managers like to maintain discretionary control over inventory levels so that they can take into account subjective factors such as prospects for future demand. Sales and production personnel also make significant input into decisions of this type.

In the case of raw materials inventories, purchase agents often have a weekly or monthly budget for purchases, and they can exercise discretion as to which items to buy at any given time. If an opportunity arises to make an advantageous purchase of one item, they may defer the acquisition of other items that are not critical.

Perpetual inventory records are verified at the time of the physical count, which may be made just once per year to coincide with the annual audit or more frequently for control purposes. Discrepancies between the records and the results of the physical count can arise for one of several reasons. The most common reason is that there are errors in the inventory records themselves. Receipts or issuances may not have been properly recorded, or there may have been unreported loss, waste, shrinkage, or breakage. But shortages may also be due to theft, and some types of inventory are obviously more attractive to thieves than are others. The reasons for the discrepancies between the records and the physical count must be investigated so that appropriate action can be taken to prevent recurrence. Also, the records must be adjusted to bring them into line with the results of the count.

Inventories, whether of raw materials or of finished goods, are normally valued at historical cost—either the cost of acquisition or the cost of manufacture. But accounting conservatism dictates that if an impairment of value is identified, the items in question must be written down, or even written off, so that inventory values will not be overstated. An impairment of value can result from deterioration or substandard manufacturing quality, or it may arise from a decline in market value. Inventory values must not be allowed to exceed market values on an individual basis or on a global basis for the whole of the current inventory.

Various types of adjustment are required either to reconcile reported quantities with the physical count or to reduce inventory valuations. These adjustments are usually entered in the form of transactions, sometimes together with receipts or issuances and sometimes as a separate type of transaction. The adjustment entries are subsequently posted to the master files in the normal manner.

Accounting Transactions

Formal accounting transactions are the receipt and issuance of raw materials; the accumulation of manufacturing costs, including the costs of materials, labor, and overhead; the transfer of completed goods out of production; and the final sale of finished goods inventory. The recording of these transactions is central to the valuation of raw materials, work-in-process, and finished goods inventories and to the determination of cost of sales.

As noted, the recording of inventory transactions requires either that a standard cost system be adopted or that a suitable cost flow model be selected to account for the receipt of items at different costs. There is a trend toward the increasing popularity of LIFO because of its favorable tax implications in times of rapid and continuing inflation. On the other hand, the use of LIFO complicates the recording process by making it necessary to maintain multiple cost layers for a single inventory item. It will be seen later in this chapter that the file structure may need to be radically altered if a change is made from, say, the weighted-average model to LIFO.

The acquisition of raw materials forms an interface between the production cycle and the purchasing cycle. The associated accounting transaction incurs a payable and its subsequent liquidation at the time of payment. Correspondingly, the sale of finished goods forms an interface with the revenue cycle (Chapter 22), and the transaction establishes a receivable to be collected at a later date.

The accumulation of production costs is the most complex set of accounting transactions. These include the issuance of materials to production, the distribution of direct labor charges, and the application of factory overhead. The accumulation of overhead costs represents a further complication.

Overhead may be applied to the product on the basis of either a plantwide or a departmental rate, but in both cases, provision must be made for the disposition of any residual under- or overapplied overhead remaining at the end of the accounting period. Production costs may be traced to their product cost object by way of a job order or process costing system, according (as discussed earlier) to the quality of the accounting information that is required and the price that can be justified in terms of bookkeeping costs. If a standard cost system is not used, there must be a proper accounting for variations in unit costs from one unit of product to another. If standard costs are used, variance accounts must be established to handle the discrepancies between actual and standard costs for materials, labor, and overhead, and provision must be made for the disposition of the variances when the books are closed.

STRUCTURE OF THE PRODUCTION CYCLE

Inputs, Files, and Outputs

A summary of the inputs, files, and outputs associated with the production cycle is presented in Table 21.1. The input source documents consist of receiving reports, production orders, time cards or labor tickets, and sales orders or picking tickets. The receiving reports form an interface with the purchasing cycle, and the sales orders and picking tickets from an interface with the revenue cycle. Other inputs include adjustment entries to the raw materials and finished goods inventories, engineering specifications, and overhead allocations. Intermediate documents include materials requisitions, which are an output from the production control application and an input to raw materials inventory and work in process, and completed production cards, which are outputs from work in process and inputs to finished goods inventory.

Output documents (aside from the intermediate documents already mentioned) include work orders, job cards, and purchase requisitions. Purchase requisitions form an interface with the purchasing cycle. The principal output reports consist of the stock status report and reorder report for each type of inventory, and a number of reports associated with production control and work in process. The output from production control includes the production schedule and the bill of materials. That

TABLE 21.1 Summary of the Inputs, Files, and Outputs Associated with the Production Cycle

Application	Inputs	Files	Outputs
Raw materials inventory	Receiving report (Materials requisition) Adjustments	Raw materials inventory Receiving file Issuance and adjustment file	Stock status report Reorder report Purchase requisition
Production control	Production order Engineering specifications	Production data file	Production schedule Bill of materials Materials requisition Work order
Cost accounting (Work in process)	(Materials requisition) Time card, labor ticket Labor distribution Overhead allocation	Open job file Standard cost file	Materials and labor usage report Variance report Scrap report Production status report Job card Completed production card
Finished goods inventory	(Completed production card) Sales order Picking ticket Adjustments	Finished goods inventory master file Completed product file Shipment and adjustment file	Stock status report Reorder report Production order

from work in process, or cost accounting, includes the materials and labor usage report, the materials waste and scrap report, the production status report, and variance reports required in a standard cost system.

The principal files are the master files for both inventories and the open job (or work-in-process) file. The open job file is analogous to the open purchase order file in the purchasing cycle (Chapter 20). Its records remain open until individual jobs are completed and are transferred out of production. Transaction files include the receiving file, the raw materials issuance file, the production data file, the completed product file, and the shipment file. The production data file accumulates materials, labor, and overhead costs prior to their posting to the open job file. Additional transaction files may be required for adjusting entries to both inventory master files if these adjustments are not combined with either the receipt or issuance transactions.

In a standard cost system, a further master file is required for the standard allowances for materials and labor, the standard materials prices, and labor and overhead rates.

Processes

System flowcharts of the principal processes in the production cycle are presented in Figures 21.1 through 21.4. Figure 21.1 shows the processes associated with the management of raw materials inventory. Goods are received from suppliers, and the receiving transactions may be stored in a temporary transaction file prior to posting or may be posted immediately in a real-time system. Materials are issued to production upon the submittal of materials requisitions, and these transactions also are posted to the master file. Adjusting entries are shown combined with issuances in Figure 21.1; they could equally well be combined with receipts or be treated as a third type of transaction and stored in a separate transaction file.

The purpose of inventory posting is to update the on-hand balance and possibly one or more activity fields in the master file. The master file data are then available for query or interrogation by the operator or are listed to form the stock status, or inventory status, report. The reorder report lists the subset of inventory items requir-

FIGURE 21.1 Raw materials inventory management: batch (upper left) and real-time (lower left).

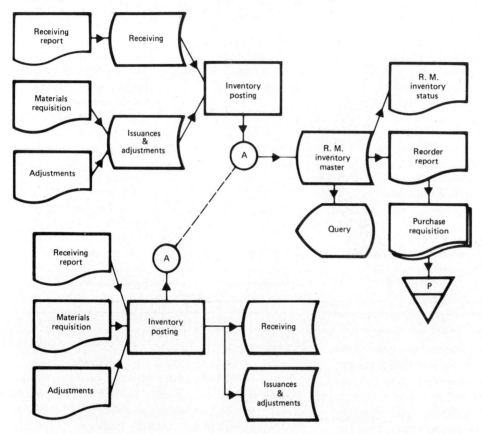

ing replenishment. Upon authorization by management, purchase requisitions are issued to initiate the ordering of the items from suppliers.

Figure 21.2 shows the activities surrounding the production control application. Production is initiated by the issuance of a production order and by the provision of a set of engineering specifications outlining what materials are to be used and how the product is to be made. In the case of products manufactured routinely, the specifications may be stored in a production master file and accessed each time the particular product is to be made. From the specifications, a schedule of production is prepared, together with the bill of materials and a set of work orders listing the operations to be performed in the

conversion process. The bill of materials is subsequently used to prepare materials requisitions as the batches of materials are needed.

Figure 21.3 shows the activities associated with the work-in-process, or cost accounting, application. Materials, labor, and factory overhead entries are accumulated in the production data transaction file. Various reports are prepared detailing the use of materials and labor and including comparisons with standard cost figures. In a job order system, cost data are posted to the open job file, which takes the place of the work-in-process master file; paper job cards are updated with the same data. The production status report shows the current status of all jobs currently in production.

FIGURE 21.2 Initiation of the production process.

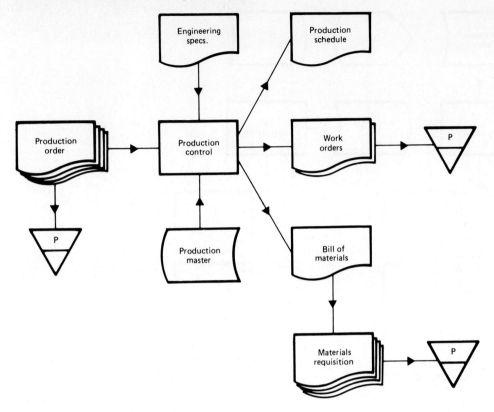

Figure 21.4 shows the processes connected with the management of finished goods inventory. It is broadly similar to Figure 21.1, which pertains to raw materials inventory, except that completed products may be shipped directly from the factory instead of passing into the finished goods warehouse. Two transaction files are shown; again, a third could be established if it were desirable to segregate inventory adjustment entries from either receipts of finished goods or issuances to shipping.

The reorder report for finished goods is used as a basis for issuing production orders for the routine replenishment of inventory items for sale.

The flow of paperwork in the production cycle is clearly shown by a document flow chart, as illustrated in Figure 21.5. Only a single factory department is shown, although in real life, several departments may be involved in manufacturing the particular product. The production order is shown as originating in the finished goods warehouse. This would be appropriate in the case of the routine replenishment of finished goods inventory, but production orders can also originate from other areas, such as sales. Similarly, the completed product is shown as passing to the finished goods warehouse; instead, the product may be shipped to the customer directly from the warehouse.

Key Documents

Production Order. The production order initiates the production process by authorizing the allocation of factory resources to the manufacture, construction, repair,

FIGURE 21.3 Accumulation and distribution of production costs.

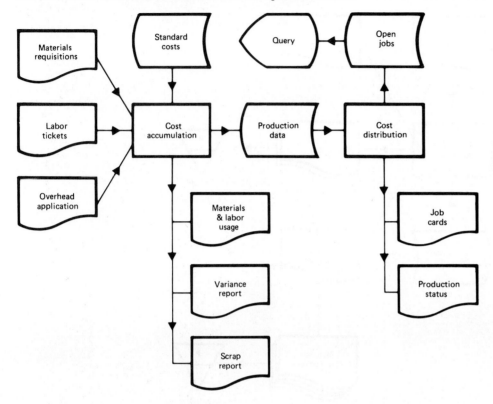

or servicing of goods or capital items. If goods are to be produced for stock, the production order will usually be issued by a responsible individual in the finished goods warehouse; otherwise, it may be issued by sales or engineering. If the goods are to be produced for immediate sale, a copy of the sales order (see Chapter 22) may be used in place of a separate production order. In highly automated systems, production orders and other documents in the production cycle may be replaced by machine-readable records.

The production order form normally contains information such as the following:

- Form name and number
- Order number
- Job number assigned
- Date of order
- Date required
- For sale or stock

- Contract number
- Customer number (if any)
- Sales representative code (if any)
- Warehouse reference
- Destination
- Shipping instructions
- Responsible department
- Quantity ordered
- Unit of measure
- Specification reference
- Shop routing
- Shop scheduling
- Tool and materials requirements
- Disposal of scrap
- Special instructions
- Authorization

Production order forms should be prenumbered for control purposes. Multiple copies are usually prepared for

FIGURE 21.4 Disposition of completed production and finished goods inventory management.

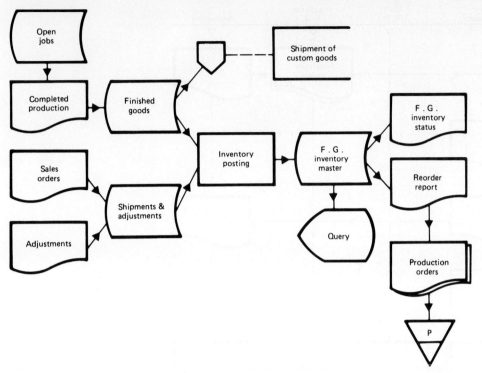

distribution to production control, inspection or quality control, tooling, and accounting. One or more copies will be retained by the issuing department for its permanent records.

Materials Requisition. The materials or stores requisition authorizes the release of raw materials to production and forms the basis for identifying materials costs. It is prepared from information contained in the bill of materials, is issued by the factory department responsible for production, and is submitted to the stores. Cost data are normally entered by the stores clerk. The content of the materials requisition may be

- Form name and number
- Materials requisition number
- Job number
- Contract number (for billing purposes)

- Department
- Date
- Authorization
- Filled by (stock clerk)
- Received by (representative of responsible department)
- Checked by

These items appear only once. In addition there are repeated line items:

- Part or item number
- Description
- Unit of measure
- Quantity required
- Quantity issued
- Unit cost or transfer price

Requisitions should be prenumbered. Multiple copies are required for distribution to the stores and to accounting; one or more copies will be retained by the issuing de-

FIGURE 21.5 **Flow of documents associated with the production cycle.** Note that the production order may be issued by sales or by engineering.

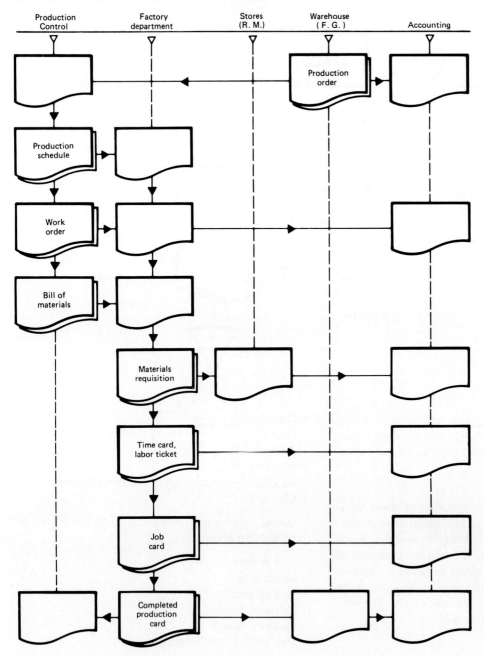

FIGURE 21.6 Stores requisition form, provided by a large U.S. manufacturing firm.

STORES ISSUE REQUISITION

Order Taker _____   Issue Date _____

Stockkeeper	Qty./Dimension	Unit	Group/Part No.	Part Description/Location	BOM No.	BOM Item No.

Charge Account _____   Deliver To _____   Time Needed _____
Requisitioner: Name _____   Employee No. _____   Company _____
Who-Code _____   Shop _____

partment. An example of a stores requisition is presented in Figure 21.6.

Work Order. The work order authorizes the allocation of labor resources to production; it is the labor counterpart of the materials requisition. Work orders are often prepared by production control, but they are authorized by the factory department responsible for production. Work orders are also used in service departments such as physical plant and equipment maintenance. A single work order usually refers to some identifiable task, or group of tasks, forming part of the total production effort.

A typical work order contains the following data:

• Form name and number
• Work order number
• Job number
• Contract number (for billing purposes)
• Department

• Date
• Authorization
• Task identification (group of tasks)

with repeated line items:

• Task number
• Description
• Applicable labor grade
• Number of hours

The estimated completion time or, in the case of a standard cost system, the standard labor allowance for that task, may be included. Copies of the work order are prepared for production control, accounting, and the factory department in question. Figure 21.7 shows a typical work order used by a repairs and maintenance department.

Job Card. The job card, or job sheet, is used in manual or semiautomated job order costing systems to ac-

FIGURE 21.7 Work order form, provided by a large U.S. manufacturing firm.

Approval is governed by SAP

WORK ORDER

DEPT.	CLASS	UNIT	OR	JOB	OTHER

T 029400

Re ed by ______ Phone ______

Assign/Deliver to ______ Bldg. ______

Location of Equipment ______ Bldg. ______

Priority A B C D

	MO.	DAY	YR.
Date Ordered			
Date Wanted			

Order Description – Enter in blocks a sufficient description to identify the job on an IBM report. *Please Print*

Est. Cost

$

Description of Job & Symptoms ______

Shut Down Required ☐ Yes ☐ No Date ______	PERMITS REQUIRED: ☐ Open Flame ☐ Safe Work ☐ Other ______	Estimated Cost ☐ Under \$2500 ☐ \$2500 to \$7500 Approved by ______	☐ Annual Work Order

Materials & Tools Required ______

☐ Closing Notice Will be Submitted

Estimated Material Cost

$ ______

Date Wanted	PRI	EMP	Employee Hours

T 029400

Remarks: ______

☐ Identify as Direct Charge

Crew No.

WORK SAFELY

T 029400

Sub-Work Orders: ______

Corrective Action, Comments & Probable Cause of Job ______

Completed by: ______

Date Completed Mo.	Day	Yr.	EMP	Employee Hours

PRIORITY:
A – Urgently needed today
B – Needed for efficient operation (within 1-3 days)
C – Non-critical in nature (as soon as practical)
D – Must be performed during next shutdown

Copies: White, Green, Blue and Manila to Maintenance Department

Pink – Retain to plan job and/or record correction
Retain bottom portion of Manila to tag equipment.

(Use back of white copy if additional space is required.)

cumulate production costs by individual unit or batch of goods. It receives data from the materials requisitions and the time cards or labor tickets; factory overhead will also be applied at the departmental or plantwide rate. Job cards normally accumulate cost data by department:

- Form name and number
- Production order number
- Job number
- Contract number (if any)
- Date placed in production

- Finished goods part or item number
- Batch size
- Expected completion date

with repeated line items:

- Date of cost incurrence
- Department
- Time card or labor ticket reference
- Direct labor hours (regular)
- Direct labor hours (overtime and special)
- Direct labor cost
- Materials requisition number
- Direct materials cost
- Factory overhead cost
- Other costs
- Total cumulative cost to date

Overtime and special hours are segregated from regular direct labor hours to provide a basis for analyzing costs at a later stage. Overtime and other labor premiums are often charged to the product, despite the theoretical preference for including them in overhead. Premiums may arise because of tight production schedules requested by the customer or because of internal scheduling problems.

Upon completion of the production process, the information on the job cards is used to prepare a completed product card, which in turn may be used for customer billing purposes or to update finished goods inventory records.

Principal Files

Inventory Master File. The master files for both raw materials and finished goods inventories should be maintained in a random access medium to provide for operator query of inventory levels and other data. In manual systems, card files are almost invariably used because of their convenience. In automated ones, magnetic disk media are most suitable. Some very large inventories are maintained on magnetic tape so as to reduce storage costs, but the loss of random access capability can be a serious disadvantage. Typically, the master files contain descriptive data on the items, on-hand and related balances, and summarized activity data:

- Part or item number
- Description
- Warehouse location
- Shipping weight or packaging instructions
- Unit of measure
- Quantity on hand
- Quantity on order
- Quantity on reserve
- Unit cost
- Unit price (or transfer price)
- Reorder point
- Order quantity
- Date of last order
- Date of last delivery
- Average monthly usage
- Year-to-date usage
- Recommended vendor
- Production specification code
- Delivery lead time

In some cases different units of measure apply to the same inventory item. Items may be purchased and sold by the case or in individual units or, if liquids are involved, by the drum, quart, or gallon. Reserve quantities are sometimes earmarked and set aside for favored customers or for designated production orders; items on reserve are not available for general use.

Special consideration must be given to the unit cost field. If the weighted-average cost model is used, a single-unit cost field will be sufficient and the cost will be updated every time a new batch of units is received. Similarly, if the specific identification model is used, a single field will be adequate, but each differentiated unit, or batch of units, is stored in a separate master record. Thus, in an inventory of rare coins, mint-quality silver dollars are stored separately from lower-quality ones and are given a different inventory number. The more difficult problem arises if the FIFO or LIFO model is used, because of the need to store multiple cost layers for each item.

If the particular system supports variable length records, all that is required is to assign a pair of fields—a quantity and a cost—to each new cost layer that is established. But if there is a restriction on fixed-length records, some other strategy must be found. One is to allocate a sufficiently long record to accommodate the maximum number of cost layers likely to be encountered on any item, but this usually wastes storage capacity because some items are probably more active and have many more cost layers than do others.

Another strategy is to have multiple master records for a single item, one for each cost layer. This wastes storage space and may also complicate the retrieval process.

A third strategy is to leave the cost data and quantities in a separate file, possibly the receiving file. Individual records in this separate file are associated with each cost layer for each inventory item. The records remain open until the particular cost layer is liquidated; in the case of the LIFO model, this may not occur for a long time, perhaps not for many years. Data base management systems use a modified form of this strategy. Groups of data elements representing the cost layers are owned by each master record.

Receiving file. The receiving file can form an interface between the purchasing and the production cycle. But to serve this purpose, it must contain detailed line-item records, not just a summary of the overall purchase. The file can be maintained on a sequential access medium, such as magnetic tape. However, as noted, some FIFO and LIFO inventory systems rely on the receiving file to hold the quantity and cost data relating to each cost layer; in this case, random access would be required to support the inventory status query activities. The following fields are usually included:

• Purchase order number
• Requisition number
• Vendor number
• Date of receipt
• Complete/partial shipment flag
• Payment terms
• Comments
• Part or item number*
• Quantity received*
• Unit of measure*
• Unit cost*
• Condition*
• Repeated fields*

The receiving file is usually maintained in chronological order. If it is to be used as the repository of cost layer information, the file can be sorted by inventory item number to facilitate retrieval of on-hand dollar balances and also to facilitate the matching of receipt and issuance records, as the cost layers are progressively liquidated.

Open Job (Work-in-Process) File. The open job, or work-in-process, file records data on all jobs currently in production. It applies most directly to job order costing systems, but it can be used with some modifications in process costing systems; in the latter case, a "job" may be identified with a department and a time period (usually one month). The file should preferably be maintained in a random access medium, such as cards or magnetic disk, to support interrogation or query activities. In manual systems, the file is sometimes made up of copies of the job cards themselves. The file typically contains the following fields:

• Job number
• Production order number
• Date placed in production
• Finished goods item or part number
• Batch size
• Customer or contract number
• Expected completion date
• Responsible department
• Direct labor hours (regular)
• Direct labor hours (overtime and special)
• Direct labor cost
• Direct materials cost
• Factory overhead applied
• Other costs (if any)

In some types of service enterprises, there are no materials costs, and so the corresponding field can be omitted. On the other hand, in the construction industry, additional cost fields are often included to hold subcontract and equipment-lease costs. If custom products are involved, additional fields may also be required for accumulated progress payments and possibly retentions. The open job file is normally sorted by assigned job number or production order number.

Production Data File. The production data file, or cost accounting transaction file, is intended to accumulate cost data prior to posting to the open job file. It can be maintained in a sequential access medium because file interrogation is rarely needed in this case. The fields included should match those in the open job file:

- Date of cost incurrence
- Job number
- Department identification
- Direct labor hours (regular)
- Direct labor hours (overtime and special)
- Direct labor cost
- Direct materials cost
- Factory overhead applied
- Other costs

If fields are omitted from the open job file, the corresponding ones can be omitted from the production data file. Conversely, if additional fields are included in one, they must be included in the other for consistency. The file may be ordered chronologically.

Completed Product File. The completed product file is the finished goods analog of the receiving file. It records the emergence of the goods from production and either their passage into finished goods inventory or their readiness for shipment if they are already earmarked for a particular customer. The file can normally be maintained in a sequential access medium. Its content may be as follows:

- Production order number
- Job number
- Date of completion
- Responsible department
- Customer or contract number
- Finished goods item or part number
- Batch size
- Unit production cost

The completed production file can be ordered chronologically or by job number, production order number, or part or item number.

Selected Reports

Inventory Reorder Report. Reorder reports are usually prepared for both raw materials and finished goods inventories. The reorder report is a status report that lists the items that require replenishment, either from outside vendors, in the case of raw materials, or from in-house

production, in the case of finished goods. The need for replenishment is normally indicated when the quantity on hand falls below a predetermined reorder point. For each item listed, a recommended order quantity may be shown, and additional data may be provided to indicate the urgency of placing an order. Useful measures of urgency are the quantity currently on hand, the expected rate of usage, and the expected replenishment lead time. A reorder report for raw materials may also include the names of recommended vendors, whereas one for finished goods may refer to production specifications that are kept on file. Figure 21.8 shows a typical report layout for finished goods inventory.

Materials and Labor Usage Report. The materials and labor usage report is one of several activity reports prepared for analyzing production costs and their inputs. Various report formats are in common use, and various combinations of data may be included. Figure 21.9 illustrates one format. For each active job, the major categories of materials are listed, together with the quantities used and wasted. Also, the number of labor hours expended on the job is shown, with a breakdown by labor grade and a division into regular hours and overtime or special hours.

In some cases, the usage report lists only the materials used in production, and waste or scrap is shown on a separate report. In other cases (as in Figure 21.9), waste is included in the same report. Waste may be divided into normal and abnormal waste; the latter is regarded as a controllable item, and any significant amount of abnormal waste is treated as a sign of inefficient production or poor workmanship. The division of labor hours into regular, overtime, holiday, and other special hours provides a basis for the analysis of scheduling effectiveness and of any labor rate premiums charged to the particular job. Lost time associated with sickness, personal business, blood donations, attendance at Christmas speeches, and the like may also be included in the usage report to provide further information on overall labor efficiency.

Production Status Report. The production status report shows the accumulated costs expended on each job in production, with a breakdown by cost element—typically, materials, labor, and factory overhead. Labor

FIGURE 21.8 Illustration of a reorder report for finished goods.

Item number	Description	Quantity on hand	Quantity on reserve	Reorder point	Order quantity	Lead time	Monthly demand	Production reference
		ZEUS MANUFACTURING COMPANY FINISHED GOODS REORDER REPORT As of 9/30/XX						Page 1
A - 2391	2 - in. copper pipe	1200 ft.	0	1500 ft.	2000 ft.	2 wks.	1000 ft.	42 - H - 337 - 1
A - 3684	6 - in. copper pipe	500 ft.	100 ft.	1000 ft.	1000 ft.	2 wks.	1000 ft.	42 - H - 360 - 3
A - 8850	4 - in lead tubing	9150 ft.	0	10000 ft.	5000 ft.	3 wks.	5000 ft.	33 - J - 490 - 1
B - 1244	1 - in. alum. conduit	0	0	5000 ft.	5000 ft.	1 wk.	1000 ft.	57 - A - 112 - 2
C - 5506	12 - in. ducting	2500 ft.	500 ft.	30000 ft.	15000 ft.	4 wks.	5000 ft.	12 - R - 000 - 1
C - 5507	14 - in. ducting	1000 ft.	0	10000 ft.	10000 ft.	4 wks.	5000 ft.	12 - R - 001 - 1
D - 0224	End plates	300 ea.	0	500 ea.	600 ea.	1 wk.	200 ea.	00 - D - 355 - 0
D - 0381	R - H bends	620 pr.	0	1000 pr.	500 pr.	1 wk.	500 pr.	00 - D - 206 - 0
D - 0382	L - H bends	45 pr.	0	1000 pr.	500 pr.	1 wk.	500 pr.	00 - D - 207 - 0
D - 0673	4 - way junctions	1100 ea.	400 ea.	1500 ea.	1000 ea.	6 wks.	500 ea.	56 - A - 115 - 3
E - 5640	3/8 AF bolts	250 doz.	0	300 doz.	1000 doz.	1 wk.	300 doz.	12 - C - 000 - 4
E - 6190	5/16 screws	0	0	1000 doz.	1000 doz.	1 wk.	500 doz.	12 - D - 132 - 1
E - 9000	3/4 Af bolts	100 doz.	0	1000 doz.	500 doz.	2 wks.	600 doz.	12 - G - 005 - 2

Report number 666 / A

hours may be included (possibly divided into regular and overtime hours) to permit the computation of average labor rates or average labor productivity.

Figure 21.10 shows the corresponding report for a construction company: the construction status report. It conforms to the general format, but it includes the additional cost elements of subcontract and equipment lease costs, cost items that are often substantial in the construction industry.

Some organizations extend the scope of the production (or construction) status report to include estimates of degree of completion for each job, and sometimes even projections of expected costs to complete the job. The projections are normally based on comparisons between actual and budgeted figures for the work done to date. To make reliable projections, it is usually necessary to have separate estimates of degree of completion for each of the major cost elements involved. The reason for this is that expenditures on one cost element, say, materials, may not be maintained in step with expenditures on another element such as direct labor. In particular, materials may be issued, but the associated conversion work may not be done until some time later. In the case of construction companies, large quantities of materials may be purchased for a given project long before any work is performed. Similarly, large subcontracts may be placed—and paid for—at various stages during completion of the overall project.

FIGURE 21.9   A materials and labor usage report.

										Page 1

SATURN INCORPORATED

MATERIALS AND LABOR USAGE REPORT

For Week Ending 12/4/XX

		Materials :					Labor :			
Job #	Order #	Type	U / M	Used	Spoiled	Scrap	Grade	Reg.	O / T	Holiday
352	J - 99012	Sheet	sq. ft.	40000	200	500	Unskilled	500	20	0
		Rolled	ft.	6500	0	380	Semi-sk'd.	1200	600	40
		Extruded	ft.	30200	15000	640	Machinist	800	100	0
							Tool & die	200	0	0
353	H - 23404	Rolled	ft.	800	0	50	Unskilled	440	0	0
		Section	ft	1600	400	180	Semi - sk'd.	2000	0	0
		Wire	ft.	29000	150	60	Finishers	320	30	8
354	J - 40820	Sheet	sq. ft.	15000	1100	650	Unskilled	840	40	20
		Extruded	ft.	4550	0	300	Skilled	520	0	0
		Castings	ea.	5	0	0	Painters	100	24	16
		Misc.	–	360	20	20				

Form # 40. Revision 5/80

INTERNAL CONTROLS

Control Objectives and Risks

The main control objectives relating to the production cycle are as follows:[1]

- Inventory costs are assigned in accordance with prescribed methods of valuation and reflect the lower-of-cost or market rule.
- Usage and movement of inventory is recorded correctly as to account, amount (quantity and dollars), and accounting period.

- Recorded balances of inventory accounts are periodically substantiated and evaluated.
- Access to inventories is permitted only in accordance with management's authorization.
- Production is planned in accordance with management's authorization.
- The use of resources in production and the associated costs are accurately and promptly recorded and reported.
- Materials, labor, overhead costs, and related adjustments are accurately classified, summarized, and reported.
- Completed production and its associated costs are accurately and promptly recorded and reported.

The associated concerns center on the risk that inventory items could be diverted to unauthorized use, that inventory valuations could be misstated, and that computed production costs could be in error. In addition, there is

[1] See, for example, Arthur Andersen & Co., *A Guide for Studying and Evaluating Internal Accounting Controls*, Publ. no. AA 2880, Item 1 (Chicago, Arthur Andersen & Co., January 1978). Also, see Ernst & Whinney, *Evaluating Internal Control: A Guide for Management and Directors*, Publ. no. 39078 (Cleveland: Ernst & Whinney, 1979).

FIGURE 21.10 A cost status report for a construction company.

Job number	Description	Labor hours	Labor cost	Materials	Overhead	Sub-contract	Eqpt. lease	Total cost
1201	1st. Nat. Bank Bldg.	21,300	220,180	115,490	220,180		45,000	600,850
1202	Hound Creek Bridge	960	7,200	10,350	7,200	31,800	9,200	65,750
1204	Moon County School	41,820	316,670	425,000	316,670		341,000	1,399,340
1205	St. Diana's Church	1,540	17,080	54,310	17,080	105,000		193,470
1207	Callisto Turnpike	30,700	210,240	894,060	210,240	1,350,200	880,000	3,544,740
1208	Iris Co. Warehouse	2,390	18,400	351,300	18,400		15,450	403,550
1210	Minerva Apartments	7,480	82,310	67,950	82,310	9,400		241,970
1211	Paris Mall	17,300	135,500	276,000	135,500		75,700	622,700
	Total	123,490	1,007,580	2,194,460	1,007,580	1,496,400	1,366,350	7,072,370

JUNO CONSTRUCTION COMPANY
CONSTRUCTION STATUS REPORT
As of 5 / 31 / 19XX

Page 1

Report no. 9041

the risk that production could be planned and initiated without management's approval.

Inventory costs may be improperly determined or classified, or errors made in cost allocations affecting inventory valuations. Cost flow models, such as FIFO and LIFO, may not be applied in accordance with approved procedures. Total inventory values may be correct, but errors may exist in the distribution of total value by individual item or among raw materials, work in process, and finished goods inventories. Errors in the perpetual inventory records for individual items can in turn result in unnecessary purchases of materials or production of finished goods; the end result may be the overstocking and obsolescence of certain items and shortages of others.

In terms of irregularities, inventory adjustments—or inventory valuations—may be intentionally manipulated to conceal misappropriations of materials or goods. Alternatively, inventory values may be manipulated by management to improve operating performance or to reduce tax liabilities. Standard costs may be changed without management authorization, possibly to conceal unfavorable variances; as a result, period costs could flow into inventory.

Inventory values may be inflated owing to obsolete, slow-moving, or overstocked items. Failure to identify such items may allow purchases or production of unusable, unsalable, or unprofitable goods to continue. Loss of market value may not be properly reflected by a write-down or write-off of inventory costs. This could be the result of negligence; alternatively, it might result from management's reluctance to recognize a large loss or its desire to conceal previous errors of judgment in purchasing or production decisions. A premature or unwarranted write-down of inventory items may conceal misappropriations of assets or be part of a scheme to facilitate bargain purchases.

A number of risks surround the physical safeguarding of inventories. Loss, shrinkage, or deterioration of inventory items may go unnoticed, with the result that perpetual inventory records are overstated. Issuance of materials to production may not be reported or recorded correctly, leading to a mismatch between raw materials and work-in-process inventories. Alternatively, the same materials may be shown as part of both inventories. Scrap, spoilage, and waste may not be correctly recorded and accounted for, or the sale of scrap may not be reported.

Inventory may be stolen by employees, management, or outsiders, for personal use or for unauthorized sale.

Scrap may be stolen, or the proceeds from the sale of scrap may be misappropriated. Inventory may be scrapped without management's knowledge, possibly in an attempt to conceal shortages or to facilitate bargain purchases of useful goods or materials. Attempts may be made to falsify the physical count of inventory. Fictitious or nonexistent items may be included, resulting in a misstatement of inventory and cost of sales. Similarly, goods held on consignment may be included in inventory.

Failure to regulate production in accordance with management's plans may result in excessive production and inventory levels, on the one hand, or underutilization of capacity and shortages, on the other. Excessive investment in inventories and abnormally high carrying costs may be incurred along with unwarranted charges for overtime premiums. Unauthorized products may be produced that cannot be sold by the company or are intended to be stolen upon completion of production. Other production requirements may be neglected, or customer service levels may be sacrificed in the process.

Materials, labor, and overhead costs may be expensed when they should be charged to the product or included in product costs when they should be expensed. Overhead may be incorrectly allocated either from service departments to production cost centers or from production centers to the product. Period costs may be improperly included in manufacturing overhead or depreciation charges incorrectly determined.

Completed production may not be recorded correctly or not recorded at all, resulting in an apparent but spurious shortage of finished goods inventory. In turn, there could be an unwarranted repetition of production orders, or there could be a loss of sales from the apparent inability to meet demand. Errors may be made in the transfer of quantity and cost data from work in process to finished goods. Deliberate modifications might be made to conceal shortages or theft.

Control Measures

Much of the burden of safeguarding inventories obviously falls on physical security measures. Securely locked storerooms or warehouse buildings, external fences, burglar alarms, electronic sensing and monitoring devices, fire and smoke detectors, security guards, and surveillance cameras all play an important role. Access to stores and warehouses should be restricted to authorized persons, who should identify themselves with badges, identification cards, or magnetic keys. Issuance of magnetic and other keys should be carefully controlled and recorded against the bearers' signatures. Employees in sensitive positions should be bonded. Insurance coverage should be carried and be regularly reviewed for adequacy.

The inspection process and the physical inventory count are additional components of physical control. They ensure, on the one hand, that inventory asset values are not impaired by poor quality, and, on the other, that items appearing in the accounting records are physically on hand.

However, the information system also bears a large part of the burden of internal control in relation to the safeguarding of inventories and more broadly throughout the production cycle. Maintenance of perpetual inventory records is an important control measure and is preferred over the periodic inventory method; comparisons can be made at any time and indeed should routinely be made between the actual and the recorded quantities on hand. Any significant discrepancies should be investigated to determine whether they result from errors or irregularities. Also, the perpetual inventory records provide detailed data for subsequent costing of work in process and sales. A standard cost system represents a further important control measure because of the ability to compare actual and standard data. The standards provide a reference by which judgments of reasonableness can be made. Significant variances should be investigated promptly, first, to determine whether errors or irregularities are involved and, then, if the data are found to be valid, as a basis for strategies for corrective action.

Separation of Duties

Responsibility for custody of inventory items should be carefully separated from the responsibility for maintaining perpetual inventory or other accounting records. Similarly, the receipt or issuance of inventory items should be separated from the preparation of receiving or shipping documents and from the preparation of materials requisitions or completed production cards. Responsibility for handling and accounting for scrap should be separated from each other as well as from responsibility for the disposal or sale of scrap.

Responsibility for reviewing inventory valuations and approving write-down or write-off of inventory values should be separated from the maintenance of perpetual inventory records and from authority to dispose of unsalable or obsolete items.

Control of Documents

All sensitive documents, including production orders, materials requisitions, work orders, and completed production cards, should be prenumbered and issued in sequence. Routine document control should be carried out to account for any gaps or duplicates in document sequence; any deviations from continuous, unbroken sequence should be listed on an exception report for investigation.

Prenumbered forms should also be used for the approval of inventory adjustments; subsequent adjustments should reference the authorization number. Prenumbered forms should be required for the disposal of any asset, including inventory or scrap.

Supplies of prenumbered forms should be kept in a secure place and be made available to authorized persons only.

Authorization of Transactions

Authority to accept raw materials for inventory lies with the receiving department, and authority to transport finished goods lies with the shipping department; both activities fall outside the normal boundaries of the production cycle.

Authorization of production orders should be made in accordance with clearly stated management criteria relating to maximum permissible inventory levels and to acceptance of sales orders or contracts. Any deviation from those criteria, to alleviate layoff situations or for other reasons, should be approved in writing by man-

agement. Due attention should be given to production priorities established by management. All production orders for custom goods should be carefully compared with sales orders or contract specifications prior to approval.

Authorization of materials requisitions for the issuance of raw materials to production lies with the responsible factory department. As noted earlier, work orders are also authorized by the supervisor of the factory department in question. The same supervisor subsequently approves the time cards or labor tickets that report the performance of the work. Overhead rates, whether plantwide or departmental, are approved by higher-level management and usually remain in force for a 12-month period. Any deviation from predetermined overhead rates should be approved in writing. Similarly, standard costs and allowances are approved by higher-level management as part of the budget process and should remain in effect until written exception orders are issued.

Written procedures should be established for the accumulation of materials, labor, and factory overhead costs on job cards or otherwise.

A written authorization should be required before any item of equipment, materials, goods, or scrap can be removed from the plant facilities. All such disposals should be reported and independently reviewed.

Other Input Controls

The usual batch controls can be adopted for all materials requisitions, time cards, labor tickets, and completed production cards submitted for processing. Batch-balancing techniques, hash totals, and control logs should be used to verify the completeness of the input data and subsequently to ensure that the posting of appropriate data to master files has been completed.

Special attention must be given to the security of interactive computerized systems, particularly to those operating in a real-time mode that is highly sensitive to error contamination. Access to interactive terminals should be controlled by physical controls over terminals and by password. Transaction entry should be accepted only upon submittal and verification of a user identification code. Access logs should be routinely reviewed to determine the origin of transaction input data. Point-of-entry editing of data should be carried out where appropriate. All inventory part or item numbers should be validated by check digits or by reference to a table or master file. Validity and limit checks should be made of key field entries such as quantities and dollar figures.

File Controls

Care must be taken to maintain the currency of data relating to inventory quantities, costs, and prices, in raw materials and finished goods master files. Fast-moving inventories demand the use of real-time–processing modes.

File maintenance activities should be controlled, particularly when cost or price fields are exposed to modification or update. Edit logs should be prepared and reviewed independently of the file maintenance activities themselves. As noted, any adjustments of inventory values must be approved in writing and documented for review. Furthermore, such adjustments should be entered as transactions and not treated as a file maintenance activity.

Data security measures are particularly important to the production cycle because of the size of the files that may be involved and because of the volatility of their data content. The reconstruction of production cycle files after a system crash may be extremely difficult unless provision has been made for frequent backup.

Processing and Output Controls

Independent comparisons should be made between production records and production orders to ensure that all production orders are duly completed and that all completed products resulted from a properly authorized production order. Outstanding production orders should routinely be followed up to determine their production status. Production orders and job cards, and job cards and completed production cards, should be compared to verify the integrity of the audit trail.

The number of outstanding production orders and the number of jobs currently in production should periodically be reconciled. The number of spoiled jobs reported should be correlated with the issuance of spoilage reports, the return of spoiled materials to the stores, and the final disposition of scrap. Quantities of materials used in production should be compared with data contained in the bill of materials, and if a standard cost system is used, actual and standard figures should be compared. Perpetual inventory records should be reconciled with balances in the general ledger control accounts.

Periodic checks should be made to determine that the computer programs and processing procedures used conform with current documentation and authorizations. Processed test data should also agree with precomputed results. Computer programs or manual procedures should be developed for routinely analyzing inventory status so as to identify slow-moving, overstocked, or obsolete items. Actual inventory levels and maximum-level criteria established by management should be compared.

SUMMARY

The production cycle accounts for the conversion of input resources—materials and vendor and employee services—into distributable products. It is also concerned with the costing of stores of inventoried resources. In manufacturing organizations, where it is most conspicuous, the production cycle includes the applications of production control, cost accounting, and the management of raw materials and finished goods inventories. The accumulation of manufacturing costs may use either a job order or a process costing system, and standard cost allowances may permit the periodic analysis of variances.

In merchandising organizations, production cycle activities are present in the management of merchandise inventories. In both manufacturing and merchandising organizations, the maintenance of inventory records provides information for the effective control of inventory levels and also the traditional cost-accounting data for asset valuation and cost of sales. The choice of inventory flow model (FIFO, LIFO, and the like) is important to the design of the accounting system, aside from its importance for tax planning purposes.

In service organizations, production cycle activities may survive in the costing of services. Particularly in organizations that perform contract services, the accumulation of costs and the tracing of costs to contracts are important accounting functions.

The principal documents in the production cycle are production and work orders, materials requisitions, and job cards. The principal files are the inventory master file (or files), the receiving file, the open job file, the standard cost file, the production data file, and the completed product file. Major reports are the inventory status report, the reorder report, the materials and labor usage report, standard cost variance reports, and the production status report.

Internal control in the production cycle emphasizes the need for the physical protection of inventories, proper control over the manufacturing process, and the provision of reliable cost-accounting data.

BIBLIOGRAPHY

Arens, Alvin A., and D. Dewey Ward. *Systems Understanding for Auditing*. Haslett, Mich.: Systems Publications, 1981.

Arthur Andersen & Co. *A Guide for Studying and Evaluating Internal Accounting Controls*, Publ. no. 2880, Item 1. Chicago: Arthur Andersen & Co., 1978.

Bodnar, George H. *Accounting Information Systems*. Boston: Allyn & Bacon, 1980.

Ernst & Whinney. *Evaluating Internal Control: A Guide for Management and Directors*, Publ. no. 39078. Cleveland: Ernst & Whinney, 1979.

Forms for the Key Operations of Business. Glenview, Ill.: Moore Business Forms, 1977.

Hax, Arnold. C., and Dan Candea. *Production and Inventory Management*. Englewood Cliffs, N.J.: Prentice-Hall, 1984.

Kollaritsch, Felix P. *Cost Systems for Planning, Decision, and Controls: Concepts and Techniques*. Columbus: Grid, 1979.

Pescow, Jerome K., ed. *Encyclopedia of Accounting Systems*. Englewood Cliffs, N.J.: Prentice-Hall, 1976.

DISCUSSION QUESTIONS AND PROBLEMS

1. Define and discuss the following terms:

- Bill of materials
- Completed product file
- Completed production card
- Conversion
- Cost accounting
- Finished goods
- Inventory management
- Inventory master file
- Inventory (stock) status
- Job card
- Materials and labor usage report
- Materials requisition
- Materials waste scrap report
- Open job (work-in-process) file
- Perpetual inventory records
- Physical inventory count
- Production control
- Production cycle
- Production data file
- Production order
- Production status report
- Raw materials
- Receiving file
- Reorder report
- Standard costs
- Unit of measure
- Work in process
- Work order

2. The bill of materials prepared by Widget Manufacturing Co. for the production of long widgets lists materials required at two points in the manufacturing process. The first point (A) is at the commencement of production; the second (B) is after the completion of the stamping and drilling processes:

Part number: 1234

Description: Long widget

Materials per batch of 100 units:

Materials Item No.	Unit of Measure	Quantity at Point A	B
9136	lb.	48	25
9218	ea.	6	0
9337	ea.	0	180
9382	ft.	20	0
9506	ft.	200	0
9671	ft.	6	40
9724	pr.	0	50

Required

a. Design a materials requisition form suitable for Widget Manufacturing Co.

b. Insert the information necessary to obtain the materials necessary to start production of 300 units of long widgets.

3. Black Company uses a system of work orders to authorize repair work on items of machinery returned by customers. Work order no. 1234, for the repair of a small pump, lists tasks to be undertaken by three labor grades:

Task	Labor Grade	Time Allowance (hours)
Degrease pump	Unskilled	0.1
Disassemble	Semiskilled	0.5
Repair motor	Skilled	3.0
Clean bearings	Semiskilled	0.8
Reassemble	Skilled	1.0
Test	Skilled	1.0

Labor tickets submitted later indicate the actual time spent on a number of jobs performed on the day in question:

Grade	Work Order No.	Hours
Unskilled ($4.00/hr.)	1233	4.3
	1234	0.2
	1235	3.5
Semiskilled ($6.00/hr.)	1234	1.5
	1236	2.0
	1237	4.5
Skilled ($8.00/hr.)	1232	3.0
	1234	4.5
	1235	5.0
	1237	3.5

Materials costing $24 were used in the repair of the pump, and overhead was applied at the rate of $7.50 per direct labor hour.

Required

a. Determine the total cost to complete work order no. 1234.

b. Evaluate the efficiency of labor usage in connection with that job.

4. The data in the table at the end of this section appeared on the raw materials stock status report for a small woodworking shop.

Required

a. Identify the items that would be listed on the corresponding reorder report.

b. Review the reorder points prescribed for the various inventory items, and recommend any necessary changes.

5. Prepare a systems flowchart relating to the management of finished goods inventory in an organization that manufactures automobile spare parts. No custom orders are accepted, and all completed products are

21

transferred into inventory. A real-time information system is employed, and interactive terminals are provided in the warehouse and at four remote locations, for status query. A computer program automatically generates a production order whenever the quantity on hand falls below the predetermined reorder point for a particular item.

6. Design a production order form for Red Container Corporation, which accepts custom orders for corrugated products. Cardboard and other containers are produced in multiples of 1,000 units to specifications provided by the customers. Each order requires the product to be routed through a particular combination of processing operations. Eight processes can be carried out (designated A through H), but any one order requires a maximum of four operations. No goods are produced for stock.

7. White Textile Company maintains a raw materials inventory of cloth and related products for the production of men's suits. Its computerized information system includes an inventory master file that contains the following fields:

Stock number
Description
Color
Mill supplier (name and telephone number)
Stockroom location
Unit of measure (bolts, yards, etc.)
Quantity on hand
Quantity on reserve
Unit cost
Extended cost

Currently a weighted-average cost model is being used, but management is interested in converting to a LIFO model to minimize taxes. Initial estimates indicate that over a two- to three-year period, up to ten cost layers might be accumulated for any one inventory item. The system does not provide for variable-length records.

Required
a. Prepare a design for the existing inventory master file.

b. Make a suitable recommendation to management for converting to a LIFO model, and show the design of any additional records or files required.

8. Orange Steel Products, Inc., uses a job order cost system to accumulate its manufacturing costs. Prime cost inputs are materials requisitions and time cards; overhead is applied at the rate of 125 percent of direct labor cost. Job 5678 was in production for two weeks, and during that time the following accounting events took place:

Date	Event
5/3	Forty ft^2 of 1/2" steel plate (stock no. P-2604/K) and 10 ft of extruded section (no. H-9123/C) were issued to production; unit costs were $2.25 per sq. ft. and $1.20 per ft., respectively.
5/9	Reported direct labor costs on job 5678 consisted of 15 regular and 4 overtime hours of skilled labor, at $9.00 per hour; time and a half is paid for overtime.
5/12	Fifteen ft of steel tubing (no. J-1974/M) was issued to production; unit cost was $1.60 per ft.
5/16	Ten regular hours of skilled labor and 8 regular hours of unskilled labor were reported; the rate for unskilled labor was $7.50 per hour.
5/17	Job 5678 was completed and transferred to finished goods inventory without additional expenditure of materials or labor

Required
a. Design a job card suitable for Orange Steel Products and illustrate the design with the data for job 5678.
b. Design a production status report for Orange Steel, and include as one line item the data relating to job 5678 as of the close of business on May 16.

9. Audit of the books of the company referred to in Problem 4 (see the data) showed that posting errors had been made over a six-month period. A detailed analysis revealed that issuances of item 4003 had been posted to 4002 and that receipts of item 4006 had been posted in error to 4007. As a result, there were substantial discrepancies between the inventory records for these items and the quantities determined in the physical inventory count:

| Item No. | Quantity on hand: | |
	Records	Actual
4002	800 ft.	45,000 ft.
4003	32,800 ft.	1,600 ft.
4006	—	20,400 ft.
4007	24,800 ft²	2,800 ft²

The apparent overage of items 4003 and 4007 had not previously been noticed; however, the corresponding shortages of items 4002 and 4006 had come to light some weeks earlier, and a part-time worker had been fired on suspicion of theft.

Required

a. Discuss the implications of the errors that were detected.

b. Suggest internal controls that would have reduced the likelihood that the errors could have gone unnoticed for so long.

10. Jill Johnson is a first-level manager of a production department at Acme Electronics, Inc. She is concerned that excessive lost time, caused by labor problems in her department, will result in abnormally large labor efficiency variances for the current quarter. It is a particularly crucial time for her, as she is hoping for a promotion to corporate headquarters, and she wants to avoid any suggestion of mismanagement of her department.

To conceal the problems, she accesses the standard cost master file from an interactive terminal in her office and increases the labor-hour allowances for several of the jobs she supervises. Two weeks later, when the quarterly analysis of variances is produced, it shows only small unfavorable, or significant favorable, variances in the area for which she is responsible. Shortly afterward, she receives her long-awaited promotion and is transferred to California.

Required

a. Discuss the implications of the irregularity that Johnson was able to perpetrate.

b. What internal control weaknesses must have been present for Johnson's actions to have gone undetected?

11. The main plant of Alexis Manufacturing Co. in Reno, Nevada, and four satellite production plants are located in neighboring cities. Production cost data are captured and accumulated at the satellite plants on microcomputers that can operate in a stand-alone mode and that have individual floppy disk devices for storing small files. All data verification and correction are performed locally. The machines can also operate as intelligent terminals and communicate with a host computer in Reno. The main computer has extensive disk and tape storage on which central files are maintained of production data, work-in-process and finished goods inventories, and standard cost allowances.

Every Friday current data from the satellite plants are transmitted to Reno and accumulated into companywide totals. Inventory files are updated, and management reports are prepared. Standard cost production and variance reports are transmitted to the satellite plants to be printed locally, while summary reports are printed at the central facility. Monthly inventory status reports are prepared for use by management at the Reno plant.

Required

a. Prepare a system flowchart showing the accumulation and processing of data at one of the satellite plants and the Reno facility. Indicate all relevant local and companywide files.

b. What are the principal controls that should be incorporated into the system to protect data from contamination or loss during accumulation at the local plants and transmittal to the central facility?

12. A new administrator at City Hospital is trying to improve operating efficiency and slow down spiraling health care costs. She has established five responsibility centers: Emergency, Obstetrics and Gynecology, General Surgery, General Medicine, and Pharmacy. To accumulate cost data for each responsibility center, the administrator has developed worksheets to be completed by each physician, surgeon, or paramedic. The worksheets record the tasks performed, the responsibility center to which it relates, and the time spent in hours and fractions of hours.

The system is working well except that the doctors are reluctant to take the time to complete the worksheets. In some cases, floor nurses have been told to fill out the forms; in others, doctors have hurriedly filled them out without due care to see that the entries are correct. The administrator is concerned that the system's effectiveness is being frustrated by negligence by the medical professionals and is seeking ways to solve the problem.

Required

As a consultant to the hospital, analyze the problem and suggest ways in which reliable labor data can routinely be gathered.

13. During the design of an inventory management system, the following specifications were proposed for the transaction file and master file:

Inventory Transaction File	Inventory Master File
Transaction date	Product number
Transaction type	Description
Source document reference	Location
Product number	Unit of measure
Description	Quantity on hand
Unit of measure	Unit cost
Quantity	Extended cost
Unit cost	

The transaction file is to be used for all three types of inventory transaction: receipts, issuances, and adjustments. Transaction records are to be retrieved by date, and master records are to be retrieved by product number or product name.

Required

Analyze these file specifications to provide a normalized logical data structure defining the schema of a relational data base management system. Provide tables and relationships to describe your final normalized form, and also draw a data access diagram showing how data elements would be retrieved.

14. a. Prepare a HIPO overview diagram describing the accumulation of direct materials and labor costs in a job-cost system.
  b. Prepare a HIPO detail diagram describing the application of manufacturing overhead to production. In the system in question, overhead is to be applied on the basis of direct labor hours.

15. A pertinent internal control objective for the production cycle is

Inventory values are to be assigned in accordance with generally accepted methods of valuation.

Required
a. List the risks (the things that could go wrong) if this control objective were not achieved.
b. List applicable controls to reduce the risks referred to in (a).

Data for Problem 4

Item No.	Description	On Hand	Reorder Point	Order Quantity	Delivery Lead Time (weeks)	Monthly Usage*
4001	2″ × 1″ white pine	2400 ft	3,000 ft	4,000 ft	1	10,000 ft
4002	2″ × 2″ white pine	800 ft	6,000 ft	4,000 ft	1	12,000 ft
4003	4″ × 2″ white pine	32,800 ft	6,000 ft	4,000 ft	1	3,000 ft
4004	8″ × 2″ white pine	2,000 ft	3,000 ft	4,000 ft	1	16,000 ft
4005	4″ × 4″ cedar	1,200 ft	3,000 ft	3,000 ft	2	8,000 ft
4006	8″ × 4″ cedar	—	2,000 ft	3,000 ft	3	8,000 ft
4007	96″ × 48″ plywood	24,800 ft^2	2,000 ft^2	2,000 ft^2	1	2,000 ft^2
4008	48″ × 48″ plywood	1,600 ft^2	2,000 ft^2	2,000 ft^2	1	3,000 ft^2
4009	$\frac{1}{2}$″ molding	—	10,000 ft	10,000 ft	2	20,000 ft
4010	$\frac{3}{4}$″ molding	44,000 ft	10,000 ft	10,000 ft	2	5,000 ft
4011	$\frac{13}{16}$″ molding	60,400 ft	10,000 ft	10,000 ft	2	2,000 ft
4012	$\frac{1}{2}$″ dowel	2,200 ft	3,000 ft	3,000 ft	1	12,000 ft

* Average for the previous year.

22

The Revenue Cycle

LEARNING OBJECTIVES

After studying this chapter you should be able to

- Describe the major activities of the revenue cycle.
- Explain the principles of sales order processing and credit screening.
- Explain the principles of shipment of goods.
- Explain the principles of customer billing and collection.
- Identify the principal inputs, files, processes, and outputs in the revenue cycle.
- Identify the content of major documents, files, and reports in this cycle.
- Identify the main control issues in the revenue cycle.
- Discuss the main control measures in this cycle.

CHAPTER OUTLINE

OVERVIEW OF THE REVENUE CYCLE

Receipt of an Order
Credit Screening
Shipment of Goods or Provision of Services
Billing and Collection
Accounting Transactions
Sales Analysis

STRUCTURE OF THE REVENUE CYCLE

Inputs, Files, and Outputs
Processes
Key Documents
Principal Files
Selected Reports

INTERNAL CONTROLS

Control Objectives and Risks
Separation of Duties
Control of Documents
Authorization of Transactions
Other Input Controls
Processing Controls
Output Controls

SUMMARY
BIBLIOGRAPHY
DISCUSSION QUESTIONS AND PROBLEMS

OVERVIEW OF THE REVENUE CYCLE

The revenue cycle consists of the receipt and processing of sales orders, the shipment of goods or the provision of services to customers, and the associated billing and collection activities. It is sometimes referred to as the *selling cycle* or the *selling and collection cycle*. The revenue cycle typically consists of the following activities:

- Receipt of an order
- Credit screening and approval
- Shipment of goods or provision of services
- Customer billing and servicing of accounts receivable
- Collection of cash
- Recording of the accounting transactions
- Sales analysis

Related activities include the setting of sales prices, costing of sales, provision for bad debts, write-off of uncollectibles, and provision for warranty expenses.

Receipt of an Order

The sales order may originate from various sources. A customer may walk into a store or sales office and buy something. A customer may send in a purchase order by mail or Telex. An order may be received by telephone, either directly from a customer or from an outside sales representative, possibly to be confirmed in writing later. A sales representative may submit a number of orders upon returning from a sales trip. An independent broker or agent may close a sale and forward the order to the client company. A standing order may be in effect for goods or services to be supplied at regular intervals or according to some other determinant of frequency.

In wholesale organizations, it is customary for a sales order to be written up listing the items required, their prices, and all terms and conditions relating to the sale. If custom goods or services are involved, a negotiated contract may accompany the sales order. In retail enter-

578

prises, a sales ticket or sales slip may take the place of the sales order. Sometimes the sales ticket is imprinted with information from a credit card and is signed by the customer to authorize payment.

Credit Screening

Cash sales are normally acted upon at once, as are orders supported by a letter of credit from a bank or other guarantor. But most credit sales—including credit card sales for more than about $50—are contingent on the outcome of some form of credit screening. In the case of regular customers, credit information is usually stored in the customer master file or credit file. The credit information can be expressed in one of two ways, as a credit rating or a credit limit. A credit rating is a ranking of customers by creditworthiness: from those who enjoy virtually unlimited credit all the way to those who are denied credit altogether. A credit limit is a dollar ceiling up to which credit sales are automatically authorized. A credit rating or limit is a means for routine screening by sales clerks acting under a general authorization. In borderline cases in which the programmed decision would yield a negative result, credit can always be extended on a case-by-case basis by a specific authorization.

The establishment of credit arrangements may precede the placement of the first order placed by the prospective customer, or it may be initiated some time later after a number of cash sales have already been completed. The credit arrangements will be reviewed periodically and either be improved as the relationship between the two parties becomes stronger or be further restricted if the relationship deteriorates. A delinquent customer may be placed on a "credit hold" until payments are received.

The level of the credit limit that is set, or the leniency of the credit rating that is established, depends on the reputation and financial stability of the customer, on the customer's previous payment record, and on the general eagerness of the organization to do business with that customer. New businesses, or newly qualified professional people such as physicians or lawyers—even with little current financial credibility—are often given favorable credit arrangements because the seller organization wants to secure their business in anticipation of future growth and financial stability. In the case of consumer credit, a number of criteria are used to assess creditworthiness: age, ownership of a home or automobile, subscription to a telephone service, stability of employment or place of residence, level of income, existing credit arrangements or indebtedness, and any relevant history of financial responsibility (or otherwise). A points system is often used in which each criterion is given a prescribed weighting, and the total score determines the credit rating. Criteria other than those just mentioned used to be employed but have now been declared illegal. For example, it is no longer permissible to discriminate on the grounds of race or to discriminate between men and women. Credit references from banks or from other suppliers doing business with the particular customer are relied on to a large extent in the establishment of retail credit and commercial or trade credit.

Shipment of Goods or Provision of Services

If credit is approved or cash terms are agreed to and prices quoted by the customer are verified, an acknowledgment or confirmation will be sent to the customer to indicate acceptance of the order.

If the sale of goods is involved, shipment may be promised immediately or scheduled for some time in the future. In the simplest case, the goods are supplied from inventory, but this may not always be possible. Inventories may currently be depleted and the items backordered. Records of backorders are often kept on file until new supplies become available; at that time, the items may be shipped, or the customer may be notified and invited to submit a new order. In other cases, no inventories are maintained at all, and the goods are acquired from a supplier or are placed in production specifically to fill the particular order. This is a common practice when sophisticated or expensive products are involved, and it is the only feasible approach if the goods have to be produced or configured to the customer's specifications. If it appears that there will be an abnormally long time before delivery can be made, the customer may be asked to confirm the order; alternatively, the customer may be offered a substitute product.

If services are to be provided, the acknowledgment usually indicates the duration of the period over which the services will be provided and the date on which the provision of services is scheduled to commence. Details of the services may be contained in a separate agreement or contract.

Frequently, an order for goods extends to several different items. To facilitate the retrieval of the items from inventory, a picking ticket is often prepared. It identifies the items and quantities required, and it gives the warehouse location, aisle number, shelf position, bin number, or other reference to the location of the items. This information is particularly helpful if extensive inventories of many different items are maintained and if the inventory is spread throughout a large warehouse or among a number of separate buildings. If the inventories are smaller and are confined to a small area, information on the location of the items may not be needed, and a copy of the sales order may be used in place of a picking ticket.

Some form of paperwork must accompany the goods in transit. This paperwork may be a copy of the sales order or a copy of the invoice (possibly with price data omitted), or it may be a separate shipping document. The goods may be shipped by road, rail, air, or water, or they may be conveyed by the U.S. mail service, by parcel service, by the company's own delivery trucks, or by a common carrier. The choice will depend on the size and weight of the items, on their susceptibility to damage, and on the length of time available for shipment. Shipments may normally be made by river barge, but one that has to be expedited may have to send by air freight. Insurance must be arranged for the shipment, and if a common carrier is involved, a bill of lading usually has to be prepared. The bill of lading is the contract between the shipper and the common carrier.

Billing and Collection

An invoice normally is prepared at about the same time as the goods are shipped. If goods are supplied or services are provided over a period, invoices for progress payments may be submitted during the period and a final invoice at the end of the period. The pattern of progress payments, if any, must be agreed to when the sales contract is drawn up.

The invoice specifies the terms of payment, including the date on which the amount becomes due. A discount may be offered for earlier payment or a service charge imposed if payment is delayed beyond the due date. Prompt collection from customers has always been important, but it becomes vital in times of high interest rates; organizations simply cannot afford to finance a high level of accounts receivable that represent "free credit" to their customers. In some situations, payment is not expected until a monthly (or other periodic) statement is sent to the customer, but more commonly, the invoice itself represents the request for payment.

The customer statement lists the invoices issued during the current month and the payments received. Most organizations send out statements only when there is current activity or an outstanding balance; some send them out only if the balance is overdue.

There are two principal types of accounts receivable systems: the balance forward type and the open invoice type. The former considers payments to be applied against the outstanding balance rather than against particular invoices; there is no attempt to match individual payments and invoices. Invoices are regarded as "open" only during the current period, and the corresponding records are removed from the open invoice file and archived at the end of the period. On the customer statement, amounts associated with invoices from the previous and earlier periods are collapsed into a balance forward. In the latter, payment are correlated with individual invoices, and although the statement may not show invoices that remain open from previous periods, the associated records stay in the open invoice file until payment is received. One consequence of the difference between the balance forward and the open invoice types of accounts receivable system is in the ability of customers to make payments on a selective basis. The open invoice type of system allows the customer to withhold payment on one invoice—perhaps a disputed one—while settling a later one. The balance forward type does not provide that capability because the invoices and payments (to the extent that they are matched at all) are matched on a FIFO basis without regard to the wishes of either the customer or management.

When payment is received, a receipt may be sent, but an increasing number of organizations no longer routinely prepare receipts. Instead, the canceled check serves as a permanent record that payment has been made and can be produced by the customer should a dispute regarding payment ever arise.

Statements provide the normal means of notifying the customer that a balance is outstanding. But if payment is delayed for an excessive period of time, a delinquency notice, or dun, may be sent. The delinquency notice may be a preprinted business form, or it may consist of a letter from the credit manager or some other individual. The letter often spells out what action the organization proposes to take to secure payment and may also notify the customer that further sales will not be approved until the amounts are paid.

If the customer is not satisfied with the goods that have been provided, part or all of them may be returned; alternatively, the customer may keep the goods and seek an allowance or adjustment of the invoice amount. The seller organization can either approve the allowance or refuse to do so and insist on the original amount. Ultimately, a court may have to decide whether the goods were indeed defective or whether the invoice should stand as originally prepared. Cancellation of an invoice, or adjustment of the amount due, is normally formalized by means of a credit memorandum, a copy of which is sent to the customer in question. If there is an ongoing relationship between the customer and the organization, the credit memo may merely serve to reduce the amount of future payments. Otherwise, a voucher must be prepared, and a refund check sent to the customer.

There are several possible variations from the basic billing pattern described. One is the case of the retail organization that accepts credit cards serviced by an independent finance company. The seller organization submits a copy of the sales slip and receives immediate payment by the finance company. The finance company then assumes responsibility for collection from the original customer, usually in the form of installment payments with interest.

Somewhat the same situation arises when an organization discounts or factors its receivables with a finance institution. Again, the finance institution assumes responsibility for collection, and the seller is relieved of the burden of preparing invoices and statements and receives immediate payment. The price paid for receiving immediate cash by organizations accepting credit cards, and organizations that borrow against or sell their receivables, is a service charge that can be as high as 10 percent of gross sales and commonly is about 4 percent. Except when sales margins are high, these levels of service charge can be a substantial burden on the organization's profitability.

Another variation arises when a sales tax is collected. The laws of some states permit companies to remit the sales tax either when the sale is closed or when payment is received. Many companies choose the latter option because it has more favorable cash flow implications. However, when this is done, care must be taken to match properly the amount of the sales tax liability with the amount of the original sales. Whichever approach is adopted, provision must be made for handling sales to exempt organizations from which no sales tax is collected.

Accounting Transactions

The formal accounting transactions in the revenue cycle include the sale and the establishment of the receivable, the adjustment of the invoice amount to reflect a return or allowance, the recognition of sales discounts or sales tax, and the final collection of cash. There may also be formal transactions relating to the provision for doubtful accounts and the provision for future warranty expenses. The receipt of the sales order is not a formal transaction, but it is of obvious importance from an internal management standpoint. The payment of sales commissions or bonuses is another accounting transaction.

The shipment of goods, or the provision of services, forms an interface between the revenue cycle and the production cycle. Similarly, the collection of cash forms an interface with the investment cycle. The cash receipts journal can be regarded as part of either the revenue cycle or the reporting cycle.

TABLE 22.1 Summary of the Inputs, Files, and Outputs Associated with the Revenue Cycle

Application	Inputs	Files	Outputs
Sales order processing	Sales order Sales slip, retail Customer purchase order	Open order file	Picking ticket Acknowledgment memo Sales register Open order report
Shipping	Sales order (Picking ticket)	Shipment file	Shipping document Bill of lading Shipment register Shipment report
Accounts receivable	Sales order (Shipping document) Customer check Return memo	Customer master file Open invoice file Payment/credit file	Invoice Customer statement Delinquency notice, dun Schedule of aged receivables Credit memo Receipt
Sales analysis	(Management request)	Sales history file	Management reports, various Screen displays, various

Sales Analysis

Many organizations include a sales analysis application as part of the revenue cycle. Sales history is accumulated for subsequent analysis to meet management's requests for planning and control information. Sales recorded over some period of time may be analyzed by customer, customer type, region or territory, product type, dollar amount, and so forth. Frequently, some subset of the data is isolated for analysis, such as all sales that exceed a specified dollar threshold. By this means, it is possible for management, for instance, to obtain information on the breakdown, by customer, of all sales exceeding $5,000, made in the southwestern United States.

Sales analysis is an important example of the way in which data accumulated as part of the operational data-processing function provide the basis for retrieving decision support information. Sales analysis has become much easier with the emergence of interactive terminals and personal computers that can be operated by managers themselves. It has also been greatly facilitated by the growth of data base management systems and query languages (see Chapter 9). But, in all cases, the key to successful sales analysis is the use of a comprehensive system of transaction coding that permits the identification and association of transaction data with the required characteristics to meet the particular request. In the example mentioned in the previous paragraph, the transactions would have to be coded with the customer identification, the sales amount, and the territory in which the sale took place.

STRUCTURE OF THE REVENUE CYCLE

Inputs, Files, and Outputs

A summary of the inputs, files, and outputs associated with the revenue cycle is shown in Table 22.1. The main input documents are the customer purchase orders, sales order forms, return and allowance claims, and customer payments. The output documents include acknowledgment memoranda, picking tickets, shipping documents, bills of lading, invoices, customer statements, and delinquency notices. Picking tickets and shipping documents also serve as intermediate documents: picking tickets are outputs from the order-processing application and inputs to the shipping application; copies of shipping documents are outputs from the shipping application and inputs to accounts receivable.

Output reports include the sales register, the open order report, the shipping register, the open invoice report, the schedule of aged accounts receivable, and the various management reports produced by the sales analysis application.

The principal files are the open order file, the shipment file, the open invoice file, the payment/credit file, and the customer master file. All except the last are formal transaction files; however, the records in the open order and open invoice files are not automatically purged at the end of the posting operation. Records remain in the open order file until the goods are shipped or the services rendered. Similarly, in open invoice accounts receivable systems, the records in the open invoice file remain active until payment is received or until a credit memorandum cancels the invoice. In balance forward systems, the records in the "open invoice" file are usually purged at the end of the month, in conformity with the classic posting cycle. The shipment file and the payment/credit file are transaction files in the classic sense and are purged when posting is complete. The former represents an interface between the revenue cycle and the production cycle.

Processes

Systems flowcharts of the main processing activities associated with the revenue cycle are presented in Figures 22.1 through 22.3. Figure 22.1 shows the processing of sales orders and related credit-screening activities. Sales orders are prepared from customer purchase orders or from some other source, and credit is checked against data contained in the customer master file. Upon ac-

FIGURE 22.1.   Processing of sales orders for shipment.

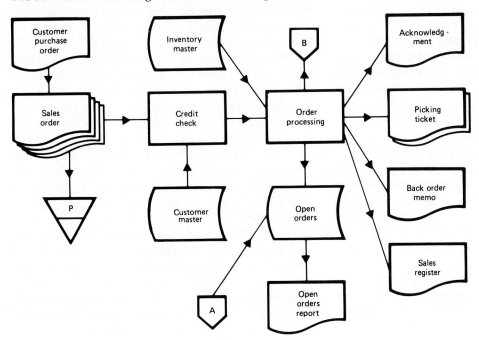

FIGURE 22.2. Preparation of goods and paperwork for shipment.

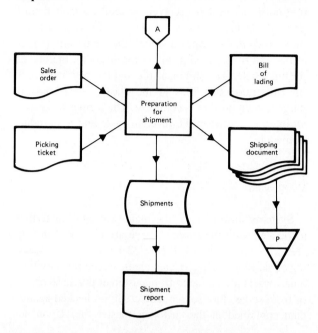

ceptance of the order, an acknowledgment is sent to the customer either confirming the availability of the goods and scheduling their shipment, or advising the customer that the goods must be backordered. In the latter case, a backorder memorandum is sent to the purchasing department or to production control requesting replenishment of the items in question. If the order can be filled immediately from inventory, a picking ticket will be prepared for the retrieval of the items from the stockroom or warehouse. Order data are entered in the sales or order register, and associated records are written to the open order file. An open order report may periodically be prepared listing all orders that are awaiting the shipment of goods or the provision of the services involved.

Figure 22.2 shows the preparation of shipment paperwork. Data from the order form and the picking ticket are used to prepare the shipping document and, if it is required, the bill of lading. Appropriate records are also written to the shipment file and may be listed in the shipment register or shipment report.

Figure 22.3 shows the billing and collection

processes. Invoices are prepared from information contained in the sales order and the shipping document. Summary data are written to the open invoice file, which then forms the basis for subsequent preparation of the open invoice report, the customer statements, the schedule of aged accounts receivable, and any delinquency notices required.

Data on collections and returns may initially be logged into a payment/credit file and subsequently posted to the open invoice file. Alternatively, they may be entered directly into the open invoice file. This latter practice will be acceptable if complete payments are the norm. If partial payments or frequent returns and allowances are likely to be involved, it is preferable to establish a separate transaction file. Approved returns and allowances are confirmed by a credit memorandum, a copy of which is sent to the customer.

For clarity, the flowcharts as presented here commonly show reports being generated from their associated transaction files. In most cases, customer names and product descriptions are omitted from the transaction files in the interest of minimizing storage capacity. It would therefore be necessary for the appropriate master files to be accessed to retrieve the descriptive data for inclusion in the reports. The customer master file would be accessed to retrieve customer names, and the inventory or product master file would be accessed to retrieve product descriptions.

Figure 22.4 presents a document flowchart showing the normal movement of paperwork in the revenue cycle as it relates to the sale of goods. Sales returns and allowances are not shown, but they could be incorporated by including the receipt of the claim from the customer and the issuance of a credit memo by accounts receivable or sales. With minor modifications, the same flowchart could be made to apply to the sale of services. The warehouse and shipping columns would be replaced by the organizational unit providing the services, and of course, there would be no picking ticket.

Figure 22.5 shows the basic elements of the sales analysis process. The sales history file is accumulated from records written in the order-processing application. Certain types of analysis may be carried out routinely, whereas others are initiated in response to a specific request for information from management. The results of

FIGURE 22.3. **Customer billings, collections, and returns.**

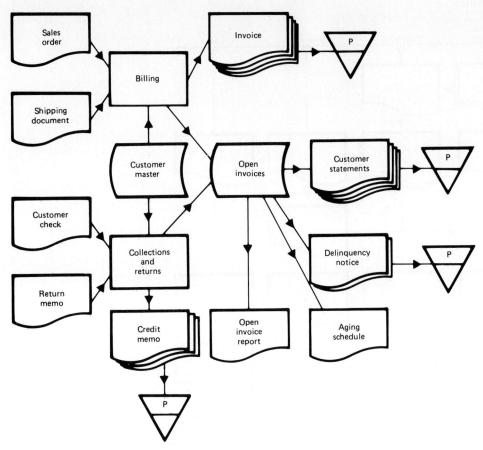

the analysis may be displayed on a video screen or delivered in the form of printed output, according to the needs of the user and the amount of data involved.

In addition to the processes already described, file maintenance provisions must be made for the update of records in the customer master file. Update is normally confined to name and address fields and to other fields not involved in transaction posting. In some systems, data relating to customer balances are excluded from the customer master file and are stored in a separate accounts receivable master file. Here, it is assumed that all permanent and semipermanent data, including balances, are put in the single customer master file. Figure 22.6 shows a screen menu suitable for maintaining the customer master file.

Key Documents

Sales Order. A sales order form records the receipt of an order from a customer. A single sales order may contain a number of separate line items. A typical sales order should contain some or all of the following types of data:

- Form number and description
- Name and billing address of customer

FIGURE 22.4. Document flowchart showing the movement of paperwork in the sale, shipment, and collection activities.

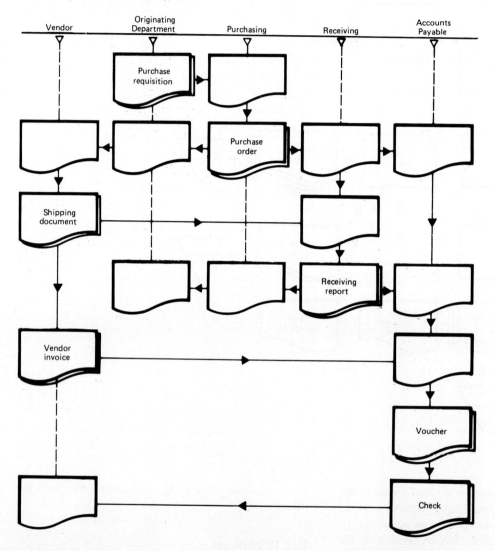

· Shipping address
· Customer number
· Order number
· Date of order
· Required delivery schedule
· Terms and conditions
· Shipping instructions
· F.O.B. point
· Responsibility for damage

· Billing instructions
· Sales tax status/exemption number
· Sales representative's code
· Special instructions

These items appear only once. In addition there are repeated line items:

· Item number or code
· Description

FIGURE 22.5. **Analysis of sales in response to management requests for information.**

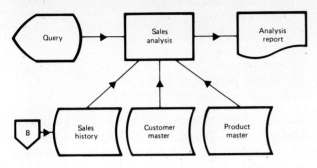

- Quantity ordered
- Unit of measure
- Unit price
- Extended price
- Line-item discount
- Net extended price

Sales order forms should be prenumbered. Multiple copies should be provided for distribution to shipping and accounting. Additional copies may be sent to the warehouse and the customer. One copy is retained by the sales department. Copies of the sales order sometimes replace the picking ticket, the shipping document, and even the customer invoice.

Picking Ticket. A picking ticket is used to facilitate the location and retrieval of the items from the stockroom or warehouse, in readiness for shipment. It is prepared from the information contained on the sales order. No more than two copies are usually needed: one to go to the shipping department and one to remain in the warehouse or stockroom. The typical content of a picking ticket is

- Form number and description
- Customer number
- Order number

FIGURE 22.6. **Screen form for customer master file maintenance.**
(Courtesy of Management Science America, Inc.)

```
    COMPANY: 01                ACCOUNT    MAINTENANCE
    CUST NO: 00000000000101     INVOICE                    ALPHA
    NAME:     ABC APPLIANCE & FURNITURE CO     ABBR NAME:  ABC APPLIANCE
    ADDRESS 1: 1976 PEACHTREE ROAD N.E.        CONTACT:    SAM HOFFMAN JR.
    ADDRESS 2: ATLANTA                         USER CODES: S6L
    ADDRESS 3:           GA 90601-1324         TELEPHONE:   404  475-9564
    OPT ADDR 1:                                ALT ACCT NO:00000000000100
    OPT ADDR 2:                                EXEMPTIONS: 3EB4    TYPE: 0

     * * * * * * * * * * * * * * * * * *  C R E D I T    I N F O R M A T I O N *
       FINANCE CHARGE  *   CASH TOLERANCE   *  CREDIT LIMIT:   80000      C/L % 0500-
     POLICY:    1      *  POLICY:    1      *  REVIEW CODE:    R          RISK CODE: 2
     ANNUAL %: 1800+   *  NET CHK %: 0100+  *  CREDIT ANALYST: 01         SALESMAN:  JGS
     MINIMUN:  0100+   *  MAXIMUM:   000500 *  OPEN DATE:      1276
                       *                    *  D & B CODE:     5A2
     * * * * * * * * * * * * * * * * * *  *  D & B DATE:      0681
       LATE PYMT CHARGE *  ANTICIPATION     *  D & B NUMBER:   0024250328
     POLICY            *  POLICY            *  NACIS CTGRY:    0000
     ANNUAL %: 0000+   *  ANNUAL %:  00000+ *  NACIS DATE:     00000
     MINIMUM:  000+    *                    *  NACIS DESCRIP
                       *                    *  SIC CODE:       5702   TERMS:   010
     * * * * * * * * * * * * * * * * * * * * * * * * * * * * * * * * * * * * * *
                       ** EDIT ERROR. CORRECT HIGHLIGHTED FIELD
     REQUEST: -                                          ACTION: ----
```

- Date of order
- Required delivery schedule
- Special instructions

With repeated line items:

- Item number or code
- Description
- Warehouse number and location
- Aisle number
- Shelf position or bin number
- Quantity ordered
- Unit of measure
- Availability (Y/N)

Shipping Document. The shipping document or packing slip accompanies the goods in transit to the customer. It contains largely the same information as the sales order, except that any variances between quantities ordered and quantities shipped should be identified. It also is customary to exclude any price data. If a copy of the sales order is used in place of a separate shipping document, the part of the form where price data would appear is left blank (by means of a "window" in the interleaving carbon) or overprinted to make it illegible. Figure 22.7 shows a typical packing slip; the company in question uses a separate invoice form.

Invoice. The invoice is prepared from the information on the sales order and shipping document and is sent to the customer to initiate the collection process. A typical invoice contains the following data:

- Form number and description
- Name and address of issuing organization
- Invoice number
- Invoice date
- Name, billing address, and shipping address of customer
- Customer number
- Sales order number
- Date of shipment
- Sales representative's identification
- Mode of shipment
- Freight and handling charges
- Sales tax
- Terms

With repeated line items:

- Item number and description
- Quantity ordered
- Quantity shipped
- Unit price
- Extended price
- Line-item discount (if any)
- Net extended price

Invoices should be prenumbered for control purposes. Multiple copies should be prepared for distribution to the customer (two copies) and to sales; one or two copies may be retained by accounting.

Customer Statement. The customer statement, developed from information in the open invoice file, is prepared at regular intervals, usually monthly. The content of the statement is normally

- Form number and description
- Name and address of issuing organization
- Name and billing address of customer
- Customer number
- Statement number
- Date of statement
- Sales representative's code
- Current balance
- 31- to 60-day balance
- 61- to 90-day balance
- Over-90-day balance

With repeated line items:

- Invoice number, date, and amount
- Payment date and amount
- Credit memo number, date, and amount

Principal Files

Customer Master File. The customer master file should provide for random access of records for interrogation and credit-screening purposes and for routine retrieval of data for processing invoices and payments. In a manual system, a card file is appropriate; in an automated system magnetic, disk storage is most suitable. The typical content of the file is as follows:

FIGURE 22.7. Packing slip. (Courtesy of Healthdyne, Inc.)

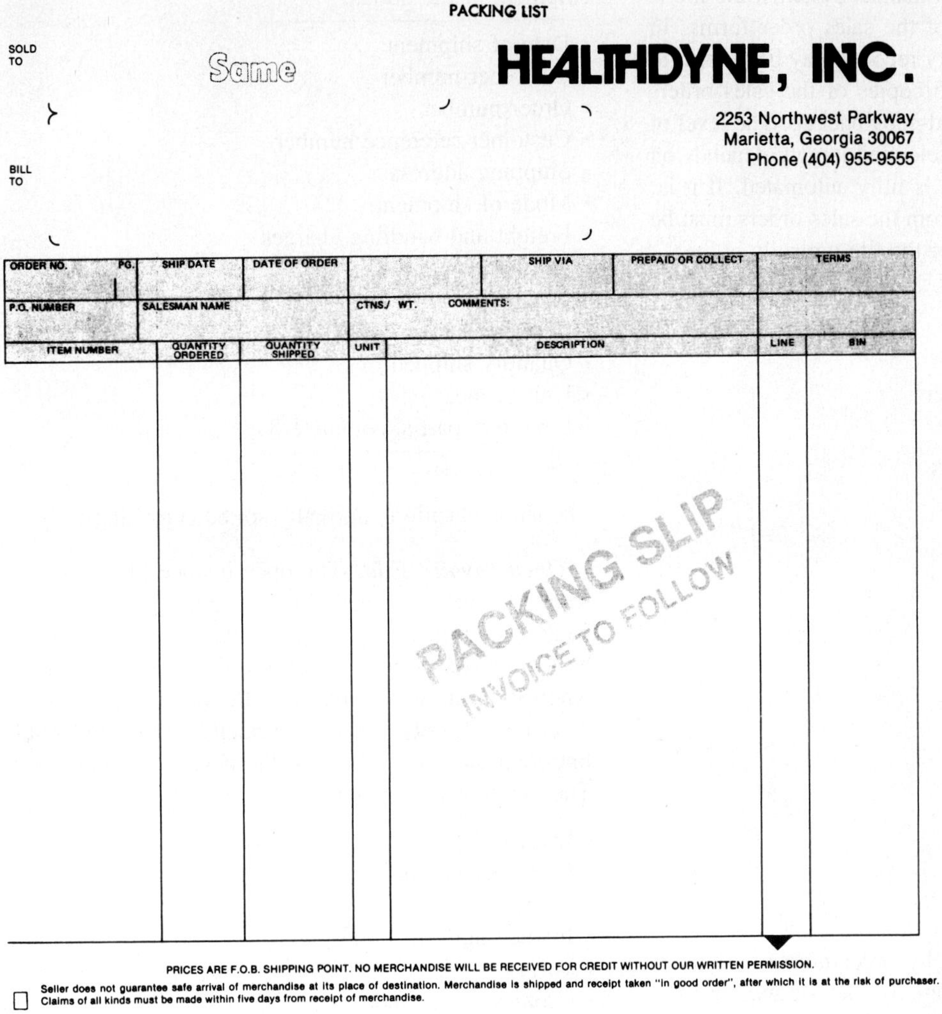

PACKING LIST

SOLD TO Same

HEALTHDYNE, INC.

2253 Northwest Parkway
Marietta, Georgia 30067
Phone (404) 955-9555

BILL TO

ORDER NO.	PG.	SHIP DATE	DATE OF ORDER		SHIP VIA	PREPAID OR COLLECT	TERMS
P.O. NUMBER		SALESMAN NAME		CTNS./ WT.	COMMENTS:		

ITEM NUMBER	QUANTITY ORDERED	QUANTITY SHIPPED	UNIT	DESCRIPTION	LINE	BIN

PACKING SLIP
INVOICE TO FOLLOW

PRICES ARE F.O.B. SHIPPING POINT. NO MERCHANDISE WILL BE RECEIVED FOR CREDIT WITHOUT OUR WRITTEN PERMISSION.

Seller does not guarantee safe arrival of merchandise at its place of destination. Merchandise is shipped and receipt taken "in good order", after which it is at the risk of purchaser. Claims of all kinds must be made within five days from receipt of merchandise.

- Customer number
- Customer name and billing address
- Regular shipping address
- Contact name and telephone number
- Sales territory
- Credit rating or limit
- Sales tax percentage, or exemption number
- Current balance
- 31- to 60-day balance
- 61- to 90-day balance
- Over-90-day balance
- Year-to-date sales
- Year-to-date collections
- Comments

The aged balance fields are sometimes omitted in open invoice systems if the transaction records are readily accessible, as in a data base configuration. The file is normally sorted by customer number, which also serves as the primary retrieval key. If the file volatility is high, an ISAM structure may be used.

Open Order File. The open order file can be accessed randomly or sequentially. In manual systems, the file is often composed of copies of the sales order forms. In automated systems, summary records may be written to the open order file, and the copies of the sales orders maintained as a separate hard-copy backup. The level of summarization that can be tolerated largely depends on whether invoice preparation is fully automated. If it is, the detailed line-item data from the sales orders must be included. The full content of the file typically is

- Date of order
- Customer number
- Order number
- Customer reference number
- Sales representative's code
- Terms and conditions
- Sales tax percentage
- Requested delivery date
- Shipping instructions
- Special shipping address
- Actual shipment date
- Partial/complete flag
- Open/closed flag
- Comments
- Item number or code*
- Quantity ordered*
- Unit of measure*
- Unit price*
- Line-item discount*

*Repeated fields

The file is normally sorted by order number. If order numbers are assigned sequentially, the file will also automatically be sorted chronologically.

Shipment File. The shipment file can be accessed sequentially if this is most convenient. In manual systems, the file may be composed of copies of the shipping documents. In automated systems, the copies of the shipping documents are kept as a separate hard-copy backup. As with the open order file, the shipment file must contain line-item data if full automation is desired. In particular, the line-item data are required if the file is used to post issuance data to the inventory master file. The content of the shipment file is similar to that of the open

order file, except for the data specifically related to the shipment of the goods:

- Date of shipment
- Customer number
- Order number
- Customer reference number
- Shipping address
- Mode of shipment
- Freight and handling charges
- Partial/complete flag
- Comments
- Item number or code*
- Quantity shipped*
- Unit of measure*
- Line-item partial/complete flag*

*Repeated fields

The shipment file is normally sorted chronologically.

Open Invoice File. The open invoice file preferably should be accessed randomly, but sequential access can be adopted if necessary. In a manual system, the file can be composed of copies of the invoices themselves, whereas in an automated one, the file consists of summary records only. There is normally no need to include line-item data, regardless of the degree of automation. The file content typically is as follows:

- Invoice date
- Customer number
- Order number
- Invoice number
- Terms
- Gross invoice amount
- Sales tax
- Freight and handling charges
- Discount amount
- Net invoice amount
- Date of payment
- Amount of payment
- Check number
- Partial/complete flag
- Open/closed flag

The open invoice file is normally sorted by invoice number; it is also in chronological order if the invoice numbers are assigned sequentially.

FIGURE 22.8. An open order report.

AIS ASSOCIATES
OPEN ORDER REPORT
As of 2/28/XX

Page 1

Order date	Order number	Customer number	Customer name	Sales-man	No. of items	Gross amount	Comments
1/07/XX	1024	323	Jasper Company	PDQ	4	$17,050	Expedite
1/10/XX	1027	187	Saphire, Inc.	EFA	2	9,460	
1/18/XX	1034	229	Chalcedony Bros.	BHJ	17	27,580	Reference J93-B
1/22/XX	1035	290	Emerald Co.	AMP	8	12,300	Needed 3/1/XX
1/30/XX	1039	124	Sardonyx Assoc.	GIM	5	23,850	
2/08/XX	1043	87	Sardius. Ltd.	MCD	11	5,440	Yes
2/12/XX	1050	301	Chrysolite Co.	DEF	3	2,870	
2/20/XX	1052	208	Beryl Bros.	HAP	7	3,130	Follow up
					Total	$101,680	

Form no. 666/Rev. 6.

Sales History File. The sales history file provides permanent summary records of all sales for subsequent analysis. It is most commonly maintained in automated systems because of the difficulty of performing analysis by hand.

The large volume of data involved makes magnetic tape an attractive storage medium; however, the data would have to be transferred to a random access medium for analysis. Ideally, the data should be stored on magnetic disk from the outset. Line-item data must be included if product preferences are to be analyzed. The content of the file may be

- Date of order
- Customer number
- Territory
- Sales representative code
- Gross amount of sale
- Item number or code*
- Quantity ordered*
- Unit of measure*
- Unit price*

*Repeated fields

Records are purged from the sales history file when the data are no longer considered relevant. The period of retention may vary from about three months to five years, depending on management's needs, the cost of file storage, and the ability to process and perform meaningful analysis on a potentially very large volume of data.

Selected Reports

Open Order Report. The open order report is a status report prepared from the open order file (possibly with customer names retrieved from the customer master file). The report may be sorted chronologically or by order number[1] or customer; the last has the advantage that orders placed by the same customer are grouped together. The specific information included in the report depends on management's needs. Figure 22.8 illustrates one possible form.

Shipment Report. The shipment report is an activity report prepared from the shipment file, with customer names and product descriptions recovered from the customer and product (or inventory) master files. In some

[1] As noted earlier, these will be the same if order numbers are assigned sequentially.

FIGURE 22.9. A shipment report with detailed line items. In an alternative form of the report, only summary data are included.

PQR INCORPORATED
SHIPMENT REPORT
for week ending 12 / 8 / XX

Page 1

Date of shipment	Order number	Customer number	Customer name	Mode of shipment	Item number	Description	Quant. ordered	Quant. shipped	Unit of measure
12 / 02 / XX	1962	23	Red Co.	Our truck	2061	2in. widget	14	14	Each
					2064	4in. widget	8	8	Each
					2068	6in. widget	1	1	Box
					3020	Thin lubricant	2	1	Drum
12 / 05 / XX	1970	46	Blue Co.	U . P . S .	2061	2in. widget	3	3	Case
					1022	Short stand	60	60	Pair
					1024	Long stand	72	60	Pair
					3040	Thick lubricant	6	6	Drum
					3060	Solid lubricant	2	2	Quart
12 / 08 / XX	1978	19	Green Co.	U . S . Mail	2064	4in. widget	20	20	Case
					2068	6in. widget	15	12	Each
					3020	Thin lubricant	5	5	Pint

Report no . S / 20

FIGURE 22.10. A schedule of aged accounts receivable.

ABC COMPANY
SCHEDULE OF AGED ACCOUNTS RECEIVABLE
As of 10/31/XX

Page 1

Customer Number	Customer Name	No. of invoices	Total	Current	31-60 day	61-90 day	Over 90 day
666	Mercury Associates	2	$3,792	$1,230	$2,562		
667	Venus and Sons	3	1,455	1,455			
668	Earth Corporation	5	4,817	1,924	1,800	$1,093	
669	Mars, Incorporated	8	9,006		3,545	5,461	
670	Jupiter Brothers	13	16,380	9,932	6,448		
671	Saturn Enterprises	11	12,255		4,687	5,580	$1,988
672	Uranus Unlimited	5	4,760	4,760			
673	Neptune, Inc.	3	2,085		2,085		
674	Pluto Partners	1	890				890
		51	$55,440	$19,301	$21,127	$12,134	$2,878

Form no. 65536

cases, the report takes a summary form, just listing complete shipments; in other cases, the detailed line items are included. Figure 22.9 illustrates the latter form. The detailed report can become quite lengthy if numerous shipments have been made during the period, each consisting of many line items. The summary form may be more appropriate in such situations.

Schedule of Aged Accounts Receivable. The schedule of aged receivables, or aging schedule, is a status report prepared from the open invoice file, with customer names retrieved from the customer master file. The total balance due from each customer is shown, together with a breakdown of the balance by age category. The number of invoices outstanding may also be shown. A typical layout of the report is shown in Figure 22.10.

Sometimes the individual invoices are listed on the schedule, each placed in its proper age column. This form is a combination of the schedule of aged receivables and the open invoice report.

INTERNAL CONTROLS

Control Objectives and Risks

The main control objectives pertaining to the revenue cycle and its component applications require that[2]

- Customer orders receive proper approval of credit and terms before acceptance.
- Goods shipped or services rendered are properly billed and are in the correct amounts.
- Sales are properly recorded as to account, amount, and accounting period.
- Customer returns, allowances, and discounts are properly approved and recorded.
- Customer receipts are properly recorded as to account, amount, and accounting period.
- Cash receipts are properly applied to customer balances and deposited.

[2] Ernst & Whinney, *Evaluating Internal Control: A Guide for Management and Directors,* Pub. no. 39078 (Cleveland: Ernst & Whinney, 1979).

These objectives address a number of concerns relating to the unauthorized extension of credit; the failure to record, or improperly record, sales; and the improper recording or misappropriation of cash receipts.

Credit may be extended to poor credit risks, thereby damaging future cash flows and possibly leading to the overstatement of collectible accounts receivable. Excessive discounts may be offered, or unwarranted allowances granted, either through negligence or as part of a deliberate irregularity. Departures from management policies relating to credit terms, discounts, or allowances may be enacted to facilitate "side deals" or kickbacks.

The failure to bill customers properly for shipment of goods or provision of services will result in the understatement of revenues and accounts receivable. Correspondingly, the failure to record the associated outflow of inventory will result in the overstatement of inventory and the understatement of cost of sales. A deliberate failure to record sales may reflect attempts by dishonest individuals to obtain goods or services without being billed.

The preparation of invoices using unauthorized prices may damage the organization, regardless of whether the prices are higher or lower than the correct ones. Prices that are higher than the authorized ones may antagonize customers and possibly lead to damage suits; prices that are lower than the authorized ones will damage the organization's revenues and cash flows. Irregularities can be perpetrated in which certain individuals receive goods or services for less than the proper rates; illegal payments or kickbacks may be involved in the irregularities.

Sales may be improperly recorded or not recorded at all. Improper recording can include application to the wrong general ledger account and recording in the wrong amount. A deliberate attempt may be made to suppress earnings and therefore taxes; alternatively, an attempt may be made to exaggerate the performance of the organization by overstating revenues. Sales may be recorded at less than the amount billed, and the additional revenue may be misappropriated upon remittance by the customer. Sales may also be attributed to the wrong accounting period, so that a mismatch—in either direction—occurs between recorded shipments and sales. This may result from an attempt to smooth income.

Returns and allowances may be misclassified or not

recorded at all, thereby overstating revenues and accounts receivable. Customer credits may be granted in excess of those permitted under management policy. Credit memos may be issued but not sent to the customers; subsequently, the additional amounts remitted by customers may be misappropriated. Similarly, customer payments made in full after the expiration of the discount period may be improperly recorded as though the discounts had been taken, and the additional amounts misappropriated.

Cash receipts from customers may be lost, misappropriated, or not recorded. Collections and deposits may be incorrectly recorded or recorded in different accounting periods. Entries may be made to the wrong general ledger accounts. Mismatches may occur between the amount collected and that deposited, possibly as part of an irregularity. Also, attempts may be made to misappropriate cash and to conceal the defalcation by making debits to other accounts (e.g., expense accounts) or by issuing fictitious credit memos.

Cash receipts may be posted to the wrong customer's account; this will leave total accounts receivable correct while misstating the individual account balances. Accounts that are collectible may be written off without proper authorization, and the customer's remittance misappropriated. Postings may be delayed to conceal the misappropriation of a float of cash; this irregularity is sometimes referred to as *lapping*.

Separation of Duties

There should be adequate separation of duties between the review of creditworthiness and the acceptance of sales orders; otherwise, the zeal for closing sales may interfere with caution in avoiding poor credit risks. Many organizations have a separate credit department that approves the initial credit rating assigned to new customers and routinely reviews the ratings of existing customers in the light of level of sales and payment history. Credit policies must be reduced to writing, and any deviations from those policies must be approved by the credit manager in advance of the sale.

There must also be separation of duties among the shipment of goods, the granting of credits for returns and allowances, the receiving of cash, and the associated accounting functions. Customer billing should be separated from shipping and inventory control. The responsibility for writing off uncollectible accounts should be independent of the servicing of accounts receivable.

Control of Documents

Sales order forms, shipping documents, and invoices all should be prenumbered for control purposes. Transactions should be logged into the respective journals or registers in numerical sequence, and any gaps or duplication of numbers promptly investigated and resolved. Shipping documents should be reconciled with sales orders and invoices reconciled with both. This is to ensure that all orders are shipped and all shipments are billed. No sales orders should be processed unless a formal sales order has been written up and logged into the sales register. Similarly, no goods should be shipped without a formal shipping document. The transfer of responsibility for goods from the organization to the shipper or common carrier should be evidenced in writing by means of a bill of lading or otherwise.

The inventory of sales order forms, shipping documents, and invoices should be controlled to restrict access to them to authorized persons.

Authorization of Transactions

Proper authorization must be given for the approval of credit terms, the setting of prices, the shipment of goods or the provision of services, the granting of credits for returns for allowances, the determination of discounts, and the writing off of uncollectible accounts receivable.

Authority for establishing credit policy lies with the credit department and upper management. The credit manager has the responsibility for screening new customers for creditworthiness and for granting nonstandard credit terms to individual customers. Credit can be extended to existing customers by the sales department within the guidelines of established policies.

Prices are set by the sales or marketing departments and are approved by top management. Formal price lists should be drawn up for routine use and be routinely reviewed. Care must be taken to ensure that no obsolete price lists remain in use. Similarly, policies relating to volume and other discounts should be put in writing. Any deviations from standard price lists or standard discount policies must be properly authorized. An exception report should be prepared, listing all such deviations together with the identification of the person who approved them.

Credits for returned goods must not be granted until the goods have been received and checked. The approval of credits for returns and allowances must be independent of the billing function.

A formal policy must be established for the write-off of accounts receivable as uncollectible. All reasonable measures of collection should have been exhausted before accounts are deemed to be uncollectible. Delinquent accounts should be identified and followed up independently from the routine servicing of accounts receivable and cash receipts. Sales commission should be adjusted for actual or estimated bad debts.

Other Input Controls

Control of cash receipts frequently begins in the mail room. Incoming mail should be opened by personnel who are independent of the treasury and accounts receivable functions, and a complete list immediately should be made of currency and checks received for subsequent reconciliation with the cash receipts journal. In all cases, receipt of cash must be segregated from the accounting function. If currency is involved, employees should be bonded and closely supervised. In retail organizations, cash register tapes should be reconciled daily with the amount of cash in the register drawers.

From a control standpoint, the open invoice accounts receivable system is superior to the balance forward system because of the routine matching of payments with specific invoices. This procedure helps reduce the likelihood that payments are posted to the wrong customer's account. Posting to the accounts in both types of systems should be independently checked against the total of cash receipts.

Processing Controls

Independent checks should be made that prices charged to customers conform with current standard price lists. Quantities listed on the invoices should also be checked against the corresponding quantities appearing on the sales orders and shipping documents. Individual accounts receivable balances should be reconciled with the total shown for the accounts receivable control account. The bank reconciliation provides a further check that all cash receipts have been properly deposited.

Output Controls

Each day's cash receipts must be deposited promptly and deposit slips maintained on file for subsequent independent reconciliation with entries in the cash receipts journal.

Controls must be in place to ensure that all invoices and credit memos are mailed to customers. Customer statements provide a useful—if one-sided—check on the correctness of accounts receivable records. Customers can be relied on to challenge extraneous invoices charged to their accounts or inflated amounts due; on the other hand, they are unlikely to report missing invoices or understated amounts.

SUMMARY

The revenue cycle refers to the distribution of resources, in the form of goods and services, to parties outside the organization, and to the collection of revenues for these resources. The revenue cycle embraces the operational applications of credit screening, sales order processing, shipping, and accounts receivable, and the decision support application of sales analysis.

Sales order processing covers a range of activities, including order taking and order tracking. In both manufacturing and merchandising organizations, it interfaces with the shipping function. In service organizations, it may interface with contract-tracking activities.

The approval and extension of credit vary considerably in form, from the traditional pattern of commercial credit arrangements to the issuance and use of credit cards. The accounts receivable application, as the direct result of credit sales, includes both billing and cash collections.

The principal documents in the revenue cycle are customer purchase orders, sales orders, picking tickets, shipping documents, invoices and statements, credit memos, and customer checks. The principal files are the customer master file, the open order file, the shipment file, the open invoice file, and the sales history file. Major reports are the sales journal, the open order report, the shipment report, the open invoice report, and the schedule of aged accounts receivable.

Internal control in the revenue cycle emphasizes the need for proper authorization of credit terms, correct recording and recognition of revenues, and the careful control of cash receipts. Related areas include the proper valuation of accounts receivable and the write-off of uncollectible accounts.

BIBLIOGRAPHY

Arens, Alvin A., and D. Dewey Ward. *Systems Understanding for Auditing*. Haslett, Mich.: Systems Publications 1981.

Briegel, Louis R. *The American Dream*. Marietta, Ga.: Ad-Vision, 1981.

Ernst & Whinney. *Evaluation Internal Control: A Guide for Management and Directors*, Publ. no. 39078. Cleveland: Ernst & Whinney, 1979.

Forms for the Key Operations of Business. Glenview, Ill.: Moore Business Forms, 1977.

Gelinas, Urie J. "Using an Illustration of a Conceptual Information System to Improve Pedagogy in MIS Courses." *MAS Communication*, vol. 5, no. 3, October 1981, pp. 17-27.

Pescoe, Jerome K., ed. *Encyclopedia of Accounting Systems*. Englewood Cliffs, N.J.: Prentice-Hall, 1976.

DISCUSSION QUESTIONS AND PROBLEMS

1. Define and discuss the following terms:

- Acknowledgment
- Balance forward system
- Bill of lading
- Credit hold
- Credit limit
- Credit memorandum
- Credit rating
- Credit reference
- Credit screening
- Customer invoice
- Customer master file
- Customer statement
- Delinquency notice
- F.O.B. point
- Open invoice file
- Open order file
- Open invoice report
- Open invoice system
- Open order report
- Partial payment
- Partial shipment
- Payment/credit file
- Picking ticket
- Returns and allowances
- Revenue cycle
- Sales analysis
- Sales discount
- Sales history file
- Sales order
- Sales register
- Schedule of aged receivables
- Shipment file
- Shipping document
- Shipping register

2. An independent computer repair and maintenance company offers contractual services to users of several brands of computer hardware. Describe the steps that the company would probably take to secure a contract, provide the services, and obtain payment.

3. A retail department store uses a points system to assign credit limits to new applicants for its revolving credit plan. Applicants scoring over 100 points are assigned a credit limit of $2,000; those scoring between 50 and 100 points are assigned a limit of $1,000; those with 30 to 50 points are given a limit of $500; those between 20 and 30 points are given a limit of $200; and those scoring fewer than 20 points are rejected. Points are contributed toward the total score according to various attributes taken from the application questionnaire:

Attribute	Points
Is in regular employment	20
Earns between $10,000 and $20,000 per year	10
Earns over $20,000 per year	20
Is a professional person	20
Has lived at present address for at least six months	10
Is married	5
Owns a home	10
Subscribes to telephone in own name	5
Owns an automobile	5
Has bank checking account	10
Has bank savings account	5
Has one or more major credit cards	10
Has previously declared bankruptcy	−30

Required

Determine the credit limit to be assigned to Miss Mary Black, a certified public accountant who has just moved into the neighborhood. She has earned over $30,000 a year for the last five years, owns a car, has recently established checking and savings accounts at a local bank, and has three national credit cards. Currently she lives in an apartment and has a telephone both at home and at her office.

4. Cistern Company is a wholesaler of plumbing fixtures and related products. The company's large inventory extends thoughout three warehouse buildings designated A-Shed, B-Shed, and C-Shed. Inventory records include a 15-digit item number and a 30-character description.

One of the warehouse buildings (C-Shed) is divided into bays, numbered 1 to 50, for the storage of large items such as bathtubs, prefabricated shower stalls,

sinks, toilets, and lengths of pipe. The other two buildings are lined with four-tier shelves for the storage of small items such as faucets, elbow joints, ball cocks, and cans of jointing compound. The aisles are numbered 1 to 20 in each building. The position of an item along any given aisle is designated by a location code consisting of the tier and the shelf position. For example, "B-25" corresponds to the B-tier (second from the top) and position 25.

Required

Design a picking ticket to be used by the company for the retrieval of inventory items. Quantities of items ordered typically lie in the range 1 to 50.

5. During August, the following invoices were issued by One Company to its customer, Another Company:

Date	Invoice No.	Amount
8/3	9508	$ 350
8/10	9583	1,750
8/13	9665	800
8/21	9697	1,230

There was one outstanding invoice as of August 1—no. 9267, dated 7/13, for $500. On August 28, Another sent a check for $2,250, in payment of invoices 9267 and 9583. Invoice 9508 had been returned earlier because of a dispute regarding one of the items listed. The invoices dated 8/13 and 8/21 were not due until sometime in September.

Required

a. Show what records would be maintained by One Company as of August 31 if its accounts receivable function were structured on (i) a balance forward basis and (ii) on an open invoice basis.
b. Late in September (before any further sales or payments were made involving Another), the controller of Another Company telephoned to report that part

of his company's payables records had been destroyed in a fire. To help him reconstruct Another's records, he needed to know which invoices had been paid from August 1 onward and which remained open. What information could be provided to the controller, assuming that One's receivables system was of each type mentioned in (a)?

6. Roy's Office Supply company sells stationery and a range of office products to several local businesses. An analysis of its sales and collections records revealed the following data:

Order No.	Net Invoice Amount	Date of Sale	Date of Payment
203	$210	3/2	3/12
204	75	3/4	3/20
205	375	3/5	5/16
206*	280	3/8	3/21
207	125	3/12	4/29
208	160	3/18	4/1
209	380	3/25	(written off 7/1)
210	145	3/28	4/15

* Sale to an exempt organization

The outstanding balance as of March 1 was $760. Of this amount, $320 was collected in March and the remainder in April; none represented sales to organizations that were exempt from sales tax.

Required

Determine the amount of sales tax, figured at 4 percent of net sales, to be remitted to the state revenue authority for the month of March, assuming that (a) the company recognizes sales tax at the time of sale and (b) it recognizes sales tax at the time of collection.

7. The sales history file of P-Company contains the following data for the months of June and July:

Order Date	Customer Number	Territory	Product Number	Gross Amount
6/5	25	SE	136	$25,000
6/11	13	NE	101	15,000
6/15	19	NE	105	5,000
6/19	8	NW	122	40,000
6/25	21	NE	103	35,000
6/28	35	SE	101	20,000
7/1	2	NW	118	25,000
7/7	6	NW	101	10,000
7/12	18	SE	120	45,000
7/19	13	NE	101	5,000
7/21	25	SE	103	15,000
7/27	35	SE	122	30,000
7/30	8	NW	103	30,000

Required

a. Determine total sales for (i) June and (ii) July in each of the three territories: SE, NE, and NW.

b. What customer made the largest dollar purchases in the group of products that includes nos. 118, 120, and 122?

c. Show a breakdown of sales of product no. 101 by territory, for the two-month period.

d. What was the product with the lowest dollar sales during (i) June and (ii) July?

e. In which territory were the highest dollar sales made of the product group that includes nos. 101, 103, and 105?

8. Draw an expanded document flowchart, similar to that in Figure 22.4, for the flow of paperwork involved in the sale and shipment of goods and the associated collection activities. Include the documents relating to the return of substandard or damaged goods, to the claim for allowances, to the issuance of credit memos, and to the receipt of partial payments. Also show the preparation and dispatch of customer statements.

9. Design an invoice form for Ace Cleaning Company, which offers janitorial services to industrial clients. Most of Ace's work is done under ongoing contracts, in which the same amount is billed each month. But one-time cleaning jobs are also undertaken, both for regular clients and for others, and these are billed according to the number of labor hours spent on the particular job.

Ace does not offer discounts for prompt payment, but it does impose a penalty of 1.5 percent per month on accounts more than 30 days overdue. The basic invoice terms are net 30.

The invoices must show the name and telephone number of the crew leader.

10. Jason Research, Inc., is a small consulting firm that undertakes research and development contracts for the U.S. Army. Most of Jason's contracts are of the "cost plus fixed fee" type. One of these contracts, no. 123456789, is for a total estimated cost of $125,000 and a fixed fee of $6,250. The contract covers a 12-month period.

Billings for progress payments, covering costs only, are prepared monthly. Quarterly billings are submitted for the portion of the fee that has been earned. This portion is calculated according to the following formula:

$$\text{Portion of fee earned} = \frac{\text{Actual costs for the quarter}}{\text{Total estimated costs for the contract}} \times \text{Total fixed fee}$$

Required
a. Design an open invoice file for Jason Research suitable for storing invoice records relating to progress payments and fee payments.
b. Insert records corresponding to the first quarter's billings under contract no. 123456789, given that costs for the first three months were $8,570, $10,350, and $9,210, respectively.

11. Ross Company, a distributor of light manufacturing parts, has been having difficulties with the increasing size of its accounts receivable balances and slow payment by customers.

Presently all billing is done out of the home office in Chicago. Each week the 12 branch offices, which extend over a 20-state territory, submit details of shipments

made to customers from their local distribution points. Invoices are prepared and mailed to customers after each sale, and bimonthly statements are sent to delinquent accounts. All sales are made on terms of 1/20, n/60.

Billings and collections are processed on a computer that has been in operation for about nine months. Eighteen clerks are employed in the accounts receivable department. The supervisor had frequently complained about the low morale of the clerks, and there is increasing employee turnover, absenteeism, and tardiness in the department. There was resistance to the introduction of the computer, and management has more than once remarked that the company was better off under its old manual system.

Required
You, an MAS specialist with a national public accounting firm, have been called in as a consultant to advise the company. Draw up two separate proposals for dealing with the problems, to be submitted first to your own manager and then to the management of Ross Company.

12. What internal controls would be effective in preventing the following problems?
a. A customer claims that an invoice does not reflect a special discount negotiated with the sales representative who closed the sale. The sales person is no longer with the company.
b. A customer claims that a shipment of goods never arrived. The shipping clerk says that he remembers that the shipment was picked up by a common carrier about three months ago.
c. A customer complains that the price of a certain item has suddenly jumped by 30 percent. An investigation shows that there has not been a price increase but that the customer has been underbilled for the last nine months.
d. A customer calls to inquire why a credit for returned goods has not been granted. The company's books show that a credit memo was issued six weeks ago and that a refund check was issued and cashed.
e. Upon receipt of a delinquency notice referring to an overdue amount, a customer produces a canceled check in the amount of the invoice.

13. A new computerized sales order-processing system is being developed for a corporate client. During the initial design process, the following specifications were proposed for the sales transaction file and the open sales order file:

Sales Transaction File	Open Sales Order File
Date of sale	Sales order number
Sales person number	Sales person number
Sales order number	Customer purchase order number
Customer purchase order number	Date of sale
Customer number	Customer number
Customer name	Customer name
Customer shipping address	Customer shipping address
Customer billing address	Customer billing address
Product number*	Product number*
Description*	Description*
Unit of measure*	Unit of measure*
Quantity*	Quantity*
Unit price*	Unit price*
Extended price*	Extended price*

* Repeated fields

The two files are identical except for their retrieval keys and usage characteristics. Transaction records are to be retrieved by date of issuance of the sales order, whereas open sales order records are to be retrieved by sales order number. The transaction file is to be purged once per month. The open sales order file is a permanent file, although individual records will be purged 30 days after shipments have been completed.

Required

Analyze these file specifications to provide a normalized logical data structure suitable for defining the schema of a relational data base management system. Provide tables of data elements to describe your final normalized form, and also draw a data access diagram showing how the data records would be retrieved.

14. a. Draw a HIPO overview diagram for the process of cash collection.
b. Draw a HIPO detail diagram for the preparation of a bank deposit slip.

15. A pertinent internal control objective for the revenue cycle is

Customer receipts are properly recorded as to account, amount, and accounting period.

Required
a. List the risks (the things that could go wrong) if this control objective were not achieved.
b. List applicable controls to reduce the risks referred to in (a).

Glossary

absolute value The value attached to the symbols used in a numbering system, as distinct from that attached to the relative positions of those symbols in the number.

acceptance report A report issued to confirm that services procured from an outside vendor have been completed satisfactorily.

access controls General controls concerned with restricting to authorized persons physical or electronic access to computer resources.

accessibility The ease or difficulty of accessing the data in a storage medium, as measured by the time or cost to enter or retrieve a record.

accounting applications Subsystems of the accounting information system. Examples include accounts receivable, accounts payable, general ledger, inventory management, payroll, purchasing, and sales order processing.

accounting controls The subset of internal controls concerned with the integrity of the accounting data and the protection of the company's assets.

accounting information system A subsystem of the business information system associated with the types of information and information processing that fall within the province of the accounting function.

accounts payable The amounts owed to vendors and others, arising largely from purchases of merchandise or raw materials. The accounting application involving such data.

accounts receivable The amounts owed by customers and others, arising primarily from credit sales. The accounting application involving such data.

acknowledgment A document sent to a customer confirming that an order has been received and the proposed terms of sale accepted. A signal returned from a receiving station to the transmitting station, indicating that a message has been received.

acoustic coupler A simple type of modem in which an acoustic carrier wave is used for data transmission.

action document A document that gives rise to an economic event as well as records a transaction. An example is a purchase order.

activity ratio A measure of file activity, equal to the percentage of records accessed during a prescribed period.

activity report A report listing the transaction activity that has occurred during a prescribed period. It corresponds to the listing of a transaction file.

address A reference to the physical location of a data element or record in a storage medium or device.

administrative controls The subset of internal controls primarily concerned with enforcing management policies and procedures and encouraging operational efficiency.

aged receivables (schedule of) A status report in which amounts owed by customers are classified into different age categories. The categories typically used are current, 30 to 60 days, 60 to 90 days, and over 90 days overdue.

ALGOL (Algorithmic Oriented Language) A high-level programming language used primarily for scientific applications.

alphabetic data Data consisting of only the letters of the alphabet.

alphanumeric data Data consisting of both alphabetic and numeric characters and special symbols such as punctuation marks and certain mathematical symbols.

analog computer A computing device that operates by measuring and comparing voltage level. Analog computers are not normally used for business applications.

analog signal An electrical signal with a continuous waveform.

analytical review A series of reasonableness tests performed in a financial audit engagement and aimed at analyzing relationships among the data. Various statistical techniques are typically used to perform the analytical review.

ANSI flowcharting standards The flowcharting standards established by the American National Standards Institute.

applications See **accounting applications**.

applications controls A subset of accounting controls that relate to specific applications within a computerized information system rather than to the system as a whole.

applications software The user-oriented part of the computer software that performs specific information-processing activities such as processing the payroll. It contrasts with systems software that is machine oriented.

arithmetic/logic unit (ALU) A component of the central processor unit that performs arithmetic and logical operations.

ASCII code A code, formally known as the American Standard Code for Information Interchange, that assigns numerical equivalents to commonly used symbols, including the letters of the alphabet and the numbers 0 through 9. It is a widely used standard for the storage and transmission of data by computers.

assembler A systems software package that translates mnemonic or assembly code into machine code. An assembler is a rudimentary form of compiler.

assembly code A low-level symbolic programming language using mnemonics for the applicable operation codes.

asynchronous transmission A form of serial transmission in which no attempt is made to synchronize the clocks in the transmitting and receiving devices. Instead, start and stop bits are interposed between each byte.

audit committee A standing committee of the board of directors charged with monitoring control and audit matters in the organization.

audit objectives The set of general and specific objectives established by an auditor that determine the procedures to be performed during the audit engagement.

audit opinion A formal part of the audit report in which the auditor either attests or declines to attest to the fairness of the financial statements.

audit procedures Combinations of techniques performed in particular areas of the accounting system to support the audit opinion.

audit reliance The reliance placed on audit procedures to achieve the objectives of the engagement.

audit report The means by which the auditor communicates the conclusions of the audit to management and others.

audit risk The risk that material errors may exist in the financial statements and not be detected by the audit procedures.

audit software Computer programs used by an auditor to assist in performing audit tests.

audit techniques The activities of observation, inquiry, examination, inspection, confirmation, and testing on which audit procedures are based.

audit testing A major class of audit techniques customarily divided into compliance testing and substantive testing.

audit trail A path through the information system that can be traced to verify the correctness of transaction processing.

auditor An external auditor is an individual, independent of the organization, who is responsible for attesting to claims made by management or others concerning the fairness and integrity of financial information. An internal auditor is an employee responsible for monitoring and improving the effectiveness of the the internal control system.

authorization A directive issued by management to perform a specified procedure or procedures.

autodial modem A type of modem capable of automatically dialing the telephone number of a host computer or data service.

Bachman diagram A diagrammatic means of representing the relationships among data elements in a logical data structure.

background task A low-priority task executed by a computer when resources are available.

backup file A duplicate copy of a file made for security reasons in case the original is damaged or destroyed.

balance forward system A type of accounts receivable system in which cash collections reduce the customer's unpaid balance but in which no attempt is made to match them against particular invoices. This type of system contrasts with the open invoice system.

bar chart A chart that depicts the values of discrete variables by means of the lengths of horizontal or vertical bars.

BASIC (Beginners' All-Purpose Symbolic Instruction Code) A simple high-level programming language commonly used on micro- and small minicomputers. BASIC was originally conceived as an interpretive language, but BASIC compilers are now available.

batch controls Accounting controls concerned with the integrity of a batch of transactions before, during, and after processing.

batch processing The simplest mode of computer processing in which transaction data are accumulated into batches and processed all at one time.

baud rate   A measure of the data transmission speed, now superseded by measurement in bits per second.

BCD (binary coded decimal)   A code used for data storage and transmission of numeric characters. This code is now largely obsolete.

bill of lading   A document evidencing the contract for shipment of goods executed between a seller and a common carrier.

bill of materials   The list of materials required to manufacture either a single unit or a batch of a given product.

binary search   An efficient method of record retrieval by content in which the records in the file are sampled in a prescribed sequence until the desired one is targeted. The binary search procedure is applicable only to ordered files.

binary system   A numbering system with a base of 2 and using the symbols 0 and 1. All digital processors use the binary system at their basic electronic level.

bit (binary digit)   The most elementary unit of data. It can take one of two possible values, usually designated 0 and 1.

bit dropping   The unintended conversion of a bit in semiconductor memory from a 1 to a 0, or (by extension) from a 0 to a 1, caused by random electronic interference. The phenomenon is sometimes referred to as bit toggling.

block diagram   A simplified flowchart in which the elements are depicted by rectangular blocks. An example is an organization chart.

block layout   A report or display format in which the data associated with a single record are presented in a block rather than in a line across the page or screen.

blocking factor   The ratio of the length of the physical record to that of the logical record. The term is used most commonly in connection with magnetic tape media.

bottom-up design   A system design strategy in which the lowest-level subsystems are designed first and then are integrated into the overall system.

bottom-up programming   A program development strategy in which the lowest level program modules are written first and then are integrated into the overall program. This approach is consistent with bottom-up systems design.

bubble chart   A simple form of data flow diagram in which information processes or entities are represented by circular symbols.

budget tracking   The process of comparing actual and budget data as a basis for management control.

buffer   A storage area set aside as a temporary place of residence for data being transmitted (in either direction) between the central processor and a peripheral device.

bus topology   A network topology in which all devices are connected to a single linear conductor, or bus.

byte   An aggregate of eight bits that can take a total of 256 different values. Often it is regarded as the equivalent of a character.

canned programs (or canned packages)   Applications software developed and marketed to multiple users having similar requirements.

caption   The explanatory label attached to a column or stub in a table or to a chart or diagram.

card reader   The on-line counterpart of the keypunch machine, used to read punched card media for processing by the computer.

card verifier   An off-line device used to verify the content of punched card media, involving reentry of the original source data and automatic comparison with the encoded data.

cash requirements forecast   A report listing amounts necessary to pay outstanding accounts payable falling due within a specified period.

cassette   A magnetic tape medium in which two reels of tape are enclosed in a small plastic cartridge.

central processor unit (CPU)   The heart of the digital computer in which the processing intelligence resides. It contains the control unit, the arithmetic/logic unit, main memory, and various interface units for communicating with peripheral devices.

centralized system   A computer system in which processing facilities are concentrated at a single geographical location or in a single device.

change listing   A listing of changes to a master file made during file maintenance activity.

channel capacity   The capacity of a telecommunications system, measured in either frequency bandwidth or bits per second.

character printer   A printing device that prints one character at a time, like a typewriter.

character set The set of characters available to an output device, including the letters of the alphabet, the numbers 0 through 9, and certain special symbols.

chart A graphical tool used to communicate information in a qualitative but easily comprehended manner.

check digit A digit appended to an account number as a control measure. An associated edit check is programmed to reject invalid account number/check digit combinations.

chief information officer An executive-level manager responsible for all information services activities within the organization.

chip A small slice of silicon on which are etched large numbers of transistors and associated circuits, used as either a digital processor device or a memory device.

classification The process of separating data into meaningful categories, such as assets, liabilities, revenues, and expenses.

clerical procedure A manual-processing operation performed by clerks. A set of directives informing clerical personnel how to carry out such an operation.

closed system A system that has no significant interaction with its environment. It contrasts with an open system.

coaxial cable A telecommunications medium consisting of a central electrical conductor surrounded by a concentric metal shield.

COBOL (Common Business Oriented Language) A compiler-oriented high-level programming language used primarily and extensively for business applications.

coding A general term for the assignment of symbols to transactions, accounts, or other entities. Translation of processing activities into the statements of a computer program.

column chart A form of bar chart in which the values are represented by vertical bars.

columnar flowchart A flowchart in which the symbols are arranged in vertical columns, usually corresponding to areas of responsibility within the organization.

command file A file containing brief coded instructions. It can be regarded as a rudimentary form of program file.

communications channel The connecting link between a given pair of devices or nodes in a telecommunications system.

communications device A peripheral device providing for the transmission of data over a distance. The most common communications device is the modem.

communications medium The nature of the communications channel used in a telecommunications system. Examples of communications media are telephone lines and fiber optic cables.

comparison The process of comparing items of data to determine the degree of similarity among them. The process may be designed to ascertain whether items are similar, to determine their relative positions in an ordered sequence, or to compare their numerical values.

compiler A computer software package providing for the one-time translation of program source code into executable machine or object code.

completed production card A document listing relevant cost data prepared when production of a unit or batch of goods has been completed.

completed production file A transaction file containing records of costs and other data related to production jobs that have been completed.

compliance testing Audit testing designed to ascertain the degree of reliance that can be placed on the internal controls.

computed addressing A strategy for record storage and retrieval in which the primary key is translated into the record address by means of a suitable algorithm. It is also referred to as hashing.

computer A device (normally electronic) providing the capability for processing data in response to programmed instructions.

computer crime Illegal activities committed with the aid of a computer or otherwise involving computer resources.

computer generations Distinct phases in the historical development of automated information processing.

computer operating controls Internal controls intended to provide for the reliable operation of computer facilities. An example of a computer operating control is the installation of an uninterruptible power supply.

concentrator A communications device that allocates

channel capacity to two or more users in proportion to their respective traffic densities.

conceptual design   The phase of systems design in which major design decisions are made.

confirmation controls   Internal controls that confirm accounting records by comparison with independent evidence. An example of a confirmation control is the physical inventory count.

control   A general term refering to the objectives for which a system is intended, or to constraints that tend to limit its ability to achieve those objectives. In an information system the controls are intended to safeguard the system and the enterprise against errors or irregularities and to further the objectives of management.

control consciousness   The intangible factors consisting primarily of management attitudes that provide either a favorable or an unfavorable environment for the success of internal control measures.

control environment   The environment of tangible and intangible factors provided by the organization and other outside influences, that determine the effectiveness of specific internal controls.

control objective   A specific statement concerning the controls needed to counter a particular threat from errors or irregularities.

control principle   A general statement concerning the controls needed to reduce a particular type of risk to an acceptable level. A single control principle may embrace a number of control objectives.

control unit   A component of the central processor that controls the operations of the other components of the central processor and the peripheral devices attached to it.

controller's manual   A manual containing copies of all procedures in effect in the organization.

conversion   The process of converting from the old to the new system during system implementation. The process of converting raw materials into finished products.

conversion cycle   See **production cycle**.

core memory   A type of main-memory technology in which data are stored in the fields of small toroidal magnets. Core memory devices are now largely obsolete.

cost accounting   A branch of accounting concerned with the accumulation of costs, in order to assign costs to departments and products, determine inventory values, and measure income.

CPU   See **central processor unit**.

credit hold   A restriction on extending further credit to a customer because of a poor payment record.

credit limit   A dollar ceiling up to which credit will automatically be extended without the need for further credit screening.

credit memorandum   A document issued to a customer indicating a reduction of the amount owed. It is often associated with returns or allowances.

credit rating   An index or code reflecting a customer's creditworthiness.

credit reference   A letter or other communication attesting to the creditworthiness of a customer; usually prepared by a bank or another company with whom the customer has done business.

credit screening   The evaluation of a customer's ability and readiness to pay if credit terms are extended.

critical path   The path (or paths) through the network representing a complex project and connecting tasks that have no slack.

critical path method (CPM)   An application of network theory to the scheduling of complex projects with multiple component tasks.

critical success factor (CSF)   One of several identified factors on which the success of an organization depends. Examples of CSFs are product styling, customer satisfaction, and employee loyalty.

CRT (cathode ray tube)   An alternative term used for a video screen.

custom software   Applications software developed to meet the requirements of a particular user.

customer file   A master file containing relevant narrative data on all active customers and, sometimes, accounts receivable balances and associated summarized transaction data.

daisy-wheel printer   An impact printer that prints characters by means of hammers arranged around the periphery of a wheel, resembling the petals of a daisy.

data   The raw material of facts and figures from which useful information can be extracted to meet user needs.

data access diagram   A block diagram showing how

data elements are retrieved in a relational data base management system.

data aggregate A collection of elementary data elements that conveys more useful information than the individual elements do.

data and procedural controls General controls to ensure that data input to the system is current and that it is processed promptly and accurately.

data bank See **data base**.

data base A general term for the totality of stored data in an information system.

data base administrator An individual responsible for maintaining the data base, securing its content, and advising users on all matters relating to data storage and retrieval.

data base controls Internal controls intended to protect the security, integrity, and processing of the whole data base. The term is used primarily in connection with data base management systems.

data base management system (DBMS) A combination of computer hardware and systems software providing centralized data storage and retrieval.

data base software Computer software used to interface applications programs with a DBMS.

data base system An information system that uses a DBMS.

data capture The initial formalizing and recording of source data for subsequent processing by the information system.

data capture controls Internal controls relating to the classification, identification, entry, and verification of transaction data.

data definition language Part of the data base software in which are defined the data elements used in application programs. The data definition language is invoked when the application software is compiled.

data dictionary A systemwide catalog of data elements, their meanings, and attributes, commonly used in connection with a DBMS.

data element The smallest unit of data that has meaning to a user. Examples are a name, account number, or dollar amount.

data entry controls Application controls concerned with protecting the system from entry of invalid or erroneous input data.

data flow diagram A free-form graphical representation of information systems. A bubble chart is one type of data flow diagram.

data manipulation language Part of the data base software interfacing applications software and the DBMS at execution time.

data preparation device An off-line device used in a pure batch process to encode transaction data onto an input medium.

data processing The routine processing of numeric, alphanumeric, and other data to provide information to various users.

data-processing librarian See **information services librarian**.

data-processing steering committee See **information services steering committee**.

data redundancy A situation in which the same data element is stored in more than one file or more than one physical location.

data service A commercial data retrieval service provided to end users and available over telephone lines. A popular data service provides up-to-the-minute securities prices on major exchanges.

data structure The arrangement of data elements and records to meet prescribed objectives relating to storage and retrieval.

DBMS See **data base management system**.

debug To correct errors in a computer program.

decentralized system A computer system in which processing facilities are placed at a number of separate locations.

decimal system The conventional numbering system with a base of 10 and using the symbols 0 through 9.

decision support system (DSS) A functional subsystem of the business information system supporting management's needs in planning, control, and decision making, and supplying information in response to specific requests from management.

decision table A table showing the outcome of a programmed decision for a range of specified conditions.

decision theory A body of theory that attempts to reduce to a mathematical calculation rational decision making under conditions of uncertainty. The calculation involves the available alternatives and the probabilities of occurrence of the corresponding outcomes.

decoding The process by which machine-readable data are translated into human-readable form.

delinquency notice (dun) A formal notification to a customer that payments are overdue and that the organization intends to take action to collect them.

deliverable items Goods or other items that must be delivered to a customer to meet contractual obligations.

departmental computer A medium-sized computer capable of supporting several interactive terminals and suitable for use in a single department of an organization. It is a newer term for a minicomputer.

detail diagram A columnar block diagram showing the inputs, processes, and outputs in a low-level information subsystem.

detailed design The phase of systems design involving detailed decisions relating to the system inputs, files, processes, and outputs.

digital computer An electronic computer that operates on the principle of counting discrete electrical pulses corresponding to binary digits. Virtually all computers used today for business applications are digital computers.

digital signal An electrical signal consisting of a sequence of discrete pulses.

direct access See **random access**.

disaster planning Contingency planning conducted to ensure that the information system can survive large-scale damage to, or failure of, computerized processing facilities.

disk cartridge A rigid magnetic disk medium that can be removed from the disk drive. Sometimes referred to as a *disk pack*.

disk directory A machine-readable directory of the files stored on a magnetic disk.

disk drive See **magnetic disk drive**.

diskette An alternative term for a flexible (floppy) disk.

display System output in the form of an image on the screen of a video terminal or monitor.

distributed-processing system A type of computer system in which processing intelligence is distributed among a number of different devices. A type of system in which linked processing facilities are located at different geographical locations.

document A paper medium (or its equivalent) on which are recorded details of a single transaction or a small number of related transactions.

document flowchart A derivative type of systems flowchart that emphasizes the flow of paperwork through the information system.

documentation The body of written material describing the system, how it was designed, and how it works.

documentation specialist An individual trained in the preparation of documentation.

documentation standards A set of standards regulating the preparation, authorization, dissemination, and use of documentation in an organization.

dot-matrix printer An impact printer that forms the characters by printing closely spaced dots arranged in a rectangular matrix.

download To tranfer files from a host device into a personal computer.

downtime Time during which computer facilities are inoperable because of either equipment malfunction or preventive maintenance.

early finish date The earliest date by which a task in a complex project can be completed, corresponding to the early start date.

early start date The earliest date on which a task in a complex project can be started, as determined by the earliest date by which all predecessor tasks can be completed.

EBCDIC (Extended Binary Coded Decimal Interchange Code) A code used for data storage and transmission, comparable to the ASCII code.

edit checks Application controls that ensure that input data conform to certain anticipated characteristics. Typical edit checks include checks of data type, length of data element, numerical magnitude, and internal consistency.

editor A system software package providing for editing of on-line files via an interactive terminal.

EDP (electronic data processing) An obsolete term relating to the processing of data in a computerized information system. It is also known as ADP or automatic data processing.

EDP controls An obsolete term referring to the subset of accounting controls concerned with computerized information systems, including general and application controls.

EDP steering committee See **information services steering committee**.

electronic spreadsheet A rectangular matrix provided

by a computer software package, into which an end user can insert data, textual legends, or computational formulas. The stored versions of electronic spreadsheets are referred to as *templates*.

employee file A master file containing relevant narrative data on each active employee and, sometimes, summarized payroll and deduction data.

encoding The transcription of data into machine-readable form for subsequent processing by a computerized system.

encryption The process of scrambling transmitted messages to prevent eavesdropping.

end-user computing Computerized processing performed by an end user rather than by a computer professional. End-user computing typically uses interactive terminals or personal computers.

error contamination The contamination of stored data arising from the input of erroneous data or from processing errors.

error controls Internal controls dealing with the prevention, detection, and correction of errors.

error recovery The process of recovering from erroneous or invalid data processing caused by human error or computer malfunction.

event-driven system See **real-time system**.

exception report A report listing items deemed unusual with reference to established norms.

exchange sorting A class of methods of file sorting in which successive pairs of records are interchanged until the record keys are ordered in the desired sequence.

execution cycle The cycle (or portion of a cycle) during which a machine code instruction is executed by the arithmetic/logic unit.

expert system A software system that simulates the role of a human expert in solving problems. Expert systems typically operate interactively by asking the user a series of questions and then, on the basis of a computerized analysis of the facts, proposes a diagnosis and/or recommends a course of action.

false origin A characteristic of a scale used on a graph when the value zero does not lie within the range plotted.

FASB (Financial Accounting Standards Board) The private-sector organization responsible for setting rules and standards relating to external financial reporting in the United States.

fatal error An error that causes execution of a computer program to terminate prematurely.

feasibility study A study conducted to determine whether a proposal is technically, practically, or economically feasible.

feedback The capture of part of the system output as a basis of modifying the inputs or controls. The usual objective is to make the system self-regulating.

fiber optic cable An optical communications medium consisting of a thin transparent material through which light waves can be transmitted.

field The portion of a record accommodating a data element.

file A general term for a collection of records related to a particular application and stored for subsequent retrieval and use.

file listing A printed copy of the content of a file.

file maintenance The modification of file content by direct intervention by the user. File maintenance activities include adding new records and editing or deleting existing records.

file maintenance controls Controls that ensure that file maintenance activities are performed in accordance with management authorization.

file medium The medium in which the file data reside. Examples are printed cards, punched cards, magnetic disk, and magnetic tape.

file-processing controls Internal controls relating to the routine processing of stored data.

file query The process by which a user accesses information contained in a data file.

file security controls Internal controls relating to the security of stored data.

file volatility A measure of file activity equal to the number or percentage of additions, deletions, or updates to a file within a prescribed period.

finished goods Manufactured products awaiting sale and shipment to customers. The costs assigned to those products.

fixed disk A magnetic disk medium that is permanently mounted in the disk drive and cannot be removed. The Winchester drive is a popular variety of fixed disk.

flexible (floppy) disk An inexpensive form of removable magnetic disk medium in which data are encoded on the magnetic surface of flexible plastic disks.

flowchart   A graphical depiction of a system for analysis, design, evaluation, or control.

flowcharting template   A template or stencil used to draw flowcharting symbols.

flowline   A line segment drawn on a flowchart to show the association of two symbols, in particular the flow of data or logic between them.

FOB (free on board) point   The point at which the title to goods passes from a seller to a buyer. It normally determines which party is responsible for shipping charges and for the safety of the goods in transit.

foreground task   A high-priority task executed by the central processor ahead of lower-priority tasks.

FORTRAN (Formula Translation)   A compiler-oriented high-level programming language used primarily for scientific and engineering applications.

friendly system   See **user-friendly system**.

fully connected topology   A network topology in which all devices are connected in pairs to one another.

Gantt chart   A horizontal bar chart used to present the schedule for a complex project.

gateway   A communications device that connects a network to some other computer system such as a host computer, another network, or a data service.

general authorization   An authorization that pertains to a whole class of transactions and that provides for the routine delegation of management responsibility within the constraints of the situation to which it applies.

general controls   A subset of accounting controls concerned with all aspects of computerized processing. They are systemwide controls that form the environment in which application controls function.

general processing controls   Internal controls relating to basic features of manual or automated processing in the accounting system. An example of a general processing control is the use of prenumbered documents.

general systems theory   A body of theory providing for the analysis of complex systems in terms of a common framework of inputs, outputs, processes, and environment.

generalized software   Software that can perform various related applications functions and that can be tailored to a particular task by means of user-selected instructions.

gigabyte   1,073,741,824 (i.e., 2^{30} bytes).

graph   A graphical tool for representing the relationship between pairs of variables.

graphics   The use of charts, graphs, or other diagrammatic means for communicating information.

hard copy   Data residing on durable, nonvolatile media such as paper.

hardware   A general term for the equipment components of a computer system.

hardware and system software controls   General controls addressed to the security of computer hardware and systems software and restricting the use of those facilities to authorized purposes.

hardware key   A security device in the form of a hardware component that must be inserted into, or attached to, a computer before associated software can be operated.

hashing   See **computed addressing**.

header label   A machine readable label at the beginning of a magnetic tape used for file identification.

heading   The title of a table, report, or chart. It may also contain a subtitle, reference number, and headnote.

headnote   A disclosure placed near the top of a tabular form, usually limiting or qualifying the generality of the data presented in the table.

hexadecimal system   A numbering system with a base of 16 that uses the symbols 0 through 9 and A through F. It is used to represent data in most small and some large computers.

hierarchical block diagram   A type of block diagram that emphasizes the vertical or hierarchical relationships among information subsystems.

hierarchical model   A type of structural model in which there is a distinct hierarchy of data; data elements at one level own those at the next lower level. It can support one-to-one and one-to-many relationships, but not many-to-many relationships without incurring data redundancy.

HIPO (Hierarchical plus Input, Process, and Output)   A documentation convention for structured systems design, consisting of a hierarchical block diagram or structure chart and a set of overview diagrams and detail diagrams.

holographic reader   An optical input device, often used for reading Universal Product Codes, that involves a process of three-dimensional holographic images.

host computer   A large computer to which smaller individual computers or local area networks may be connected.

human readability   The ability of data to be read by human beings as distinct from machines. It contrasts with machine readability.

impact printer   A printing device that forms characters by the impact of a hammer or a set of wires on an inked ribbon.

incompatible duties (or responsibilities)   Combinations of activities that, if performed by the same individual, could result in undetected errors or concealed irregularities.

index file   A file whose records contain pointers to records in another data file.

information media   The media—typically, documents, displays, reports, and files—on which information resides.

information processing   The processing of numerical, graphical, textual, and other types of data with the objective of providing meaningful information to a user constituency.

information services department   A department in an organization providing services in the area of information processing.

information services librarian   An individual in an information services department who is responsible for the custody of program files, data files, and documentation when not in use.

information services steering committee   A high-level committee charged with making recommendations to top management on all matters relating to the information services activities in the organization.

information system   A combination of people, facilities, technology, and media intended to provide quantitative information to a user constituency.

information theory   A body of theory that attempts to attach a quantitative value to the information contained in a communicated message. It is also known as communications theory.

initial costs   The costs incurred to develop an information system, as distinct from the ongoing costs required to operate and maintain it.

input   The signals representing the effect of the environment on a system. Data entered into an information system for intended processing.

input device   A peripheral device used to enter input data into a computer system.

input-file matrix   A matrix showing the relationship between input and file data elements.

input-output matrix   A matrix showing the relationship between input and output data elements.

input prompt   A caption or brief message displayed on the screen to assist a user in entering data into an interactive system. Most prompts are in the form of a request for a certain data element.

insertion sorting   A simple method of sorting in which a new file is built record by record. The records are inserted in the new file in their appropriate positions with respect to the sort key.

integrated software   Computer software that combines several distinct processing capabilities otherwise packaged separately.

intelligent terminal   An interactive terminal that has a significant level of programmable intelligence and storage capacity and that can perform useful preprocessing or postprocessing tasks on the data. Some intelligent terminals can function as small stand-alone computers.

interactive batch processing   A mode of interactive processing in which input data are entered into a transaction file through an on-line terminal but in which the update of master files is performed by a batch process.

interactive processing   A mode of computer processing using on-line terminals, in which a dialogue can be maintained between the user and the system.

instruction   An elementary computer command executed by the arithmetic/logic unit.

instruction cycle   The cycle (or portion of a cycle) during which the next instruction is loaded into a register in readiness for execution.

instruction set   The repertoire of instructions available to a given central processor.

interactive system   A computer system supporting an interactive processing mode.

interpreter   A system software package providing for line-by-line translation of program source code into machine code at execution time.

interview   A face-to-face encounter between an individual and an audience of one or more others for the purpose of gathering information.

interviewee The person or persons being interviewed.

interviewer The person conducting an interview.

inventory The stock of goods and supplies maintained to support the ongoing production and sales activities of an organization. The costs assigned to those items.

inventory file A master file containing descriptive data, quantities, and dollar balances for all items currently in inventory.

inventory management (or **inventory control**) The custody of goods in inventory and the process of monitoring inventory levels in conformity with management's authorization. A major objective is usually to maintain the supply of goods while minimizing inventory costs.

inventory status report A status report listing inventory items, their quantities on hand, and other pertinent data; also called a stock status report.

inverted file An index file sorted by some key other than the one on which the main data file is ordered.

investment cycle The transaction cycle dealing with the investment of resources in the organization and with the management of those resources. Typically it includes the applications of cash management, fixed-asset management, and debt and equity management.

invoice A document stating the details of a sale, the amount owed by the customer, and the terms of payment.

ISAM (Indexed Sequential Access Method) File A type of ordered file structure in which records are divided into blocks. The address of the first record in each block is listed in an accompanying index file. ISAM files are useful in situations involving high volatility.

job card A document used in a job order accounting system for accumulating labor, materials, and overhead costs for a batch of goods in production.

job control language (JCL) A set of commands used to control the automatic loading of programs and files in a batch process.

job station A small organizational unit or subsystem in which specific tasks are performed. An example is the section of the accounts receivable department where customer statements are prepared.

job station analysis An in-depth study of the work of a job station, forming part of a systems analysis exercise.

journal A chronological list of transactions that have occurred during a specified period; also called a register. Examples are the general journal and various special journals.

key A data element or field used to identify records in a file and typically used as a basis for retrieval by content or for sorting the file.

keying Entry of data through a keyboard.

keypunch machine An off-line data preparation device in which input data are encoded onto punched cards. Keypunch machines are now obsolete.

key-to-disk machine An off-line data preparation device in which input data are encoded onto magnetic disk media.

key-to-tape machine An off-line data preparation device in which input data are encoded onto magnetic tape media.

kilobyte 1,024 (i.e., 2^{10} bytes.)

labor usage report An activity report presenting details of labor usage and expenditures during a specified period.

large mainframe computer See **mainframe computer**.

laser disk An optical storage device in which data are imprinted on a rotating disk by a laser beam. The data are also read by a laser beam. Laser disks typically have higher capacities than do magnetic disks, however, the technology necessary to erase data on laser disks has been slow to emerge.

laser printer A high-technology printing device that forms characters by means of a laser beam.

late finish date The deadline imposed on the completion of a task in a complex project so as to avoid delaying successor tasks.

late start date The latest date on which a task in a complex project must start, corresponding to the late finish date.

ledger A list of the accounts corresponding to the whole or a part of the chart of accounts, together with their balances and sometimes supporting summary data. Examples are the general ledger, subsidiary ledgers, and the factory ledger.

line graph   A type of graphical representation of data in which data points are connected by straight lines.

line printer   A printing device that prints a whole line of characters at a time.

linear scale   A scale used on a graph in which equal intervals of distance correspond to equal values of the associated variable.

linked list   An array of data elements or records containing pointers indicating the next (or previous) key in a sequence.

local area network (LAN)   A configuration of networked computers covering only a limited geographical area, such as a single building.

logarithmic scale   A scale used on a graph in which equal intervals of distance correspond to equal ratios of the associated variable.

logical data analysis   A step-by-step process by which data structures can be expressed in optimal form for use as relational data base schemas. Logical data analysis involves simplification and removal of redundancy.

logical record   The configuration of related data elements of significance to the user or programmer. It does not necessarily correspond to the configuration of data elements in the physical medium or storage device (the physical record).

logical structure   The data structure in a data base as perceived by the user.

machine code   A computer program consisting of binary instructions directly executable by the arithmetic/ logic unit.

machine-generated code   Applications software produced as the output from certain types of generalized computer programs.

machine language   See **machine code**.

machine readability   The ability of data to be read by a computer input device.

magnetic disk   A storage medium in which data are encoded on the magnetic surface of a rotating disk. Magnetic disk media support random access to data.

magnetic disk drive   A peripheral storage device providing for the use of magnetic disk media.

magnetic drum   An obsolete type of storage device in which data are encoded on the magnetic surface of a rotating drum.

magnetic ink character recognition (MICR)   Machine recognition of data magnetically encoded on paper media.

magnetic tape   A storage medium in which data are encoded on the magnetic surface of metalicized plastic tape in reels or cassettes. Magnetic tape media support only sequential access to data.

magnetic tape drive   A peripheral storage device providing for the use of magnetic tape media.

magnetic wand   A small portable input device used to read magnetically coded data from a product or other item; frequently used in connection with point-of-sale systems.

main memory   A storage device within the central processor that provides high-speed, addressable, random-access memory.

mainframe computer   A large computer providing substantial processing capability.

management by objectives (MBO)   A technique of management control in which individuals negotiate performance targets with their superiors and then are evaluated with respect to those targets. MBO is used chiefly within the ranks of professional and management personnel.

management controls   A general term encompassing all policies, procedures, operating techniques, and organizational mechanisms that management uses to run the organization.

management fraud   Fraud perpetrated within the organization by individuals with management responsibility.

manual controls   The subset of internal accounting controls concerned with manual procedures.

manual system   A type of information system in which no more than rudimentary computing facilities (such as adding machines or calculators) are employed.

many-to-many relationship   A characteristic of a logical data structure in which a number of data elements mutually own a number of others. An example is the relationship between educational courses and the students registered for them.

many-to-one relationship   A characteristic of a logical data structure in which a number of data elements mutually own a single common data element. An example is the relationship between line items on a materials requisition and the requisition number. It is the inverse of the one-to-many relationship.

master budget   The primary quantitative tool of short-run management planning. The budget documents management's revenue, cost, assets, liabilities, and equity targets for the coming year. The budget then provides a benchmark for measuring progress toward those targets.

master file   A data file containing permanent or semi-permanent data, corresponding to a ledger.

material control weakness   A weakness in the internal controls that exposes the organization to a significant degree of risk.

materials requisition   A document authorizing the issuance of materials to production of a specified job.

materials usage report   An activity report presenting details of all materials issued to production, and related costs incurred, during a specified period.

materials waste (or **scrap**) **report**   An activity report presenting details of all material wasted or scrapped during a specified period.

megabyte   1,048,576 (i.e., 2^{20}) bytes.

menu   A list of processing options displayed on a screen of an interactive system, from that a particular process can be selected.

merging   The process of combining two or more files into one. Normally the term is used for source files that are ordered on the same key and when the resulting file is similarly ordered.

message integrity controls   Internal controls protecting the integrity of messages transmitted over a telecommunications system.

message security controls   Internal controls providing for the security of messages transmitted over a telecommunications system.

microcomputer   A computer that uses a microprocessor as its central processor and that typically provides a level of processing capability lower than that of other types of computers.

microfilm printer   An output device that prints to microfilm media.

microprocessor   A central processor based on a single large-scale integrated chip.

microsecond   One millionth of a second.

minicomputer   A computer providing processing capability between that of a microcomputer and a large mainframe computer. Sometimes referred to as a *departmental computer*.

minuend   The number from which another number is subtracted.

mnemonic code   A programming verb, such as ADD, that stands for a binary operation code. It is used in assembly code programming.

mnemonic variable name   A variable name used in a computer program, that reminds the programmer or user of the meaning of the variable.

modem (modulator-demodulator)   A communications device in which digital signals are converted into analog signals at the transmitter and converted back at the receiving station.

multiplexor   A communications device that allocates channel capacity equally between two or more users.

multitasking   A mode of automated processing in which two or more tasks or jobs are executed concurrently by the central processor.

nanosecond   One billionth (10^{-9}) of a second.

narrative description   A textual description of part or all of a system for the purposes of system development or documentation.

network architecture   A conceptual overview of the various subsystems of a telecommunications system and their mutual relationships. The network architecture proposed by the International Standards Organization consists of layers representing such subsystems as the physical communications medium, interface devices, and communications software.

network model   A type of structural model in which there is no distinct hierarchy; data elements can have several owners and can own several other elements. It can support many-to-many relationships as well as one-to-one and one-to-many relationships.

network server   A communications device that controls message traffic in a network.

network system   A computer system involving communications among multiple linked computers.

network topology   A schematic representation of the arrangement of communications channels and nodes in a network system.

nonfatal error   An error in a computer program that does not cause premature termination of execution.

normal form   An intermediate or final stage in the logical analysis of a data structure. The three normal forms are referred to as the first, second, and third normal forms. The third normal form is regarded as the optimal form of the data structure.

normalization The process performed in logical data analysis in which a data structure is expressed in its third normal form.

numbering system A system of counting or of assigning quantitative values that uses a set of symbols and corresponding rules of association. The number of symbols required is equal to the base of the system. The most familiar numbering system is the decimal system that has a base of 10 and uses the symbols 0 through 9.

numeric data Data consisting of only the decimal numbers 0 through 9 or their equivalents.

object code The binary machine code instructions produced when programs written in high-level programming languages are translated by a compiler.

octal system A numbering system with a base of 8 that uses the symbols 0 through 7. It is used for representing data in many large computers.

off line A general term applied to a file or a peripheral device that is not under the control of the central processor. An off-line file cannot be accessed unless some operator action is taken, such as mounting a tape.

off-page connector See **on-page connector**.

on line A general term applied to files or peripheral devices that are under the control of the central processor. An on-line file can be accessed upon execution of a suitable machine instruction without operator intervention.

on-page, off-page connectors Flowcharting symbols that indicate the association between pairs of entities that cannot be joined by a flow line.

one-to-many relationship A characteristic of a logical data structure in which one data element owns a number of other elements. An example would be the relationship between vendor and voucher number.

one-to-one relationship A characteristic of a logical data structure in which there is a unique relationship between one element and another. An example is the relationship between badge number and employee name.

ongoing costs The costs, primarily maintenance and operating costs, incurred over the life of an information system. Lease costs of hardware and software or depreciation charges represent an addition to the ongoing costs.

open invoice file A file used in an open invoice system containing records of all invoices that remain uncollected.

open invoice report A report listing all invoices outstanding as of a specified date.

open invoice (or open item) system A type of accounts receivable system in which invoice records remain on file until payment is collected.

open job file A file containing records of jobs currently in production.

open job report A report listing all jobs in production as of a specified date.

open order file A file containing records of all customer orders that remain unfilled.

open order report A report listing all customer orders unfilled as of a specified date.

open purchase order file A file containing records of all purchase orders for which the goods or services have not been received.

open purchase order report A report listing all purchase orders outstanding as of a specified date.

open system A system that has significant interaction with its environment; virtually all business systems must be regarded as open systems.

open voucher file A file containing records of all vouchers that remain upaid.

open voucher report A report listing all disbursement vouchers outstanding as of a specified date.

operating cycles The three transaction cycles most directly associated with the operation's day-to-day affairs: the purchasing, production, and revenue cycles.

operating system The principal component of systems software that provides supervisory control over the operations of the computer.

operation code Part of the machine code instruction that causes execution of the desired processing activity.

operational data processing The routine processing of data in an information system. It includes the processing of general ledger, accounts receivable, accounts payable, payroll, and inventory transactions.

operator documentation Instructions and background information provided to a computer operator to assist in operation of the system.

optical character recognition (OCR) The process of machine recognition of printed characters or text.

optical wand A small portable input device for reading optically coded data from a product or other item; frequently used in connection with point-of-sale systems.

ordered file A data file whose records contain keys that form an ordered sequence. Examples are an alphabetical file and a chronological file.

organization change symbol A flowcharting symbol indicating the transfer of processing responsibility, or custody of data, from one organizational group to another.

organizational controls Internal controls dealing with the responsibilities of personnel within the organization.

organizational environment The social, geographical, and structural environment in which the information system must function.

output The signals representing the effect of a system on its environment. The processed data delivered by an information system to its users.

output controls Application controls concerned with the proper preparation, distribution, and use of system output.

output device A peripheral device used to communicate processed output data from a computer system to its users.

output specifications A detailed statement of the outputs required from an information system and the format in which those outputs are to be prepared.

overlay A program module that occupies the same main-memory space previously occupied by another module.

overview diagram A columnar block diagram showing the inputs, processes, and outputs in a high-level information subsystem.

ownership of data A term used primarily in connection with data base management systems to designate the association among data elements in a logical data structure.

page printer A hard-copy output device that prints a whole page at once. Page printers operate in much the same way as does an office copying machine.

paper tape punch An off-line data preparation device in which input data are encoded onto paper tape media.

paper tape reader The on-line counterpart of the paper tape punch used to read paper tape for processing by the computer.

parallel transmission A telecommunications mode in which the eight bits comprising a byte are transmitted simultaneously.

passive terminal A video terminal that has only rudimentary buffer space and processing capability and that relies on central processor commands for essentially all interactive operations.

payroll A general term referring to the body of employees to whom wages or salaries are paid. The accounting application dealing with the payment of wages and salaries.

payroll deductions Amounts deducted from employee gross pay to cover such obligations as medical insurance premiums, union dues, and tax withholdings.

perpetual inventory system A system of record keeping in which inventory records are updated each time goods are issued or received.

personal computer A microcomputer intended to be operated by a single individual, often an end user.

PERT (Program Evaluation and Review Technique) A scheduling method, similar to the critical path method (CPM), in which the completion times of individual tasks can be expressed probabilistically.

petty cash system An arrangement whereby small expenditures can be made in currency at the discretion of an appointed custodian.

phased conversion A strategy for successful systems conversion in which one application at a time is brought to operational status.

physical inventory count The determination of inventory quantities and values by direct examination and count of the inventory items.

physical record The configuration of related data elements or fields as it resides in the physical storage medium or device.

picking ticket A document indicating the description, quantity, and warehouse location of goods ordered by a customer. Its purpose is to assist in filling orders for multiple items from a large warehouse.

pie chart A type of graphical representation of data in which allocations or proportions of some total are depicted by the relative sizes of sectors of a circle.

PL/1 (Programming Language 1)   A high-level programming language that attempts to combine the best features of COBOL and FORTRAN.

planning and control cycle   The cycle of transactions associated with the planning, control, and management of economic resources within the organization. Typically it encompasses the budgeting and budget-tracking processes.

planning sheet   A schedule of tasks to be performed during a systems analysis or audit engagement.

plotter   An output device designed to produce two-dimensional graphics material on paper media.

plug compatibility   A general term indicating the ability to interface computer hardware components sold by different manufacturers.

point-of-sale system   An online system that automatically records sales transaction data. The device often uses a magnetic or optical wand or a holographic reader for reading encoded inventory data on product tags.

pointer   A field in a record containing the address of another record.

point-to-point topology   A network topology in which two devices are connected to each other by a communications channel.

positional value   The value attached to the relative position of the symbols in a number rather than to the symbols themselves.

postimplementation review   A review of the systems development activities conducted after conversion has been completed to evaluate the success of the systems project.

posting   The process of updating master file records to reflect accumulated transaction activity.

posting cycle   The cycle of events associated with the accumulation of transaction data and the periodic posting of those data to a master file. The term describes a batch process but not a real-time process.

predecessor activity   A task in a complex project that must be completed before some reference task can be started.

prenumbered documents   A control in which sensitive documents are preprinted in a numerical sequence that permits an accounting for all numbers at successive stages of processing.

primary key   The key used most frequently for identifying records in a file.

printer   An output device that delivers data in printed form.

printer terminal   An interactive terminal that incorporates a keyboard and a printer monitoring device.

procedure   A manual operation intended to accomplish some objective. The formal directive to perform such an operation.

process   An activity or course of events occurring in accordance with an intended purpose.

processing controls   Application controls concerned with the accuracy and completeness of automated processes.

production control   The process of developing production plans and scheduling and monitoring production operations.

production cycle   The cycle of transactions in the conversion of raw materials into finished goods, the maintenance of inventories, and the provision of services. Typically it includes the application of production control, cost accounting, and inventory control.

production data file   A transaction file containing records of costs relating to each job in production incurred during a specified period.

production order   A document authorizing the expenditure of company resources on the production of a specified batch of goods.

production status report   A status report listing all jobs currently in production, the accumulated costs related to them, and sometimes the estimated degree of completion or the estimated costs to complete.

program evaluation and review technique   See **PERT**.

program file   A file containing the source or object code of a computer program.

program flowchart   A type of flowchart that depicts the flow of logic through a process, often used in the development of computer programs or for documentation of programs.

program structure   The logical pattern inherent in a computer program required by the rules of the particular high-level programming language.

program syntax The structural characteristics of a computer program required by the rules of the particular high-level programming language.

programmed decision A highly structured decision that can be reduced to a set of formal statements indicating which course of action is to be adopted under specified conditions.

protocol The set of rules regulating the transmission of messages across the interfaces between adjacent parts of a telecommunications system.

prototyping A technique used in systems development in which users are allowed to experiment with simulated portions of a new information system in order to evaluate the effectiveness of the system and to provide feedback to the designers.

purchase order A document sent to a vendor requesting delivery of specified goods or services on the understanding that payment will be made upon delivery in accordance with applicable terms.

purchase register (or journal) An activity report listing purchases that have been made during a specified period.

purchase requisition A document requesting and authorizing the purchasing department to procure specific goods or services from an outside vendor.

purchasing cycle The cycle of transactions related to the acquisition by the organization of resources in the form of goods and services. It normally encompasses the applications of purchasing, receiving, accounts payable, and payroll.

purchasing department An organizational unit through which all purchasing activities are channeled.

pure batch system A mode of processing in which transactions are encoded off line and processed in a batch without user interaction.

query language A programming language normally using plain English commands entered through an interactive terminal, providing for user selection and analysis of different configurations of data elements from a data base.

questionnaire A document normally sent to a number of individuals soliciting responses to a number of questions required for data gathering.

random access The capability of accessing individual file records without having to read earlier records in the same file; also known as direct access.

raw materials The materials, parts, and subassemblies that form the basic ingredients of the manufacturing process.

real-time processing A mode of processing in which master records are updated when a transaction occurs, rather than at prescribed intervals of time.

reasonable assurance The situation in which the risk of loss due to errors or irregularities is balanced by the cost of the controls designed to minimize those errors or irregularities. The corresponding situation in which audit risk is balanced against the cost of the audit procedures.

receiving document (or report) A document confirming that goods have been received and inspected and either accepted or rejected on stated grounds.

receiving file A transaction file containing records of all goods received during a specified period.

record The aggregate of related data elements or fields forming the building block of a file.

record retention policy A management policy providing guidance on the required period of retention for records of different types.

reference pointer A flowcharting symbol used to draw attention to a particular feature of a flowchart, often referencing a comment in accompanying narrative documentation.

register Another name for a journal. A temporary storage location for data or instructions being executed in the central processor unit.

relational matrix A matrix used to show the relationships between pairs of variables in a logical structure.

relational model A type of structural model in which the logical structure can be represented in the form of simple tables consisting of a key and associated data elements. The same data may be perceived in different tables according to the key selected.

remote job entry (RJE) A mode of processing in which batch jobs are entered into a computer through remote terminals.

removable disk A disk cartridge or disk pack that can be removed from a magnetic disk drive.

report An output medium usually printed on paper and containing a summary of significant numbers of transactions or containing data from nontransaction sources.

report generator A generalized program providing for

the printing of reports from file data in accordance with user-supplied formatting commands, headings, and captions.

reporting cycle   The cycle of transactions associated with the reporting of financial information to internal and external users. Typically it encompasses the general ledger application and all activities related to the preparation of external financial statements.

request for proposal   A solicitation to prospective vendors to submit proposals on how specifications relating to a required goods or services can best be met, and to submit a bid price for supplying the proposed resources.

request for quotation   A solicitation sent to prospective vendors inviting bids on required goods or services.

responsibility accounting   A system of internal reporting in which the content and format of accounting reports are tailored to the responsibilities of individual recipients.

responsibility matrix   A matrix showing the organizational assignments related to the tasks comprising a project.

retrieval by address   Retrieval of a record residing at a specified physical location in a file, storage medium, or device.

retrieval by content   Retrieval of a record that contains a specified key or data element.

returns and allowances   Amounts rebated or deducted from customer accounts because goods are found to be damaged upon receipt or are otherwise unacceptable.

revenue cycle   The cycle of transactions in the distribution of resources, in the form of goods and services, and the collection of revenues for those resources. Typically it includes the applications of sales order processing, billing, cash collections, and sales analysis.

ring topology   A network topology in which all devices are connected to a circular conductor.

risk   A general term describing the uncertainty of business and the possibility of loss from a variety of contingencies.

risk of incorrect acceptance   The probability that financial information might contain material errors that were not detected by the audit examination.

risk of incorrect rejection   The probability that finan-

cial information is correct but nevertheless is believed to be misstated as the result of the audit examination.

RPG (Report Program Generator)   A high-level programming language that was originally intended primarily for producing reports from file data but that has developed into a general purpose business language.

sales analysis   The analysis of sales history to provide information to management for planning, control, and decision making.

sales discount   The amount by which a normal sales price is reduced to reflect the favored status of the customer, the large volume of the sale, or prompt payment of the invoice.

sales history file   A file containing summarized sales data for analysis.

sales order   A document authorizing the sale on prescribed terms of specified goods or services to a customer.

sales order processing   The processing of customer orders leading to the production and shipment of goods or the provision of services.

schedule of aged receivables   See **aged receivables (schedule of)**

schema   The description of the whole data base in terms of its component data elements and the relationships among them.

scratch file   A temporary file established during a processing operation and subsequently purged.

screen formatting   The process of programming screen forms, often with the aid of generalized utility programs.

secondary key   A key other than the primary key that may be used for identifying records in a file.

secondary storage   On-line data storage external to main memory, usually in the form of magnetic disk media.

sector   A portion of the track on a magnetic disk corresponding to a physical record.

semiconductor memory   A main-memory medium in which the data are encoded in the form of electric charges in transistor devices; also referred to as metal oxide semiconductor (MOS) memory.

separation of duties   The assignment of different individuals to pairs of mutually imcompatible duties or responsibilities.

sequential access A mode of access to a file in which records must be accessed in turn, starting with the first record. Magnetic tape files are restricted to sequential access.

sequential search A strategy for retrieving records by content in which each record is examined in turn until the desired one is located.

serial file A file whose records are stored in arrival order; new records are simply added to the end of the file.

serial transmission A telecommunications mode in which the eight bits comprising a byte are transmitted one after the other.

service bureau An organization that offers for a fee data-processing services to user customers.

service contract An agreement with an outside vendor to provide for an ongoing fee service and maintenance support for a computer system.

shakedown The final adjustment or tailoring of a new system to ensure that it is fully operational.

shipment file A transaction file containing records of all shipments made during a specified period.

shipping document A document accompanying goods in transit, usually indicating the descriptions and quantities of the goods.

shipping register (or **journal**) An activity report listing all shipments made to customers or others during a specified period.

simulation The portrayal of business activities by a mathematical model. The recomputation of the client's financial data as part of an audit procedure.

slack A measure of the flexibility in starting or completing a task in a complex project, equal to the difference between the late start and early start dates.

smart terminal A video terminal device incorporating a larger buffer space and more processing capability than a passive terminal does.

software A general term for the sets of programmed instructions entered into a computer to perform desired processing activities.

software house An organization that specializes in the development and marketing of computer software.

software transportability The ability to use software developed for one computer system on another system.

source code The original version of a computer program written in a high-level programming language.

specific authorization An authorization that applies only to a specific transaction.

speed degradation The decrease in processing speed that occurs in the face of increasing demands on central processor resources from competing on-line terminals.

spooling A scheme in which sets of ouput are written to secondary storage and queue for the attention of the printer. By means of spooling, a single printer can service concurrently the needs of several tasks or jobs.

standard costs Normative measures of the materials, labor, and overhead costs that ought to be expended in the manufacture of a product or the provision of a service.

star topology A network topology in which all devices are connected to a central node.

statement of objectives A formal statement of the informational objectives of a given organization as approved by management.

status report A report listing balances and other pertinent data as of a specified point in time. It corresponds to the listing of a master file. An example is the balance sheet.

string A set of characters stored or processed as a unit without any numerical or logical values being attached to the component characters. Strings may contain textual material such as a name.

structural independence A term used to characterize the independence between the logical and physical data structures in a data base management system.

structural model One of several broad propositions that serve as a model of the logical data structure in a system.

structured interviewing A strategy for successful interviewing in which a set of prescribed and pretested questions is put to the respondent in a prescribed order.

structured programming A strategy for effective and efficient development of computer programs, normally involving division of the program into modules.

stub The data element that identifies the subject of a line item in a table. As an example, the name of the subscriber forms the stub in a telephone directory.

subschema   The description of the part of the data base of interest to a given user, in terms of its data elements and the relationships among them.

substantive testing   Audit testing designed to verify classes of transactions and the correctness of individual account balances.

subsystem   A system within a system. One of the interacting components that comprise a system.

subsystem structure   The arrangement of subsystems within a system and the interrelationships among them.

subtrahend   The number that is subtracted from another number.

successor activity   A task in a complex project that cannot be started until some reference task is completed.

summarization   The process of reducing a larger volume of data to a smaller volume for more economical storage and easier comprehension.

superminicomputer   A minicomputer with superior processing capability.

supervisory program   An early and rudimentary form of operating system used for controlling the operation of a computer.

synchronous transmission   A form of serial transmission in which the clocks in the transmitting and receiving devices are synchronized with one another.

system   An assemblage of interacting components united at least to some degree in pursuit of common goals.

systems analysis   The process of defining systems objectives, evaluating existing information systems, and recommending improvements.

systems analyst   An individual trained in systems analysis and design.

systems design   The process of producing a complete paper model of a proposed information system.

systems development   The process of analyzing existing information systems and designing and implementing major systems changes or new systems.

systems development controls   General controls concerned with systems development.

systems documentation   Technical documentation describing the system, its development history, and its operation. Systems documentation is addressed to systems analysts, programmers, auditors, and other systems professionals.

systems flowchart   A type of flowchart that emphasizes the flow of information through a system.

systems implementation   The process of translating a systems design into a working information system. It includes the acquisition of data-processing resources and the conversion from the old to the new system.

systems overhead   The use of systems resources, in the form of processing capability or memory storage capacity, for what the user would regard as nonproductive purposes.

systems penetration controls   Internal controls intended to protect an information system from unauthorized access via a telecommunications network.

systems project   The project established to organize the development of a new or substantially modified information system.

systems proposal   A formal proposal listing recommendations for enhancing an existing information system or developing a new one, presented for consideration by management.

systems security controls   Internal controls providing physical security (and other related types of security) for the information system.

systems software   A set of program packages, normally supplied by the hardware manufacturer, that perform essential tasks in the operation of the computer and in the development and execution of applications software.

table   An information format in which data are presented in columns.

tagging and tracing   A computer audit technique for identifying transaction paths, and for making an indepth study of the flow of data along them.

tape drive   See **magnetic tape drive**.

task description   Narrative documentation of a manual or automated process in an information system.

tax tables   Tables supplied by revenue authorities indicating amounts required to be withheld from employees' gross pay in a range of income brackets.

tax withholdings   Amounts withheld from employees' gross pay to cover periodic tax deposits required by federal, state, or local revenue authorities.

tax-withholding report   A report listing amounts deducted from employee gross pay to meet the requirements of tax-withholding laws.

telecommunications The technology by which messages can be transmitted from one location to another.

telecommunications administrator An individual responsible for the operation and control of a telecommunications system.

telegraphic style The communication of information as concisely as possible using key words, as in a telegram or a newspaper headline.

tertiary storage Off-line data storage, usually in the form of floppy diskettes, disk cartridges, or magnetic tape.

test deck An obsolete term used to designate sets of simulated transaction data prepared for conducting audit tests on a client's system.

text file A file containing textual material, usually with no more than a loose structure of identifiable records.

thermal printer A printer device that uses a heated print head and prints on thermally sensitive paper.

threat A specific contingency that could expose the organization to loss.

throughput A general term describing the volume of data processed by an information system.

time card A document indicating the hours worked by an employee during a specified time period and, sometimes, the jobs on which the employee was working. It is typically used by hourly employees and often punched at a time clock.

time sharing A scheme in which several interactive terminals are connected to a single central processor. A service offered by a commercial computer company in which many user customers can access a host computer via interactive terminals.

time sheet A document indicating the hours worked by a salaried employee during a specified time period and the jobs on which the employee was working.

top-down design A strategy for systems development in which the system and the highest-level subsystems are defined first in terms of the functions they will serve. Development then proceeds to progressively lower subsystems, but the objective is to defer detailed design decisions to as late a stage as possible.

top-down programming A strategy for program development in which program modules are designed in general terms and then developed in progressively

greater detail. This strategy is consistent with top-down design.

transaction The formal representation of an event that has accounting significance. The data analog of an economic event.

transaction cycles The highest-level subsystems of the accounting information system. Each cycle consists of a number of accounting applications.

transaction file A file containing details of transactions accumulated during the posting cycle, usually in chronological order.

transaction flow The movement of transaction data through the processing stages of an information system.

transaction log A control report listing the summary content of transactions that have occurred during a specified period.

transaction origination controls Application controls concerned with the authorization and creation of transactions.

transaction path The path through the processing stages in an information system taken by a specified transaction.

treasury cycle See **investment cycle**.

true origin The characteristic of a scale used on a graph when the portion of the scale plotted contains the value zero.

turnaround document A document serving as both an output and an input document. An example is a punched card that is sent with an invoice to a customer and is returned with the payment.

turnkey system A computer system that is supplied with all necessary software and documentation and that can be operated by personnel with little computer training.

unit of measure The unit by which quantities of goods are measured. Examples are units, pairs, dozens, gallons, feet, cases, and drums.

user documentation Documentation prepared for users of the system, explaining how they should interact with the system and sometimes containing instructions on the operation of on-line terminals.

user-friendly system An information system intended for use by nonspecialists and designed to operate in a nonthreatening manner.

utility programs Programs performing frequently used

processes, such as file sorting, supplied as part of the systems software.

variable name   The name assigned to a numeric, logical, or string variable in a computer program.

vendor file   A master file containing relevant narrative data on all active vendors and, sometimes, accounts payable balances and summarized pertinent transaction data.

verifier   An off-line device used for verifying the encoding of input media by automatic comparison with reentered input data.

video display terminal   An interactive terminal incorporating a keyboard and a video screen monitor.

virtual memory   A strategy for increasing the apparent size of main memory by automatically transferring program segments and data back and forth from secondary storage.

voice recognition   The process by which audible speech is transcribed automatically into machine-readable data.

volatility   See **file volatility**.

voucher   A document authorizing the disbursement of cash in payment of an amount owed.

wide area network (WAN)   A configuration of networked computers extending over a substantial geographical area.

word processing   The input, storage, composition, editing, and printing of textual material—including reports, proposals, letters, envelopes, and mailing lists—with the aid of computer facilities.

work in process   Goods currently at various stages of completion in the production process. The costs assigned to those goods while in production.

work order   A document authorizing the expenditure of labor resources to the production of specified goods or the provision of specified services such as repairs and maintenance.

zero-based budgeting (ZBB)   An approach to the budgeting of discretionary items in which expenditures must be justified each year as though they were new items. ZBB seeks to overcome the ''inertia'' associated with ongoing expense items.

Index